A2

Applied Business

for EDEXCEL

Single and double awards

John Evans-Pritchard ● Margaret Hancock
Rob Jones ● Alan Mansfield ● Dave Gray

CP Causeway Press

endorsed by
edexcel

Acknowledgements

Dedication

To Sheila, Amanda Jane, Oscar and Cleo, Jan, Natalie, Holly, Jack and Ellen.

Cover design by Caroline Waring-Collins. Illustration © Tiit Veermae/Alamy.

Graphics by Caroline Waring-Collins and Kevin O'Brien.

Photography by Andrew Allen and Dave Gray.

Proofreading by Sue Oliver, Heather Doyle and Mike Kidson.

Reviewer - Stuart Kneller.

Typing - Ingrid Hamer.

Acknowledgements

Belbin® Associates pp 76-77, Corel pp 204, 263, 295(b), Digital Vision pp 9, 22, 59, 76, 81, 85, 91, 95, 97, 100, 120, 197, 201, 205, 231, 279, 289, 332, 339, 345, 411(l), Digital Stock pp 118, 230, Foreign & Commonwealth Office p 72, Hillingdon Times (Clive Tagg) p 63(b), Image 100 pp 79, 103, 169, 223, 411(r), Nottingham City Council p 63(t), Photodisc pp 14, 20, 29, 32(l), 32(r), 39, 41, 43, 48, 49, 55, 71, 96, 99, 105, 107, 130, 145, 152, 181, 183, 193, 206, 208, 209, 214, 220, 274, 295(t), 298, 311, 312, 323, 327, 340, 379, 392, 397, 403, 424, Quality Villas p 86(r), Rex Features pp 54, 64, 65(l), 65(r), 136, 150, 211, 252, 256, 261, 278, 283, 287, 317, 334, 353, 367, 391, Stockbyte pp 26, 50, 344, 151, Stockdisc pp 80, 89, 164, 408, Topfoto pp 74, 86(l), 115, 333, 337.

Office for National Statisitics material is Crown Copyright, reproduced here with the permission of Her Majesty's Stationery Office.

British Library Cataloguing in Publication Data

A catalogue record for this book is available from the British Library.

ISBN-10: 1-4058-2116-7
ISBN-13: 978-1-4058-2116-2

Contribution © John Evans-Pritchard, Margaret Hancock, Rob Jones, Alan Mansfield, Dave Gray.

Pearson Education, Edinburgh Gate, Harlow, Essex, CM20 2JE.

First published 2006
Third impression 2006
Typesetting by Caroline Waring-Collins and Anneli Griffiths, Waring Collins Ltd.
Printed and bound by CPI Bath

Contents

Preface

A2 Level Applied Business for EDEXCEL (Single and double awards) is one of a series of books written to follow the EDEXCEL Advanced Subsidiary GCE and Advanced GCE in Applied Business (single and double awards). Other books in the series include:

- **AS Level Applied Business for EDEXCEL (Single award)** containing Units 1-3;
- **AS Level Applied Business for EDEXCEL (Double award)** containing Units 1-7;
- **Applied Business for EDEXCEL Teachers' Guide**.

A2 Level Applied Business for EDEXCEL (Single and double awards) contains Units 8-14 of the specification. Units have the following features.

Content coverage Units provide comprehensive coverage of 'What you need to learn' in Units 8-14 of the EDEXCEL specification. They give the content knowledge for Units 8 and 10 external assessment and essential background information for internally assessed Units 9, 11, 12, 13 and 14.

Meeting the assessment criteria Unit 8 provides suggested responses and guidance at Mark Bands 1, 2 and 3 to produce a business plan for the externally set assignment. Units 10 contains sample questions in the style of the external examination, with sample marks. They clearly show the expected answers and how marks are allocated in the externally assessed examination. Understanding how questions are answered and marked will enable students to achieve examination success. Units 9, 11, 12, 13 and 14 provide suggested student responses or guidance for internal assessment at Mark Bands 1, 2 and 3. Understanding the type of response required for different Mark Bands will allow students to meet the assessement criteria effectively. Answers and suggestions are not meant to be comprehensive, reflecting all of a student's internal assessment, just the part that relates to the content covered in that section.

Examination practice Units 10 provides sample questions which reflect the style of question asked in the externally assessed examination. Completing all the examination practice questions will allow students to practise and develop the skills for examination success.

Portfolio practice Units 9, 11, 12, 13 and 14 provide questions which allow students to practise the knowledge, application, analysis and evaluation skills which they need to demonstrate in internal assessment.

Research activity Units 9, 11, 12, 13 and 14 provide suggested research and investigation activities. They allow students to practise the research skills required for their internal assessment.

Business examples Many examples are given of actual businesses to illustrate how their operations relate to the EDEXCEL specification.

The publication has been endorsed by EDEXCEL.

Author team for the series

- **John Evans-Pritchard** is Chief Examiner with a major awarding body and an experienced author and teacher.
- **Margaret Hancock** is Principal Examiner with a major awarding body and an experienced author and education consultant for Business Studies.
- **Rob Jones** is an Examiner with a major awarding body and an experienced author and teacher.
- **Alan Mansfield** is Principal Examiner with a major awarding body and an experienced business and education consultant.
- **Dave Gray** is an experienced author and teacher.

The authors would like to thank Stuart Kneller for acting as a reviewer and for his comments and advice in the development and production of the series of books. They would also like to thank all those business representatives who spent time researching and supplying information for use as case studies.

Business plans

A business plan is an important document for a business. Essentially, it is a detailed report that gives the background to the business idea or concept. It will usually include aims and objectives for the business supported by marketing research, a marketing plan, resource requirements and plans, together with financial data and analysis. It should also include forecasts and information that will demonstrate that the business idea will be viable. A detailed timetable for key stages in the plan will be required along with details of how the plan will be measured and monitored. It is also usual to include a brief section on the credentials of the person or team that have put together the business plan, which will support the idea for running a business and reassure potential lenders or investors that the originator of the business plan knows what they are doing.

A business plan is an essential tool when thinking about starting a business. It has a number of important functions including:

- to check and confirm that the business idea is realistic and viable;
- to demonstrate to stakeholders that a business idea is worthwhile, viable and attractive;
- to raise finance that will be required for development, start-up, and the launch or introduction stages of a business;
- to be used as a working plan for management to follow once a decision to go ahead has been made;
- to provide some protection for stakeholders through contingency planning for a scenario that if, for whatever reason, the business plan fails utterly.

In business jargon a business plan should be SMART, as shown in Figure 1.

Although most business plans will share a similar structure and format, and will include some common features and information, the precise make-up of a plan will vary according to the needs of the business, the needs of stakeholders and the expectations and standards of the market. So although there will be similarities in structure, the content and information in the business plan of a furniture manufacturer, a website designer, a food retailer or an importer of cycle parts are likely to be different.

A business plan should always be clear, objective and easy to understand, as the audience for a business plan is unlikely to be as expert as the people putting together the plan in the specifics of the product or market involved.

Why start a business?

Starting a business is not for everyone. Some people perform much better and are much happier or more satisfied when working as part of a team in a business that is owned, run and managed by someone else. They never aspire to owning and running their own business. They are quite happy to let someone else take the responsibility for providing them with a regular income. The responsibility to make the business a success and to protect employees and other stakeholders from failure can produce great stress. Starting a business will place many stresses on an individual and the relationships they have with family and friends as the business becomes the most important thing in the life of the entrepreneur, the person starting the business. There is an increased responsibility, especially when the business starts to grow and employ people. Starting a business also involves risk, mainly personal and stakeholders' financial risk, but there is also the risk of personal failure, which can be devastating for some people.

With all this negativity, why start a business? The reasons can be many and varied, but the main reasons include:

- the challenge – because they want the stimulating experience of creating a business from scratch;
- a sense of personal achievement – proving that a business idea can work and will generate money;
- personal freedom – not working for someone else and not tied to corporate working hours or a corporate ethos;
- financial freedom – not relying on someone else to produce the money;
- the opportunity to generate and earn more money than an employer would pay as a salary;
- to generate a greater return on personal savings than if they were deposited in a savings account;
- employment – if, for whatever reason, a person finds themselves without a job or has become unemployable, starting their own business will provide employment and an income.

Not everyone who starts their own business succeeds, but even if a business does not succeed, what the entrepreneur has learned from the experience will be very valuable, for personal development, for the next new business idea or for future employers.

Figure 1 *A SMART business plan*

- Specific – stating exactly what the plan should achieve.
- Measurable – providing details of what can be measured and monitored and how this will be carried out and reported.
- Agreed – that everyone who is party to the business plan and expected to make it work has 'signed off' in agreement with the aims and objectives.
- Realistic – that the aims and objectives can be achieved with the product as described in the market targeted with the resources that have been forecast, requested or planned.
- Time specific – a detailed timetable for key stages in the plan for launching activities, for measuring achievements and for decision making.

Choosing the right name for the business

This may not seem very important compared with having a business idea or getting the product right. However, it is often the name of a business that is the first point of contact for customers and other stakeholders so it is important that you choose a good one. The name of the business will become the identity and the brand, it will create an impression of the business and it will be used by anyone who tries to contact the organisation. In addition, it will be a key element of any marketing communication materials that are produced, from letterheads and business cards to advertising and promotional material. Figure 2 shows key questions to be considered when choosing a business name.

Figure 2 *Choosing a business name – questions to consider*

What do you want the name to do?

- Identify you/yourself as the business.
- Describe the business – building, plumbing, cleaning or designing.
- Evoke an image, create an impression or be fashionable.
- Be quirky and memorable.
- Be versatile so the name can be applied to a range of products or services.
- Be good for communications, websites and e-mails.

What makes a good name?

- Do you want to use your own name?
- Should the name reflect the product or service provided?
- What image do you want the name to convey?
- Will it work on marketing communications, letterheads, business cards and advertisements?
- Will it make a memorable and easy to use web address?

What to avoid.

- Names that are too long and complex.
- Names that are difficult to pronounce.
- Names that are rude or offensive.
- Names that limit or restrict use.
- Names that are already in use or too similar to other businesses.

What kind of business to start?

All businesses start with an idea. A financially viable idea is vital. The business idea and how it is presented in the market place is very important. It will define a business so far as its customers are concerned. But there is more to a business than just an idea and how it appears. The decision of what type of business to set-up is also important, so that it is appropriate for the market place, does not waste resources and is a legal entity.

There is a number of different types of business that can be started. Each has particular characteristics and a defined legal status. Which type of business you decide to start will depend on a number of factors, such as the business idea, your aspirations, your resources, the risk that you want to take, the requirements of stakeholders and what is appropriate in the market place.

Many small businesses or SMEs (small-medium sized enterprises) start up as small operations. Many begin as either sole traders or partnerships although there are other forms of business organisation, as explained later.

Sole trader

As the name suggests, a sole trader, in the eyes of the law at least, is a single individual who owns and operates a business and is responsible for all business and financial decisions. A sole trader is responsible for organising resources and raising finance to fund the business. Being a sole trader does not prevent the business from employing people and many sole traders build up quite large business organisations. Although based on an individual, businesses run by sole traders still have to operate within the same legal framework as all other businesses in respect of employment, discrimination, data protection, consumer protection, trade descriptions and health and safety. But as a sole trader, all business and financial decisions are ultimately their own individual responsibility. This means that sole traders have **unlimited personal liability**.

Examples of sole traders can be found in just about every sector of every market. Wherever there is scope for good business ideas, and individuals willing to take a chance of making money out of their idea, there will be sole traders. Examples include service providers such as plumbers, painters and decorators and gardeners, individual workers such as artists and designers, small manufacturers such as printers and bespoke clothes makers, and small retailers, although there are many more. Table 1 shows the benefits and drawbacks of being a sole trader.

Partnership

A partnership is a type of business organisation that has two or more people trading together as a single entity. Each partner has equal status and equal responsibility, in a legal sense anyway. A partnership operates under the **Partnership Act, 1890**, full details of which can be found on the HM Revenue & Customs website http://www.hmrc.gov.uk/manuals/bimmanual/bim72505.htm.

Although it is not a legal requirement it is a good idea when forming a partnership for the members of the partnership to sign a **Deed of Partnership**. This is a document, drawn up by a solicitor, that defines the legal and business relationship of the partners. A Deed of Partnership will include issues such as the division of profits, the responsibilities of each partner, and other factors that may be specific to the nature of the business sector in which the partnership operates. Although it may not seem necessary when the business starts and everything is going well, a Deed of Partnership could prove to be very valuable in the future for resolving any disagreements or disputes that may arise out of the partnership. The benefits and drawbacks of partnerships are shown in Table 2, although many of the problems that could affect

Table 1 *Sole traders*

Benefits

- As a sole trader a business is easy to start and easy to close. There is minimal paperwork to start-up – the only organisation that needs to be informed officially is HM Revenue & Customs, the tax office, to change the tax status of the individual starting the business. HM Revenue & Customs will also require an annual income and expenses account, presented to its own specification, on the sole trader's annual tax return.

- It could also be very useful to let the bank know. Many sole traders start to operate with a personal bank account but this can cause problems if payments are received that are clearly in the name of a business as it could appear that it is an attempt to avoid paying bank charges. It can be equally problematic when applying for an overdraft of business proportions or if a supplier seeks references from the bank. For these reasons it is good practice to open a dedicated business bank account.

- Perhaps the most attractive reason for starting a business as a sole trader is to have access to all of the profit that is generated by the business. Once all creditors have been paid, what is left belongs entirely to the sole trader to save, spend or distribute as they see fit.

- A sole trader can work whenever they want, for as long as they want, as hard as they want or take time off or a break from work – so long as they are satisfied that the business is meeting their own individual aims and objectives. All decisions are ultimately the responsibility of the sole trader. This is attractive to people who like to be in total control of their own destiny. There is no limit to what a sole trader can achieve, but there is no safety net should things go wrong.

Problems

- The risk of unlimited personal liability if anything goes wrong with the business. The finances of the business and the personal finances of the sole trader are considered to be one and the same. This means that all creditors of the business will have a claim on the personal assets of the sole trader if payment of debt is not met. At its extreme, it could mean that the sole trader could lose house and home as well as all the assets of the business.

- Status, linked to risk. Some suppliers, customers and even potential employees may not consider that a sole trader has the financial stability of other types of business. From their point of view a sole trader could be a risk. They may also perceive it as being a small player. This can affect status in the market place.

- Unless the sole trader is independently wealthy or has built up a sufficient fund of savings before the business starts there will always be a great deal of pressure on finances. Although it may not cost a lot to start a business as a sole trader it will still need to be funded with working capital until it starts to generate sufficient income and profit to be self funding. Many sole traders find that they do not have sufficient financial resources to fund growth and expansion, which can be limiting and frustrating. It is also common for sole traders to decide not to draw a salary when the business is in the start-up phase. This could mask the fact that the business is not viable or that the costing, pricing and other finances have not been adequately planned to generate sufficient profit for the business to pay its own way.

- Raising finance can also be a problem for sole traders as lenders tend to view sole traders as small businesses with a degree of risk. Although there is unlimited liability, any responsible lender will only provide money that they think there is a reasonable chance of getting back should the business fail. This can lead some sole traders to use 'loan sharks', organisations that do not restrict lending to responsible levels, charge extortionate levels of interest and have no compunction about liquidating a business or an individual's assets to collect the debt.

- In order to succeed, many sole traders also find that they tend to work very long hours to make sure that the business succeeds.

partnerships can be overcome by a well-worded Deed of Partnership.

Partnerships are commonly found in legal and professional services, such as solicitors, architects, dentists, and accountants and retailers and manufacturers who require more finance than a single person can provide, although there are many other examples.

Limited liability partnership

The limited liability partnership (LLP) is a new form of business entity with limited liability that was introduced in 2001. The idea is to retain the attractions of a partnership and at the same time extend some of the protection afforded to limited companies. The business is still owned by the partners, but the main difference is that, as the name suggests, partners in a LLP have some financial protection in the form of limited liability – rather than the equal financial responsibility and liability shared by members of a

traditional partnership check out www.companieshouse.gov.uk/infoAndGuide/llp.shtml. The benefits and drawbacks of limited liability partnerships are shown in Table 3.

Other business organisations

The assessment of unit 8: Business Development is based on a business plan for a sole trader or partnership. However, there are other business organisations.

Private limited companies Some small businesses set up as private limited (Ltd) companies. The organisation is treated in law as a single individual entity in that it is separate from the people who own it and run it. A private limited company must have at least one director, although there can be more, and one company secretary. Directors and other company officers are employees of the company. Limited companies must be registered at Companies House and each year must submit an annual return and set of

Table 2 *Partnerships*

Benefits

- The attraction of a partnership lies in the strength of two or more people working together, pooling their skills and resources to create a successful business in which the partners all share the rewards. This sharing can reduce the pressure on individuals and the reliance on the performance of just one person to keep the business going. Decision making can be shared and time out of the business for holidays can be covered by the partners, which means that customer service levels can be maintained.
- Being able to draw on a range of skills from different partners means that a partnership can have some very strong competitive advantages, particularly when compared to a sole trader working alone.
- Capital within a partnership is also likely to be greater than from a sole trader, as most partnerships will pool resources.
- Like being a sole trader, partners will have access to all of the profit that is generated by the business to spend or distribute as they see fit. Sharing the rewards of the hard work involved in running a business can be very attractive and worthwhile, as can the camaraderie of a small number of people working together creating a successful business.

Problems

- Many partnerships start out because two people like each other and want to work together. They may be friends or spouses and the idealised image of a working partnership sounds very attractive. However, the pressures of starting and running a business can create pressures on even the strongest of friendships or relationships.
- Decision making becomes difficult and there may be times when partners have to choose between making decisions that will preserve the friendship or decisions that will protect the business. This can be very hard.
- A partnership also provides an opportunity for blame if the business does not achieve the aims and objectives that have been set. It is easy to blame one's partners for failings which may be due to other factors, such as the product is not very good, that competitors are providing a better service, or that there has been a downturn in the market. Blaming partners can lead to resentment and the danger that the partnership could break down and affect the business adversely.
- Partnerships rely on mutual trust, but where money is concerned temptation can sometimes become more powerful than trust. Having equal access to the bank account has been known to be just too tempting for partners. Less then honest partners have been know to drain a business of money and leave the remaining partners to make up any losses or to pay for any debts.
- There is also the issue of unlimited liability. In traditional partnerships each partner has equal and unlimited responsibility for the liabilities of the business. But in the eyes of the law a partnership is treated as an individual. This means that if one partner absconds, the remaining partner could find that they have total responsibility for liabilities, such as debt and tax, that is owed by the other partner.

Table 3 *Limited liability partnership (LLP)*

Benefits

- The attractions of a partnership, but with some protection from unlimited liability is undoubtedly the main attraction of an LLP.
- The main difference, and perhaps attraction, that makes a LLP different to a limited company is that an LLP has the organisational and structural flexibility of a partnership and is taxed as a partnership, as opposed to being taxed as a company. In other respects it is very similar to a company, certainly in the way that it operates and is perceived by its customers. Like a limited company, all LLPs must be incorporated at Companies House. The name of all limited liability partnerships must end with the words 'Limited Liability Partnership' or the abbreviation 'LLP'.
- This business structure is particularly attractive for large professional practices, such as law firms, dental surgeries and accountancies as it means that individual members of the partnership are protected from the total financial liabilities of the entire partnership which could be considerable if the business has a large number of partners.
- As an LLP the partnership can trade just like a business even though the partners within the organisation may change.
- An LLP retains many of the attractions of a traditional partnership – the shared responsibilities, mutual trust and understanding and the strengths associated with working as partners rather than in an employer-employee relationship, the details of which should be defined in a Deed of Partnership.

Problems

- The will be similar reservations as those that apply to a traditional partnership – pressures such as the reliance on mutual trust and responsibility, issues surrounding the ability for a partnership to make changes or investments without the agreement of all partners and difficulties created by the reliance on individual partners who are each expected to show a similar commitment to the business.
- Raising capital for large investments or developments may also be more difficult than if the business was established as a limited company.
- Partners may also find that the benefits of partnership are outweighed by the legal requirements of an LLP and that there is little advantage in this type of business when compared to running a limited company.

annual accounts to Companies House. Capital is raised from private investors who are sold or allocated shares in the company. Profit is paid to shareholders in the form of a dividend based on the number of shares held.

Public limited companies

This type of company, known as a plc, is only really suited to large operations. The main difference between a private limited company and a public limited company is that the public limited company may raise capital by offering to sell its shares to the public. Before it can start trading a PLC must satisfy Companies House that at least £50,000 worth of shares have been issued and that each share has been paid up to at least a quarter of its face value. Shares may be traded publicy on a stock exchange.

Co-operatives

Sometimes known as a worker's co-operative, this is a type of business that is owned by its employees. Each employee has equal responsibility and say in the way in which the business is run, and an equal right to a share in any profits. A co-operative must have a minimum of three members and must satisfy the Registrar of Companies that it has a bona fide reason to be a co-operative. To set up a co-operative it must be registered at Companies House under the Companies Act as well as being registered under the Industrial and Provident Societies Act with the Registrar of Friendly Societies.

Meeting the assessment criteria – examiners' guidance

When studying unit 8 it is important to remember that the means of assessment is different to the way that all the other units in the Edexcel GCE in Applied Business specification are assessed. The assessment evidence for unit 8: Business Development is based on:
- producing a fully developed business plan;
- for a small business which is a sole trader or partnership;
- presented as a viable business idea;
- suitable to support a request for finance;

which will be externally set.

The background scenario and brief for the business plan will be issued to learners who must then complete set tasks relating to the given scenario, under set conditions. The production of a business plan is designed to measure the degree of students' business understanding. This means that students will need to draw on learning that has been covered in other units, as well as the content that is specific to this unit.

Each section of this unit deals with a particular aspect of the business plan. The following shows an example of the type of information that could be included in a business plan to justify the choice of business organisation.

Sharon Lee jewellery

Sharon Lee graduated from university with a degree in jewellery design. She has also learned the craft of jewellery making by attending various training courses and working part time repairing jewellery for a local shop.

Sharon now has to start earning a living. There is no opportunity for additional repair work from the shop. She believes that with her skills and training she should be able to design, manufacture and sell her own range of necklaces and costume jewellery. It has always been Sharon's ambition to run her own business, but she needs start-up finance so that she can rent a workshop, buy equipment and materials, build up a stock of necklaces to sell and pay for her living costs until the business takes off. She has savings of £1,000 and has asked her bank about the possibility of a £10,000 loan.

The bank is pleased to help her, but has asked for a business plan that it can consider before formally committing to give her finance. The bank provides her with some leaflets about starting your own business and a basic business plan form, which she starts to complete.

Title: Ms
Surname: Lee
First name: Sharon
Address: 15 Allerton Close, Liverpool, L14 5NX
Nationality: British
Country of residence: Great Britain
Date of birth: 26/02/1984
Telephone: Home: 0151 155 4081
Mobile: 07000 554081

'This information is required in the business plan so that it is easy for the bank to make contact with me whenever it needs to and so that before it lends me any money, it can check that I have a fixed address. This will provide the bank with some kind of reassurance.'

Education
GCSE in English Language, Art, Geography, D&T
GCE A-Level in Art
Wigan College of Art – foundation year
University of London – BA (Hons) Jewellery and Silversmithing

'This information is required in the business plan to provide some credentials, to show the bank that I have some skills and training that will be relevant to the business that I want to start.'

Relevant work experience

For the three years that I was at University I worked for a local jewellery shop, doing repairs for customers. This gave me a wide range of experience in different materials and solving many different problems. I have also been making necklaces for sale at craft fairs. This has shown me what sells and what does not sell – information that will be very important when making stock for my own business.

'This information provides additional support to my plan for a jewellery making business. It shows the bank that I already have some experience in the trade sector that I have chosen.'

Training

In addition to my degree course I have attended practical courses in silversmithing run by the Crafts Council. I have also attended a Business Link course for business start-ups.

'This provides additional information to show the bank that in addition to any academic qualifications, I have undertaken some practical training that will be relevant to my chosen business.'

Business idea

I want to produce and sell my own range of high quality jewellery.

'This section is only short and to the point but it provides the bank with the basic idea for the business and does not commit me to any particular items. It confirms that in addition to making the jewellery I am determined to make money from it by selling it myself. Note the reference to "high quality jewellery". This shows that I have set standards and that I aim to produce quality products which will attract customers. All this is very reassuring in just a few words.'

What resources, expertise and/or equipment will you need?

To run my business I will need a small workshop unit, approximately 400sq feet. Space in a managed suite of units will be ideal as this means that I will have access to toilets and catering facilities. The equipment I need to start the business will include: workbench and lights for close-up work and a safe for storing raw materials and stock securely. I will also need to buy-in some raw materials for making the initial stock. I already have the basic tools that I need.

'This section outlines the basic requirements for the business. The bank has not asked for it to be costed at this stage in the business plan, but it wants to have some idea of the scale of the requirements for the business.'

Name of business

My Sharona – I have decided to trade under this name because jewellery is a very personal choice and by using the word 'My…' it implies personal ownership. Shorona is a play on my own name and many of my customers associate me directly with my jewellery.

'A business plan needs to include the name of the intended business for a number of reasons. First, the business needs a recognisable and memorable identity and second, by providing the name the bank can check that no other businesses are using the same name.'

Start-up date

2nd April 2008

'The start-up date provides the bank with the timescale for starting the business. It will give an indication of when the finance will be needed, but it also shows that when writing the business plan I have understood the concept of time and deadlines in a business sense. It will also show if I have allowed enough time to research the market.'

Type of business

Sole trader

'I have decided that it would be most appropriate for me to run the business as a sole trader for a number of reasons.
1) I want to work on my own, running my own business with the minimum of interference.
2) I am attracted by the idea of retaining all of the profit for my own use;
3) The start-up will be relatively low cost and therefore low risk, so I am not likely to run up huge debts or liabilities that would jeopardise my personal assets.
4) I understand that the business will start out in a relatively small and modest way and that it would not be appropriate for me to attract the additional costs involved in setting up a partnership or company.'

Overall, I have provided the basic information required by the bank. I could also add information on the size of the market, potential customers and any competitors. The bank would probably require detailed financial information and evidence that the business would be viable. This would be included in another section of the business plan.

Mark Band 1 This would include the choice of potential idea, giving basic reasons for choice, viability and strategies. It might include details under a number of headings. The details shown under the heading 'Type of business', with a reason for this idea, and details under the heading 'Business name', giving the name as a feature to attract customers, demonstrate strategy. Viability would be shown in a financial section of the business plan.

Mark Band 2 This would include information on the business, idea supported by evidence of viability and detailed strategies with some justification of proposal. Details might be shown on many areas of the business including business idea, relevant experience, the choice of the name, and type of business and relevant resources. These would be supported by commentaries justifying choice.

Mark Band 3 This would include comprehensive and original ideas with fully supported and justified evidence and proposals. It would show all data presented here on the business plan with comprehensive commentary justifying the choices that were made. It would also include reference to data shown in other parts of the plan, as dealt with in other sections, such as the degree of competition.

2 Identification of a business opportunity

Why generate a business idea?

Which came first, the chicken or the egg? In business whatever you think about this question one thing is certain, a business always starts with an idea. A good, original idea may sound preferable, but even a simple idea can be turned into a successful business if there is a market. A business idea is really the identification of an opportunity that could be developed into a viable business. Viable in this case means that it is capable of generating sufficient profit from sales to meet realistic financial aims and objectives.

To be viable the business idea will need to 'pay its own way' and generate profit for the entrepreneur to draw as wages, reinvest to help the business grow, or start other businesses. Unless someone is independently wealthy, there is little point in starting a business for its own sake or a starting a business that will not produce a better return on money invested than interest from a bank account. The whole point of running a business is to make money. The actual amount may vary depending on aims and objectives, but a business must make money to be viable.

Sources of business ideas

There is a number of different ways that people come up with a business idea. Some may seem obvious, some cold and calculating and others may appear to be fortuitous – the right idea at the right time. Some examples are shown in Figure 1.

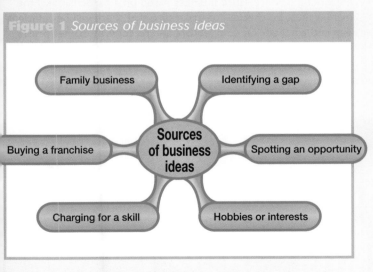

Figure 1 *Sources of business ideas*

Family businesses

It may be that there is already a family business or business connection that will lead to a new business idea, as shown in Figure 2. Similarly, if there are already business premises, another member of the family could use some of the space for their own enterprise. In this situation the new business would only need to

contribute to the fixed overheads rather than bearing the full overhead costs of setting up in separate premises. The existence of a family business should also mean that there are experienced people around who can mentor the new business. Despite the family connections, people should not let sentiment get in the way of business and any new enterprise should be worthwhile and viable in its own right.

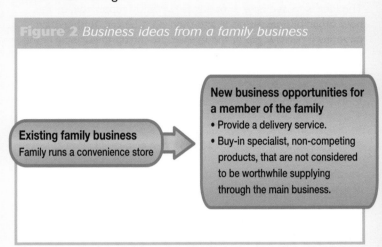

Figure 2 *Business ideas from a family business*

Existing family business
Family runs a convenience store

New business opportunities for a member of the family
- Provide a delivery service.
- Buy-in specialist, non-competing products, that are not considered to be worthwhile supplying through the main business.

Identifying a gap in the market

It may be possible to spot a gap in the market – a segment within the overall market that is not currently being served. This 'gap' could be found as a result of trying to buy a particular product and finding it unavailable or difficult to acquire. The business opportunity is that you recognise that there may be other people in the same situation and that you could fill the gap by starting a business to provide the missing product. The danger is that you may be in a minority and that the market that you choose to enter is too small to develop into a viable business. Market research will provide data to answer this question, but even if the figures are small you could decide that the opportunity is big enough for your own aims and objectives.

Many sole traders have created good businesses in segments that are considered by large companies to be too small for them to bother with. This is the basis of **niche marketing**. A more scientific approach to filling a gap in a market is to use marketing research to survey a chosen market and identify any gaps, either statistically or from consumer feedback. Once this has been done the opportunity will need to be quantified by assessing the size of the gap. The gap will also need to be researched in terms of the ease and cost of access compared to the opportunity, to decide whether starting a business to fill the gap will be both possible and viable. If not, a gap will need to be found that does meet these criteria. Table 1 shows some 'gaps' that businesses have been able to exploit.

Table 1 *Gaps in the market*

Product	Opportunity
King of Shaves	Shaving cream with skin protection
Benecol	Butter substitute that reduces cholesterol
Saga holidays	Holidays for over 50s

Spotting an opportunity

This is a bit like spotting a gap, but perhaps on a broader scale. The idea is to see how a market is currently supported, to see how other businesses do it, and then do it better. Rather than targeting a narrow gap in the market, an entrepreneur may come up with a money-making idea, an overall concept, that seems to indicate a business opportunity. This is the point when some marketing research becomes essential to:

- see how the market is being satisfied, or not, at the moment;
- assess the size of the opportunity;
- check out competition;
- investigate ease of access and the overall cost of entry into the market.

Another aspect of this would be to pick a market segment that a larger business does not consider to be worth supporting and do it better to win the market. Conversely, this is what leads to the long-term erosion of brand leading businesses if they do not maintain their marketing support. Whilst many a small business will be striving to find the elusive 'million pound product', there will also be some large companies that decided to focus on extremely large product sectors and have decided to drop products that do not exceed their multi-million pound targets. This is how many of the famous brand names from the past have moved from the company where they originated to being owned and marketed by venture capital groups or trading companies.

Turning a hobby or interest into a money making business

It is not unusual for someone who has a passion or interest in a hobby to think that they would like to work in the same area of interest. Some examples are shown in Table 2.

But are any of these real business ideas? Using the criteria of viability, if the hobby develops to the point when it generates sales and a profit level that is at least the equivalent to a wage plus money to invest, it could be considered to be a business. However, it is quite a commitment to move from secure employment to the full-time pursuit of a hobby or interest. Before taking this step the idea and the market will need to be checked, using marketing research. The danger of turning a hobby into a business comes when commercial interests start to take precedence over personal interest. This can happen when a collector has to part with a treasured item to make sure that turnover targets are met, or when a collector realises that what they would pay as a collector would not leave sufficient margin for profit when the item comes to be sold. Other people have realised that what was interesting in small doses, as a hobby, becomes just as boring as any other job when they are forced to deal and trade in the market full time.

Charging for a skill that you have or a service that you can provide

Some people have a natural skill or talent that other people are willing to pay for, such as actors, singers, artists or craft workers. Other people can acquire a skill through education or training. Both routes could result in establishing a business or at least a freelance opportunity based on the sale of these skills. Before embarking on a freelance business based on a particular skill the market must be checked to make sure that there will be sufficient demand, to check on competitors and to confirm market pricing. Viability and long-term sustainable opportunity is the key, rather than trying to start a business on a one-off job that just happens to pay well. Hard work and determination will also have an important part to play.

Table 2 *Turning interests into a business idea*

Interest	Business
Playing games	Computer games shop.
Good food	Restaurant.
Hiking	Guided tours of the Lake District.
Collecting	Buying and selling antiques.
Playing guitar	Guitar repair technician.

Buying a franchise

Although this option means that you will be buying a business idea that someone else has had, and has been able to market successfully, it may be that operating a franchise in a market that you have chosen is your business idea. A franchise is usually a business idea that has been so successful that the owner, the franchisor, will be in a position to sell not just the concept but the whole package of product and marketing mix so that other people will be able to replicate the business itself, usually in a defined location or geographic area. A franchise will usually allow some scope for entrepreneurial flair, but within tight parameters established by the owner of the franchise. Operating as a franchisee still means that you will need to run it as a bona fide business – the market will need to be researched to establish size, ease of access or local competition. A business plan for a franchise will still need to include detailed projection for sales and cash flow forecasts. Before a franchise is granted, i.e. sold to you, the franchisor will need to be reassured that not only is there a market where you propose to trade with the franchise, but that you are capable of running a business. This is to protect their brand name and reputation in the market place. Marketing research plus experience or perhaps working in a branch of the franchise you are considering could cover both of these issues. Having bought a franchise, a franchisee will usually have to make a decision on their legal status.

If your own business idea is strong enough, if it has a distinctive product and brand, and if you are able to demonstrate that you have a successful marketing mix, then there is no reason why you should not be able to offer your business idea as a franchise for potential franchisees to buy from you and run in the way that you have defined.

Ideas generation techniques

You may have heard the terms 'thought shower' or 'word storming'. These are where a group of people meet and just suggest ideas, in this case for a business or a product, in an open forum where no one is right, no one is wrong and most importantly no one laughs at or ridicules an idea. No matter how way out, all ideas are written down for consideration. The aim is to produce as many ideas as possible. No ideas should be rejected until they have been evaluated. This open-minded thinking technique can throw up new ideas that would not emerge in a formal business meeting. This does not mean that a session is disorganised or casual - it is an important ideas generation technique that has proved its worth in many businesses that are willing to give it a try.

Once the ideas have been produced, similar ideas are grouped as common threads emerge. Common ideas are then evaluated in their own right and against company objectives to see which are feasible. These are then subjected to an opportunity assessment to estimate the size of the market opportunity and the ease and cost of entering that market. Like most of the different sources of business ideas covered in this section it is important to test them using marketing research to check feasibility and viability before

they are pursued, through test marketing or small scale trials before a full-blown launch.

Analysing the business idea

Without carrying out large amounts of marketing research, there is a number of simple analysis techniques that can be applied to a business idea to see if it could be developed. First, list advantages and disadvantages, and compare them with your own aims and objectives, or the objectives for the business. This will soon help you weigh up the idea before going much further, and will quickly identify non-starters. SWOT analysis techniques could then be usefully applied to business ideas that emerge or are generated from any of the sources of business ideas that have been mentioned. SWOT analysis means considering the Strengths, Weaknesses, Opportunities and Threats as they apply to the business idea, see section 25.

- Strengths – are all the good, positive things that will accrue from the business idea and all the positive aspects of the qualities of the business idea.
- Weaknesses – are things that might make a business vulnerable, such as negative aspects of the qualities of the business idea.
- Opportunities – represent potential, what the business could achieve.
- Threats – are external factors, outside the direct control of the business. Threats could include competition, government legislation, the contraction of a market and customers having different needs to those that had been assumed or identified.

A SWOT is just a snapshot of a situation at a given point in time. To remain relevant and useful it may need to be updated as the situation or circumstances change.

As the business idea develops there will be a point when a PESTLE analysis will provide useful support, or at least raise issues that need to be considered before the business is launched. A PESTLE analysis is based on applying Political, Economic, Sociological, Technological, Legal, and Environmental criteria to the business idea, or seeing how the business idea is likely to be affected by each of these issues, see section 25.

Whilst it is good practice to carry out detailed product development, and to research the market thoroughly before starting a business, there is no point in spending too much time on these activities. While doing this a competitor may come along and steal the market by launching first and your business may always have to catch up. Many good ideas have been researched to death and entered the market too late or too expensive because they have been 'improved' and tinkered with as a result of feedback from consumer research groups. It is too easy to waste time, tweaking a business idea or product, waiting for it to become perfect or for conditions in the market place to be just right. There comes a point when it is not worth improving any more. If the idea is good, it should be introduced into the market as soon as possible, or when there is an opening or opportunity. Then, if necessary, it can be modified. An old saying in marketing circles is that a good idea, launched with vigour today, is better than a great idea tomorrow.

Meeting the assessment criteria - examiners' guidance

Each section of this unit deals with a particular aspect of the business plan. The following shows an example of the type of information that could be included in a business plan to justify the choice of business idea.

Business example - Guy Townshend

Guy Townshend is a keen golfer. He plays every weekend and is an active member of the local golf club. If asked, he would say that golf is his passion and that in an ideal world he would win the lottery and spend every day playing golf to improve his game.

He works currently for a firm of investment accountants. His job is to recommend portfolios of shares for people to invest their savings or lump sums of cash in the stock market. He also sells private pension schemes. The firm he works for makes its money from commissions paid on these investments and pensions. Guy is bored with his job and has thought up a number of different ideas for running his own business.

At the golf club, Guy is quite well known and is often asked by other members about suggestions for their savings and investments. Before he hands in his notice Guy needs to consider his business ideas.

Aims and objectives
1. To start my own business and work for myself – to be my own boss.
2. To work in a business in which I am really interested.
3. To earn enough to pay the mortgage and have enough over to spend on the family, on holidays, on my interests and to

save for the future.
4. To maintain contact with people – I like the office environment.
5. To spend as much time playing golf as possible

'It is important to have aims and objectives before starting a business, or indeed before generating business ideas. Although my list may seem short and perhaps simplistic, it sums up adequately my aspirations at this moment in time.'

Ideas for my own business
1. Become a professional golfer.
2. Set up as an independent financial adviser with office in town.
3. Set up as an independent financial adviser with office at the golf club.
4. Set up as an independent financial adviser working from home.
5. Start importing Titleist golf clubs and equipment to sell to other golfers.

'I complied this list from ideas I have had over a number of years and also from ideas suggested from friends and relatives who know me. Although items 2, 3 and 4 appear to be very similar, in my mind they are quite different because the different locations will affect my status, access to potential clients and the opportunity to meet my objectives for the business. I have decided that to help me make a decision I will consider the advantages and disadvantages of each business idea.'

Business idea	Advantages	Disadvantages	Score
1. Become a professional golfer.	• Will mean that I can play golf all of the time. • I could travel the world. • I have the opportunity of winning lots of money. • I could live the glamorous lifestyle.	• I am not that good a player. • Too much competition. • I would be away from home and family for most of the time. • I would have to fund all of my own travel and other expenses with no guarantee that I would make any money.	On balance, may not be realistic.
2. Set up as an independent financial adviser with office in town.	• I know the business sector and should be able to offer the same products as I do at work but take the commission for myself. • Most clients expect to come to an office in the town so I would be meeting their expectations. • Central for all business services. • Could generate passing trade.	• Direct competition with old firm. • High overheads as rent in town centre is likely to be expensive. • Clients could make direct comparison with competitors. • I would be doing the same job as I do at the moment, which bores me, but with no guaranteed salary.	Feasible, but disadvantages seem to outweigh advantages.
3. Set up as an independent financial adviser with office at the golf club.	• Members of the club seem to have plenty of money to invest. • I could talk to them and sell to them in a relaxed, informal environment. • No direct competition. • I could be on the golf course playing and still making business contacts.	• Clients may not like seeing financial services in a golf club environment, clients will have gone to relax and not talk about business. • Golf club may change policy and I may lose the office. • The golf course will be a great temptation and I may spend time playing when I should be selling.	• Like the idea – if it does not work then I will not have lost too much. • Being on the spot should, on balance, bring me into contact with a lot of potential customers. • Need to do some research before making final decision.
4. Set up as an independent financial adviser working from home	• Low overheads. • Will not have to sell so much to pay for overheads or before business is in profit. • Will not have to get up so early to get to work. • If there is no work I could get on with decorating and doing the garden.	• Will need to find office space in the house – could be difficult. • May not appear to be professional in eyes of clients. • Difficult to focus and get motivated when not in a work environment, too may distractions. • Risk that I will not be able to make any sales.	• Lowest cost, but maximum upheaval at home. • Does not strike me as being most professional way of doing this – especially as I will be asking clients to trust me with a lot of their money.

Business idea	Advantages	Disadvantages	Score
5. Start importing Titleist golf clubs and equipment to sell to other golfers.	• Titleist is one of the best brands of golf equipment in the world. • Would be able to get a set for myself at trade prices. • Lots of other players would like to buy Titleist but cannot get them easily which means that there should be a good market. • Good profit margins.	• Titleist may already have a UK distributor and may not want to trade with me. • Would be expensive to buy in stock – high capital investment for start-up. • Will need somewhere secure to keep stock – high overheads. • Not all golfers believe in Titleist as the best make.	A dream job – but may not be feasible. I do not really know the import and selling game, would need to learn. Investment in stock puts me off.

'The table above has not only listed advantages and disadvantages, but summed up my thoughts about each business idea. I feel this is vital before I make any final decision. Whilst each idea has merit, the downside risk, that I will not make any money, is quite realistic. However, this kind of exercise will help me identify potential problems and potential business ideas that could be developed further. It has helped me to identify what is probably the most suitable option - set up as an independent financial adviser with office at the golf club – although further research is now necessary.

To support the business idea I could have added some market research data to quantify the size of the market, potential customers. I could also have added some estimates of the financial opportunities for each of the ideas. More detailed financial information and evidence that the business would be viable would be included in another section of the business plan.'

Mark Band 1 Potential idea selected giving basic reasons for choice and viability. This would involve the choice of an idea, its potential advantages and disadvantages, and whether the choice is realistic, viable and better than, say, another.

Mark Band 2 Sound information on business idea supported by evidence of viability. This would involve a number of ideas suggested, indicating advantages and disadvantages, with a judgement of the most realistic and viable of the ideas.

Mark Band 3 Comprehensive and original ideas with fully supported and justified evidence. This would involve a consideration of many ideas, with clear advantages and disadvantages of each, and a judgement taken based on the viability and realistic chances of being a success, also taking into account business objectives.

3 Research

Market researching

Before starting any business it is essential to learn as much about the market place as possible. This will help to identify and understand some of the issues and challenges that will be faced, and provide information to help decision making. Marketing research also forms a valuable part of a business plan, where the research findings are used to support business aims, objectives, recommendations or decisions.

Like any research project, you need to start with the aims and objectives for the research – why am I doing it and what do I want to find out? Once the aims and objectives have been set, the next question is where to get the information or answers that are required. There are two principal approaches to marketing research - primary research and secondary research. More details are provided in section 26.

Primary research

This is the origination and collection of research data that has not been collected before. It means starting from scratch and designing original research that is specific to a particular project. The main advantage is that this should provide precise information that will relate directly to your own business idea. As a result it should provide strong support for any decisions that are made. Primary research is a powerful addition to a business plan for a number of reasons.

- It demonstrates that you have been responsible, conducting research before committing resources.
- It should be able to support any decisions or assumptions that you have made in the business plan.

- It is difficult to challenge, as the research will have been conducted to meet the specific needs of the business plan and facts are much more powerful than opinion in this situation.

Some formal primary research methods are shown in Table 1.

These different research methods will produce **quantitative** and **qualitative data**, depending on the method used. There will also be a range of cost implications, again depending on the method used. You will need to decide which method is most appropriate to meet the needs of your business plan, within the resources available.

There may also be a role for informal primary research. This could just involve talking to people involved in business, discussing ideas to see what other people think. It will be primary because the questions that are asked will relate directly to your business idea and it will be the first time that these questions will have been asked. Although informal, you will at least be seeking the opinion of independent people which is better than no research at all. Informal research like this may give new ideas or help to rethink plans that might avoid making basic mistakes.

Secondary research

This is the use of data that has already been collected, analysed and presented or published. Secondary research data is widely available in the form of reports and articles and can be very useful for painting a picture of the background to a business idea, to set the context of the idea within the overall market place. The main advantages of secondary research are that it is usually easy to obtain and is quick to carry out. It is also likely to cost much less than conducting

Method	Examples
Structured observation	Watching and recording behaviour or events.
Surveys that involve direct questioning using a structured questionnaire	Street interviews, postal surveys, online surveys and telephone interviews.
Hall tests and product tests	Inviting people to try a product or look at a business concept and record their opinions on a questionnaire.
Focus groups	Using small groups of people to consider and discuss a product or business idea, recording and analysing the comments and discussions to learn what they think, making the assumption that these opinions will translate into the wider market.
Test marketing	Trying out the business idea in a small and controlled area that replicates, on a smaller scale, the situations that it will face in the wider market. This can be very valuable as it means that any mistakes that are made are likely to be smaller, easier to correct and less expensive that they would be in the wider market place.

Table 1 *Primary research methods*

primary research, although this is not always the case as buying some commercial research reports outright can be very expensive. Some sources of secondary research data are shown in Table 2.

Table 2 *Sources of secondary data*

Source	Examples
Internal data	Data that is already collected and held by businesses, such as financial and accounts information, sales figures, customer records and old reports on primary research that may have been conducted for another project but can provide background information for a new business idea.
Library and Internet sources	Quick and easy to access, they include government reports and statistics, copies of commercial research reports, and trade journals that are up-to-date with what is happening in the market place.

When using secondary research it is important to note:
- when it was collected and published – this will give an indication of how old it is and lead to a judgement about how much the market will have changed since the original research was conducted;
- who produced the research – this may be the government, a research organisation, or a business that is already trading in the market. Who produced the research will give an indication of how much reliance can be placed on the findings, and how much bias, if any, may be included;
- why the research was done – this may help explain the findings, will provide a context, and will show the motives behind the findings or conclusions of the research. It will again provide an indication of any bias that may be inherent in the report.

Any marketing research included or used in a business plan should be identified and credited clearly with its source and the date.

Researching the business idea

This is required to see if a business idea has any merit and if anyone else thinks that the idea could work. More formally, a business idea needs to be researched to show, in the business plan, that the idea is worth the proposed investment of resources. It needs to be an objective piece of research that will stand up to scrutiny by stakeholders who may not know much about the idea being considered, but could be required to support the idea or provide resources, such as finance, for product development or the launch.

It would be usual to first research the concept, the idea itself, before committing resources. If there is sufficient market data to support the concept, then it may be worth investing resources to produce more developed marketing materials or samples of the product itself and conduct further research. Secondary and primary research can be used for this.

Primary research If the business idea really is new, and no secondary research exists, then primary research will be the only option. This allows tailored questions that should meet the aims of the research precisely to be asked. Researching concepts can be difficult, as most respondents find it hard to answer questions or provide information about something that they have to imagine. As a result findings can be negative, not because it is a poor idea, but because the respondents have no point of reference to use for their answers. In this case sample products or concept boards which present and explain the ideas in a simple way can be used. The actual research method used will depend on the resources available and the type of response that are needed – quantitative or qualitative. Again, primary research can be tailored to meet your aims.

Secondary research This can be used in a number of ways.
- It can provide information about whether the idea already exists in the market and, if so, what it is, how it is presented, what consumers think and how they are responding. If not, it could indicate that that no one has had the idea before or that it is a poor idea and that there is no interest and consequently no market.
- It could be used to establish the background to a market that you want to enter. Even if there is no precise data that fits a business idea, you could draw parallels using similar ideas or products as examples or comparisons. For example, a business idea may be to open a shop selling satellite radios. If there was no secondary data about retailing these hi-tech products, secondary data about radio listening in general or about sales of personal audio devices could be used to demonstrate that a market exists for listening to radio and that the market has not yet caught up with satellite radio technology.

The more support that can be provided for the research the better will be the quality of the response from respondents. As noted, concepts are difficult to research, so concept boards will help, sample products are better and actual products are even better still as they are likely to be cheaper than producing a few samples just for research purposes. These comments apply equally to business ideas. The more realistic the idea or business being researched, the better the quality of the research findings, because the respondents will have more to work with.

Once there is research about a business idea, you must decide how much to put into the business plan and how much you analyse and interpret the findings. Bear in mind that the audience for the business plan may not be as familiar with the business idea or the use of marketing research as you. It may be better to put in just enough to support your plans, rather than provide every piece of research that you have done.

Supporting the business plan

Marketing research is often used to support business plans because it is harder to argue against facts and figures from good quality research than it is to challenge opinions. Most people who read a business plan will be reassured by the inclusion of supportive research for two reasons.
- It shows that the plan has been put together by someone who understands business and how a business plan is used and that

they are serious enough about the plan to conduct research to find out more about the market.

- It provides supporting evidence to the plan, which should reassure and help reduce the risk involved. All new business ventures have an element of risk. Stakeholders who are looking at a business plan when providing resources will feel more positive towards the plan if research shows that the risk is understood or reduced by positive research that supports the idea.

What research and how much you include in the business plan will depend on the audience and how hard you need to prove that your business idea is a good one. Someone who is experienced in reading and interpreting business plans may be able to take in more sophisticated research data than someone less experienced or who is looking at the plan from one particular angle, such as the finances. Research to support a business plan does not need to be complicated. It just needs to show the reader that the plan is good and is likely to succeed. As a rule of thumb it is usual to include just the basic facts and figures that support the plan, but keep any additional research findings readily available should anyone ask for clarification or for more information.

Researching the market

Understanding the size, scale and scope of the market will enable you to judge whether your business idea will stand a chance and whether there is any real opportunity. Without this kind of background knowledge you will be guessing and may over or under-estimate the business opportunity and your chances of success. Equally, a stakeholder reading the business plan will need to know what is happening in the market that they are being asked to support. Unless the market is particularly small or unusual, secondary research can be used to to provide background data shown in Table 3.

The PESTLE model may provide a useful framework for building up a picture of a market using research data. A PESTLE analysis is based on applying Political, Economic, Sociological, Technological, Legal, and Environmental criteria to the market and commenting

Table 3 *Market data used in a business plan*

- The size of the market, any trends, whether it is growing or shrinking and the volume and value of sales in the market.
- The main players, the companies, the products, the brands and market shares.
- Who are the buyers and users – trade buyers and consumers, how many, how much they use and buy and any other consumer data?
- How is the market likely to change in the future?

on how the market is likely to be affected by each of these issues.

Researching competition

This is needed to identify likely competition to the business idea. It will help not just to identify the number of competitors, the size and the scale or scope of their business, their location and the extent of their distribution, but also to forecast how the business idea is likely to be affected by competition in future. Taking research of competitors still further, it will enable you to gauge the market and consumer opinion of competitors. This can help you develop a marketing mix for your own business that will avoid or overcome problems that competitors are having in the market place. A good way of collecting research about competitors, to compare them like for like and against your own business idea, is to use the marketing mix as a model, as shown in Table 4.

From this information it should be possible to make an estimate of competitors' marketing strategies, which can be evaluated against their achievements, and the marketing strategy that you have adopted for your own business idea. Competitors' tactical marketing plans and activities can also be identified and evaluated.

Any marketing research included or used in a business plan should be identified clearly, attributed and credited with its source and the date.

Table 4 *Using the marketing mix to research competition*

For each competitor, draw up a profile based on the following.
- Product – what is their product or product range, what are the brands involved, what variety of products do they sell (styles, sizes, colours), what market are they in, where are the products positioned in the market, what are the sales or market shares?
- Price – what are the selling prices, retail prices, discounts, what are the estimates of cost price by deconstructing the products, what are the estimates of the margin they must be making?
- Place – where are they based, where is their product sold, how does it get from the business to the consumer, which channels of distribution are utilised, what is the distribution chain, how much does it cost a competitor to distribute its products?
- Promotion – which promotional tools are being used, which types of promotion, which media, how much promotion, how long does the promotion run, how much is it likely to cost, is it effective, what do consumers think about it and what is the reaction in the market place?

Meeting the assessment criteria - examiners' guidance

Each section of this unit deals with a particular aspect of the business plan. The following shows an example of the type of information that could be included in a business plan about marketing research.

Business example - Oona Joyner

Oona Joyner has been working as a beauty therapist at a health spa in a local hotel since she obtained her Level 3 NVQ in Beauty Therapy, 5 years ago. Oona is aware that the products she uses are chemical based and that sometimes clients will experience an allergic reaction. She has the business idea that she could develop a small range of products that use only natural ingredients that are less likely to cause a skin

reaction. Based on what she has read in the beauty therapy trade press and the comments from her clients she thinks that there will be a market for such products. Oona has contacted a family friend who works in a trade laboratory that formulates cosmetics. She says that the laboratory will produce formulae for any beauty therapy products that Oona wants and will mix up small batches for trial.

To turn the idea into a business Oona needs to raise money from the bank or get investment from other stakeholders. This will be used to pay for the production of a small run of trial products that she can use for a test market before committing to the expense of full-scale production of these products. As part of her business plan Oona includes some marketing research.

The Market

Executive Summary

Skincare: Market Size
- The UK market for skincare grew by 6.8% in 2004 to reach a value of £929.8 million (US$1,690.5 million).

Skincare: Market Sectors
- Facial care was the largest sector, accounting for 75% of sales in 2004, worth £703.4 million (US$1,278.9 million).

Skincare: Share of Market
- Procter & Gamble was the dominant player in the skincare market in 2004, with a share of 12.9% based on their Olay, Total Effects and Regenerist brands.

Skincare: Marketing Activity
- UK marketing activity for skincare is dominated by expenditure on television advertising.

Skincare: Corporate Overview
- With so many large names present in the market, the skincare market remains highly competitive and relatively fragmented.

Skincare: Procter & Gamble
- Procter & Gamble increased its turnover by 18.5% over 2003 to US$51.4 billion in 2004, with operating income reaching US$5.9 billion.

Skincare: L'oréal Group
- Between 2003 and 2004, L'Oréal Group increased its turnover by 3.6% to reach €14.5 billion, with profits before tax reaching €2.1 billion.

Skincare: Beiersdorf AG
- Beiersdorf AG increased its turnover by 2.5% in 2004 to €4.5 billion, with net profits reaching €492 million.

Skincare: Unilever Group
- Unilever decreased its turnover by 5.9% in 2004 to €40 billion, with operating profits reaching €3.4 billion.

Skincare: Distribution
- Pharmacies/drugstores represented the key distribution channels, accounting for 41.2% of sales, principally because of the activities of two chained retailers, Boots and Superdrug.

Skincare: Consumer Profile
- Per capita expenditure in the skincare market grew exponentially over the review period, fuelled by top-line anti-aging product development.

Skincare: Market Forecasts
- The market for skincare is forecast to grow by 53% from 2004 to 2009, to reach a value of £1.4 billion (US$2.6 billion).

Skincare: Sector Forecasts
- Facial care is expected to remain the largest sector, accounting for 73.6% of the market in 2009, reaching sales of £1.0 billion.

Source: adapted from *Skincare in the UK*, Euromontor 2005, http://www.majormarketprofiles.com/report_summary.asp?docid=35526.

'The inclusion of this Executive Summary from a Euromonitor report will be useful for a number of reasons.

1) It has been produced by an authoritative researcher with a good name and reputation.
2) The general data about the size of the UK market should add weight to my argument that there is a market for my proposed products.
3) Data is based on UK, which is where I am operating currently.
4) It notes the main players in the market, i.e. my biggest competitors, noting their relative size within the overall market.
5) It provides some distribution data.
6) It is positive about the future, noting that per capita expenditure has grown and that the sector forecasts future growth.
7) Because I found this information on the Internet it has not cost me much money.

However, there are some reservations about including this research, which I need to address.

1) It is now out of date, being published in 2005 and with figures from 2003 and 2004 – what has happened in the market since then?
2) Being secondary research it is very general and not at all specific about the type of products that I am proposing.
3) It raises the question of whether it is realistic for a small start-up business to try to compete directly with such multinational brands as Procter & Gamble etc.

This data is likely to provide background information but I need more data more specific to my own products and plans. So I have decided to carry out my own primary research.'

My product ideas

In order to get some consumer reaction to my idea for a range of beauty therapy products based on natural ingredients I have conducted some primary research. I have asked 120 clients over the past 4 months the following questions.

(1) If a range of beauty therapy products was available that used only natural ingredients, would you use it?

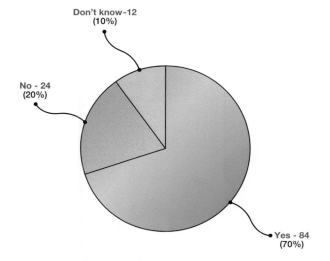

Don't know-12 (10%)

No - 24 (20%)

Yes - 84 (70%)

'Whilst this is primary research, it is somewhat limited. Only one basic dichotomous question with the 'Don't know' option is used, but it does indicate a positive reaction to the business idea, or at least the product. I could have asked whether the clients would buy such a product, but that leads into questions about price,

which I may not have investigated at this early stage. In addition to asking clients, I asked a manager of the hotel a series of questions about the concept of natural beauty products and whether they would consider using them at the spa. Because this research relates to just one manager, I decided to report the research findings in the form of a report.

Interview conducted 26/2/2006

During my interview with Ms. Durrant, facilities manager of the Straith Hotel, she made the following comments.

- We only use top quality products in our spa.
- We would be prepared to use your natural products if they cost no more than our existing range and if our clients want them.
- We would only use your natural products if they work.
- We would only use these natural products if they have passed all the testing required.
- The hotel does have an environmental policy and natural products would certainly fit in with this providing they come from renewable resources.

'These responses fit loosely in the PESTLE structure and although they are not all positive they do indicate that I would have the opportunity to test market the products at the hotel where I work. This would provide valuable data to help me make decisions about moving to the next stage in the business plan – a regional launch.

The inclusion of both secondary research and original primary research provides sound information and helps to show a more comprehensive analysis and evaluation of the market and my business idea.'

Mark Band 1 The potential idea will be selected, giving basic reasons for choice and an outline of marketing strategies and identification of competitor information will be given. This would include an indication of the product chosen, backed up by some basic market research information, such as some points from the Euromonitor report and any primary research. This would also indicate the level of competition.

Mark Band 2 Sound information on business idea will be supported by evidence of viability and detailed strategies, with some justification of the proposal. Sound information on competitors will also be included. This would include detailed information from both primary research, such as interviews and questionnaires, and the secondary research report. The research would be used to justify the product choice, the type of strategies used and the degree and nature of competition.

Mark Band 3 Comprehensive and original ideas with fully supported and justified evidence and proposals will be given. Comprehensive and original information on competitors will also be given. This would require an extensive analysis of the information from both primary and secondary research. It should indicate not only the likely success of the product, but the degree and nature of competition, the nature of the market, likely strategies to be used and the effect of PESTLE factors. A judgement would also be made on the extent to which the market research information can be said to be reliable and representative of the market facing Oona Joyner's beauty care products and therefore its potential effect on the success of the business.

ST. MARY'S UNIVERSITY COLLEGE

4 The marketing mix

The choice of product and the marketing mix

Having an idea for a business, as explained in section 2, is all very well. However, at some stage you will need to clarify and define your 'product' and make it easy for potential customers and consumers to see precisely:

● what a business has to sell;
● what they can buy from the business.

When the word 'product' is used in this unit, and in general in marketing, it can apply to either physical goods bought by customers and used by consumers, or to a service that is bought, received or experienced by customers or consumers.

The marketing mix is the combination of variables that make up the marketing strategy and plans of a business. The main variables are shown in Figure 1. This section looks at how the elements of the marketing mix affect the business plan. Further details on the marketing mix are given in section 25.

Figure 1 *The marketing mix*

What have you got to sell?

Many people have bright ideas for products, but not all of the ideas are realistic or can be made into something to sell and make money. The 'product variable' in the marketing mix is about specifying and defining precisely what is being sold or more importantly what it is that customers will pay for. The 'product' is likely to have been constructed from many variables, as shown in Figure 2.

However, even when you think that you have defined your product, it may not have been identified from the point-of-view of customers and the market. An example, is shown in Figure 3.

Producing or selling a physical item is likely to be more straightforward as the customer can see what is for sale. But even here perception between seller and buyer may be different. A farmer may grow a cauliflower and think that is a fine vegetable. The customer buying that same vegetable may see it in terms of the meal that the cauliflower will produce. To the farmer the

Figure 2 *Variables that form part of the product choice*

Product

What it is
What it does
How much it costs
How it performs
The flavour or colour
What it looks like
The size
The shape
How it is packaged and presented

Figure 3 *Parties Galore*

Parties Galore provides services as a party organiser. This means that it will take a brief from a customer and carry out all the organising and arranging required for a party or event tailored to the precise needs of the customer. The owner of Parties Galore thinks that the customer is buying a service based on what the business does, i.e. find and book suitable venues and arrange catering, entertainers, decorations and flowers, etc.

From the perspective of the customer, the 'product' that they are buying is a 'hassle free' party that everyone will enjoy and remember for a long time. It is the same event, but viewed in different ways. Identifying what your customers buy is very important, as it will give you a focus for your marketing activity, in particular marketing communication. If you create awareness and promote what the customer buys then the message will be more direct and more likely to be recognised by the customer, which could lead to a sale. Confuse customers with long detailed description of what you or your product does and they are likely to look elsewhere for a simpler solution to meeting their needs.

vegetable is only worth a few pence, but to the buyer a good meal is likely to have a considerably higher value. Recognition of differences in perception could lead to an opportunity, in this case for the farmer, to raise prices and make a higher margin.

A quick test to help identify your product is to imagine bumping into someone at a party who asks 'So, what is it that you do… ?' Answer that in a clear and concise way so that they instantly understand and you will have a short and simple description of your 'product'. This description should be clear enough for someone to recognise as something that they may want to buy or could imagine someone else buying even if they are not in the target market.

Why would anyone want or buy the product?

This question needs to be answered to confirm that there is indeed a market, or at least a demand that could be turned into a market, for the product that you are selling. The answer should come from marketing research, as subjective opinion can be very misleading when it comes to estimating the size of a market. Secondary sources are a good place to start, as they should help to find background information on the market that can be used to set the scene in a business plan.

If you are trying to establish the size of a niche market or a market that is not covered adequately by secondary research, primary research may have to be carried out to establish if a market exists and, if so, what is the scale of the opportunity. This information will be very valuable in a business plan.

If demand for a product cannot be identified, there could be two main reasons:

- there may not be a market for the product – it is something that no one wants to buy;
- there is no market yet and a market may have to be created through marketing activity to raise awareness and demand.

Why would they buy it from you?

There is a number of factors that affect why people might buy a product.

Quality Quality is an important factor when it comes to the actual product or business idea.

- the absolute quality of the materials that are specified and used;
- the quality of the work;
- the quality of the way the product is finished, packaged and presented – how good the product looks;
- performance quality – how well the product performs, how quickly the service is supplied and, whether it is within the timescale expected by the customer, on time and at the right price.

Quality may be actual or it may be a subjective perception that a customer creates, based on the experience of dealing with a business. In this way quality can affect the reputation of a business. Most customers will expect a certain quality standard, or even take it for granted and only comment when the standard falls below what they were expecting. When this happens it may be too late to alter their perception that the quality standard is poor. Once a reputation for quality is lost, it is very difficult to regain.

So how are quality standards set?

- First, the quality standards and expectations that are operating within a chosen market must be identified. This means marketing research.
- Then consider whether you need to meet or exceed these quality standards in order to be competitive. Quality is rarely free, so if you find that you do have to raise quality standards, in terms of product, materials or service, then estimate the cost and add it into the equation used for costing the product. This will show how quality will affect the selling price and the profit margin.

If it is possible to raise quality and remain competitive, all well and good. If not, you will need to see where savings can be made to maintain a competitive price, protect margins and maintain a level of quality that is acceptable to the market. Alternatively a high quality can be used to establish a price premium - a higher price than the rest of the market. Adopting this strategy will mean that features of the product that are a direct result of its high quality will need to be presented and explained to customers in product performance or marketing communications in order to justify the higher price. Conversely, it may be that in your chosen market that you can adopt a lower standard and it will still be acceptable to customers. In this case you can either lower prices to reflect the lower quality, or treat the lowering of quality as a way of reducing the cost and take this saving to boost profit levels.

Price This is another factor that affects why customers will buy from you. A pricing strategy must be right for the product and the market. Pricing strategies include those shown in Table 1. Quality assurance is dealt with in section 6.

Table 1 *Examples of pricing strategies*

Strategy	Effect
Price leadership	Dictating the price to the market so others follow.
Price skimming	Charging a high price at the start and then lowering as competition increases.
Market penetration pricing	Charging a low price to break into markets.
Competitive market based pricing	Charging similar prices to those of competitors.

Depending on the pricing strategy that is adopted for a business plan, you may be the lowest, the highest or the best value. Whatever pricing strategy chosen, the crucial factor for the business plan is that it will generate both sales and profit for the business. The pricing strategy needs to make sure that the business will be viable. Section 25 gives more details on pricing strategies.

Place The place variable in the marketing mix will affect why people will want to buy from you. Having the product in the right place at the right time is usually no accident, but has occurred through careful research and planning. A business plan should give some indication of how you plan to make sure that your product is in the right place at the right time. It is important to target distribution by:

- market;
- segment;
- named chain of retailers if appropriate;

and explain how you intend to secure this distribution and the timescale involved. Your route to market is a fundamental part of the business plan. Section 25 gives more details on place/distribution strategies.

Promotion How much promotion there is and how effective promotion is will influence why anyone would want to buy from you. Creating awareness of the business or product is vital. Without awareness no one will have seen or heard about your business. This can put you in a difficult position when it comes to selling the product or services. You will have to do two jobs – first sell the idea of the business, then sell the idea of its product – doubling the task and risking frustrating the customer.

Awareness can be created using a range of different types of marketing promotion, from public relations through to paid for advertising. In parallel with raising awareness, promotion should be designed to either create demand or show that your product meets a demand that already exists in the market. Stating what type of promotion is planned, how much it will cost and the forecast effect of the planned promotion should be included in a business plan. Section 25 gives more details on promotion strategies.

So the marketing mix (product, place, price and promotion) is a good model to use when preparing information for a business plan. A SWOT analysis will also help you to check that you have got the product right, or as right as it can be given your resources. Highlighting any weaknesses or threats in a business plan is not itself a sign of weakness. It will demonstrate that you have considered not only the positive points about your business idea but are realistic enough to identify any risks, and hopefully have defensive plans in place.

There are also other factors that might affect why people might buy from you.

Relationship between buyer and seller It is often argued in selling that 'people buy people'. This means that no matter how good a product, a major factor in selling is the personal relationship that is established between yourself and the customer. This also applies when dealing with other stakeholders in the business, such as suppliers, distributors and potential sources of finance, like banks. In a one-to-one selling or presentation situation this is done through personal communication, but the way in which you present yourself will have a bearing. If you look professional and conduct yourself in a business-like manner this will set the standard and establish you as someone who is serious about the business plan.

USPs You must consider any 'unique selling points' (USPs). These are distinctive points that make your product different, in a positive way, to all other products in the marketplace, points that identify your competitive advantage. To get some idea about USPs and how they work just look at examples of advertising done by leading business organisations, as shown in Figure 4. Analyse the claims they make and you will quickly see that most advertisements contain one or two fundamental claims about the business or its products that are designed to make it stand out in the market place and make it distinctive from all of its competitors.

A USP may be:
- actual, based on measurable differences – speed, performance or strength;
- implied, based on promises or potential;
- mythical, based on a magical or secret ingredient that enhances performance.

A USP needs to be clear, distinctive and, above all, truthful. Many products have disappointed their customers through over-claiming and as a result have been discredited and lost out ultimately to competition.

Figure 4 *Examples of vehicle USPs - function and style*

The marketing mix and business objectives

However a business decides to construct its products and however it applies the marketing mix, it needs to make sure that the overall business objectives will be met. These should be clearly stated in a business plan so that the marketing aspects of the plan can be brought in and shown to support the overall objectives in a cost-effective way.

The timing of plans is also linked to meeting objectives for two reasons.
- First, anyone reading the business plan, such as potential stakeholders, must know when things are likely to happen, when decisions will be taken and when they will know if the business has been a success or not.
- Second, the business must have some parameters within which to work and measure performance against the objectives that it has set.

Each section of this unit deals with a particular aspect of the business plan. The following shows an example of the type of information that could be included in a business plan about a choice of product and an appropriate marketing mix.

Business example - Teddy Bear Child Care

When she was a health and social student, Geena Mason started evening and weekend work as a baby sitter for friends and relatives. Awareness of her service spread by word of mouth. She built up a good reputation in the area in which she lives and has a small number of regular customers. Having achieved the health and social care qualification and a qualification in childcare, Geena decided that she liked the baby sitting work and that she would like to do it as a job. Based on the hours she had being doing though informal means she thought that she could do it full time as a business if she offered a professional babysitting service. Geena produced the table below to show the marketing mix and other factors that might influence customers.

	My business Teddy Bear Child Care.	Competitor 1 Mrs Jones, child minder.	Competitor 2 Smiths Child Minding Agency.	Competitor 3 Relatives.
Product	First class, professional baby sitting service.	Registered childminder who offers some baby sitting in the evenings.	Baby sitting and child minding.	Baby sitting and family support.
Price	• £5 per hour from 8.00 to midnight weekdays. • £6.00 per hour from 8.00 to midnight weekends. • £10.00 per hour after midnight any night.	• £5.00 per hour 9.00-17.30. • Ad-hoc pricing during weekends and evenings.	• £6.00 per child per hour.	• Often free. • Sometimes a low token charge, like pocket money.
Place	• I will travel to customers' homes within 10 mile radius of where I live. • I use my own transport.	• Has no transport so can only operate within walking distance of her home. • Unless parents deliver and collect children from her home.	• Has a network of baby sitters to whom they subcontract the work so can operate over a wide area.	• Based at home of child/parent.
Promotion	• Posters in doctors' surgeries. • Business cards handed to customers and any parents that I meet. • Word of mouth by existing customers.	• Word of mouth only.	• Small advertisement in local newspaper.	• None.
USPs	• Professionally qualified.	• Has a mother's experience.	• Provides service any time, anywhere.	• Already in the family and on the spot. • Always available.

	My business Teddy Bear Child Care.	Competitor 1 Mrs Jones, child minder.	Competitor 2 Smiths Child Minding Agency.	Competitor 3 Relatives.
Strengths	• Level 3 Child Care. • Level 3 Health & Social Care. • First aid certificate. • Already have a good reputation with existing customers. • Have a small but regular customer list.	• Good reputation locally. • Well known round local schools. • A mother herself so has learned how to deal with children from practical experience.	• No problems with capacity and has lots of people on their books. • Operates over a wide area.	• The commitment that only a member of the family can give.
Weaknesses	• First job. • May not have enough customers to survive. • Could seem expensive compared with free baby sitting done by relatives.	• Not professional. • No professional qualifications. • Treats it as more of a hobby.	• Poor reputation. • Do not always turn up as promised and can let down some customers. • Low commitment from baby sitters as the agency takes a high commission and pays a low rate.	Family issues may make relatives reluctant to keep baby sitting.

'I need to prepare a business plan to raise a loan to pay for a car so that I can keep the business mobile. I also have to pay for the posters and business cards and need some cash as start-up capital to give me something to live on until the business gets started and an income is generated.

I have included this table in my business plan to show the bank manager that I am serious about setting up as a professional baby sitting service which I intend to call Teddy Bear Child Care. The table compares the proposed marketing mix of my business, Teddy Bear Child Care, with those of the main direct competitors. This demonstrates that I am aware that I will not have the market to myself and that I will need to identify positive differences which could be used to market and promote my business. I have also added USPs, plus some strengths and weaknesses. They show that, although there is competition, there are still possibilities for me to make my business successful.

The table also indicates suitable strategies that I might use. For example:
- *product – I would stress the quality of the caring service that would be provided given my qualifications;*
- *price – the pricing structure is flexible and matches or betters local competition with the exception of relatives minding children;*
- *place – I can offer convenience by travelling to customers' homes;*
- *promotion – I will advertise in a number of areas, which targets the market more extensively and effectively than competitors.'*

In summary I would argue that although there are local competitors, some of which have advantages that I do not possess, they do not match the overall quality of the service I am providing, nor my marketing mix which meets customers' needs.

Mark Band 1 Potential idea is selected giving basic reasons for choice and viability, outlining marketing/promotion strategies and identifying competitor information. This would include a justification for the product based on qualifications, an indication of the type of strategies to be used, such as matching or bettering prices, and the number and nature of the competitors.

Mark Band 2 Sound information on business idea will be given, supported by evidence of viability and detailed strategies, with some justification of proposals. Sound information on competitors will also be given. This would include the main reasons why the business will be successful compared to the competition. Details will be given of the strengths of the business compared to the competition and the possible weaknesses. Details will also be given and justified for the approach to the marketing mix, such as the type and reason for price, product, place and promotion strategies.

Mark Band 3 Comprehensive and original ideas will be fully supported and justified and evidence and proposals will be given. Comprehensive and original information on competitors will be given. This would require a justification of all the reasons why the product and business idea has been chosen, an extensive SWOT analysis, including data in the table, and a detailed comparison of the marketing strategies to be used, compared to those of competitors. An overall evaluation of the business against rivals will also be provided.

5 Scale and structure of the business

Business size

Although most businesses start small, the small start often paves the way for development and growth. How fast and how far the business expands is determined by the aims and objectives of the proprietor as much as the opportunities that exist in the market.

When preparing a business plan it is worth giving an indication of how you expect the business to develop. This may be a formal projection based on market research data or it could be based on your own personal aspirations. Personal aspirations, aims and objectives may be sufficient if the business is a sole trader. However, if the business is a partnership there will be two or more sets of aims and objectives, each based on different aspirations of the partners, who may or may not agree. The aims and objectives of stakeholders, such as financial providers or customers may also need to be taken into account.

Measurements of scale

Scale can be measured in a number of ways as shown in Figure 1.

Figure 1 *Measurement of scale*

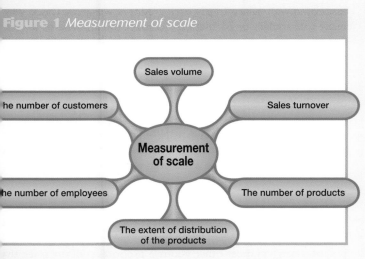

An expansion in any of these will result in a change in the scale of the business. Small changes and fluctuations can usually be coped with without putting too much pressure on the business. If required, additional resources, support and services can usually be drafted in for a short-term solution. At some point the scale of the business could have grown so much that temporary support and services may not be available or may not be able to cope with the additional demand. At this point decisions may have to be made about increasing resources. This could be larger premises or more employees depending on what is required to make sure that the business maintains a good standard of customer service. This decision will have to be fully costed and carefully planned as additional resources will increase the business overheads and will have to be paid for from increased income to maintain profit margins and keep the business viable.

Projecting the scale of a business

It is up to those writing the business plan to forecast the scale of the proposed business, rather than leave it up to the reader of the plan to guess or make their own estimates. This forecast should be based on an assessment of the opportunities in the marketplace, tempered by a realistic appraisal of the experience, skills and resources that will be used by the business team to launch and run the business. The opportunity assessment should be based on solid primary and secondary market research, together with any supporting evidence that can be obtained from potential customers. Notes of interviews with potential customers and promises to buy are all very well, but they remain speculative until a firm order is placed. Even then, nothing is certain until the product has been paid for.

Forecasts should be as realistic as possible. A wise person once said 'if it sounds too good – it probably is'. In this situation, if it sounds too easy to hit a sales target, or to reach a targeted turnover figure, then it probably is. Many people fall into the trap of extrapolating a single sales success into a bigger picture. They assume, usually incorrectly, that if sales for a given period such as one week have been £1,000, then sales for the year will be £52,000, ignoring seasonal factors or the effects of promotion. You need to be very careful when making forecasts and any forecasts made should be supported by hard evidence, or at least be based on certain assumptions, so that anyone reading the plan and its forecast can check the figures.

Supporting any forecasts should be a realistic appraisal of the experience, skills and resources of the business team or the person writing the business plan. This will reassure and add credibility to any forecasts of scale. It would look very optimistic if a person with no business experience produced a plan for a multi-million turnover. It could happen, but it would be a rarity. However, inexperience should not stop you from planning and starting a business. If the idea is good and if the market exists, there is no reason why a business should not be started by someone with enough enthusiasm, which will in many cases more than makes up for cynical experience.

Planning changes to the scale of a business

When planning and forecasting, there may be certain points in the life cycle of the business that will cause a step change to the scale of the business. It may be that for the first two years a business plans to trade in a small, discrete area, say, just one city, and then roll out the business across a larger area of the country until it operates on a national basis. This expansion could be accomplished slowly and gradually, but competitive pressures and customer demands may mean that one week a business is city based and the next customers expect it to be national. If this is the case then the change in scale needs careful planning to keep up with demand, so that customers are not let down and the business does not over-stretched any of the resources. It will be far better for a business to plan any changes in scale and to carry them out when it is certain that resources are in place, rather than be forced into changes by pressure from the market. Changes in scale can affect many different aspects of a business. Some examples are shown in Figure 2. Figure 3 shows how a businesses has changed as it has expanded.

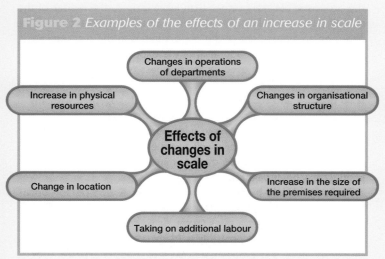

Figure 2 *Examples of the effects of an increase in scale*

Figure 2 *Changes in scale*

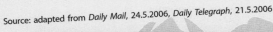

In 2006 Marks & Spencer was 'booming'. It unveiled a 35% increase in profits of £751.4 million. Food and women's clothing in particular showed spectacular improvements. This was helped largely by successful advertising campaigns featuring Twiggy and the use of the 'Your M&S' catchline. As a result the company aimed to continue the modernisation of its 307 stores and the opening of more Simply Food outlets and roll out hot food take away outlets under its Go Deli brand. It also aimed to expand in Asia and Europe and as part of this strategy it planned to open new buying offices in Delhi and Shanghai as part of the drive to increase efficiency. This would allow M&S to increase the volume of goods that it sourced directly from overseas suppliers.

Source: adapted from *Daily Mail*, 24.5.2006, *Daily Telegraph*, 21.5.2006

Scale and risk

As a business grows in scale, some of the risks associated with running a business grow also.

Marketing risks If a small company supplying a local market introduces a new product that does not sell, the risk is likely to cost less than a major national organisation that launches a product that fails, although in terms of relative importance the failure could still hit the small company very hard. A small business advertising locally may risk losing a few hundred pounds if the advertising campaign does not work. A large, national advertiser, however, would stand to lose many thousands of pounds.

Security risks Scale also has a security risk. For example, the wage bill for a business employing three people will be much less than a business with three hundred employees. This means that there is greater scope for theft of the payroll and for fraud. Opening new branches will mean more places need to be kept secure.

Financial risk There may also be a personal risk associated with expansion. A sole trader and businesses in traditional partnership have a personal liability for the debts of the business. As a business expands, the scale of its commitments is also likely to grow. For example, it may need to hold higher stocks, with the consequent higher cost and higher value. Advertising and other promotional expenditure could grow. As credit increases so the personal risk associated with failure to pay back creditors will grow. This is why many sole traders or partnerships convert the business to a limited company when they reach a certain size, when the personal financial risk becomes too great a threat to their home and personal life.

When reading a business plan most potential stakeholders, especially those expected to invest money in the business, will be interested in the proposed scale of the business. This will help them to check that the plan is within the capabilities of the person proposing to run the business and to gauge some idea of the scale of financial risk that may be associated with the plan.

VAT implications of scale

Value added tax, VAT, is applied to most goods and services bought and sold in the UK. When you buy a computer, a cinema ticket, a pair of shoes and most other goods, a proportion of the price that you pay is VAT. Similarly with services, transport, delivery and building, VAT will have been applied. HM Revenue & Customs states, 'VAT is a tax on the final consumption of certain goods and services. VAT is a tax on consumer expenditure. It is collected on business transactions, imports and acquisitions.'

A business that reaches the turnover limit for VAT registration set by HM Revenue & Customs is legally obliged to charge VAT on the goods and services that it may sell, where VAT is applied, no matter who or what the customer. In 2006 the standard VAT rate was 17.5% and the limit for registration was £61,000, a figure which has increased each year. Depending on the scale of the business and the forecast growth, it may not take long to reach this limit. Conversely, many small businesses manage to trade profitably under the VAT limit.

For most established businesses charging, collecting and paying

VAT is not a problem. It will have become an automatic part of the financial system within the organisation. However, if competitors have a turnover below the VAT registration threshold, but a business has a turnover taking it over that threshold, it may face a situation where its prices are uncompetitive. It will need to add VAT, whereas competitors will not. This situation is common amongst small, service-based businesses that provide a local service for customers with only a small discretionary income, such as painters, decorators and gardeners. The addition of 17.5% VAT to prices will soon be noticed by customers in this type of market.

It is illegal to avoid charging or paying VAT, where applicable, no matter what the circumstances. Faced with the requirement to register for VAT, and the prospect of becoming uncompetitive, a business has few choices – to charge the VAT and cover the price increase with increased added value, absorb the VAT and lose margin, or hold the price and margin by making savings.

Full details on VAT can be found at http://customs.hmrc.gov.uk/.

Meeting the assessment criteria - examiners' guidance

Each section of this unit deals with a particular aspect of the business plan. The following shows an example of the type of information that could be included in a business plan about the scale of operation of the business.

Business example - Party Gift Bags

Lesley Leonard has started a business, based on producing and selling ready-made, party bags for children's parties. Her business idea is to take the pressure off busy parents that make all the arrangements for the party by producing her ready-made bags filled with gifts and activities. The precise content of the bags will be decided by Lesley, depending on how much the parents want to pay for each bag.

This is an extract from Lesley's business plan.

Year 1
Projected sales, £15,000, gross profit £10,000, Net profit £5,000
Working from home, plan to provide party bags in the town where I live. By limiting my operation to this single town I should be able to confirm if there is a market for my products and a viable business opportunity, without risking too much. I have been left sufficient money in a grandparent's will to cover my living costs for one year so even if the business does not succeed I should be able to survive.

'I have been very careful not to over-forecast my performance in year 1. At this stage the business will be run from home. I will live on an inheritance until the business produces sufficient profit to pay my wages.'

Year 2
Projected sales, £25,000, gross profit £16,666, Net profit £8,333
I plan to continue working from home throughout this year but aim to expand my area of operating into the nearest town. This should be possible as it is only 10 miles away and the local newspaper that I plan to use for advertising circulates there also.

'Year 2 shows a proposed increase in sales based on careful local expansion – nothing too drastic. Although gross profit as a percentage of sales has remained the same as in year 1, the increased turnover generates a greater amount of profit.'

Year 3
Projected sales, £50,000 gross profit £33,000, Net profit £3,000
This year I plan to operate across the whole of the county in which I live. This should expand my market considerably.

However, it will mean that I will need to move from home to run the business from a factory unit. The lease will cost me £20,000 which will affect my net profit severely. Once established, I should be able to build the business and expand in the future. Despite this expansion I intend to remain a sole trader.

'Year 3 is the year of change. I plan to expand the operation greatly. This should increase the potential market and consequent demand for party bags. This increase will necessitate moving into larger, purpose built factory premises for storing stock and raw materials. Consequently, this planned expansion will hit cash flow and profit for this year, but this should increase in future years.'

'I have presented my forecast for the first three years of trading in such a way that anyone reading the business plan will see that I have justified all of my forecasts and assumptions. However, anyone doing a critical reading of this part of the business plan may ask for additional supporting evidence for the sales projections. This would include a comprehensive breakdown of the sales and marketing support that would be given to make sure that it grew as forecast. This may include a list of potential customers or at least further information about why expanding my geographic area of operation will automatically result in additional sales. This will be presented in another part of the plan.

Mark Band 1 Resource requirements and quality issues are dealt with here at a basic level. This would simply state the effect on resources of staying at the same size and possible effects of growth.

Mark Band 2 Resource requirements soundly presented with examples and application. This would include an analysis of the effects on the business of remaining the same, with examples, and the effects of growth. It would include financial issues, such as where the money will come from in the initial period (the inheritance), the fact that profit will fall as a result of the lease payment, as well as other issues, such as the need to move premises and the changes in stock required.

Mark Band 3 Resource requirements comprehensively presented with supported detailed evidence. This would provide a detailed analysis of the position of the business in years 1, 2 and 3, as it grows. It would include a financial analysis of the effect on profits, cash flow and the assets and liabilities of the business, with detail shown in another part of the business plan. It would also include an evaluation of the overall effect of growth on changes in resources, premises, organisation and strategy.

6 Resource requirements

Resources

In addition to describing the business idea and indicating the scale and scope of the proposed business, a business plan also needs to outline the resources required at various stages in the life cycle of the business. A resource is anything that is required to start-up and run the business. For planning and management, resources are usually grouped together as shown in Figure 1.

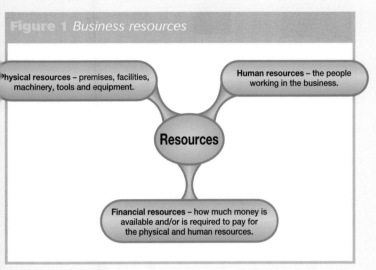

Figure 1 *Business resources*

Physical resources – premises, facilities, machinery, tools and equipment.

Human resources – the people working in the business.

Resources

Financial resources – how much money is available and/or is required to pay for the physical and human resources.

When planning resource requirements it is also worth identifying the suppliers of materials, products and the range of services that the business will need, as these will all have an impact on the financial resources and the way that physical and human resources are utilised.

Resource planning starts with forecasting requirements, moves to specification, and then to decisions about acquisition. Planning will also need to take into account the change in resource requirements at different stages in the life cycle of the business and for different size businesses. Resources required for start-up may be quite different from the resource requirements for a business that has been up and running for a number of years. A sole trader who aims to keep the business small will have different resource requirements to someone who aims to expand their business.

Physical resources

Physical resources can take different forms.

Location, premises and facilities The starting point for physical resources is – where are you going to work from and where will the business be located? Many small businesses start out being run from home. This is fine, so long as there is sufficient space and the space is suitable for running the business safely. Space requirements will be based on another physical resource – the equipment that will be used by the business and the space that is required to house and use the equipment. If the only physical

resources are a PC, printer and scanner, then it would be relatively easy to set up in a spare room at home. If the physical resources include tanks of liquid, a mixing machine, a bottle filling line and space to store the finished products, then it may be essential that the business is located in a purpose-built factory unit. Sometimes this aspect of physical resources in an industrial setting may be referred to as 'plant', as in power plant or a production plant.

Deciding where to locate the business and the type and size of premises required will depend, mainly, on what the business does, as explained in the previous example. Facilities available at the premises are another factor that depends on the type of business. For example, a physiotherapist may need a waiting room and shower facilities for customers, but a manufacturer may need production and storage facilities. There is also the cost. Working from home is likely to be attractive from a cost point of view. You already have the premises, you know how much it costs to live there and, by not having to pay for additional premises to work from, overheads will be kept down. As soon as you agree to move in to an office, a shop or factory unit, the overhead costs will shoot up and will need to be funded by additional sales and profit. Location will also be influenced by local government restrictions. For example, land can be designated as residential or commercial space, which can influence the building of new premises.

Before deciding on where to locate the business, a SWOT analysis may help. You can consider the Strengths, Weaknesses, Opportunities and Threats of a location, from your own point of view as the person running the business. Then do SWOT from the point of view of customers and see what, if anything, changes. It may be that your home is a great place to work from for you, but it could be a unsuitable if others are employed or if you expect customers to visit your workplace. You must also consider personal safety and security. Although you may be working from home you will still have responsibilities under the **Health & Safety at Work Act**. Working from home can also appear amateurish and may give the completely wrong impression to customers. In this instance, these SWOTs will almost be risk assessments of working from home compared with working from designated premises. Even simpler would be to list the advantages and disadvantages of different premises or locations to help with decision making.

Machinery, tools and equipment These are other physical resources that may be required. Depending on the type of business, these physical resources may range from office machinery and equipment to specialised machinery necessary for production, printing or packaging. Tools to perform the job or service are another type of physical resource. Forecasting and planning resource requirements will be based on the type of business, its products or outputs and the scale of the business. Transport would be another physical resource. Some uses of transport by businesses are shown in Table 1.

A vehicle could be much more than just transport. For example,

Table 1 *Reasons for transport*

Use	Businesses or employees
For deliveries to customers	Printer, component manufacturer, shop
Carry customers	Taxi firm
To carry out the job	Sales representative
Market research	Researcher
Transport and storage of equipment	Plumber, electrician, painter and decorator

Figure 2 *Materials, stocks and services*

Materials
Raw materials or components needed for manufacturing.

Stocks
Products that have been manufactured, a supply of goods to sell or resell or consumables such as paper or ink cartridges.

Services
Electricity, gas, water, telephones, mobile phones, specialist skills, IT repair or maintenance services, banking, accountancy, legal services, design, printing or publicity.

a car could affect the image of a business. A new car might indicate success and pride in the quality of presentation, whereas an old or dirty vehicle might suggest that the business was failing. Some vehicles could be used to promote the business, for example a van with full contact details of the business could act as a mobile poster. A business must consider what it needs, how the vehicle will be used, and how much it could earn or lose by not having transport before making a decision. Again, a SWOT analysis and lists of advantages and disadvantages could be used.

Materials, stocks and services Linked closely to physical resources are the materials, stocks and services required by a business. Examples are shown in Figure 2. With business services there is a crossover between physical resources and human resources, as most services will be performed by a human being.

In addition to planning how necessary and how many of these resources will be needed, the business must establish where these materials and services are to come from. This is a **sourcing** exercise based on criteria such as quality, price, availability and lead times.

Human resources

These are the people working in the business and for the business. Depending on the size and scale of the business, this could range from one person working alone as a sole trader, through to medium sized businesses that employ a small number of people or hire in specialist staff and service providers when necessary, to large organisations that employ tens, hundreds, even thousands of people.

Human resources need careful planning like all resources. Unlike physical resources, however, employees have rights under employment legislation and require a safe working environment, as well as being expected to observe good practice under health and safety legislation themselves.

Human resources are frequently cited as the greatest cost for a business for certain reasons, including the following.
- They need to be paid a wage, ranging from the legal minimum to the market rate for the job, a direct cost taken from profit.
- Human resources lead to indirect costs, such as National Insurance contributions, pension contributions, sick pay, holiday pay, and other costs associated with worker's rights legislation.
- Depending on the size of the human resources employed an employer may also need to provide facilities, such as toilets, a restroom or catering facilities.
- Depending on the labour market situation, availability and the market pay rate, and the particular skills that are required by an employer, human resources may attract other costs, which take the form of employee benefits.
- Employee benefits may need to be paid, such as private medical cover, additional pension contributions, membership of gyms or sports clubs, and other privileges that are only available to employees.

This means that acquiring human resources is a big decision. Every employee taken on will have to be justified in terms of increased sales turnover and income to pay for the employee.

In addition to the financial cost of employing people, there are other effects that human resources have on a business. Each employee should be aware that they have certain responsibilities. The basic responsibility is for health and safety, making sure that the work place is safe for themselves and others. There is the responsibility to meet the terms and conditions in their contract of employment, such as adhering to start times and hours of work. There is a corporate responsibility, as employees represent the business and how they are perceived by customers and suppliers can have an effect on the image and reputation of the business.

Planning human resources will be based on forecasting requirements at different stages in the life cycle of the business and changes as a result of increased or decreased demand from customers. This will be based on skill requirements and the numbers of employees that have those skills. For example, a small IT service provider may need a small number of highly trained staff. However, a distribution warehouse or a fruit farm may need a high number of unskilled staff, or at least staff having a different set of skills to those required for an IT service. Human resources planning is covered in detail in unit 9.

Financial resources

This is the money that is in business or the money that will be required to start-up and run the business. Most start-ups will usually have money, such as savings, that is available to invest to get the business up and running until it becomes viable to the point that it is generating sufficient income and profit to pay for wages. However, it is common for a start-up, and as well as businesses at other stages in the life cycle, to need additional financial resources. This may be for expansion, for the purchase of premises, machinery or equipment, or for some other project linked to the business that is beyond the financial resources that are available directly. Sections 7 and 32 have information about different sources of finance.

Perhaps the most pressing financial resource requirement for businesses is **working capital** (see section 33). This is money that is readily available to pay for the day-to-day bills associated with running the business, such as paying wages or buying materials. This may come from cash inflow, the money that comes into the business. But sometimes it may be necessary to seek additional finance for working capital. For example, a business needs to buy raw materials to cope with a sudden upturn in demand. Additional working capital could be made available via an overdraft facility at the bank, but this comes with a cost. Savings built up from profits generated by the business could be used. If this is not available, the business may need outside finance from a bank, investor or other stakeholder.

Financial resource requirements over and above working capital will need to be forecast, planned, and costed carefully, based on the overall plans and objectives for the business.

Resource planning

Resource planning is essential for the efficient and effective running of the business. Getting resource requirements wrong could make running the business difficult. Examples might be:

- being in the wrong premises;
- not having sufficient staff to meet customer needs;
- paying for 1,000 square metres of office space when you only need 100 square metres;
- buying and holding stock that will last for one year at current rate of sale rather than working on a 'just-in-time' system;
- employing five people when the sales only justify one person.

Resource planning should cover the basic stages in the life cycle of the business, based on the overall objectives in the business plan as shown in Figure 3.

Figure 3 *Resources planning over the life cycle of a business*

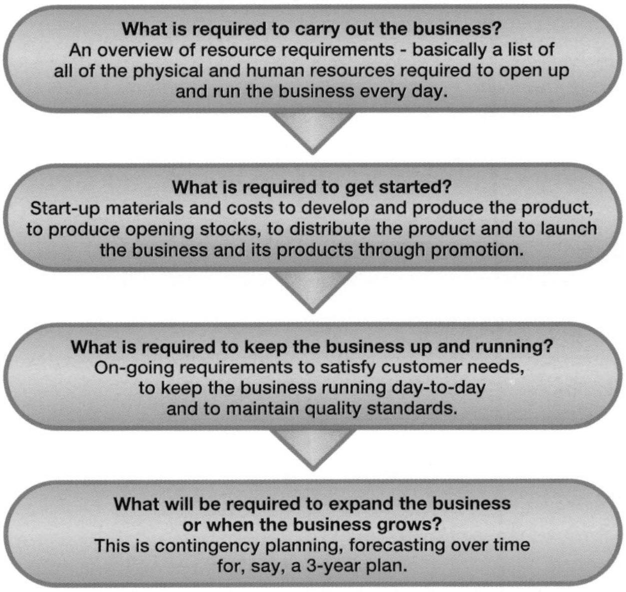

What is required to carry out the business?
An overview of resource requirements - basically a list of all of the physical and human resources required to open up and run the business every day.

What is required to get started?
Start-up materials and costs to develop and produce the product, to produce opening stocks, to distribute the product and to launch the business and its products through promotion.

What is required to keep the business up and running?
On-going requirements to satisfy customer needs, to keep the business running day-to-day and to maintain quality standards.

What will be required to expand the business or when the business grows?
This is contingency planning, forecasting over time for, say, a 3-year plan.

Considerations to take into account when planning resource requirements include:

- how necessary – does the business really need a new car? Do we need to advertise in that magazine? Do we need a year's supply of ink cartridges for the printer?
- how much or how often – should the business hold large quantities of stock, or should it operate on just-in-time deliveries from suppliers? Is this resource likely to be used every day, or will it only be used one a month?
- allocation – where should the financial resources be allocated, how should they be spread across the different needs of the business? Is it more important to spend money on improving deliveries or on improving production?
- prioritisation - what is the most important and the most immediate need for the business? What is required first to meet customer needs and what could be left until later? What can be afforded now, what will have to be left until finances improve and how will this affect the business?
- what is the best form of acquisition - buying, renting, hiring or leasing?
- which type - human resource or physical resource – man or machine? Which is the most useful? Which will be the most cost-effective?

- when will the resource be required – immediately, in the future, at start-up or when running the business?
- costs – what will all of the resources cost in the short term, on-going running costs, and in the long-term?
- timing – when will the resources be required? Immediately? In the future? All of the time? Only occasionally?

Acquiring resources

As with any acquisition there will be a number of options to consider, the main ones being outright purchase or renting, hiring or leasing options. When developing the business plan you will need to research and consider the advantages and disadvantages of these options. They are shown in Table 2.

The two options in Table 2 may seem to apply exclusively to physical resources, but they have their equivalents in human resources – taking on permanent staff and taking on staff, or acquiring the skills, under a temporary arrangement. These are shown in Table 3.

Including a section on resources in a business plan is vital. It demonstrates to potential stakeholders that you have considered the scale and the scope of the business and forecast your needs,

Table 2 *Acquiring resources*

Outright purchase	
Advantages	Disadvantages
<ul><li>You will own the resource.</li><li>It will be an asset of the business.</li><li>You can do what you want with it.</li><li>You could hire it to other businesses when not in use, to raise additional money.</li><li>You can sell it to raise money in the future.</li></ul>	<ul><li>May have a high initial cost.</li><li>Could hit cash flow badly.</li><li>Could land the business in debt.</li><li>May have high maintenance costs.</li><li>It could become a limiting factor to the development of the business.</li><li>It could go out of date or become obsolete (a feature of technical resources).</li><li>Replacement or updating could be costly.</li></ul>

Renting, hiring and leasing options	
Advantages	Disadvantages
<ul><li>No large capital cost.</li><li>Cost is spread over low regular payments, helps cash flow.</li><li>Usually competitively priced.</li><li>Can be replaced and updated easily, with no capital cost.</li><li>Resource will be maintained by actual owner/hiring or leasing organisation.</li></ul>	<ul><li>You will not own it.</li><li>It will not become an asset of the business.</li><li>Failure to pay could result in resource being taken away.</li></ul>

Table 3 *Advantages and disadvantages of permanent and temporary staff*

Permanent staff	
Advantages	Disadvantages
<ul><li>Always available to the business (based on contract of employment).</li><li>Can build up loyalty and a team spirit.</li><li>Will become known by customers.</li><li>Can act as good ambassadors for the business.</li><li>Can develop some commitment to the business.</li></ul>	<ul><li>Wage becomes a fixed overhead.</li><li>Additional indirect costs start to add up – National Insurance, pension and employee rights.</li><li>Difficult to get rid of if business takes a downturn or if dissatisfied with performance.</li><li>May require management skills that are not within the business.</li></ul>

Temporary arrangement	
Advantages	Disadvantages
<ul><li>Can be hired or released to meet fluctuating demands of the business.</li><li>Can bring specialist skills to the business to meet short-term or project-based needs.</li><li>Will not be a permanent/fixed overhead that needs to be paid for.</li></ul>	<ul><li>Low level of loyalty/commitment to the business.</li><li>Skills may not be available when required, or not available immediately.</li></ul>

based on the overall objectives and plans for the business. It will show whether you will have the right support and business structure is able to run the business and make money. It will also help potential stakeholders get some idea of the financial requirements and the commitment that they may be expected to make towards the business.

Quality and resources

Quality is very important for any business because this is how customers and consumers will ultimately judge the business, its products and its services. It is also one of the most direct ways of comparing competitors. However, there are very few, if any, absolute measures of quality within a business. All quality measures will tend to be relative, measured against standards set internally by the business itself or based on external standards. **Quality control** can involve checking products after manufacture or service provision to make sure that no faults exist. Many businesses today, however, use **quality assurance** procedures designed to identify problems before they occur. This means ensuring quality is taken into account at all stages in the production process, that everyone in the business is responsible and can involve taking into account customers' views in the production stage.

Internal quality standards These will be set by management and all employees will be expected to work to these standards as part of their normal job. On a personal level they could range from the time that employees are expected to start work, through dress codes to the way that employees communicate with customers. On a business level they will tend to relate more closely to the specific products and services of the business.

External quality standards These can take a number of forms.

- Industry standards. These will either be set or established by an organisation that represents an industry, such as the Engineering Council, or the Institute of Grocery Distribution. Alternatively, they could be set by the market leading business in a particular industry or sector, for example Microsoft in IT, Tesco in grocery retailing, Coca-Cola Enterprises Ltd. in soft drinks, News Corporation and News International in publishing. Industry standards are often translated into competitive standards, i.e. the standard to which a business must operate if it wants to be competitive in a particular market.
- British and European quality assurance standards. This would include British Standards Institution (BSI) and International Standards Organisation (ISO) standards for materials, goods, services and management.
- Legal standards. These will be outlined in Acts such as the **Health & Safety at Work Act** and the **Consumer Protection Act**.

Ways of establishing and maintaining quality in a business

Setting clear and consistent standards for products and services, that are recognised and applied by all employees is essential for a business concerned with quality. This can be achieved through the use of published specifications and comparing all production against established standards. This approach will also have an impact on suppliers who will be expected to apply similar quality standards to goods or materials that they provide. In a service industry supplies in the form of associates or sub-contractors will be expected to work to the same standards as set by the business employing them. Having clear and consistent working standards that are recognised and applied by all employees. This can also be achieved through the use of clear specifications, backed up by including a quality requirement in job descriptions.

Working to British and the International standards Most materials, goods and services will have been subjected to BSI assessment, product testing, certification and inspection. The BSI website states that 'BSI Standards exist to make life safer and more efficient and to facilitate trade'. Associated with this are the ISO 9000 series of standards which have been written to help businesses and organisations implement effective quality management systems. Check out http://www.bsi-global.com/News/Information/index.xalter for more information about British Standards and ISO standards.

Benchmarking Businesses often benchmark their operations against those that are considered 'best' in an industry in order to compare themselves. This can help a business to identify quality it is achieving and where it can make improvements.

Some methods may be introduced as businesses grow larger.

Total Quality Management (TQM) This is the application of quality standards to all functions within a business to ensure that 100% of output is at the highest quality. It can be applied by making sure that everyone in the business has clear responsibilities and recognises the responsibilities that they have to customers, both internal and external to the business. TQM is focused on the efficient management of the process of running the business rather than just focusing on products or outputs. The introduction of TQM could include changing working practices, such as using more efficient shift patterns, flexitime, moving to team working or the introduction of regular training sessions for employees. TQM could be extended to suppliers. For example, the introduction of just-in-time inventory control linked to just-in-time manufacturing is usually done to improve efficiency in a business. In addition, this tighter management of supplies and resources may also have a positive effect on quality.

Quality circles This is the use of multifunction teams, drawn from all levels of employees, who meet regularly to discuss quality, health and safety, and any other issues that could affect the quality of output from the business. Quality circles are encouraged to come up with new ideas and solutions to any quality problems that are raised.

Measuring and monitoring quality

Having set quality standards it is up to the business to measure and monitor quality standards to make sure that standards do not slip and that quality is not eroded. This can be done in a number of ways, including the following.

- Customer research, such as the use of customer feedback forms, or telephoning customers to ask them about the quality of goods or service that they received. More formally, an independent market research agency could be employed to interview and gather data and opinions on quality from customers. Mystery shoppers are often employed to gather information about the quality of service that they receive from a business.
- Statistical sampling. This involves looking at a representative sample of goods drawn from normal production and comparing them with a previously set quality standard and checking that they conform to the specification and standards set.

The cost of quality

Everything comes at a cost and quality is no exception. Higher quality materials, goods and services tend to be more expensive than lower quality equivalents and a business must decide how much quality is worth. As a business improves quality, overheads can increase as higher cost resources are employed. Can this cost be absorbed in the business overheads, is the profit sufficient to pay for an increase in the works cost created by the cost of increasing quality or will the price have to be increased to maintain the profit margin, will customers be prepared to pay more for a higher quality product? These are not always easy questions to answer, but if a business is serious about setting and maintaining quality standards then the cost of achieving quality is a cost that it must pay.

Each section of this unit deals with a particular aspect of the business plan. The following shows an example of the type of information that could be included in a business plan about the resource and quality requirements of the business.

Business example - Mistry Games

Sunil Mistry has put together a business plan based on his idea for running a business based on renting out computer games. He plans to operate from home, marketing the business to students at the schools and colleges in the town where he lives. As part of his business plan Sunil has outlined his resource and quality requirements.

Physical and financial resources

Resource required	Start-up costs	Running costs year 1
PC – to manage the customer database – to manage rentals – to run my accounts	£500 (includes processor box, monitor and keyboard)	Electricity, included in overheads for house Estimate service once a year at a cost of £100
All-in-one printer, scanner, copier	£100	Ink cartridges Black 1 every month @ £18.99 each Colour 1 every three months @ £19.99 each Total for year = £307.84
Wireless network system	£60	Electricity, included in overheads for house
Broadband	Installation of connection, £50	£15.99 per month = £191.88 for year
Internet security software	£34.99	None
Microsoft Office Small Business Edition	£215.97	None
Secure filing cabinet to store computer games when not out for rental	£114.99	None
Games for rental	Two copies of each game in Top 10, £400.00	Two copies of each new game to enter Top 10 throughout year, estimated at £500.00
Total	£1,475.95	£1,099.72

Human resources

I have no plans to take on any employees. If I need skilled help to sort out any IT problems I will pay a local specialist at the going rate, currently £75.00 for first hour, £50.00 per hour thereafter.

I have estimated the start-up cost based on the current purchase price from high street retailers. The running cost for year 1 is estimated, apart from the cost of broadband, which will be the same per month as I am currently paying.

I have guessed at the consumption of ink cartridges, as I do not really have any idea how many I will be using.

'The table over provides a simple business plan showing my resource requirements. Greater detail showing, for example, a comprehensive breakdown of how the resources will contribute to the running of the business, full costs and financial projections for the business, will be shown in financial statements in other parts of the business plan. As the business develops I will need additional resources, such as dedicated customer relationship software. Developments such as this would be included in later years of a 3-year forecast.

Looking critically at this part of the business plan, I wonder whether two copies are enough for a really popular game. It could restrict the business if I had loaned out both copies and started to lose business because customers requested the game and there were no further copies to lend. A solution is to buy more copies but I must be aware that this would increase costs and I could be left with a lot of obsolete games if I am not careful. Also there is no reference here to insurance. Working from home I had assumed the business would be covered automatically by the household contents insurance. This may not be the case and so I have decided to contact my insurance company and explain the situation. This could result in additional premiums or insurance dedicated to the business. However, this would mean that any claims made against the insurance would be more likely to be honoured as the insurance company has been kept informed, has estimated the risk and made any covering charges as appropriate.

I must also carry out further research into the need for financial resources to pay for any fees, charges or licences required for this type of business. These would need to be built into any calculations of profit shown in other parts of the business plan.'

Mark Band 1 Resource requirements are dealt with here at a basic level. It might include parts of the table with some simple comments about the type of resources used and their quality. Simple evaluation would be given on whether the resources and quality are satisfactory.

Mark Band 2 Resource requirements soundly presented with examples and application. This would show all the details in the table, with comments on their need in the business. It would be supported by other parts of the plan, which would show detailed costings of resources and forecasts. Any constraints would be outlined. The plan might also include some comments on how the business proposes to ensure quality in its service and evaluate how resources and quality are managed.

Mark Band 3 Resource requirements comprehensively presented with supported detailed evidence. This would take each part of the table above and justify exactly why the resources are required. Detailed support would be provided of costings and financial plans this year and in future and any legal and technical constraints would be identified. The methods of quality control and assurance that the business will attempt will be explained. There would also be some attempt to critically evaluate the plan, making improvements, and suggesting how this could provide efficient management of resources.

Sources of finance and the start-up budget

Finance and the business plan

One of the most important parts of the business plan is the section outlining the financial requirements of the proposed business idea. What might this involve?

- Calculating the amount of money needed to set up the business. This is the money needed to buy essential resources so that the business can begin to operate.
- Calculating the working capital requirements of the business. This is the money needed to fund day-to-day business activity in a future time period.
- Identifying the different sources of finance that the business proposes to use.
- Preparing a start-up budget. This shows how the money raised will be spent when setting up the business.
- Preparing a cash flow forecast statement. This shows the planned inflows and outflows of cash for a future time period – usually twelve months.
- Calculating the break-even level of output.
- Preparing a projected profit and loss account and a balance sheet for the first year of trading. Accounts for the first three years of trading may be prepared to show how the business might look in the future.

Sources of finance

Raising money to start a business is often very difficult. Money lenders are likely to be very cautious when approached by entrepreneurs with requests for start-up capital. This is particularly the case when people are setting up a business for the first time. However, there is a range of possible sources that may be considered. They are summarised in Figure 1 – both long-term and short-term sources are included.

Choosing appropriate finance

Entrepreneurs are likely to consider a number of factors when choosing between different sources of finance. A brief summary is provided below and a more detailed account is given in section 32.

Cost When raising money costs are incurred. For example, money borrowed from a bank incurs an interest charge. Other costs may be administration, promotion and legal fees. Entrepreneurs will prefer those sources of finance which cost the least.

Legal status Many new businesses start life as a sole trader or partnership. These tend to be small and have a limited choice of finance sources. They are likely to rely on mortgages, personal capital and bank overdrafts for their needs. Companies have a wider selection to choose from, for example shares. As businesses grow in size they are likely to find it a lot easier to raise finance. Money lenders feel more secure when lending money to established businesses with a proven record and a documented trading history. Such businesses are also likely to get better terms when borrowing money because they are less of a risk.

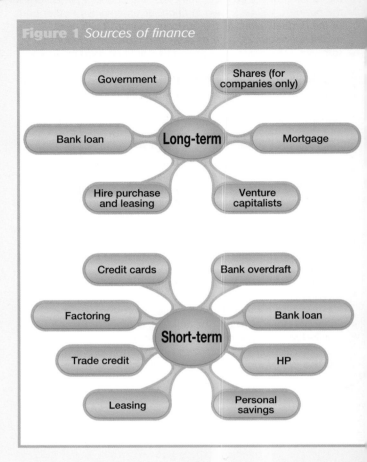

Figure 1 *Sources of finance*

Use of funds Generally, short-term sources are used to fund revenue expenditure. For example, a bank overdraft may be used to pay for raw materials and utility bills. On the other hand long-term sources are preferred when funding capital expenditure. For example, a mortgage is likely to be used to pay for business premises and expensive plant and machinery. However, in recent years a number of financial experts have suggested that a lot of businesses are undercapitalised and that business owners should raise more long term and permanent capital. This would help to avoid cash crises and may be more cost-effective since long-term sources are often cheaper.

Control Sometimes business owners can raise money if they are prepared to share control. For example, a sole trader may decide to take on a partner. The new partner will provide some fresh capital, but will also take a share of the profit and may participate in decision making. Business angels and other venture capitalists may also provide funding in exchange for a stake in the business. Generally, businesses can often raise more money if they are prepared to relinquish some control.

An example of the sources of finance used by a new business is shown in Figure 2. Mayate was able to get a £10,000 bank loan because she produced a comprehensive business plan and was

Figure 2 *Appropriate sources of finance for a new business*

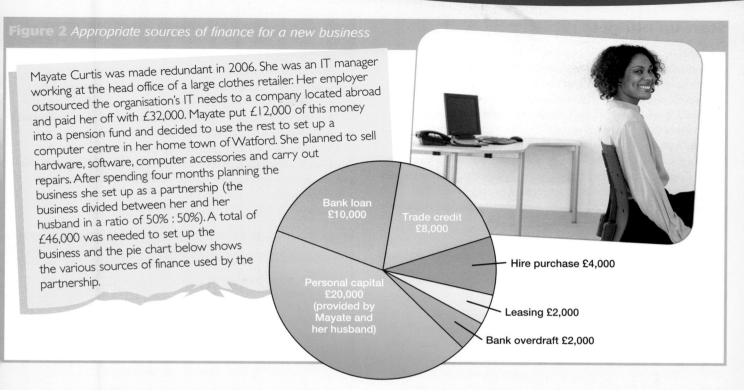

Mayate Curtis was made redundant in 2006. She was an IT manager working at the head office of a large clothes retailer. Her employer outsourced the organisation's IT needs to a company located abroad and paid her off with £32,000. Mayate put £12,000 of this money into a pension fund and decided to use the rest to set up a computer centre in her home town of Watford. She planned to sell hardware, software, computer accessories and carry out repairs. After spending four months planning the business she set up as a partnership (the business divided between her and her husband in a ratio of 50% : 50%). A total of £46,000 was needed to set up the business and the pie chart below shows the various sources of finance used by the partnership.

Bank loan £10,000

Trade credit £8,000

Hire purchase £4,000

Leasing £2,000

Bank overdraft £2,000

Personal capital £20,000 (provided by Mayate and her husband)

Figure 3 *Source of finance for Brand Xposure*

[B]rand Xposure was set up by Sarah Sayed and Tessa Meade. They [w]anted to develop a promotional merchandise company creating [c]ustom-made, unique promotional materials. They began trading in [2]001 in a unit in the Bon Marché centre in Brixton. However, even [t]hough their business idea showed a great deal of promise Sarah [a]nd Tessa struggled to raise the necessary start-up capital. Various [m]ajor banks turned them down on the basis that they didn't have a credit history.

Eventually they got support from Business Link for London and its local provider in the area, oneLondon. They placed Sarah and Tessa on a one-day course on setting up a business. This introduced them to a business adviser, who gave them finance, business planning and marketing advice, as well as details of the oneLondon loan fund. The loan fund panel was impressed with Brand Xposure's suggestions, commitment and dedication to the business idea, and awarded them a loan of £3,000 in April 2002. This was a big relief for Sarah and Tessa, who had so far struggled to convince every financial institution they had seen to take their business seriously. 'One bank manager even asked us who had written the proposal, doubtful that we had written it ourselves,' says Sarah. 'Although all of the bank adverts make it sound easy to get funds and open bank accounts, we did not find this the case. No one would give us an overdraft facility for a relatively small amount of money and to actually get our account up and running took three months.'

A year later, the business now nets an income of over £100,000 and Brand Xposure is already looking to expand to bigger premises. Both Sarah and Tessa love running their own business and are grateful to oneLondon for helping them through the tough times.

Source adapted from www.gle.co.uk.

able to convince the manager that her business idea and aims were viable. The manager was also impressed with her knowledge of the market and products. £15,000 was needed to decorate and fit out some premises in a retail park near Watford. About £20,000 was invested in stock of which £8,000 was funded by trade credit. Mayate hoped to buy all stock on trade credit in the future once she had an established trading record. A van was purchased for £4,000 using hire purchase and some equipment was leased. The bank overdraft provided some extra working capital in case sales were below expectations at the beginning. The sources of finance used by Mayate are highly appropriate. She has used long-term sources to buy fixed assets and short-term sources (where possible) to fund revenue expenditure.

Difficulties raising start-up capital

One of the most difficult tasks when setting up a business is raising sufficient capital to buy the resources needed to start trading. An example highlighting this problem is outlined in Figure 3.

The importance of the business plan when raising finance

Entrepreneurs are not likely to attract funding unless they can produce a well written and professionally presented business plan. They are not likely to be taken seriously if they cannot provide documented proof of careful thought and planning. Figure 4 shows an extract from the website of a business advisory service which outlines the importance of the business plan when raising finance.

Start-up budget

A budget is a plan which shows the different items of income and expenditure for a future time period. Budgets are usually presented on spreadsheets and show items of expenditure and income in columns. Each column usually represents one month or perhaps a week. The start-up budget will focus on planned expenditure for the period up until trading begins. Income is not likely to feature in the start-up budget because trading will not have begun. One of the benefits of producing a start-up budget is that it helps to calculate the amount of money that a business will need to set up. It will also help to identify exactly when the money will be needed. An example of a start-up budget is shown in Figure 5.

Figure 4 *The importance of the business plan when raising finance*

No business plan (BP), no finance. Poor BP, no finance. Unrealistic BP, no finance. Naive BP, no finance. Your BP says, 'this is what I know about my business, myself and my future'. When looking at BP's the financier is sometimes quoted as saying, "I use the '50% rule'. I take 50% off the projected income, and add 50% to the projected costs, and if the BP still stands up it has passed the first stage".

So, if you have any doubt about your ability to write a targeted BP that is a working blue print for your enterprise, pay someone to do it. There are probably more people per capita who know how to write a BP than at any other time: the Internet entrepreneur being responsible. This does mean that £500 can get you a 'professional' BP. The key to choosing who will get your £500 is in how many questions you are asked: the more questions asked the more targeted the BP will be.

Source: www.bizhelp24.

Working capital requirements

Working capital is the money a business needs to trade with. It is the money needed to meet revenue expenditure and is the difference between current assets and current liabilities. When a business first starts trading working capital requirements can be quite demanding. This is because the business is not yet established and revenue is likely to be relatively low and patchy. Day-to-day trading costs such as rent, utility bills, wages and stock will continue to be incurred so money is needed to cover them. If a business does not have enough working capital it will struggle to survive. Therefore when setting up it is important to make sure that careful thought goes into calculating the businesses working capital requirements.

In the example shown in Figure 5, Paul and Irene Simmons need a minimum of £12,200 to set up their online business. However, they will also need a further amount of money for their working capital. It may actually be quite difficult to estimate the precise needs of the business. It will obviously depend on unknown factors such as early sales levels. It will also depend on whether sales are for cash and whether the business can get trade credit. However, it is important to include in the business plan such an estimate. Some business advisers would suggest that working capital needs should be provided from start-up capital. This may avoid undercapitalisation. However, in practice a lot of businesses begin trading by using a bank overdraft to contribute towards working capital. One of the advantages of a bank overdraft is flexibility. This will help overcome the problem of estimating the precise amount of working capital needed. Working capital is explained in detail in section 34.

Figure 5 *Start-up budget for Biker Gear*

Biker Gear is being set up by a couple who have decided to extend their mutual passion in motorcycles to a business interest. Paul and Irene Simmons are going to sell motorcycle accessories online. They have spent six months planning the business with the help of a local business adviser. They plan to buy motorcycle accessories such as rain suits, helmets, helmet bags, cycle alarms, chain wax, sprocket kits, battery chargers, panniers, tank bags, lubricants, specialist magazines and heated handlebar grips. Stock will be purchased from a range of manufacturers and stored in a lock-up garage which they plan to rent and orders will be taken on their website. Their adviser encouraged them to produce the start-up budget which is shown below. The budget is for a four month period and the business will begin trading on 1st July when their website goes 'live'. The budget shows that they will need a minimum of £12,200 to set up the business.

Start-up costs	February	March	April	May	£ Total
Website design		200	200	200	600
Internet charges				150	150
Utilities connections				250	250
Market research	400				400
Rent				500	500
Stationery			200		200
Stock			1,000	3,000	4,000
Drawings	500	500	500	500	2,000
Advertising				300	300
Legal fees			100	200	300
Van			2,000		2,000
Signage				150	150
Packaging				150	150
Fittings			300	400	700
Other costs	100	100	100	200	500
Total	1,000	800	4,400	6,000	12,200

Each section of this unit deals with a particular aspect of the business plan. The following shows an example of the type of information that could be included in a business plan to justify the choice of finance and show how working capital requirements were determined.

Business example – Total Beauty

Julia Cairns and Samantha Campbell both worked part time for a large department store in the cosmetics section. They also attended a local college where they studied health and beauty care. It was their dream to leave college and set up their own beauty salon. They hoped to open a small salon in their local town selling a range of cosmetics and beauty products and offering facial and body treatments, electrolysis, waxing, Indian head massages, reflexology, aromatherapy and nail treatments. If this was successful, in the future, they might develop an online retail service. This was the way things were moving and they felt it would give them a much larger potential market and may help to keep costs down.

However, their main problem was a lack of finance to meet the start-up costs. The most they could raise was £2,000 each. They knew that the key to raising more finance was to produce a sound and realistic business plan and to impress potential money lenders with their experience and knowledge of the market, positive personalities and commitment to running their own business. Julia and Samantha calculated that they would need a further £7,000 to get their business up and running.

Sources of finance

It is planned to raise a total of £15,000 to meet the start-up costs and provide some initial working capital for the business. This includes £4,000 provided by the owners. The pie chart below shows the planned sources.

'The personal capital provided is quite low and ideally would be higher. However, this is all that could be raised given our personal circumstances. Assuming that a bank will provide funding, it has been calculated that £6,000 could be borrowed and repaid easily within four years. £5,000 would be used to convert a small shop into a beauty salon in a less expensive part of the town. The rest of the bank loan and personal capital will be used to meet the setting up costs shown in the start-up budget. The £1,000 bank overdraft would be used to provide some initial working capital when the business starts trading. However, it was hoped that this would not be needed. The main advantage of this source is its flexibility. A credit card would also be used to provide working capital. This was surprisingly easy to obtain and although the limit is £4,000 we only plan to use up to £2,000. We also plan to repay the amount owed on the credit card promptly to avoid interest charges.

A lot of the stock will be purchased on sale or return. The supply of cosmetics and beauty products is highly competitive and we can benefit from favourable supply terms. Around £3,500 of stock will be purchased in this way with a further £500 bought using trade credit. Some essential equipment for beauty treatments and aromatherapy will be purchased using hire purchase. We feel that these sources of finance are suitable for the types of expenditure outlined.'

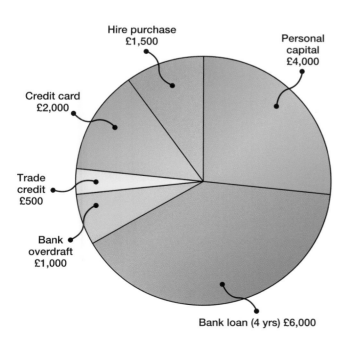

Start-up budget

Costs	May	June	July	£ Total
Conversion costs	1,500	1,500	2,000	5,000
Rent	400	400	400	1,200
Equipment	500	500	500	1,500
Utility charges	50	100	50	200
Advertising		100	300	400
Telephone	40	40	40	120
Uniforms			200	200
Stock			1,000	1,000
Stationery			100	100
Party expenses			400	400
Other costs	300	300	600	1,200
Total	2,790	2,940	5,590	11,320

'It is planned to spend three months setting up the business. Most of this time will be spent preparing the salon. The start-up budget is drawn up for these three months. The business will be launched on 1st August 2006. A small launch party is planned which will be advertised locally. Some free treatments will be given away in the first month of trading.'

Mark band 1 The plan would need to include a list of the sources of finance that are being used. It would also explain briefly why these sources have been chosen. A simple start-up budget should be included and a basic comment about how working capital requirements will be met.

Mark band 2 The plan would need to include a detailed list of the sources of finance that are being used and the start-up budget. The sources of finance chosen must be justified. There will also be comments on the implications of the start-up budget and a detailed explanation of how the working capital requirements of the business will be met. There is a need to show independence of thought and a clear understanding.

Mark band 3 The plan needs to be comprehensive and professionally presented. It should include an analysis of the sources of finance that have been selected explaining the reasons why you think they are suitable. It should include a detailed start-up budget and a detailed explanation of the implications of the key entries. The working capital requirements should be outlined in detail including an explanation of how they are going to be met. There is a need to show originality, independence of thought and clear understanding.

The importance of cash flow and the business plan

Cash is the lifeblood of a business. Without cash a business cannot trade. It is therefore crucial for new business owners to demonstrate that they understand the importance of effective cash management. One way in which this can be achieved is by including an accurate cash flow forecast in the business plan. Money lenders and other stakeholders will want to be sure that the owners have given careful thought to the cash position of the business, particularly in its early and vulnerable stages.

In 2005, 18,122 businesses collapsed. The main reasons why new businesses often fail are down to:

- a lack of entrepreneurial qualities, i.e. a lack of organisational, communication and business management skills;
- a lack of information, about the market, competitors, business practices, resource availability and management techniques, for example;
- a lack of planning, i.e. failing to look into the future and undertaking essential business tasks at the appropriate times.

Figure 1 *Kelly's Cattery*

Elaine Kelly left her job as a carer in a local care home to undertake care of a very different kind. She planned to set up a cattery to look after people's cats while they were away from home. The idea came to her when she was asked by a neighbour to look after a kitten for a month while they visited relatives in New Zealand. The neighbours were so pleased with the care given by Kelly that they gave her £200. This seemed rather a lot to Kelly and suggested that owners were prepared to pay good money if their pets were well looked after in their absence.

Kelly spent a lot of time researching her business idea. She also took animal care courses to gain some useful qualifications. For example, she visited a couple of catteries in towns further afield to look at how the places were managed. One of the final stages in the planning process was to produce a cash flow forecast for the first six months of trading. The following information will help to understand the forecast:

- the cash sales are based on market research and inquiries from adverts placed in February;
- the expected payments are based on actual costs quoted, such as vet's insurance and rent, and estimations based on sales levels;
- the £5,000 bank loan was granted to provide some initial working capital;
- the business has negotiated a £2,000 bank overdraft;
- the negative opening cash balance (£1,200) arises as a result of setting up costs exceeding the capital raised (setting up costs are not shown in this forecast because they were incurred before trading began in March).

The cash flow forecast prepared by Kelly shows that the cash position of the business improves strongly in the first six months of trading. However, it must be remembered that the £5,000 bank loan has done a lot to boost the cash position. Elaine also knows that during the winter months sales will drop quite considerably because people take fewer holidays.

£	MAR	APR	MAY	JUNE	JULY	AUG
Receipts						
Bank loan	5,000					
Cash sales	2,000	2,500	3,000	4,000	6,000	4,000
Total receipts	7,000	2,500	3,000	4,000	6,000	4,000
Payments						
Rent	500	500	500	500	500	500
Pet food products	200	250	300	400	600	400
Electricity	30	30	20	20	20	30
Loan repayments	350	350	350	350	350	350
Leasing charges	540	540	540	540	540	540
Advertising	300	300	200	200	200	100
Vet's insurance	400	400	400	400	400	400
Other operating costs	200	250	300	300	350	300
Drawings	600	600	600	600	600	600
Total payments	3,120	3,220	3,210	3,310	3,560	3,220
Net cash flow	3,880	(720)	210	690	2,440	780
Opening balance	(1,200)	2,680	1,960	2,170	2,860	5,300
Closing balance	2,680	1,960	2,170	2,860	5,300	6,080

NB – brackets equal negative numbers.

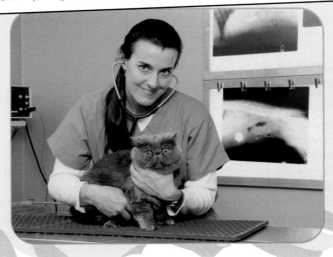

Compiling a business plan is obviously part of the planning process and will help business owners to set their business in motion and achieve specific aims. The cash flow forecast in the financial section of the plan will show the anticipated flows of cash into and out of the business for a future period of time. It will also show the expected cash balance at the end of each month. This will 'flag up' times when cash might be short and indicate to the owners in advance that measures will be needed to raise more cash or reduce spending. If the cash flow forecast is accurate, future cash difficulties can be identified and business failure avoided.

Sources of information for the cash flow forecast

Cash inflows In the top section of a cash flow forecast the planned cash inflows are recorded. Some of the money may come from injections of capital or a bank loan. These values will be known for certain. However, the main problem will be predicting the cash inflows from sales. New business owners must find a way of predicting future sales levels. The information may come from another section in the business plan where market research information or sales forecasts have been presented. Once this information has been generated it can be used to produce monthly entries for cash inflows. In some business plans more than one cash flow forecast may be presented – one showing the best case scenario for sales and another showing the worst case scenario. This approach may help business owners to see what happens to the future cash position if things turn out for the best, or perhaps more importantly, the worst.

Cash outflows The middle section in the cash flow forecast shows the items of expenditure anticipated by the business in the future. Some items will be known with certainty. For example, fixed costs such as rent, insurance, advertising and business rates will be known in advance. These can be entered confidently in the forecast. Variable costs such as materials, fuel, labour costs and packaging depend on the level of sales. These are more difficult to predict because sales levels are uncertain. However, they can be based on the sales forecasts made in the marketing section of the business plan.

Figure 1 shows an example of a cash flow forecast produced by a business that is about to start-up.

Cash flow forecast as a management tool

The cash flow forecast is not just a financial statement that is presented in a business plan. It is an important financial management tool. Cash flow forecasts should be produced on a regular basis throughout the life of a business. They are used to monitor the flow of cash in the business at all times. They should also be updated if certain entries change. This is simple to do if forecasts are produced using spreadsheets. It will also be helpful to carry out variance analysis. By calculating **cash variances** business owners can identify differences between planned expenditure and actual expenditure and take corrective action, such as increasing an overdraft with a bank or arranging a short-term loan, if necessary.

Break-even

The level of sales or output where total costs and total revenue are exactly the same is called the break-even point. For example, if a business produces 1,000 units at a total cost of £20,000 and sell them for £20 each, total revenue will also be £20,000 (£20 × 1,000). At this level of sales, the business is making neither a profit nor a loss, it is breaking even.

The break-even point can be calculated in two ways. One approach is to use the contribution method (where contribution = selling price - variable cost). The break-even level of output is shown in Figure 2.

Figure 2 *Break-even output*

$$\text{Break-even} = \frac{\text{Fixed costs}}{\text{Contribution (price - variable cost)}}$$

For example a business has fixed costs of £36,000 and variable cost of £8 per unit. If price is £20 per unit, break-even output will be:

$$\frac{£36,000}{£20 - £8} = \frac{£36,000}{£12} = 3,000 \text{ units}$$

Another approach is to use the total revenue and total cost equations where total costs (TC) = fixed costs (FC) + variable costs (VC) and total revenue (TR) = price (P) × quantity (Q=output). Using the same information from Figure 2, break-even is calculated in Figure 3.

Break-even and the business plan

Most business owners will want to include some break-even analysis in their business plan. It is helpful to know what sales levels must be achieved in order to cover total costs. It will also show stakeholders when the business is likely to begin making a profit. Another purpose of break-even is to set targets. Many new businesses aim to break-even in a certain time period. For example, a business might aim to break-even in the first year of trading.

The break-even point will also help to clarify the viability of a business idea. For example, if calculations show that a business will break-even when 3,000 units have been sold, it would be viable if sales were 4,000 units. In this case the margin of safety is 1,000 units, as shown in Figure 3. The **margin of safety** is the difference between the current and break-even output over which the business makes a profit. It would not be viable if total capacity was only 2,000 units. Neither would the business be viable if market research suggested that only 1,000 units could be sold.

Owners might include some break-even calculations or present a break-even chart. A break-even chart provides a visual means of analysing a firm's financial position at different levels of output. For

Figure 3 *Break-even output*

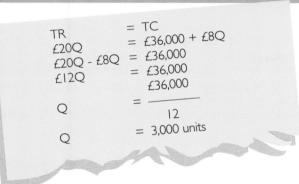

$$
\begin{aligned}
TR &= TC \\
£20Q &= £36,000 + £8Q \\
£20Q - £8Q &= £36,000 \\
£12Q &= £36,000 \\
&\quad £36,000 \\
Q &= \frac{}{12} \\
Q &= 3,000 \text{ units}
\end{aligned}
$$

£ Revenue/costs

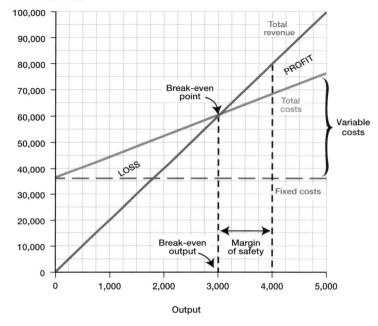

Output

Figure 4 *Profit target*

$$
\frac{\text{Profit target + fixed costs}}{\text{Contribution}}
$$

example, stakeholders can see at a glance the amount of profit or loss that will be made at different levels of output. The margin of safety can also be shown. This is the difference (measured in units of output) between current sales levels and the break-even level of output. The margin of safety provides business owners and other stakeholders with an assessment of risk. It shows by how much sales can fall before a loss is made. It therefore gives an indication of the business's ability to withstand unfavourable trading conditions.

Figure 5 *The Fellowship of Sound*

Ben Fellows hopes to set up a mobile DJ business, the Fellowship of Sound, providing sound entertainment at parties, weddings and other functions. He has compiled a list of costs and divided them into fixed and variable. They appear in the extract from his business plan as two pie charts shown below. Ben thinks he will charge £180 per booking on average.

The number of bookings that the Fellowship of Sound would need to break-even is:

$$
\text{Break-even} = \frac{£10,000}{£180 - £80} = \frac{£10,000}{£100} = 100 \text{ bookings}
$$

According to market research at least two bookings per week would be possible in the first year. Therefore, the business is likely to break-even in its first year of trading. Indeed, if bookings exceed two per week a profit will be made.

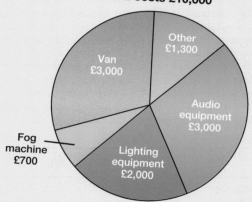

Fixed costs £10,000

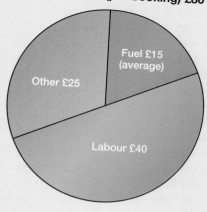

Variable costs (per booking) £80

Break-even analysis can also be used when setting profit targets. For example, it is possible to calculate how much needs to be sold in order to reach a specified profit target. The formula in Figure 4 could be used. Figure 5 shows how a new business used break-even analysis in its business plan.

Drawbacks of break-even analysis

It must be remembered that the use of break-even analysis as a financial management tool has its limitations. They are summarised briefly below.

- Some of the assumptions made are a little unrealistic. For example, it is unlikely that all output will be sold.
- Businesses operate in a dynamic environment. Unfortunately break-even charts cannot cope with changes in a range of business variables such as technology.
- If the cost and price information is inaccurate or out of date the break-even calculations will be wrong and misleading.
- In reality, total cost and total revenue equations are not linear (as they are shown to be here).
- Break-even analysis becomes very complex for multi-product businesses.

Meeting the assessment criteria - examiners' guidance

This section focuses on the cash flow and break-even forecasts in the business plan. The following shows an example of the type of information that could be included in a business plan in relation to cash flow and break-even.

Business example - Saffron City

In 1998, Muhammad Yunus and Kamal Ahmed moved from Chittagong, Bangladesh to London. They both got jobs in the same restaurant in Brick Lane in East London, famous for its Asian restaurants, and worked for seven years. During that time they saved hard in the hope that one day they would have enough money to open their own restaurant. In June 2006, their dreams were realised. They opened Saffron City, a restaurant specialising in Bangladeshi cuisine in north London. They spent £30,000 of their own savings converting an old Italian restaurant into a modern 'high class' establishment. Before beginning work on the conversion and preparing for the

opening, Muhammad and Kamal spent several months planning and drew up a business plan. The extracts below show the cash flow forecast and some break-even analysis.

Cash flow forecast June 2006 – May 2007

- The forecast does not include the £30,000 spent setting up the business.
- The opening cash balance is £300. It was left over from the £30,000 spent setting the business up.
- It is assumed that a £2,000 bank loan (repayable over 18 months) will be granted. Repayments are included in 'other fixed costs'.
- Normal sales are based on estimates from market research. For example, in June when the business first opens, it is expected to be quiet, with just 100 meals being sold.

£	JUN	JUL	AUG	SEP	OCT	NOV	DEC	JAN	FEB	MAR	APR	MAY
Receipts												
Bank loan	2,000											
Normal sales	2,000	4,000	5,000	5,000	5,000	5,000	6,000	4,000	4,000	5,000	5,000	6,000
Functions					2,000		3,000					
Total receipts	4,000	4,000	5,000	5,000	7,000	5,000	9,000	4,000	4,000	5,000	5,000	6,000
Payments												
Rent	700	700	700	700	700	700	700	700	700	700	700	700
Fixed labour costs	2,500	2,500	2,500	2,500	2,500	2,500	2,500	2,500	2,500	2,500	2,500	2,500
Advertising	100	100	100	100	100	100	100	100	100	100	100	100
Insurance	60	60	60	60	60	60	60	60	60	60	60	60
Other fixed costs	140	140	140	140	140	140	140	140	140	140	140	140
Food produce	200	400	500	500	700	500	900	400	400	500	500	600
Variable labour costs	100	200	250	250	350	250	450	200	200	250	250	300
Other variable costs	100	200	250	250	350	250	450	200	200	250	250	300
Total payments	3,900	4,300	4,500	4,500	4,900	4,500	5,300	4,300	4,300	4,500	4,500	4,700
Net cash flow	100	(300)	500	500	2,100	500	3,700	(300)	(300)	500	500	1,300
Opening balance	300	400	100	600	1,100	3,200	3,700	7,400	7,100	6,800	7,300	7,800
Closing balance	400	100	600	1,100	3,200	3,700	7,400	7,100	6,800	7,300	7,800	9,100

Note - brackets equal negative numbers.

'The cash flow forecast shows that the business will have a sound cash position over the first year of trading. The cash balance is positive throughout the period and rises from £400 to £9,100. However, the forecast does not include any drawings. It is also based on estimates for sales. The forecast does not include any of the £30,000 set-up costs. It is drawn up for the first year's trading. The costs have been divided into fixed and variable costs which will help when constructing a break-even chart.'

Break-even chart

* It is assumed that the average price per meal will be £20.
* Variable costs will be £4 per meal.
* Fixed costs for the first year will be £72,000. This **does** include the £30,000 setting up costs.

'The break-even chart shows that the business will break-even when 4,500 meals have been sold. This means that the business will not break-even in the first year of trading. According to the cash flow forecast, the business will generate sales of £61,000. This means that a total of 3,050 (£61,000 ÷ £20) meals will be sold. At this level of sales Saffron City will make a loss of £23,200. This is shown on the break-even chart. Although this seems like a large loss, it must be remembered that £30,000 of the fixed costs were 'one-off' costs and will not be incurred again. We are relatively happy with this predicted financial outcome of the business for the first year. Businesses often do not make a profit in their first year and we intend to draw up a 3-year plan to show that sales will expand and profit will be made in years 2 and 3. Our aim was just to get the business running and then expand sales later through promotion and word of mouth.'

Mark Band 1 The plan needs to include a simple cash flow forecast. A twelve month forecast should be drawn up using a spreadsheet if possible. It would also include some simple break-even analysis. A break-even chart could be included to show when the business expects to break-even.

Mark Band 2 The plan needs to show a detailed cash flow forecast. This should be for at least twelve months and be produced on a spreadsheet. It should explain the main details in the forecast. Some break-even analysis is also required. It should be presented as a break-even chart showing where the business will break-even. It could show the margin of safety and any profit targets that you have been set. There is a need to show independence of thought and clear understanding.

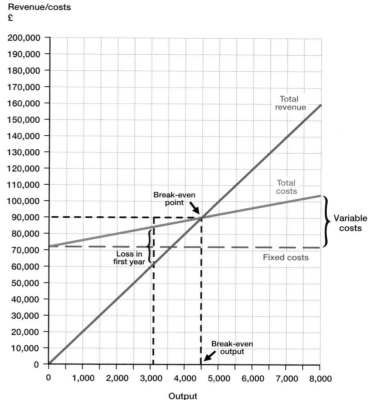

Mark Band 3 This requires a comprehensive and professionally presented cash flow forecast. This must be produced using a spreadsheet and cover at least a twelve month period. There would also be a clear explanation of the expected cash position of the business over this period and comments on any other important details in the forecast. A break-even analysis will also be included, presented as a break-even chart for the first year of the business, showing any profit targets that have been set. There is a need to show originality, independence of thought and clear understanding.

The profit and loss account

Businesses commonly produce financial statements at the end of the trading year. They are used to clarify the performance of the business and provide a record of the firm's financial position. In particular, the profit and loss account is used to show how much profit the business has made. It contains information on revenue and costs based on the transactions undertaken by the business during the year. The information contained in profit and loss accounts may be of interest to a range of stakeholders. Examples are given below.

- The owners will want to know how well their business has done. They will be interested in the amount of profit made and might use the information to decide how much profit to retain and how much to withdraw.
- Tax authorities such as HM Revenue and Customs will need information contained in profit and loss accounts to calculate the tax liabilities of companies and business owners.
- Suppliers and money lenders will want to know whether a business is financially stable before granting trade credit or providing funds.
- Potential partners or providers of finance are likely to be interested in the performance and financial position of a business before investing in a company.

Profit and loss account and the business plan

It is common practice to include a profit and loss account in the business plan. However, since the business plan is drawn up before trading begins, the financial information presented in the profit and loss account cannot be based on actual transactions. Therefore, business owners must prepare a projected profit and loss account. This means that all the entries in the account must be estimated. In practice they are likely to be based on information in the cash flow forecast. Figure I shows a projected profit and loss account for a new business.

The balance sheet

The balance sheet provides a summary of a firm's assets, liabilities and capital. It highlights some important financial information about a business.

- It shows the value of working capital (net current assets). This helps to assess how easily a business can meet its immediate debts.
- The capital structure of the business is presented. This shows all the different sources of finance used by the business. For example, it shows the balance between loan capital and owners' capital.
- It shows the asset structure of the business. This illustrates how the money raised has been spent. For example, it shows the balance between fixed and current assets.

Figure 1 *Projected profit and loss account for Café Barr*

Sarah Hemmings plans to open a small café in the Birmingham suburb of Great Barr. She thinks she has spotted a gap in the market and found an ideal location near to a bus terminus in a small shopping complex. Sarah plans to invest £25,000 of her own money setting up a high quality café offering a range of hot drinks, fresh smoothies and healthy snacks. The projected profit and loss account shown below was presented in her business plan.

Café Barr
Projected profit and loss account y/e 31.7.07

	£	£
Sales		74,000
Cost of sales		
Opening stock	0	
Add purchases	36,700	
	36,700	
Less Closing stock	1,200	
		35,500
Gross profit		38,500
Expenses		
Wages	16,000	
Leasing	6,000	
Interest	2,000	
Advertising	2,000	
Other expenses	10,000	
Depreciation	6,000	
		42,000
Net loss		3,500

The projected profit and loss account shows that Sarah expects her business to make a small loss in the first year of trading. However, this may not be a problem if she has enough cash to continue trading. It is not unusual for a new business to make a loss in the first year. It takes time for a new business to become established. If Sarah was using her business plan to support an application for funding she may also include a projected profit and loss account for the second trading year. If this account showed that the business had become established and moved into profit, this would provide the necessary support. However, the further she project accounts into the future the less reliable they become. This is because it is so difficult to predict revenues and costs so far into the future. There are so many external factors, such as competition and the state of the economy, that can affect trading conditions. It is generally accepted that projected accounts provide only limited information.

- The net asset entry in the balance sheet provides a guide to the value of the business. Also, if net assets rise over time, this suggests that the business is growing.

The balance sheet and the business plan

A business plan is likely to contain a balance sheet. On the first day of trading a business will already have a number of assets, liabilities and some capital. For example, it will have purchased some resources such as equipment and stock. These would be shown as fixed assets and current assets in the balance sheet, respectively. The business might also have a bank loan which would be shown as a long term liability and the stock might have been purchased using trade credit which would be shown as a current liability. And the owner's capital would also be shown. However, a balance sheet drawn up before the business starts trading is not particularly helpful. A business plan is more likely to present a projected balance sheet. For example, a projected balance sheet for the end of the first year of trading would be more helpful. This will show the firm's financial position after a full year in business. Like the projected profit

and loss account, much of the information shown will be estimated. Figure 2 shows a projected balance sheet for a new business.

Limitations of the balance sheet

It must be remembered that the balance sheet has certain limitations.
- The value of fixed assets is only estimated (cost - depreciation). Consequently they may be worth less if resold.
- Intangible assets, such as goodwill, are not recorded on the balance sheet. Thus, the true value of the business may be understated.
- The balance sheet is a static statement. The values shown are only accurate for the day that the balance sheet is published. When the business begins trading again the value of assets, liabilities and capital will change.
- Projected balance sheets contain estimated information. The further they are projected into the future, the less reliable they are.

Figure 1 *Projected balance sheet for Easy Fit*

...o Sartori left his job at a ...retailer as a kitchen fitter ... up his own kitchen and ...oom fitting business. He ...ed up with the service he ...om his employer. He was ...tantly being let down ...h supplies failed to arrive ...customer's address leaving ...to deal with a potentially ...easant situation. He ...ared a business plan to ...port an application for ...ding. He wanted to borrow ...,000 to buy some essential ...ources so that he could ...in trading alone, fitting ...hens and bathrooms for ...ople who had already ...ught their own units and just ...nted them fitting professionally. Calvino had decided to operate at the top end ...the market where he would be working with high quality materials and earning ...her fees. The projected balance sheet below is an extract from his business ...an.

...he projected balance sheet shows that Easy Fit is expected to be in a financially ...able position at the end of the first year of trading. It shows that the business:
- has working capital of £2,100;
- has £4,000 cash in the bank;
- is fairly highly geared (more than half of the capital is raised from a bank loan);
- made a profit of £2,600 in the first year of trading;
- is valued at around £12,600.

Easy Fit Balance sheet as at 30.9.07	
	£
Fixed assets	
Tools and equipment	18,000
Vehicle	7,500
	25,500
Current assets	
Stock	1,200
Debtors	2,000
Cash at bank	4,000
	7,200
Creditors: amounts falling due in one year	
Trade creditors	3,700
Accruals	400
Other creditors	1,000
	5,100
Net current assets	2,100
Creditors: amounts falling due after one year	
Bank loan	(15,000)
Net assets	12,600
Capital	
Opening capital	10,000
Retained profit	2,600
Closing capital	12,600

Meeting the assessment criteria - examiners' guidance

This section focuses on the projected accounts in the business plan. The following shows an example of the type of information that could be included in a business plan in relation to the profit and loss account and the balance sheet.

Business example – Luke Carter

Luke Carter plans to start his own driving school. He has been on a course and is now a qualified driving instructor. He has been given a £10,000 interest free loan by his parents and plans to offer driving lessons in his home town of Banbury, Oxfordshire. He will also use £10,000 of his own savings and expects to get a small bank overdraft to provide some working capital if needed. His father insisted that he should produce a business plan before granting him the loan. He wants him to prove that he is capable of planning and understands the difficulties in running a business. He also feels that producing a business plan will improve the chances of success for his son. The business plan extract in Table 1 shows the projected profit and loss accounts. The extract in Table 2 shows the projected balance sheet. Luke wants the business to break-even in the first year.

Table 1 *Projected profit and loss accounts for Luke Carter's driving school*

Luke Carter Projected profit and loss account y/e 31.7.07		
	£	£
Turnover		33,000
Cost of sales		12,800
Gross profit		20,200
Expenses		
Insurance	4,200	
Advertising	2,500	
Repairs & maintenance	3,700	
Garage rent	1,000	
Admin. costs	1,300	
Other costs	3,200	
Depreciation	4,000	
		19,900
Net profit		300

Luke Carter Projected profit and loss account y/e 31.7.09		
	£	£
Turnover		73,000
Cost of sales		28,200
Gross profit		44,800
Expenses		
Insurance	4,400	
Advertising	2,000	
Repairs & maintenance	4,100	
Garage rent	1,100	
Admin. costs	1,500	
Other costs	5,000	
Depreciation	4,000	
		22,100
Net profit		22,700

'The first projected profit and loss account presented in the business plan shows that I meet meet my aim of breaking-even in the first year of trading (a small profit of £300 is made). The projected turnover is £33,000 and gross profit is £20,200. The list of expenses is consistent with those a business operating a driving school would incur. I have not employed anyone yet since there is not an entry for wages in the list of expenses.

The second profit and loss account shows the projected figures for 2009. The account represents the expected performance of the business in three years' time. By this time I expect to increase turnover to £73,000 enjoying a profit of £22,700. Cost of sales and expenses have increased but not in the same proportion as sales. This suggests that many of the costs are fairly fixed. I am satisfied with this level of profits given my aim to get established and make a profit in 3 years.'

Table 2 *Projected balance sheet for Luke Carter's driving school*

Balance sheet Projected balance sheet at 31.7.07		
	£	£
Fixed assets		
Vehicle	20,000	
less depreciation	4,000	16,000
Current assets		
Prepayments	2,000	
Cash at bank	4,300	
Cash in hand	200	
	6,500	
Current liabilities		
Trade creditors	1,300	
Accruals	900	
	2,200	
Net current assets		4,300
Long term liabilities		
Loan		(10,000)
Net assets		10,300
Capital		
Opening capital		10,000
Profit and loss		300
Closing capital		10,300

'The projected balance sheet presented in my business plan shows that the driving school business is in a fairly sound financial position. There is £4,300 cash in the bank and the only real debt is the interest free loan from my parents. However, there is no evidence of any drawings from the business. This is because I have a part-time job and shall be living at my parents until the business becomes established. In the long term this arrangement can not go on. I have chosen not to produce a projected balance sheet for three years time. This is because it would probably have very limited use at the moment.'

Mark Band 1 There is a need to show a projected profit and loss account and balance sheet for the first year of trading. Any important points arising from these projections, such as whether targets have been met and whether the business is in a sound financial position, should be stated.

Mark Band 2 There is a need to produce a projected profit and loss account and balance sheet for the first year of trading. Some simple analysis on these accounts should be carried out (ratio analysis is not needed here) and you should explain any findings. For example, whether turnover and profit targets have been met, how well costs have been controlled and whether the company is in a sound financial position could be explained. There is a need to show independence of thought and a clear understanding.

Mark Band 3 There is a need to produce a projected profit and loss account and balance sheet for the first year of trading. It could help to produce a projected profit and loss account even further into the future (perhaps three years) to show that the business has been sustained over a period of time. There is a need to analyse the accounts (not using ratio analysis) and draw some conclusions about the financial position of the business based on this analysis. For example the analysis may comment on whether any financial targets have been met, how much working capital and debt the business has and whether the business is financially sound. There is a need to show originality and independence of thought and a clear understanding.

10 Reality checks and evaluation

Reality checks

It could be argued that writing a business plan is the easy part, but making it happen in line with the plan is more tricky. When writing a business plan, an important question to ask is 'Realistically, can it be achieved?'

It is easy to get carried away with forecasts and projections. Just because sales in the first day are £100, it does not mean that sales for the year will be £36,500, i.e. 365 days × £100. There are reasons why this sales figure may not be realistic.

Constant sales The forecast assumes that £100 will be received 100% of the time, which is unrealistic.

Number of days worked The total may only be £22,000, not £36,500. This lower total could be based on 220 days, the number of working days available in a year when weekends and public holidays are deducted from the total 365 days. A businessperson may work more than this, such as additional weekends, but without risking health there will be a limit to the maximum number of days he or she can work in the business.

Test, local and national markets Another example of this unrealistic 'grossing up' would be taking a figure for sales in a limited area and multiplying it up to forecast potential sales nationally. This is one of the dangers with test marketing or using a pilot before launch. Unless conditions are replicated precisely as a scaled-down model then it is important to be careful about projecting the figures on a larger scale. This does not only apply to sales figures. An example is shown in Figure 1.

> **Figure 1** *Unrealistic forecasts as a result of different levels of marketing spending*
>
> A test market is run in an area that represents 10% of the population. Sales are supported by media spending of, say, £10,000. If national spending is not at least £100,000 then the level of support in the test market will be excessive and could result in sales at a level that cannot be replicated nationally. A business may achieve fantastic results in a test market, but struggle to achieve anything like the same level nationally. The problem can often be attributed to overweighting marketing support and general enthusiasm in the business to a degree that cannot be sustained on a larger scale.

Conversion rates Experienced salespeople say that 'selling is a numbers game …'. What they mean by this is that from the total number of sales calls they make, only a number (or percentage) are converted into sales, with a certain sales value. There is a limit to the number of sales calls or direct marketing contacts that can be made in a day. Therefore using these numbers or percentages will only crudely forecast what can be achieved realistically. Turning round these numbers and applying an average sales figure to an average day will give a better indication of what sales are realistic in a given period of time. This calculation can then be used as a **reality check**.

For example, if a business plan forecasts sales of £330,000 in the first six months, 110 business days, this anticipates a minimum average daily sales of £3,000. For some businesses this may be realistic, but is it for all businesses? If yes, fine, but if not, what can be done about it?

It is better to be realistic and make forecasts using figures that are achievable, rather than include numbers in a business plan that look great, but are unlikely to be achieved. **Over-forecasting** can lead to problems for a business, as shown in Table 1.

> **Table 1** *Problems of over-forecasting*
>
> - It will create disappointment and feelings of failure.
> - It could result in overstocks and the consequent costs involved in storing excess stock or disposing of unsold stock which may have become unsaleable.
> - It may mean that a business has arranged large premises or warehouse space that is no longer appropriate – another cost.
> - It may lead to the hiring of more labour than is necessary.
> - Over-forecasting and the underachievement of sales and income will affect cash flow and the ability to pay creditors.

Before finalising figures for a business plan it is important to pause and give them a reality check. Realistically, can they be achieved? If not, think again. Lower forecasts are more likely to be met, will give a sense of achievement, and it is usually better for a business to scale up to meet demand than to have to scale down because targets have not been met.

Self-evaluation

Not everyone is cut out to run their own business. It does not suit everyone and many people prefer to have the relative stability of being an employee and knowing that they will receive a regular wage.

Before accepting the challenge of running your own business you need to consider a number of questions, including:
- is there a worthwhile market for my business idea?
- is my product good enough for the market?
- do I have the skills to turn my idea into a business?
- do I have the resources to turn my idea into a viable business?
- do I have the commitment to do what it takes to get the business up and running, such as long hours, working alone, cold

calling and potential disappointment, and worrying whether the business will make enough money to pay creditors and wages? These are all aspects of **personal self-evaluation**.

You also need to conduct a self-evaluation on the facts and the figures and the resultant plans. This can be achieved by comparing what you are planning against the norm in the market.

- Compare your plans with competitors. Are they similar, inferior or better than the way in which competitors run their business?
- Compare your product offer with competitors. Is it the same, comparable, inferior or better?
- Are your sales projections realistic when compared to other businesses in the same or a similar market? Are you anticipating exceeding the sales produced by a long established business or are you only looking at a small percentage of sales when compared with similar sized businesses in the same market?
- Are your targets realistic? If your plans are based on making 50 direct selling telephone calls a day, can you actually do this? If you need to contact 1,000 potential customers each month, can this really be achieved?

Thorough market research before the business plan is launched will help identify the standards and levels of achievement operating within your chosen market. If you can meet all of the targets in your plans realistically, then fine. If not it may be better to scale down the plans and operation to more realistic levels, succeed, then start to scale up the business.

Use of SWOT analysis

One relatively objective way of evaluating yourself and your business plan is to use a basic SWOT analysis. Try to truthfully complete each section, identifying Strengths, Weaknesses, Objectives, and Threats. The emphasis should be on being truthful. If you are not truthful there is only one person that you are fooling and that is yourself. One major benefit about conducting a SWOT analysis on yourself is that you can do something about any Weaknesses that you identify, such as training or research. Even Threats can be moderated by planning if you can see them coming. The danger in self-evaluation is that Strengths and Opportunities are over-stated, either in an attempt to impress or through self delusion, trying to make the situation seem better than it really is. Details on how to carry out a SWOT analysis are given in section 23.

External evaluation

There is a number of different organisations that will look at a business plan and give an objective opinion of the realism of the figures and the chances of success. Some will even give advice and suggestions for improving the plan and making it more realistic. Such organisations will include the following.

Business Link This is a government agency dedicated to providing advice and support for starting, maintaining and growing a business. The Business Link service is part of the government's campaign to promote enterprise and to make the UK the best place in the world to start and grow a business. It is primarily funded by the Department of Trade and Industry, supported by a number of other government departments, agencies and local authorities. To find more information and to locate your local Business Link look at the website www.businesslink.gov.uk.

Banks Most banks are very keen to attract business customers and most banks are keen to support existing and new business. As a result, they often have a business adviser available at a branch to talk to customers and provide advice as required. The focus of the advice is likely to be financial but most banks will also be able to advise on broader business issues. Local banks will also have local knowledge which can be very helpful.

Development agencies In some parts of the country the government operates development agencies that are responsible for encouraging and developing economic recovery. Part of this will be to encourage new business to start up in the area, often supported by grants or other financial assistance. Just put 'development agencies' in a search engine and you will see if any are operating in your area.

Professional services This would include accountancies and management consultants. Usually expert in particular aspects of business, these are commercial organisations that are likely to charge for reviewing and advising on business plans, but they are another option.

Downside analysis

Downside analysis means that you need to consider what would happen if things did not go according to plan, sometimes known as looking at the 'worst case scenario'. Typical situations to consider for downside analysis are shown in Table 2.

The ultimate downside is the cost of the business failing. What would be the total cost resulting from setting-up the business, attempting to run it for a given time, then it failing and having to close? Although this may sound negative, it is a figure worth estimating and keeping in mind just in case. It may help to keep things in perspective and help with the decision to close down sooner rather than later, which could compound the financial problems.

Having identified the downsides, you will then be in a position to make **contingency plans**. These are plans that kick-in when problems occur to avoid the situation getting any worse.

'What if?' scenarios

The use of 'What if?' scenarios, based on the speculative 'What if? question is a useful way of testing plans and, if necessary, changing plans or identifying where contingency planning may be required. The idea is, once a plan has been formulated, to consider alternatives that could affect the plan. As a result of 'What if?' testing you may decide to do nothing, as the scenario that you have considered will not affect the original plan too much. Alternatively, it may be that a particular weakness needs to be addressed to avoid problems or a previously unforeseen catastrophe is highlighted.

'What if?' scenarios can take many forms. You need to consider scenarios that relate to the plans that you developing. As a starting point it may be useful to base 'What if?' questions on the variables of the marketing mix, as shown in Table 3. These are just examples. In practice, 'What if?' testing could cover all aspects of the

Table 2 *Downside analysis*

Scenarios	Important questions
Sales targets not being met by a huge degree	Missing a sales target by a few points can be overcome, but what if sales were only 10% of those forecast? How would this affect the business, its employees and the stock being held?
Stock not being available	What if production could not keep up with demand? What if promised deliveries do not arrive from overseas? What if all the stock is found to be faulty and unsaleable?
Distribution targets not being achieved	What if targets are not met and you only manage to achieve a handful of stockists in one area? This is bad enough on its own as this limited distribution will affect sales directly. But what if national advertising is about to start and generate demand from all across the country and you end up with consumers whose demand cannot be met, resulting in no sales and a ruined reputation?
Marketing problems	What if advertising does not work, does not generate sales, or worse, offends or alienates the market and puts customers off buying? What if you cannot keep up with demand for the product or service? What if customers want their money back, for whatever reason?

Table 3 *What if? scenarios*

What if ...	Possible outcomes	Solutions or contingency plans
the product is not ready by the launch date?	• Customers are let down. • Planned distribution is not required on original dates. • Promotion may have to be delayed.	• Increase resources to make sure that product is available. • Try to establish when product will be ready. • Inform all parties that may be affected by delay. • Revise plans based on new dates.
the product does not work/does not do what it promises?	• Product will have to be withdrawn. • Under the Trade Descriptions Act the business may be sued. • Customers may want their money back.	• Withdraw product. • Estimate cost of withdrawing product and make sure that future products work. • Contingency plans to cover possible costs. • Change claims/product description.
sales do not reach forecast?	• Negative cash flow. • Profit forecast not achieved. • Overstock. • Resources are not fully utilised and start to cost more than forecast.	• Change promotional strategy. • Cut the price. • Incentivise sales team. • Make contingency plans based on lower sales/income.
sales exceed forecasts?	• Run out of stock. • Deliveries cannot be met. • Customers are let down. • Resources are depleted.	• Make contingency plans for additional stock/resources. • Ration deliveries and raise price to slow sales.
the price is too high?	• Customers do not buy. • Sales are lower than forecast. • Competitors use this for their own advantage.	• Cut prices, but watch effect this will have on profit margin. • Add value. • Run a promotion to offset perceived high price.
the price is too low?	• Sales exceed forecast. • Profit margin is depressed. • It starts a 'price war' in the market.	• Raise price to appropriate level. • Adopt competitive pricing strategy. • Reduce product/service to level appropriate to price.
distribution targets are not met?	• Consumers cannot buy product. • Sales targets are not met.	• Consider other distribution channels. • Scale down production/resources/promotion until distribution improves.
distribution achieved exceeds targets?	• Resources not available to service wider distribution. • Stocks are spread too thinly across wider distribution, leading to high levels of out-of-stock.	• Plan to increase resources to meet demands of increased distribution. • Contingency plan for possible increased demand for product.
the advertising does not work?	• Product does not sell. • High stocks need to be stored until they do sell. • Management unhappy as sales/financial targets are not met.	• Investigate alternative means of promotion which could be used tactically if required. • Make changes in marketing mix to compensate.
the promotion costs more than planned?	• Budgets are blown. • Management is unhappy as demand on financial resources is above forecast.	• Make savings in other areas. • Keep a financial contingency fund to pay for emergencies like this.

Figure 2 *Disaster planning*

Figure 3 *Disaster effects*

In 2006 two major Hemel Hempstead businesses committed their future to the town following the explosion at the Buncefield oil depot after striking a deal to move into the Peoplebuilding in Maylands. Northgate Information Solutions and 3Com, both IT firms, were forced to move out of their Hemel Hempstead offices after the buildings were devastated by the December 2005 blast. The two firms have shifted operations to the futuristic Peoplebuilding while a decision is taken on whether to rebuild their old offices. Earlier in 2006 distribution firm Lane Group announced it was leaving the town because of damage done to its premises in the blast. The announcement left up to 85 jobs hanging in the balance.

Source: adapted from www.hemelhempsteadtoday.co.uk, 26.4.2006.

business. It is closely associated with many aspects of forecasting, planning and downside analysis, and should be viewed as an important part of planning to avoid problems down the line.

Risk assessment

Linked to downside analysis would be a **risk assessment** - what risks are attached to the business plan. The most immediate and sensitive risk is financial risk - how much money would be lost if everything went wrong or if targets were not met. The most direct effect would be on cash flow and very quickly this would affect ability to pay creditors and employees, followed by potential closure of the business. Financial risk is compounded in a sole trader or traditional partnership, where risk is unlimited and creditors could attempt to recover their loss through the courts or by using debt collection agencies. Ultimately businesses could file for bankruptcy, although this will not necessarily guarantee that they will get paid. Risks are also attached to other resource issues, such as what would happen to all the stock did not get sold, what to do with the rented office if the business folds and what happens to employees if there is no work?

Some businesses take risk assessment even further and think of it in terms of **disaster planning**. What this means is that the business tries to consider the worst disaster that could befall the business, and make plans for recovery should such a disaster strike. Typically, disaster planning would include the factors shown in Figure 2. There could be many more, different, disasters that could strike a business, more than could be realistically listed here. What needs to be considered in disaster planning is likely risks, the chances of them happening and contingency plans that can be

applied should disaster strike. Figure 3 shows an example of the impact of a disaster on businesses and their contingency plans. Section 53 explains risk assessment in terms of organising an event.

There will always be risks associated with starting a new business and no one would be expected to identify and make contingency plans for every single risk that could possibly occur. However, it is worth acknowledging the greatest potential risks in your business plan to show anyone reading it that you have been realistic and sensible and have not assumed that everything will go as planned. For some entrepreneurs the risks associated with business are what they love, the challenge, but most of all the pleasure in the knowledge that they have overcome the risks and as a result have a good business that stands to make a lot of money. But the risks have got to have been worth it in the end.

Meeting the assessment criteria - examiners' guidance

Each section of this unit deals with a particular aspect of the business plan. The following shows an example of the type of information that could be included in a business plan to evaluate the success of the business idea and operation.

Business example - Jane Forth ironing service

Jane Forth was working at a bank as a counter clerk, dealing face to face with customers paying in and drawing out cash. She liked some aspects of the job, such as meeting people or having a chat, but was fed up with working for a large faceless organisation that did not recognise her potential.

She has had an idea for setting up her own business – an ironing service. She has been listening to colleagues at the bank, complaining about one of the most boring and arduous household chores, ironing clothes, and thought that there could be money to be made by ironing for other people. Her secondary market research indicated that in the current UK society there is a group of households that are cash rich and time poor, meaning that they have relatively high incomes as a result of working long hours, but consequently have fewer hours to spend with the family and on leisure pursuits. Jane intends to target this kind of family as she thinks that they will be prepared to pay her for ironing to take the pressure off the household and free them up for leisure activities.

Jane has prepared a business plan which she intends to use to raise the capital required to pay for premises, ironing equipment and a van for collection and delivery. However, as she has no experience of running a business she is getting worried. She has been looking at the Business Link website for guidance (www.businesslink.gov.uk) and spotted a 'reality check'. Jane decided that it would be useful to try to answer all of the questions on the web page before finally deciding to give up her job at the bank.

Jane's notes on her self-assessment are as follows.

Are you ready to start up?

Personal sacrifice

I am quite prepared to give it a try, I can see no future in my job at the bank, but I am a hard worker, keen and enthusiastic to do something for myself.

Financial insecurity

This does worry me. I am still living at home, but I make a contribution to the household costs. Once I no longer have a regular salary from the bank I will not know how much I will be earning each month, not in the early days at least. The loss of a regular wage will also mean that I may not be able to go out clubbing with friends as much as I like. This will be hard. Hopefully, the business will give me a good wage once it gets going. All of my research shows that there is a demand for my ironing service.

Loss of company perks

At the bank I get plenty of paid holidays, I also get free membership of the bank's gym, and I have been able to join the banks health insurance scheme. Once I work for myself I will have none of these 'perks'. Again, this will be hard to come to terms with as I have enjoyed these extras since I left school. I suspect that the worst thing will be trying to take a holiday, because unless I take on help I will not be able to carry on the business if I take a break. This is something I need to think about carefully.

Pressure on close relationships

I am not in a close relationship at the moment, so this is not currently an issue.

Isolation

I cannot answer this. I really like working as part of a team at the bank and I like meeting all of the customers that come in. I will still be meeting people when I collect and deliver their clothes, but when I am ironing I will be very much on my own unless I take on extra help. I suspect that I will feel a bit lovely and isolated, but I will have the radio on which will keep me company. I will then have to see how I cope.

'I feel that I have been very honest in my self-assessment. It has identified some potential weaknesses. However, I feel that I have identified how to overcome these weaknesses – take on additional help, having the radio playing to ease the isolation.

In addition to this brief set of self-assessment questions I would carry out a SWOT analysis in another part of the business plan to check that I was ready for the start-up and use market research to confirm that there really was a demand for the business idea. This would demonstrate a comprehensive analysis and evaluation of my present position and improve the quality of my business plan.'

Mark Band 1 A simple evaluation of the business position. This might include a basic self-assessment, highlighting some strengths and weaknesses of the business/entrepreneur and an

Are you ready to start up?

The day-to-day reality check

Setting up your own business requires your full commitment. A valua way of finding out about the day-to-day realities is to talk to people who have already experienced them. However, there are some matte which anybody hoping to start up should be aware of.

Personal sacrifice

The physical and emotional demands of starting up in business shoul not be underestimated. Starting a business is a life-changing event ar will require hard work and long hours, especially in the early stages.

Financial insecurity

There can be times of financial uncertainty, and this may have a knod on effect for both you and your family, for example, you may have to forgo holidays. You may have invested personal savings or used your family home as security and in the worst case scenario you risk losing your investment or even your home.

Loss of company perks

Setting up your own business means that you will no longer be able take advantage of the usual benefits associated with a permanent job This includes the loss of "safety net" benefits such as pension rights, s pay, paid holiday and other company perks.

Pressure on close relationships

You will need the support of your family and friends. They should be aware from the outset of the effect starting up a business will have o your life and it is crucial that they are right behind you. Their emotional backing may also need to be complemented by a practical "hands on" approach. Discussing these issues before they arise will help.

Isolation

Being your own boss can be a satisfying experience. However, shouldering all the responsibility for the success of the business can prove lonely. Unless you develop a network of contacts, there will be one there to bounce ideas off.

Source: adapted from www.businesslink.gov.uk.

indication of the likelihood of success based on this information.

Mark Band 2 Sound analysis of the position showing independence of thought. This would include a detailed evaluation of the position of the business/entrepreneur. It would detail all the potential strengths and weaknesses and give suggestions on how any weaknesses can be dealt with, and an evaluation of the extent to which this might improve the success of the business.

Mark Band 3 Comprehensive analysis of the position, with detailed recommendations and justified conclusions. This would include a comprehensive evaluation of the position of the business/entrepreneur – including both self-assessment and SWOT analysis. It would detail all the potential strengths and weaknesses, suggest how any weaknesses can be dealt with and justify these changes. An overall evaluation will then be given, stressing which strengths and weaknesses are most important and the extent to which strengths outweigh weaknesses, or otherwise.

11 Planning and forecasting

The need for planning

Much of unit 8 has dealt with making plans for starting a business. This includes planning for research, the product, pricing and financial plans, distribution plans and promotion and other marketing plans. But planning does not end with the launch of the business. A business needs to organise how it will develop the next day, the next week, the next month and if possible for the next few years.

The idea of projecting forward and planning how the business moves into the future is part of good management practice. It is usual for a new business to concentrate on the launch and the immediate growth period after the launch. At the time the launch seems like the most important thing in the world and everything is focused on that one date. Suddenly the day arrives, the business is launched and a vibrant and exciting phase will begin – the product is ready, marketing activity starts, customer communication starts, customers make contact and customers start to buy the product.

It may seem that everyone is chasing the business for information, decisions and the product. The danger is that all available time will be spent on the launch and its immediate after-effects. However, a business is more than just the launch. It has to be sustainable and have a viable life after the launch, as it moves into the next stage in its life cycle. With a new business it is easy to spend all the time 'doing the business', i.e. contacting customers and supplying the product, and not devoting sufficient time to running the business. Without forward planning there will be a point when customers start to run out and when the telephone does not ring quite so often. There will then be a sudden realisation - 'Where is the next order coming from? How can I pay the bills next month? Where has the cash flow gone?' This is why it is so important to plan ahead and to build-in time for running the business.

Forecasting and business projections

Sometimes considered one of the 'dark arts' associated with marketing, like statistics, forecasting can be used and interpreted in many ways. The basic idea of forecasting is to use your best skill and judgement to predict what is most likely to happen. This may sound like 'crystal ball gazing', but forecasting in business is rarely done by guesswork alone. It best done using as much supporting quantitative data or qualitative opinion as is available.

Usually associated with numbers, such as sales forecasts, production forecasts, income forecasts or profit forecasts, forecasting can be used in many different ways in business and marketing. It is often used to predict in the areas shown in Figure 1. Forecasting draws on certain features including the following.

Use of historical data The starting point for most forecasting is usually history. A business must take into account what happened in the same period last year or the years before, and then consider what is likely to happen this year, next year and beyond if

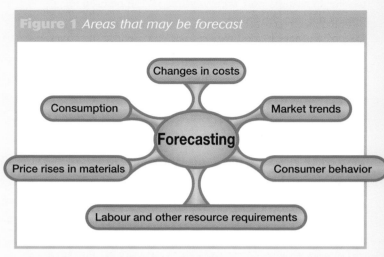

Figure 1 *Areas that may be forecast*

- Changes in costs
- Consumption
- Market trends
- **Forecasting**
- Price rises in materials
- Consumer behavior
- Labour and other resource requirements

nothing changes. This last statement is important because, as the financial services industry says, 'past performance is no guarantee of future performance.' Why? Because things are bound to change – markets are subject to and affected by so many external forces that they are bound to change. Changes in the market place include:

- the progress of businesses and products through their life cycles;
- changes in competitors' activities;
- changes ineconomic trends and the economy;
- changes in fashion;
- the influence of marketing activity such as advertising.

All of these and more will affect the future of a business.

Use of statistics Statistics can be used for forecasting. Most statistical forecasting methods rely on historical trends. This is known as **extrapolation**. It is the use of statistical data to project trends forward. Again, this method will need to be treated with some caution or at least moderated in the light of subjective information about changes in the market place.

Use of targets or objectives The targets or objectives of planned marketing activity can be used to add to statistical forecasts. If advertising is planned it should have an objective, such as raising consumer sales by x%. This percentage is then applied to the statistical forecasts during the period that the advertising is likely to be effective. The danger is that the advertising may not be effective, or may be more effective than forecast. Both eventualities will affect the actual sales and create a variation from the forecast. However, applying such anticipated changes to past performance is valid or why bother to advertise or promote in the first place?

Use of market research Market research is often used to help make forecasts or projections. Questions can be included on questionnaires that ask respondents about their future intentions. Focus groups can be organised to discuss current behaviour and opinions and the groups can be led through to the future to get the respondents to think about how their behaviour or opinions might change. Two of the most useful methods of market research for predicting future changes are the use of continuous auditing data and the use of regular research panels. Continuous audit data will build up trend information that can be used for projections. Panels that are researched on a regular basis are very good at picking up changes over time, which again can be used for projections into the future.

Use of experts Market experts and experienced members of the team can be useful as they can use their skill and experience to consider how a market might change and how this would affect business in the future. Although this is subjective opinion, personal skill can be very sensitive to picking up trends and changes in the market place. There are even specialist commercial agencies that predict future changes. Figure 2 shows an example. Similar organisations operate in other markets, making forecasts that will affect entire industries. These commercial forecasting agencies rely heavily on market research and the behaviour of market leaders and trendsetters that have an effect on wider consumer behaviour. The further ahead a company wants to project or forecast, the more it will cost as the research become more detailed and sophisticated.

Figure 2 *Use of experts' information for forecasting*

The International Colour Authority (ICA) is one of the world's leading colour forecasting organisations. Its services are used by paint companies, décor companies and fashion industry companies that need to know what will be 'the' colour for next season, so that they can gear up production and stocks to meet the demands of the market.

Justification When presenting forecasts or including them in business plans it is important to justify and qualify them with any information, assumptions or supporting data that has been used to arrive at the forecasts. Doing this will give anyone reading the marketing plan the opportunity to agree or disagree with the assumptions and, if necessary, apply their own interpretation to the assumptions to test the conclusions.

The launch plan

This is an outline of what needs to be done to start the business and to get it up and running. All of the financial planning should have been done during the early stages, when the original idea for the business was being considered and checked to make sure that the idea was worthwhile and viable. All of the planning based on the variants in the marketing mix will have been finalised. These include:

- product – what it is and what business is being launched;
- price – how much its products will sell for;
- place – where is the business being launched, its location plus where and how the product will be sold;

- promotion – how the business will be supported with promotional activity.

Overlaying all of this will be the dates and timings, showing when it is all going to happen.

A launch plan will usually be supported with financial data and any marketing research that supports and justifies the actions being planned. It is also worth including a calculation based on the premise that the launch may not go as planned and that in fact it goes disastrously wrong – 'What would be the cost of total failure, or deciding not to go ahead with the launch?'

The 3-year plan

There is nothing intrinsically 'magic' about a '3-year plan'. It is not a guarantee of success. But it does mean that a business is looking forward and planning the stages in its development, at its own pace, rather than leaving things open to chance, the whims of the market place, or worse, being led by competitors.

A 3-year plan will give a business a structure to work within. It may decide that the plan needs changing. In fact a plan should be a dynamic, living thing that is used actively rather than a document that is the result of an academic exercise that just gathers dust on a shelf. A 3-year plan need not be a huge document. It needs to be sufficient for the business and any stakeholders to see where the business is going, based on its aims and objectives.

Typically, a 3-year plan will draw together information about the financial and sales forecasts of the business and the dates or timings of any significant events or changes to resource requirements that will impact on the business. It should also include changes or initiatives based on the variants of the marketing mix:

- product plans, new products, product developments;
- pricing and financial objectives;
- place – distribution objectives and any changes in the route to market;
- promotion – planned marketing activity, dates and media.

Some businesses may produce 3-5 year plans, 5-year plans or plans for longer periods if they need to plan ahead for longer periods.

Timing of business plans

This refers to when things are expected to happen or, more directly, when the business will make things happen. Timing and deadlines are very important. Few businesses are not bound by time constraints. Individuals within a business will also be directly affected by timing, if only to know when to turn up in the morning and when to go home.

When adding timings into a business plan, like all other forecasts and projections, it is important to be realistic. It is no use planning to launch the business in three months when you know that it will take longer than this to get stock shipped from the Far East or for premises to be ready. Shortening timings or setting unrealistic deadlines will only lead to frustration and worry as they are missed, with the consequences that all other deadlines are missed. You will always be running, trying to catch up from the start. This can have a negative and depressing effect on someone trying to start a business.

Monitoring

Built into the plans for running the business should be regular monitoring to make sure that it keeps on track, that it continues to meet the aims and objectives, so that if it does not the business can change plans or make new plans to bring itself back into line. Monitoring will also enable a business to revise its objectives and plan the necessary changes. Monitoring should take place in a number of areas, as shown in Figure 3.

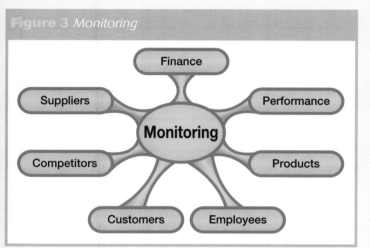

Figure 3 *Monitoring*

Finance Financial monitoring is perhaps the most necessary. Keeping track of money coming into the business and money going out will soon show if any problems are occurring. The use of a cash flow forecast can be useful in this respect. A rolling monthly annual figure will highlight trends, up and down. It will also smooth out any peaks and troughs in the financial figures, which could distort, raise false hopes or make you unduly worried. This means adding together monthly figures for twelve months to give the annual figure, then as each month passes adding the figures for that month to the total and subtracting the figure for the same month in the previous year. In this way the annual figure will be up-to-date, but be moving to show any trends.

General performance Regular monitoring of sales data against objectives or forecasts will, like the analysis of financial data, highlight any problems before they become too great to overcome. A business needs to be aware if it is growing, static or declining. It can then make decisions about whether to do something about it.

Products It is useful to monitor just what products or services are selling. Keeping on top of product sales patterns will help forecasting and planning and may highlight opportunities for developing or expanding a market. In addition, a business needs to know what are the best sellers, which are performing poorly, which customers keep asking for and which they are ignoring. Overall, are products still meeting customer needs? Monitoring products is an important part of the quality assurance process. It is no good setting quality or performance standards at the start of a business and assuming that they will remain static. A business needs to keep on top of product quality to make sure that customers remain satisfied with the product or service that they receive. Customer feedback research is a useful tool for this.

Customers Who are the customers? Are they the same or changing? Is the business attracting new types of customers from different markets? Is a business retaining all of its old customers or is it losing them? Monitoring the customer base will help answer each of these questions.

Competitors Who are they? Are they changing? What are they doing? What are their marketing plans and what product plans have they launched? A business needs to monitor and keep up to date with competitor activity so that it can protect its own business.

Suppliers In this situation a business is a customer and needs to make sure that it continues to receive good customer service from suppliers. If they let a business down, it may lose customers' trade. Keeping records and monitoring the performance of suppliers is another aspect of quality control.

Employees This may not apply to all businesses, but where there are employees or a team working together in a business there is an opportunity for monitoring performance. This can be used for staff development, training, or even discipline in some cases.

Regular monitoring will mean that a business will be able to evaluate its position at any time or when a stakeholder asks for an update of the current position of the business. If you can demonstrate that you are on top of things, this will greatly add to the confidence that stakeholders will have in you as a person who can run a worthwhile, well planned and, most importantly, a viable and profitable business.

Each section of this unit deals with a particular aspect of the business plan. The following shows an example of the type of information that could be included in a business plan to forecast the position of the business.

Business example - Demont Jordan

Demont Jordan intends to start trading as a marketing and advertising consultant. He is planning to launch the business from the start of the next calendar year. In addition to his main business plan he has added a 3-year plan, which includes the following details:

	Notes	End Year 1	Year 2	Year 3
Sales	1	£17,600	£35,200	£66,000
Business costs	2	£15,000	£7,000	£10,000
Gross profit	3	£2,600	£28,200	£51,000
Customers	4	Six	Eight	Ten
Working area	5	Essex	Essex	Essex
Promotion	6	Direct mail Listings in directories	Direct mail Listings in directories	Direct mail Listings in directories
Promotion costs	7	£1,000	£1,000	£1,000
Net profit	8	£1,600	£27,200	£50,000

Notes.
1. Assumes starting in Year 1, working 20% of available time (maximum 220 days a year) at full rate of £400.00 per day, growing to 30% and 40% of available time as awareness grows and I get more busy through Years 2 and 3. I have not planned any increase in my daily rate as my overheads are not forecast to increase. Will need to monitor sales as Year 3 may reach VAT threshold, which will have major implications.
2. Business costs in Year 1 are for start-up costs, a new computer and printer, and the deposit on the car. In Years 2 and 3 the costs will come down as I am not planning to buy new capital equipment. Costs will therefore be mainly consumables.
3. Gross profit in Year 1 is very modest as a direct result of high start-up costs. Years 2 and 3 will see gross profit rise as cost will not increase as much as income. This means that although I will need to rely on savings during Year 1 for my living costs I will be able to draw a real wage in Years 2 and 3.
4. Year 1 starts with the six clients that I have already contacted. As I am a sole trader I do not want to have too many clients. I aim to maintain a high quality of service and do not want to let this slip by having too many clients to deal with.
5. My plan is to just operate within the borders of Essex. This will mean that I can concentrate my modest marketing budget in media that only circulate in Essex, and that my travelling costs will be kept down as I will not be having to drive too far, although I will be prepared to travel further if the clients are prepared to pay.
6. I intend to keep my promotion very simple. Directory listings to create a general awareness, plus direct mail to targeted businesses in Essex will be used.
7. I do not plan to exceed this promotional cost and do not foresee that it will increase over the years.
8. Net profit is gross profit less promotional cost. As mentioned in Note 3, no wage to be drawn until Years 2 and 3.

'I have chosen to do the projections across three full years. Some business start-ups will wait until they have figures for the first year, then project three, even five years on from that point. It all depends on the requirements of the business and for whom the plan is being written. However, I feel confident that I have realistic projections based on accurate data.

As a sole trader, without any projected need for a large capital investment, this forecast gives me confidence that I should be able to make money from my chosen business idea. If I needed to go to a bank or other stakeholder in order to raise capital I may have forecast Year 1 and then project on for three years from the end of Year 1. In this way any high start-up costs will (hopefully) be out of the equation and the projection will present a more realistic picture of the way that the business is forecast to run, its likely income, profit margins, and other targets.'

Mark Band 1 A simple evaluation of the business position at the end of year 1 and a 3 year projection. This would show the basic figures in the table and statements on its likely success over the period, giving reasons.

Mark Band 2 Sound analysis of present and projected position showing independence of thought. This would include all the figures in the table, supported by calculations and forecasts in other parts of the business plan. Independence of thought might include changes made to the projections in changing circumstances, such as the need for extra finance.

Mark Band 3 Comprehensive analysis of present and projected positions, with detailed recommendations and justified conclusions. This would require an extensive business plan showing all aspects and calculations of financial positions in Year 1 and to Year 3. This would be supported by calculations such as revenue and costs, profit, budgets and cash flow and the strategies used to achieve these. Changes that may need to be made to the business operation would be highlighted and justified.

12 Motivation

What is motivation?

In general terms motivation is the force which drives individuals to behave in a particular way or take a particular action. For example, students at college may be motivated to work hard at their exams because they want to secure a good job, medical patients may be motivated to lose weight because they have been told their obesity is life-threatening or athletes may be training hard because they are motivated by the desire to win medals.

In the context of business, the term motivation is usually used in terms of developing strategies to achieve the best output from staff – to get them to work as hard and effectively as they are able. Workers who are hard working and productive make a business more efficient and productive.

Indicators of a well-motivated workforce

Figure 1 shows some indicators of a well-motivated workforce.

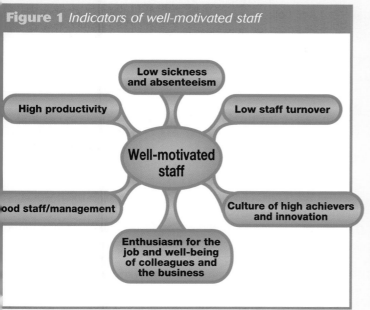

Figure 1 *Indicators of well-motivated staff*

- Low sickness and absenteeism
- High productivity
- Low staff turnover
- Well-motivated staff
- ...ood staff/management
- Culture of high achievers and innovation
- Enthusiasm for the job and well-being of colleagues and the business

High productivity High productivity comes from effective and efficient use of equipment, resources and personnel. A supermarket, for example, may have productivity targets linked to customer loyalty or wastage. When employees and management have little interest in their work the supermarket is unlikely to be able to meet targets of this type. To enjoy customer loyalty or see minimum wastage, a supermarket needs to have staff who are:

- happy in their work;
- making sure the shelves are topped-up regularly;
- checking that there is continual supply of trolleys available;
- keeping the retail area safe with spillages cleared up quickly and

who go out of their way to help customers and experience customer loyalty.

The importance of developing people in improving productivity is highlighted in Figure 2.

Figure 2 *Developing people and productiivity*

The key to organisational success is the development of people, creating a more skilled confident and motivated workforce capable of improving not only a company's bottom line but its shareholder value and output too. People-based strategies enable organisations to execute better business planning and focus companies' aims, increasing productivity.

Source: adapted from www.investorsinpeople.co.uk.

Low absenteeism and sickness In all businesses, at any one time or another, there are likely to be a few members of staff who are absent or off due to illness. High levels of absenteeism, high levels of sickness or simply a failure to report in to work can be indicators of a poorly motivated workforce.

Dissatisfaction in the workplace may be from any number of reasons such as:

- the stress of the work;
- poor working conditions - perhaps the building is too hot, too cold or too crowded or there is no-one to talk to;
- management has an uncaring attitude towards personal circumstances such as child care responsibilities;
- pay is too low.

A study of 250,000 employees by Lancaster University and Manchester Business School in 2005 found that workers who are unhappy in their jobs are more likely to become ill. Workers who are satisfied by their jobs are more likely to be healthier, as well as happier

Others may just not make an effort to come into work when they feeling 'under the weather' or simply take a 'sickie', claiming to be unwell when they are not. Workers who generally find most aspects of their work satisfying and fulfilling would be less disturbed by problems or be happy to put in the effort to find a solution. An example is given in Figure 3.

Low staff turnover Staff turnover measures the number of people that leave a business during the year as a percentage of the total number of people employed. It is important to keep staff turnover low because it is expensive to recruit and train new staff. The Royal Bank of Scotland, for example, has found that a one percentage point reduction in staff turnover can save the group over £20 million a year.

A high level of staff turnover is an indicator of poorly motivated

Figure 3 *Stopping the sickies: the carrot*

Standard Life Healthcare, an insurance company based in Guildford, has taken a carrot approach. It decided that finding ways to encourage people to stay healthy and come to work was the best approach. It has set up a range of ways to support employees.
- Fitness classes.
- Massages at your desk.
- Online health checks and guidance.
- Healthy meals in the restaurant.

The outcome of these strategies has been just as Standard Life Healthcare hoped: absenteeism has fallen and productivity has risen. Staff are happier, healthier and enjoy coming to work.

Source: adapted from http://news.bbc.co.uk/1/hi/programmes/working_lunch/3644234.stm, September 2004.

Figure 4 *Feeling valued*

'Good employers recognise that their staff are going to have problems from time to time and are flexible about how they dea with it,' the trades union organisation's spokesman said. 'Staff working for an understanding employer with flexible working practices are more likely to feel valued and be more productive'. TUC - March 2005

Source: adapted from http://www.bbc.co.uk/news.

Figure 5 *Staff creativity*

Media Agency MediaCom, relies heavily on the creativity of its st As part of its strategy to attract, retain and motivate innovative personnel it offers a range of exciting benefits which include a visiting manicurist, generous pension contributions, opportunity t use a free holiday apartment in Cyprus, free cappuccino and fabulous prizes for new ideas.

Source: adapted from *The Sunday Times 100 best companies to work for 2005*.

---

staff. Furthermore, high staff turnover in itself can lead to poor motivation as social bonds are less likely to be created and there will be fewer people in the organisation who feel a sense of 'ownership' through long service or company loyalty.

Organisations therefore will be keen to see a low level of staff turnover and will aim to achieve this by helping workers, for example, achieve job satisfaction, or having working conditions that suit their personal needs, such as a comfortable environment, flexible working hours or sufficient remuneration for a comfortable lifestyle.

Good staff/management relations Managers who meet the needs of their staff in terms of, for example, providing good working conditions, being sympathetic to their grievances or offering good career development opportunities, are likely to enjoy a good relationship with their staff. In turn, staff are more likely to show commitment and flexibility. This is illustrated in Figure 4.

Culture of high achievers and innovation Workers who are highly motivated will work to the best of their ability, striving to do well both for themselves and the business. They will be seeking ways to improve and refine their own working environment. They are likely to be thinking about their work even at times when they are not in the workplace and will be keen to find solutions to problems that may be making their own work or the work of

others more onerous than they feel it should be. Well motivated workers will also be interested in the forward progress of the business and will be much less likely to resist change than the unmotivated worker. An example is shown in Figure 5.

Enthusiasm for the job and well-being of colleagues and the business Highly motivated staff will be keen to do well, wor for the good of the business and will look forward to going to work. They are more likely, where the job permits, to show initiative and choose to do extra tasks, rather than waiting to be instructed. Even in a working environment where there would appear to be little opportunity for taking initiative, such as on an assembly line, well-motivated workers would be concerned about potential problems such as faulty products coming through or hold-ups in supplies, and would suggest solutions. Others may choose to run social events for their workmates in the interests of creating good working relationships.

In 2005, for example, Nottinghamshire City Council introduced an award scheme for staff who are 'Going the extra mile' as explained in Figure 6.

How to motivate

It may be possible for an organisation to identify factors that sho that its workers are demoralised. It may be less easy to find ways to raise the level of motivation. Finding the right balance could be critical for a business experiencing poor industrial relations, or facing rising costs due to excessive wastage or careless work practices, or suffering low productivity.

Organisations will employ a variety of incentives to raise motivation. Figure 7 shows some of these incentives.

Figure 6 *Nottingham City Council – Going the Extra Mile Award*

Barbara Kirk, a Senior Home Care Worker is the first winner of the GEM Home Care Award. Barbara was nominated for the Go the Extra Mile award after putting together a presentation for Worcestershire County Council, which is setting up its own specialist dementia team. Barbara said: 'It is lovely to be recognised but certainly all my team, the managers and I believe all the Home Care Service "Go the Extra Mile" regularly. We're very supportive of each other and dedicated to our service users.'

Source: adapted from Nottingham City Council.

Money Organisations that seek to recruit and retain the best staff in terms of qualifications and commitment may feel they need to attract them with high salaries. Money may also be a motivator through the awarding of bonuses which may be paid, for example, when production deadlines or sales targets are met. They may even be paid for reduced absence or to encourage staff retention. In August 2004, British Airways announced that it would pay a £1,000 bonus to staff who claimed fewer than 16 days' sick leave over two years.

Share options, where employees are rewarded with shares in the company, are becoming an increasingly popular means of motivating staff. Some argue that share options have the double benefit of not only being seen as a financial reward which earns

the owner dividends, but also gives the employee a vested interest in the success of the company. Employees who own shares are more likely to be motivated and show flexibility if they see it as beneficial to the organisation. They may also be less likely to take industrial action. On the other hand Figure 8 shows that this may not always be the case.

There are drawbacks, however, to using money as the sole motivator in an organisation. People who are motivated by money may not show loyalty to a company through difficult times if they see that they are likely to be denied a pay rise or bonus, which is the very time when the organisation is in need of their best talent.

Figure 8 *Deferred shares as an incentive*

Deferred shares - which can only be sold in future years - can be used as a way of both motivating staff to keep on performing and to encourage them to stay put. Shaun Springer, chief executive of executive search firm Napier Scott, thinks such handcuffs are a waste of time - a new employer will simply pay an even higher package to buy them out.

Source: adapted from www.guardian.co.uk.

Money, or the absence of it, may even be perceived in some circumstances as a demotivator. The theorist, Frederick Herzberg, (see section 13), considered money not to be a motivator, but a hygiene factor. He believed that while money in itself is not a motivator, the absence of it can be a demotivator. For example, when bonuses or pay rises are awarded, those that don't receive them will feel they have been treated unfairly. An example is given in Figure 9.

Figure 7 *Incentives*

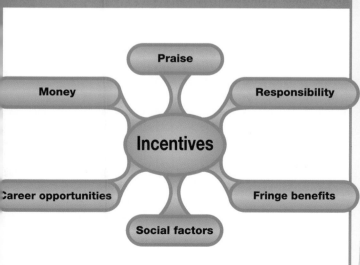

Figure 9 *Heathrow workers strike over bonus*

Workers at Heathrow's Terminal 5 staged a walkout last week over pay. The action on Monday, January 23, was the fourth in a series of strikes that started in December last year. Workers for Laing O'Rourke who are building the £4.2billion Terminal 5 at Heathrow Airport are in dispute over an extra £1 per hour in workers' bonus schemes. Workers wanted the extra money in their bonus scheme, which has not been reviewed in three years, and is lower than other workers on the site.

Source: adapted from *Hillingdon Times*, 1.2.2006.

Praise Everyone enjoys being told they have done well. Even if we have never been lucky enough to receive a prize, certificate or trophy most of us have times when we can remember being told 'well done' or being praised for a piece of work and how it made us feel good. Many effective businesses and managers recognise this need to be valued and have strategies in place in the workplace to ensure that workers feel praised and valued. Crew Clothing, a chain of outdoor leisure clothing suppliers, has reward schemes which include Manager of the Year and Team of the Year which are presented by the Managing Director.

However, effective managers recognise that praise has to be given carefully. For example, it is important that people are singled out for their achievements in team situations. If people are routinely included in whole-team praise, the high performers are at risk of being demotivated. Effective managers are also mindful of the fact that they should not praise people for doing everyday assignments that they should be completing anyway otherwise they are unlikely to strive to achieve more.

Responsibility Giving workers responsibility encourages a sense of ownership and empowerment. If they have the power, for example, to make even minor changes in their work situation, those changes are likely to be for the better. If they are given responsibility for results, such as meeting production schedules, or successful marketing, they are more likely to be striving for positive outcomes, as shown in Figure 10.

Figure 10

Honda UK, car, motor cycle and power equipment suppliers, encourages the workforce to contribute to marketing. All members of staff, regardless of their role are invited to help out at motor shows or boat shows.

Source: adapted from *The Sunday Times 100 Best Companies to Work For 2005*.

Strategies that include devolving power down the hierarchy are, of course, likely to lead to a loss of direct control by management and can lead to stress and demotivation of those who are ultimately accountable for the actions of those below them in the hierarchy. An organisation which employs a strategy of giving more responsibility to production workers may, for example, be involved in costly training packages to raise awareness of Health and Safety issues. Or if they are encouraging all staff to be involved in marketing, it may be necessary to ensure that they are trained in the necessary technical and interpersonal skills.

Career opportunities Employees who see that they may have a future with the company and can progress up the career ladder are more likely to be working to the best of their ability. On the one hand they want to be seen to be worthy of promotion and on the other they want the company to succeed because they see themselves playing a part in its future growth and profit and being rewarded accordingly. Thomson Directories, for example, gives excellent opportunities for progression. In 2004, of the 49 managers or supervisors who were appointed, 41 were as a result of internal promotion. An organisation which offers these opportunities is likely to see a high level of loyalty from its staff.

However, organisations may not always be able to offer a robust career path for all employees. This may be due to the uncertainties of continually changing technology, proposed changes in objectives or business strategies or because that particular industry is 'worker-heavy' with a relatively high unskilled or semi-skilled workforce and small management base such as in the catering or production industries. Such organisations would need to look to other methods of motivating staff.

Social factors Workers who get on well with their colleagues and enjoy a good relationship with management are likely to feel less stress in the workplace. They will feel supported and relaxed and enjoy going to work. It is also recognised that many important and potentially innovative strategies or policies are often first suggested and discussed at informal social gatherings. Many organisations understand the importance and potential impact of good interpersonal relationships and encourage this. For example, staff at WPA Health insurers enjoy Chinese meals together after work, weekends in Normandy and Bruges, theatre trips, ten pin bowling and taking part in football matches.

One difficulty of encouraging social factors within the workplace is achieving a balance between too much or too little social interaction. Too little and the workers feel alienated, too much and no work gets done. Further, the manager who has fostered a good relationship with and amongst staff may then find it difficult to take disciplinary measures or to handle staff when they are required to show greater commitment to completing projects.

Fringe benefits Benefits in addition to pay and working conditions can have a significant financial advantage for workers and have an important impact on staff recruitment, commitment and retention. Visualfiles, for example, a computer software company, offers **free private health care**.

Flexible work programmes are often seen as a fringe benefit. Some features of a flexible work programme may include workers having the freedom to set their own starting and finishing times, facilitating job sharing so that single parents can spend more time with their children, allowing some work to be carried out at home, shift swapping where workers arrange their own shifts. This allows workers to achieve a better **work-life balance**. Other fringe benefits may include

- pension schemes;
- company car;
- in-house nursery or subsidy towards child care;
- subsidised canteen;
- a staff-friendly policy on compassionate leave for personal

emergencies such as elderly parent care or a child in hospital;
* works buses or subsidised travel to and from work;
* in-house sports facilities.

Fringe benefits, however, can present the potential for conflict. Flexible working hours, for example, can have an adverse impact on effective communication in the workplace. It was suggested earlier in this section that money may be seen as both a motivator and a demotivator. In the same way fringe benefits can provide the organisation with a dilemma. They are often the first things to be considered for cutbacks when the business is facing financial constraints and when such benefits are taken away workers can face financial difficulty and feel more demoralised than if they had never been offered them in the first place. Figure 11 shows an example.

Figure 11 *Harrods shutting pension scheme*

famous London department store Harrods is notifying its staff about closing its final salary pension plan to new and existing employees. It proposes the final salary pension scheme will be closed to existing and new employees at the start of April. Harrods has said the decision was 'not taken easily' and that a new money purchase scheme will be introduced. The Transport and General Workers Union said staff were 'shocked', and that it wanted talks on the issue with Harrods. The union said there were currently 1,500 members of the pension scheme who will be directly affected by the change.

Source: adapted from http://www.bbc.co.uk.

Psychological factors Many workers will often be working in organisations which are not in a position to offer huge pay packets or other financial incentives. Sometimes the working conditions may not even be that favourable. The staff who do show commitment are motivated by the work itself. They feel valued and consider they are fulfilling a worthwhile and an important role in their workplace and society as a whole. This type of worker is often seen in the public service industries such as health care, education and the fire services. The staff at St Joseph's Hospice in East London, for example, who care for the dying, consider the work to be a privilege.

The potential for conflict

The examples of incentives that businesses could introduce to increase motivation, given in Figure 7, often appear to be relatively simple. If poor pay is identified as leading to low morale the organisation could simply increase the wages. Or staff who are unhappy with mobile snack service could be provided with kitchen facilities. Staff expressing concerns about poor career progression may put pressure on the business to review its career structure.

However, all business decisions have to be made taking account of the organisation's aims and objectives. It follows therefore, that proposals to meet workers' needs may conflict with one or more of the overall business objectives. Some examples are:

* an increase in wages may conflict with the aim of the organisation to reduce costs because of poor profit performance;
* a decision to improve working conditions by refurbishing may conflict with longer term plans to re-locate;
* a review of the career structure to provide clearer career progression may conflict with a plan to re-structure and cut out layers of the hierarchy.

Resolving conflict of objectives

Matching the needs of the individual with the needs of the organisation always brings the potential for conflict. Business has to devise strategies to deal with such conflict. This may, for example, be by seeking out some compensatory alternatives or involving staff in the decision-making to raise awareness of the constraints the business is working under. Two further examples are given in Figure 12.

Figure 12 *Resolving conflict*

56% of staff who work for the Asda Supermarket feel they are low paid. Asda operates on very thin profit margins which means that a small increase in costs, such as an increase in pay, can have a significant impact on profitability and therefore objectives linked to future investment. Asda addresses this conflict between staff's personal objectives and company objectives by providing additional benefits (e.g. colleague discount card, share options, flexible working options) estimated to be worth an extra 50p per hour. The HSA group, a personal medical plan provider, recognises the conflict employees can experience between meeting their own needs and the needs of the company. Amongst other benefits, they offer a day's paid leave for moving house and a day's paid leave when a child starts a new school.

Source: adapted from company information.

On its website, http://www.inchcape.com, Inchcape, distributors of new and used cars, lists discounted car purchase, employee car leasing schemes, a 'Save As You Earn' (SAYE) share option scheme and discounted gym membership amongst the benefits it offers for employees.

Research the websites of other large organisations and list the benefits that two of them offer to their employees. If is often helpful to look for the 'corporate information' or 'company information' section of the website to find this type of information. Outline the strengths and weaknesses of each benefit.

Research task

Portfolio practice · Eversheds

'Eversheds was the first UK law firm to introduce a flexible working programme and now has 277 people working flexibly, including 12 job sharing and 45 with reduced hours each day. Although the workload is high, 72% think their work is stimulating and nearly seven out of 10 staff are excited about where the company is going.'

Source: adapted from *The Sunday Times 100 best companies to work for 2005*.

(a) **Explain the likely advantages to Eversheds of introducing the flexible working programme.**
(b) **Explain why the flexible working programme is likely to improve motivation in the organisation.**
(c) **Suggest a business objective that a business such as Eversheds may have set itself and explain how meeting the needs of individuals through a flexible working programme may conflict with that objective.**

Meeting the assessment criteria - examiners' guidance

For your assessment you are required to write a report on the factors that affect motivation in an organisation with which you are familiar. This involves a description and explanation of motivation methods used by the business and their strengths and weaknesses. It also requires the understanding of conflicts that may arise and suggested solutions.

Business example - Snowdrop Park Hospice

Snowdrop Park Hospice is a charity which provides care for patients suffering terminal illness. Staff are expected not only to care for and support patients but to create an environment where everyone is considered as family.

Mark Band 1 *A basic description of the motivational strategies of the organisation.*
Staff felt that communication is very good at Snowdrop Park Hospice. The hospice manager has an open door policy which means that staff can go at any time to talk to her when she is free without having to make an appointment. She also makes frequent visits to all parts of the hospice. Staff felt that their concerns were listened to and acted upon. Staff were given up to five days' leave for personal emergencies.

Mark Band 2 *A good explanation of the organisation's motivational strategies. Strengths and weaknesses of the strategies are identified. Understanding and examples of potential/actual conflict between individual and organisational needs are clear.*
When staff were interviewed they all felt very confident of the procedures and who to contact at times of emergency. It is important in an organisation like Snowdrop Park Hospice that staff feel comfortable that there is quick and effective communication between staff and management because if they are suffering anxiety or uncertainty this will affect their relationship with patients and their families. However, this may put management under stress if they are continually faced with staff problems and it reduces the incentive for staff to develop the skill to use their own initiative.

The staff particularly appreciated the leave they were offered for personal emergencies. For example, one member of staff had her credit cards stolen and was given time off to arrange replacements. It was critical that she did that immediately and the organisation understood that she would not be working

effectively if she was worrying about her financial affairs. This attitude helps to improve management-staff relations. Staff are more likely to cover for absent staff if they know that they themselves may benefit from this policy at some time. However, planning can be difficult if staff expect to have time off at short notice. Also, if this fringe benefit is cut back in times of financial difficulties, staff could become demotivated.

The low pay scales are an area for potential conflict. As a charity the organisation needs to keep its costs to a minimum and be seen to be using resources wisely, but individuals will be seeking enough to cover their basic needs and perhaps would wish to be earning the amounts they could earn in other sectors.

Mark Band 3 *Relevant examples of how the conflict between individual and organisational needs may be resolved or avoided are given and justified.*
Taking account of the financial constraints the charity works under, the solutions to potential conflict between the organisation's need to keep costs down and individual needs to enjoy a comfortable lifestyle must necessarily be low cost or even non-financial. There are incentives that could be offered to staff which would not incur large outlay of expenditure. Perhaps a link could be made with a local company which has gym facilities for the hospice staff to use their facilities. The charitable nature of the organisation would make this type of arrangement possible and there would be the added benefit that the profile of the charity would be raised. This would not cost the hospice anything but staff would have the financial benefit of free gym membership.

The management could organise low cost social events. This would meet the staff's social needs and would play an important part in the creating the family atmosphere that the hospice seeks.

Staff could have a greater involvement in decision-making, for example on shift hours, stock control or family liaison. This would help meet their status and self-esteem needs which were not being met by high wages and would raise awareness amongst the staff of the financial constraints the organisation is working under and possibly reducing the demands for higher pay. However, this could conflict with patient care as staff would be taken off those duties for the consultative process.

Motivation theories and managing human resources

Section 12 looked at the importance to an organisation of having a well-motivated workforce. Extensive research has been carried out to examine what motivates people to work harder and to help businesses devise strategies and policies that would inspire their workers. This research has led to a number of important motivational theories.

Many successful businesses now apply the results of these findings to their human resources management programmes and use motivational theories to help manage their employees. Of course, every organisation has its own individual set of circumstances and it cannot be said that any one of these theories is able to offer the perfect solution. However, the work of these psychologists and management experts has been very influential in the way that businesses manage their staff.

Taylor

Frederick Taylor adopted a scientific approach to motivation. He believed that the main factor which motivated people was money. Taylor argued that providing workers with the opportunity to earn more money would increase output and productivity. This approach is often successfully adopted in industrial processes where pay is directly related to rate of production, such as:

- when workers are paid by the number of items they process (piece rate);
- where work is monotonous and repetitive or where, through the payment of bonuses, workers need to be encouraged to meet deadlines.

Taylor's approach, sometimes referred to as the Scientific Management approach, often demands strict autocratic-style management, as described in section 16. This is particularly the case where peformance payments are dependent on the performance of others such as on a production line. Autocratic managers tend to make their own decisions with little reference to the views of others.

Figure 1 gives an example of an organisation that has successfully given financial incentives as a motivator.

Critics of this approach believe that it does not recognise that poor productivity may be influenced by other factors and ignores the human side of production. Nor would it be an appropriate formula for industries where creativity is a key resource. Further, there are many industries, such as the hospice described in section 12, where there are financial constraints and low pay yet staff are highly motivated and dedicated and so clearly money is not the main motivator.

Mayo – the Hawthorne Effect

Elton Mayo argued that people respond not only to financial rewards, but also to other factors, such as working environment and social interaction. His ideas were developed from studies at the Western Electric Hawthorne Works in Chicago, which led to

Figure 1 *Royal Mail incentives*

In August 2004 the Royal Mail introduced a scheme to reward postal workers with new cars and holiday vouchers if they do not take any sick leave. Staff who went six months without a day off sick were entered in a prize draw. Attendance levels have risen by 11% - some 1,000 workers a day - since it was launched, the firm said.

Source: adapted from http://news.bbc.co.uk/.

Figure 2 *Whittard of Chelsea – tea and coffee specialists*

'There is a great, friendly family atmosphere in Whittard's shops. Everybody makes an effort to get to know each other well and we work brilliantly as a team. The company is fun and fulfilling and I hope I never leave. My job means a lot to me and has taught me a lot of valuable lessons.'

Source: adapted from www.whittard.co.uk.

the phrase 'the Hawthorne Effect' being used to describe the findings.

Today, this approach, sometimes referred to as the Human Relations school, recognises that workers need to perceive that they are valued by management to be motivated. Managers that want to maximise productivity must serve all employees' needs, including, importantly, the need for recognition and belonging. An example is given in Figure 2. This approach may also involve the use of teamwork and recognise that good communication is also recognised as being essential.

A typical management style for a leader following Mayo's theory would be a more relaxed, democratic style, allowing interaction amongst the staff. Management would be approachable themselves and be willing to listen to grievances.

McGregor's Theory X and Theory Y management styles

Douglas McGregor's ideas provide a guide to management styles in different business situations. However, they also give some insight into factors that may motivate employees and leadership approaches that may be taken by managers to effectively motivate employees. McGregor compared two different styles of managers - Theory X and Theory Y managers – each having particular views about the factors that are likely to motivate workers.

McGregor argued that a Theory X manager believes:

- employees are essentially lazy and will avoid work if left to their own devices;
- workers need to be closely supervised and directed and threatened with sanctions or punishment;
- employees will show little ambition and dislike reponsibility;
- workers dislike work and are only motivated by money.

This corresponds with the scientific management approach and so Theory X managers are likely to adopt autocratic management styles.

Alternatively, Theory Y managers tend to take a more human relations view of employees. They argue that many factors, not simply money, can motivate workers. They will often have a more democratic leadership style.

Table 1 shows features of a Theory Y management style and how they have been applied at the Fire Services National Benevolent Fund, a charity which organises fundraising events to provide services for serving and retired fire service personnel and their families.

Maslow's hierarchy of needs

Abraham Maslow's theory of motivation argued that people are motivated because of their desire to satisfy their needs. These needs are often shown in order of priority in the form of a pyramid, as illustrated in Figure 3. Maslow suggested that people have a **hierarchy** of needs that must be satisfied in order. People have to meet one set of needs before they can satisfy the next and higher order needs.

Maslow's hierarchy illustrates the following needs of employees.

- Physiological needs. These are basic human needs such as survival, the need for shelter, food and air to breathe. In work this might include the need to earn a basic wage to feed a family.

Table 1 *Theory Y management style*

The Theory Y manager believes:	Fire Services National Benelovent Fund
• Employees are ambitious and self-motivated and satisfied by doing a good job. • Workers are anxious to accept greater responsibility, and are able to exercise self-control and self-direction. • Workers enjoy work and will be imaginative and creative if given the opportunity. • Workers want to be trusted. • Workers can organise themselves. • Workers should be rewarded appropriately.	• The training programme includes the chance to study for professional qualifications. • There are opportunities for advancement. • There is a secure and warm working atmosphere. • 86% of staff feel they make a valuable contribution to the success of the organisation. • Staff gain satisfaction from knowing they do a job that benefits firefighters.

Source: adapted from *The Sunday Times 100 Best Companies to Work For 2005*.

Figure 3 *Maslow's Hierarchy of Needs*

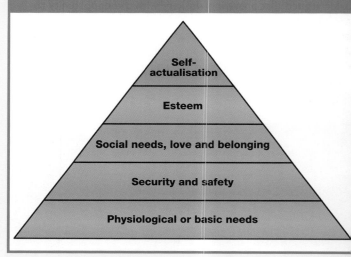

- Security and safety. This is the need for security, safety and protection against danger. In work this might include a safe environment and job security.
- Social needs and love and belonging. This is the need to feel accepted and part of a group. In work it might include working in a team or developing work friends.
- Esteem. This is the need for recognition, praise, self-respect and status. In work it might include rewards for achievement, such as promotion.
- Self-actualisation. This is the need to fulfil potential. In work it might include being given the opportunity for workers to be

Figure 4 *Maslow's hierarchy of needs and Bacardi Martini*

Drinks manufacturer, Bacardi-Martini, was ranked number nine in the 2005 *Sunday Times* list of 100 best companies to work for. Certain factors at Bacardi-Martini would suggest that the needs on Maslow's hierarchy are being met for most workers.

Need	Bacardi Martini
Physiological	Employees are offered a free lunch every day.
Security and safety	Workers have free health insurance and a non-contributory pension scheme.
Social – belonging and love	There is a close-knit feeling and a family atmosphere.
Esteem	91% are proud to work for Bacardi-Martini; trust has replaced clocking in for shift workers; managers express appreciation for a job well done. There is a monthly meeting where staff representatives put forward ideas and have their concerns listened to.
Self-actualisation	People are given responsibility; 82% feel they can make a valuable contribution to the company's success. The company has an open door policy and employees are free to approach any level of management, up to the managing director, with their ideas.

Source: adapted from *The Sunday Times 100 Best Companies to Work For 2005* and company information.

innovative and carry out their own ideas.
An example of how these needs might be met in business is shown in Figure 4.

The follower of Maslow's theory is likely to adopt a democratic or paternalistic management style. They will be concerned for their workers' needs and encourage two-way communicatiion. They are likely to be willing to delegate appropriately and give opportunities where possible for personal development and progression.

Herzberg's hygiene factors and motivators

Frederick Herzberg's ideas suggested that there are two factors which might affect the motivation of employees at work, which led to the development of his two factor theory.

- **Motivators** please people and encourage and motivate people to a higher level of performance.
- **Hygiene factors** are features of the work and workplace which displease, or dissatisfy, people if they are not met. In themselves they do not motivate, but, if not present, they can lead to dissatisfaction.

Motivators and hygiene factors are summarised in Figure 5.

Herzberg stated that if employers and managers want their employees to be motivated, they must first meet their basic requirements in terms of hygiene factors and then provide the motivators. Figure 6 shows news reports which demonstrate how workers can be affected by the presence or lack of good hygiene factors and motivators in their workplace.

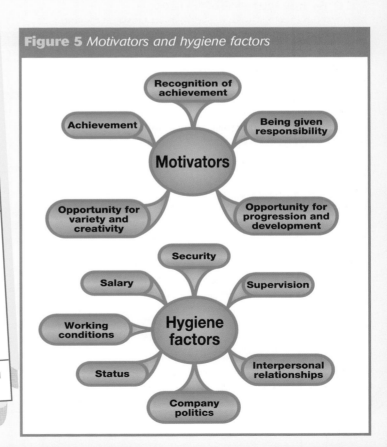

Figure 5 *Motivators and hygiene factors*

Figure 6 *Impact of hygiene factors and motivators in the workplace*

Working conditions
Our office is really stuffy we have three fans and an air cooler, but even with these the temp this afternoon was getting above 33 degrees - everyone just feels so lethargic and can't concentrate. Workers should be able to go home as we aren't very productive at the moment. Plus the air cooler is so loud we can hardly hear anyone speaking a few feet away let alone on the telephone, and we can't have the windows open too much as the blinds then fall apart, and we can't not have the blinds drawn because then we can't see our screens.

Status A survey has suggested that, of all the different jobs in the UK, those who are happiest are hairdressers. Emma Martin has been a stylist for 22 years and many of her clients have become friends after years of her preening their locks. She is still enjoying it and believes the profession is gaining esteem - TV shows like *The Salon* and *Cutting It* might be making a difference.

Interpersonal relationships Bullying is seen as an increasing problem in the UK workplace. The TUC believes that unless the problem is tackled, stress and ill-health can become part of the daily life of those being bullied, resulting in working days lost through sickness.

Responsibility The results of a study from the University of Kent has found that employees are becoming less and less happy in their jobs. Workers feel like robots, with little responsibility and little scope for innovation. Hours are longer and job satisfaction is lower.

Source: adapted from http://news.bbc.co.uk.

Applying the ideas of one motivational theorist you have studied, ask five people in full-time or part-time work to:
- place in rank order the motivating factors identified by that theorist;
- identify strategies used by their employer which could be matched to any of the factors.

The five people you interview should come from a range of ages, from teenagers to people close to retirement.

Research task

Portfolio practice · Incentives

Figure 7 is an extract on 'Being a good boss' from www.bcentral.co.uk.

For one business which you have investigated, evaluate:
(a) the effectiveness of the incentives they use to motivate staff;

(b) whether the introduction of additional incentives similar to those described in Figure 7 would be possible and effective.

Figure 7 *Improving motivation with incentives*

Remuneration is about far more than an employee's basic pay package. Using incentives such as bonuses, commission payments, company cars, pensions and private health care schemes could all help to motivate your team and boost your business's productivity.

To use pay as an effective incentive, you need to decide what you want from each employee and reward them for reaching goals which will really benefit the business. These targets should be challenging - but not impossible to achieve.

Source: adapted from www.bcentral.co.uk.

Meeting the assessment criteria - examiners' guidance

For your assessment you are required to write a report on the factors that affect motivation in an organisation with which you are familiar. It should include reference to theories and techniques used by the organisation and an evaluation of their effectiveness and suggestions for alternative strategies.

Business example - Jeffersons Bulk Buy

Jeffersons Bulk Buy provides a professional wholesale service for independent retailers and caterers. Table 2 shows the results from a questionnaire recently completed by 125 members of staff. An employee has suggested to the management strategies to improve motivation at Jeffersons Bulk Buy.

Table 2 *Survey of 125 staff at Jeffersons Bulk Buy*

	Agree
My work gives me opportunities to be creative	23%
I am paid a fair salary	12%
I get on well with my colleagues	82%
My line manager praises me	35%
My line manager is approachable	34%
My appraisal meetings are worthwhile	23%
I like coming to work	65%
The company has a good health and safety policy	77%
I am ambitious	64%
I have enough training to do my job well	42%

Mark Band 1 *Links are made to a recognised theorist. Strengths and weaknesses of the techniques used by the organisation are identified.*

Over three quarters of the staff at Jeffersons Bulk Buy are satisfied with health and safety so they feel secure, which meets the requirements for the second level on Maslow's hierarchy of needs. My research showed that they are also given plenty of opportunities for social interaction and there is a monthly get-together organised after work with tea and biscuits. 82% of staff felt they got on well with colleagues. These factors would suggest that the third level – social needs – is also met. The first level of Maslow's pyramid is physiological needs, but only 12% of the staff feel that they are paid a fair salary.

Mark Band 2 *Clear links and references are made to a recognised theorist. There is a suggestion of an alternative or additional motivational technique.*

Maslow said that for staff to be well motivated they should have achieved one level before the next can be met. So although there is evidence that the second and third levels of the hierarchy can be met at Jeffersons, 88% being unhappy with their pay would suggest that the first level, basic needs, is not being met. The feeling of security and good social interaction in themselves are unlikely to lead to well motivated staff if staff are dissatisfied with their pay and so cannot get beyond the first level.

The company is not in a position to offer increased pay because its had a poor financial performance last year and one of its business objectives is to reduce costs. Perhaps it could look at offering staff opportunities to buy bulk products at a discount – this would be a very good financial opportunity because, as a wholesaler, it already sells its products cheaper than in retail stores and a discount would bring the price down even more. This would help staff with the weekly shopping bills, in effect giving them an indirect pay rise.

Mark Band 3 *There is clear evaluation of the techniques used by the organisation. The suggestion of an alternative or additional motivational technique is supported and justified.*

Jeffersons is not in a position to offer more pay, but there are opportunities to increase motivation which would cost little in financial terms. The monthly tea and biscuits meeting is meeting the social needs of employees. However, there are other areas of motivation which could be met at these events. Only 35% felt they received praise. Management could take the opportunity to praise employees who have done particularly well that month. This would give them status, which is identified as one of Herzberg's hygiene factors. They could also seek their views on an informal basis on ways to solve problems – this would give staff a sense of achievement if the suggestions are carried through, another of Herzberg's motivators, and would address the fact that only 23% of the workers feel they are given opportunities to be creative. The appraisal system could be reviewed to include opportunities for training which at present doesn't seem to be a main feature of the appraisal. Although training may be expensive, if it addressed the conflict between 64% of staff being ambitious but only 42% feeling training was sufficient and 23% feeling the appraisals were worthwhile, it may improve motivation and consequently productivity.

14 Working in teams

Groups and teams

Groups and teams exist in all organisations. They can be informal or formal.

Informal groups In most organisations informal groups are formed because they meet the needs of one or more of the individuals in those groups. They may include, for example, the need:

- for social interaction;
- to discuss grievances about the management;
- to exchange ideas on a common interest or career progression.

People in informal groups are likely to be from a mix of departments and even across the lines of hierarchy. While informal groups will not have been set up by management, they can form a useful purpose. They may meet social needs, which increases motivation, or management may use them to gain or disseminate information 'through the grapevine'.

Formal groups In most organisations there will also be formal groups. These are groups that have been formed to meet short-term and long-term objectives of the organisation.

It is often considered that the terms 'group' and 'team' are synonymous. However, while groups are a collection of individuals who are working towards a common goal, teams:

- are superior, in that team members feel a sense of ownership and commitment, and respect each other's talents;
- tend to be more established, with a clear set of aims and objectives;
- will be committed to their common goals as it is likely that they will have helped to establish them;
- have team members who feel empowered.
- are usually formed with a reason or purpose at work or to undertake an activity.

Effective teams will have been carefully selected, with balanced and complementary membership of employees.

The benefits of working in well-structured teams

Section 15 explains the ideas of theorists who have studied team dynamics and their theories about what leads to a successful team. However, whichever theory is applied when the team is brought together, an organisation will enjoy significant benefits if the team is well-structured, as shown in Figure 1. Figure 2 gives an example.

Boosts morale The social interaction of any type of team working has the potential to make individuals feel part of a close-knit circle. Membership of a well-structured team, in particular where it is likely that individuals have been selected because of particular skills or characteristics necessary for the team's effectiveness, will make workers feel they are playing an integral part of the whole process and have the confidence that they can influence decision making. This will meet the social and esteem

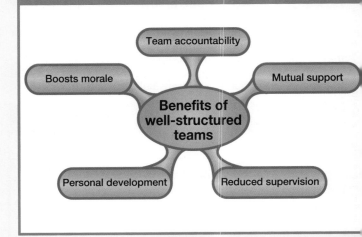

Figure 1 *The benefits of working in well-structured teams*

needs of the individual and, from the organisation's point of view, achieve good levels of motivation.

Mutual support Members of an effective team will have an understanding of each other's strengths and weaknesses and will strive to minimise those weaknesses, giving support where necessary. There will be minimal competition between individuals as there is good understanding of the destructive effect that internal conflict can have on the performance of the team. This w

Figure 2 *A well-organised team structure*

When the UK took over the presidency of the EU in July 2005 British officials unveiled a logo of swans flying in the V-formation.

'The idea is a metaphor for leadership, teamwork and efficiency, which is particularly appropriate for the EU, given the system of rotating leadership,' says Kate Thomson of the Cabinet Office' European Secretariat.

'Migrating birds fly in a V formation. This is highly efficient, because all the birds in the formation, except for the leader, are in the slipstream of another bird.

Periodically the leading bird drops back and another bird moves up to take its place.'

Source: adapted from http://news.bbc.co.uk.

create a good working environment for the individual who will feel comfortable about seeking support from other members of the team. The business also benefits in that there will be fewer issues presented to management to deal with, as potential problems are often resolved within the team. Where issues need to be taken outside the team to management, the team is likely already to have discussed them and will propose potential solutions.

Personal development An atmosphere of mutual support will also lead indirectly to opportunities for personal development. It is in the interests of the team as a whole that individual members, who are lacking in knowledge or experience in any area that is seen as vital to the team's success, are given opportunities for personal development in those areas. Whether this training takes the form of on-the-job training from within the team itself or needs to be delivered by other means, the team is in a good position to carry out an accurate skills assessment to ensure the most effective training is delivered. This, of course, is beneficial both to the individual and the organisation.

Team accountability In many team projects, the short-term objectives are likely to have been set by the whole team itself and not imposed from outside. As a result individuals in that team will feel ownership of the goals and targets. They will see failure to meet those as a whole-team failure, even if in the event it may be identified that it is the failing of one individual in particular. In a creative industry in particular, such as advertising or design, this security will foster an atmosphere of **innovation and creativity** which will be of benefit both to individuals, for their own career development, and to the organisation for robust product development and **productivity**. This sense of accountability felt by individuals will also enhance the effective use of resources and subsequent control of costs.

Reduced supervision The setting of its goals by the team itself will mean that the team will feel ownership of them and will strive to achieve them. Furthermore, individuals within the team will have a good understanding of the importance of their own contribution. Individuals within a well-structured team will be self-motivated and minimal supervision will be needed. This clearly is an advantage to management, whilst at the same time raising the self-esteem and feeling of personal fulfilment amongst individual employees.

Limitations of team working

Setting up effective teams requires time and commitment from management, as shown in Figure 3. When the time and effort is not spent on carefully planning the team there can be problems.

Planning the team One of the greatest limitations of teamwork is where the importance of careful structuring of the team with a balance of skills and characteristics has not been recognised. This is covered in section 15. It is simply not enough to group a set of individuals together and assume they will work as a team. The setting up of an effective team requires time, thought and planning from management.

Size of the team If the size of the team is not appropriate for the task there will be problems with its effectiveness. A

Figure 3 *Teamwork*

'The task is to convince staff members of the excitement of teamwork. In a shared model, everyone on the team initiates things, rather than waiting to be told what to do by the leader. They have a part in creating the values and the vision of the organization.'

Source: Kathleen Allen, Senior Fellow at the University of Maryland's Burns Academy of Leadership.

supermarket, for example, will have small teams for different product sections who work very well together. It will be more difficult to see the entire personnel of 100 or more functioning as a team. If nothing else, effective communication and exchange of ideas will be difficult.

Communication An individual who finds him or herself in a poorly structured team is likely to experience poor communication. The team will lack focus and fail to understand the priorities and needs of its members. There will a lack of clarity about objectives and deadlines. Successful teams can still operate effectively even if team members are not all necessarily working in the same location such as on the same floor, in the same building or even in the same geographical area. However, if when the team's objectives are set, consideration has not been given to providing adequate time and opportunities for exchanging ideas and reviewing progress it is unlikely to be a cohesive entity.

Group dynamics Section 15 examines how a balance of characteristics and skills has been shown to contribute to the effectiveness of a team. However, there may still be personality clashes as well as conflict between team and personal objectives. If the 'chemistry' of the group is not right, the team has the potential for failure.

Leadership problems Too often it is assumed that the most senior person in the team should be the team leader when they may not necessarily have the correct skills for that particular role in that particular project. The style of leadership is also an important consideration to take into account. For example, an autocratic leadership style, a leader who expects complete obedience and does not allow free exchange of ideas, would be totally inappropriate for a team whose remit is to propose designs for the company's new website. Leadership styles are examined in detail in section 16. Ineffective or inappropriate leadership can cause a team to fail. Frustration with unclear goals and lack of progress will cause exclusive cliques to form.

Conflict of interest Where there are no clear group goals, the team is poorly managed or the team is appearing to fail, personal goals will predominate. Individuals will be seeking to disassociate themselves from group responsibility and will fail to give support to other members or accept group accountability. Competition to be the one to succeed and the achievement of personal objectives will predominate.

Team balance Earlier in this section the issues of personal development and mutual support were shown to be significant benefits of team working, both to the individual and the organisation. However, a downside of that is, when an individual is selected for a team because of a particular set of skills or characteristics, he or she may feel that the balance for them is being tipped too far in the direction of contributing rather than benefiting and that no personal progression or development is taking place. Equally, the issue of team accountability can be contentious for hardworking and conscientious workers who may feel that their personal achievements are threatened by the errors of others. All of this will lead to lack of motivation and poor job satisfaction.

For this task you need to work with a set of people who are working together on a particular project. It may, for example, be a group or team in your part-time work or a set of people in your college or school. Interview members of that team and then:

- assess whether the set of people may be classified as a group or a team;
- recommend and justify one change that may improve the effectiveness of that team.

Research task

Portfolio practice · Claridge's

Figure 4 is an extract which describes how Sara Edwards, HR director at the Savoy Group, embarked on a programme of modernisation at Claridge's hotel.

(a) **Explain why Sara Edwards may have felt it was important that the company should have a mission.**
(b) **What is Sara Edwards likely to have meant by the sentence 'It was essential that the hotel's managers felt part of the process and started working as a team'?**
(c) **Assess the likely impact of the 'performance' activity described in the second paragraph of Figure 4 on the ability of the members of the senior executive to work effectively as a team.**

Figure 4 *A new direction*

It became clear that the company had no clear direction and desperately needed a mission that its people could unite behind and work towards. The senior executive team worked together to create the new vision: 'Claridge's will be the first choice of any guest coming to London looking for style and quality service, and the first choice employer by the year 2005'. Its mission is to constantly achieve excellence by always striving for perfection. The environment for success was to be created by embracing a philosophy of 'one team, one hotel' and following a set of seven values.

But this was just the beginning of the journey. It was essential that the hotel's managers felt part of the process and started working as a team. During a management retreat, cross-dimensional teams were given one of the values to 'perform' to their peers before performing to their teams back at the hotel. A prize was given to the best performance.

This dramatic move away from the previous stiff, restrained culture helped encourage fun and demonstrate that the executive team were committed to change.

Source: adapted from http://www.melcrum.com.

Meeting the assessment criteria - examiners' guidance

For your assessment you are required to write a report on a group activity that you have investigated. It should include the benefits and limitations of team working and consideration of the leadership style.

Business example - Murtons Flyers

Jake has a part-time job with Murtons Flyers who arrange door-to-door deliveries of free newspapers and leaflets. His particular job is to accompany the van drivers and drop the bundles of papers outside the homes of the paper boys and girls. Just recently there have been complaints of bundles being dropped at the wrong houses and delays. His job is informally called the 'dropper'. Sarah, another worker, was a checker - someone who rings or calls at houses randomly to check that the deliveries have been made.

Mark Band 1 *A basic description of the benefits and limitations of team working together with an outline of the structure of the operation of the team activity.*

Jake was asked to be a member of team analysing the whole of the delivery network of the area. There were five members in the team, one from each level in the distribution chain: the regional supervisor, one of the drivers, the area distribution manager, Jake as a 'dropper', and Sarah, the checker. One of the benefits of this group of people being formed into a team was that they all had knowledge of one stage of the delivery chain. However, as they were from all levels of the hierarchy there may not be the free exchange of information. As a younger part-timer, Jake felt quite intimidated to be at the same meeting as the regional supervisor.

Mark Band 2 *Show understanding that individual roles within a team have a significant outcome on team activity.*

Sarah had direct communication with customers. She rang or called to check that the deliveries had been made and was a useful source of feedback to the rest of the team. Sarah would often take comments from customers to team meetings. When there were favourable comments about delivery this boosted team morale. Sarah's role helped support managers who had limited time for customer research. If there were many unfavourable comments, Sarah suggested that team meetings would need to be held more regularly to address the issue. Despite the criticism, team members felt motivated they were at least making plans to address the problem. Sarah was also able to make other suggestions. For example, customers made comments about delivery times and features such as inserts. As a result of Sarah's feedback managers changed the procedures of deliveries, such as times of day and days of the week, or the number of inserts placed in magazines.

Mark Band 3 *Individuals may have objectives and needs different from those of the team as a whole.*

Individual members of the team were all aware that any changes in the procedures would impact on their own jobs. At one point, for example, it was suggested that the deliveries should be made earlier in the day but Jake knew that he wouldn't be able to do that as he would still be at college. Even if he thought for the delivery process as a whole that an earlier delivery would meet the objectives of streamlining the delivery system, he was unlikely to support that argument as it meant he would have to find another job. A second suggestion was that smaller delivery drops should be combined, with the paper boys and girls going to collect their bundles from a central point. This was well supported and it was generally felt that this would also fulfil the company objective of attracting more paper boys and girls because paying them the extra time involved in collecting their bundles meant the job would have the potential for them to earn more money. The area distribution manager, however, was concerned about the security of bundles being left on street corners, didn't want the stress that would be involved and was concerned about the impact on the budget.

Teamwork

Section 14 looked at the nature of teams and the benefits and limitations of teamwork. This section examines the ideas of four management theorists whose work on teams has been significant and explains how their ideas can affect the approach of businesses to the management of human resources.

Belbin

A team role, as defined by Dr Meredith Belbin, is:

'A tendency to behave, contribute and interrelate with others in a particular way'. (www.belbin.com)

Dr Belbin's research showed that there are nine types of behaviours or team roles which are adopted naturally by the various personality types found among people at work. These are shown in Table 1. The accurate categorising of individuals against these team roles and ensuring representation of all the role types within the team is critical in success of any management or work team.

Belbin identified three personality groups.
- Action-oriented – people who like to get on with things and enjoy seeing projects through to completion.
- People-oriented – people in this category are aware of the impact of their actions on others and have good communication skills.
- Cerebral – the definition of cerebral is 'relating to the mind'. People who are cerebral are less likely to be affected by emotions and will understand the requirements of the task in hand.

While everybody is likely to show characteristics of all of these groups, Belbin suggested that most people will predominantly fall into one group. Within those groups, Belbin then identified three personality types all of whom are needed for a successful team. These personality types are shown in Table 1.

Organisations which find it useful to take account of Belbin's theory could set their employees a **behavioural test** to assess which type of role each fits into. This will help to ensure there is a balance of role types in teams. A behavioural test, which would usually be in the form of a questionnaire, measures the way people behave in any given situation. Tests can be self-assessment or may be completed by an observer. Once the results are analysed a team can be set up with the ideal mix.

It is important to remember that the categories that Belbin identified are personality and characteristic types and not job roles. People are unlikely, certainly over a short period of time, to change from one category to another. Businesses that are frequently changing the structure of their teams, perhaps to design different marketing strategies or fulfil different projects, may therefore find it difficult to apply Belbin's theory unless they have a large pool of labour to move around. Smaller workforces would

Table 1 *Belbin's team role types*

Action - oriented roles	SHAPER	Enjoys pressure and a challenge. Has the courage to overcome obstacles.
	IMPLEMENTER	Reliable and efficient. Enjoys seeing ideas through.
	COMPLETER FINISHER	Keeps to schedule. Pays attention to detail. Checks for errors and omissions.
People - oriented roles	CO-ORDINATOR	A good chairperson. Identifies goals, encourages decision making. Good delegator.
	TEAMWORKER	Avoids conflict. Co-operative. Listens well.
	RESOURCE INVESTIGATOR	Seeks out opportunities and contacts. Enthusiastic. Good communication.
Celebral roles	PLANT	Creative, imaginative, solves difficult problems.
	MONITOR EVALUATOR	Sees the whole picture. Judges roles accurately.
	SPECIALIST	Self-motivated and single-minded. Has skills particular to the project.

Source: www.belbin.com.

only have a limited number of each behavioural type with the knowledge and skills required for the job.

An example of a business which makes use of Belbin's ideas is shown in Figure 1.

Figure 1 *Edison Personal Developments and Belbin's ideas*

Edison uses a number of diagnostic tools to assess learning needs and produce appropriate development pathways. The Belbin Team Roles model is one such tool that we use for team selection and development. We use Belbin particularly because, in our experience it has a high degree of validity, that is the traits identified can be seen clearly in each individual who takes the assessment. We use the original software produced by BELBIN® and as such we are licensed to carry out Team Role modelling.

Source: adapted from Edison Personal Developments - www.edisonuk.com/project_management.htm.

McGregor

Douglas McGregor's Theory X and Theory Y management styles were discussed in section 13. Some argue that succesful teams will be led by Theory Y managers who allow involvement in decision making, assume that the members will be self-motivated and give opportunities for creativity and imaginative output. Indeed, in many organisations the team leader may not necessarily be the most senior person or may be a rotating position. An example is shown in Figure 2.

Blake & Mouton Managerial Grid

Team leadership styles can also be examined through the ideas of Robert R Blake and Janse S Mouton. The Blake & Mouton Managerial Grid plots leadership style along two axes. The attitudes of an individual manager towards people and towards the task are assessed on a scale of 0-9 on each axis.

- 'Concern for task' is scored from 0-9 along the horizontal axis.
- 'Concern for people' is scored from 0-9 along on the vertical axis.

Most people's style of leadership will be plotted around the middle of the two axes. Blake & Mouton's Team Leader type was their perception of the most appropriate style for managing teams. The Team Leader type scores 9,9 on the scale (see Figure 3) and shows commitment both to the task and to the people he or she is leading.

However, no two business situations are the same and some teams may flourish under different styles. Figure 3 also shows the three other extreme types, and while they are generally not perceived as being appropriate for leading teams, there are circumstances under which those types may be appropriate. All of the extreme types are shown in Table 2 with examples of when the style may be appropriate.

Figure 3 *The Blake & Mouton Managerial Grid*

9	1,9 Country Club									9,9 Team Leader
8										
7										
6										
5										
4										
3										
2										
1	1,1 Improverished									9,1 Authoritarian
0	1	2	3	4	5	6	7	8	9	

Concern for people (vertical axis)

Concern for production (horizontal axis)

Figure 2 *WL Gore*

Teams at W L Gore, manufacturers of products such as waterproof clothing, 'elect' their own leaders.

The company has a team-oriented atmosphere. There are no status-oriented divisions, such as executive dining rooms or plush corner offices. Each employee has the same title, Associate, and is compensated on his or her contribution to the company's results. There is a lattice organisational structure instead of a hierarchy. This allows leaders to emerge instead of assigning managers. There are no bosses, only sponsors, who help employees get started with a new job or assignment, recognized for their work and paid fairly.

Source: adapted from *The Sunday Times 100 Best Companies to Work For 2005* and AB *Insight*, March 2004.

Table 2

Type	Score	Characteristics	Appropriate for:
Team Leader	9 on task, 9 on people	Leads by positive example, encourages members to reach their highest potential and encourages members to achieve goals.	Leading productive teams, particularly where there is a requirement to meet targets or deadlines.
Authoritarian	9 on task, 1 on people	Task-orientated, expects people to do what they are told, has no consultation and wants human elements to interfere to a minimum degree.	Leading teams of new or inexperienced workers or where strict regulation is needed, for example on assembly lines where health and safety may be an issue.
Country Club	1 on task, 9 on people	Uses rewards to encourage people to achieve goals. Relationships are important to the Country Club leader, although the friendly organisational atmosphere can lead to poor discipline.	Leading a team of highly-motivated, ambitious individuals who require little direction.
Impoverished	1 on task, 1 on people	Delegates, has a relaxed style and allows members free rein.	Leading teams where there is a requirement to generate creativity or develop self-reliance.

Adair's Action-Centred Leadership Model

John Adair's Action-Centred Leadership Model identified three functions for a leader.

- Achieving the task – setting aims, identifying resources, planning, reporting, reviewing.
- Managing the team or group – setting standards of behaviour, maintaining discipline, boosting morale, fostering team spirit, facilitating communication.
- Managing individuals – giving support, training, praise, responsibility, status, opportunities to reach potential.

Figure 4 gives a summary of how Adair believes the three functions of an effective team leader could be achieved.

Some examples of the types of activities an effective team leade would need to carry out in order to meet John Adair's ideal are shown in Table 3. Many organisations make use of Adair's concept and practical philosophy as the foundation of their leadership development. These include the British Army, Royal Navy, Royal Ai Force, Scottish Police Service, Kraft Foods International, United Airlines and World Scout Association.

Figure 4 *How the functions of an effective team leader can be achieved*

You will have worked, or are working now, in a team. It may be a sports team, a study team, a team to organise an activity or a team at your part-time or full-time job.

1. Applying Belbin's approach, identify factors in the characteristics of the individuals within the team and the way it was led that contributed to its success or lack of success. If possible survey other members of the team to give you further research material.
2. Identify six different activities performed by the leader of your team to match each of the six activities suggested by John Adair (see Figure 4) which should be carried out by an effective team leader. Describe those six activites and explain how they match John Adair's model.

Research task

Table 3 *Activities required of an effective team leader*

Initiating
- Define the task.
- Identify aims and objectives for the group.
- Identify resources, people, processes, systems, budget, communication systems and IT.

Planning
- Set time line.
- Determine strategies and tactics.
- Establish individual responsibilities, objectives and accountability.

Controlling
- Monitor progress.
- Identify reporting schedules.

Supporting
- Monitor and maintain discipline.
- Anticipate and resolve group conflict.
- Assess and change, as necessary, the balance and composition of the group.
- See the team members as individuals.
- Be aware of skills, strengths, needs, personal objectives and concerns.
- Give recognition and praise.
- Where appropriate, give extra responsibility.
- Identify training needs.

Informing
- Report on progress towards group aims and objectives.
- Give feedback to the group on overall progress.
- Seek feedback from the group.

Evaluating
- Review, re-assess and adjust plans, methods and targets as necessary.

Portfolio practice · Flintocks Associates

Flintock Associates is a successful engineering research and development consultancy based in the Midlands. It specialises in studying combining new materials with traditional building methods. 60% of working time is spent working in teams discussing ideas for new materials and designs. Creativity and innovation are high on the agenda for Flintock Associates.

82% of employees say that people in their team go out of their way to help them, and more than 80% say their team cares for each other. There is a weekly team briefing where team members are encouraged to talk openly about any concerns that they have.

Flintock Associates has just taken on a large new research project and has recruited a large number of new staff to cover this project.

(a) **Identify and explain the features of teamwork at Flintock Associates that would suggest that the teams are likely to be working effectively.**

(b) **Suggest an appropriate leadership style for managing the teams at Flintock Associates, giving your reasons.**

Meeting the assessment criteria - examiners' guidance

For your assessment you are required to write a report on the consideration of team structure and leadership style.

Business example - Riverboat Clothing

Li Mei is the owner of Riverboat Clothing, a clothing store in Cheshire. She leads a team of 10 sales assistants. It is important to the business that team meetings, which take place each week to decide on activities for the week ahead, are carried out effectively. Li Mei wants to incorporate some of the ideas of Dr Belbin to help the team function as well as possible.

Mark Band 1 *A basic description of the operation of the team activity with reference to the work of a recognised team theorist.*

Riverboat Clothing is a retail outlet. Apart from the face-to-face interaction with customers in the store, there are plenty of other functions that have to carried out. As Riverboat is an independent store there are no constraints on the layout of the shop, the window display or colour schemes, so the weekly meeting where the focus for the week ahead is decided is very important. As this involves creativity and then implementation it would be ideal if the team consisted of the personality types that Belbin identified in his team roles. For example, a plant would bring ideas for window designs and an implementer would make sure everything is in place, such as getting flowers for the window ordered, or identifying when the latest styles are in, so that the window is dressed in a way that would catch customers' eyes.

Mark Band 2 *Understanding that individual roles within a team have a significant impact on the outcome of the team activity.*

The team has a lot of tasks to carry out each week. There is stock to be ordered and checked, special orders to be made up for customers, returns to be processed. Riverboat Clothing also has a mailing list that needs to be maintained and mailshots sent out from time to time. At the end of the day the takings have to be counted and banked, the shop cleaned and tidied and someone has to be responsible for locking up and setting the alarms. Applying Belbin's theory, if there were not all types in the team, the group would not function effectively. At Riverboat Clothing, Li Mei could set everyone a psychometric test and then identify how they fit into Belbin's roles. So, for example, she would see that, if she assigned the jobs of stock ordering or monitoring the cash till to someone who was identified as a resource investigator, mistakes may occur as it would be more appropriate to assign it to a completer finisher who is someone who pays attention to detail and checks for errors and omissions. The resource investigator, as a seeker of opportunities and contacts and have good communication skills, may be more usefully used investigating new suppliers.

Mark Band 3 *An explanation, using references to at least one theorist, which demonstrates that individuals may have objectives and needs different from those of the team as a whole.*

Li Mei has a weekly meeting every Wednesday after the shop has closed when staff are required to stay for an hour to discuss the next week's focus and displays. It is important to Li Mei that these topics are covered. The team therefore has objectives in terms of the everyday running of the store, such as ensuring that the store looks well presented at all times. In addition, last year had not been a particularly successful year and so Li Mei has also set some objectives about cutting waste and reducing unnecessary expenditure.

However, some of the individuals within the team have objectives which conflict with those of the team as a whole. While members of the team understood the need to reduce costs, individuals in the team felt that it would be beneficial for their own professional advancement to be able to use a variety of materials and textures to decorate the window. This was agreed by the team as not being possible due to the expense.

Danny, as deputy manager, usually did the balancing of the till at the end of the day. He is reliable and efficient and would probably be identified, if he took Belbin's psychometric test, as an implementer. The team recognised that using Danny in this way was probably the most effective way to meet its objectives. However, there are individuals who had objectives of enhancing the variety and enrichment in their work who would have liked the opportunity to learn how to do that job. This therefore may influence them when discussions are carried out for the work of the week ahead.

Management and leadership styles

Section 15 looked at how the management of teams can affect their performance and how the work of management theorists can be applied to teams. Effective management does not of course only apply to team work. The human resources function in an organisation is just one of many resources it uses to achieve its aims and objectives. The management and leadership styles adopted across the whole work place are crucial to the effectiveness of the organisation as a whole and to the motivation of its staff. Figure 1 shows an example. Figure 2 shows some management and leadership styles that are adopted in the workplace.

Figure 1

ll leaders know that their organisations are only as good as their aff. Improvements in services cannot be achieved without an fective people management strategy that links the management f a council's largest resource – its workforce – to the chievement of its priorities.'

r Sandy Bruce-Lockhart, Chairman, Local Government ssociation,
he Local Government Pay and Workforce Strategy 2005: Transforming our authority – creating real and lasting change.

ource: adapted from www.employers.gov.uk.

Figure 2 *Management and leadership styles*

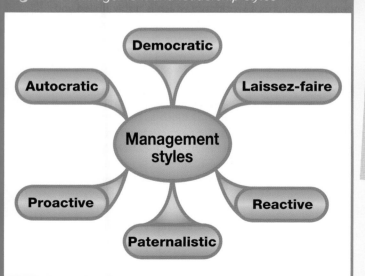

Autocratic styles

There are certain features associated with an autocratic management and leadership style.

- Autocratic managers alone set objectives and allocate tasks.
- He or she expects workers to do exactly what they are told to do and only when they are told.
- There is no consultation and no participation in decision-making.

The second paragraph of Figure 3 is an example of the leadership style of an autocratic manager.

Figure 3 *A move to an autocratic management style*

Elspeth ran her own dry cleaning business. In the first few years, she had four trusted employees whom she allowed plenty of input and her business had a close-knit friendly atmosphere. The employees were committed to the business often doing more than they were expected to do.

However, as the business grew, its customer base increased and it took on more employees. Elspeth began to feel it imperative to have tight control in order to maintain the reputation and standards that had been the cornerstone of her business. She was reluctant to relinquish any of her control of the business and she gradually started being more authoritative and insisting that staff completed projects quickly and without consultation. There was no time for discussion and she no longer welcomed opinions. She became very dismissive when her decisions were questioned.

A major drawback of an autocratic style is that it can lead to poor motivation. As workers do not have an opportunity to put forward views and make suggestions, they are not likely to feel involved in the running of the business and therefore feel no sense of ownership nor personal commitment. The business may subsequently find that it cannot rely on workers to put in that bit extra when it is under pressure, perhaps to meet deadlines, or raise the standard of service. It is also likely that creativity or new ideas for improvements to processes and procedures, which would normally have the potential of being beneficial to the company, would be stifled.

While many businesses may claim to be taking a softer approach, in practice this style can still often be seen in the workplace and in some situations an autocratic management style may still be appropriate. Most sections of the police or the armed forces, for example, have to be run on autocratic style – decisions need to be made quickly and situations can become very dangerous if everyone is not quite clear what is expected of them.

Other examples where an autocratic approach could be appropriate include the following.

- Where health and safety issues are vitally important. No one would want to be in the situation, for example, where a manager would start consulting with the staff about the best exit from the building when the fire alarm is ringing.
- Where there is a high proportion of new or inexperienced employees who are unfamiliar with routine systems and procedures. In this instance, an autocratic style may raise motivation as those who are lacking in confidence know precisely what is expected of them and exactly what they have to do to meet their obligations.

Paternalistic styles

A paternalistic style is a more benign style of autocratic leadership. While still expecting complete control and dictating what workers do, the paternalistic manager also has concerns for workers' social and physical needs A paternalistic manager feels a 'parent-like' attitude towards workers. When making decisions a manager taking this approach will tend to feel that these should always be made in the best interest of the workers. Not only does this style have the drawbacks inherent in any autocratic style, it can have the additional disadvantage that as the manager strives to treat everyone individually there will be inconsistencies, which may cause bad feeling.

A significant benefit, however, is that workers are more likely to feel looked after and valued, and accordingly will show a higher level of motivation and loyalty.

Paternalistic management can typically be found in the fast food industry. Strict adherence to company policies and procedures regarding consistency and speed of service, the need to maintain high profile product brand standards and the high proportion of young, unskilled labour demand a firm controlling hand and offer little opportunity for individual vision. These are features of an autocratic style. However, where this differs from an autocratic style is that very often, it is coupled with a package of incentives, personal development opportunities and employee support which treats each worker as an individual.

Democratic styles

Democratic leaders include workers in the decision making. Workers are consulted and their views influence the final decision. In a truly democratic environment, management will have had to

put into place opportunities for the consultation process which has implications for production time – taking time to talk to people takes time away from being productive. It can also mean that decisions will take much longer, particularly if the consultation process involves several levels of the hierarchy. This style of management is clearly, therefore, particularly time-consuming. A further significant drawback is that, as in any democracy, there will be winners and losers. It would be unusual to have unanimous agreement on issues, and those who were in the minority can feel disgruntled. If, for example, the decision to take on a new order which involved staff being required to put in a large amount of overtime, had been voted in by a majority of the workforce, those that voted against it would feel a great sense of injustice when they were eventually expected to do the overtime.

On the plus side, a democratic style of leadership can be very motivating. Workers feel a valued part of the organisation and it establishes an environment where ideas of potential benefit to the company are seriously listened to. Furthermore, when staff themselves have been part of the decision-making they feel a commitment to making that decision succeed. An example is shown in Figure 4.

Figure 4 *Longbridge International*

When new initiatives are considered at recruitment consultancy, Longbridge International, they are discussed and agreed collectively. Almost 89% of the staff believe they make a valuable contribution to the company and 88% feel they make a difference.

Source: adapted from *The Sunday Times 100 Best Companies to Work For 2005*.

Laissez-faire

The laissez-faire manager has minimum input, giving the staff a free rein – a 'hands-off approach' with no clearly defined plan. This generally requires a workforce which is highly skilled and experienced, with the drive to achieve success, otherwise laissez-faire style would often lead to poor co-ordination, a lack of focus and a low level of discipline. However, it can be appropriate in industries where creativity and freedom to take risks with potentially innovative outcomes are sought.

Businesses that encourage a laissez-faire style in their managers need, therefore, to consider, as much as the personal qualities of the managers themselves, the characteristics of their workers and the work itself and would need to ask certain questions.

- Can the workers be relied upon to work unsupervised?
- Do they have the skills and resources to work unsupervised?
- Does the work lend itself to being operated in a free and easy atmosphere?
- Do we need creativity and originality to flourish?

Laissez-faire styles will typically be found in creative industries, such as advertising, design or entertainment. An example of this style and its benefits and problems is shown in Figure 5.

Figure 5 *Ron Atkinson – football manager*

Ron Atkinson's managerial strategy was to recruit players of an established pedigree and then to let them get on with the job at hand. He trusted their professionalism and dedication and treated them like adults who did not need an overbearing manager to ensure high performance … . In the latter part of his career, Atkinson became known as something of a turnaround specialist. Coventry, Wednesday and Forest all appointed him mid-season when they were in real danger of being relegated. He succeeded in saving Coventry and Wednesday … . His unwillingness to intervene much in the everyday activities of his players also resulted in a collapse of club discipline at Manchester United. His successor, Alex Ferguson, was left to clamp down on a drinking culture that had been allowed to develop.

Source: adapted from www.growingbusiness.co.uk.

Figure 6 *Strategies for tackling anti-social behaviour*

The police have a significant role to play, in proactively working to build safer, more cohesive communities. We aim to improve our existing relationships with a full range of agencies to tackle the environmental and social issues that can result in isolation and prompt anti-social activity.

Devon & Cornwall Constabulary Strategic Plan 2005-2008

Source: adapted from www.devon cornwall.police.uk/v3/publrep/annstratplan0506/files /stratplan/stratcontent/03stratplanning.htm.

Proactive and reactive styles

Management styles can also be proactive or reactive.

- The **proactive manager** anticipates issues and plans ahead for them, both short and long term. He or she will tend to work closely with staff to determine potential problems and opportunities.
- **Reactive managers** will wait until problems manifest themselves and act accordingly. They are not innovative, preferring to follow the example of other managers.

As an example, the proactive manager might identify that a planned project will highlight the need for additional staff and will start the recruitment process at an early stage. The reactive manager is more likely to wait until staff start complaining that they are overworked or deadlines are missed.

While generally proactive managers may be seen as more successful, as they anticipate problems and work to avoid them, this style can lead to increased stress for staff who may be faced with constant change, which in the short term they see as unnecessary. Although reactive managers may be seen as constantly 'fire-fighting' they may well enjoy a good relationship with their staff as they would generally address their concerns and work for a solution. In addition, a characteristic of reactive managers is that they often simply follow in the steps of proactive managers, introducing initiatives they have observed working successfully elsewhere in the organisation. While lacking originality, this can benefit their staff in that teething problems may already have been identified and ironed out.

The way that the police operate illustrates very well the difference between proactive and reactive. Responding to reports of crimes and investigating the crimes is a reactive approach. Police authorities are now increasingly looking towards proactive measures to identify the sources of crime and preventing those crimes being committed in the first place, as in Figure 6.

In business, the management of technology departments often require a proactive approach. Network managers and those responsible for IT systems need to be one step ahead of problems and put in place strategies to ensure they are avoided. A department in this area with a reactive management approach faces the risk that their staff will be spending time rectifying faults and facing criticism from senior management.

Meetings

Meetings are an integral part of the management process and the leadership style used in a meeting is crucial to its effectiveness. Figure 7 shows some types of meeting that may take place. They can be used for various purposes.

- Consultation - to gather the views of people in an organisation. Examples might include a meeting to find out views about a possible takeover or a consumer panel to get views about a potential new product.
- Dissemination of information – to pass information to people in the organisation. Examples might include a health and safety meeting on new procedures or a meeting to outline new work practices.
- Investigation – to find reasons that an occurrence has taken place. Examples might include a production meeting to identify why targets are not being met or a marketing meeting to find out how the target market has changed.

Figure 7 *Types of meeting*

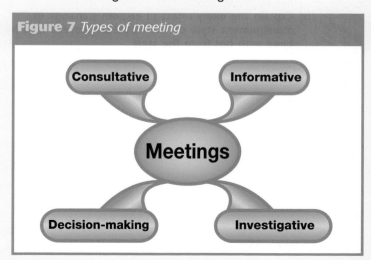

- Decision making – to choose a course of action. Examples might be a strategy meeting of managers or a shareholders' meeting to vote for a director.

The style of leadership is likely to vary depending on the purposes of holding the meeting. Some leadership styles that may be appropriate for managing the types of meetings in Figure 7 are shown in Table 1.

Research task

For a meeting that you have been involved in or observed, analyse the styles of leadership that were adopted during the meeting and evaluate whether the styles of leadership used were appropriate.

Table 1

Meeting	Appropriate style of leadership
Consultative	<ul><li>Democratic – seeking views from participants, providing clear opportunities for everyone to contribute.</li><li>Laissez-faire – allowing free discussion, minimal direction to generate ideas.</li><li>Proactive – setting agenda, providing discussion topics.</li></ul>
Decision making	<ul><li>Democratic – give opportunity for all members to put forward ideas, ensure consensus on final decision.</li><li>Reactive – allow open discussion, follow and respond to discussion threads.</li></ul>
Investigative	<ul><li>Autocratic – set strict agenda to ensure all issues are addressed.</li><li>Laissez-faire – allows open forum of ideas.</li></ul>
Informative	<ul><li>Autocratic – disseminating information, no discussion necessary, opinions of recipients irrelevant.</li><li>Reactive – invite comments, offer to follow up concerns.</li></ul>

Portfolio practice · The autocratic manager

Refer to Figure 3, which illustrates how Elspeth, the owner of a dry cleaning company, became an autocratic manager.

(a) Suggest and explain the style of management that Elspeth had adopted in the first few years of running her business.

(b) Explain the likely effect of Elspeth's change in management style on the FOUR employees who had been with her from the start.

(c) (i) What problems might Elspeth face as a result of her autocratic management style?
(ii) Suggest and explain an alternative management style that Elspeth might adopt which will overcome these potential problems, while at the same time meeting her need to maintain the reputation and standards that had been the cornerstone of her business.

Meeting the assessment criteria - examiners' guidance

For your assessment you are required to write a report on the leadership styles featured in a group activity.

Business example - CD-2-U

CD-2-U is an Internet shopping site for music CDs. It is a private limited company run by Darren Holland. Darren has four members of staff working for him who all have particular roles although they are expected to help out in other areas, particularly when the two people processing orders get behind.

Mark Band 1 *A basic description of the benefits and limitations of management styles*

Usually Darren adopts a democratic management style. This gives the opportunity for staff to put forward their views and generates ideas. It also makes the staff feel involved in the business. However, it does waste time because every time a major decision has to be made he has to call a meeting. With an autocratic management style he would be making all the decisions himself which would be much quicker. On the other hand it could be demotivating to the staff because they don't have any influence in how the business is run.

Mark Band 2 *Examples of how different leadership styles are appropriate for different circumstances.*

On its website, CD-2-U has a promise to customers that they will receive their CDs within 48 hours. Sometimes Darren has to be really strict with his staff to make sure those targets are met and insists that they help with getting orders despatched. This means he sometimes has to tell them to leave other tasks such as updating the website design or checking the stock. This is an autocratic way of managing his staff. Usually, though, he lets them decide for themselves what needs doing. Darren has complete trust in the two website designers and interferes very little in what they are doing. This would be a laissez-faire style.

Mark Band 3 *Acknowledgement that different leadership styles are appropriate for different circumstances.*

It is important for CD-2-U to meet its delivery targets and so, if the staff are not voluntarily helping out with the despatch, it is appropriate for Darren to adopt an autocratic style. However,

this is more like McGregor's Theory X style of management which is considered to be demotivating. Darren is generally democratic, which gives the staff opportunity to be involved in decision making. This is particularly valuable in the music supply industry because fashions and styles change very quickly and a range of views on what type of stock should be promoted would be valuable. It is also a small business and if some staff began to feel sidelined it could be very damaging to morale. The time factor in involving staff in decision making is an issue, however. No work at all would be done for the period of time they are discussing and they have the 48-hour turnaround time for orders to consider too.

The laissez-faire style of management is appropriate for the website designers. They are specialist and Darren knows they are highly qualified and very committed to the work and so need little control. If they spent a lot of their time playing games on the Internet or sending e-mails he would then need to have more control over them. The laissez-faire style of management also allows them to be creative which if he kept imposing his thoughts on them would restrict their own ideas. However, it does mean that Darren himself may experience more stress as he has the final responsibility but little control.

Reasons for training

The human resource function in an organisation ensures that personnel are used and developed in the most productive way. The driving force behind training and development will be the need to meet organisational objectives. An example is shown in Figure 1.

Figure 1 Training at Marks & Spencer

All the buyers and merchandisers have recently completed a course to learn about the new buying processes M&S is about to introduce. It was very thorough, which was great for me considering how little I knew about buying and merchandising when I started. Also, as well as providing me with a great insight into these areas, the course gave me the chance to interact with other people in the team who, between them, have loads of knowledge and experience to share.

Harry – Marks & Spencer plc.

Source: adapted from www2.marksandspencer.com.

When organisations are recruiting staff they will seek out the person who has the most appropriate skills and qualifications for the job. Nevertheless, however well qualified an individual may be, the organisation is still likely to need to provide training. For example, there will be few organisations which will not have their own particular procedures and systems of which staff need to be aware and, for most large organisations in particular, it is important that all employees have a good understanding of the corporate aspects for a new employee when starting work are usually covered in an **induction programme**. Induction training aims to ensure that new employees settle into their work and become as productive as possible as quickly as possible. An example is shown in Figure 2.

Even where new and existing employees are well qualified for the job, there may be areas of subject knowledge that the business feels they would benefit from refreshing or learning from scratch. An example is shown in Figure 3.

In other cases, such as where businesses offer graduate training

Figure 2 Induction training at a University

The induction process for new staff at the university aims to give individual members of staff the opportunity to:
- understand the organisation and the section in which they work;
- become fully effective in their role in the shortest possible time;
- establish effective working relationships with their customer colleagues and their line manager.

Their detailed programme includes information on
- personnel matters, e.g. pay, holidays, pensions;
- structure and procedures of the employee's own work section;
- duties;
- legal issues.

Figure 3 Health and safety training at Quality Villas

When Dan Thompson started work at Quality Villas in Berkhamsted he was sent on Health and Safety training. Although Dan had been appointed because of his qualifications and wide experience in the travel industry he had moved from a travel company which booked holiday accommodation in hotels to a company which provides top-quality villa accommodation. Part of his job is to go on trips abroad to view and rate the villas. Dan needed training to understand what to look for to make sure the facilities, such as swimming pools or kitchen areas, complied with safety regulations.

Source: adapted from company information.

schemes, Apprenticeships, day release or NVQ opportunities, recruits may simply have been appointed for their personal and intellectual characteristics. The organisation then needs to put in place a plan to provide them with all the skills and qualifications for the job, right from the basics often through to a final qualification.

Figure 4 shows an extract from information about a course being run in 2006 at Kingston College which offers a hairdressing Apprenticeship for someone already employed by a hairdresser.

Figure 4 *Hairdressing Apprenticeship*

Curriculum Area	Hairdressing
Duration/Mode of Study	Up to 2 years depending on student's ability. I day a week at college, 3 days minimum employed in a hairdressing salon.
Entry Requirements	No formal qualification although 3 GCSEs or equivalent at or above Grade D is desirable. Willingness/desire to work in the hairdressing industry. Applicants must be employed in a hairdressing salon. All applicants will be interviewed to judge their suitability for enrolment on the programme.

Source: adapted from www.kingston-college.ac.uk.

Figure 5 *Adavantages and disadvantages of Apprenticeships*

Home - Apprenticeships
Young people
Partners
Apprenticeships on offer

Employers
About Apprenticeships
How will it help me?
Business benefits
Success stories
Your questions
Awards
Next steps
Employ over 5000 staff?

Business benefits
Real value for money

Whole site ○ this section Go

Your business will benefit from Apprenticeships in the following ways:

Improved productivity

Apprenticeships equip young people with the skills and knowledge to do the job better. And because they are motivated they work harder and more effectively for your business.

Motivated people

Apprentices are motivated people who are keen to learn. By offering Apprenticeships you will find it easier to recruit and retain able young people.

Relevant training

Apprenticeships are designed by businesses in your sector to meet the needs of your business. This means the training is always relevant and it is tailored to the needs of your sector by people who genuinely understand what you do.

Avoid skills shortages

Apprenticeships allow you to invest in your business's future. By taking on an apprentice you can acquire specialist skills for your business that allow you to keep abreast of new technology.

Further reading

Apprenticeships Task Force: Final Report July 2005

The Apprenticeships Task Force was an employer-led body established by the Chancellor, Secretary of State for Education and Skills and the Chair of the Learning and Skills Council in 2003.

Apprenticeships are a major component of the education and training system and one that is crucial for raising the skill levels of our workforce to those attained by our main competitor nations.

Source: www.apprenticeships.org.uk.

Figure 5 shows an extract from the website www.apprenticeships.org.uk, a government funded website giving advice and support on Apprenticeships. This extract describes the advantages to an organisation of offering an Apprenticeship.

Training methods

Training may be delivered through both on-the-job methods (training while carrying out the job) and off-the-job methods (training at a location, whether in-house or externally, away from the work station).

Table I shows some of the training methods that organisations

will use. Most training programmes and courses are likely to include a combination of several of these methods.

Business examples are given later in this section of how businesses choose the most appropriate training method to take account of the skill being enhanced and the business objectives behind the training. An additional consideration is that whichever training method is used, as with any business activity, it will bring both costs and benefits to the organisation. Businesses need to weigh up these costs against each other and against the benefits when making the final decision. Some of these costs and benefits are shown in Table 2.

Table 1 *Examples of training methods*

On-the-job training	Off-the-job training
• Coaching/instruction – trainee is guided through the processes and equipment while actually carrying out the job. • Observation (commonly referred to as Sitting-next-to-Nellie) – trainee observes an experienced employee at work. • Mentoring/buddy – worker has a nominated employee to whom they can go and ask questions when needed.	• Lectures – a talk with visual aids. • Role play – practical simulation of the workplace activity, often used when interaction with others, such as customers, is an important element of the work. • Courses – these may range from one or two day programmes of lectures and activities covering one specific aspect of the work, such as learning a new computer program, to university courses where the workers may be sent away for a period of time to gain a specific qualification. • Computer simulation package – the worker works through modules and games representing the work situations. • Videos. • Adventure/activity weekends.

Table 2 *Costs and benefits of on-the-job and off-the-job training*

On-the-job training	Off-the-job training
Costs • Risk of expensive errors in terms of, for example, customer service, materials or product quality. • Loss of productivity of equipment while training is carried out, e.g. a piece of machinery or a delivery van. • Can be distracting, e.g. a potential drop of productivity of others affected by the training or everyday activity in the workplace may mean concentration is lost and training is ineffective. **Benefits** • Trainee is faced with real life scenarios. • Likely to be cheaper in terms of financial costs – no need to send the employee on expensive external courses or buy special equipment and materials. • Can be motivating because workers feel they are hands-on from the start.	**Costs** • May often be unsupervised or away from control of supervisors – increases risk of ineffective training if worker not self-motivated. • Financial costs, such as the cost of skilled trainers or travel. • The worker is unproductive while training takes place. **Benefits** • Employer likely to be training with others in same circumstances – this can be motivating as it raises confidence and meets social needs. • Opportunity to use specialist trainers and centres which can raise standards and/or lead to economies of scale. • Raises awareness of the importance of the training.

Even after the costs and benefits have been weighed up, there may also be constraints on delivering the training, for example the financial costs of delivering the training may be beyond the company budget or there may be lack of suitable expertise. These constraints are examined in section 18.

In the same way as the need for the training itself will have been identified to meet business objectives, the decision on which method used to deliver that training will also be focused around meeting business objectives. Most businesses these days also recognise that improved motivation, both towards the training itself and to its subsequent application in the workplace, will arise if the training and the method used also help meet the individual's personal needs.

Even in areas where the choice of training methods is limited, meeting objectives is still likely to be a driving force. For example, an organisation which needs to train its new customer service employees in the features of its customer database clearly has to have the employees sitting in front of a computer and operating the program. However, choices available may include:

• delivering training in a classroom situation with a simulated program;
• trainees observing an experienced member of staff;
• trainees being observed and instructed whilst carrying out the work live.

Examples of **business objectives** which will influence the choice as to which of those methods is used may be:

• improve level of customer service – method 1 is likely to be the most popular choice as trainees are not dealing with customers until they are fully trained and methods 2 and 3 have the potential to delay the processing of customers' transactions;
• need to cut costs – method 2 is likely to be the most cost effective as work is still being carried out as usual and the trainee is not holding up production whereas methods 1 and 2 are expensive in terms of staff time and resources;
• increase staff motivation – methods 2 and 3 give existing workers the chance to have an added dimension and interest to their work through involvement in the training of new employees. This has the potential to increase motivation. Method 1 is likely to be led by someone whose main job is to run the training courses and therefore does not provide an opportunity for existing experienced shop floor workers to extend their skills.

Examples of **personal needs** which may also influence the choice as to which of those methods is used may include:

• social needs – method 1 offers the opportunity to interact with other new trainees;
• esteem needs – method 2 has the potential to give employees confidence and make them feel valued because they are interacting with a senior or experienced member of staff;
• responsibility needs – method 3 has the potential to make employees feel an integral part of the organisation from day one.

Aims of training

Some typical business objectives which lead to the need to offer training are given below in Figure 6.

Technological innovation Technology is moving ahead all the time. New software willrequire staff to be trained on how to use it. The introduction of an intranet system, or automation on a production line, for example, will necessitate staff being given support with adapting to significant changes in their working procedures. Figure 7 shows how the need to introduce new technology may have affected training.

Diversification Businesses will often require staff to become multi-skilled in order to have the flexibility to move staff around as work pressures demand, or to be able to offer a variety of products. Figure 8 shows how the need for diversification can affect training.

Figure 6 *Examples of business objectives which can raise the need for training*

Figure 7 *Technological innovation and training*

Business objective
During 2004 and 2005 most retail businesses are likely to have set themselves the objective to install successfully a chip and pin system. This objective would have been set because after 1 January 2005 they were liable for any credit or debit card fraud which could have been prevented by installing chip and pin. This objective created the need for training.

Training
One training method that may have been seen as appropriate would be role play. This would not only have ensured that staff understood the procedures but would also meet their personal needs in that it may resolve concerns about explaining the system when dealing directly with customers.

Increased productivity If it has been identified that a member of staff, or a team or section, or indeed the whole workforce, could be working more effectively, the organisation is likely to decide to give training to raise the level of performance. Raising productivity might need improvements in product knowledge or customer service skills for a sales assistant who has been the subject of customer complaints, or improvements in technical expertise for skilled workers. Of course, wishing to raise the level of performance of an employee may not always be simply due to ineffective working practices. The employee may be performing extremely well and the organisation may decide to move them to

Figure 8 *Diversification and training*

Business objective
Marcus runs Tops Cars, a mobile car repair company. He employs four staff each of whom runs a van which goes out to customers to service their cars at their homes or workplaces. He has set himself the objective to introduce a car valeting service. While he wanted the service to be available to any of his clients at any time in the week, he knew that there was not enough business to employ someone else full-time.

Training
This objective therefore raised the need to send one of his mechanics on a training course run by one of the cleaning products companies so that he could be used both as a mechanic and to do car valeting as needed. Marcus decided to offer this opportunity to Akashi. Although Marcus could have trained him himself, he decided to send Akashi on the course which led to an NVQ in car valeting because he knew that Akashi was anxious to improve his qualifications and would therefore feel a sense of achievement.

the next level. Sports people are continually training to raise the level of their performance. Figure 9 shows how the need for increased productivity can affect training.

Improve employee motivation Section 12 investigated the importance to a business of having a well-motivated workforce and there will be few organisations which do not feel it is important to see high motivation. Evidence of particular indicators of low motivation such as high levels of sickness or staff turnover may make an organisation keen to introduce measures to raise motivation amongst its staff. There will also be times when the business may already enjoy a good level of motivation but feels that the staff should feel a particular commitment to the well-

Figure 9 *Increased productivity and training*

Business objective
A DIY company wished to improve productivity by reducing costs and identified that a significant outlay each year went on repairs to the racks in the warehouse where heavy items were stacked. The damage was as a result of carelessness by the forklift truck drivers. In order to meet the objective 'to reduce costs by minimising damage to the warehouse racks' the DIY company arranged for drivers to have a refresher course with an instructor. The training, and the training method, one-to-one training with a qualified and competent teacher, would also meet the employees' safety needs in the workplace, giving them skills to avoid personal accidents.

Figure 10 *Employee motivation and training*

Business objective
A manufacturing company has decided to move to just-in-time production. This has implications for employee motivation because the lower stock levels provide less of a cushion against wastage and absenteeism and require co-operation between sections. One objective the business set in this connection is to restructure the workforce with an emphasis on teamwork.

Training
In order to encourage the unity of the teams the company has decided to send some of them on an adventure course. One employee said 'the course was great. It was at an outward bounds centre and we spent two days in the most beautiful setting, admittedly in the pouring rain. We did a variety of group exercises, such as raft building and shooting videos. It was great fun and we learnt a lot about team building and leadership.' A course of this nature would help meet individuals' social needs with the potential to make them feel more a part of the organisation.

Figure 11 *Increasing market share and training*

Business objective
A supermarket has identified through research that it has recently lost loyal customers due to disappointment at the level of help, advice and politeness they receive from the staff. One objective it has set to address this problem is to improve customer service.

Training
One strategy it has employed to improve customer service is to give training to all shop floor staff who deal directly with customers. Part of the training programme will include a computer software package, with a range of interactive activities based on scenarios covering customer questions and circumstances. Staff were able to organise amongst themselves which times during their shifts they could log-on to one of the two work stations in the staff rest room. This was an innovative way to bring training to the staff who had not experienced this style of training at this company before. This therefore met the personal needs of the employees by offering them variety in the workplace. It also met their esteem needs because it demonstrated that the company trusted its workers to be self-directed.

The Investors in People Standard helps organisations to improve performance and realise objectives through the management and development of their people. Visit the 'Case Studies' section of its website www.investorsinpeople.co.uk.
1. Identify, giving examples, two companies which have good standards of staff development.
2. Explain the strengths of their programmes for individuals and businesses.

Research task

being of the company. Examples of such circumstances would include impending structural or procedural changes, poor market performance or necessity for wage constraints. Figure 10 shows how the need to improve employee motivation can affect training.

Increase market share Market share is the proportion of total sales in a particular market. To ensure survival, effective businesses will constantly be analysing market share and reviewing objectives in that connection. Figure 11 shows how the need to increase market share can affect training.

Portfolio practice · A training course

Interview a tutor, lecturer or teacher in your college or school about a recent training course in which he or she has taken part.

(a) **Identify the college or school objective that raised the need for the training.**
(b) **Describe the training method that was used to deliver the training.**

(c) **Explain the personal benefits to the tutor, lecturer or teacher of taking part in the training.**
(d) **Evaluate the costs and benefits to your college or school of the training opportunity and the method used to deliver the training.**

Meeting the assessment criteria - examiners' guidance

For your assessment you are required to write a report on a recent training programme for one individual. It should include a description of training methods and reasons for training and the costs and benefits to the organisation of training the researched individual. Your report should show an understanding of the potential impact on motivation of ineffective training provision.

Business example - Castle Star Hotel

Jenny is a hotel receptionist at the Castle Star, the flagship hotel of Marchwood Hotels, a chain of 23 hotels across the British Isles.

Mark Band 1 *Reasons for training, the costs and benefits to the organisation of training the researched individual.*

Jenny had been given training in interpersonal skills and customer service after she had been working at the Castle Star for six weeks. There had been some complaints from guests that her manner was off-hand when checking them in. Colleagues and management had also observed that she was unwilling to go out of her way to help guests when they were making enquiries. Marchwood Hotels is a chain of five-star hotels and customer service ranks highly in its priorities. Most of the guests at the Castle Star are regular visitors and many guests stay at other hotels in the chain. Jenny and her colleagues on reception are the 'face' of Castle Star and Marchwood Hotels, and there are therefore direct financial benefits of the reception staff being well trained, as guests who feel they have been treated well will return. Good training is also motivating for staff as they feel that they are valued. The financial costs of training Jenny include the cost of bringing in a trainer and having to pay other workers on reception overtime to cover for her while she is being trained.

Mark Band 2 *A description of training methods. An explanation which shows clear understanding with examples of the motivational aspects of effective training.*

One of the activities on Jenny's training course was a role play where she had to deal with a customer making enquiries. She had previously been told to study a manual which listed typical questions that customers might ask, with a range of answers, such as times, details about room service, cost of telephone calls and Internet connections, directions to local attractions and transport. Because she had the experience of having practised and then been observed, assessed and given feedback her confidence was improved and she performed better when she returned to her job. Jenny was also more committed to her job after the training because she realised that the management had a choice of whether to train her or move her

to a less responsible job. She was pleased that they valued her enough to keep her and give her training which was motivating and gave her increased job satisfaction.

Mark Band 3 *An understanding of the potential impact on motivation of ineffective training provision.*

Jenny was quite surprised to be told she had to go on a training course and was upset when the reasons were explained. It was important therefore that the training was effective otherwise not only would Jenny's skills not have improved, but she would be demotivated because she had lost self-esteem.

If her training had been ineffective it would have an adverse impact on her work. She would have felt demoralised that her skills had not improved and would be worried about retaining her job which would raise her stress. She would also be wondering whether the company valued her if they couldn't take the trouble to arrange a good course for her. It would also make her feel that it didn't actually matter very much whether she dealt with guests properly because the hotel didn't think it important enough to train her properly.

Jenny's colleagues would also have been affected. They had been complaining to management about her attitude and would have been very optimistic that when she returned to her job she would be better with the guests. If that had not happened they would have felt frustrated and annoyed that the hotel had not taken their concerns seriously. This would have affected their motivation and may possibly have led to increased staff turnover in future.

Constraints on training

Section 17 looked at how the provision of training is driven by business objectives. It also examined how businesses are likely to carry out a cost benefit analysis when making decisions regarding the training. However, once the organisation has identified the most effective and efficient training programme to meet its objectives, there are still likely to be constraints on whether that programme represents the best option, or is even accessible to the organisation. These factors would also inevitably play a part in the decision making. An alternative strategy might achieve the desired outcome without the constraints that the training presents. Examples of constrainsts an organisation may encounter would include the identified training package being too simple or expensive or that the training may raise unreasonable expectations amongst the staff about promotion or increased pay opportunities.

Figure 1 gives some examples of the types of constraints that businesses will experience when drawing up a training programme.

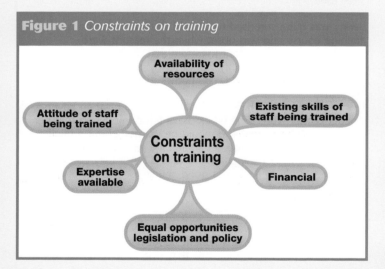

Figure 1 *Constraints on training*

Financial constraints and the availability of resources

Training is expensive. Some courses, such as group courses for IT, cost as little as £50 per person a day. Other types of training can cost many thousands of pounds if specialist programmes have to be devised and several trainers recruited, as in the introduction of a new software system across a large company. An example is shown in Figure 2. Figure 3 illustrates some of the areas that are allocated funds in a typical training budget.

Of course, there is not only the cost of the course itself. There are also the short-term costs of the personnel who are undergoing training due to the fact that they are unproductive during that time and a temporary replacement may have to be paid.

Businesses would therefore need to determine whether the training they have in mind to offer to staff is value for money. Even

Figure 2 *Southdown Housing Association, training cost*

In 2004 Southdown Housing Association, based in Sussex, spe
almost £100,000 on training.

The size of the training budgets varies ... from £2,000 to £9C
million. The average size of the training budget ... is £621,162
and the average spend per employee ... is £607.11.

Source: adapted from *2005 Annual Survey Report - Training & Development*, Chartered
Institute of Personnel and Development.

where a business has decided that the training is affordable, there would be other analyses it would need to carry out. For example

- a training programme intended to raise productivity would be foolish not to analyse the expected cost of the training in relation to the expected short and long-term financial gains;
- sending the entire workforce on an adventure weekend to encourage the unity of teams would be an extremely expensive option for a large manufacturing company. It may be more cost-effective in the long term to give each team a smal seating area and drinks machine. The Honda car manufacturin plant at Swindon provides rest facilities for tea breaks where team members can meet during the working day and form social bonds.

Attitude of staff being trained

The level of motivation of those being trained will have a significant impact on the effectiveness of training. People are ofte resistant to changes in their working practices, whether through

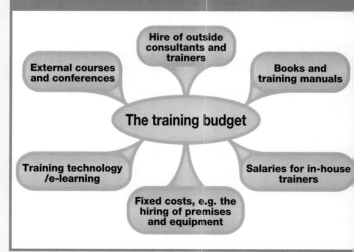

Figure 3 *Areas allocated funds in a training budget*

anxiety caused by feeling that it may be too stressful or demanding, because it may increase their workload, or simply because they are content with things the way they are. Poor communication in an organisation may have led staff not understanding the reasons for the training programme.

Training undertaken by staff who are enthusiastic about taking part is more likely to be effective than where staff are disgruntled. Again, an organisation would have to consider whether the method of training is appropriate. Under these circumstances, for example:

- a computer package requiring trainees to work through modules may not be appropriate if it requires a level of self-motivation which may not exist amongst the staff;
- using mentors or buddies from existing staff members to raise the level of skills may generate more problems than it solves as disaffection may be spread through the organisation.

Equal opportunities legislation

Constraints presented under equal opportunities legislation can have a profound effect on the provision of training. Various legislation prevents discrimination on certain grounds when deciding on employees to be trained.

- The **Sex Discrmination Act, 1975** makes it unlawful to discriminate on grounds of sex or marital status. So a business that deliberately chooses a male rather than a female or a single rather than a married person for training is likely to be contravening legislation.
- The **Race Relations Act, 1976** prevents discrimination on grounds of race, colour, nationality or ethnic, national or religious origin. Choosing not to select an employee for training simply because he or she was born in another country is likely to contravene legislation.
- The **Disability Discrimination Act, 1995** makes it illegal to discriminate against employees with disabilities unless there are justified reasons. Choosing not to select an employee with hearing difficulties because he or she may not hear a lecture, although audio facilities are provided, is likely to contravene legislation.
- In 2006 the UK had to introduce age legislation to comply with EU regulations. This would make discrimination on the basis of age illegal. So a business must allow all age groups to be eligible for training to comply with legislation.
- The **Employment Equality (Sexual Orientation) Regulations, 2003** protect employees from direct and indirect discrimination, harassment and victimisation in employment and training on the grounds of sexual orientation.
- The **Employment Equality (Religion or Belief) Regulations, 2003** protect employees from direct and indirect discrimination, harassment and victimisation in employment and training on the grounds of religion or belief.

Few businesses these days are likely to deliberately attempt to contravene the law by denying an individual training simply on the grounds of colour, race, sex or disability. However, there are other considerations that may have an impact. Two examples illustrate this.

- It may have been identified that sending staff on a course provided by an outside agency may present the best option.

However, if that results in discrimination because, say, a disabled person cannot enter the building because no suitable access facilities or fire exits are provided, that could be discriminatory. In-house training would therefore be a better option.

- A video would not be appropriate if there was not access to a British Sign Language interpreter for anyone undergoing the training who was deaf.

Figure 4 shows how taking into account legislation can affect the recruitment of employees for training.

Figure 4 *Managers and training*

General assumptions that certain groups of people are not suitable for management posts and therefore do not need training must be avoided. Managers should:
- encourage all staff to develop their skills and gain experience;
- make sure that promotion opportunities are accessible to all who qualify;
- ensure everyone is considered fairly for training opportunities, including part-time employees.

Source: adapted from Bracknell Forest Borough Council Development and Training Programme.

Existing skills of staff being trained

For a training programme to be effective it must be at the correct level for the trainees involved. Section 20 explains about 'skills audits' which help organisations identify existing skills of staff in order to tailor appropriate training programmes for them. The existing skills of those being trained, and the level at which the proposed training is to be pitched, will be important factors in the success of any training package.

- Any course involving computer packages, e.g. a Computer Aided Design (CAD) course is unlikely to be effective for a person who lacks basic IT skills. An introductory IT course would need to be followed beforehand.
- Where the training is addressing aspects of dealing with people, such as interpersonal skills or customer service, everyone is likely to be at different levels and have different areas of expertise. Watching videos or listening to lectures may be less effective than arranging discussion groups where ideas, experiences and strategies can exchanged.

Expertise available

It may be possible to train employees by making use of in-house expertise. However, if a company decides to offer in-house training through mentoring or off-the-job courses, it is not only the technical expertise – the knowledge of the work itself – that should be taken into consideration. This type of training may prove to be inappropriate due to the deliverer not being proficient in other areas of expertise which may be important for effective training, such as communication skills, the ability to inspire confidence or efficient record keeping.

If companies need to maintain a continued service or level of production, the training may be constrained by the expertise available to cover for staff undergoing the training. In these cases on-the-job training programmes may be more attractive to organisations than off-the-job.

Figure 5 illustrates how an organisation can be faced with having to train a large number of personnel, but may not have the expertise within the organisation to do so.

Figure 5 *Relocation and training*

A major UK DIY chain was planning a move of its head office from South West London to the Midlands and expected to lose a sizeable proportion of its personnel skilled in the buying and merchandising aspects of the business. It needed to bring new recruits up to speed quickly but did not have within its remaining personnel those with the right level of business knowledge. The new recruits would need to operate to the same level of experience as its existing buyers and merchandisers if the business was not to be put at risk.

The DIY chain's solution was to call in a specialist retail sector training company, First Friday, which had the people with the business knowledge and the resources to deliver an intensive training programme in a short space of time to match the recruitment of new starters into the business.

Training review and evaluation

When an organisation has invested in training, it would need to know whether it was a success. Although the trainee may report that the training was useful, these days it is seen as increasingly important that the amount of improvement is measurable and that the training activity is assessed to help decide whether it was value for money. Some questions that an organisation will ask itself are shown in Figure 6.

How to evaluate training

Training will usually be evaluated at several levels.
(i)   The learners will report how valuable the training was to them.
(ii) The trainers will report whether they felt the training was successful and pitched at the right level.
(iii) The intended new or improved skills of the learners will be reported on through observation, tests or survey.
(iv) What is the outcome for the business?

The last level is the most difficult for businesses to analyse. There are several tools which may be used by senior management. These include the following.

Assessing business objectives Section 17 explained that the need for training will arise out of a need to meet business objectives. An organisation will be able to assess the value of the

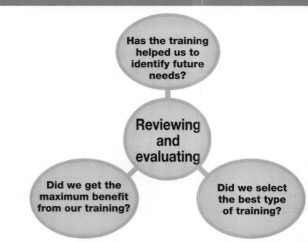

Figure 6 *Reviewing and evaluating training*

training if those objectives have been achieved within the time frame it has set itself. However, this may not seem as easy as it would appear if several strategies have been put in place to achieve a business objective. For example, a hospital may have set itself an objective to reduce the occurrence of post-operative infections. This is likely to have resulted in a range of training targeted at different individuals - training to raise awareness of the necessity for cleanliness around the wards, training in effective waste disposal, training in personal hygiene - as well as other strategies such as increasing the number of times day wards are cleaned or imposing new rules on visitors. If the objective of reducing post-operative infections was achieved it would be very difficult to identify which area of training was the most effective.

Analysing benefits and costs It was explained earlier that there is a need to analyse the expected cost of training in relation to the expected short and long-term financial gains. Caterpillar Tractor Company's training programmes, for example, advertise that

Figure 7 *SMART targets and training*

Business examples of SMART targets may be:
● Specific – 'To answer 95% of 999 calls within 10 seconds' – Northamptonshire Police 2002/3.
● Measurable – '... achieve sales of $10.4 billion to $10.6 billion for the quarter ended December 2005' – Intel.
● Achievable and Realistic – 'The target has been increased from 13 days in 2002/03 to 20 days as a realistic and achievable target for 2003/04' – Wigan & Leigh Housing Report – Target for response times for repairs.
● Time-related – 'Building plans must be completed by 2007 so that work can begin in 2008' – London Olympics 2012.

Source: adapted from www.northants.police.uk, http://blogs.guardian.co.uk/technology/ www.wiganmbc.gov.uk, http://news.bbc.co.uk.

ffective training can result in longer equipment life and reduced maintenance and repair costs. The expenditure on equipment and maintenance can be measured in relation to the cost of the training.

SMART targets Organisations may have targets towards achieving their objectives. One target setting tool is **SMART** targets would be set for the trainee that are **Specific** (identify the desired level of performance), **Measurable** (offers a robust way of comparing pre-training performance against post-training) **Achievable** and **Realistic** (that the trainee or team is capable of achieving the target taking account of their ability and the resources available) and **Time-Related** (a deadline is set to carry out the evaluation). An example is shown in Figure 7. An example of the evaluative process involved in a training activity is shown in Table 1.

Research task

You are required to research the costs to an organisation of providing a recent training opportunity for an individual or group training course or programme.
1. In order to find this information it may be helpful to interview the member of staff responsible for staff development at a business you have researched or have worked in or at your local college or school.
2. Your research should investigate the total costs, not just the direct cost of the training itself. The indirect costs may include items such as travel, accommodation, staff cover and potential loss of business while the trainee is away.

Table 1 *Evaluation of training for sales assistant*

What do we want to evaluate?	How can we evaluate it?
What are the objectives of the training?	• Sales assistant to improve product knowledge.
How can we measure whether objective has been achieved?	• Observation of customer satisfaction. • Reduction in number of enquiries passed by sales assistant to colleagues and manager.
Was the training effective?	• Obtain feedback after training from trainee, colleagues, line manager. • Are customers' questions answered accurately? • Do customers seem satisfied? • Is the sales assistant dealing with more enquiries on his/her own than previously?

Portfolio practice · Training and organisational objectives

For the training opportunity that you researched above in the 'Research Task':

(a) state the objective which identified that training needed to take place;
(b) identify the methods by which the training was evaluated;

(c) make recommendations for improving the way that training is evaluated;
(d) taking account of the costs that you identified in your research, make ONE recommendation for an alternative use of those funds which has the potential to achieve the same objective.

Meeting the assessment criteria - examiners' guidance

For your assessment you are required to write a report giving a comparison of the strengths and weaknesses of a training programme, taking account of the constraints of the organisation and an evaluation, with alternative recommendations, of the effectiveness and appropriateness of the training programme.

Business example - Getting Back

Steve was a trained engineer, but enjoyed a variety of sports, including skiing and water sports. He spent his weekends coaching and providing first aid at a local outdoor centre. Last year he was given the opportunity to join a friend, Ben, who was running his own private sports injuries clinic, Getting Back. Getting Back had been extremely successful and Ben wanted to expand. Taking on Steve was an attractive proposition for him because Steve had good knowledge of sports and sports injuries. Because he was new to the particular type of client that Getting Back has, Ben felt he could hire Steve on a lower salary than someone who had more experience. Steve was delighted at the opportunity. He had thought about getting into this field for some time. The first thing he had to do was to go on a part-time diploma course in Sports Therapy which Ben let Steve do in company time.

Mark Band 1 *An identification of the strengths and weaknesses of the training programme.*
Ben had suggested that Steve did the course part-time so that he could also be working straight away for Getting Back. It also meant that the topics that Steve was studying had more meaning because it was likely he would be seeing examples in his every day work. A weakness of the programme was that Steve found it stressful trying to study and work at the same time, particularly around the time that assignments were due in. A further issue was that because their clients included some top level sports people, Steve occasionally had to miss lectures or tutorials because of the pressure on him to give his consultations at times that suited the customers.

Mark Band 2 *A comparison of the strengths and weaknesses of the training programme taking account of the constraints on the organisation.*
If Getting Back had funded Steve in full-time study, although the course would have been completed quicker, it would have been a very expensive option. It may also have caused cash flow problems because Steve would be costing the business money but not generating any income. Getting Back is at a time of expansion when lack of finance has the potential to cause significant problems. However, by studying part-time Steve was productive right from the start and Getting Back could begin increasing its client base and therefore increase turnover.

Having the opportunity to see real examples in his work of the theory he was studying at college meant that Steve's training would be meaningful and effective. It also meant that he was bringing in new ideas which Ben found valuable because up until then he had been the only one in the business. It also impressed the clients because they were able to say that Steve knew all the latest techniques. On the other hand, the pressure on Steve to juggle work and study meant

that sometimes he was tired. On one occasion he spoke sharply to a client. Getting Back cannot afford to lose clients at this time when trying to attract more clients.

Mark Band 3 *An evaluation with alternative recommendation of the effectiveness and appropriateness of the training programme.*
Although Steve was productive right from the start, there were problems as occasionally he had to make the choice between seeing clients or attending lectures. If he chose the former he risked missing vital information on his course and then had to catch up later. But if he attended his lectures Getting Back was not meeting its clients' needs, which was particularly important at this time. The issue of stress on Steve should also have been taken into account because his attitude towards clients is an important factor in the survival of Getting Back, particularly when there are only two people dealing with the clients and they are trying to attract more. However, costs are an important issue for Getting Back and in the short-term this seemed a good option to make sure that there was the potential to see more clients from the first day that Steve joined the business.

A more appropriate method may have been to have employed Ben full-time in the business for a year, with him following the diploma course part-time in the next year. In this way Getting Back could fit in even more clients and although Steve may not have had the right qualifications for all of the work, he still had quite a bit of experience with his coaching and first aid in the outdoor centre and there would have been a lot that he could help Ben out with. As an engineer he was probably also quite good with equipment and could have taken responsibility for maintaining that. In addition, he could have been doing paperwork so Ben could increase his client contact time. This would have helped the company generate more income which could have been put aside for Steve in the second year. By the second year Steve would be much more knowledgeable about some of the issues and so the course would be less challenging. It would also put less pressure on the business finances. He also may have built up a relationship with the clubs and clients he was working with. This may have made them more receptive to taking appointments at times that suited Steve rather than at unsuitable times.

19 Identifying individual development needs

Development needs

Section 21 explains the importance of Personal Development Plans (PDP) in the management and development of people in a business. A PDP forms the basis of training and career development of an individual within an organisation. However, before an individual in an organisation, with the support of management, can draw up a personal development plan, his or her development needs will have to be identified.

For example, individuals in an organisation who have ambitions to progress up the hierarchical ladder will need to analyse what skills and qualifications they need to be striving for in order to be considered for promotion, and to plan for the future accordingly. Equally, management may have plans for the development of staff. If it is intended to bring in a new computerised system, for example, the staff will need training. Their present standard of skills will have to be analysed and their future needs established.

Figure 1 shows the range of tools available for training needs analysis.

Job analysis

Job analysis helps determine what the demands of a particular job are in order to achieve effective performance. A job analysis can identify the:

- duties;
- responsibilities;
- equipment used;
- work relationships;
- work environment.

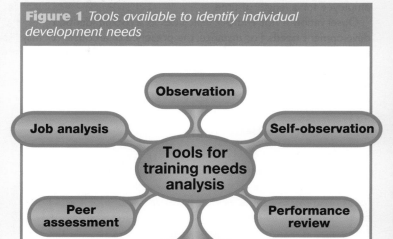

Figure 1 *Tools available to identify individual development needs*

The most common use for a job analysis report would be when drawing up a **job description**, which outlines the duties associated with a particular job, what the job entails and the skills needed by the job holder. The skills of an individual can be compared against the job analysis report and areas of weakness can form the focus of an individually-tailored training programme.

Figure 2 shows an extract from a typical job analysis checklist completed by Raj, an administrative assistant at Special Spreads, a catering company.

Figure 2 *Job analysis checklist for an administrative assistant*

Activity	Occasionally	Monthly	Weekly	Daily
Type letters, envelopes and labels				✓
Type and distribute minutes of meetings		✓		
Prepare meeting rooms			✓	
Open, sort and distribute post				✓
Maintain signing-in-and-out-register of keys for filing cabinets	✓			
Record event bookings on the database			✓	
Deal on the telephone with suppliers and customers				✓

Equipment
Please tick the equipment that is needed for your job

Calculator		Photocopier	✓
Computer	✓	Camera	
Word processing package	✓	Fax machine	✓
Scanner		Laminator	
Secure storage Facility	✓	Mobile phone	

Observation

Observation would normally be carried out by a line manager who would report on the skills and performance of the individual during the course of their everyday contact. Occasionally a formal observation may take place, where the observer sits with the employee for a length of time.

Observation is not without difficulties as a tool in identifying development needs. For instance, the presence of an observer may affect the way the individual works. The individual may feel under pressure and not perform in a typical way. This could lead to inaccurate measure of performance and therefore inaccurate identification of training needs, for example.

Self-observation

In a system of self-observation, the worker is asked to identify their own strengths and weaknesses and suggest areas for training. A significant advantage of such a method is that, as the training will focus on areas which the worker has suggested, he or she is likely to be committed to that training and be keen for it to be successful. A downside, of course, is that the worker may not be honest about an area of weakness if it is an aspect of the job that is dull or particularly challenging. Equally, a less confident employee may underestimate his or her skills. Either way, an inaccurate assessment may result.

Peer assessment

Peer assessment to collect data for identifying training needs is often attractive to businesses. It involves using the views of those who work with an individual in identifying development needs. Those who are working alongside are often in the best position to judge their colleagues' performance and identify their strengths and weaknesses. Furthermore, knowing that you are going to be the subject of report back from your peers is often a significant motivator, leading both to improved performance and confidence that the training needs will be accurately assessed.

However, for the training needs to be accurately assessed, the observers themselves will have to be trained before-hand. Another difficulty is that the whole process can often prove to be overly bureaucratic and time-consuming.

Peer assessment can take place in a number of ways, as shown in Figure 3.

Appraisal and performance reviews

The one-to-one discussion involved in appraisal and performance reviews provides a vehicle for developing ideas and identifying training needs. Goals and targets are often set at appraisals and these can be compared with actual performance. When targets have not been met, this could form the basis of a discussion over whether further training is needed. An example is shown in Figure 4.

Figure 4 *Learning from feedback at Eversheds law firm*

We believe that feedback is one of the best ways of helping you to develop your skills. We have a structured performance and development review process that involves continuous coaching and the chance to regularly review your performance.
Every staff member (even our managing partner) has an annual personal development review. It's an opportunity for you and your manager to have an open, constructive discussion about how you are getting on in your current job and your future aspirations. It is also used to set personal business related objectives (often challenging) for the year ahead and to identify your learning and development needs.

Source: adapted from www.eversheds.com.

While the terms appraisal and performance review are often used in the same context and may therefore be seen as interchangeable there is a distinction.

- An annual **performance review** would generally be focussed on comparing performance and progress against an agreed plan of action and targets and then setting plans and targets for the coming year.
- Comparisons of performance against targets are often a feature of **appraisal**, but that is not always necessarily the case. An appraisal, in addition to discussions on personal performance, usually aims to review the whole development of the individual, giving, for example, opportunities to discuss progression, pension rights or how working relationships affect performance.

Identifying training needs in practice

The most accurate assessment of training needs is likely to comprise a combination of several of the above processes. For example, data gathering is usually a feature of appraisal and that data may have been generated from peer assessment or observation. And there will be few appraisal systems where the employee is not expected to assess their own performance in some way. An example is shown in Figure 5.

Figure 3 *Methods of peer assessment*

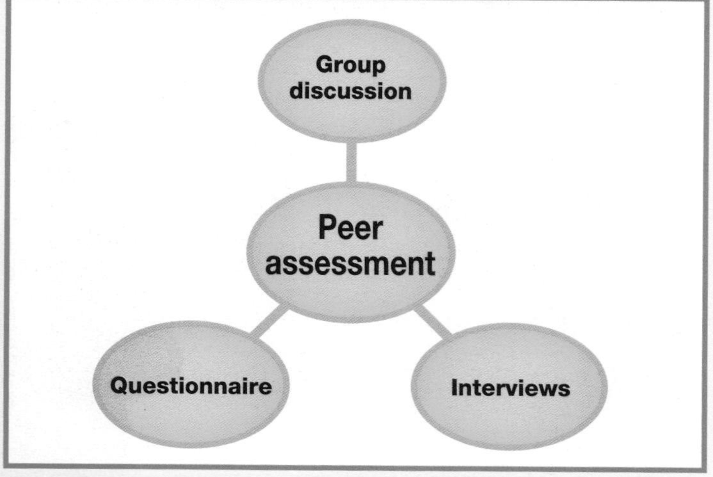

- Group discussion
- Peer assessment
- Questionnaire
- Interviews

Figure 5 *Price Waterhouse Coopers – training and development*

Working with your own career counsellor, and taking on board the feedback of your colleagues, you will for the most part be responsible for identifying your own relative strengths and weaknesses and ambitions, and developing a plan to address them. We'll help you choose the right course to meet your ambitions, and will make sure you have all the support and resources you need to come through with flying colours.

Source: adapted from www.pwc.com/uk.

Interview a person who is in full-time employment to investigate their appraisal process. Write a report on:
● what data is collected prior to the appraisal interview and how it is collected;
● whether targets are set and, if so, what they focus on;
● whether training needs are identified and, if so, how are they identified and what plans are put in place for those needs to be met;
● any other features of the appraisal process.

Research task

Portfolio practice · J M Computing

J M Computing is an IT/Internet consultancy business. There are 88 employees. Formal appraisals are held annually and all staff meet their line managers monthly to discuss progress and feedback. 86% say they receive support from managers when they need to learn new skills.

The firm spends an average of £227 per person on training – even though most training is provided free by product suppliers. A number of other courses are considered essential for individual roles but the firm does allow employees a degree of flexibility when selecting those relating to personal skills.

Source: adapted from *The Sunday Times 100 best companies to work for 2005*.

(a) **Identify ONE feature of an appraisal system which would support J M Computing's policy on training.**
(b) **Suggest and explain, from the data, why it is likely that staff at J M Computing will be highly motivated by their training opportunities.**
(c) **Recommend, with justification, ONE method for J M Computing to identify possible training needs of its 88 employees.**

Meeting the assessment criteria - examiners' guidance

For your assessment you are required to write a report giving a comparison of the strengths and weaknesses of training. This should include an analysis of the effectiveness of training both for the individual and the organisation, taking account of the constraints on the organisation, and an evaluation, showing independent thought, with alternative recommendations, of the effectiveness and appropriateness of the training.

Business example - J & J Balfours, engineering company

The human resources department at J & J Balfours, a medium-sized engineering company, has installed some new software to manage the personal data held about employees, their shift rotas and the monthly salary payments. The six members of the human resources staff have been sent on a course run at a specialist training centre to learn the software.

Mark Band 1 *An identification of the strengths and weaknesses of the training.*

With the training being held at a specialist centre the trainers were expert in their knowledge of the software and experienced at running this kind of training. Also, taking staff away from their workplace meant they would not be interrupted by the everyday queries they would feel they needed to answer. However, the training was using a simulated programme and the trainees did not get an opportunity to use the actual data they would be handling at work. Also, two or three members of staff felt uncomfortable being in a classroom situation – they felt they were 'back at school'.

Mark Band 2 *A comparison of the strengths and weaknesses of the training programme taking account of the constraints of the organisation.*

Using a specialist training centre with the courses run by experts meant that the trainees and management of J & J Balfours had confidence that the information they were being given was accurate and up-to-date. The experienced trainers were used to anticipating the types of questions and problems people would experience, handling them appropriately.

The course was expensive as in effect the business was paying not only for the trainer but the hire of premises as well. It would have been cheaper to have had the training on site but J & J Balfour don't have the facilities to run the training course on the premises and sending staff outside the organisation on a course, at a nice location with a nice lunch, made them feel valued and emphasised the importance of the training.

It was a big drawback that staff were doing the training with simulated data and were not able to start setting up their own database with the personnel whose details they were actually recording. Some staff felt this would have saved time because they still had to enter all the data when they got back. However, using simulated data meant that any errors were not important. In the workplace they were dealing with 'real' people and any errors in personal data, the hours that someone had worked on a shift or in calculating the monthly pay would be damaging to the organisation. If they made errors on the training in the simulated environment this did not matter and it highlighted areas where they would have to be cautious in the workplace. Also, starting the database from scratch back at the office would help reinforce learning.

Mark Band 3 *An analysis of the effectiveness of training both for the individual and the organisation, taking account of the constraints on the organisation, and an evaluation, showing independent thought, with alternative recommendations, of the effectiveness and appropriateness of the training.*

The training was essential for the organisation. The software program itself is efficient and accurate and cost-effective in terms of staff time. The printouts and automated salary payments also give a more professional image. Payments are made straight into bank accounts which saves considerable paperwork. It was important therefore that the training was

carried out effectively, which the use of trained personnel ensured it was. It was not practical to run the training on the premises – there were only four computers as not all of the six staff who were being trained worked in that area at the same time. The room was quite small and not of a suitable layout for training. Taking staff out of the office provided variety and job interest, and gave them self-esteem.

However, a single day's training meant that everything was being learned in one day. By the end of the day the six trainees were very tired and did not fully understand all the information they were given. This was evident from two serious errors which became apparent in the system a fortnight later. They had been given a manual which was useful for reference but, as it simply listed processes and did not explain how errors could be rectified, it was not as effective as it might have been. A Frequently Asked Questions (FAQ) section would be useful in the manual. Although these problems were sorted out and eventually the staff managed the system, they went through a period of frustration and were quite demoralised.

A more effective training process may have been to have broken the training into modules over a period of time, with both systems, the traditional paper-based system and the new software, running alongside for a time with the emphasis gradually shifting from one to another. For example, the first training session could have been half a day and explained about data entry. The trainees could then have had the next session some time later when all the data had been entered. They would then be able to ask questions based on their actual experience and searching and managing the data could have been the focus of the training. This would have given the trainees job satisfaction because they were likely to have felt a sense of achievement with less to remember and apply, and they would be enthusiastic about the next round of training. However, this would be a more expensive option as the training would probably take more hours and the process of introducing the software would be longer.

What is a skills audit?

Section 19 looked at the range of ways an organisation will collect data in order to identify individual development needs. It is not uncommon for this data to be collated formally into a skills audit. A skills audit is a means by which a business assesses the skills needed for a particular job and evaluates whether the employee who is the job holder has these skills.

The data collected in a skills audit will be one of the underpinning elements of a Personal Development Plan. This is illustrated in Figure 1. Personal Development Plans are examined in detail in section 21.

Figure 1 *The relationship between skills audits and Personal Development Plans*

Individual skills audits

An individual skills audit evaluates whether individual employees have the skills and knowledge required for a particular job. Individuals can be:

- assessed by others in the business;
- asked to make a self-assessment on the skills they have.

Then these are be matched against the job role currently being carried out.

An individual skills audit is often a common feature of an **induction programme** for new personnel and is used to identify where that individual needs training or individual support. For example, to be an effective call centre operator there will be a range of skills that are seen as essential, e.g. good keyboard skills, good telephone manner, careful attention to detail, punctuality and good listening skills. Once appointed the employee's competency across all the necessary skills would need to be measured. If an individual has been assessed at, say, 1 on a scale of 1 (low) to 5 (high) at keyboard skills, keyboard training could be seen as an essential part of the Personal Development Plan.

It is possible, of course, that the skills audit may highlight that an individual has a skill which is not being utilised in his or her present role but is in short supply elsewhere. The call centre operator described in the paragraph above, may, on the other hand, have a very high level of IT skills and the organisation may be short of people to work on their IT support systems. The employee could be offered the opportunity to change jobs.

Group skills audits

There will be occasions when organisations may decide to carry out a skills audit across a team, department or the whole organisation. The organisation may, for example, have decided to take responsibility for training away from individual sections and offer centralised training to enjoy economies of scale. In order to do this it would be essential to identify what areas of training are needed across the whole organisation.

Some other examples of occasions when an organisation may decide to carry out a skills audit are shown in Table 1.

Table 1 *When might a group skills audit be necessary?*

Activity	Reason for audit
Takeover or merger	Horizontal integration (the joining of firms at the same stage of production, such as two manufacturing firms or retailers) in particular is likely to mean that a duplication of skills and job roles exists across the newly formed company. The new management will wish to assess the skills available in the whole workforce for effective forward planning and restructuring.
Restructuring	An organisation may have decided, for example, to delayer or downsize. It will be important to assess all the skills that individuals have in the organisation in order to be certain they are keeping the personnel who have the skills which are most valuable.
Diversification	One factor in the decision about whether to enter new markets is whether the organisation has the skills and expertise amongst its existing personnel to be able to do this.
Introduction of new processes or automation	Any new process or the introduction of automation will require staff to be trained. The business will wish to ascertain the level of training needed. Some staff, for example, may already have knowledge and skills that they acquired with a previous company.

Collecting the data

The methods for collecting and recording data for assessing skills will be no different from collecting data for other purposes, such as marketing research, customer feedback or carrying out a job analysis. The difference with collecting data about personal performance to identify current and future needs, is, of course, the human element. Inaccurate data, or data collected in an insensitive manner, has the potential to have seriously adverse effects on motivation. Consideration has to be given, as well, to who collects the data. If it is not to be a self-assessment, the employee needs to have the confidence that the person collecting the data has the necessary knowledge of the task to make informed judgements and is of appropriate status to make them feel that accurate and meaningful data will be produced. Ofsted inspectors in schools, for example, are usually subject specialists in the areas they are investigating in depth and would normally have had senior management experience.

Methods of collecting the data may include observation, formal written questionnaire or a test. Alternatively, it may simply feature as part of the appraisal process with face-to-face questioning.

Recording and analysing the data

It may be that a skills analysis has taken the form of a simple questionnaire or interview with just one or two key areas being identified which can be easily addressed through existing training packages. In those cases it is unlikely that any formal or complex recording and analysis process needs to take place.

In other circumstances, such as in the examples in Table 1 when group skills analyses need to take place, a more formal approach required. Data needs to be produced which can be analysed in an objective way, perhaps by using a computer program or through mathematical processes to show trends, percentages and comparisons. There are several tools which can be use for this purpose. Two examples are given below.

Likert Scale This gives the respondent the opportunity to give levels of agreement with a statement, as shown in Figure 2.

Semantic Differential Scale Respondents are asked to grade themselves on a scale of, typically, 1 to 5 or 1 to 7, as shown in Figure 3. Some organisations will use a more simplified version giving just two or three worded options such as in Figure 4 in th portfolio practice section.

Using businesses you have researched, are familiar with, that you may work at, or your school or college, find and analyse three different formats for drawing up a skills audit. The different formats may cover, for example:

- scales of measuring levels of skills (e.g. Likert Scale, Semantic Differential Scale) or
- different methods of collection (e.g. observation, appraisal, questionnaire)

Research task

Figure 2 *Example of Likert Scale*

Put a tick in the box that shows how much you agree with each of the statements					
	Strongly agree	Agree	Neither agree nor disagree	Disagree	Strongly disagree
I am good at information technology	✓				
I am good at speaking in public				✓	

Figure 3 *Example of Semantic Differential Scale*

Observation of Customer Services Operative

Please ring the number which most closely matches the operative's skill

Scale: 1 = Good, 5 = Poor

Handling routine questions	1	②	3	4	5
Handling difficult questions	1	2	3	④	5
Politeness to customer	①	2	3	4	5

Portfolio practice · Special Spreads

Figure 2 of section 19 showed a job analysis checklist completed by Raj, an Adminstrative Clerk at Special Spreads, a catering company. Figure 4 below is an extract from the skills audit data that has been collected on Raj.

(a) Suggest, with reasons, how the skills audit data may have been collected.

(b) Using the data from Figure 2 in section 19 and Figure 4, analyse the suitability of Raj's skills for the job.

(c) Recommend, with justification, TWO training activities that Raj should be offered.

Figure 4

	Good	Satisfactory	Weak
Information technology: Competence in			
Word processing	✓		
Spreadsheets			✓
Database		✓	
Powerpoint		✓	
Interpersonal skills			
Telephone skills		✓	
One-to-one discussions		✓	
Group discussions			✓
Running meetings			✓
Organisational skills			
Filing	✓		
Record keeping		✓	
Collating		✓	

Meeting the assessment criteria - examiners' guidance

For your assessment you are required to write a report giving a basic description of the reasons for carrying out a skills audit. Your report should show evidence of good research into common formats for skills audit collection and realistic short and long-term targets identified.

Business example - Alan – Foreman of safety operatives

Alan is foreman in charge of safety operatives at a petro-chemical plant. He is carrying out the annual skills audit.

Mark Band 1 *A basic description of the reasons for carrying out skills audits.*
Because of the potential dangers of errors or failures at a petro-chemical plant, safety is a high priority. It is essential to confirm regularly that all the staff who are involved in the health and safety procedures at the plant have the necessary skills to:
- apply health and safety regulations correctly;

- operate the machinery safely;
- wear and maintain the correct protective clothing;
- evacuate staff as safely, quickly and efficiently as possible in an emergency.

Mark Band 2 *Evidence of good research into common formats for skills audit collection.*

Some of the skills were assessed by a test. The trainee was asked questions about the protective clothing and a tick list was completed by the trainer. The correct operation of machinery is assessed by observation. Alan, the foreman, goes round and checks the operatives when they are operating the machinery and he also uses peer observation by asking them all to keep an eye on each other and report back to him. They work in teams so this is an effective way of data gathering for assessing skills. One drawback of peer observation is that it can be influenced by personal relationships but Alan felt that this wasn't very likely as operatives know that mistakes in this industry can cost them their lives. Operatives have a six-monthly appraisal with Alan where they discuss training needs, so this is an additional data gathering tool for a skills audit.

Mark Band 3 *Realistic short and long-term targets identified.*

Alan helps new operatives set their short-term targets on their two-week induction course and most operatives can meet all their short-term targets during that period. Short-term targets for a new operative would include those shown below.

Short-term target	Reasons
Read the health and safety manual	New operatives must become familiar with the procedures right from the start because their own and their colleagues' personal safety depend on their correct application. They also need to be able to refer to the manual quickly if they have a query. They will be asked about the manual at their first follow-up training session.
Understand the reasons for each item of protective clothing	It is essential that they wear their protective clothing correctly from the start as they will not be allowed on site without it. Learning the function of each piece of clothing is likely to make them more motivated to wear it.
Lead the team in (a) operating the hose reels (b) checking the monitors	Being expected to take the initiative and successfully lead the team will motivate the trainee to learn the necessary procedures. It will raise their self-esteem and the achievement will encourage him or her to move on to the next stage in operating the machinery.

Personal Development Plans

A plan of action

Throughout the sections in unit 9 the steps that businesses and individuals take in order to ensure that the right skills are available and most effectively used in the organisation have been examined. Increasingly, organisations are using Personal Development Plans as a tool to form the basis of training and career development of the individual. Students hoping to continue studies into higher education, are likely to be expected to complete a Personal Development Plan (PDP) or Career Planner, for example.

While the layout, content and amount of detail in Personal Development Plans will vary from organisation to organisation there are three underpinning questions that form the basis of career and personal development planning, as shown in Figure 1.

Figure 2 shows how these questions are addressed in a typical Personal Development Plan. Figure 3 shows an example of how these might be applied to an employee and Figure 4 shows an example of an extract from a typical Personal Development Plan for a Customer Adviser at Skipton Building Society.

Figure 1 *Personal Development Plans - key questions*

Where am I now? → Where do I want to go? → How am I going to get there?

Figure 2 *Features of a Personal Development Plan*

Where am I now? → Identifying strengths | Identifying weaknesses | Identifying existing skills/qualifications

Where do I want to go? → Identifying long-term aims | Identifying future required skills/qualifications

How am I going to get there? → Setting time line | Setting short-term goals

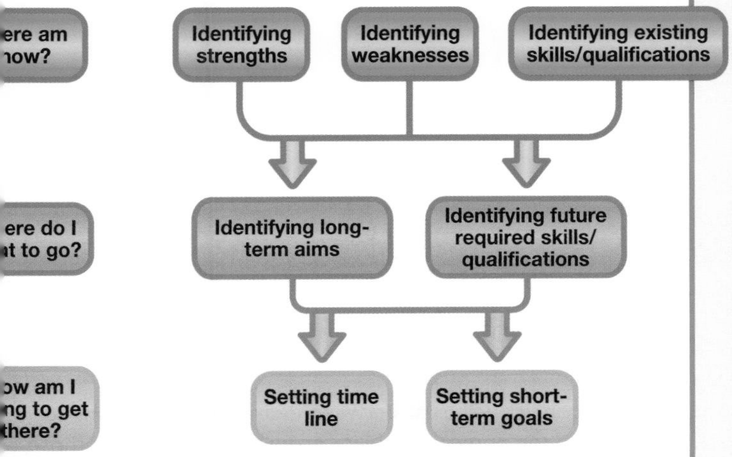

Figure 3 *An employee's Personal Development Plan*

In July 2006 Gemma was accepted on the Graduate Training Programme at Trees Garden Centres. Below illustrates how the features shown in Figure 2 may be applied to Gemma.

Strengths	Good interpersonal skills. Fair organisational skills. Excellent IT skills.
Weaknesses	Gets very nervous about giving oral presentations. Dislikes group work.
Existing skills/qualifications	Degree - 2.1 in Geography.
Long-term aim	Manager of a Trees Garden Centre.
Future required skills/ qualifications	Get certificates for all in-house courses recommended by Trees, e.g. Health and Safety, Communication and Presentation Skills, Legal Issues, Product Knowledge, People Management.
Time scale for long-term goals	2007 – Section Manager. 2007/2010 – Courses recommended by Trees. 2011 – Garden Centre Manager.
Short-term goals next year)	• Certificate in Product Knowledge to qualify for section manager. • Enrol on course at evening class to improve communication and presentation skills. • Get more used to working in a group and improve organisational skills by joining the social committee. • Record all appointments and meetings in the calendar facility in Microsoft Outlook.

Figure 4 *Skipton Building Society Personal Development Plans*

Skipton is the 7th largest UK building society. On its website Skipton Building Society states 'Our aim is to offer customers the very highest standards of service. One vital ingredient is the professionalism of our staff. Our commitment to their training and development is recognised by the fact we have achieved the prestigious "Investor in People" award'.

Source: adapted from http://www.skipton.co.uk/ and company information.

PERSONAL DEVELOPMENT PLAN
Name: Shirley Smith   **Role: Customer Adviser**

Date Set	Learning Policy	Specific Actions	By When	Desired Outcomes	Review Da
	Know key features and benefits of the Society's current range of mortgage products.	• Read product leaflets. • Read relevant circulars. • Discuss with colleagues/manager.	Next sales meeting.	• Able to articulate features and describe corresponding benefits to customers. • Achieve a pass mark on product knowledge test.	
	Be able to conduct an effective telesales call.	• Attend telesales workshop. • Observe colleagues making calls.	Within 6 months. By next maturity campaign.	• Competent to make own calls. • Appointments/leads being generated.	
	Use effective questions when using the enquiry form with customers to ensure all information fully completed.	• Attend Module 2 of 'My Famous Future' programme. • Observe colleagues using the enquiry form. • Role play using the form with colleagues/manager.	Within 3 months.	• Enquiry forms always fully completed with relevant customer information.	
	Know what specific activities need to be completed in what timescales for audit checks.	• Read relevant recipe cards/manual sections. • Check audit sheets.	Within a week.	• All audit checks completed on time.	

Personal Development Plans – the benefits and risks

There are both benefits and costs of Personal Development Plans for a business as shown in Figure 5.

There are benefits for both the individual and the employer.

• From the individual's point of view Personal Development Plans can also be a significant motivating factor, with employees becoming focussed on self-improvement and understanding the long-term implications of their efforts.

• From the employer's point of view supporting Personal Development Plans and encouraging employees to be proactive about their career planning is a valuable tool for developing good staff/management relationships and fostering loyalty.

However there are also risks. Businesses will be constantly assessing whether raising expectations of the opportunities that may be presented to employees could cause more damage than not offering a PDP programme at all. Section 12 explored the potential for conflict between individual and company objectives.

Figure 5 *Weighing the risks*

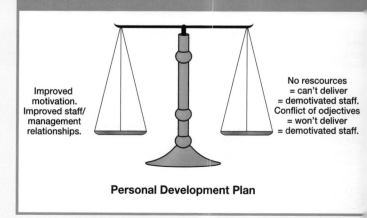

Improved motivation. Improved staff/ management relationships.

No rescources = can't deliver = demotivated staff. Conflict of odjectives = won't deliver = demotivated staff.

Personal Development Plan

The same conflict will exist between individual's aspirations to progress and the company's ability or willingness to meet those aspirations. An example is given in Figure 6.

Figure 6 *Glorious Villas*

Ashley works at Glorious Villas, a holiday company offering self-catering villas and chalets for rent throughout Europe.

Glorious Villas is owned and run by Maggie who had started the business from scratch fifteen years ago. Besides Maggie, there are eight staff who are all under 30. Six months ago, a new trainee started. She had just finished college and brought her Personal Development Portfolio with her. Maggie was impressed by how motivated the trainee was and the fact that she had her next five years mapped out. She felt that the trainee would be working hard because she had given serious thought to what she needed to do to progress and had already identified what training she needed. Maggie thought the opportunity to develop this excellent set of documents should be offered to all the staff.

Ashley was delighted. He hoped one day to run his own holiday company. 'Maggie is right' he thought 'I really need to plan out my future.' He drew up a detailed action plan which included acquiring diplomas in Cyclical Effects of Tourism, Brochure Design and International Emergency Management. He asked Maggie if he could take responsibility for overseeing the Italian market which she agreed. He also felt he needed to improve his Italian and enrolled on an evening class.

A month ago Ashley heard about a three-day course on Presenting your Product through Brochure Design and Websites. He went to Maggie and asked if she would send him on it.

'I'm really sorry' said Maggie 'you know that we had a bad season last year and we just don't have the funds to send you on that training – it is very expensive. And with our target of improving response rates to customer enquiries I can't spare anyone out of the office for a whole week'.

Maggie was also a little anxious that Ashley seemed to be very ambitious. What if he went off and set up in competition to her?

Portfolio practice · **Glorious Villas**

Look at the case study in Figure 6.

(a) **Identify and explain the conflict of objectives that existed between Ashley's aspirations and Maggie's business objectives.**

(b) **Suggest and explain the impact that Maggie's reaction to Ashley's request may have on motivation at Glorious Villas.**

(c) **Assess whether Maggie made a wise decision to encourage her staff to produce Personal Development Plans.**

Draw up a skills audit which could be used at a workplace with which you are familiar or at your school or college. For example, you could identify the skills needed and suggest how the performance could be measured at those skills for:

- successful completion of your course;
- a good performance in your own full or part-time job;
- an individual in an organisation you have researched as part of your studies.

Research task

Meeting the assessment criteria - examiners' guidance

For your assessment you are required to draw up a Personal Development Plan for yourself together with short and long-term targets in your career and/or educational development and how you intend to achieve them.

The following guidance is given for students meeting this part of the assessment evidence.

Mark Bands 1 and 2 *Evidence of good research into potential further/higher education and career routes.*
Students may find it useful to research the following websites.

- Hobsons Springboard – Education Search
  http://www.springboard.hobsons.co.uk/educationsearch.jsp

- Video interviews giving career advice
  http://www.kidzonline.org/streamingfutures/

- Online careers service
  http://www.careers-portal.com -

- Need 2 Know Learning
  http://www.need2know.co.uk/learning

- DFES – Information to young people
  http://www.dfes.gov.uk/youngpeople/index.shtml

- UK Active Map of Universities and HE Institutions
  http://www.scit.wlv.ac.uk/ukinfo/uk.map.html

Mark Band 3 *Evidence of sound and appropriate research into potential further/higher education and career routes for the individual learner.*
To obtain the marks in Mark Band 3 for this Assessment Objective, students should show evidence that they have researched routes appropriate to their own qualifications, experience and ambitions.

If, for example, the student hopes to start up his or her own business the Personal Development Plan would need to show a draft business plan linked to his/her own training and personal development, and sources of support.

If the student is planning on a career following on from further or higher education, the research needs to show evidence that courses are appropriate to the chosen career (possibly, say, by a record of a conversation or exchange of correspondence with a human resources manager in that sector) and that the entry level qualification is a realistic match to his or her own expected attainment.

The Personal Development Plans show targets and time scale for achieving academic qualifications e.g. GCSE, AS, A Level or a degree. It should also show goals set to exploit or improve personal attributes which may not always be measured by academic achievement and which may have been identified as strengths and weaknesses, e.g. working with people, numeracy and literacy, presentation skills, organisational skills, knowledge of IT.

22 Influences on marketing decisions

Decision making in business

People make decisions in everyday life. They range from the mundane (shall I have a cup of coffee or not?) to the life changing (shall I try for this job or another job?) Even the simple decision about coffee can lead to other decisions (shall I have the cappuccino at home or in a coffee bar, or in a cup or a mug?)

Business decisions In business, people also make decisions. The difference is that these decisions are made for the good of the business – the product, the brand and the company. People can find decision making difficult. They worry and ponder and may be forced by circumstances or time pressures into rushing a decision. Sometimes they make no decision at all and miss an opportunity. No one can be expected to get every decision right, but the cliché is that so long as you get at least 51% of your business decisions right, you are doing well and will have beaten the odds. This presumes that the outcome of a decision is a simple 'right or wrong'. This is a simple way of considering decision making, because sometimes a decision may not be actually wrong, it is just that another decision may have achieved a better result.

A decision is a commitment to a particular course of action. It may be an action in itself or the choice that has to be made. It is often based on the allocation and commitment to use resources. In business, decision making is based on a range of factors, usually with a desired outcome in mind or based on a particular need that will make sure that an organisation operates successfully. Examples include the need to:

- follow a strategy or course of action;
- achieve an aim, objective or target;
- avoid or overcome a problem.

Marketing decisions Marketing decisions are similar to business decisions, but they are linked to marketing strategy, plans and the marketing mix. Like business decisions, marketing decisions will also be prompted by the need to follow a strategy or course of action, achieve a marketing aim, objective or target, or to avoid or overcome a problem.

Every marketing decision taken will be different. Even though it may be a decision that appears to be familiar, the factors will be different – at a different time, under different conditions, in different circumstances, or with different variables. For this reason it is important to consider each decision carefully and conduct research or collect supporting information before the decision is made. This helps to support the decision, and, if necessary, to justify a course of action. Experience counts when making marketing decisions, but this must be supported by data that can be analysed, measured and monitored.

Businesses have both **strategic** and **tactical** marketing objectives which they try to achieve through decision making.

- Strategic marketing objectives tend to be long-term marketing goals.
- Tactical marketing objectives are short-term goals that may be

achieved through marketing.

Strategic and tactical marketing is covered in section 25.

Information about business and marketing decisions can be found from many sources. Some examples are shown in Table 1.

Table 1 *Business and marketing decisions*

Found in	Business decision
News	A car manufacturer has decided to close a plant.
Trade press	A perfume manufacturer has decided to change its production methods.
Contacts in organisations	The personnel department has decided to change its recruitment agency.
Work experiences	The health and safety training has changed to improve reactions to emergencies.

Found in	Marketing decision
News	A car manufacturer announces it will launch a new design at a high premium price.
Trade press	A perfume manufacturer has decided to sell through a restricted range of retail outlets.
Contacts in organisations	The marketing department has decided to use its own surveys rather than a research agency.
Work experiences	The sales of a product increase during summer as a result of a sale.

Reviewing the current situation

Before a decision can be made from a position of knowledge, rather than just taken randomly or guessed at, it is important to consider the current situation that exists before the decision is made. There is a joke that when someone asks for directions to get from A to B, the reply is 'Well, I wouldn't start from here …'. Sometimes planning marketing activity is a bit like that. You know what you want to achieve, and the theoretical ways of implementing the marketing activity, but real life gets in the way and in an ideal world you would not have started from the situation where you now find the business. This is quite important for marketing decision making. Businesses have to deal with the 'now' rather than what might have been.

The current situation will be made up of internal and external factors, as shown in Figure 1. It is this kind of information that is usually included in the 'background' section of a marketing plan.

Figure 1 *External and internal factors affecting marketing decisions*

External factors
For example, shape and dynamics of the market, competition and the economy.

Internal factors
For example, corporate strategy, ethos and internal competition for resources.

External factors influencing marketing decisions

External factors are factors outside the business that might influence its decisions, such as its marketing planning. Before implementing a marketing plan. a business needs to estimate the size of the market and understand the influence of external factors such as:
- customers and consumers – what is their profile and how many there are;
- competition – what is it and how many businesses are involved;
- distribution – what is the supply chain, how many distributors there are, what type of distributors there are, where are the distributors and how they distribute the goods.

There are other external factors that a business may have little or no influence over. Using a SWOT or a PESTLE analysis will help the business to identify external factors that influence marketing decisions, and help judge what can influence in any given situation. These are covered in section 23.

Customers and consumers Customers are the people or businesses that buy a product. Consumers are those that actually use up, consume, the product itself. Sometimes the customer may also be the consumer if they buy something which they then eat, read, listen to, or use up in any way.

Alternatively, a customer may be a distributor that operates between the producer and the consumer, distributing the product to the consumer on behalf of the producer. The classic example of a distributor is a shop. The shop may not actually produce the products it sells, but it buys them, as a customer, from the producer/supplier and makes them available for the consumer. The route along which a product travels to reach the consumer is the supply chain. It may be short – direct from producer to consumer – like the apples sold at the farm gate to the consumer, or it may be long and complex, involving a number of different distributors – carriers, warehouses, wholesalers, retailers – like most manufactured consumer goods.

When measuring a market it is useful:
- to understand who are the customers, who are the consumers, and who are the distributors;
- to have a profile, a description, of each;
- to have an idea of the numbers involved.

It may require **primary research** to find this out, see section 26 but for most markets there is likely to be some **secondary research**, which will provide some idea of the customers and consumers. It may be published in a commercial report on a market, or as a report in the media. Depending on the quality and reliability of the secondary research and how it is to be used, it may or may not be necessary to conduct primary research to confirm the findings.

Competition Few people have the opportunity of starting with a brand new product in a brand new market that is just waiting to buy that product. In reality, competitors and competition may already exist and can be of influence in a number of ways.
- **Direct competition.** These are direct, product for product, competitors that sell a range of goods or services similar to your own, or at least similar from the perspective of a customer. These competitor products are an alternative that a customer can buy, instead of your product. A business can create differences between its product and a competitor through brand values, by changing the specification, the price, added value features or a combination of the above to make their product more desirable for the customer and consumer. Direct competition is generally a good thing. It generates innovation, stimulates interest and dynamism in the market and usually provides the consumer with better quality or better value products. Direct competition may make a marketing manager's life difficult, but it can be addressed through managing the marketing mix and making sure that the product offered is more attractive than those of the competition.
- **Indirect competition.** There is another form of competition that is less easy to deal with. This is indirect competition in the form of competition for the different ways that consumers can spend their money. For every pound of disposable and discretionary income that ends up in the hands of a consumer there are a million ways to spend it, and every pound that is not spent on one business's product will have been spent on competitors' products.

Disposable income This is the amount that is left after personal income has been reduced by statuary deductions such as income tax. Using Maslow's hierarchy of needs as a model, see section 13 consumers may be said to spend in an order of priority.
- First will be spending on basic essentials such as food, drink and accommodation. Expenditure on accommodation may include mortgage payments or rent, and council tax payments. There is little that marketing can effectively do to change or reduce expenditure in these areas as it will be set and influenced by national and local economic factors.
- Next will be expenditure on items that make the consumer's life comfortable, safe and secure, such as heating, lighting, transport, motoring expenses, insurance and education. Marketing and competition is starting to have an influence in these areas although they are still regarded by many consumers as the essentials of life. For instance, within transport and motoring there are choices about the type of transport - public or private, the type of vehicle and the fuel used. Oil companies compete for the brand of fuel that is used and filling stations and supermarkets compete to sell the fuel to consumers. Within the insurance industry marketing and competition can

Table 2 *Effects of some economic factors on disposable income and marketing*

Economic factor	Change	Disposable income and confidence	Marketing
Unemployment	Rise in	Fall	May have to offer discounts
Trade cycle	Move into boom	Increase	May be able to charge higher prices
Interest rates	Fall	Increase	May be able to charge higher prices

influence consumer choice of the policy that they choose and company that runs the insurance scheme. Consumers may choose to turn down heating or use fewer lights in their homes. Even within education, marketing is starting to have an effect as centres compete for students and students are offered an ever widening range of courses. All of these expenses of life and the family will reduce the consumer's disposable income.

There are other external factors that affect disposable income. Changes in factors affect consumer attitudes to life, security, happiness and willingness to spend money. In turn, this economic cycle may be affected by local, national, European or worldwide events that have an effect on the UK economy. This effect on consumer expenditure can be seen whenever there is a change in interest rates, for example. These can have a direct influence on attitudes to consumer confidence and consumer expenditure and the economy in the UK. Table 2 shows some examples. The effects of changes in the economy on marketing plans are explained in section 26. Sections 68 and 69 of this book give background information on how changes in the economy can affect business.

- It is only once expenditure on all life and family matters has been met that consumers end up with a budget that they can spend on things that make their life better, easier, more comfortable, more enjoyable and fun. This is discretionary income and this is where competition for the consumer's spending really starts to get tough. There is a truism that people can only spend a pound once. No matter how many things you want to spend your money on, once it has been spent on one thing, then that same pound cannot be spent on something else. Consumers need to make a decision as to how and where that pound is spent.

How is this competition for the product of a business? If a consumer has only a pound to spend and it is spent on going to the cinema, then it cannot be spent on the product of the business. In these terms, competition for a business is anything that stops a consumer spending money with that business on its products. Viewed in this way, fashion clothing competes with soft drinks, computer games compete with luxury chocolates, charity appeals compete with DVDs. From an overall marketing perspective every product in every market is a potential competitor. How does a business cope? In reality, marketing strategy and activity should be based on raising awareness of the business or product with the target market. This will mean that when the consumer is 'in the market' to spend money, especially on the product that is offered, then there will be an

increased chance that it will be the product or brand of a particular business on which they choose to spend money.

Distribution For a business that is mainly involved in production, the supply chain and the distribution points along that supply chain will be a vital lifeline to its consumer base. Any problems that affect the supply chain will have a direct effect on the producer's ability to supply its customers, and may also affect its income and profit. This is why it is important to understand the distribution chains that operate in any market and to be able to identify the main distributors in the market. Information about a supply chain will include how many distributors, what type of distributors, where are the distributors located, and how they distribute the goods.

Information about distributors and the supply chain may be available in published secondary research. However, there is no substitute for actually researching distribution directly. This is so

Figure 2 *Sainsbury's supply chain*

In the mid-1990s Sainsbury's had an outdated supply chain structure. It had 2,000 suppliers and 800 million cases of product each year and it still circulated its warehouse pick lists on paper. Its IT system was old and inefficient. This often led to stock shortages. Between 2000 and 2005 Sainsbury's overhauled its IT system. The new system had many benefits. Sainsbury's could handle greater volumes and mixes of products and the business benefited from a more accurate view of all activities within its supply chain. Store consignment inaccuracy fell from 0.6% to 0.25%. Depots saw timely delivery and notification of vehicle arrivals. Shelves were replenished more rapidly and there was good visibility of inventory from incoming truckload to supermarket shelves. Costs also fell. Sainsbury's achieved a best-in-class 'cost per case' and an in-store availability of 97%.

Source: adapted from *Supply Chain Management Review*, 7.5.2004.

that a business can not only identify the distribution, but can get close enough to understand the distribution. This will be vital information that will be required when putting together marketing plans, so much so that some businesses will have separate marketing plans for each element in the distribution chain, to make sure that they are all supported and prepared for the launch of a new product or a new marketing initiative. A business may have problems if it started an advertising campaign without making sure that the products being advertised were available and stocked in sufficient quantities in its distributors. If this was not done, there would be a lot of angry consumers that could not get hold of the products, a lot of frustrated and annoyed distributors that had no products to sell, and a producer that was not maximising the sales opportunity generated by the advertising, with the subsequent failure to generate income and profit.

The supply chain is also important for retailers. Figure 2 shows an example.

Internal factors influencing marketing decisions

These are influences that are produced from within the business itself. Like external factors, internal factors that can influence marketing decisions need to be identified and a judgement made as to how relatively important each is to the success of the business.

Corporate strategy Corporate strategy will be the way that the business has chosen to run itself, to meet its long-term aims and corporate objectives. Corporate strategy is likely to have been established by the senior management of the business, or it may be dictated by the business owner, whether an individual or a corporate group. Corporate strategy is designed to provide the business with a set of guidelines within which the overall business is run, with the aim of meeting its business objectives. It is usual for all functions within a business to operate with its corporate strategy. A corporate strategy may be kept securely within the organisation, parts of it may be issued as required, such as trading terms and conditions that are issued to suppliers and customers. Sometimes aspects of corporate strategy are published and promoted in the

form of a **mission statement**, as shown in Figure 3.

Corporate ethos Corporate ethos is about the ethical stance that the business has taken, how it intends to run itself, and what it will consider from a business point of view. But perhaps more importantly it is also about what it will not do in its pursuit of business. It is the moral code which is applied to the business and the moral code which all aspects of the business will be required to operate. This will include marketing planning and decision making. For example, ethical businesses may refuse to advertise with organisations that invest in arms or sell in countries with a poor record on human rights.

An example of how a mission statement establishes not only the corporate strategy but also the ethos of a business can be found on the website of ice cream manufacturer Ben & Jerry's, shown in Figure 4.

Resources and business priorities Internal factors may be resource based. For example, a business may need to consider if there is sufficient money, product, materials, skills or human resources to support the marketing plans.

Another internal factor could be based on the priorities of the

Figure 4 *Corporate ethos of Ben & Jerry's*

Ben and Jerry's statement is broken down into;
* product mission;
* economic mission;
* social mission;

with a brief explanation for each section. The business is making it very clear how it intends to operate, and this will have an enormous impact on its marketing plans.

www.benjerry.com/our_company/our_mission/index.cfm.

Figure 3 *Google's mission statement*

A good example of a mission statement can be found on the Corporate Information page of the website produced by Google, the Internet search engine. It states:

'Google's mission is to organize the world's information and make it universally accessible and useful.'

This simple mission statement sums up in one sentence who the business is, what it does and why it does it, all in very clear language. Whilst it may appear to be simple, these few words have an impact on everything that Google does, the way it runs its business, the products it offers, the way it interacts with its customers.

Source: adapted from www.google.com/intl/en/corporate/.

business, or at least the priorities that are set by influential managers within the business. For example, if there is a fixed budget for spending on sales promotion, a sales director may argue the case at board meetings for spending the budget direct with the sales team, a marketing director may argue the case that the money would be better spent on advertising. A decision will have to be made and in this situation a powerful and influential sales director may be more persuasive than the marketing director when presenting a case for spending money to the board of directors, or vice versa.

Sometimes the situation may be even more complex and the decision about how to spend or invest resources within the business becomes more difficult. An example would be when different functions within a business are competing for resources,

for example when the production team wants a new packing machine, the finance team needs a new ICT system, the distribution department needs a new fleet of lorries, and the sales and marketing teams also make a bid for the money for sales promotion or television advertising. Like consumer spending, the business can only spend money once and the management of the organisation will have to make a decision as to how to spend the money and get the best return on the investment for the benefit of the business. Simple calculations, such as return on capital employed, will not be that useful in this situation. The return, such as sales that result directly from advertising, may be able to be measured, but how can the return on new lorries or a new ICT system be measured and compared directly?

Examination practice · Precision Timepieces Ltd

Precision Timepieces Ltd is an old, long established importer of high value wristwatches. Most of its product range is manufactured in Switzerland. The Precision Timepieces range of watches can be found on sale in a limited number of independent jewellers and watch specialists, probably just one in each major city in the UK.

The marketing team has been offered a range of low-priced watches manufactured in China. Before any business decisions are made it needs to evaluate the market for low-priced watches and investigate how the new range will impact on the

business and its retail customers. This new range will be very different from the existing ranges, which are premium priced.

(a) State TWO different internal factors that could affect the decision whether to sell the watches from China and explain how each factor could affect Precision Timepieces' decision. (6 marks)
(b) Discuss the effect that selling low-priced watches could have on the competitive position of Precision Timepieces Ltd. (4 marks)

Meeting the assessment criteria - examiners' guidance

Mondo Fashion is a high-class clothing store in the centre of London. Each day a group of protesters gather outside with posters denouncing the fact that some of the items on sale use real fur.

(a) Discuss how this external influence could affect the business commercially. **(4 marks)**

Exemplar responses
• *Business sells fewer items/sales turnover/income declines – profitability is reduced.*
• *Business could lose direct sales – customers are put off by protesters and will not enter shop - consequently do not buy, so income/profit is lost.*
• *Pro-fur customers are unlikely to be put off/may be more determined to buy fur – business could increase income/profits.*

Mark allocation
1 mark for how business could be affected commercially (maximum 2 marks).
1 mark for how external influence is linked to commercial effect on business (maximum 2 marks). **(4 marks)**

(b) State ONE business decision that Mondo Fashion will need to make if it is faced with continued protests. Explain the

potential consequences to the business of this suggestion. **(3 marks)**

Exemplar responses
To stop selling fur products.
Potential consequence
• *Could lose a valuable product range – will no longer have a range that will sell to people who want fur.*
• *Will need a replacement product range – will need to make up loss of revenue/profit by other means.*

To continue to sell fur products.
Potential consequence
• *Protests will continue – so will need to make it easier for customers to shop/may need to have special opening arrangements.*
• *Protests will get worse – will need to address security issues – for staff/premises/customers.*

Need to find out what customers think.
Potential consequence
• *Will need to conduct market research – be prepared to make changes/stick to current range as suggested by customers.*

Mark allocation
1 mark for appropriate business decision.
1 mark for potential consequence.
1 mark for explanation. **(3 marks)**

23 SWOT and PESTLE analysis

Situation analysis using planning tools

There is a number of ways in which a business situation can be analysed and considered before deciding which action or route to take, or which plan to implement.

These methods can be used to analyse both the current and future situation of the business. Two main methods are considered in this section – SWOT and PESTLE analysis.

SWOT analysis

A SWOT analysis is a useful tool for assessing and evaluating a situation as part of the decision making process for a business. SWOT is an acronym that stands for Strengths, Weaknesses, Opportunities and Threats, as shown in Figure 1. It is with reference to these factors that SWOT analysis is made.

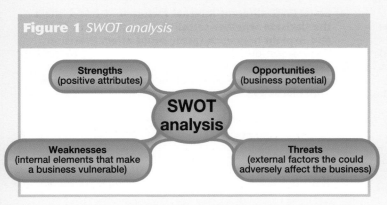

Figure 1 *SWOT analysis*

SWOT analysis can be used for analysing many different situations, both internal and external to a business. It is very useful for checking market needs, business opportunities and marketing plans against the ability of the business to deliver and satisfy the needs. It can be applied from the position of the business itself, or from the perspective of customers, consumers or even competitors. The simplicity of SWOT analysis makes it relatively quick and easy to apply, and the results of such analysis can be easy to understand and are usually readily accessible to most people. But although apparently simple, its value should not be underestimated.

Strengths These are all the good, positive attributes that can be identified or quantified. Strengths come from within a business or organisation, or are positive aspects of the qualities of a product.

Weaknesses These are the elements of the situation that make a business vulnerable. Again, they come from within the business or organisation, or may be negative aspects of the qualities of a product.

Opportunities These represent potential - what the business could achieve. This could be as a result of changes in the market or changes in customer needs. Sources of opportunity could include existing needs that are not being satisfied, or changes that

could be made to create new needs. Opportunities are not strategies in themselves. They reflect potential which will remain whether or not a decision is made to exploit it.

Threats These are external factors, outside the direct control of the business, that potentially can adversely affect the business. Threats could include competition, government legislation, the contraction of a market, or customers having different needs to those that had been assumed or identified.

Conducting SWOT analysis

It is often a good idea to conduct a general strengths/weaknesses and opportunities/threats analysis on a business before getting into the detail of a more focused situation analysis. This will provide a useful background to the business against which other SWOT analyses may be carried out. The reason for this is that no matter how big an opportunity may appear, it may not be possible to exploit it if the business does not have the right strengths or has weaknesses that prevent the opportunity from being exploited fully, or if it is devoting all of its resources to fighting off threats.

For example, a 'strong' new product may fail because the business does not have a strong enough sales team to develop its potential, or a business may not be able to exploit a growing market because it does not have resources that can develop a product that is right for the new market.

Examples of the questions that might be asked when carrying out a general strengths/weaknesses and opportunities/threats analysis are shown in Table 1.

Ways to improve a SWOT analysis might include the following.
- Be honest.
- Be objective.
- Use marketing research where available.
- Decide what situation is to be analysed.
- Decide on the perspective for the analysis.
- Think laterally, around the situation.
- Try not to be subjective, biased or too flattering.
- Use the 'So what?' question to critically analyse SWOTs.

The importance of point-of-view perception in a SWOT analysis

What is considered to be a strength from the point of view of the business may actually be considered to be a weakness from the point of view of its customers.

For example, a number of banks have opened customer support centres in low cost areas such as India. Figure 2 shows how a SWOT analysis may be carried out for this aspect of the business. This illustrates that a SWOT analysis applied to the same situation from two different perspectives can result in very different findings.

Table 1 *Strengths/weaknesses/opportunities/threats*

Checklist for conducting a strengths/weaknesses analysis of a business situation	Checklist for conducting an opportunities/threats analysis of a business situation.
<ul><li>What are the USPs (unique selling points)?</li><li>Are there any special skills that can be called upon?</li><li>Is there any technological advantage that can be used?</li><li>What marketing information/marketing research is available?</li><li>What distribution does the product/business enjoy?</li><li>What is happening in each distribution sector?</li><li>What history and heritage can the business call on?</li><li>What resources are available to support marketing plans?</li><li>Which bits of the business generate the most/least gross profit (GP)?</li><li>Can pricing be controlled and, if so, how well?</li><li>How is the current product range performing against the competition?</li><li>What is the market share?</li><li>How loyal is the customer/distribution base?</li><li>What is the image of the product/business?</li><li>What is the production/output capability?</li></ul>	<ul><li>Which needs has the business been satisfying?</li><li>Will these needs continue to exist?</li><li>Can we continue to satisfy them?</li><li>What needs are likely to change?</li><li>Do we actually want to satisfy these new needs?</li><li>Do the existing products satisfy the new needs? If so, what is the potential?</li><li>Can we continue to satisfy these new needs with the current products? If not, how can these new needs be satisfied?</li><li>Can the existing marketing mix be changed/modified to satisfy the new needs?</li><li>Is there a new product opportunity?</li><li>Which needs are likely to remain unsatisfied?</li><li>Could a competitor satisfy these new needs?</li><li>What are our penetration objectives in this market?</li><li>What are the market opportunities that we could exploit – short term/long term?</li></ul>

Figure 2 *SWOT analysis of customer support centres by a bank from the business and customer perspective*

SWOT analysis from the perspective of the business, the bank

Strengths
- Lower wage bills.
- Lower overheads than in the UK.
- Quality of staff is improved as can afford to employ graduates.
- Management of the staff and telephone system is someone else's problem.

Weaknesses
- Management of service could become remote, due to distance.
- Could lose touch with day to day issues/problems.
- Staff are not on the spot for briefings or updates.
- Communication of business plans to telephone team could take time.

Opportunities
- If move of customer support to India is successful could move other service functions, such as ICT, book-keeping or accounts.
- Could sell buildings previously used by UK-based customer service team.
- Can spend more time focusing on main business rather than have to manage the day-to-day issues of a large telephone team.

Threats
- Technical breakdown of telephone/communication system.
- Changes in policy of overseas government that may affect customer support team.

SWOT from the perspective of customers of the bank

Strengths
- Customer support staff available 24/7.
- Lower bank charges (as a result of lower wage bills).
- Staff left in UK should be able to concentrate on improving overall business to the advantage of customers.

Weaknesses
- Cannot talk to someone who is local/understands local needs/problems.
- Telephone team members may not always have perfect command of English usage. This means that some subtleties of language and colloquialisms may be misunderstood.
- Regional accents not always understood.
- Customer support team cannot relate to concerns that apply in UK only.

Opportunities
- Few, if any, positive opportunities for customers as telephone team is far away across the world.
- Can complain, argue and harangue person on end of telephone without fear of reprisal.

Threats
- Higher telephone bills, such as having to have long telephone conversations just to sort out a simple matter.
- That other banking services may be transferred overseas.
- That other banks may follow suit.

Benefits and problems of SWOT analysis

A SWOT analysis can be applied to any business, business situation, product, brand situation, task, or decision. It can even be used for self-analysis by applying the criteria to a person or a team. But it is important to remember when conducting SWOT analysis that a business and the market are dynamic - things change. SWOT analysis is just a snapshot of a situation at a given point in time. To remain relevant and useful it may need to be updated as the situation or circumstances change.

To be useful, all analysis needs to be honest and objective. A good plan can fail if a weakness is ignored. A weakness is unlikely to disappear or suddenly improve and become a strength overnight. Equally, a business would be deluding itself if strengths were over-stated. But it would be just as bad if the strengths were not recognised and the business failed to capitalise on them.

This can mean facing up to some harsh realities that may not be liked or agreed with by other members of the team. It is easy to focus on the positive aspects of an analysis, but if it is to protect itself and survive a business must face up to realities and deal with the real situation rather than ignore any problems and hope that they will go away.

Another factor is that strengths and weaknesses should be considered as being relative, rather than absolute. For example, a marketing team may consider its resources to be weak in some areas when compared with what it believes are required to launch a new product. However, compared with other businesses in the marketplace its resources may be significantly better than the competition.

Perception also has a part to play. When conducting SWOT analysis, a decision must be made about which perspective the strengths and weaknesses are being considered from. For example, a 78% brand share may be perceived as a strength by customers, as it means that the brand can be sold at a premium price, and by competitors, as it would be difficult for them to sell against as it dominates the marketplace. The business itself may be very proud of its high brand share, although it might also consider aspects of high share as a weakness, including:

- it makes the brand vulnerable to erosion;
- it will cost a lot to maintain such a high share;
- it means that the business is unlikely to have much opportunity for growth in the market as it already has the highest share and the cost of further growth is likely to be unprofitable.

PESTLE analysis

A PESTLE analysis is a useful tool for assessing and evaluating external influences on a situation as part of the decision making process. PESTLE is an acronym that stands for Political, Economic, Sociological, Technological, Legal and Environmental, as shown in Figure 3. It is with reference to these factors that PESTLE analysis is made.

The analysis should include an assessment of the different factors under each of these headings that will affect or influence the business, its marketing plans or the situation that is being analysed. Like SWOT analysis, it pays to think laterally and around the situation, to consider it from every angle to try to estimate how each of these headings will impact on the situation that is

Figure 3 *PESTLE analysis*

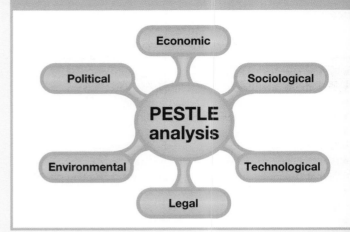

being analysed. Under each heading the consideration could be both the impact of the situation being analysed on the heading, and/or the impact of the subject of the heading on the situation itself. There may be some areas of overlap between headings, such as when economic changes are being brought about for political ends, or when an environmental issue starts to have a social impact. There may also be advantages and disadvantages under each heading, which makes the PESTLE analysis more detailed and a useful tool to aid decision making and to help provide background to the development of the marketing mix and marketing plans.

Political This would include actual and potential political pressure from initiatives and enforcement from central, regional and local government, and directives from the EU. It would also include lobbying and pressure from bodies that can assert political influence or that operate within a political framework, such as government agencies and non-government organisations (NGOs) like international charities. Political pressure and influence can also emerge at a local level, from district and town councils and other local politically oriented organisations. Figure 4 shows an example

Figure 4 *Political influences on marketing*

In 2005 tighter rules affecting broadcast and non-broadcast adverts came into force in response to public concerns about under-age and irresponsible drinking. In 2006 a Young's beer advert was banned by the Advertising Standards Authority as breaching these rules. The advertisement showed a man with ram's head surrounded by women. with the line 'It's a ram's world'. The ASA said the advert linked alcohol with social success. The ASA told Young and Co's Brewery to ensure it did not link its product with success at a social occasion in future adverts.

Source: adapted from news.bbc.co.uk.

Table 2 *Economic changes and the marketing planning process/marketing mix*

Economic change	Possible change in marketing plans
Rise in inflation/prices	Look for lower cost **promotion** or **distribution** methods
Rise in value of the pound/ change in exchange rates	Makes UK goods more expensive abroad. Switch **promotion** to the UK market.
Rise in interest rates	Makes borrowing more expensive – may have to cut back on **marketing plans**.
Rise in employment levels	Develop top of the range **product** with a **premium price**, change **promotional** methods and **target** ABC1 groups
Recession in trade cycle	Reduce **prices** of products

Economic This will relate to both micro and macroeconomic pressures, activity and dynamics. This means local and market based issues, as well as regional, national and the effects of world trade agreements. The impact of economic issues may be purely financial or may translate into the effects of economic measures, such as employment levels, imports/exports, balance of trade, investment and consumer spending patterns.

The effect of changes in economic factors on consumer spending was dealt with in section 22. Table 2 shows the possible effects of some major economic changes on the marketing plans of a business. Background information which may help in the understanding of how economic changes affect a business are in sections 68 and 69.

Sociological This is how the situation being analysed will impact on the way that people live and behave in society, or how sociological issues will impact on the situation being analysed. Here, attitudes and opinions as much as actual social behaviour will be important. These include issues of lifestyle, family size and structure and other patterns of social behaviour. The actual and forecast changes in society will also be included under this heading.

Technological This includes issues that relate to the application of scientific developments to products and the market place as explained in sections 74-76. This will include actual and new or emerging technologies. Technological issues do not necessarily have to be new in absolute terms, but can be just as important if they are new to a business or new within the marketplace that is being analysed. For example, wireless telecommunications had been known for many years before they were applied to small hand-held devices, which brought about the massive mobile telephone market.

Legal This includes how existing or forthcoming legislation is likely to affect the product, the market and marketing plans as explained in sections 65-67. Legislation governs the implementation of marketing plans, the way that the product is described, and the way that it is packaged, distributed and promoted. Legislation also affects the customers and consumers in the marketplace. Legislation is far-reaching and could be local, national or international in its origin or its impact.

Environmental Like political and economic issues, environmental issues may be local, regional, national or international in their effect or impact as explained in sections 72 and 73. It could be how environmental issues are likely to affect the situation being analysed, or how the subject or outcome from the situation has an impact on the environment. Like sociological issues, environmental issues may be based on perception, opinion and attitude as much as the actual facts of the situation, but all are important parts of the analysis.

What is included under each heading of a PESTLE analysis can be determined by knowledge of the market or the situation being analysed, but will be strengthened if the information can be based on market research facts, rather then subjective opinion. There is, however, a place for subjective or speculative opinion in this type of analysis because the impact of a marketing plan may not always be felt by people that have access to market research or have an understanding of the issues involved. This is all about perception, and although a piece of information may be genuinely supported by market research based facts, if it is not perceived as such by a sector of the audience then they will never believe that it is true. It is often worth considering what other people think rather than just relying on what you know. This can help determine how certain plans are presented, in such a way that they are understood and appeal to the audience, rather then trying to convince it of the facts.

Ways to improve a PESTLE analysis might include:
- being honest;
- being objective;
- being as thorough and as broad as possible when considering each heading;
- using marketing research where available;
- deciding what situation is to be analysed;
- thinking laterally, around the situation;
- trying to anticipate likely challenges to the analysis and collecting data as appropriate to your needs;
- using the 'So what?' question to critically analyse PESTLE.

Like a SWOT analysis it is important to remember that a business and the markets are dynamic - things change. A PESTLE analysis is just a snapshot of a situation at a given point in time. To remain relevant and useful it may need to be updated as the situation or circumstances change. Figure 5 shows an example of an actual PESTLE analysis. This example has taken a high-profile situation in a major industry. It is extreme and much more far reaching than most business situations or decisions. However, it does illustrate how a PESTLE analysis can be used to explore many of the external issues surrounding a situation.

Figure 5 *PESTLE analysis of nuclear power*

There is some debate in the UK about whether nuclear power should be used to generate electricity in the future. This will mean building new nuclear power stations. A PESTLE analysis of this situation might look like the following.

Political

- The national government has to make sure that there is sufficient energy being generated to keep industry running and be sufficient for consumer needs based on long-term projections.
- The national government has made international commitments to reduce the amount of greenhouse gasses being produced by the UK; one major source of greenhouse gasses is the generation of electricity. Using nuclear power to produce electricity will reduce the reliance on coal, oil and gas fired power stations and consequently produce less greenhouse gasses.
- The decision to return to nuclear power will have to be addressed as a political issue to be covered at local, regional, national and international levels.
- Nuclear power is unpopular, if it wants to be re-elected the government will need to make a good argument to support nuclear power that will persuade the majority of the population to vote for them
- At a local level the siting of a nuclear power station will be extremely unpopular. This will have a major impact on local politics.

Economic

- The country is forecast to need ever increasing amounts of electricity.
- Nuclear power is a relatively low cost way of producing electricity.
- A new power station will provide jobs when it is being built and will become a major (local) employer in the long-term once it is up and running.
- Local business and support services will benefit from the work created at a new power station.
- Local housing prices may fall, as few people will want to live near a nuclear power station, or they could rise as high paid technical staff move into the area and need somewhere to live.
- The area will attract fewer visitors or tourists, which would affect the local economy.
- Nuclear power could enable the UK to become an exporter of electricity, which will boost the economy and help offset the international trade balance.
- The management of waste from nuclear power stations could

support an industry that has been under severe economic pressure for many years, it could become another way of attracting businesses from overseas, by selling its services to other countries that have nuclear power stations.

Sociological

- A new power station will provide many long-term jobs at every level of skill.
- Some communities may be affected by nuclear workers moving into the area.
- Some communities may be affected by people moving out of the area to get away from the power station.
- Some families may lose their homes if large areas of land need to be purchased.
- Protests against the building of the power station may disrupt local towns and villages during construction.

Technological

- Nuclear power technology has developed a long way since the last nuclear power station was built in the UK during between 1988 and 1995, this should mean that a new power station will be safer, more efficient and less polluting than its predecessors.
- Given the environmental lobby and government commitments to reducing waste emissions, a technological solution will have to be developed that meets the needs of the industry as well as the country.
- The technology required for the safe storage and disposal of nuclear waste will continue in an effort to reduce the risks associated with nuclear power.
- Technological developments in the industrial and consumer markets will rely even more on electricity for power, which will maintain demand and increase the pressure for affordable energy.

Legal

- A determined government would make sure that there was no legal impediment to the development of nuclear power stations before embarking on such a course of action.
- Groups against the development and building of nuclear power stations would equally seek legal support for their opposition.

Environmental

- The storage and disposal of nuclear waste will have a long-term effect on the world/environment.
- There may be health and safety risks local to a new power station, as well as worldwide.
- With fewer visitors, there will be less erosion on the environment surrounding a new power station; this will benefit native plants and wild animals.
- Environmental lobby groups claim that even if the problem of what to do with radioactive nuclear waste were solved, there would still be the risk of Chernobyl-type accidents.
- The use of nuclear energy will reduce the reliance on fossil fuels and consequently reduce the impact that the extraction of fossil fuels has on the environment.

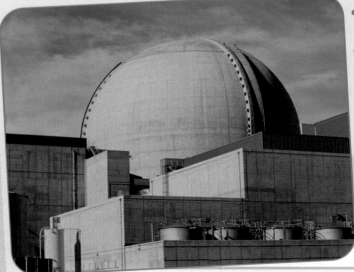

Uses of SWOT and PESTLE analysis

SWOT and PESTLE analysis can be applied to any business, part of a business or a business situation, and used to analyse the impact of marketing plans or decisions. Table 3 shows some examples.

Together, SWOT and PESTLE analysis can be very powerful tools for a business. For example, having conducted a PESTLE analysis the lists under each heading will probably include both positive and negative factors that are likely to affect the situation being analysed. It should also include factors that are having an impact now, and those that are likely to have an effect in the future. All of this will need to be considered and taken into account before any firm decisions or plans are made. It is also worth interpreting the findings of a PESTLE analysis in the light of a SWOT analysis. For example. a PESTLE analysis may indicate that all of the signs are right for the introduction of a new product or service – an opportunity for the business. A comparable SWOT analysis will highlight the ability of the business to make the introduction with any success by analysing the strengths, the weaknesses and threats that are likely to have an impact on the new product introduction.

Table 3 *Effects of SWOT and PEST analysis on marketing decisions*

Marketing decision	Example
Launching or developing a product	A mobile phone business may wait until a new technology (T) is researched before launching a new product.
Strategic or tactical decisions	A food manufacturer may identify an opportunity (O) in future to develop a strategy to move over to organic production methods.
Competitive advantage	A sandwich shop's strength (S) may be that it is the only one in the area which offers a business delivery service, giving it a competitive advantage over rivals.
Timing of decisions	A retailer may wait to see if interest rates rise (E) before it decides if it needs to discount products.
Correctly targeting markets	A business may identify a weakness (W), finding sales are low of a clothing range because its clothes are targeted at too young an age group.

Meeting the assessment criteria - examiners' guidance

Rosario Diggs manages The Place, a leisure centre in the Manchester area. She is fully qualified as a facilities manager but has only limited experience of selling and marketing. The leisure centre is owned and financed by the local council, which employs all the staff and pays all the running costs. It has four different areas with facilities designed to attract a wide range of users.

The Public Library
Run as a public service. Provides free information and Internet access, lends books, videos/DVDs and CD's without any direct financial charges.
Open Monday - Saturday, 09.00 to 18.00, late night Thursday until 21.00.

Skate 'n' Disco
Combination sports and dance-club venue, where roller skates can be hired and customers can skate, exercise and have fun to a background of loud music.
Open Tuesday - Saturday, 19.00 to 23.00.
Entrance - adults/over 16 years £2.00; under 16 years and concessions £1.00.

The Theatre
Equipped to put on plays and shows and for showing films. Currently only used for a pantomime during December and to show films on the Friday and Saturday evenings on first weekend of every month.

A Coffee Bar
Serves non-alcoholic beverages and snacks only.
Open Monday - Saturday, 10.00 to 17.00.

The leisure centre is well known to adults who live in the area. Among students and other young people there is only low awareness of the range of facilities at the centre.

The Place is within easy walking distance of a main shopping centre. There is a bus stop right outside the main entrance. Ample car parking is available on site. There is direct competition from a nearby commercial cinema and other leisure activities such as restaurants, fast-food outlets, pubs and clubs, and sport and home based activities like television and computers.

As part of her commercial management of The Place, Rosario wants to prepare a SWOT analysis.

(a) From the scenario identify ONE commercial weakness for each of the facilities offered by The Place. **(4 marks)**

Exemplar responses

Library
• *Information provided free by library.*
• *No charge made at library for Internet access/loaning videos, DVDs or CDs.*

Skate'n'Disco
• *Only open in the evenings.*
• *Only open Tuesday-Saturday/missing opportunities on Sunday and Monday.*
• *Relatively low prices/could charge more for service.*

Theatre
• *Under-utilised.*
• *Overheads must still be paid for even if not used.*
• *Only used for pantomime in December.*
• *Films only shown two days each month.*

Coffee Bar
• *Only open during day/10.00-17.00.*
• *Not open when Skate'n'Disco open.*
• *Sells snacks only.*
• *Sells non-alcoholic beverages only.*

Mark allocation
1 mark for each commercial weakness. **(4 marks)**

(b) State the difference between a 'weakness' and a 'threat' in a SWOT analysis. **(1 mark)**

Exemplar responses
• *Weakness relates to an internal issue and a threat relates to an external issue.*
• *One is internal to the organisation and the other is external.*

Mark allocation
1 mark for difference. **(1 mark)**

(c) Explain why the Theatre could be perceived as a commercial opportunity for Rosario. **(4 marks)**

Exemplar responses
• *Building already exists and is equipped for theatre productions/film projection – it is available for theatre productions for 11 months – Rosario could stage/promote her own productions in the theatre – and generate income from sales of tickets.*

• *Could rent theatre facility to theatre production companies – they would bear the risk – Rosario would receive the rent relatively risk free – which would be highly profitable.*
• *Cinema is a popular leisure activity – theatre equipped for film projection – only used two days a month – potentially 28 further days each month available to show films/attract an audience for films.*

Mark allocation
1 mark for why it is a commercial opportunity (maximum 1 marks).
1 mark for development points (maximum 3 marks). **(4 marks)**

Examination practice · **The Place**

Read the scenario for The Place in 'Meeting the assessment criteria'.

Rosario wants to widen the range of products sold at the Coffee Bar to include the sale of alcoholic beverages. She thinks that a PESTLE analysis will help her make the right decision.

(a) **Based on the situation in the scenario, give ONE factor for each element of a PESTLE analysis relating to the proposed sale of alcoholic beverages at the Coffee Bar.** **(6 marks)**

(b) **Give ONE source of information that Roasario could use to find out more about the legal issues surrounding the sale of alcoholic beverages, and explain why it would be appropriate.** **(3 marks)**

Effective planning

Effective planning needs careful thought and preparation. There is a number of tools that a business can use to identify where it is with a product, what its options are, and what are the likely outcomes of different strategies that could be applied to the product or the business itself. This section examines three planning tools:

- the product life cycle;
- Ansoff's Matrix;
- the Boston Consulting Group (BCG) Matrix.

The product life cycle

Before deciding on marketing strategies, formulating marketing plans and changing the marketing mix, it is important to identify precisely where a product or business is, in terms of its potential and its projected life cycle.

This is an important factor in marketing and product development. It is based on the observation that all products, and indeed most businesses, pass through a series of stages from initial concept and development through to the time when they are withdrawn from the market. The main stages of the product life cycle are shown in Figure 1.

Figure 1 *The product life cycle*

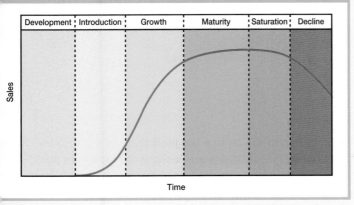

Some products, such as those based on fads and fashions, or those based on technologies that are quickly replaced, can have a relatively short product life cycle. Examples are shown in Table 1. They reach maturity and peak quickly after launch and decline equally quickly. Others, as shown in Table 2, have a long life cycle that extends the maturity stage through continuous marketing activity. This can maintain sales and keep a product profitable and prevent it from declining for many years. These products receive regular marketing activity and have enjoyed relatively long life cycles, which show little or no signs of declining. This illustrates that managing the life cycle of a product is an important skill in marketing.

Table 1 *Products with relatively short life cycles*

Brand	Reason for short life cycle
Fashion garments	Seasonal changes in item, style and colour.
Paint colours	New ranges launched each year.
Pop music acts	Meteoric rise, sells lots of music, highly popular until the next one comes along.
Computer software	Versions updated and replaced on a regular and ever quickening cycle.

Table 2 *Products with relatively long life cycles*

Products	Examples
Confectionery	Cadbury Dairy Milk chocolate (early 1900s), Mars Bars (1923), KitKat (1937).
Drinks	Coca-Cola (1886), Pepsi Cola (1903).
Publications	*The Times* (1788), *Radio Times* (1923).
Brands	Sainsbury (1869), Kodak (1888), Marks & Spencer (1894), Ford (1903), Kellogg's (1902) Persil (1909), Disney (1923).

Stages in the product life cycle

As Figure 1 shows, the product life cycle passes through a number of different stages over time. During each stage the sales, in units and value, will change. They rise during the early stages before reaching a steady level, plateauing and eventually declining. Net profit will also vary. Most of these changes occur because marketing activity applied to the product will be different at each stage throughout the life of a product.

Development This stage occurs pre-launch and pre-introduction to the market. It is the time when all of the research and development (R&D) required to get a product ready for the market is carried out. This may include activities such as marketing research of product concepts, product design and specification, technical development and testing. Other development activities will include production planning, designing and sourcing packaging, and arranging storage and distribution. During this stage the marketing team will be planning the marketing mix, getting everything ready for the product launch, such as planning the various elements in the marketing mix, such as pricing, and the design and production marketing and promotional materials. In

Figure 2 *Using the break-even point to forecast sales and time period before a new product will start to show profit*

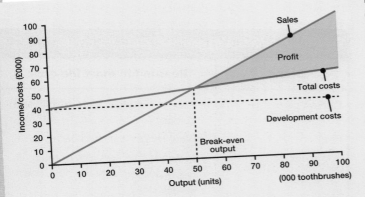

The break-even point can be seen by drawing the graph above. Alternatively the break-even point can be calculated by using this formula:

$$\text{Quantity of product required to sell to reach the break-even point} = \frac{\text{Total costs incurred during development stage}}{\text{Contribution per unit}}$$

where
Contribution = selling price – works cost
Works cost = fixed cost per unit + variable cost per unit

An example would be, a business spends £40,000 on the R&D required to bring a new toothbrush to the market. This development cost includes design, model making, research and tool-making. In production, each toothbrush has a fixed cost of 10p plus a variable cost of 10p for the plastic and Nylon, which makes a works cost of 20p. Each toothbrush will be sold to distributors for £1.00. The number of toothbrushes that must be sold before the business reaches the break-even output to cover its development costs is:

$$\frac{£40,000}{£1.00 - 20p} = \frac{£40,000}{80p} = 50,000 \text{ toothbrushes}$$

Having calculated the quantity of product that needs to be sold before breaking-even, a forecast of rate of sale will give an estimate of how long the business must wait before the break-even point is reached, how much time before the business will be able to show a real profit on the sales of the product.

$$\text{Time} = \frac{\text{Break-even sales volume}}{\text{Forecast sales per week or month}}$$

Using the previous example.

$$\text{Time} = \frac{50,000}{2,000 \text{ per week}} = 25 \text{ weeks}$$

This calculation shows that if sales of the toothbrushes are forecast at 2,000 per week, it means that the business will have to wait for 25 weeks before the break-even point is reached, before the new toothbrush goes into profit. This is assuming that the sales forecast is correct.

addition to actual product and marketing development, the development stage will also include all of the lead times required for production, things like sourcing and commissioning capital equipment, sourcing raw materials and packaging. The initial production of sales samples and the sell-in stock will also need to be done.

During the development stage the business will be investing time, money and other resources and not receiving any income or profit as sales have yet to start. There may also be some capital investment in machines and equipment to make the product, or in the case of a service, equipment that may be required before the service can be delivered to customers. The costing and pricing work that is done at this stage may show a healthy profit on paper, but until the product achieves some actual sales, and the consequent income, profitability remains theoretical at this point. Many businesses will treat each new product, or range of products, as a new profit centre that will need to make its own contribution to the income and profitability of the business. More importantly, this tactic will enable the money spent on the development of the new product to be identifiable as a figure against which to calculate how many or how much of a product must be sold before the initial investment in R&D is recovered, and forecast how long this may take. These are important pieces of information for the business, potential investors and other stakeholders, as they indicate the break-even point and points after which the product should be in profit. An example is shown in Figure 2.

Introduction This is the launch and sell-in period, when a new product is literally 'introduced' to the market. It will be a period of feverish, but hopefully well-planned activity based on implementing the marketing mix. Most important will be the need to generate awareness of the launch with potential customers and consumers in the target market.

During this period the business will still be investing resources before the product starts to show a net profit. The investment will be in the form of sales and distribution costs, sell-in promotion to the trade and the start of consumer promotion. For a manufactured product that is sold through the usual supply chains, launch stock will be delivered to distributors to await purchases by consumers. Services will start to generate initial interest and early orders as awareness increases, but like products, the supplier is unlikely to see any income in the early days unless sales and deliveries are dependent on direct payment.

How long the Introduction period lasts will depend on the forecast life of the product. A product that is destined to have a very short life during which it will be expected to generate maximum sales is likely to have a relatively short period of introduction. The business will want to get it into the trade and selling as quickly as possible and so will concentrate marketing resources in the launch. This will be typical of a product that enters a fast moving market where it will quickly become outdated as the market moves forward. A product being launched into a highly competitive market, where there is a large number of suppliers bringing out new products on a regular basis with little product differentiation, would also aim for a short, but high impact introduction. Some examples are shown in Figure 3. In each of these markets the producer will want to gain maximum sales as quickly as possible, and this can be achieved by a very high-profile introduction.

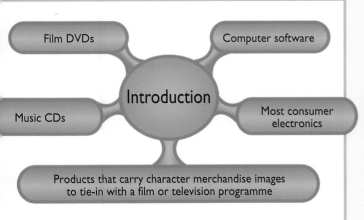

Figure 3 *Products aiming for a short but high impact introduction*

A product that is destined to be around for a relatively long period can afford to have a longer and slower Introduction. Sales and distribution can be taken at a more measured pace, perhaps region by region or on an area by area basis rather than attempting to hit the whole market in one go. This would be typical of when using a test market before rolling out a product across a wider area. This strategy is often used in markets when a manufacturer has only limited supply and wants to secure solid distribution and high levels of customer satisfaction rather than stretch a few products across a wide market and risk upsetting distributors that cannot get stock or frustrating consumers that cannot buy the product. Examples may be found in the car

market, in markets for household goods, such as furniture, or trade markets like printing machinery where the product is expected to be useable for a long period of time.

Growth During this period in the product life cycle distribution will continue to grow and sales will start to generate income and profit for the business. Distribution growth can be sustained by using tactical marketing strategies to build on existing distribution. Alternatively distribution can be increased by turning to a new market or sector of a market that has yet to be targeted or exploited for distribution.

As distribution grows, awareness of the product within its target market should also grow. This, combined with marketing activity that continues to raise and create demand, should lead to a growth in consumer sales. As consumer sales grow, distributors become more willing to stock the product, and increase stock levels to meet consumer demand. Increased distribution and higher stocks lead to more exposure to consumers and the target market, which, in turn, lead to increased sales. In some sectors, especially products in retail distribution, there is also likely to be a growth, or at least an increase in 'facings' - the amount of product exposed to consumers for sale. Increasing facings is a good way of raising awareness and increasing sales. The way that success breeds success during the growth period is an example of a 'virtuous circle'.

To avoid the product growth stalling or failing to meet its full potential, the marketing mix will need to be managed carefully to make sure that growth is sustained. There will need to be a careful balance between resources invested in maintaining growth such as advertising and other promotional support, and the profit that can be generated from the growth in sales, to make sure that the marketing support is financially viable. Other areas of a business will also need careful management during the growth period. Sales will need to be forecast so that the business can buy-in raw materials, packaging and other materials required for manufacturing the product. Alternatively, for a bought-in product the buying team will need to be able to source sufficient stock to support the growth in demand. This could be affected by suppliers' deadlines, delivery transport, and other factors outside the direct control of the business. Finance may need to be raised to fund the purchase of goods and materials as sales and deliveries may exceed payments back into the business. Other departments within the business may also need to be geared-up to support growth, such as dispatch, customer support services, and the accounts team.

But just looking at the statistics associated with growth, sales into the trade/deliveries out from the business can sometimes be misleading. The growth period is also a period of 'pipeline filling'. This means that before the target market can buy a new product it must pass along the supply chain to reach the consumer. Getting a product into the distribution trade so that there is sufficient product ready and available to meet consumer demand is known as 'filling the pipeline'. These sales into the trade, into the distribution outlets, is one way of measuring growth, but far more important is the measure of sales out of the distribution outlets and into the hands of the consumer. Sales out of the trade will determine future orders and hopefully repeat orders as the product takes off. A new product that just sells into the trade and does not achieve sufficient consumer take-off will not generate sales or profit for the distributors and will quickly be perceived as a failure. This will result in the distributors selling-off the product, not reordering, and bringing about a very short and unsuccessful life for the product. This in turn can lead to bad publicity for the manufacturer or the supplier of the product, and is likely to lead to trade resistance to stocking new products from this business in the future.

The growth period in the life of a product can be very exciting, but it also needs to be managed as carefully as any other project.

Maturity Eventually, the rapid growth in sales following the launch or introduction of a new product will start to slow down. Opportunities for growth will decrease as all potential distribution is achieved and the distribution pipeline has been filled with stock. Sales will find their natural level, based on the size of the market, and on consumer need and replacement as a product is consumed. This level may be satisfactory to the manufacturer, supplier and distributors in terms of generation of income and profit, but if not, sales will need to be boosted or at least stimulated by promotion.

The maturity stage is when profit will be maximised, when a product will start to pay back all the investment that has been made during the development, introduction and growth stages. It is a period when a business, and its distributors, will want to 'milk' the product, that is take as much profit from its sales with the minimum of investment and expenditure.

During this period a business may decide that there is little to be gained by attempting to grow any more. If a product were market leader with, say, an 80% market share, the cost of attempting to gain the remaining 20% of the market could be prohibitive, or at least unprofitable.

It is during the maturity stage of its life that a business can start to extend the life of a product by the use of marketing activity designed to maintain sales and keep interest in the product alive. This can be achieved through the use of promotion, relaunches and other marketing activity. There is no fixed rule about the length of a product life cycle, it may be short in products that are based on fads and fashions, or those based on technologies that are quickly replaced or superseded. Such products will have had a relatively fast introduction, followed by rapid growth and a short period of maturity before they peak, reach saturation and decline. However, there are examples of products where the business has successfully maintained and extended the maturity stage for many years

Sales may be maintained at a satisfactory level until something happens to change and upset the equilibrium. This change may be in the form of technological development, which renders the earlier product obsolete, or at least outdated when compared with products that feature the new technology. Changes in fashion can also make a product look dated as new, better looking products come into the market and consumers tire of the 'old' look, or 'old' way of doing things. The most frequent change in the equilibrium of a market is likely to come from competitive activity. A competitor could use any of the elements of the marketing mix to affect the market. It may launch a new product, incorporating a new look, a new specification or utilising new technology. It could cut prices, offer new and improved terms and conditions of sale,

adopt a new pricing strategy. It could make a breakthrough in terms of distribution, such as getting product into new places, increasing facing in stocking outlets. It could invest in promotional activity, such as advertising, generate press coverage using PR techniques or offer free gifts. To combat competitor activity a business will need to manage its own marketing mix to avoid losing sales and market share to the competitor if it wants to maintain or extend the life of the product.

Many businesses seek to maintain the maturity stage of their products for as long as they remain profitable, but at some point this may change and the product enters a new stage in its life cycle.

Saturation This is the point in the life of a product when everyone who wants one has bought one, and new customers/consumers are falling, or slow to enter the market. It may be that the product has become dated or has been overtaken by newer models and competitors. It may be that tastes and fashion have changed as new fads and fashions come along.

Market penetration, the percentage of households, customers or consumers that have the product, is high or as high as it is ever likely to get without massive investment in promotion. At this point the business may decide that further promotion is not likely to be profitable and a decision will be taken to just service the market and take the sales without further investment.

It is certainly possible to make good profit margins from products that have reached saturation point. All investment in marketing activity is cut and the business just supplies the market, hoping that the product will just continue to sell under its own momentum and distributors will not notice that sales have slowed or started to decline.

Extension strategies such as limited promotion to extend the product life, or at least slow its decline, may still be employed during the saturation stage, but they are less likely to be effective than during the maturity stage. Some examples are shown in Table 3.

Table 3 *Possible extension strategies*

Strategy	Example
New varieties	All Bran and All Bran Yogurty, low fat versions of products.
New models	PlayStation. X-box, car models, mobile phones.
New formulas of products	Soap powders.
New packaging	Coca-Cola in bottles or cans.
New markets	Sports shoes used as fashion footwear, bite sized versions of confectionery.
Relaunch	Mini launched in 1957, new Mini in 2001.

Decline This is when sales really start to fall, distribution starts to shrink and the few consumers left will start to find it increasingly difficult to obtain the product. However, it is important for a business to manage the decline of a product, rather than let it free-fall out of the market. A managed decline can still be relatively profitable as the remaining consumers are likely to be willing to pay a premium to continue to have access to the product that they have known, used and liked throughout its life cycle. An example is shown in Figure 4. Another reason to support and manage the decline is so that a business is seen to be supporting its distributors, important if you want them to continue trading with you and to take any new or replacement products in the future.

Figure 4 *Sales of non-digital cameras, 2006*

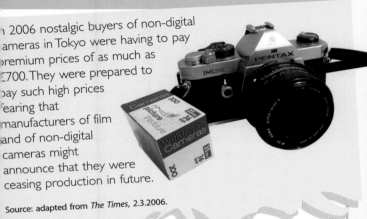

In 2006 nostalgic buyers of non-digital cameras in Tokyo were having to pay premium prices of as much as £700. They were prepared to pay such high prices fearing that manufacturers of film and of non-digital cameras might announce that they were ceasing production in future.

Source: adapted from *The Times*, 2.3.2006.

In one sense a product in the decline stage starts to become a niche product, as it is only being bought by a minority market. Such consumers can still be supplied through the development of specialised distribution and stockists. The development of specialist websites to supply products that have only a small market or become a minority interest is one way that products in decline can continue to generate income as sales decline.

There will be a point at which it is no longer viable to produce and supply a product, and it is withdrawn from the market. The ideal situation is that well before the point of withdrawal the business has already introduced a new or replacement product, rather than leave this to a competitor to fill the void.

Ansoff's Matrix

Igor Ansoff was founder of the strategic marketing organisation Ansoff Associates International. His name is now synonymous with the product-market growth matrix, which bears his name.

Ansoff's Product-market Growth Matrix, shown in Figure 5, is a tool that is used by business to identify which, of a number of options, a business could adopt to increase its sales. It is based on comparing the relative merits of selling existing products and new products in existing markets and new markets.

Depending on the aims and objectives of the business, and the strategy it wants to adopt, Ansoff's Matrix will suggest one of four

Figure 5 *The Ansoff Product-market Growth Matrix*

	Existing product	New product
Existing market	*Market penetration strategy*	*Product development strategy*
New market	*Market development strategy*	*Diversification strategy*

options.

- **Market penetration**, the safest option, based on selling more to existing customers, or taking sales from competition.
- **Market development**, seeking new channels of distribution or selling in different geographic areas - a slightly higher risk to the business.
- **Product development**, selling new products into the existing market, with all of the risks associated with new products.
- **Diversification**, the highest area of risk - almost like starting a new business, based on developing new products for new markets, two sets of unknowns which could cause problems.

To make use of the Ansoff Matrix, a business will need to set objectives for its products or for the business itself. It must then apply these objectives to the Ansoff Matrix and see what its options are for achieving the objectives.

Based on the options indicated by the Ansoff Matrix, the business can decide if its objectives are realistic in the current circumstances, or whether it will need to make changes to its product mix or its marketing mix to move it closer to achieving the objectives. Thus it will start to develop a cohesive marketing strategy. Once it has a strategy it can start to make plans for its marketing activity and for the business itself.

Conversely, a business could look at its current position, based on its products and the characteristics of the markets where it is currently trading. This will locate the business and/or individual products or product ranges in one of the segments of the Ansoff Matrix. Based on the location, the business can consider its options, based on what it wants to achieve, or what it could achieve with its current products. Again, the outcome will be a strategy for the business to pursue.

Market penetration The starting point for most businesses will be to establish whether it can continue to grow by following a market penetration strategy, i.e. selling more of its existing product into the markets where it is currently trading. This is a relatively low risk strategy as the market and the products to service the market will already exist. It is a strategy that requires relatively less investment than the higher risk strategies. If this can be achieved, all well and good and the marketing mix will need to be planned to support this strategy.

A business may adopt this strategy for a number of other reasons, for example:

- if the market is growing sufficiently to enable the business to increase its own sales just by holding market share and growing with the market;
- if the business has no other options, due to limited resources, but to keep going with its existing products;
- if direct competition is declining as businesses leave the market for whatever reason, the gap they leave can be filled with existing product;
- if the business is a strong/dominant market leader it can force competition out of distribution. This is the tactic behind the category management strategy adopted by market leaders.

Market penetration can be achieved in a number of ways, as shown in Figure 6.

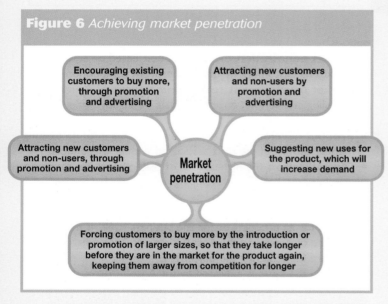

Figure 6 *Achieving market penetration*

If growth cannot be achieved through direct market penetration then the business will need to consider which other strategy it can follow, or indeed wants to follow, as suggested by the options on the Ansoff Matrix.

Growth based on existing products in existing markets may also be possible through internal efficiencies – cost cutting, more efficient production and more effective selling. In reality, internal efficiencies should be an ongoing activity, rather than a strategic decision.

Market development Opening up new opportunities for existing products is a strategy that raises the risk level just slightly. Broadly the strategy is to seek new channels of distribution for the product or to sell it in different geographic areas.

A business may adopt this strategy for a number of other reasons, for example:

- the product or brand is so strong that it will readily and easily find acceptance and sales in new markets - the Virgin brand and the Coca-Cola product are examples of this;
- the business may have made a very heavy capital investment in

plant or equipment that will only produce one type of product. In this situation it may only be able to achieve payback by selling more of the same product and if existing markets have reached saturation level then the only option is to seek new markets;

- market research identifies that new markets are emerging or seen to be opening up and there is a need for the existing product.

In practice, market development can be achieved in a number of ways, as shown in Table 4.

Table 4 *Achieving market development*

- Moving into geographical areas where the business is currently not trading, for example western businesses moving into China and the emerging Eastern Europe countries.
- Geographical expansion may not necessarily be national or international. A business may identify that there are regional opportunities that could be exploited. Even towns or counties where the product is not currently on sale would represent a new geographic market.
- A strategy based on entering new channels of distribution may also represent a new market. For example a business that starts trading over the Internet whilst retaining its distribution in high street retailers would be developing a new market opportunity for its existing products. Trading direct with a national chain of shops would be a new market for a business that previously restricted its distribution to the independent sector.

Product development Here a business is selling new products into the existing market. To do this successfully it will need to be confident that its name is sufficiently strong to get its customers and consumers to buy the new products that it introduces. In addition, it needs to be confident that all the new products will be as good as its existing products and that there is actually a market for the new products. Each of these is an area of risk and failure in any of these areas will make it harder to introduce new products in the future as the customers and distribution trade will not be confident of their potential and may not buy them.

This strategy is often adopted by a business that:

- has very strong distribution and a grip on its customers, and is confident that any product that carries its brand name will be successful in its existing markets. Sony is a good example of this strategy;
- is trading in a market where there are not many products, where there is limited choice for consumers;
- is in a market that is segmented very finely, with little product differentiation, but the small differentiation that does exist will have an appeal for a different segment of the market, almost a niche marketing strategy;
- has a wealth of new product ideas that have been generated by a positive new product development (NPD) strategy. In this situation the business may decide that it is worth the risk of flooding the market with new products on the premise that some of them will become successful and that unless they try to sell them they will never know;

is operating in a market where the products have a very short product life cycle. The fashion industry thrives on introducing new products every season, moving on and introducing more next season and so on.

n practice, product development can be achieved in a number of ways, as shown in Figure 7.

One final word of caution about a product development

Figure 7 *Methods of product development*

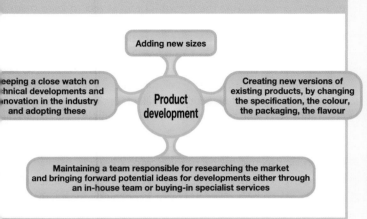

trategy is the reported high failure rate for new products. This an be mitigated, however, by extensive market research, gap nalysis, thorough product testing and careful test marketing or iloting before huge commitments of resources are made.

Diversification This is the highest risk strategy of all – moving nto two unknowns – new products and new markets. Despite his, it is a strategy that has been pursued by many businesses, ome of them successfully.

Although it is not a strategy to be taken lightly, the main reasons why a business may decide that diversification is the only way orward are shown in Table 5.

Success through diversification can never be guaranteed, but the hances of success can be increased by:

- thorough market research into the product and the market opportunities;
- total commitment through every level of the business;
- firm management of resources, especially finances.
- honesty, and a willingness to quit or pull back if the new products or new market do not meet targets, rather than trying to make them work by throwing more and more money at a project.

Boston Consulting Group (BCG) Matrix

Most successful businesses will have a mix of products. Some will be big sellers that generate the most income and profit, some will be new products that need lots of promotion, and some will be products that are past their 'best by' date but are kept in the ange for completeness or sentimental reasons. The aim is to maintain a balance between the products to make sure that as one moves along the product life cycle and into decline, there are other products being introduced to replace it.

The Boston Matrix is a useful tool to identify the status of each

Table 5 *Reasons for diversification*

- The product range and existing markets in which it operates no longer offer any opportunity for expansion or growth.
- Existing products may be growing old or becoming outdated as they move from the saturation into the decline stage of the product life cycle.
- At the same time the markets themselves may be in decline as customers age or drop out of the market for different reasons.
- A business may decide that the opportunities for diversification are worth the risk, especially if it is successful and cash-rich in its existing markets and is willing to take the gamble because the reward will outweigh the potential loss through failure.
- A business may decide that it does not want to keep all of its eggs in one basket, i.e. that it does not want to depend on just a limited range of products in one market for its future.
- A business may believe that its business model is so successful that it could be applied equally successfully to different products in different markets.

product and to help planning resource allocation and marketing requirements. This is known as 'portfolio analysis'. This means that a business can assess each of the products or product ranges that it currently offers to make comparisons and judge where they sit in relation to each other and in the marketplace. Products are compared, based on market share, growth of the market they are in, and how much they contribute to, or cost, the business. This will enable the business to start to make some decisions about each product and its consequent marketing requirements.

The Boston Matrix is based on a square, divided into quadrants, with a vertical scale based on the rate of market growth, usually a percentage, and a horizontal scale based on market share, as shown in Figure 8. Where a product is positioned within the Boston Matrix can indicate whether it is worth keeping, and if so what marketing support it may need, whether to withdraw it from the market place, which products to leave to decline naturally and which products may need more than just marketing support to survive and develop, and earn its place in the range on offer. Used together with the product life cycle, the Boston Matrix can help an organisation understand more about its products in a business sense.

The principles of the Boston Matrix are not limited to individual products. It can also be used to analyse a brand, product groups or ranges, or discreet profit centres or income streams within a business. However the management decides to define and measure within organisation. Even the entire business itself could be located somewhere on the matrix. This will help management identify precisely where it is in the market place and its potential in the future. To keep things simple, this section will refer to 'product' when using the Boston Matrix, but in practice, 'product' could refer to individual products, product ranges, brands or businesses.

The Boston Matrix was developed in the USA in the early

1960's by Bruce D. Henderson when he established The Boston Consulting Group as the consulting arm of the Boston Safe Deposit and Trust Company, a major banking firm. The concept is very simple - categorise each product or product group as either a Question Mark, a Star, a Cash Cow, or a Dog, according to its growth rate and its market share. The amount of cash and profit generated by each product, and the amount each product costs to either maintain or grow its market share is another factor when using the Boston Matrix, and making decisions about products.

Figure 8 *The Boston Matrix*

		Market share	
		High	Low
Market growth rate	High	Star	Question Mark (?)
	Low	Cash Cow	Dog

The portfolio concept can be very useful as it helps a business recognise just what it has got, in terms of the performance and potential of its products. In this way the business can recognise that within its total operation each product or product group has its own dynamic and requires its own management strategy in order to maximise its potential and to make the most effective use of resources available.

Question Mark Such a product has only a low market share, but is in a market that is growing fast. A business must decide what to do with such a product (hence a question). This is a scenario that is typical of a new, innovatory product that is struggling to gain market share, or is in a new market that has yet to grow and develop. Should a business invest in tactical marketing plans that will increase its market share and catapult it into the Star sector? Or will investment and resources required to promote the product outweigh its growth and profit potential? If plans are delayed there is the risk that it will never achieve sufficient market share even though the potential is there. A business is unlikely to be able to invest in all of its products all of the time and there will be some that are just not worth investing in, and these will have to be cut or left to decline naturally. There is no easy answer for a Question Mark product – just gather as much market research information as possible and try to make the decision from an objective position of strength, rather than a subjective or sentimental position. In some examples of the Boston Matrix, the

Question Mark is referred to as a 'Problem Child'. It means the same thing, it is just another way of describing products in this

position on the matrix.

Star This classification is a good reflection of its description and its position in the portfolio. Stars are products that have a high market share that is growing fast, in a market that is itself growing. They generate high income for the business but will require an equally high level of investment in terms of marketing support. Typically this would equate to a new product in the growth stage in its life cycle and are sometimes referred to as Rising Stars. These products will require high investment of resources in order to sustain and maximise the growth potential, and to keep them ahead of competition. Eventually, growth will slow as they enter the Maturity stage of the product life cycle. At this point a business will usually reduce its support to a level that is just sufficient to maintain market share. The business will now want to start to take profit from sales. Thus, the Star will turn into a Cash Cow for the business, where it will be kept and 'milked', until it is no longer generating sufficient profit in relation to the investment required. As the once Star product declines, through the Cash Cow quadrant, it will eventually become classified as a Dog. This shows the circular dynamic nature of the Boston Matrix.

Cash Cow Every business is likely to have a Cash Cow. It will probably be the best seller, the most important product, the one that has the largest share of the market and the one that generates most of the income and profit for the business. It will be relatively stable and well established and consequently requires relatively less marketing support than other products, certainly less than it generates in profit. Growth will tend to be low-level, but market share will be high. It will be in a market that is relatively large and stable, but is showing little or no growth and may be in long-term decline. Cash Cows are very important and need to be protected as they provide the business with its main income. They will pay the overheads of the business and provide cash for investment in other products. In this sense they will be attractive to competitors and therefore potentially vulnerable to competitive pressures. To make the most out of Cash Cows, they will need to be protected from competitors and managed carefully so that they continue to generate the strong cash flow. It is this flow of income from the Cash Cows that will be needed to promote the Stars of the business, or to offset investment in supporting Question Marks until a decision is made about their future.

Dog This classification should not necessarily be considered as negative, as in 'bad dog', a common mistake. The original BCG classification views it more as a 'pet dog' – something that is small and vulnerable and needs looking after. Dogs, like pets, will be totally dependent, in this case, dependent on the success of other products within the portfolio. Products identified as Dogs have a low market share and low growth prospects, but they may still have a role to play in the business as they may complete an overall product offer, or provide an alternative to competitors' versions of similar products. Without them the business may be perceived as having an incomplete range of products. But looking after a Dog comes with a price - low sales and low figures for absolute profit although the percentage profitability on these products may be acceptably high on paper. Any investment in marketing is unlikely to be recouped unless it is sufficient to make the market grow or increase the market share enjoyed by the Dog to the point that it starts moving towards becoming a Star. A Dog will be a drain on the business and the business may decide that it would be better to withdraw the product, or sell it, and invest the money saved elsewhere in its portfolio.

Using the Boston Matrix

Simply locating products on the Boston Matrix is relatively easy. Just define each product in terms of its market share and market growth and decide where it sits. This position may be central to one of the quadrants, or closer to one or other of the axes, again depending what is decided about the market share and rate of market growth, supported by marketing research.

More difficult is deciding what to do with each product as a result of its location on the Boston Matrix. Depending on the aims and objectives of the business, the potential offered by each product and the resources available, there is a number of options to consider.

Do nothing Here the product is left to rise or fall and find its own position and level in the market place and then the situation monitored. This will mean that a decision, whether to support or withdraw the product, will still have to be made at some point in its life. In some cases this will mean delaying the inevitable, i.e. to cut losses and withdraw the product. In other cases it may prove that there is a market, that the product could start to earn its place in the portfolio by generating income and profit. The decision in this case is based on potential, whether the product will sell enough to generate a satisfactory income and profit to justify future investment, and whether the cost of support will be worth the investment.

Keep it where it is This is where the business provides just enough support to maintain the product in its current position. This is one step on from doing nothing. In the case of a Cash Cow this strategy aims to keep the income and profits rolling in with minimum investment. For a product that has been classified as a Dog, the objective of maintaining it in the current position will need to be judged against what its presence contributes to the business in terms of range completion or competitive offer, as well as income and profit generated. Again, the product and its position in the marketplace will need to be monitored to confirm whether this strategy is right, whether to cut all support or to increase support.

Increase support This will mean promoting, growing market share or helping the market develop and grow. This strategy has the objective of turning a Question Mark product into a Star. It is a potentially expensive option as the amount of investment required will be difficult to forecast. However, it can be managed to some degree by setting targets and measuring achievement against these targets. In this way a business can control the amount of money it invests, and take decisions about how much more to invest, in stages rather than make an open-ended commitment to expenditure. At some point the product being supported will 'peak' or the market will plateau, reaching a level above which it is unlikely to grow any further. This will be the maturity stage in the product life cycle and some of the Star products will (hopefully) turn into Cash Cows. However, this may not happen for products that have a short life cycle, characterised by extremely rapid growth, followed by an equally rapid decline – typical of short life fashion products, or products in markets where technology is advancing rapidly to the point that a product is virtually obsolete from the moment it is launched, for example computers. In this situation the Star will fall back to become classified as a Dog.

This shows that once placed in the Matrix a product need not stay in the same position forever. It is therefore advisable to review the product portfolio on a regular basis. The product life cycle as well as the marketplace will be dynamic. A business can take steps to grow the market share of its products through investment, promotion and other marketing activity. Although the rate of growth of the market is often outside the direct control of a business, it may be able to exert some influence through its marketing activity. The movement of a product round the Boston Matrix is essentially anticlockwise. A product starting life as a Question Mark can be moved into the position of a Star, given sufficient investment and support. A Star will reach its peak then tend to move downwards to become a Cash Cow as it reaches its maximum market share and the market growth rate slows, or may plummet quickly and soon become a Dog, depending on the length of its life cycle. Dogs, nice as pets, will starve the business of income, drain the business of profit if supported for too long and should be withdrawn unless there is a strong strategic reason for keeping them in the portfolio.

Meeting the assessment criteria - examiners' guidance

Having completed an MBA at Edinburgh University, Griff Shepherd returns to Slough to work in the family business, Shepherd's Paint Products Ltd. (SPP) as its marketing manager. The business was founded over 50 years ago by Griff's grandfather. It manufactures a small range of specialist paints for the building trade. Before he can make any plans for the business Griff needs to learn more about the market for trade paints and product ranges produced by SPP.

To learn about the product ranges produced by SPP he asks for a report from the sales manager. He is told:

- the best seller is White Metal Finish, accounting for 80% of sales and profit earned by SPP;
- the Coloured Metal Finish paints are not selling very well, there is a large range of 25 different colours which in total only account for 10% of sales and profit;
- the biggest surprise has been the new product that has been developed - Textured Finish. It has only been on the market for one year but is already generating 10% of sales and profit for SPP.

To learn about the trade paint market he buys market research data in the form of a report produced and published by the *Financial Times*. It shows that the Specialist Paint Market in which SPP trades breaks down as shown in Tables 6 and 7.

Griff decides to use a Boston Matrix to help him plan the business strategy for SPP.

Table 6 *Specialist Paint Market 2005 – Sales*

	Sales volume in '000 litres			Sales value in £'000		
	000 Litres	% total	% change year/year	£000	% total	% change year/year
Damp Proof Paint	105.0	4.1	8.8	862.6	2.9	2.5
Floor Paint	697.4	27.2	5.9	5,294.6	17.8	5.8
High Gloss	341.0	13.3	-7.9	5,711.0	19.2	0.8
Metal Finish White	820.5	32.0	-13.1	11,005.7	37.0	-9.3
Metal Finish Colour	51.3	2.0	-43.0	386.7	1.3	-30.9
Radiator Paint	171.9	6.7	-2.4	2,439.1	8.2	3.2
Textured Finish	376.9	14.7	7.8	4,045.3	13.6	20.5
Total Market	2 564.0	100	-4.0	29,745.00	100	-0.6

Source: adapted from AMMS.

Table 7 *Specialist Paint Market 2005 – Market Share*

Market Shares – value £%

Manufacturer	Metal Finish White	Metal Finish Colour	Textured Finish
Andrews	0.4	13.7	10.7
Housey	0.0	0.0	42.0
Muirs	0.4	7.8	10.8
Shepherds	90.1	52.5	6.4
Tritex	1.6	10.2	18.8
Zephyr	7.5	15.8	11.3
	100	100	100.0

Source: adapted from AMMS.

(a) **(i)** On the Boston Matrix, Figure 9, show where each of the current SPP product ranges should be located.

(3 marks)

Figure 9 *Boston Matrix*

		Market share	
		High	Low
Market growth rate	High	Star	Question Mark (?)
	Low	Cash Cow	Dog

Exemplar responses

		Market share	
		High	Low
Market growth rate	High	Star	Question Mark (?) *Textured Finish*
	Low	Cash Cow *White Metal Finish*	Dog *Coloured Metal Finish*

Mark allocation
1 mark for each correct position. **(3 marks)**

(ii) Using the information in Table 6 and Table 7, justify each location in the matrix that you have selected.
- White Metal Finish.
- Coloured Metal Finish.
- Textured Finish. **(6 marks)**

Exemplar responses
White Metal Finish
- *SPP has large/largest share of market – market is large/growth is slow/negative.*
- *SPP holds 90.1% value share of market – market has declined -13.1% volume/ -9.3% value year on year.*
- *accounts for 80% of sales and profit earned by SPP – this, combined with market share/market growth information describes a classic Cash Cow.*

Coloured Metal Finish
- *SPP holds over half of market – but market for coloured metal finish is small and has declined dramatically over year.*
- *SPP holds 52.5% of market – market has declined -43% volume/ -30.9% value year on year.*
- *Only accounts for 10% of sales and profit – combined with market share/growth defines a Dog.*

Textured Finish
- *SPP has only small share of market – but market is fastest growing in terms of value.*
- *SPP holds only 6.4% of market – market has grown 7.8% volume/20.5% value.*
- *New product for SPP – in market that is small/growing fast defines a Question Mark.*

Mark allocation
1 mark for justification based on market share (maximum 3 marks). 1 mark for justification based on market growth rate (maximum 3 marks) or 1 mark for justification based on position of product within SPP.

(1 + 1) x 3 = (6 marks)

Examination practice · Shepherd's Paint Products Ltd (SPP)

Use the information provided about Shepherd's Paint Products Ltd (SPP).

(a) Explain how a business like Shepherd's Paint Products Ltd (SPP) can use the Ansoff Product-market Growth Matrix to help it develop a marketing strategy based on market penetration. **(4 marks)**

(b) Give TWO reasons why a market penetration strategy would be appropriate for SPP. **(2 marks)**

(c) Based on the Ansoff Matrix, describe the strategy that SPP must have followed to arrive at the introduction of its Textured Finish. **(4 marks)**

25 Developing a marketing strategy

Strategic marketing decisions

Strategic decisions tend to be based on the need to achieve the long-term objectives that the business has set. Because of the time scales usually involved in changing consumer behaviour or attitudes to a business or its products long-term, in this sense, can be taken to mean anything from two to five years. Any shorter and it would be difficult to measure whether a marketing strategy has had the desired effect on a market, anything longer is unlikely because of the fast moving nature of most markets. A marketing strategy will be the over-riding approach to marketing that the business decides to adopt, based on meeting the overall aims and objectives of the business. It will be the general approach to the way that the business plans to run its marketing programme to meet its mission statement.

Product strategy

There are many different product development strategies that a business might consider using.

Continuous innovation This strategy means that a business will have a high commitment to research and development (R&D) in order to be able to bring new and innovative products to the market in a continuous, but managed, stream. The object is to demonstrate to both **trade**, i.e. **business to business (B2B)** and **consumer** markets that the business is a technological leader and as such will always produce excellent products and is better than its competitors because it makes available the latest technology. It will also provide an opportunity for price skimming, to generate maximum sales and profit for itself and its distributors.

Continuous innovation is often associated with businesses that have an overall strategy for continuous improvement, sometimes known by the Japanese term **kaizen** or the kaizen philosophy. Such businesses seek to maintain leadership in a market and maximise productivity through continuously seeking improvement in working practices as well as technology. This so-called Japanese industrial and manufacturing philosophy is often contrasted with the approach that used to be followed by Western industries, exemplified by one-off developments and improvements which would be exploited until forced to make the next improvement. However, this old approach has become outmoded as European and American businesses compete increasingly in international markets.

Category dominance This means that a business attempts to dominate a product category, market or market segment with its products and to exclude or force out competition. This often happens in a market where a small number of manufacturers dominate, each selling a number of brands, each brand having a number of variants to meet the needs of every type of consumer, thus seeking to dominate a category and give the consumer no reason to buy a competitor product.

Although category dominance may be sought, and sometimes

Table 1 *Product strategies*

Strategy	Industry examples
Continuous innovation	High tech industries, such as electronics, computers and pharmaceuticals (Apple, Intel, Microsoft)
Category dominance	The washing powder market, the household paint market and garden chemicals (Procter & Gamble, Unilever)
Niche marketing	Organic foods and wine, hairpieces, activity holidays (West Country Organics, Exodus walking holidays)
Mass marketing	Motor car manufacturing, printing and publishing popular newspapers and magazines, packaged foods, and popular entertainment products on DVDs and CDs (Ford, Nestlé, Warner Bros)
Quality products or services	Watches (Rolex) and Michelin Star restaurants
Standard product	Drinks manufacturers (Coca-Cola) and paint (Dulux, Crown)
Tailoring products	Couture fashion market and other craft based businesses that make products to specific orders (Madetoorder a – manufacturer of t-shirts, garments and signs)

Figure 1 *Safeway sale*

When the Safeway supermarket chain was sold, the Competition Commission favoured the stores going to Morrison so that it would provide competition for Tesco, Sainsbury's and ASDA, each of which would be considered to be unfavourably dominant in the market had the Safeway stores gone to either of them.

Source: adapted from media reports.

achieved, by some manufacturers within retail stores, there are some constraints. For example, in the UK the Competition Commission polices markets where category dominance by a limited number of businesses is against the public interest. The aim of the Competition Commission in this situation is to try to maintain consumer choice by making sure that there is sufficient competition in a market. An example of this is shown in Figure 1, showing limits set for the share of the market that can be held by one supermarket.

Niche marketing This is a product segmentation strategy based on marketing research identifying a gap in the market or a group of consumers/customers whose needs are not being met by the main suppliers. Alternatively it can work when a business decides that it is worth specialising and concentrating marketing activity on the gap, the niche that has been identified.

Before this strategy is adopted the business must decide whether the niche identified is large enough to be worth concentrating on, and likely to be profitable. In addition, it must decide whether it has a product to meet needs of customers in the niche, if it is worth developing a product to meet needs of these customers, whether it has the resources to support marketing plans aimed at the niche, and whether the niche marketing strategy will be viable and profitable. One advantage of a niche marketing strategy are that costs can be kept low, so a small business may grab a big share of the market/niche and become a major player within the niche. Competition may also be less, as a niche may be too small and likely to be ignored by large mass marketing organisations. Within a niche a business can become a specialist, marketing communication messages can be focused, a business can really satisfy its customers and this situation can be exploited through higher prices which can increase profitability.

Mass marketing The opposite to niche marketing, where a business decides that it will focus on supplying products in high volumes to large 'mass' markets. This strategy is usually linked to a business that has facilities for mass production, which requires high levels of investment in fixed production lines that can produce goods in extremely high volumes at the lowest possible unit price within the overall price structure of its target market. Mass markets are usually highly competitive as businesses seek to maximise productivity and output. Because of this, margins in mass markets are often relatively low – relying on high volume sales to generate a worthwhile income and profit. As a result they also tend to be vulnerable to small changes in cost, which in high volumes can make a major difference to profit or loss.

Some businesses have recognised that although they operate in

what would be defined as a mass market, they can differentiate products. They tailor products to meet the needs of different consumers by applying small changes to the products. Examples can be found in electronic goods for home entertainment and the white goods market, where the basic product is manufactured in mass/high volumes, but batches are made different by the use of minor changes to the specification, using differentiators like colour, finish and styling. This can also be seen in the motor car market where manufacturers have the same basic vehicle in a variety of colours and styles, and just give them slightly different names or badges.

Always having the best quality product on the market/to provide the best service to customers This is an example of a strategy that is likely to be adopted by a new business that wants to enter a market, has done its research and identified weaknesses in the products currently on the market. By striving to provide the 'best' product or the 'best' service a business is coming close to continuous innovation, although it may use changes to specification, such as product strength, durability and speed of delivery as improvements rather than technical innovation to maintain its lead as the 'best'. The term 'best' is a subjective concept which may need to be qualified through research amongst customers to see what they would classify as being the 'best', sometimes called benchmarking.

Supplying a standard product to all markets This strategy may seem to be similar to mass marketing, but it can be used equally well by smaller organisations aiming to supply small or niche markets. The key is that the business has a policy of producing a standard product. This simplifies manufacturing, packaging, stock holding and distribution as only one, or a limited number, of standard products is being made. As with mass marketing, even standard products can be customised for different markets by making simple changes to the external appearance of the product whilst maintaining a standard body. Figure 2 shows an example.

Tailoring products to individual customers, markets and sectors This strategy can be seen in action by studying small specialist businesses that pride themselves in providing personalised or tailored products or services to meet the particular needs of individual customers and markets. Small businesses often use this strategy but large businesses will tailor products if the volumes are sufficient or if there is sufficient financial or competitive advantage. Some manufacturers never sell

Figure 2 *Ford car production*

Ford is a manufacturer of motor cars. Two of its brands are the Ford Mondeo and the Jaguar X-type. The Jaguar X-type, launched in 2001, is sold as a relatively up-market brand. Ford management revealed that the X-Type was based on a Mondeo so that the car could be in showrooms as soon as possible. If Jaguar developed a new platform, the X-type would have been delayed another year and Ford didn't want to wait. The X-type shares the same, although modified, chassis as the Ford Mondeo.

Source: adapted from www.drive.com.au and www.brandrepublic.com.

products under their own brand name but just manufacture on behalf of larger organisations that market the products with their own brand name on it. For example, most 'own brand' and 'own label' goods sold by retailers will have been produced by a specialist business that manufactures to the specification set by the retailer. Often, one factory will be turning out similar products for a number of different retailers, each with its own packaging and branding. Another way that a business may use this strategy is if marketing research identifies a particular niche or need in a market that can only be satisfactorily met by the production of something tailored to meet that need. Before going ahead with this strategy the business will need to be satisfied that the tailored product will meet the criteria set for volume, sales and profit margin.

Pricing strategy

Business can adopt different pricing strategies as part of their marketing strategy.

Maintaining price leadership This may mean that the business decides that it wants its products to be the highest priced products on the market at any given time. Price leadership is a bold statement, usually made by confident, established businesses that have sufficient 'muscle' in the market, through market leadership, brand leadership or weight of advertising, or have a unique product that can command a premium price.

However, it can also mean to be the lowest priced. For example, a chain of petrol stations may decide that it wants to establish a reputation for selling the lowest priced petrol and adopt a 'lowest price in the area' policy to undercut competitors and attract customers. This approach is very similar to market based competitive pricing. Some food supermarkets have adopted a low-pricing strategy, which often goes hand-in-hand with a 'best value' strategy, although best value does not necessarily equate to having the lowest prices. An example of low price strategy is shown in Figure 3.

Market skimming This means to set a high price to maximise

profitability before a business is forced, usually by competitive pressure, to reduce the price to a level closer to the norm for the market. This pricing strategy is often used when a new, innovative, fashionable or high-tech product is launched. There are two main reasons why a business may adopt the strategy of 'skimming the market'.

- To recoup investment in new product development (NPD) as quickly as possible, before competitors bring out a similar, inevitably lower-priced, product, and the innovator is forced, by competitors to lower prices. An example might be pharmaceuticals companies that charge high prices before competitors enter the market and often lower prices after patents expire.
- If the product is particularly fashionable, the manufacturer will know that a segment of the market will be prepared to pay a premium for the privilege of getting early access to the product before the mass market catches on. An example might be clothes from designers after Paris or Milan shows, which are later copied by mass market chains.

Market penetration pricing This means that a business will set the price of a new product deliberately low to undercut competitors and force its way into a market. The idea is that this will achieve high volume sales and boost market share in a very short time, at the expense of margin, which it will hope to build up later on the back of repeat sales and brand loyalty. This strategy is particularly appropriate for products that may have only limited advantages over similar products in the market. Or it could be used for a business that wants to make a major impact on a large, but relatively sluggish market that is dominated by a small number of complacent businesses with large market shares, that are not investing in the development of the market, i.e. they are 'milking' it and taking as much profit as possible without investing in growing or developing the market. An example is shown in Figure 4.

The downside of this strategy is that it may mean that profitability is low during the sell-in period, certainly lower than would normally be expected for a product selling at the market price. It may also mean that it is difficult to increase the retail price at a later date as consumers assume that the introductory price will be the usual selling price. Penetration pricing may also attract a competitive response in the form of increased discounts or promotions. It is also difficult to judge the success of a launch

Figure 3 *John Lewis Partnership pricing strategy*

The John Lewis Partnership (a retailer) has a 'Never Knowingly Undersold' policy, which is backed up with the offer to refund the difference to customers that find an identical product on sale in the UK at a lower price.

In addition to constantly monitoring retail prices in other stores, this policy is protected by the careful selection of own label products and products that are made to specifications set exclusively for the John Lewis Partnership.

Source: adapted from various sources.

Figure 4 *Penetration pricing*

In 2006, the sports chain Sports Soccer followed Asda by selling England World Cup shirts ahead of their official launch Sports Soccer said it was undercutting Asda by selling away shirts in its 300 stores for half the recommended retail price of £44.99. Asda released 5,000 shirts in 42 of its superstores at £28.00 for an adult's and £23.00 for a child's, and was to release another 22,000. Its shirts come from the 'grey market' (surplus stock legally bought in Europe from third party distributors) rather than from Umbro, the Football Association's licensed supplier for the away kit. In response, Sports Soccer was aiming to sell England adult shirts for £22.49.

Source: adapted from *The Observer*, 26.2.2006.

based on penetration pricing because it creates an artificial rate of sale and pricing structure in the market which may not continue when the price reverts to the normal selling price.

Competitive market based pricing With this strategy a business sets its prices based on the price of similar competitor products. This means that the business must monitor the prices in the market to keep up-to-date. In a crowded market where there is little product differentiation, like the petrol or washing powder markets, competitive market pricing is used because no one brand will want to be out of line with the others as this will have a negative effect on sales. Table 2 shows some examples. This strategy is often used in a market that is dominated by a strong price leader brand. To compete effectively a business may decide to undercut the price leader to attract sales. This is similar to the strategy of being the lowest price in a market, but being the most competitive does not always mean being the lowest priced, as added value can be created using promotions or improvements to service levels.

Place/distribution strategies

Businesses can adopt different distribution strategies as part of their marketing strategy.

Dealing directly with retail customers This means that a business has decided that it will not rely on a distribution chain that includes distributors and wholesalers, or cash and carries, but instead will aim to supply customers direct, using its own resources. The advantage is that it reduces the number of mark-ups that will be applied along the distribution chain, allowing the business to either make a greater margin itself, or enable it to be in a position to pass on some additional margin to the retailer in the form of a low selling price or additional discounts. This strategy works best when dealing with a limited number of retail customers, ideally shipping into the retailer's own warehouses for them do distribute to their own stores as required. One downside of this strategy is that the business will have to devote some resources to distribution, which may distract it from its main business.

Dealing with retailers indirectly, using wholesalers and distributors This is the converse of dealing direct with retail customers. It is often used because a business does not have the resources, or because it does not have the desire to get involved with making deliveries to every store that orders its products. It would rather pay for another, specialist, business to carry out the distribution or deliveries. This used to be the most common way for manufacturers to distribute products, but pressure on margins and the demands of major retailers has forced many businesses to deal direct.

This is also the preferred policy for some large retail groups when buying a limited number of product lines from a small supplier. It is better for the major retailer to have 100 products delivered on one lorry from one wholesaler, than have one product delivered by one hundred individual lorries from a range of different manufacturers.

Cutting out all retail customers and selling the product to the consumer direct This strategy means that the supplier has access to the full retail margin for itself – a very attractive proposition for many businesses. Examples of this strategy can be seen in direct sell advertising magazines and newspapers or on television, where the product is advertised and the consumer is invited to pay the manufacturer direct. One obvious danger here is that this immediately puts the manufacturer in competition with its retailers, so some businesses are reluctant to adopt this strategy, or will only do it in a relatively low-key way to avoid upsetting the retail customers. This is also a common strategy for small, start-up businesses, particularly if they are producing specialist, craft-based products. Examples would be artists, jewellery makers and other specialist businesses that sell from stalls at craft markets. The growth in Internet trading has also helped increase the incidence of selling direct to customers, but here it is not limited to just small businesses. Figure 5 shows an example.

Trading from a designated/chosen location A business may decide that it will only trade from premises in high streets, or in shopping malls, or in out-of-town retail parks. The strategic choice of location will depend on the space requirements for the business and access to its target market. A good example of location strategy in practice can be seen by studying how food supermarket chains select locations for stores. At one time there was a desire for a presence in high streets. As retail parks expanded and food supermarkets opened ever-larger stores there was a movement out of the high streets. Having saturated out-of-town sites and as access to new out-of-town developments became

Product type	Product	Price
Newspapers	The Guardian	70p
	The Independent	70p
	The Telegraph	65p
Tabloid newspapers	The Daily Mirror	38p
	The Sun	35p
	The Daily Star	30p
Womens' magazines	Cosmopolitan	£3.20
	Red	£3.20
	Vogue	£3.60
	Eve	£3.10
Golfing magazines	Golf International	£3.80
	Today's Golfer	£3.60
	Golf Punk	£3.50

Table 2 *Competitor-based pricing of newspapers and magazines, March 2006*

Figure 5 *Internet distribution*

In addition to attracting major manufacturers that are happy to take the full retail margin, selling direct over the Internet is a strategy that has been used successfully by musicians, such as Prince or the White Stripes. They have a loyal fan base which is prepared to buy limited edition products that are only made available direct from the artist's Internet site. This has had the effect of shifting the power and control over product release, as well as the profit margin, from the record company to the artists themselves.

more difficult, food supermarket chains have returned to high streets by buying-up existing chains of smaller, convenience stores.

Some fast-food and some specialist coffee outlets also have a strategy that takes into account where they open branches. They will combine criteria for the physical location with the market size – the numbers of shoppers or visitors that visit that location. Another example of an aspect of this strategy is when a business decides that it will only open a branch where the population meets certain criteria for size and profile. This would be typical for a fast-food outlet franchise that knows, to produce sales sufficient to get its minimum level of return on investment, it needs, say, a population of 20,000 households within a 3 mile radius of a new store.

Holding the maximum shelf space available in outlets that stock the product This involves switching the emphasis from the physical location of a business to the physical location of a product within a retail outlet. This is a strategy that is likely to be set by a market leading business that wants to maintain its presence and dominance in-store, on-shelf, to squeeze out competition and present consumers with a limited choice, i.e. the choice of the one major brand.

Being positioned as an impulse buy in all stockists A business may rely on impulse buys for its sales. In this case it will want its products positioned where they will be seen by the maximum number of people, picked up, and purchased. A visit to any retail store will provide examples of impulse buy products, but they are not always positioned in the best place for maximum impulse. Competition for space in-store means that whilst some products can be positioned in the best location, at the till, on a gondola end, or on a site that is in the maximum flow of customers, inevitably some products will be found pushed to the back.

Only providing a service within a limited radius of premises This would be a strategy typical of a service business that understands the limits of its own resources for providing the service. It would be no good offering a national service if it was a small business with only one means of transport. Equally, this strategy will have implications on the choice of promotion and media that are suitable, as it could not support customers who

were attracted by advertising outside its area of service.

Promotion strategies

Businesses can adopt different promotion strategies as part of their marketing strategy. Decisions that a business must consider when choosing a promotional strategy include:

- what to tell customers – what image will be conveyed and what unique selling points (USPs) will be stressed?
- how to convey the information – will information be given or persuasive images be used?
- what use will be made of **above the line** (advertising using paid for media) or **below the line** (other promotion) methods (see Figure 6)?
- how much will be spent – what is the size of the budget for the promotion?
- the timescale of the promotion – will it last for a short or extended period?
- what mix of media will be used – will the business concentrate on just one media or more than one?

A business may make use of different promotion strategies.

Using 'added value' and avoiding promotion based on cutting the price (and consequently the profit) This is a strategy that would help a business maintain its margins as well as its reputation. In this case, adding value means adding something to the product that is attractive to customers/consumers but is less costly to the business itself than using cash to discount.

Promoting 'flagship' products This is a strategy adopted by a business that has a wide range of many products, so many that it would not be cost effective to promote or advertise every single one. Instead, it will select one or two important, innovative or otherwise high-profile products and give these the maximum level of promotion that it can afford. In this way, it should sell the product promoted, and will have a 'halo effect' – promotion by positive association – on its other products. Businesses that adopt this strategy often find that in consumer research respondents will swear that they have seen advertising for a wide range of its

Figure 6 *Above the line or below the line methods of promotion*

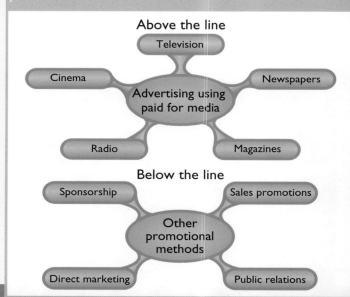

products, when in reality it has just concentrated advertising on one or two.

Promoting the brand name With this strategy the business will promote its brand name to the exclusion of individual products, again relying on the 'halo effect' of the brand to promote and sell any product that also bears that same brand. This is the very effective policy that is used by businesses which operate in many different markets and although having some product promotion, their main strategy is promoting and reinforcing the brand values associated with the company. This strategy enables a business to try many different markets and apply its brand to a wide range of diverse products.

Table 3 *Promotion strategies*

Promotion strategies	Example
Using 'added value'	Free postage and packing, an extended warrantee or a telephone helpline for technical enquiries.
Promoting 'flagship'	Sony (TVs), Mars (Bars), Kellogg's (Cornflakes), Renault (Clio).
Promoting the brand name only	Nike, Philips, Virgin, Barclays.

Tactical marketing

Tactical marketing tends to be related to turning a marketing strategy into an action plan. Tactical marketing is the way that the business puts its marketing strategy into practice – the marketing plans that are used to carry out marketing activities within the overall marketing strategy, achieving short-term 'tactical' aims, gains and objectives. However they are interpreted, tactical marketing plans are usually put into place to promote the aims of the business, either in its own right or against competition. Tactical marketing can be used to maximise support for the marketing mix and include the following.

Product

- To launch a new model next season with a higher specification. This would create interest in the product and have the short-term effect of boosting sales as consumers. An alternative approach would be to replace a current model with a new product that has upgraded the technical specification. Both would create a tactical advantage to the business.
- Product relaunch. Many businesses reach the stage that they need a major change in order to stimulate sales or to bring products up to, or to take them ahead of, competition. One tried and tested answer is to 'relaunch' the business or product, so the project is treated as a new product launch. The business may change its branding, corporate image, product specification or some other aspect of itself to re-present the business or product to its customers as if it were new. This should not be seen as a purely cosmetic exercise. To be successful everyone involved needs to believe and demonstrate that it really is a relaunch and that customers will see and benefit from the changes that are brought about by the

relaunch. There are also promotional advantages from a relaunch as it gives the business a reason to mount a new advertising and PR campaign to communicate the changes that have occurred.

- To advertise a new standard of delivery. Depending on the business examples of this could include a product being with customer within 24 hours of placing an order, customers welcomed by staff within one minute of entering the restaurant or a guarantee extended from one year to three years.
- Larger size for the same price. This could be interpreted as a tactical price promotion and the unit cost will be reduced. But the emphasis here is that it is the product that has changed and the price has not been affected. More importantly, the selling price will not have been reduced. This means that the business is not seen to be eroding/degrading the price perception of the product and will not have the awkward step of having to return to the original price, often interpreted as a price increase, once the promotion ends.
- Timed access. This is a common tactic for launching new software. The consumer gets a chance to try the product for a limited time. If consumers want to continue using the product once the time limit has expired they must buy the product, or cease to be able to use it. The business is gambling on the fact that it will be so good, and that consumers will become so used to using it, that they buy it.

Price

- Short-term discounts/money off. This tactic is more or less guaranteed to have an effect, if only to prompt competition to cut prices also. It can be used in many forms, whatever is appropriate in a given situation, from advertised price reductions, to reduced prices at the till, to money off coupons and vouchers, to discounts linked to volume sales. Three-for-the-price-of-two, buy-one-get-one-free (BOGOF) and similar deals can also be interpreted as money off. The emphasis here is on 'short-term', which means that a 'close out' date should be built into the marketing plan. If this type of promotion is allowed to run for too long it will cease to have a tactical effect and will be perceived as being the norm for the product. This can degrade the image of the product and make it seem to be a cheap, low cost item. It also reduces margins at every level in the supply chain, which will not be popular with distributors unless the increase in sales more than offsets the reduction in margin created by the price cut. This can be a very difficult position from which to recover.
- Competitive market based pricing. This can be a very powerful pricing strategy, but can also be a very useful tactic to gain a short-term advantage over local competition. The reason that it is likely to be short-term is that, by its very nature, it will invite competition to match or better the price chosen. This may have a stimulating effect on the market but can also lead to a price war, something that is to no one's advantage and should be avoided at all costs.

Place

- Aiming for distribution in targeted outlets, e.g. prestige outlets, one outlet/stockist per town/shopping area. Although this may be a strategy adopted by a business, it has a tactical use if the business has a weakness in distribution in a particular area, or if it feels that distribution in a prestige outlet would help its sales into other outlets. In these situations a business may target certain distribution outlets and focus most of its marketing activity on these targeted outlets. Examples would include businesses that target the Selfridges department store so that they can benefit from the promotional opportunities afforded by positive association with this prestige outlet. Similarly, a cosmetics business may aim to get distribution in Boots outlets. Once in Boots it will be able to use this as a lever to get distribution in other pharmacists and chemist shops because if Boots is sufficiently interested in the product, the implication is that its competitors should be too.

- Sales/merchandising 'blitz' in one town/district to achieve saturation distribution. This means concentrating marketing resources in one closely defined area. This tactic can achieve dramatic increases in distribution is a relatively short time. It is often seen as a good way of utilising limited sales resources by concentrating them in one area rather than spreading them over a wide area.

- Targeting areas where there is no competition or competition is weak. This tactic needs to be based on marketing research, or at least marketing intelligence that highlights weak areas. It is a good way of making an impact and creating distribution without directly affecting competition and attracting retaliation from the competition.

- Buying prime sites in retail stores/end of gondola displays for short-term promotion. This is linked to creating impulse sales, but is achieved by moving the product away from its usual location on a run of shelves and resiting it in a place where it is more likely to be seen by consumers.

Promotion

- Topical/opportunistic advertising. Some businesses have an open brief with their advertising agency to develop topical advertising based on current news or events, so long as it is appropriate to the business or the brand. This is extremely tactical, as there can be no telling when a suitable advertising concept may come along.

- Product tie-in with film/TV show. There are many examples of this form of promotion every time a new Hollywood blockbuster film is launched. The attraction for participating businesses is that the products that are associated with the new film will benefit from the general promotion of the film and word of mouth advertising. Sometimes tie-in promotions can achieve cult status, for example the McDonald's Star Wars figures that were given free have now become very collectable items. One consideration before committing to a tie-in promotion is to make sure that the film or programme will be appropriate for the target market. It would be no use linking an 18 rated film with a product aimed at children. Also, there is no guarantee that any new film will be successful and there is always the danger that a tie-in will link otherwise successful products with a flop, something that can be hard to recover from.

- Sampling. This involves letting consumers try a small 'sample' of the product, to demonstrate how good it is and encourage consumers to buy the product next time they are in the market.

- 'Free-with' products. This is a classic promotion but one that still works, especially if the item given free is appropriate to the

main product, like a camera that is now packed and sold inside a 'free' leather case rather than a plain box, or is topical such as a tie-in with a new film. Such a promotion can be used to sell in new stock to retailers and give them a reason to mount a new display to help sell the product.

- Generating impulse sales. This may be achieved as simply as re-siting the product in a higher profile location in a shop. A more definite way of promoting impulse sales may be to change to packaging and/or produce a merchandising unit from which to sell the product. This is often done by confectionery companies to promote impulse sales of particular chocolate bars. It is also done by some newspapers that find it hard to compete when displayed alongside many other, similar, newspapers. By producing its own merchandising the newspaper can be presented in a more distinctive and hopefully eye-catching way. Examples will be found in railway stations and newsagent's shops.

These are just some examples of common marketing strategies and tactics that are used in business and which should be recorded when building up the background for a marketing plan. Other strategies and tactics will appear over time. Reading, watching and listening to business reports in the media will provide more examples. Examples can also be found by talking to business contacts that have been made through friends, family, work placement or your own job, and investigating what marketing strategies and tactics are use, which are the most effective and why.

Target markets

These are markets that have been identified through research or sales analysis as being particularly important for the business. They may have the greatest opportunity for distribution and sales currently or the potential of becoming worthwhile markets if promoted. Marketing strategies and tactics that target specific markets will have been designed to create awareness and generate desire to purchase. Typically, target markets will include the following.

Consumers and consumers Targeting will aim at communicating directly with the people that a business wants to buy and use its product. Because consumer markets tend to be large, there will be no shortage of communication options. This means that targeting within consumer markets can be very sophisticated, using media with an audience profile that matches the consumer profile for the product

Trade customers (B2B) The consumers of some products and services will be business organisations (business to business, B2B). Targeting will be based on using specialist trade press that is read by decision makers in the trade or using direct marketing techniques. Like consumer markets, targeting will be based on using media with an audience profile that matches the trade profile for the product. Some trade customers will be distributors who are important in getting the product to the consumers.

Retailers and wholesalers These are important links in the supply chain between a manufacturer or supplier and the consumer. Targeting will be based on identifying how or where consumers expect to buy the product and aiming to make sure that the product is available in those outlets. Creating awareness and targeting retailers and wholesalers with appropriate marketing activity will do this.

Large organisations These present a challenge when targeting precisely who, within the organisation, should be targeted. It is a common misconception to think that it should always be the managing director. Consider who is the decision maker with the budget and that person should be the target. Simple marketing research, such as a telephone call or e-mail, could be used to find out.

Small organisations Research needs to find out who the decision maker is and who marketing activity should be aimed at. Once a business knows this, it can use direct marketing techniques.

New customers New customers will have to be identified and researched to find out why they do not buy a product and what competitor products they may buy. Research should find out what customers like about competitors' products and promote a business's own USPs.

Existing customers Existing customers will already know and love a product. A business should find out all it can about them, develop a profile and match this profile to appropriate media.

Meeting the assessment criteria – examiners' guidance

Rizzo Products Ltd bases its marketing strategy on importing a range of pre-packed rice into the UK and distributing the 500g and 1kg packets through convenience stores. A product manager, John Gee wants to introduce a new 250g size of basmati rice. He needs to produce a marketing plan.

(a) State TWO ways that this could affect Rizzo Products' marketing strategy. **(2 marks)**

Exemplar responses
• *Product range is increased/widened/expanded.*
• *Will need to decide on selling price that is in line with current price:size ratios.*
• *Will need to justify new product to retail customers to make sure that they accept new size.*
• *Will need to decide how to inform retail customers/advertise new size to consumers.*

Mark allocation
1 mark for way marketing strategy affected. **(2 marks)**

(b) John is suggesting using a penetration price strategy for the launch. Describe and evaluate this strategy. **(5 marks)**

Exemplar responses
• *Penetration pricing means that a business will set the price of a new product deliberately low to force its way into a market – it will help achieve distribution – it will help product move off shelf as it will appear to have a price advantage – the low price will reduce retail and manufacturer margins – not likely to be able to sustain the low price over time.*

• *Penetration pricing is a very low price used to launch a new product and to undercut competitors – the low price will help generate trial sales – consumers may buy more than usual which will mean that they are not buying competitor brands for some time – difficult to raise price once established in consumers' minds – may make product appear cheap and nasty.*

Mark allocation
1 mark for describing penetration pricing.
1 mark for each positive point of evaluation (maximum 2 marks).
1 mark for each negative point of evaluation (maximum 2 marks).
(5 marks)

(c) Rizzo Products has access to a range of organically grown rice. Organic products are still a niche market in the UK. Explain what is meant by a niche market and describe how Rizzo Products can quantify the market for organic rice. **(3 marks)**

Exemplar responses
• *Discrete group of consumers/customers that exhibit similar characteristics – conduct market research – interview rice buyers/buy report on organic food market.*
• *Small part of a mass market – need to count/estimate how many/what proportion of market makes up niche – use tailor-made/ad hoc primary research/source secondary research on organic market.*

Mark allocation
1 mark for describing niche market.
1 mark for method of quantifying market.
1 mark for application to Rizzo Products. **(3 marks)**

Examination practice · Tactical marketing

(a) **Describe ONE situation that you have learned about where a business adopted a tactical marketing solution to a business problem.**
(i) **Identify the business problem.** **(2 marks)**
(ii) **Describe the tactical marketing solution that was adopted.** **(2 marks)**

(iii) **Explain why this tactical marketing solution was right for the situation that you have described.** **(4 marks)**
(b) **Discuss the relationship between tactical marketing solutions and the overall strategic marketing policies in a business.** **(4 marks)**

The need for marketing research

Some would argue that successful business decisions are made from a combination of skill, expertise, entrepreneurship and 'gut instinct'. Indeed, certain businesses are run along these lines and this may be successful, for a time at least. Problems occur when the market is moving quickly, consumer tastes are changing or if competition is adopting a more organised, managed and scientific approach. These situations are likely to require a business to become more customer-led or research driven. Many successful businesses have discovered that the only way to be as certain as possible about business decisions before a plan goes into the market place is to use marketing research to find out what the market, the customers, want and to find new products or markets to develop and move into.

Marketing research and the marketing mix

Marketing research can be used to find out many things, which can then be interpreted and used in different ways. Informing, problem solving and decision making linked to the main variables of the marketing mix are likely to be the main uses for marketing research in business.

Marketing research can be used within the marketing mix in a quantitative or qualitative way. It can be used for product decisions, pricing decisions, place decisions and promotional decisions, as shown in Table 1.

Figure 1 *Supermarkets - market size, shares, dynamics, forecasts*

Size Shares	Sales in 2005 were £134.8bn. Tesco 23.7%, Sainsbury 12.5%, Asda 11.7%, Morrison 9.7%.
Dynamics	Sales increased from £110bn to £134.8bn from 2000 to 2005. Prices fell by £1bn in 2005 compared with 2003. Food deflation was around 0.6% a year.
Forecast	It was predicted in 2005 that annual savings due to lower prices would be £1.7bn in 2006.

Source: adapted from www.just-food.com, November 2005.

Market size, shape, shares, dynamics and forecasts

Marketing research can be used effectively for measuring, monitoring and forecasting. This allows a business to identify market size, shares of the market and trends taking place, and to make forecasts. Examples for supermarkets are shown in Figure 1.

Table 1 *Marketing research and the marketing mix*

Marketing mix	Examples of qualitative and quantitative research
Product	Measure how many offices had bought a shredder to dispose of confidential documents and paperwork - quantitative data showing market penetration. Ask the employees within the offices what they thought about having to shred confidential documents and paperwork - qualitative data expressing attitudes to a recent requirement in office practice.
Price	Measure how many consumers would buy a product at different price levels - quantitative data used to inform pricing decisions. Investigate consumer attitudes to the same product that has been given different prices, whether they think that the higher price means that it will be a better product, or whether they think that the lower prices represent better value - qualitative opinion used to help decide on pricing vs product or brand image.
Place	Ask consumers where they would expect to find a product on sale - in shops, in a magazine or on a website - quantitative data that could be used to plan sales and distribution. Consumers could be asked why they think that the product would more likely be in one type of distribution outlet than another - qualitative data that could be used by a sales team to encourage different distributors to stock a product.
Promotion	Measure how many people read a particular magazine and saw a particular advertisement - quantitative data. Measure what the readers of that magazine thought about the advertisement, their attitudes and opinions, how it made them feel towards the advertiser - qualitative data.

Measuring Measuring is based on collecting data that will establish a fact at a given point in time. It could show:

- the scale of a market in terms of value or number of units bought, sold or consumed, measured by gross weight or volume;
- the size of a market in terms of value, the number of businesses/competitors trading in that market or the products that are available in that market;
- the share that any one product or supplier has in that market;
- how much is being spent on promotion in a market, how many people are aware of the promotion and how much of an effect it is having on sales.

Measurement will also show how many consumers are interested in a product, consumer attitudes to pricing, how many consumers are buying the product at different shops and what consumers think of the product. Any set of data that has a numerical basis can be used for measurement and wider statistical analysis if required.

Monitoring Monitoring is using market research to measure over time, to see what is changing in a market place and what is selling more, less, or the same. Markets are **dynamic** and whilst a snapshot of a market at any point in time may be useful, to make the data come alive the measurement needs to be repeated to see if anything is changing. By using marketing research to monitor a market or a set of consumer opinions a business can see if trends are developing and if anything has happened over time which may require the business or its products to change to retain sales and market appeal. Monitoring has a particular use for pre and post advertising awareness and sales measurement. It can be used to establish the apparent effectiveness and the cost effectiveness of any marketing or promotional plans. **Trade audits** are based on monitoring over time. They are used by businesses to monitor market share and rate of sale information.

Forecasting Forecasting is using marketing research data to predict, in as scientific a way as possible, what is likely to happen to product sales or the market in future. Consumer attitudes or opinions can also be forecast, based on what is likely to happen if a product is changed or advertised in a particular way. Another aspect of forecasting is to use marketing research to expose a sample of the target market to new products, new advertising or new packaging and ask the sample what they think. The resulting data will give a clue as to what is likely to happen if the mass market were exposed to the same new products, advertising or packaging. If the response is good, then it helps support a decision to make the change. If the response from the sample is bad, it gives the business the opportunity to pull back or make changes before a business makes a mistake on a large scale by launching into the market. Trend information and historic patterns can be very useful in this situation, but do not forget the caveat that appears on all advertisements for financial services - 'Historical trends are no guarantee of future performance'.

Planning and organising marketing research

Like all marketing activity, marketing research must be planned to be useful and effective. Without proper planning and organising,

Figure 2 *Researching the communications market*

- Background. In August 2004 the Ofcom Consumer Panel, an independent body set up to advise Ofcom (the regulator of the communications market), commissioned research into the communications market. The research would look at consumer experience of fixed and mobile phones, the Internet and broadcasting.
- Objectives. Its objectives were to find out how well consumers are informed about the range of services available in the communications market now and in the future and why consumers choose the products they do and the difficulties they face in making effective purchasing decisions.
- Type of research/sample. There would be a quantitative survey of 2,800 people carried out by Saville Rossiter-Base and a qualitative research project by MORI, using observation and 'peer' research.
- Timing. The research was due to be completed by November 2004 with publication of full results due in January 2005.
- Analysis and review. The findings would be used in areas such as advising on the switch over to digital broadcasting.

Source: adapted from www.mori.com.

research could waste resources, produce useless information, or worse, produce information that is wrong and misleading, which could result in major problems for the business or missed opportunities. There is a number of elements that the researcher must include in any marketing research proposal or plan. An example is shown in Figure 2.

Background It is always worth establishing why the research is to be done - what is the current situation in the market place. In the case of established products, it is important to investigate how they are performing and, for new products, why they are being considered. A general review of the business context in which the research is to be carried out is helpful when planning marketing research. It can help to suggest the type of research that is required and the method that would be most appropriate.

Objectives Setting objectives for the research, identifying the business problem and deciding what research answers or information are required is essential. This means that the right type and method of research can be selected. They also provide a benchmark against which to measure the outcomes - the conclusion of the research - to make sure that the objectives have been met. Without clear objectives before the research starts it will be impossible to judge whether the research has been successful or worthwhile.

Type of research How is the research linked to the marketing mix? Is the research needed for product decisions, pricing decisions, place decisions and promotional decisions? Is it seeking data-based facts, opinions, attitudes or awareness? Also, different markets may require different considerations about the type of research that is to be done. For example, research in commercial markets, looking for information about products, market shape, size and dynamics, may require a different type of research from that required in social research dealing with people, their attitudes and opinions. The type of research will be based on the objectives and will influence recommendations on sampling and the research method.

Sampling This will be based on the target population for any research activity, linked to the research method and budget. Applied mainly to primary research, a sample is the number of research elements – people or organisations – that provide data. The people or organisations that are interviewed are given or sent a questionnaire and are expected to answer questions. The sample will be drawn from the sampling frame – the list or database of people or organisations that make up the target population. It is important to be clear about identifying and defining the population that is to be sampled. This will be based on the research objectives and the type of research. The target population are the people or organisations that are to provide the research findings. Get it right and the research objectives will be met, wrong and the population wrong and the research may be incorrect. At worst it may mislead and result in incorrect business decisions being made, which could have disastrous consequences. Sampling is covered in section 27.

Research method The research method recommended may be primary, secondary or a combination of both, as dealt with later in this section.

Analysis and review Having collected the data or information it will need to be analysed to derive meaning from the raw facts and figures (see section 28). How this is analysed will be linked closely to the objectives of the research and the audience for the research. The objectives will establish what needs to be answered by the research and what precise information must be found out and presented as the conclusion. The audience will establish how the findings are to be presented, for example as a written report, a visual presentation based on tables and graphs, a verbal presentation supported by samples or other visual aids. An audience of skilled and experienced researchers will require a different style of presentation from an audience of people who are not familiar with marketing research.

There are many ways to present research findings. Researchers need to know their audience before choosing which approach to take. The actual analysis may take many forms, from the simple grouping or collation of data and the application of percentages to detailed statistical analysis. Again, the precise method of analysis will depend on the objectives and the audience for the research.

Analysis can be carried out by hand, counting and doing the calculations manually. Alternatively, the data may be entered into computer software for spreadsheet or database analysis. Even if a computer is used to do the bulk of the 'number crunching', it is worth checking using manual methods. In this way the researcher can gain more of a feeling or understanding of the findings. Errors caused by the decimal point being in the wrong place may also be spotted by a manual check. This can be useful to help avoid embarrassing errors during the presentation. A review of the

research process and outcomes is useful to help decide whether the research objectives have been met, or whether there is a case for further research or a different kind of research to meet the objectives in full.

Timing This is when the research is due to take place. The starting point is likely to be when the results of the research are required. Having set that deadline, the researcher can then work back and build in time for research development. This may include time for writing questionnaires, booking interviewers, hiring venues, recruiting respondents, the research activity (bearing in mind that primary field research will take much longer than most secondary desk research), analysis and interpretation, and presentation of findings or conclusions. Whilst timings are essential for planning, they should be flexible enough to enable the research to be carried out without compromising standards due to cutting corners. Even if timings are tight, it is the quality of the outcome of the research that is important.

Budget It is worth knowing how much money there is for a marketing research project. It would be a waste of resources to spend time setting up a detailed and extensive research programme only to find out that there was no money available to do justice to the research plan. If the budget is known, the research can be tailored as appropriate. Good research needs to be cost effective as well as being of high quality. Even with a large research budget, it is worth establishing the costs at the planning stage before the research is finally commissioned to avoid the costs growing out of all proportion to the objectives of the research.

Research methods

There are two main methods of market research.

Primary research This is the collection of original data and information for the first time. It is 'raw' data as it has not yet been analysed or interpreted. Because it is new and original, primary research can be designed to meet the precise needs of a research project. It is sometimes called 'field research' because the activity is conducted 'in the field' or the marketplace. It can also be referred to as a 'survey' when primary research is carried out to find data about a large number of people or organisations, known as a 'population'. All mean the same – that primary research is about collecting data, facts or opinions, direct from the original source of the information. People who are identified and sampled or recruited to take part in primary research are known as 'respondents'. Conducted properly, primary research should be able to provide data which can be analysed and interpreted to give answers to particular questions or to support plans, ideas or decision making.

Secondary research This is the sourcing and use of data that has already been collected, analysed and presented for use in a project or report. It uses any data that already exists and has been collected for another purpose. Investigating, analysing and using secondary data is known as secondary research. Secondary data may be quantitative, based on numbers, facts and figures or qualitative, providing views and opinion about how people think or feel. What makes it secondary data is that it already exists and has been used before. It is sometimes called 'desk research' because the activity can often be carried out at a desk or workstation as pposed to field research. Secondary research is often carried out t the start of a project to identify the main issues that need to be ddressed. It can be used to inform and to produce evidence for he marketing mix. Secondary research should not be considered nferior to primary research so long as the data is valid, is used in ontext and its limitations are understood.

Primary research methods

here are many different primary research methods.

- **Observation**. This is where data is collected by looking at and recording findings rather than by asking questions. Observations can be open, where a researcher watches a product test and records how well respondents accomplish the task and what problems they find, for example. Secret observation might involve the use of 'mystery shoppers', for example, where the behaviour of shoppers or shop staff is watched without them knowing and observations recorded.
- **Direct questioning**. Probably the most widely recognised method of primary research is the direct questioning of respondents in an interview situation, often with the aid of a questionnaire. Direct questioning is used for mass surveys, for example, interviewing lots of people in the street or over the telephone and for individual in-depth interviews. Direct questioning can take place face-to-face, such as in the common street survey, or one-to-one over the telephone (a telephone survey).
- **Postal surveys**. This is an alternative to interviews. A self-completion questionnaire is prepared and mailed by the research organisation to respondents, together with a reply-paid envelope. A small incentive is often used to encourage respondents to complete the questionnaire and return it. Postal surveys have the advantage of being able to target households and respondents fairly precisely using postal codes or to cover a wide geographic area. Although the cost of printing and mailing postal questionnaires is relatively low on an individual basis, there is usually a high degree of wastage.
- **Online surveys**. Increasingly, online resources are being used for marketing research. Although the method of delivery is different, online surveys are similar to postal surveys. Respondents are sent an e-mail to invite them to log on to the website of a research organisation. Online surveys can range from the straightforward reproduction of written questionnaires to including photographs or moving images. A problem with online surveys is consumer mistrust of the Internet, particularly regarding security. People may also be concerned that completing an online survey will result in being bombarded with advertising and spam e-mails.
- **Hall tests**. A hall test is an alternative to conducting street interviews. The research organisation books a hall or room to interview respondents rather than in the street. Respondents are often more comfortable and secure and are more likely to provide better quality answers. As the environment is relatively confidential, respondents can be shown new products or advertisements or asked to sample new flavours and give their opinions.
- **Focus groups**. Sometimes referred to as 'group discussion',

this is another form of direct questioning, but carried out with a number of respondents in a group, all being interviewed together. Focus groups are used widely to check current thinking and ideas, to monitor changes in social attitudes, to generate ideas for new product developments, to create stories for marketing, promotion and public relations purposes. A focus group is usually led by a trained psychologist. The aim is to find out the feelings from the group that may not be expressed if its members were interviewed one-to-one. Discussions will follow a 'pre-planned' route to make sure that the aim of the research is met. Focus groups may be recorded on audio or video equipment, so that results can be analysed in greater detail and so that individual quotes can be identified.

- **Test marketing**. This is a form of primary research that aims to reproduce a national sales situation in a small controlled area before launching a product to the whole country. By selecting the right area for the test market, an organisation can test sales techniques, consumer purchases and acceptance of a new product, advertising styles and levels and other forms of promotion without the high cost of a full national launch. If a product is successful in a test market, marketing plans can be reproduced nationally. Conversely, if a test market is not successful, marketing plans can be changed and tested again, or the product may not be launched on a wider scale.
- **Consumer panels**. These are fixed groups of respondents who are interviewed regularly. By recording any changes between each interview, researchers can see how attitudes or purchase levels have changed over time. These changes can be correlated against marketing campaigns to see what has been successful. Another way of using consumer panels is to establish a panel of experts or enthusiasts who will try out and test a product and report back to the business as part of a new product development programme.
- **Trade audits**. These are carried out with panels of shops or businesses in the same industry. Researchers will visit the premises of businesses on the trade audit panel regularly depending on the rate of sale of products in the market being audited. The researcher will measure stock levels and deliveries and from this calculate sales across the audit period. Trade audits are important for measuring market share or brand share and for showing seasonal trends. Trade audits can also show up long-term trends that are often missed by ad-hoc research surveys.

Secondary research

The key factor with secondary research is locating and using data from the most appropriate source. The main sources of data are likely to be either internal to the business or from outside the business.

Internal sources These will produce data that is collected and held within an organisation itself. Most businesses will collect and hold a wide range of data, which is then analysed and presented to different teams within the organisation.

- **Internal business data**. Business data can show what has been sold in a given period, how much these sales are worth and who has bought the goods. Sales may have been analysed by product, by area, by customer or by member of a sales team. This data is likely to be used first by senior management in an organisation and then stored for future use and analysis.

- **Accounts and financial reports**. Most internal business data will start with sales, particularly the value of revenue that these sales generate. The financial analysis of this data will result in one part of the business accounts. Other parts will include payments from customers, payments out to suppliers, wages and other running costs. Most organisations will be able to use ICT resources to analyse and present financial data in a variety of ways to suit the needs of the end user.

- **Customer data**. Customer data could range from the basic financial data showing sales or deliveries to trade customers such as wholesalers or leading retailers, through to specific data about the buying habits of individual domestic customers, the consumers. Data on trade customers will come directly from internal sales records. Information about consumers may have been collected from primary research, such as questioning consumers directly, or may be in a database produced from loyalty cards or credit card transactions.

- **Archives/past research reports**. Over time most organisations will create an archive, a collection, of research surveys and reports that were produced and used in the past for previous research projects. These can be a great source for secondary research for re-analysis, providing background against which to measure new findings or plan further research.

External sources These are reports and published data that have been produced by organisations other than the business itself. Most libraries will hold a wide range of secondary data in the reference section. In some areas there will be a specialist business library that collects together secondary data, commercial reports and trade journals and makes them available for public access. The Internet and search engines are an easy way to start looking for secondary data. When conducting secondary research on-line, it is important to follow good health and safety computer practice.

- **Government published data**. Governments and government departments and agencies collect a great deal of data that is sometimes referred to as 'official statistics' as they present a picture of the country itself. This could include population and demographic statistics showing, for example, how many people – social statistics – what are the living conditions of the population, health statistics – what are the most common health problems, economic statistics – how much money is generated and where is it spent, and industrial statistics – about the structure and make up of industry in the country.

- **Commercial research reports**. These are produced independently by market research organisations and made available for sale. They cover a wide range of different products, markets and industries on a regular basis. They aim to provide a comprehensive background upon which business organisations can base their marketing plans. Some manufacturers, trade associations and industry bodies produce business reports containing secondary data about their sector for stakeholders or PR purposes.

Table 2 *The benefits and limitations of primary and secondary research*

Primary research

Benefits
- Research is tailored precisely to meet the aims and objectives of the business.
- It is planned and constructed to answer any questions, solve problems or help support business decisions.

Limitations
- There can be restrictions on access to information.
- It can be very costly and time consuming.

Secondary research

Benefits
- Access to secondary research is usually easy because there are many sources to choose from.
- Relatively low cost, as costs of collecting and analysing data will have been paid for by the organisation that commissioned the original primary research.
- Relatively quick, as access is usually easy and collection, analysis and presentation of original data has already been done.

Limitations
- Relevance, as the data has already been collected and analysed for some other purpose, which means that it will rarely meet the precise needs of the current research project.
- Research may have been carried out some time in the past and things may have changed. It may be out of date.
- The source needs to be checked and the reasons for collecting the data and presenting it in the way it appears considered, as there may be bias.
- The detail in the data must be checked. It may be partial rather than comprehensive. It may be selected and presented in such a way as to meet marketing aims or communicate a particular message. The sample size may be small and may not be suitable for further analysis.

- **Trade journals**. This is a valuable source of secondary information on specific markets, industries or trade sectors. Trade journals often include reports on the state of the industry, supported by a wealth of data and research information.

- **Other media**. The business pages in national newspapers and business programmes on TV and radio will often include secondary research to support or illustrate a particular report that is being presented.

xamination practice · **Bona Boards Ltd**

The directors of Bona Boards Ltd, a major distributor of skateboards and skateboarding equipment and accessories, have the opportunity to sell a new range of boards imported from Japan. Before they make a decision about whether or not to launch the new boards on the UK market they want to pilot sales in a test market area.

(a) Describe what is meant by a 'test market' and explain how it could offer some protection for the business at Bona Boards Ltd. **(4 marks)**

The marketing research team at Bona Boards Ltd has to complete the background section for the test marketing plan.

(b) (i) Explain how secondary research could be used in this project. **(3 marks)**
(ii) State TWO relevant sources of secondary data that they could use, justifying the use of each source. **(4 marks)**

Meeting the assessment criteria - examiners' guidance

The Roxie is an independent cinema in Bradford. During 2005 its owner, Percy Quill, notices that income for the business is slowing down. Before he can decide on a marketing plan he needs to find out if it is the market for cinemagoing that is declining or if it is a problem with The Roxie itself. He has only a small budget to spend on marketing research.

Percy visited the local reference library and found a copy of the British Film Institute Film and Television Handbook 1997. The British Film Institute (BFI) is one of the leading authorities on film, cinema and television in the world. It exists to promote understanding and appreciation of Britain's rich film and television heritage and culture. It publishes a wealth of research and information on the cinema industry.

Table 3 *UK consumer spending on feature films, 1984-1995*

Year	UK Box Office (£m)	Video Rental (£M)	Video Retail (£m)	Movie Channel Subscription	Total (£m)
1984	103	425	40	-	568
1985	123	300	50	-	473
1986	142	375	70	-	587
1987	169	410	100	-	679
1988	193	470	175	-	838
1989	227	555	320	-	1,102
1990	273	550	365	47	1,235
1991	295	540	444	121	1,400
1992	291	511	400	283	1,485
1993	319	528	643	350	1,840
1994	364	438	698	540	2,040
1995	385	457	789	721	2,352

Source: adapted from BVA/EDI/BSkyB.

(a) Table 2 and Figure 3 are from the *BFI Film and Television Handbook 1997*. Assess the usefulness of these tables for this marketing research project. **(6 marks)**

Exemplar responses
Useful
• *Source is a highly regarded organisation in the film industry/secondary research so very low cost/Percy has only a small budget for research.*
• *Could use the data to compare with his own sales/income records to see if the pattern of business at The Roxie follows national trends.*
Not useful
• *Hopelessly out of date/1984-1995 and question set in 2005.*
• *No data since 1997 and the market could have changed radically in that time.*
• *Both tables show rising figures which could give a false sense of well-being if projected.*
(Question based on assessment so must be argued from both sides.)

Mark allocation
1 mark for each reason why useful (maximum 3 marks).
1 mark for each reason why not useful (maximum 3 marks). **(6 marks)**

(b) Describe ONE appropriate primary research method that Percy could use for this research project. Justify your answer. **(4 marks)**

Exemplar responses
• *Ask customers about their cinemagoing habits/what they think of The Roxie – produce a questionnaire and hand it out when they buy a ticket/collect it when they leave – low cost as it only involves writing/printing a questionnaire/no mailing or distribution costs – research should produce findings direct from existing customers.*
• *Percy to conduct street interviews with local people – will be able to ask them whether they visit The Roxie, if so/if not why – will get immediate answers/will not have to wait for research – Percy needs to protect his business so immediate feedback will be useful and he could put in place a marketing plan sooner rather than later.*

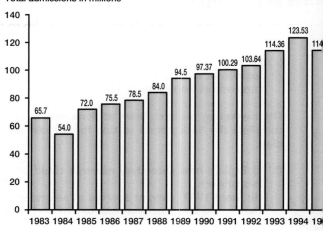

Figure 3 *Cinema Admissions, 1983-1995*

Cinema Admissions 1983-1995

Total admissions in millions

Source: adapted from EDI/Screen Digest/Screen Finance.

Mark allocation
1 mark for appropriate primary research method.
1 mark for description.
1 mark for justification.
1 mark for application to given research project. **(4 marks)**

27 Sampling

What is a sample?

The aim of marketing research is to be as accurate and up-to-date as possible and to discover the facts, figures or opinions required to meet the research objectives. Accuracy in quantitative research relies on statistics. Statistical theory involves the application of mathematical formulae and theories in the collection, organising and analysis of numerical data produced from research, to bring some kind of order, meaning and understanding to that data. Statistics are numbers and the use of statistics means the use of numbers to provide objective information that will identify facts or features from research. Statistics can also refer to the numbers that will generate ideas, plans and initiatives, or numbers that will support or disprove a theory.

Within statistical theory, the bigger the numbers in the research, the more accurate the data is likely to be. The bigger the numbers, the more the data can be analysed and split into smaller units or 'cells', each of which will provide an individual piece of information. Taking this to its logical extreme, to be sure that a research project is really accurate, data will need to be collected from every single source - from 100% of the population.

In reality, researching 100% of a population is rarely possible. It is likely to be too expensive and cumbersome to achieve. Researching 100% of a population, however, is seldom necessary. Within acceptable levels of accuracy and confidence, research data collected from a proportion or **sample** of the total population will often exhibit the same groupings, behaviour and trends as if collected from the total population. This means that, for most research, a total population can be 'sampled' – taking a small part of the total and treating it as if it represented the whole population.

Preparing a sampling plan

Having decided that primary research is appropriate to help meet business objectives, researchers must decide who to survey, who to include in the research, the total population and the sample size. This is the basis of a sampling plan. A sampling plan has three main parts:

- selecting, identifying and defining the target population;
- setting the sample size;
- selecting the appropriate sampling technique. This can be random/probability sampling or non-probability sampling.

Sampling is often used for surveys as it is usually impossible and impractical to consider researching an entire target population, unless the total population is small and there is an accessible number of respondents, or there are extensive resources or a national requirement. The most important aim in any sampling exercise is that the actual sample chosen is as true a reflection of the target population as possible.

The target population

In marketing research, **population** has a wider meaning than in common usage. A population in research terms does not just relate to people, but to the total 'universe' that could be researched in a survey. The population may be the total number of individual people or the total number of other **sampling units** (households, businesses or shops) that are the subject of the research. For example, a research survey may need to investigate shoppers in a town. In this case the population of the sampling unit would be the total number of people who shop in that town. If the survey were based on the shopping behaviour of households, the population of the sampling unit in this case would be the total number of households in that town. If it were a business-to-business survey, the population of the sampling unit would be the total number of shops or businesses that are based in the town. The source of the sample (the database) - the total list of shopper's names, the list of addresses of all the shoppers or the list of all the shops or businesses - is known as the sampling frame. It is from the **sampling frame** that the actual sample will be drawn. The choice of sampling frame will depend on what information exists or the researcher has access to which meets the objectives of the research.

Within each sampling unit that is used to make up the total population there may still be **sampling elements** - the actual individual people that are chosen to take part in the survey. For example, if the sampling unit is 'households', the persons within each household that are chosen to actually provide the information and answer the questions would be the sample element. In the case of the sampling unit being 'individuals', each individual selected will have a dual role, as both the sampling unit and the sample element. Care must be taken when defining the population for a sampling unit, to make sure that it takes in all the sampling elements, the different types of people or organisations, that must be included in the research. To do this researchers must be clear about the aims of the research – what do they need to find out and from whom? If the population is incorrect, then the sample chosen will be wrong, which could produce data that is not accurate, may not meet the needs of the research, or is misleading.

Sample size

The decision about how many people to include in the sample will depend on resources – how much is in the budget to spend on the research – traded off against the level of accuracy required. In practice it is better to sample as many people as can be afforded. The higher the number, the more chance of the research being accurate and believable. Whilst a low number like 25 interviews will produce some data, the danger is that when respondents who answer a question in a particular way fall to a tiny number, their opinions may not be representative of the total population. It would be advisable to aim for a sample of at least 100 for a mini survey, up to 10% of a population or as many as can be afforded. Samples taken to gain views about politics, for example, at general elections, are usually around 1,000 people.

Sometimes it may be necessary to collect research data from the whole population. This is known as a **census**. At one extreme is the National Census, as shown in Figure 1. At the other, it may be possible for a business to research the whole population if it is small enough. An example would be if a business wanted to research the opinions of, say, the fresh fruit buyers at each of the main food supermarket groups. This may be as few as 12 individuals, which means that a census would be possible in theory – although getting to every one of these busy people would present other challenges. Whilst a census may be feasible, access may prove to be very difficult and may not be worth the time or cost involved.

However, in most business situations research is likely to be based on sampling from a population. Care must be taken to try to make sure that the sample selected for the research is representative of the total population. This means that the sample needs to contain the same mix and balance of elements that occur in the total population. How to make sure that the sample is representative is another problem, which leads to selecting the sampling technique to use.

Figure 1 *The UK Census*

Since 1801, every 10 years the UK has set aside one day for the Census - a count of all people and households. It is the most complete source of information about the UK population. The latest Census was Sunday 29 April 2001. Every effort is made to include everyone and that is why the Census is so important. It is the only survey which provides a detailed picture of the entire population. It is unique because it covers everyone at the same time and asks the same core questions everywhere, making it easy to compare different parts of the country.

The information that the Census provides allows central and local government, health authorities and many other organisations to target their resources more effectively and to plan housing, education, health and transport services for years to come. In England and Wales, the Census is planned and carried out by the Office for National Statistics. Elsewhere in the UK, responsibility lies with the General Register Office for Scotland and the Northern Ireland Statistics and Research Agency. Plans are being made to hold the next one in 2011.

Source: adapted from www.statistics.gov.uk/census/ (November 2005).

Random or probability sampling

This is where each element is drawn from the population at random. This means that each element has an equal chance of being sampled, selected for the research. To be random, the

selection must be free from outside influence or subjective choic A good example is the Lotto game, which is part of the UK National Lottery. Here, 49 numbered balls are spun in a drum an 6 balls are drawn out at random to arrive at the winning combination of lottery numbers for each draw. Lotto relies on random sampling to make the draw fair and equal to all competitors.

How can random sampling be applied to a research task? The starting point is the definition and identification of the population Once this has been established a decision will need to made abou the size of the sample to be researched. The sample size must be at least 100 to achieve true randomness and will be limited by th resources to conduct the research, such as the size of budget or the availability of trained researchers. Assume a business has identified a population of 1,000 people that it wants to research and the minimum sample size of 100 has been chosen. Table 1 shows a number of ways that the actual sample can be selected a random.

Table 1 *Selecting a random sample of 100 from a population of 1,000*

- The names of all the 1,000 people in the population could be written on pieces of paper, these pieces of paper shaken in a hat or convenient vessel to mix them up and 100 pieces of paper drawn from the hat, each bearing the name of the individual to be interviewed.
- Each person could be allocated a unique number from 1-1,000, and 100 random numbers could be generated by computer or by referring to the first 100 entries in a published table of random numbers. The sample will then be the people whose names are associated with the randomly selected numbers.
- The names could be in a list and every tenth name on the list is selected for the research. This technique is very similar to a 'random walk' where interviewers are allocated a street and told to call on every tenth house and conduct an interview.

In theory, the random selection process should mean that the profile of the sample is **representative** of the total population. Statistical testing will provide a measure of how well a random sample matches the target population and reassurance of the leve of confidence that can be applied to any random sample, as well a levels of sampling error if required. In practice, it can be difficult to produce a pure random sample. There are variables, such as how well the population is mixed, whether the distribution is even and if there is any grouping or clustering of elements within the population. Another concern is what happens when one or more of the units selected for the research is not available. They may be out or decide to not answer the telephone. This can cause problems because random sampling requires that 100% of the selected elements must be interviewed. To achieve this may mean that the interviewer has to make call-backs or second visits to conduct the interview. If this is not done proportionally, more people from one element of the population or another will be interviewed. Any of these variables can upset the balance of the random sample and create bias within the data that is collected.

Despite the difficulties, random sampling is still used as the basic sampling technique for most telephone surveys. It is also used in other large-scale surveys of populations, such as research designed to provide general information, records of behaviour, estimates for sales, market share, usage and attitude surveys and opinion polls.

Stratified random sampling This is a way of improving the quality of a random sample. It can be used when the researcher already knows something about the total population and can identify different groups or 'strata' within the population before starting the research. Random sampling can then be applied within each of the strata. This will make sure that each of the strata is represented in the overall sample, rather than leaving representation purely to chance and risking that some strata will not be represented at all. An example would be if research was carried out amongst students at a college. A random sample could be selected and may contain representatives of students from each of the faculties, based on probability theory. However, by stratifying the students, the sampling units, into groups from each faculty, such as arts, science, business, ICT and engineering, and then drawing a random sample within each group of students, it would be guaranteed that every faculty would be represented. There will still be a need to choose the actual size of the sample. This may be a simple division of the total between the faculties, or a weighting factor could be applied to represent the numbers of students within each faculty. The objective is to make sure that the final sample is both representative and would achieve the objectives of the research.

Cluster sampling This technique is based on dividing a population into relatively small, self-contained, discrete areas or natural groupings of people, known as 'clusters', then deciding which cluster or clusters to choose for the research. A random selection technique will still be used within each cluster to select the actual sample to survey. For example, the population of the UK is easily divided into counties, local government areas, towns, communities and post code areas. Cluster sampling could be used to conduct research within different towns, rather than apply a simple random selection across an entire area, which would mean that interviews might be spread widely across the geographic area. This would help make a research survey more cost effective, without unduly compromising the integrity of the research. Cluster sampling may also be chosen by a business that only trades in one town, or has a particular strength in one area. The 'cluster' is the area that has been chosen because it will adequately represent a target population that has been chosen for the research. Within the 'cluster' the researcher must still decide on the sampling unit, households, businesses or individuals and the sample element within each unit, and use random sampling techniques to select the actual sample.

Non-probability sampling

Here there is no random selection. There is no need to know the probability of selection for each element of the sample. Instead the researcher (interviewer) has to create a miniature, small-scale replica of the total population to survey.

Quota sampling This is the most widely used non-probability sampling technique. The person planning the research needs to develop a profile of the target population for the research, based on the most obvious or important characteristics. These may include geodemographic segmentation, national census data or other important criteria that may relate to the market being surveyed, such as users of a particular product or other consumer characteristics. This information may come from particular knowledge of a market or from secondary research data. Once this profile has been developed the main criteria can be used for the percentage breakdown of the sample. These percentages are then applied to the total number of people to be surveyed. The researchers will then have a target number of respondents to survey, their 'quota', based on each of the different criteria. Researchers are free to select who they survey so long as they end up with the correct total number for each criterion within their quota. When they have reached their quota for one criterion, they move on to the next until the total sample has been fulfilled.

Tables 2 and 3 show data from the UK Film Council. This data can be used to calculate quotas in a sample of 500 people.

- **Independent quota control.** The breakdown of quotas in Table 4 has been calculated from the simple % of the total audience for the UK Top 20 films in 2004 in Table 3.

Table 2 *Cinema audience by gender, 2004*

	Male %	Female %
See at least one film per year (proportion of population)	73%	72%
Go to the cinema at least once a month (proportion of population)	27%	26%
Top 20 films (proportion of audience)	52%	48%
Top UK films (proportion of audience)	49%	51%
Total population	**49%**	**51%**

Source: adapted from CAVIAR 22 and Quarterly Reports.

Note: 'Top UK films' refers to the 17 of the top 20 UK films for which audience data were available in 2004. The overall UK cinema audience in 2004 had a roughly equal gender split, with males and females attending with similar frequency, as Table 2 shows.

Table 3 Cinema audience by age group, 2004

	Age 7-14	Age 15-24	Age 25-34	Age 35+
See at least one film per year (proportion of population)	92%	90%	84%	61%
Go to the cinema at least once a month (proportion of population)	39%	53%	34%	16%
Top 20 films (proportion of audience)	20%	26%	22%	32%
Top UK films (proportion of audience)	12%	27%	23%	39%
Total population	**11%**	**13%**	**17%**	**58%**

Source: adapted from CAVIAR 22 and Quarterly Reports.

Table 4 Independent quotas

Demographic characteristics	% going to Top 20 films	Quotas for interviewing a total sample of 500
7-14	20%	100
15-24	26%	130
25-34	22%	110
35+	32%	160
		500
Gender		
Male	52%	260
Female	48%	240
		500

Table 5 Interlocking quotas

	Age 7-14		Age 15-24		Age 25-34		Age 35+	
	Male	Female	Male	Female	Male	Female	Male	Female
See at least one film per year	36	34	43	39	40	37	66	61
Go to the cinema at least once a month	16	14	26	24	16	15	17	16
Target	52	48	65	63	56	52	83	77

* Figures are rounded

Researchers will be set these quotas as targets and so long as they end up with completed interviews in the numbers and proportions set as quotas they will have fulfilled the requirements of the quota sample.

- **Interlocking quota control**. More complex quotas can be developed if the profile of the target population can be broken down sufficiently. The quotas in Table 5 have been calculated by using the % of the total audience for the UK Top 20 films in 2004 to give the breakdown by age. The split into 'See at least one film per year' and 'Go to the cinema at least once a month' has been calculated from the ratios from the total population data. This will enable the researcher to break down the data produced into smaller cells. Depending on the objectives of the research, the researcher may decide that people who go to the cinema at least once a month are more important than those who go to the cinema at least once a year. In this situation the quotas can be reversed to give a heavier weighting to the more frequent cinemagoers. The individual figures have also been rounded because you cannot interview a percentage point of a person. The researcher will also have to accept that the total sample has changed to 496 rather than the 500 target in order to get the ratios to match the profile of the total population of cinemagoers. This reduction of the sample by 4 people is too small a percentage to have a great effect on the outcome of the survey.

Quota sampling is particularly useful for a number of reasons.

- The sample is constructed to represent the actual profile of the population rather than relying on probability generating the profile through random chance, which may or may not occur in a random sample.

- It is relatively quick and easy to set up and less expensive to organise and administer than a statistically based random sampling exercise.

- There is no statistical requirement for call backs to interview people who have been identified through the random selection process, all the researchers have to do is fulfil their quotas, thus saving time and travelling expense.

Judgement sampling Here the researcher selects a sample that as accurately as possible reflects the total population, based on skill and judgement. This is not just guesswork, but is likely to be informed by experience and knowledge of a particular population or market. Although the starting point is different, the sample may turn out to be based on quotas.

Convenience sampling Often confused with the common usage of the term 'convenient', convenience sampling is a valid sampling technique based upon choosing the sample from a population that is relatively easy to access. Examples would include sampling from fellow students, friends, visitors to a centre or shoppers in a local street or shopping centre. Again, it is likely that although the sampling activity may be based on convenience, the sample itself may also have a quota element as the researcher tries to reduce any bias and regain the balance of the survey by, say, interviewing men and women on a 50:50 basis, or trying to get an age profile that covers the target population.

Sampling for qualitative research

The nature of **qualitative** research methods means that the sample size is likely to be much smaller than for most **quantitative** research surveys. The smaller numbers involved and the more subjective nature of findings associated with qualitative research means that the findings are not likely to be subjected to rigorous statistical analysis like quantitative data. However, although the sample sizes for qualitative research may be smaller, it is still important to make sure that the sample of people that are interviewed for the qualitative research reflects the profile of the total population or is representative of the population that you need to survey. This is so that any findings from the research can be projected onto the total population with confidence. Desk research or experience of the market place can be used to determine the structure of the sample for qualitative research and quota sampling is probably the best method to use when selecting the respondents to take part in the research.

In terms of the sample size, although it is likely to be smaller than the numbers used for quantitative research the sample recruited for qualitative research should still be large enough to be credible and relevant. One criticism of qualitative research is that the numbers involved are so small that findings or conclusions cannot be a true representation of the whole population. It is hard to make recommendations for the number of people that you need for qualitative research to be relevant, as the sample size is again likely to be limited by resources available and how much money there is to spend on the research. The rule of thumb must again be 'as large as you can afford'. The numbers sampled must be traded off against the level of accuracy required or accepted. The higher the number, the more chance of the research being accurate and believable. Whilst a low number will certainly produce some data, the danger comes when the data is analysed

and the cell size, the individual number of respondents that answer in a particular way or have a particular attitude, starts to fall to a tiny number. In this situation data that makes up the cell will not be able to be analysed any further.

Finding the sample of respondents is another task. In qualitative research this process of identifying and choosing the respondents is usually called 'recruiting'. In qualitative research it is quite usual for interviewers to be set quotas for recruiting. A recruitment questionnaire will need to be prepared for the interviewers to use to make sure that they only recruit the profile of people that you want for the research. This will probably include gender and age criteria and may specify that the respondents recruited meet other criteria depending on the objectives of the research, such as being parents, home owners, car drivers, television viewers or theatregoers. Recruitment can take place anywhere, and the principles of convenience sampling can be very useful. For example, if shoppers were recruited for a focus group it would be easier to find these respondents if you visited a shopping centre. Similarly, to recruit a sample of sports players, starting at a sports club is likely to be more productive than just standing in a busy street. Recruitment can also take place by telephone, by going through a list of potential respondents from an address list. A business itself may have a list that can be used for recruitment, from sales records or other sources with the business. The actual method used will depend on who needs to be recruited and the resources available.

Examination practice · Gladston liquids

Gladston Liquids, a soft drinks manufacturer, is planning to launch a new low fat, cholesterol reducing drink. It is a relatively small business with limited funds for market research. It has identified a rapidly expanding and potentially very successful market and wants to carry out research quickly to find out whether to launch its new product. The business has decided to recruit a sample of customers for focus groups as it is particularly interested in the opinions of customers about this relatively new market opportunity.

(a) **Describe how the business would construct a recruitment questionnaire for selecting respondents for a series of focus groups.**
(4 marks)

(b) **Discuss whether the business should use a quota sample or a random sampling technique for choosing respondents for focus groups. Justify your decision.** (6 marks)

Meeting the assessment criteria - examiners' guidance

SkierAll manufactures ski and snow board equipment. It has 2,000 stockists in the UK which sell its products. The research manager needs to send a postal questionnaire to a sample of 200 of these stockists to gauge their views on the products they are selling and potential changes that may be made in the light of current sales, future trends and customers' perceptions of the product. The business is keen to get a wide range of views to ensure any changes it makes to its marketing strategy have as little risk as possible.

(a) (i) Outline why using a random sample would be an appropriate technique to use for this survey. **(2 marks)**

Exemplar responses
- *It should produce a representative sample – which provides an accurate reflection of the total population.*
- *It will avoid bias – other sampling techniques may contain a built-in bias which will result in the survey being inaccurate/misleading.*

Mark allocation
1 mark for reason.
1 mark for explaining why random sample appropriate. **(2 marks)**

(ii) Describe how the research manager can make sure that the questionnaires are sent to a random sample of shops. **(2 marks)**

Exemplar responses
- *Give a number to each name on list – use a random number generator/random number table to make selection.*
- *List names/store locations alphabetically – select every tenth name/location and send questionnaire to each of these names.*
- *Put names in a hat, shake names to mix them and pull out first 200 at random.*

Mark allocation
1 mark for each step in description. **(2 marks)**

(b) Describe **ONE** way that the research manager can increase response rate for the return of the questionnaires. **(2 marks)**

Exemplar responses
- *Include a stamped addressed envelope for return – respondents will not have to find their own means of returning questionnaire.*
- *Offer an incentive – this will encourage return as respondents will want to get the incentive.*

Mark allocation
1 mark for how response rate can be increased.
1 mark for application. **(2 marks)**

(c) Analyse why SkierAll made use of sampling and evaluate the sample size. **(6 marks)**

Exemplar responses
- *Sending to all shops would give the widest range of views - but this can be expensive and time consuming – reducing the size to 200 shops, which is 10% of the population, will not give such a wide range but will reduce cost and save time – 10% is usually said to give a representative sample – so its is a good sample of the population to take.*

Mark allocation
1 mark for reason for taking the sample.
2 marks for recognising that there are advantages and disadvantages of sampling.
1 mark for justification.
2 marks for evaluating sample size. **(6 marks)**

28 Results analysis

Analysis

Analysis is the process of sorting and bringing order to data collected during a research project, with the objective of making sense of the data. Once this has been done the data will yield information that can be interpreted and applied to marketing plans.

Many people approach the analysis of marketing research data from the point of view '… now we have the data, what do we do with it?' In fact, by the time the data has been collected it is often too late to consider what to do with it, certainly if you want to get full value from the research. It is better to have these thoughts at the planning stage so that the data is collected in a form that makes analysis easier. This should help make sure that the information will be in the form that is required and meets the objectives of the research plan.

Planning-in analysis before fieldwork starts

This makes sure that the data collected is of use and can be analysed in a way that meets the objectives of the research project. It has implications for deciding on the target population and the sample size, as well as the method of research and recording. For example, if analysis by age were required, the target population and sample must be selected to include the full range of ages required for analysis, suggesting quota sampling rather than random sampling. The questionnaire must be structured to take into account the full span of ages to allow the breakdown required to be made.

Considering analysis before research starts may also affect the questions asked and the way of asking them, to make sure that the answers collected actually help decision making about a particular issue. It would be little use asking dichotomous questions if the marketing team needed to know how much or how little the target population liked a particular advertising campaign, requiring a scaled question of some sort, which could provide such analysis. A good way to check whether a piece or research is likely to provide the right data for analysis and meet the objectives of the research is to **pilot** it with a small number of people to check that it will perform as required. If it does, fine. If not, then it can be changed before committing to the full survey and discovering that it has not produced the right data.

Post-fieldwork analysis

Once research has been carried out and the data is collected, analysis can take place. Although there are some differences in the way that **quantitative** and **qualitative** data can be analysed, there is a number of basic steps to follow that will be helpful for both types of data, as shown in Figure 1.

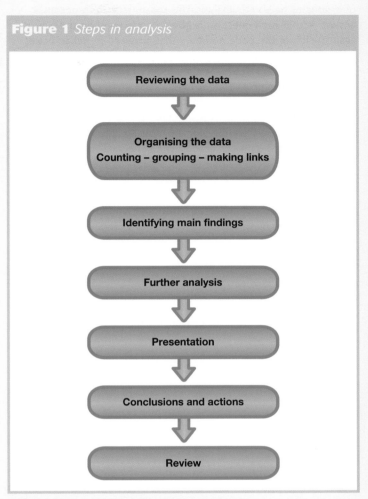

Figure 1 *Steps in analysis*

- Reviewing the data
- Organising the data
  Counting – grouping – making links
- Identifying main findings
- Further analysis
- Presentation
- Conclusions and actions
- Review

Analysis of quantitative data

Reviewing the data Data that has been collected will need to be sorted and reviewed to check what form it is in. It may be numbers, ticked boxes, scaled opinions, facts or figures. Having identified the form of the data, a decision can be taken about how it can be organised so that it can be analysed. In practice this should have been planned-in at the start of the research project and resources allocated to deal with the data.

Organising the data During this stage quantitative data will be counted and totalled, and probably entered into a computer software package, such as a spreadsheet for analysis, manipulation and presentation purposes. Depending on the size of the survey, usually indicated by the number of questionnaires, the number of questions and the number of possible answers, counting can either be done by hand or using computer software. A method of organising hand counting is to use either a **tally chart** (see later in this section) or a **blank copy of the questionnaire** to record the answers to each question. The total responses for each question and answer can then be entered into a spreadsheet for totalling, calculating percentages and more complex statistical analysis. A spreadsheet programme will also convert figures directly into charts, as required.

For larger and more complex surveys and questionnaires a professional research organisation would have 'coded' the questions to help with analysis. This means that each potential answer within each question is given a code number and it is against each of the code numbers that answers or ticked boxes will be counted. Coding answers means that data entry is easier and the software is dealing with numbers rather than words, which allows the processing to be quicker.

The counting stage will reveal the size of various groupings within the data, how many respondents said one thing compared with how many said another, for example. At this stage links may develop between different groups or segments. This can help when looking at the overall market or population, to see which groups will be affected, positively or negatively, or based on the objectives of the research.

If the data has been collected from open-ended questions, as in Figure 2, organising the data will consist of grouping together similar answers.

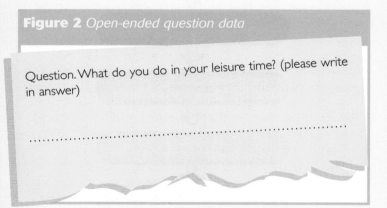

Figure 2 *Open-ended question data*

Question. What do you do in your leisure time? (please write in answer)

....

The range of possible answers to the question in Figure 2 is vast, but similar activities expressed in different ways can probably be grouped together. For example, respondents stating 'soccer, kicking a ball about, playing football with my mates, playing five-a-side' could all be grouped under a general 'football' heading. Similarly 'playing with my X-Box, using a Gameboy and spending time on my Playstation' could all be grouped as 'computer gaming'. Grouping will help to simplify the data and will mean that there are not minority subgroups, which will only complicate the data and any calculation that needs to be done. Although the actual question is open-ended and produces subjective activities, ideas or opinions, grouping these together will enable the data to be counted and presented as quantitative data.

Identifying the main findings Sometimes called 'top line' findings, these will be the most important and possibly the most obvious findings, based on the objectives of the research. The main findings will be found through basic analysis, such as totalling, calculating percentages (see later in section), identifying main groupings, looking at ratios. They may be the response from the largest group or smallest group, depending on the objectives of the research. For example, if you are seeking to discover how many

people agree with a statement or course of action, you will be looking for large numbers for support. If you are looking to show that only a minority of people dislike a product or disagree with a course of action, you will be looking for small numbers.

Further analysis The main, 'top line' findings may be sufficient for some research projects. However, there is often a need for further analysis or an in-depth look at the views or findings from one particular segment. This may involve using appropriate statistical techniques to probe and test the data to see if the findings are significant and if so to what degree. Statistical analysis will also be able to qualify research through the calculation of the level of confidence that can be placed on the findings.

When analysing research in detail it is easy to end up basing the findings on a very small number of people. For example, if 10% out of a sample of 400 disagreed with something, or their views ran counter to the majority, it would be reasonable to find out more about this minority and see why they disagreed. 10% of 400 is 40 people. If half of these were men, this brings the cell size down to 20. If these men were further broken down by, say, employment, each cell would be very small indeed. The question is then 'Are the opinions of these few men actually representative of the population as a whole?' Care must be taken to make sure that the opinions of a minority are representative and not taken out of context. This can be overcome by working with the maximum sample size that can be afforded or handled by the research team.

Presentation There are many ways in which data can be presented. These range from a simple written report, to a full-blown stand-up presentation using computers and projectors. 'A picture paints a thousand words' is often true when planning the presentation of research findings – a simple pie chart showing market share can communicate far better than a written description of the same information in some cases. Most spreadsheet software will automatically present data in a range of different charts or graphs. However, not all are appropriate for every piece of research. If charts and tables are used, Table 1 shows useful rules to follow.

Table 1 *Rules when presenting charts and tables*

Charts and tables should be:
- titled to tell the reader what is being presented and looked at and numbered to aid referencing;
- drawn to an appropriate scale, i.e. to take full advantage of available space;
- drawn with each scale labelled;
- drawn so that the sections, bars, lines, or however the data is shown are also identified using a key or labels;
- set out to include details of the source of the information and date that the data was collected.

Another consideration is the audience that will be viewing the presentation. How much do they know about the subject, how much do they understand about marketing research, can they read and understand data presented in chart form or would a written report be more appropriate? The key factor is to 'know your audience' and present the research findings as appropriate. When presenting marketing research findings it is good practice to combine verbal explanation with a written report and supporting graphics, such as charts and tables. In this way the audience can ask questions during the presentation, and will have a document to refer to and consider after the actual presentation. Table 2 shows information often included in written reports.

Table 2 *Information in written reports*

A written report of research findings will usually include:
- title and date;
- main findings, as an 'executive summary';
- a brief description of the research method, sample size, date of fieldwork, timing, and who carried out the fieldwork;
- the main body of the research and findings, based on meeting the original objectives, usually combining written narrative, supported by charts and tables as appropriate;
- any exceptional or unusual findings, with explanation;
- conclusions and actions;
- next steps, with timing;
- a copy of the blank questionnaire that has been used so that anyone reading the report can see exactly what was asked during the research.

Conclusions and actions The point of conducting marketing research is so that the findings can be used to initiate or support marketing plans. This means that it should be conducted with clear objectives in mind. This, in turn, means that for the research to be worthwhile the findings must be actionable – that something should happen as a result of the research. Research conducted for its own sake may be very interesting, but in a competitive business environment few organisations have that luxury. Having obtained the research, it will be up to the marketing team to make good use of the findings in order to get good value for money from the research. This will usually include drawing conclusions, supported by the findings, and/or identifying marketing activity/actions. Even if the research does not lead to clear marketing plans, one conclusion may be that more research is required, the action being a new research plan.

Review After the research has been completed, it is good practice to review the project and consider what went well, what went badly and what needs doing as a result of the research. This is a form of quality control that will help make the next research plan even better.

Analysis of qualitative data

Reviewing the data Qualitative data may have been produced from different types of research, such as focus groups or in depth interviews. It may be a mixture of subjective views, opinions, attitudes, motivation and so on. It will have been recorded in the form of open-ended questions, notes, audio tapes or on video/camera/DVD. Once the type of basic data has been identified, a decision can be taken as to how to organise the data so that it can be analysed. In practice this should have been planned-in at the start of the research project and resources allocated to deal with the data.

Organising the data Qualitative data will need to be read, listened to or watched, depending on the recording medium. Audio and the soundtracks from video/DVD recordings will need to be transcribed (the words from the recordings typed up in a form that can be read) so that the data is easier to access, without the need for playback equipment. In a written form, transcripts from qualitative research such as focus groups can be analysed by looking for agreement, disagreement, common themes, patterns of thought, ideas or opinions that had never been considered. The transcripts will need to be summarised, grouping together common themes, opinions or ideas.

Any really 'off-the-wall' ideas or comments should also be noted for separate consideration, to see whether they are just one-off, minority views, or whether the individual is articulating a wider view that is held by the group or other respondents. At this stage it is also useful to start making links between groups of respondents that may hold an opinion about one thing, and whether or not they hold similar opinions about other issues raised during the qualitative research. The precise links that you make will depend on what the research is expected to reveal, the main themes established in the research objectives and planning stages and the issues covered during the actual research.

Identifying main findings Like quantitative research, the main findings will usually be the things that have been said by the majority or the minority of respondents – the sample of people involved in the research. The objectives of the research will usually be the starting point against which to compare the main findings. However, one of the strengths of qualitative research is its ability to throw up thoughts or ideas that had not been considered when planning the research.

Further analysis It may be possible to analyse readings or transcripts further, perhaps reading or listening again to try to spot a particular comment or train of thought. Sometimes, if a new idea comes out of one focus group it may need to be checked by discussing it with another group or in a new piece of research. Because of the relatively low numbers associated with focus groups it is very often necessary to check to confirm findings by subjecting them to quantitative research. This will help make sure that the views expressed and collected from the groups are representative of the population as a whole and not a biased aberration of the few people that happened to be recruited for the focus group. Checking findings from qualitative research can often be accomplished by using an omnibus survey, rather than having to commission a tailor-made piece of primary research, with all the associated costs.

Presentation It is usual for qualitative research findings to be presented verbally, with supporting storyboards or charts. A verbal presentation by the researcher, usually the moderator who has run the focus groups, gives the audience a chance to ask questions raised by the findings directly to the person who has heard all of the discussion and comments from the groups. This can lead to greater insight and understanding. A written report will also be required. This will usually follow a very similar structure to reports from quantitative research surveys. They may differ in some areas, such as there will be less statistical analysis and there will be no questionnaire to file at the back of the report, although it may be useful to include some indication of the flow or direction in which the discussion was led by the group moderator. In addition to the analysis and interpretation of findings written by the moderator or research expert, reports from focus groups will usually include some verbatim statements and quotations that have been recorded from the groups as this tends to add some authenticity to the findings.

Conclusions and actions Like quantitative and all primary research, any qualitative research projects will have been done to meet a set of marketing objectives. The point of conducting marketing research is so that the findings can be used to initiate or support marketing plans. The conclusions from qualitative research are often viewed with some scepticism owing to the relatively low numbers of people involved. There is always the question of the findings being representative. However, as noted, the main findings can be tested using quantitative research methods and there should be no reason why properly conducted qualitative research should not reveal as many worthwhile conclusions as any other primary method. Again, like quantitative research, the conclusions should be actionable, or the research will have been a waste of time and money.

Review After the research has been completed, as with other marketing plans, it is always good practice to review the project, to consider what went well, what went badly and what needs doing as a result of the research, which acts as a form of quality control.

Counting using a tally sheet/tally chart

This is a quick and convenient way of counting and keeping track of numbers. It is based on drawing out a sheet or preparing a grid with the main headings of what you are counting, and using a 'five bar gate' system for counting. A tally sheet can be used, for example, in a quota sample of a survey, counting off each person interviewed in the appropriate box, as illustrated in Figure 3.

Figure 3 *Tally sheet*

Sample to be interviewed:				
	Age 18-65		Age 65+	
	Quota	Actual	Quota	Actual
Male	25	╫╫ ╫╫ ╫╫ ╫╫ ╫╫	25	╫╫ ╫╫ ╫╫
Female	25	╫╫ ╫╫	25	╫╫

The tally chart in Figure 3 shows that out of the quota of 25 respondents that meet the sampling criteria, this interviewer has completed the quota for 'Males aged 18-65', but only has 15 'Males aged 65+' and therefore needs to interview 10 more. It also

shows the interviewer has interviewed 10 'Females aged 18-65' and 5 'Females 65+' and therefore needs to interview 15 and 20 more respectively. This way of counting can also be used effective for hand counting responses to questions on a questionnaire, using a blank questionnaire as the basis for the tally chart, as for example in Figure 4.

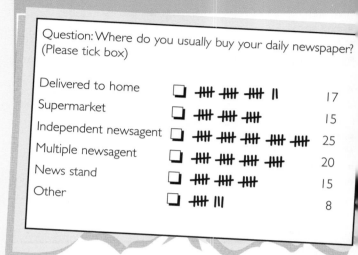

Figure 4 *Using a tally chart in a questionnaire*

Question: Where do you usually buy your daily newspaper? (Please tick box)

Delivered to home	☐ ╫╫ ╫╫ ╫╫ II	17
Supermarket	☐ ╫╫ ╫╫ ╫╫	15
Independent newsagent	☐ ╫╫ ╫╫ ╫╫ ╫╫ ╫╫	25
Multiple newsagent	☐ ╫╫ ╫╫ ╫╫ ╫╫	20
News stand	☐ ╫╫ ╫╫ ╫╫	15
Other	☐ ╫╫ III	8

Once the basic counting has been done, the 'five bar gates' can be quickly totalled and the figures transferred either manually to a graph or into spreadsheet software for more detailed analysis.

Percentages

This is a very convenient way to make comparisons between different groupings or the findings of research. The use of percentages is based on the idea of expressing the relative importance of different groups based on their share of the total – the whole sample, population or universe.

When calculating percentages, no matter how large or small the total, the total is nominally divided in to 100 parts, which equals 100%. The percentage measure is based on a share of those 100 parts. An easy way to get a feel for percentages is to visualise them as the share of a pie.

Figure 5 shows an example of how percentages can be used to show research information. Most calculators will have a button (% which will calculate percentages.

Percentages work with any size of population or total figure. It important to remember that the total will equal 100%. This means that all of the smaller segments within the total will always add up to 100%. Figure 6 shows an example. Percentages can also be expressed in bar chart form as shown in Figure 7.

Sometimes percentage calculation can be reversed. For example if a piece of secondary research reports that 5% of people have problems sleeping you may want to know how many people actually made that claim out of the total number of people interviewed. If the sample size had been 100, then the 5% would equate to just 5 people. This would raise warning signs about any

Figure 5 *Research findings in a supermarket survey, survey of 100 people*

A research survey is carried out of 100 people about supermarket shopping. If 50 were men and 50 women, the percentage of men in the survey can be found using the formula:

(Number ÷ total) × 100

So the number of men, 50, is divided by the total, 100, and converted to a 'percentage' by multiplying by 100:

= (50 ÷ 100) × 100

= 0.5 × 100

= 50%.

If 80 people out of the 100 in this survey agreed with the statement 'Service has improved' and 20 out of the 100 disagreed:
the percentage in agreement would be (80 ÷ 100) × 100 = 80%;
the percentage disagreeing would be (20 ÷ 100) × 100 = 20%.

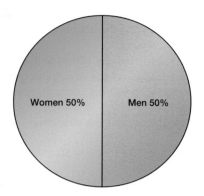

Survey amongst 100 people 50 men and 50 women

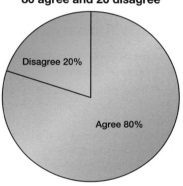

Survey amongst 100 people 80 agree and 20 disagree

Figure 6 *Calculating percentages from a sample of supermarket shoppers, survey of 440 people*

If the sample size is 440 and 176 of a sample shop in Tesco, 132 shop in Sainsbury's, 44 shop in Asda and 88 shop in other supermarkets, then the percentages would be:

Tesco (176 ÷ 440) × 100 = 40%
Sainsbury's (132 ÷ 440) × 100 = 30%
Asda (44 ÷ 440) × 100 = 10%
Others (88 ÷ 440) × 100 = 20%

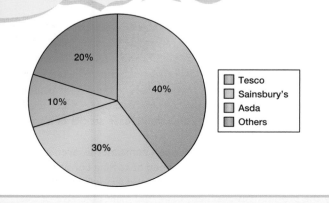

Figure 7 *Supermarket survey of 100 people*

Question 1 Parking is easy.
The percentage in agreement would be (25 ÷ 100) × 100 = 25%
The percentage disagreeing would be (75 ÷ 100) × 100 = 75%

Question 2 There are adequate trolleys.
The percentage in agreement would be (40 ÷ 100) × 100 = 40%
The percentage disagreeing would be (60 ÷ 100) × 100 = 60%

Question 3 Service has improved.
The percentage in agreement would be (80 ÷ 100) × 100 = 80%
The percentage disagreeing would be (20 ÷ 100) × 100 = 20%

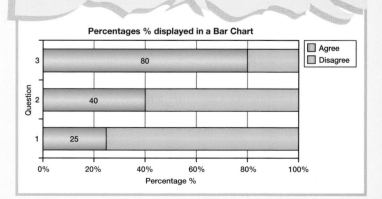

further breakdown of data from the people who had problems sleeping as it may come down to just one or two people who may not be representative of the population as a whole. However, if the sample size in the survey had been 5,000, then the 5% would equate to 250 people, a better size to start analysing and likely to be more representative of the total population.

The calculation to find the actual number represented by a percentage is as follows.

- Divide the total sample by 100 to find what 1% represents.
- Multiply the product of this calculation by the percentage you are interested in to find the actual number represented by that percentage.

In this example the calculations would be:

$$(5,000 \div 100) = 50 = 1\%.$$

So 5% is then:

$$50 \times 5 = 250$$

Basic statistical analysis

It is useful to be familiar with basic statistical analysis of data produced during a research survey.

Distribution The 'normal distribution' defines the range of probabilities of many naturally occurring events. A normal distribution will often occur in marketing research data as a series of results for a range of options in a question or survey. An example is shown in Figures 8 and 9.

Figure 8 *Normal distribution data*

Question: On average, how many days a week do you visit a supermarket?

1 day	2 days	3 days	4 days	5 days	6 days	7 days

The results were:

1 day	2 days	3 days	4 days	5 days	6 days	7 days
40	75	100	120	60	15	10

Total sample = 420 respondents.

Histograms Looking like a bar chart, a histogram is a graphical representation of a distribution. For the data in Figure 8, the resulting histogram is shown in Figure 9.

Mode The mode is the most frequently occurring value. The mode represents the largest group within a set of data, which is why the largest group is often referred to as the 'modal group'. In

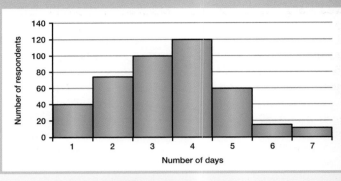

Figure 9 *A histogram*

Number of respondents / Number of days

Figures 8, 9 and 10 the modal group is represented by respondents who said '4 days', with 120 respondents.

Median The median is middle value, the central point in a distribution, 50%, the 50th percentile. For the data in Figure 8 the middle point will be represented by the 210th respondent. In the data in Figure 8 the 210th response is 3 days.

Mean Short for 'arithmetic mean', this is the statistical term meaning the 'average' within a distribution of numbers. From the data in Figure 8 the arithmetic mean is calculated by multiplying the hours by the number of respondents who ticked each respective box, adding the total together and dividing by the number of respondents, 420.

$$(1 \times 40)+(2 \times 75)+(3 \times 100)+(4 \times 120)+(5 \times 60)+(6 \times 15)+(7 \times 10) =$$
$$1430 \div 420 = 3.4 \text{ days}$$

Re-analysis of secondary data

It is often possible to analyse secondary data and extract information that meets a new research requirement. Data may have been collected and given an initial analysis to meet one particular marketing need. This does not necessarily mean that that data is of no further use. Quite often it can be re-analysed to meet a new requirement, to answer a new set of questions. Care must be taken when dealing with any secondary data by checking

- that it remains valid;
- that it is not out-of-date;
- that the sample size is large enough to stand re-analysis;
- that it will not result in tiny cell sizes which may not be representative;
- that market conditions have not changed significantly since the research was first carried out.

One common use of the re-analysis of secondary data is when research findings collected for marketing planning purposes are re analysed with the objective of supporting a sales initiative. For example, continuous audit data that has been collected to inform the marketing team about market share and used for planning can be represented in a form that can be used by the sales team to persuade retailers that they should increase stocks of a particular product.

Another example could be when consumer awareness data is collected as part of a hall test aimed at testing consumer reaction to new products. The data on new products will have been used by the product development team, the main objective of the research. The data on consumer awareness can be re-analysed and used by the sales team to encourage higher stock levels on account of greater demand from consumers, or to provide data for trade promotion, such as a press release or advertisement in the trade press, promoting the business and its brands.

Commercially published research reports on different markets can also be re-analysed and used. Again, there will have been a primary objective for the research, but there may be extracts of the data that can be used and analysed to provide different information. A published report listing the main brands in a market could be re-analysed to reveal the main manufacturers, corporate competitors, by grouping brands from the different manufacturers and seeing how the market is split once this has been done – is it the same, has it changed, which is now the most important business/competitor?

These are just examples and the usefulness of re-analysing secondary data will depend on how well it meets marketing objectives, like all marketing plans. But, it could be a very useful, low cost way of obtaining information about a market.

Using computer software for analysis

There is a number of software packages that are designed to make the manipulation, analysis and presentation of data much quicker and easier. In basic terms these will usually be spreadsheets or databases. The choice of which you use will depend on availability and access, the form of data and the ways in which the data will need to be analysed, manipulated and presented.

Most data manipulation software will enable the user to present the data in different types of chart – bar charts, columns, line graphs, pie charts, scatter graphs, stack charts and tables – whatever type is most user-friendly, so that the audience can more easily understand the data.

Examination practice · Focus groups

Having recorded five focus groups, a marketing team now has to decide how to extract the research findings from the audio tapes.

(a) **State THREE steps that will need to be followed during the analysis of this research.** (3 marks)

(b) **Explain how the findings from a focus group can be checked to increase the level of confidence in the research.** (4 marks)

Meeting the assessment criteria - examiners' guidance

Figure 10

Average Weekly Circulation of a magazine 1 July-31 December 2001- 8,448 copies
Readership: all adults total readership each week - 30,000

Readership profile
Socio-economic group

	A	B	CI	C2	D	E
%	6	53	25	7	6	3

Age group	0-14	15-24	25-34	35-44	45-54	55-64	65+
%	3.0	15.4	29.5	26.9	17.2	6.0	1.0

All parts of this question relate to Figure 10.

(a) Identify the modal group of readers in terms of socio-economic group and age group. **(1 mark)**

Exemplar responses
Socio-economic group: B
Age group: 25-34
(candidates need to get both parts correct for the 1 mark, only one part correct = no mark.)

Mark allocation
1 mark if both parts correct. **(1 mark)**

(b) Explain why the modal group could be an important piece of information for developing marketing plans for this magazine. **(6 marks)**

Exemplar responses
• *Largest group of readers – need to attract advertisers whose products appeal to this main group – can develop appropriate marketing plans – plans supported by research more likely to be successful.*
• *Valuable asset – identifies profile of the largest group of readers - can be sold as an advantage to advertisers whose customer profile matches/is a similar modal group – will help generate more income for the magazine.*
• *Shows who is currently attracted to magazine in greatest numbers – indicates who magazine should be aimed at to increase sales – this will lead to targeted marketing plans – likely to appeal more to target market.*

Mark allocation
1 mark for why should be included (maximum 3 marks).
1 mark applied to why important for developing marketing plans (maximum 3 marks). **(6 marks)**

(c) Identify **ONE** major weakness in the reliability of the data in Figure 10 and state why this could cause problems if it is used to promote advertising sales. **(2 marks)**

Exemplar responses
• *Out of date – data no longer valid.*
• *No source given – not credible/may not be believed.*

Mark allocation
1 mark for weakness.
1 mark for stating why this could cause a problem. **(2 marks)**

29 Analysing marketing campaigns 1

Marketing campaigns

A marketing campaign is usually a relatively short burst of tactical promotional activity designed to achieve specific, short-term objectives, such as increased market share, the launch of a new product or raising awareness. It may be based on just one of the variables of the marketing mix (product, price, place, promotion) or it may incorporate a number of these. Even within one of these variables, a campaign could be based on a single method, such as advertising, or even a single medium, such as television advertising. In practice, however, most marketing campaigns will be made up of a combination of methods and media, depending on how the organisation running the campaign decides to communicate with its target audience and on the budget available. Long-term marketing campaigns will usually be a result of an organisation applying different marketing plans to support its long-term business strategy.

Good marketing campaigns are based on sound marketing plans, which set out aims and objectives, outline proposed marketing activities and cost the activities against the potential returns. The key to analysing marketing campaigns is 'the more you see and experience the more you will be able to understand what is going on'. However, unless the ground rules are known, familiar structures are recognised and the language being used is understood, it may be difficult to fully 'read' a campaign. To read a campaign means looking beneath the slick surface of the media to see it for what it is, to interpret what is going on and identify its aims and objectives, and not just accept it at face value.

All marketing campaigns will have been planned by an organisation to deliver a message to the target audience. It is usually the role of an advertising agency to take a core message and present it to the target audience in a way that is attractive and memorable, and to help the organisation achieve the objectives established when the campaign was in the planning stage. There is a number of basic features to look for and identify in any marketing campaign, as shown in Figure 1.

Figure 1 *Basic features of marketing campaigns*

The main beneficiaries

The target audience

Marketing campaigns

The purpose of the campaign

The organisation running the campaign

Whose campaign is it?

Various organisations run marketing campaigns.

A commercial organisation This may be a business, such as a producer, a manufacturer, an importer or a distributor. It may also be a retailer. Commercial service providers like cinemas, theatres, music venues, banks, building societies, dry cleaners and all other private services would also fall into this category.

An official body This includes departments of central government, a local authority or a town council.

Community services These include the police, the fire service, a local health authority or a local education authority. They may also be organisations within any of these, such as schools, universities or hospitals.

Non-government organisations (NGOs) These include bodies such as charities.

Individuals Depending on the objectives of the campaign, it could be an individual who has something to market. This could range from a local advertiser with something to sell, to well-known celebrities who want to promote their name and reputation to keep them in front of the target audience.

Behind every campaign there will be an originating business, organisation or individual. Establishing the originator of the campaign is usually straightforward because most marketing campaigns promote the name or brand name behind the campaign. Often the name will be repeated throughout the campaign to reinforce it to the audience, with the aim of getting it into people's memory. However, some organisations prefer a more subtle approach and will tease the audience throughout the campaign to generate interest. But at the end, the name will still be revealed, because that is what the target audience will buy.

Who is the target audience?

Organisations and people developing their own marketing plans will need to clearly identify their target market. A fundamental part of the marketing planning is establishing who you want to receive the message from the marketing campaign and who the campaign is aimed at.

- It could be a **mass market** that sees, understands, is informed or entertained by and is expected to react to the campaign in some way, usually by buying something.
- It could be aimed at a specific, highly targeted or **niche market**.

Some organisations even create a campaign that is difficult to understand or even disliked by the mass market. However, the audience in the target market that it is aimed at will love the campaign, will identify with it and will respond positively. An example is shown in Figure 2.

Most organisations running a marketing campaign will have a core audience that it is aimed at and any other markets that see

Figure 2 *Marketing the Crazy Frog ringtone*

In the 2004-05 campaign for the Crazy Frog ringtone, research showed that a huge section of the television audience hated the advertisement, thought that it was annoying and were completely turned off. However, for the target market – young people with money to spend on mobile phones - the advertisement was perfect. It represented a challenge to authority figures (parents), was considered to be extremely fashionable, created a bond between young people who wanted to annoy their elders and link with their peers, and in so doing turned the Crazy Frog into the biggest selling ringtone of all time, and turned its creators into multimillionaires.

and react positively towards the campaign will be a bonus. It is possible to identify whether you are part of a target audience by watching a range of television commercials. Which do you like, understand and can see the point of, or which products might you buy? The chances are that you will be in the target market for these products. Which don't you understand, cannot see the point of or cannot relate to? If this is the case, you may not be in the target market for the products in these advertisements. The same principles can be applied to looking at promotions in other media, such as radio, press, cinema or poster. It is not always easy to identify the target audience from simply observing a marketing campaign. However, the marketing plan that has been produced by the organisation behind it, such as the advertiser, will state clearly who the campaign is aimed at. When trying to identify the target market or audience for other campaigns, such as a competitor, assumptions may need to be made. These should be based on skill and judgement and built up from experience. Sometimes it may be necessary to 'stereotype' and to base assumptions on pre-conceived ideas that are considered to be typical of certain audiences. There are dangers in this because stereotypes do not always behave as expected and can easily mislead. The only way to be certain is to check through marketing research.

What is the purpose of the campaign?

Any marketing campaign will have a purpose.
For a business it may be to inform about the launch a new product or to sell more of an existing product.
For a service it may be to raise awareness of the service or to attract customers.
An organisation may just want to alert the audience to something that is about to happen. For example, a Regional

Health Authority may want to inform the local population that a new walk-in health centre is to open in the area.
As with identifying the target market, looking at and comparing a range of campaigns will highlight the different products and messages that can be communicated through marketing campaigns. However, sometimes identifying the exact purpose of a campaign may be difficult. For example, a major manufacturing organisation may be running a marketing campaign. What is its exact purpose? If it has a strong brand name it could be running a corporate campaign just to promote its name. It may be trying to create an image for its brand to attract customers wherever the brand name is applied. This tactic is used successfully by businesses such as Nike and Virgin, where the brand name is used on a wide range of products with little to connect them apart from the name.

Further, whilst most campaigns will have a clear, single purpose, some will use the opportunity to send out more than one message. For example, when a new shop is about to open it may promote the date to raise awareness amongst its target audience for customers, but also use the campaign to recruit new staff. In this example it would be difficult to judge the primary reason for the campaign without additional knowledge or analysis of the timing and weight of the campaign. Whilst it is important to promote the fact of opening the new shop, without staff it would not be able to function.

When analysing a campaign it is important to keep an open mind about its purpose. It may be the most obvious 'top line' message or it may have secondary, underlying aims to meet.

Who benefits from the campaign?

There may be **direct** beneficiaries and **indirect** beneficiaries of a marketing campaign depending on the objectives of the campaign. What is superficially apparent may not always indicate the primary beneficiary of a campaign. For example, certain campaigns that appear to be promoting a new product may have the campaign paid for by the manufacturer whose products appear to be the focus of the campaign. But the most direct beneficiary is more likely to be the retail organisations that stock the product.

Similarly, press advertisements that feature a range of different goods, such as electrical items on sale at a particular retailer, could create different benefits for different organisations:
- the retailer will be raising its profile and promoting the fact that it has a range of up-to-date goods at attractive prices;
- the manufacturers of the goods featured in the advertisement will be raising awareness of their brands and products.

But who has paid for the advertisement? It may be the retailer or it could be the manufacturers because the retailer expects a contribution to the cost of advertising if it features certain manufacturers or brands. Indeed, advertising support may be a requirement that is set by the retailer for stocking a new product. In this situation the manufacturer will benefit because it has secured distribution, but this must be offset by the expense incurred by the contribution to advertising. Another example is shown in Table 1.

Identifying who benefits and by how much can get even more complex when benefits of a campaign could be created for retailers, manufacturers, brand owners, parent companies and a

Table 1 *BOGOF promotion effects*

A product is available on a 'buy one get one free' (BOGOF) offer in certain retail outlets.

Retailer benefits
- Increased sales.
- Increased turnover and profit.

Manufacturer benefits
- Increased distribution and sales out of its factory.
- Gain competitive advantage because, if its products are being promoted, the chances are that its competitors' products are not.
- Increasing the volume of consumer purchases, which will keep the consumer out of the market while it uses up the products and removing the opportunity of buying competitors' products.

wide range of other stakeholders that may be associated with the business. The network of benefits could stretch even further if associated businesses and support services, such as printers, packers, transport and distribution organisations, and creative services like designers and advertising agencies are taken into account.

Again, it pays to look beyond the obvious 'top line' beneficiaries and consider who else is likely to derive benefit from a marketing campaign.

Detailed analysis

Having established the basic features of a campaign, a more detailed analysis can be achieved by finding out the following.

Timings This includes information about:
- start dates;
- finish dates;
- duration;
- when the target audience was exposed to the campaign, i.e. daytime/night time/breakfast/drive-times/pre-watershed (before 21.00)/post-watershed (after 21.00).

Media being used Which media have been used, i.e. TV, press, cinema, poster, out of home or others? Were the media used singly, sequentially or together? What were the effects of this? Did it add strength to the campaign, or did it dilute the effect and stretch it over a long time scale?

Weighting What did the campaign achieve in terms of audience size, coverage, frequency, opportunities to see? What can you quantify?

Share of voice Share of voice can be important when trying to create an image that is perhaps larger than life. Of all the advertising or campaign activity that has occurred, what proportion was accounted for by the campaign under analysis? For example, a campaign that has an expenditure of £50,000 in a market that only spends £200,000 in a year will have a greater share of voice (25%) than if the £50,000 had been spent in a

market that has total spending measured in £millions. If advertising spots for the campaign appear in every commercial break during the period it is run, then it will have a greater share of voice than the spots have only been shown twice a day. A campaign that includes editorial coverage as well as a front cover feature and paid for advertisements in the same issue of a magazine will appear to dominate the issue and is likely to have a greater share of voice, i.e. available space, than other advertisers that may have just one page or part of a page. Share of voice can be important when trying to create an image that is perhaps larger than life.

The cost of the campaign What are the costs of the campaign and are these figures claimed or actual? To make a campaign appear to be greater than it actually is, figures can be manipulated and presented so as to make them appear more impressive. For example, an advertiser may claim to have a £1 million campaign. Analysis may reveal that the £1 million was based on 'rate card' - the top-line figure quoted by media owners when they are selling their media space. In reality, discounts could have been applied to bring the real spending down to a fraction of the figure claimed.

Another way of inflating the value of a campaign is to claim 'national equivalent'. This phrase is often used when a campaign is run in a small geographic area and the cost in that area is grossed up to what it would be if the campaign were run across the entire country. So actual spending of £100,000 in an area that represents 10% of the country could be presented as a £1 million national equivalent campaign. The only way to find out the true spending is to look at invoices or published figures.

Specific objectives Unless someone has been involved in making the decisions or has access to the stated objectives, they will have to make considered judgements about what the objectives of a campaign may be. The quality of this kind of judgement can be improved with supporting evidence or data and using reliable sources. However care must be taken when analysing objectives. Sometimes objectives may be published in mission statements or in PR/publicity announcements made about a forthcoming campaign. For example, an organisation may state that it wants to increase market share or that it wants everyone in the target market to know about its new product. In this case the stated objectives are likely to be general and obvious, but may mask an underlying set of secondary objectives, such as to defeat competitors or to deflect attention away from other activities in which the organisation may be engaged.

In addition to the declared or primary objectives there may be secondary aims or objectives. For example, a campaign may have a primary objective, such as selling-in the product to a retail chain and securing new distribution that can be built on in the future. Secondary objectives that could result could be that new consumers are attracted and try the product or that there is an increase in market share as sales increase as a result of greater distribution.

The effects of the campaign on the target audience
Whatever the stated objectives, the success of any campaign rests largely with the target audience and how it responds. Most successful campaigns will meet the objectives set to a greater or lesser degree. A **cost:benefit analysis** will help quantify this. However, the advertising world is littered with campaigns that set out with all of the right intentions, were researched well and met

Figure 3 *Marketing campaigns*

- The 1990 'Creature Comforts' animated television commercials for Heat Electric, achieved critical success, but were thought by many viewers to be for gas central heating. Ironically it was British Gas that sponsored the 2003 series of 'Creature Comforts' films.
- With a tremendous marketing campaign in 1985 the Coca-Cola Company launched a new flavoured version of its famous drink. Despite the high media spending, loyal Coke drinkers broadly rejected the drink and the launch was generally viewed as a marketing failure. However, the subsequent return to the original tasting drink with the relaunch of 'Coke Classic' catapulted the brand back to the number one slot in the carbonated beverages market. So was the 'New Coke' really a failure or just a step along the way to the prime objective of becoming the market leader?

of the criteria in the marketing brief, only to fail miserably because the target audience reacted in a way that had not been predicted. Some examples are shown in Figure 3.

When analysing a campaign you need to consider the effects on the target audience and also be aware that a campaign is likely to have an effect on an audience that may see the campaign, but is outside of the target market. This is known as a '**halo effect**'. If the response is positive, such as a sale, then it can be counted as a success, a bonus that had not been expected. However, it could also have a negative effect. This may not be a problem as the people outside of the target audience would probably not buy or respond positively anyway. If it is a negative effect on an audience that is outside of the target market at the moment, but may become the target audience later as they get older or their family relationship changes, then it could be a problem. Whilst some consumer markets are fickle, others have extremely long memories. A negative reaction at a young age could become a resistance to buying as the consumer gets older. This has been the case with many brands that focused on a narrow market, excluded the rest of the market and are now considered by a new generation of consumers to be old fashioned or too closely associated with the old market.

Outcome As a result of a campaign, what is the outcome? What is likely to happen next, as a result of the campaign? Depending on the objectives, it may be nothing - it may be that the objectives are met and that the product or organisation that was the focus of the campaign becomes a market leader. It may be that the campaign was so successful that the business can afford to repeat it. Conversely, it may have been so unsuccessful that the business fires its advertising agency or even goes bust.

Finding information

How can the information above be found? As is often the case in marketing, the solution will lie in marketing research.

Primary research Direct, primary research could be used to measure and monitor facts about a campaign, such as start and finish dates, weighting or frequency. Retail auditing could be used to measure sales in and sales out and the resulting market share. If it is important enough and if there is sufficient budget, market research could be arranged to interview people and ask what they think about a campaign.

Secondary research Secondary research will also be very useful. Trade or business press will often carry reports on marketing campaigns and give details such as a description of the campaign or advertising, where and when it will occur and the weighting or marketing spending. Post campaign reports could give details of how successful, or not, a campaign has been.

Opinion Some information can be gathered by applying subjective opinion, based on observation. This may involve just looking at and studying the campaign and recording your own or others' opinions. It may also be worth applying quantitative analysis to support these opinions. Quantitative analysis will come from measuring and monitoring and using quantitative data that have been researched from other sources.

To analyse marketing campaigns effectively involves pulling together as much information as possible to find what kind of picture it paints of the overall campaign. It is important to note sources of information to demonstrate the quality and authenticity of the data. When presenting findings it is also important to match any report to the needs of the target audience. Figure 4 shows a checklist that can be used to analyse a marketing campaign.

Figure 4 *Campaign Analysis Checklist*

Title.

Whose campaign is it? Who is behind it?

Who is the campaign for? Who is the target audience?

What is the purpose of the campaign? What are the aims and objectives?

Who benefits from the campaign?

Timings: Start dates – Finish dates – Duration.

Media used.

Weighting – Spend - Share of voice.

Specific objectives.

Constraints.

Effects.

Outcome.

Sources.

Report produced by:

Date:

examination practice · **Clinton Ltd**

Clinton Ltd, a property development company. It is interested in past, current and future trends in the housing market. In 2005 it was developing a number of properties in city areas. Most were high specification, luxury apartments. It has been running a marketing campaign for the last six months, aiming at attracting business people looking for a base near to work to buy. The campaign involved local radio advertising, billboard posters and articles in local newspapers and some national 'housing' magazines. Last month it commissioned a report to evaluate the success of this campaign.

(a) **State why it is important to date a report that is produced for a marketing campaign analysis.**
(1 mark)

(b) **Explain why it is important to try to identify the objectives of a campaign that is being analysed.**
(4 marks)

(c) **State TWO relevant sources of secondary data that the business could use, justifying the use of each source.**
(4 marks)

Meeting the assessment criteria - examiners' guidance

In the mid-2000s growing numbers of people were buying flats and apartments in city centres. Medway, a manufacturer of homeware products, has recently launched a marketing campaign to promote its products to younger couples and single people living in apartments.

(a) State TWO important pieces of information that could be included in the analysis of a marketing campaign. For each piece of information explain why it is important to the analysis. **(6 marks)**

Exemplar responses
- *Whose campaign is it – to identify who is behind campaign – puts analysis in context.*
- *Who is the campaign for – to identify target audience – help to understand objectives/measure level of success.*
- *What is the purpose of the campaign?/What are the aims and objectives? – identifies point of campaign - will enable success campaign to be measured.*
- *Who benefits from the campaign? – helps increase understanding – indicates broader issues that may result from campaign.*
(Award mark for other points from Campaign Analysis Checklist.)

Mark allocation
1 mark for each piece of information.
1 mark for why important to analysis.
1 mark for application to analysis. **(1 + 1 + 1) x 2 = (6 marks)**

(b) Describe ONE way of accessing information about Medway's objectives for inclusion in the analysis of a marketing campaign. **(2 marks)**

Exemplar responses
- *Trade press – found at local business library.*
- *Obtain copy of the marketing plan – available from business under study/own resources.*

Mark allocation
1 mark for basic source.
1 mark for description of method of access. **(2 marks)**

Analysing your own campaign

Section 29 looked at how to analyse marketing campaigns that have been carried out by other businesses. This section looks at how individuals or businesses might analyse and evaluate marketing campaigns that they have carried out themselves.

It is good practice to make sure that all marketing campaigns are based on sound marketing plans, which should set aims and objectives, outline proposed marketing activity and cost the planned activity against the potential return on investment. Analysing campaigns in any detail will be difficult unless you have direct involvement or access to the facts, figures and objectives behind a campaign. This will be more likely when working on your own marketing campaigns or campaigns where you are part of the marketing team.

The Campaign Analysis Checklist used for analysing marketing campaigns in Figure 4 of section 29 should be a useful starting point and give a structure to the analysis. It will contain the following headings.

- Campaign Analysis Checklist.
- Title.
- Subject of the campaign (product, product group, brand)
- Target audience.
- Purpose of the campaign – the aims and objectives.
- Who benefits from the campaign.
- Timings including start dates, finish dates and duration.
- Media used.
- Weighting – spending – share of voice.
- Specific, quantifiable objectives.
- Constraints.
- Effects.
- Outcome.
- Sources.
- Details of who has produced the report.
- The date of the report.

The main difference between analysing other campaigns, such as a competitor's and your own campaign, is that:

- it should be more objective as you are more likely to have access to the precise objectives, the marketing plan the campaign was based on and data relating to the results of the campaign, such as sales figures and primary marketing research;
- it should be actionable. An analysis for its own sake may be interesting, but it would be a waste of time if it did not have some actionable outcomes. These could be new objectives or recommendations for future campaigns, things that went well and/or things that did not work well and should be avoided in future campaigns, new ideas, tactics that could be used to improve the business, strategies that may need to be followed to maintain direction and suggestions for further primary research.

You will also have an opportunity of identifying any constraints that were applied to the campaign.

Figure 1 *Internal constraints on marketing campaigns*

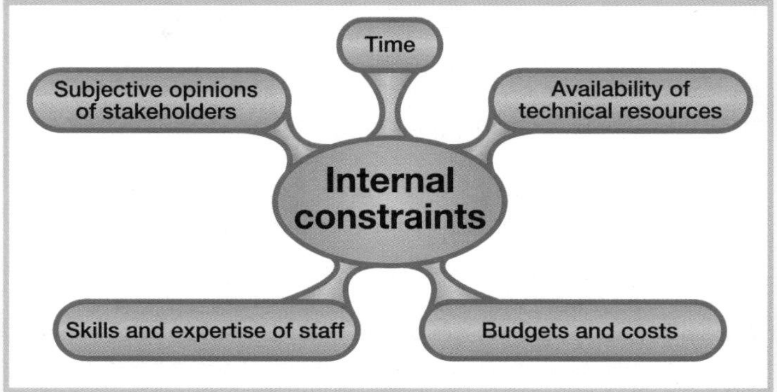

Constraints on marketing campaigns

Like all other business activity, a marketing campaign will usually be subject to constraints in one form or another. Constraints may have the effect of restricting the content or extent of the campaign to a level that can be supported, or afforded, by the business. They may also have the effect of changing planned activity. This is not necessarily a bad thing, as it is often the case that the revised marketing campaign that results from constraints is often better thought through and more focused than the original campaign.

Constraints come in many different forms and have different effects.

- They may originate from within the organisation itself – **internal constraints**.
- They may be imposed from outside the organisation – **external constraints**. You need to recognise and understand the most common constraints and how they can affect decisions regarding the marketing campaigns planned by a business.

Internal constraints

These originate and are applied from within the business or organisation itself. They are likely to be set and controlled by the senior management or influential stakeholders of the business or organisation. They may stem from the resources available, management decisions or corporate ethos. Each can have the effect of slowing, changing or halting promotional plans and campaigns. The internal constraints that have the most direct effect are based on resources, as shown in Figure 1.

Budget and costs All business activity carries a cost implication. This means that in a well-run business all activity is likely to be subject to scrutiny based on the degree to which the activity meets the aims and objectives of the business and the cost of the activity required to meet these aims and objectives. If the activity meets the aims and objectives within a budget that can be afforded, then it is likely to be judged as 'cost effective'. If it meets the aims and objectives but at a high cost, or at a cost that takes all of the profit that is generated from sales that result from the activity, then it may not be considered to be cost effective. A cost:benefit analysis is a useful way of judging whether a marketing campaign is likely to be cost effective.

Time Time may be felt as an internal constraint when linked to marketing plans and other business plans for the organisation. Once set, business plans will have a time element to them as they will have to be developed, launched and completed in line with the aims and objectives that they are designed to achieve. It would be no good running a marketing campaign over a three year period if the plans for the business wanted results within a six month period to achieve budget for the current financial year, or to meet the date for the next annual report to shareholders.

Skills and expertise of staff Whether a business has the skills and expertise to plan, produce and run a marketing campaign with its own human resources can be identified by conducting a skills audit. This will be a check on each member of the marketing team and any other team that may be involved in the promotion, such as the sales team or a technical team that is mainly employed in product development. You never know what skills exist within a team unless you make inquiries and find out. If people within the business do have the skills required, all well and good, providing they are briefed adequately on what is required for the campaign and the business is confident that whatever marketing campaigns are developed internally, they are appropriate for the market place and as good as, if not better than, those of competitors.

Availability of technical resources Quite often a business may decide that whilst it may have access to suitable creative skills internally, it does not have the technical skills to produce the support material that is required for marketing activity. For example, it would be unusual for a typical business to have its own skills and resources for the production of audio, film or television commercials.

Subjective opinions of stakeholders The internal constraints that have been mentioned so far (budgets, time, skills and expertise of staff and availability of technical resources) are likely to be objective, actual constraints that could be overcome. There is also the possibility that constraints may be less objective and positively subjective. These constraints may be based on the ideas, opinions, bias, prejudices, technophobia, previous agreements, or ethical beliefs of influential stakeholders in the business.

External constraints

These originate outside the business and are usually beyond the direct control of an organisation, but can affect the plans for marketing campaigns nonetheless. They may be set, applied and controlled by a range of organisations, such as the government, the European Union (EU), or a non-government organisation (NGO) such as a trade or industry association. External constraints are designed to protect society and individuals from being offended, cheated, misled or exploited by unethical marketing activity.

The external constraints that have the most direct effect on marketing campaigns are shown in Figure 2.

Regulation These are standards of operating and operating

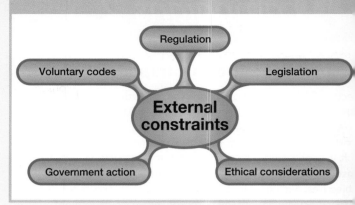

Figure 2 *External constraints on marketing campaigns*

procedures, rules, instructions and requirements that are not explicitly based on legislation, but on executive powers given to a regulator or the organisation that is setting and enforcing the regulations. Two important regulators in the marketing industry are:

● the Office of Communications (Ofcom);
● the Advertising Standards Authority (ASA).

Both can have a particular constraint on marketing plans as they regulate broadcast media and other advertising media. Also, CAP (the Committee of Advertising Practice) publishes the British Code of Advertising, Sales Promotion and Direct Marketing – the 'rule book' for non-broadcast advertisements, sales promotions and direct marketing communications.

Other examples of regulation in the context of marketing campaigns would include regulations given to exhibitors at major exhibition halls, which tell exhibitors what they can do, cannot do, must do and must not do before, during and after attending the exhibition. Legislation will always be a back-up option should a business fail to recognise the power of the regulator.

Full details of the regulation of marketing activity by Ofcom, ASA and CAP can be found at:

● www.ofcom.org.uk
● www.asa.org.uk
● www.cap.org.uk.

Legislation There is a great deal of legislation that could affect marketing campaigns. Most of this legislation has resulted from the objective of protecting consumers. The Trading Standards Central website (www.tradingstandards.gov.uk) is a good place to investigate to get some idea of just how much legislation exists to protect consumers, that could affect business and could constrain marketing campaigns.

There is no need to learn every part of every piece of legislation for unit 10. But it is useful to understand how the principal pieces of consumer protection legislation can affect marketing campaigns. Some examples are shown in Table 1.

Before any marketing plans and marketing campaigns are put into practice it is always worth checking them against current legislation to make sure that no offences are likely to occur, no legislation is broken, as a result of the campaign. Once a potential constraint has been identified, steps can be taken and plans can be changed to avoid the effect of any constraint and reduce the chance of breaking the law.

Table 2 *Effects of legislation on marketing campaigns*

Legislation	Effect
CONSUMER PROTECTION ACT 1987	Prohibits the supply of goods not in accordance with the general safety requirement or are unsafe and provides for the safety and protection of consumers, by enabling Regulations or orders to be made controlling consumer goods.
DATA PROTECTION ACT 1998	Affects the collection, storage and use of personal and financial data.
SALE OF GOODS ACT 1979 and SALE AND SUPPLY OF GOODS 1994 and SALE OF GOODS (AMENDMENT) ACT 1995	Details the rights of purchasers and the duties of sellers in the sale of goods.
SUPPLY OF GOODS AND SERVICES ACT 1982	Details the rights of purchasers and the duties of suppliers of services.
TRADE DESCRIPTIONS ACT 1968	Prohibits the misdescription of the supply of goods, and prohibits false claims for services, accommodation and facilities.

The Office of Fair Trading provides very useful general advice on consumer rights in the UK. It also provides information relating to businesses and markets (www.oft.gov.uk). Legislation in the UK is also increasingly affected by EU legislation.

Voluntary codes These are terms under which an organisation or industry agrees to operate to reduce the need for legislation or regulation. Examples include:
● the Voluntary Code of Practice for the Fast Food Industry – options for reducing fast food litter and waste in the local environment;
● the Banking Code – a voluntary code followed by banks and building societies in their relations with personal customers in the United Kingdom.

Each industry is likely to have some form of voluntary code, so it is worth investigating any that you may become involved with during your development of marketing plans or your analysis and evaluation of marketing campaigns.

Government action This external constraint is beyond the control of most businesses. It is the constraining effect of government action such as changes in the economy brought about by changes in tax, subsidies or other economic measures that affect interest rates (see section 69). Such changes can affect trade investment, consumer activity and consumer spending, and thus affect sales forecasts. Government action may also include new legislation that is brought in that had not been foreseen when planning marketing activity, such as limiting sales to certain markets, restricting advertising content, or restricting the time at which advertisements are shown. These are just examples of constraints that have happened in the past and may constrain marketing activity in the future.

Ethical considerations These are decisions or ways of conducting business that are based on how an industry or organisation believes that it should be conducting business in the best interests of its customers, employees and society in general. Ethical considerations include personal and corporate integrity, environmental responsibility, social responsibility and a general company policy or code of operating that would be considered to be good behaviour by the industry.

How this constrains marketing is that ethical aspects of a plan or marketing campaign should be considered before it is launched, to make sure that it does not cause offence or other problems that may have a detrimental effect on the ability of the campaign to meet its aims and objectives.

Ethical standards will differ within different industries and different markets. You will need to investigate each promotional activity separately, as and when they occur.

Evaluation of marketing campaigns

When evaluating a marketing campaign it is easy to become subjective and open to interpretation and excuses. However, a marketing campaign is rarely cheap and a business should evaluate it in an objective way before committing to spending the money. After the campaign has been run it must also be checked, to see if it has achieved the objectives set. Whenever possible, objectives need to be quantifiable.

Aims may start out as general ideas, for example:
● to launch a new product;
● to send information or a particular message to consumers in the market;
● to meet sales or distribution targets;
● to increase market share;
● to become market leader;
● to let the target market know that the service is now available in this area.

Depending on the business, examples of quantifiable objectives, based on these aims, are shown in Table 2.

Table 2 *Marketing objectives based on aims*

Aims may be things like	Depending on the business, examples of typical objectives, based on these aims could be
To launch a new product	to gain distribution in x'000 shops
To send information or a particular message to consumers in the market	to sign-up x'000 new customers as a result of hearing the promotional message to produce x'00 sales leads
To meet sales or distribution targets	to sell x'000 items by the end of the promotion
To increase market share	to move market share from 22% to 25%
To become the market leader	to overtake competition and grow market share to over 38%
To let the target market know the service is now available in this area	to get 10 phone call enquiries each day and convert at least one of these enquiries to an actual sale

Whether or not these objectives have been achieved can only be measured effectively by:

- monitoring and analysing business data such as sales figures, monitoring results and measuring effects such as actual rate of sales, changes in sales, sales in (to retailers) and sales out (to consumers);
- collecting primary market research data.

Methods of evaluation

The main types of marketing research that can be employed to evaluate marketing campaigns are shown in Figure 3.

Figure 3 *Evaluating marketing campaigns*

Retail audits/auditing This is the collection of sales data from a panel of retailers that represent the market. Auditors visit shops on a regular, fixed cycle, which may be weekly, monthly or bi-monthly depending on the rate of sale of the goods being audited. The auditors do a stock-count. They then add to this the figures for deliveries from manufacturers and suppliers since the last visit and compare the result with the stock-count figure from the previous visit. The difference shows how much has been sold during the period from the last visit, in either units or value terms. Retail audits are usually carried out for manufacturers and suppliers to obtain market share and rate of sale data about the market, their own goods and competitors' goods.

Continuous monitoring By auditing on a regular basis any change that occurs during the period of a campaign will be seen as

a change in market share or rate of sale. This type of research is classified as 'continuous monitoring'. Continuous monitoring can also be used to detect changes in awareness of a brand name, product or message contained in advertising, or other consumer behaviour, such as product usage or frequency of purchase. This type of research would be conducted by monitoring a panel of consumers, noting their behaviour and changes to behaviour that can be explained as a result of promotion or other activity.

Pre and post campaign measurement This method of market research is based on collecting data on the target market before a campaign starts, then collecting data using the same questions after the campaign has finished. The difference between the two sets of data should show by how much the target market has changed as a result of the campaign.

An example of this would be to measure what percentage of the target market has heard of a given brand name before a campaign, such as advertising, starts. When advertising is finished, ask the same question to measure the percentage that has heard of the particular brand name. The difference in percentage will indicate how effective the advertising has been.

This type of marketing research can be done using telephone or face-to-face interviews. It could be a tailor-made piece of primary research or it may be more cost effective to include such questions on an omnibus survey. Attitudes and opinions of marketing campaigns can also be included in focus group research. Some organisations use research panels – a fixed group of respondents that are contacted on a regular basis and used for marketing research. The fact that the panel remains relatively stable means that it can be used to measure changes in awareness, attitude and opinion over time. But to be representative of the population at large, the make up of the panel needs to be representative to start with and monitored to check that it continues to remain representative.

What is measured pre and post promotion will depend on the aims and objectives that have been set for the marketing campaign. The same technique can be used for any kind of marketing campaign so long as a measurement is taken before the campaign starts to benchmark, to establish a basic level from which any changes as a result of the campaign can be measured.

Evaluation and measurement

To mean anything at all analysis and evaluation must be measurable. At the end of the day, any analysis or evaluation of a marketing campaign will need to address some very basic questions, including the following:

- Did it work?
- Did it achieve what was planned?
- Did it meet aims/objectives?
- Are there any other benefits/problems that have arisen as a result of this marketing campaign? And if so, is there anything that needs to be done about it?

Examination practice · Avin Pettersfield

Avin Pettersfield is a manufacturer of timber-framed buildings, including outhouses, sheds and conservatories, in the South West of England. It buys in wood from both the UK and abroad and stores it in a local yard. It then produces its frames, often in bespoke sizes, to a client's specifications.

In the last year there has been a great debate amongst directors about the marketing of the business. Some want it to move forward and sell to greater numbers of people, with all the implications of financial responsibilities that this might place on the company. This might involve national promotions geared at stressing its quality against other competitors. The business has always relied on its own marketing director to handle promotions, but this type of expansion would require an advertising agency to be brought in. Other directors want the business to remain as a smaller operation, selling to a target market.

As a compromise the company has decided to expand its promotion into a wider area of the South West, instead of concentrating on towns within a 50 mile radius. Its latest promotion included advertisements in local newspapers, local radio promotions and direct mail to households within a number of cities in the area. The aim was to attract large numbers to request details about the business and to visit the website.

(a) **Describe TWO internal constraints that could have an effect on a marketing campaign designed to change the corporate image of a business.** **(4 marks)**

(b) **Explain ONE reason why it is important to consider external constraints before launching a marketing campaign.** **(4 marks)**

(c) **Discuss suitable methods that the business may use to evaluate its marketing campaign.** **(4 marks)**

Meeting the assessment criteria - examiners' guidance

You have been asked to evaluate a recent advertising campaign that has been run by the business where you work. The advertising was designed to support the sell-in of a new product into the retail trade and to generate consumer sales out of the retailers.

(a) Give TWO examples of quantitative measures that can be used to evaluate this marketing campaign. **(2 marks)**

Exemplar responses
- *Volume of goods sold.*
- *Value of goods sold.*
- *Number of retailers that take/stock the new product.*
- *Actual consumer sales out of the shops.*

Mark allocation
1 mark for each quantitative measure. **(2 marks)**

(b) Explain how marketing research could be used to analyse and evaluate the extent to which the advertising campaign has created awareness of the new product amongst consumers.

(4 marks)

Exemplar responses
- *Benchmark current level of awareness - run a series of focus groups before and after campaign – plan structure of discussion to include awareness of advertising/new product – measure actual level of awareness within focus group.*
- *Measure current level/pre-campaign of awareness – include questions on omnibus survey – repeat questions in omnibus survey after campaign – measure the pre and post campaign levels and draw conclusions.*

Mark allocation
1 mark for noting pre-campaign measure.
1 mark for appropriate method of marketing research.
1 mark for how awareness research would be included.
1 mark for noting need to measure actual awareness post-campaign.
(4 marks)

31 The need for and importance of finance

Why businesses need finance

Businesses have to pay for the resources that they use. For example, they need money to pay for premises, equipment, raw materials and components, labour, electricity and many other resources. Once a business is established, the money needed to pay for these resources will come from the revenue generated from the sale of products. However, money will also be needed before trading begins. This money will have to be provided by the owners or borrowed from organisations outside the business, such as a bank. Even when a business is trading it might need extra money to finance the purchase of some new equipment or expand its activities, for example. Mike Summers, a sole trader, runs a wine bar in Bristol called Xappers. The finance for his business is shown in Figure 1.

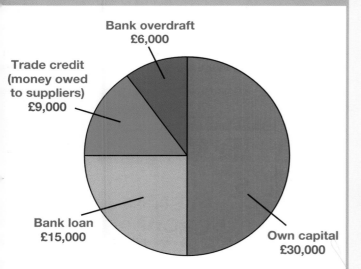

Figure 1 *Finance for Xappers*

Bank overdraft £6,000

Trade credit (money owed to suppliers) £9,000

Bank loan £15,000

Own capital £30,000

Mike Summers opened Xappers in 2004 with his own money. However, the business did well and Mike expanded by extending the premises and investing in some expensive lighting and modern furniture. To do this he used money from the bank and other sources. The current finance used by the business, including that raised for expansion, is shown in the pie chart.

Half of the money used to finance the business is provided by Mike. A bank has lent £15,000 to the business in the form of a loan and also provided a £6,000 overdraft. The business owes £9,000 to suppliers for goods such as beers, wines and spirits that have been purchased on credit.

Capital expenditure and revenue expenditure

All the money spent by a business falls into two categories.

Capital expenditure Spending on the purchase, alteration or improvement of fixed assets is called capital expenditure. Fixed assets are those assets that are intended for repeated and continued use. They are not intended for resale. Examples include premises, plant and machinery, computers and vehicles. Fixed assets are normally expected to have a life span of more than one year. Some fixed assets, such as buildings, last for many decades. It is important to remember that only the purchase of fixed assets is classified as capital expenditure. Money spent renting or hiring fixed assets is not capital expenditure. Details of capital expenditure by a business will appear on the **balance sheet**. This is because it involves the purchase of fixed assets.

Revenue expenditure Money used to meet the day-to-day running costs of a business is called revenue expenditure. Examples are wages, raw materials, fuel, advertising, accountancy fees and insurance. All revenue expenditure is spending on resources that have already been used by the business, or resources that will be used within one year. Revenue expenditure also includes the maintenance and repair of fixed assets. Details of revenue expenditure by a business will appear in the **profit and loss** account because it represents business costs or expenses.

Table 1 shows how spending by a haulage company on an articulated lorry is divided between capital and revenue expenditure.

Table 1 *Examples of capital and revenue expenditure*

Capital expenditure	Revenue expenditure
Purchase and delivery cost	Road tax
Painting logo on trailer	Insurance
Initial driver training	Fuel
	Servicing, repairs and MOT
	Drivers' wages

Long-term and short-term finance

The sources of finance used by a business can be classified as long-term or short-term.
- Money that is borrowed for less than one year is said to be a short-term source of funds.
- Money that is borrowed for more than one year is long-term finance.

However, the length of time long-term sources of finance are made available can vary significantly. For example, a bank loan may be provided for just two or three years. On the other hand a mortgage, a loan secured against property, may be for up to 30 years.

The length of time money is lent by banks and other finance providers is a key issue in business. One reason is because different sources are required for different types of expenditure. Generally, long-term finance is used to fund capital expenditure and short-term finance is used to fund revenue expenditure. For example, a business is likely to take out a mortgage to pay for a new factory but use a bank overdraft to buy raw materials. However, there are exceptions to this. Another reason is cost. Long-term sources of finance tend to be cheaper than short-term sources of finance. For example, the rate of interest on a 25 year mortgage is likely to be less than that charged on a six month bank loan. These issues are examined more closely in section 32.

Long-term sources of finance

There are different sources of long-term finance available to a business.

Owners' capital Most people who set up a business expect to use some of their own money to meet start-up costs and get established. Providing capital is part of the risk that entrepreneurs take when going into business. Unless owners risk their own money they are not likely to persuade other lenders to provide finance. Owners such as sole traders and partners are likely to use savings, redundancy payments or money obtained from friends and relatives. Once the money has been invested in a business by owners it is likely to remain there for a long time – perhaps even the life of the business.

Share capital Limited companies can sell shares to raise finance. Share capital is sometimes referred to as permanent capital. This is because it is rarely redeemed, i.e. it is not repaid by the company. In private limited companies the shares are likely to be bought by the people who set up the business, such as a family. The shares in public limited companies are traded on the stock market. This means that anyone can buy them. In the UK, shares in most public limited companies are owned by financial institutions such as insurance companies and pension funds. Shares in private limited companies are transferred privately. They cannot be sold without the consent of the other shareholders. One of the main advantages of selling shares is that very large amounts of finance can be raised.

Loan capital Loan capital is money that has been borrowed for a lengthy period of time. There are several different sources.

- **Mortgages.** A mortgage is a secured loan. This means that assets such as land or property are used as security for the loan. If the borrower cannot meet the interest and capital repayments, the lender has the legal right to repossess the assets used as security. Mortgages are often taken out for long periods of time – 20 to 30 years is common. They are a popular source of finance because interest rates are relatively low.
- **Unsecured loans.** Some financial institutions may be prepared to lend money without security although this is very rare. This type of arrangement is called an unsecured loan. This exposes the lender to more risk. If the business cannot maintain repayments the lender may not be able to recover what is owed. Consequently, the interest rates charged on unsecured

loans tends to be relatively high.
- **Debentures.** A debenture (or corporate bond) is a loan to a limited company. Debenture holders are therefore creditors of a company. They are entitled to a fixed rate of return and the loan will be repaid on a fixed date. Debentures are usually secured against property belonging to the business. Since debenture holders are not owners they do not have any voting rights.
- **Hire purchase (HP).** Businesses may use HP to buy plant, machinery and equipment. A farmer buying a tractor, for example, may make a down-payment to the dealer and borrow the rest from a finance house over a five year period. Regular instalments will then be paid to the finance house over the five year period. The tractor would not legally belong to the farmer until the last instalment had been repaid. This means that the finance house has some security if the farmer cannot keep up the repayments.
- **Leasing.** Leasing is the same as renting. Businesses can lease property, vehicles, machinery or equipment if they cannot afford to buy it outright. It is also a good way of acquiring such resources if they are only needed for a short period of time. The leasing company also meets the cost of repairs and maintenance. However, if resources are leased for a long period of time it can be an expensive form of finance. In recent years a growing trend is for businesses to sell fixed assets for cash and lease them back from a specialist company. This is called sale and leaseback.
- **Venture capitalists and private equity financiers.** A growing number of businesses are turning to specialist financial institutions called venture capitalists or private equity financiers.

Figure 2 *An example of a large venture capital deal*

In July 2005, it was announced that NCP, the car parking business founded on bomb sites after the Second World War, was being sold to venture capitalists 3i for £555m. In addition to its car parking business, NCP employs over 2,500 traffic wardens who ticket illegally parked cars for 31 local authorities. This division of the business, called traffic management, has the most potential for growth. The sale to 3i puts a value of just under £70m on the 12% stake in the company owned by the management team, led by chief executive Bob MacNaughton. The 100-strong executive team is thought to be carrying this stake into the new business where it will increase to nearer 20%.

Source: adapted from the *Guardian* 23.7.2005.

for their funds. Venture capital is usually concentrated in the newer, fast growing sectors of the economy, such as the Internet, and over half of all funds invested in the UK are in hi-tech firms. The UK venture capital industry has invested almost £50bn in up to 23,000 companies since 1983. CinVen, 3i, Alchemy Partners and Texas Pacific are some examples of established venture capitalists. Some venture capitalists specialise in management buy-outs or buy-ins. Others look to buy stakes in companies, sometimes 100%, develop the company quickly and pull out after making a healthy profit. Some of the financing deals involving venture capitalists have become quite large in recent years. An example is shown in Figure 2.

- **Business angels**. Venture capital may be provided on a smaller scale by business angels. These are individuals who invest typically between £10,000 and £100,000 in small and medium-sized businesses, often in exchange for an equity stake. Most investments by angels are made in start-up or early stage development. Business angels are attracted into providing finance because they like being part of a new business development. They may also enjoy the gamble involved and be entitled to tax relief. Some are looking for ways of using spare funds.

- **Government and European Union (EU) assistance**. Businesses may be entitled to loans and grants from the government or the EU. Most finance is obtained through applications to local authorities and businesses often have to qualify for financial aid. For example, they may have to locate their premises in a particular area. One example of government assistance is the Small Firms Loan Guarantee Scheme. This is intended for small businesses that have no track record to borrow. Banks provide the finance and the government

Figure 4 *Leasing – advantages and disadvantages*

Lowther & Co is a small parcel delivery company. It owns 8 vehicles and employs 13 staff. During December it won a contract to deliver goods to retailers for the Christmas period. To fulfil the contract it needed to increase capacity. After weighing up the advantages and disadvantages it decided to lease a vehicle for December.

Advantages
No large sums of money needed to buy or use the vehicle.
Maintenance and service costs are not its responsibility.
Leasing companies offer the most up-to-date vehicles.
The vehicle was only needed for one month.

Disadvantages
Leasing is expensive over a long period of time (although here, where the vehicle is needed just for one month, this is not the case).
Loans cannot be secured on leased assets.
Leased equipment cannot be modified.

guarantees part of the loan. Loans guaranteed are from £5,000-£100,000 for new businesses and up to £250,000 for businesses over two years old.

Short-term finance

Examples of the types of short-term finance available to a business are outlined in Figure 3.

Internal sources of finance

All of the sources discussed above are external. This means the

Figure 3 *Short-term sources of finance*

Bank overdraft
Common and flexible. Interest is only paid when the business is overdrawn. Security is not normally required.

Bank loan
A rigid agreement where capital and interest are repaid in monthly instalments over an agreed time period.

Credit cards
Increasingly common – flexible and convenient. Up to 60 days' free credit if the amount owed at the end of the month is paid on time.

Hire purchase
A finance house may also provide short-term funding, e.g. a 12 month HP agreement to buy some tools.

Short-term sources of finance

Debt factoring
Involves borrowing money from specialists called factors using sales invoices as security. Can be expensive.

Trade credit
Involves buying resources and delaying payment for up to 90 days (depending on the supplier). However, cash discounts are lost.

Leasing
Leasing can also be a short-term source of finance. It involves renting or hiring resources such as premises, equipment and vehicles for a few days, weeks or months.

money is raised from sources outside the business. However, once a business is established it might consider internal sources of finance.

Retained profit Business owners will want to take some of the profit made during the year for themselves. However, it is common to retain a proportion of the profit to develop the business in the future. It may be held in reserve or invested immediately in new activities for example. More than half of all business funding comes from retained profit. It is the cheapest source of finance with no charges for interest, dividends and administration. Retained profit will appear in capital and reserves on the balance sheet.

Sale of assets Established businesses may from time to time sell unwanted assets to raise finance. For example, land, buildings, plant and machinery can all be sold for cash if they are no longer needed. Large companies may sell off parts of their organisation to raise finance. For example, in September 2005 Ford announced that it planned to sell Hertz, the car rental business for $5.6bn. Selling Hertz was part of Ford's plans to raise finance as it lost market share in the US. Another option increasingly favoured by companies is to raise money through a sale and leaseback. This

involves selling an asset, such as machinery or property, that the business wants to continue using. The asset will be bought by a specialist and leased back at an agreed price.

Working capital Another way of raising finance internally is to 'squeeze' working capital – the money used to fund day-to-day business activity. This might involve operating a 'tighter' credit policy, reducing stocks of raw materials and finished goods or delaying payment to suppliers and other creditors. However, if this method is used to buy fixed assets the liquidity of the business will suffer.

1. Visit three small local retailers to find out what sources of short-term finance they use. Choose different types of shops so that comparisons can be made.
2. You could prepare for the visits by designing a short questionnaire.
3. Write a brief report explaining what types of finance are used and why the owners have selected these methods.

Research task

Portfolio practice · Henderson, Miyeni and Phelps

Henderson, Miyeni and Phelps is a firm of chartered accountants. It has been trading for six years and is about to expand. It plans to buy some property for £310,000 and convert it into a suite of offices. The conversion will cost a further £55,000. The partnership plans to take out a mortgage for £250,000 to help pay for the property and its conversion. The remainder of the cost will be met by internal funding. When the business moves some new computer equipment will be purchased using HP. The business also has an overdraft facility up to £5,000.

(a) **Using this case as an example, explain what is meant by capital expenditure.**
(b) **What is meant by internal funding?**
(c) **Using examples from this case, explain the difference between long-term and short-term finance.**
(d) **Discuss whether a mortgage is an appropriate form of finance for the expansion of Henderson, Miyeni and Phelps.**

Meeting the assessment criteria - examiners' guidance

You need to write a report analysing the financing needs of your chosen business including both short-term and long-term finance and an analysis of the finance used.

Business example - Greggs plc

Greggs is the UK's leading baking retailer. The company operates over 1,000 shops and two-thirds of its business is the sale of shop-made sandwiches and freshly baked savouries such as pies, pasties and sausage rolls. These products are complimented with a range of sweet products, breads and rolls. In 2004 the company made an operating profit of £44.7m. Table 2 shows some financial details from its *Annual Report and Accounts*.

During the year Greggs' capital expenditure amounted to £25m. Much of this was used buying new shops and refurbishing existing ones. For example, facilities at Leeds and Edinburgh were extended. However, it also included new vehicles, land, buildings and plant.

Greggs financed most of its capital expenditure from internal sources although it raised £686,000 from the sale of ordinary shares. A further £2,259,000 was raised through the disposal of some investments.

Source: adapted from Greggs, *Annual Report and Accounts*, 2004.

Mark Band 1 *Identify the type of business and describe in simple terms the types of finance actually being used.*

Greggs is a public limited company. This means that some of its capital is raised from the sale of shares. Share capital is permanent capital, which means it is not likely to be redeemed. Greggs does not have very much loan capital. Only £105,000 is owed by the company in the long-term. About a third of Greggs' short-term finance comes from trade creditors. This form of finance involves buying goods such as raw materials from suppliers and paying for them later. The business also owes money to the tax authorities and to shareholders. Most of Gregg's capital expenditure has been funded internally. This means the business has used its own money, such as retained profit, to fund shop refurbishment, for example.

Mark Band 2 *In your report you must distinguish between short-term and long-term finance.*

Greggs is quite a large public limited company. It owns over 1,000 shops selling sandwiches and savouries. According to the information shown in Table 2, about two-thirds of the company's finance is long-term. Capital and reserves account for £157,158,000 of the company's total capital. This means that the company's activities are funded mainly from share capital and retained profit. Share capital is permanent, which means that it is likely to remain in the company as long as it continues to trade. About a third of Greggs' finance is short term. The information shows that £74,811,000 is owed in the short-term. This money must be repaid within one year. Greggs uses trade credit as a source of finance. This involves buying goods and paying later. During the year the company has carried out about £25m of capital expenditure. It appears that this investment has been

Table 2 *Greggs financial information, 2004*	
Sources of finance	**£000**
Capital and reserves	**157,158**
Creditors: amounts falling due within one year	
Trade creditors	25,467
Corporation tax	7,685
Proposed dividend (money owed to shareholders)	7,992
Other creditors	33,667
	74,811
Creditors: amounts falling due after one year	
Deferred government grant	**105**

funded internally – probably from retained profit.

Mark Band 3 *You need to demonstrate a detailed understanding of financing needs. For example, discuss when short-term and long-term finance is appropriate.*

Greggs is a public limited company. It operates a chain of shops selling sandwiches, pies and other savouries. In 2004 it made a profit of £44.7m. The majority of the company's capital is long-term. Its activities are financed mainly from share capital and reserves. Share capital is permanent capital which means it is not likely to be redeemed. Having a lot of permanent capital may be appropriate for Greggs because most of its assets are likely to be land and buildings. Greggs has a very small amount of long-term loan capital. This is in the form of a deferred government loan (£105,000). Having a low amount of long term loan capital is good because it means that interest does not have to be paid. During the year Greggs spent £25m on capital expenditure. This is spending on fixed assets. The money was used to acquire new shops and refurbish existing ones. The money to fund this expenditure appears to have been raised internally, from retained profit perhaps. This is evident because there is very little long-term loan capital. Finally, Greggs needs to buy raw materials and other resources to operate. This appears to be largely funded by trade credit - £25,467,000 is owed to trade creditors. This is an appropriate way to finance the purchase of resources, such as flour and other raw materials and resources. Money is also owed to the tax authorities and to shareholders. All short-term finance must be repaid within one year.

Factors affecting the choice of finance

Section 31 showed that businesses have a wide variety of different financing options to choose from. The majority are external sources and can be long-term or short-term. There are also some internal sources. Generally, when a business is deciding how to fund its activities, it will prefer to use the most cost-effective option. However, there may be a number of constraints which restrict the choice of finance for a business. For example, a sole trader is unlikely to raise finance by selling debentures. Debentures are generally used by public limited companies. Also, a business cannot use retained profit if it is making a loss. The factors that influence the choice of finance are summarised in Figure 1.

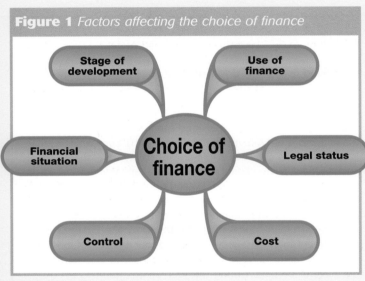

Figure 1 Factors affecting the choice of finance

Choice of finance

- Stage of development
- Use of finance
- Financial situation
- Legal status
- Control
- Cost

Legal status

Whether a business operates as a partnership or a public limited company, for example, can have an important influence on the source of finance used. Table 1 serves as a general guide to the effect legal status has on sources of finance. There are exceptions to the choices shown. For example, most government finance is intended for small and medium-sized businesses which tend to be sole traders, partnerships and private limited companies. Also, the use of debentures and sale and leaseback is more to do with size than legal status.

Public limited companies (plcs) have the greatest choice. They have access to all the different sources of finance except business angels. However, business angels may invest in small plcs. Private limited companies also have a wide choice of finance. All limited companies can raise finance by issuing shares. This is a big advantage since very large amounts of money can be raised through share issues as shown in Figure 2. Different types of business organisation may use sources of finance in slightly different ways. For example, a sole trader may use credit

Table 1 The effect of legal status on sources of finance

Source of finance	Sole trader	Partnership	Ltd Co.	PLC
Share capital	✗	✗	✔	✔
Mortgage	✔	✔	✔	✔
Unsecured loan	✔	✔	✔	✔
Debentures	✗	✗	✗	✔
Hire purchase	✔	✔	✔	✔
Venture capitalists	✗	✗	✔	✔
Business angels	✔	✔	✔	✗
Government & EU	✔	✔	✔	✔
Bank overdraft	✔	✔	✔	✔
Trade credit	✔	✔	✔	✔
Hire purchase	✔	✔	✔	✔
Leasing	✔	✔	✔	✔
Debt factoring	✔	✔	✔	✔
Credit cards	✔	✔	✔	✔
Retained profit	✔	✔	✔	✔
Sale and leaseback	✗	✗	✗	✔

cards to buy raw materials, fuel, small tools and equipment. A large plc may issue their executives with credit cards to meet travelling expenses such as hotels, flights and meals. Finally, although sole traders appear to have a fairly wide choice when it comes to raising funds, they often struggle to raise money. The reasons why are explained later in this section.

Use of finance

The type of spending for which funds are earmarked has a significant influence on the choice of finance. There are two general rules. Long-term finance is used to fund capital expenditure and short-term sources are used to fund revenue expenditure. The money used to fund revenue expenditure is often called **working capital**.

Financing capital expenditure Spending on resources such as plant, machinery, equipment and buildings generates a return for the business over a long period of time. Consequently, it makes sense to fund such spending with finance that is paid back over a long period of time. For this reason long-term sources of finance

Figure 2 Google share issue

Google, the Internet search engine, raised a massive $5.18bn in September 2005 from the sale of 14.2 million shares. Google said the money was for general corporate uses such as working capital and capital expenditure.

Source: adapted from thisisnewsandmoney.com.

re preferred for capital expenditure. Also, the amounts of money eeded to buy fixed assets tend to be quite high. Long-term ources, such as mortgages, HP, and debentures, are better for orrowing large amounts of money because more time is given for epayment.

inancing working capital (revenue expenditure) The type f finance used by firms to meet revenue expenditure is usually hort-term. This is because the resources purchased with working apital have already been used, or will be used very soon. It may ot be prudent to pay wages, for example, with a loan that will be epaid over three years. The majority of businesses use bank verdrafts, trade credit, factoring and leasing to help meet revenue xpenditure. Bank overdrafts are particularly useful to cope with harp fluctuations in revenue expenditure.

inancing growth Businesses tend to grow over long periods of me. Therefore long-term finance is usually used to finance it. irowth may be funded from retained profit, the sale of assets, nortgages, share issues and debentures, for example. Figure 3 xplains how T&F Informa issued some more shares to finance rowth. If businesses try to fund growth using short-term sources f finance they may encounter difficulties. They may end up **vertrading** and use up all of their financial resources.

ost

nevitably cost will affect a firm's choice when choosing a source of inance. Businesses will want to minimise costs, such as interest ayments and administration.

ong-term finance
- Issuing shares is expensive. Examples of costs when issuing shares include legal fees, publishing a prospectus, promoting the issue, underwriting the issue (paying an institution a fee to buy up any unsold shares) and administration such as printing, stationery, postage, data processing and processing payments. This can amount to thousands or millions of pounds depending on the size of the issue.

Figure 3 *Financing growth using a rights issue*

&F Informa is an international provider of specialist information nd services for the academic, professional and business ommunities. In June 2005 the company used a rights issue to und the acquisition of IIR Holdings, an American events business. A rights issue involves selling shares to existing shareholders. Informa offered their shareholders two new shares at 265p each for every 5 shares already held. This helped to raise £311m which contributed to the purchase cost of £768m for IIR. In a rights issue the shares are offered at a discount to encourage existing shareholders to buy them. In this case shares in T&F Informa were trading at around 360p at the time of the issue. The acquisition will help Informa to expand in the North American market.

Source: adapted from http://group.informa.com.

- At the other end of the cost scale a mortgage is relatively inexpensive. There is a lot of competition in the supply of mortgages and the interest rates charged are low compared with other types of loan capital. However, a business usually must provide security for a mortgage, such as property, and most financial institutions will only lend up to about 80% of the value of that property. There are also valuation fees, legal charges and administration costs to consider.

Short-term finance There is a lot of variation in the cost of short-term sources of finance.
- Trade credit is probably the cheapest, where payment is delayed after the purchase of resources. However, there may be hidden charges. By delaying payment a business may miss out on cash discounts for prompt payment.
- Credit cards can be a free source of finance if the amount owed at the end of the month is paid by the deadline date shown on the statement. However, once the deadline has been missed the interest rates charged are very high indeed.
- Bank overdrafts also tend to be relatively cheap, provided the overdraft limit is not exceeded.
- Interest rates charged on HP are quite high because finance houses are exposed to more risk.
- Leasing can be an expensive option if assets are leased over a long period of time.
- Factoring is becoming a popular source of finance. It is quite expensive, but many firms are forced to use this source because other sources have been denied to them.

Opportunity cost The cheapest source of finance of all is retained profit. Around half of all business finance comes from retained profit. There are no interest or administration charges and it is very convenient. However, there is an opportunity cost - a cost in 'forgone' alternative uses for the money. For example, profit is retained for business development it cannot be returned to the owners. In a plc, conflict between different stakeholders might arise. For example, shareholders might want high dividends and directors may want to retain profit to finance growth. Figure 4 shows how much profit has been retained by Carr's Milling Industries plc.

Tax issues Interest payments and other costs involved in the raising of finance are listed as costs in the profit and loss account. However, dividends are paid after tax. This is an important issue. Since interest payments can be offset against tax this reduces their true cost compared with dividend payments. This might encourage limited companies to borrow money rather than issue more share capital.

Financial situation

The financial circumstances of a business can act as a constraint when raising finance. Firms on a poor financial footing will find it difficult to raise finance and their choice of sources will be limited. It is generally the case that small and medium-sized businesses struggle to raise finance. This is because they have relatively few assets to use as security and their trading future may be uncertain. As a result they are often forced into using expensive sources of finance such as HP, leasing and factoring. Other finance providers consider them too risky. In contrast, firms that are financially sound find it much easier to attract finance and have

Figure 4 *Dividends and retained profit for Carr's Milling Industries 2000 – 2004*

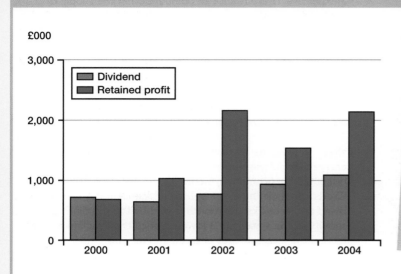

£000

Legend:
- Dividend
- Retained profit

Carr's Milling Industries is involved in a range of agricultural activities. The company produces cattle feed, fertiliser, farm supplies, machinery and cereals. Over the period shown Carr's has made a healthy profit each year. There does not appear to be a consistent relationship in this case between the size of dividends and the value of retained profit. For example, in 2000 more than half of the profit was returned to shareholders. In 2002, only about 25% was paid out in dividends. This may have been because the company wanted to use retained profit for investment purposes in 2002.

Source: adapted from Carr's Milling Industries, *Annual Report and Accounts*, 2004.

more choice. This is because they represent much lower risk to banks and other money lenders. They are also likely to be profitable which means they can use retained profit as a source of finance.

The **gearing** of a business is an important issue when considering its financial circumstances. Gearing deals with the relationship between the amount of finance raised from loans and the amount raised from shares (see section 31). Companies with a large proportion of loan capital are said to be highly geared. They may find it more difficult to attract funding because they are already heavily in debt. Highly geared companies will be particularly vulnerable if interest rates rise unexpectedly. Figure 5 shows the gearing of two companies.

Stage of development

New and developing businesses tend to be constrained when raising finance. Since they are not established their trading future is often uncertain. Consequently they present too much risk to money lenders. However, there are providers who specialise in new businesses and early stage development capital, such as business angels and venture capitalists. Unfortunately their interest comes at a cost. They will usually want a stake in the company which means they are entitled to a share in the profit. They may also want to get involved in decision making which can often impose difficult constraints. In contrast, established businesses can often attract funding more easily. They have a track record and a credit history which can be analysed by potential investors.

Figure 5 *Reg Vardy and Pendragon, gearing, 2004*

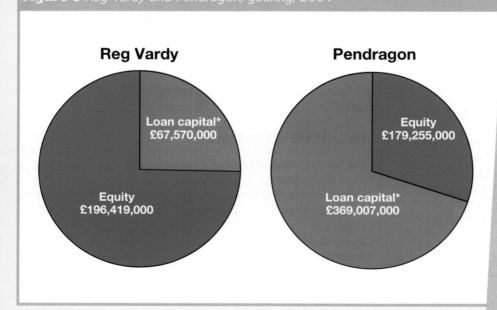

Reg Vardy

- Loan capital* £67,570,000
- Equity £196,419,000

Pendragon

- Equity £179,255,000
- Loan capital* £369,007,000

- Reg Vardy is one of the top retailers of new and used cars in the UK. It also has interests in contract hire, fleet supply and management and finance provision.

- Pendragon is also in the motor car retailing business. However, historically Pendragon has focused on the prestige car segment.

  According to the pie charts Pendragon is more highly geared than Reg Vardy. A very large proportion of its finance comes from borrowing. In contrast Reg Vardy is low geared, with only about a third of its long-term finance coming from loan capital.

* Loan capital here includes creditors; amounts falling due after one year plus provisions for liabilities and charges.

Source: adapted from Reg Vardy, Pendragon, *Annual Report and Accounts*, 2004.

Control

Raising fresh finance can have an effect on who controls a company. A limited company that raises new finance by issuing more shares dilutes control and share of profit. For example, if a company with 10,000 shares issues another 10,000, an existing shareholder with a 6% stake (600 ÷ 10,000 shares) will now only have a 3% stake (600 ÷ 20,000). The control and share of profit will fall by a half. However, there is no legal obligation for limited companies to pay dividends to shareholders. Even on a small scale control might be affected. For example, if a sole trader invites another person to contribute some capital, that person is likely to share profit and control. Using loans to raise fresh finance has no effect on the control of a business. Although in extreme circumstances, when a company is on the brink of collapse, an important creditor such as a bank may take control. Owners that use venture capitalists and business angels may also be forced into sharing profit and losing some control of their business when raising finance. Generally, business owners will prefer to raise money from loans rather than relinquishing control and having to share the profit.

Obtaining finance

Obtaining short-term finance is fairly straightforward if the business is established, solvent, and has a good track record and a bright trading future. Small companies may have to provide rather more information about their financial circumstances than larger companies. For example, a supplier may want trading references and undertake a credit search before offering trade credit.

Obtaining long-term finance can take longer. Obviously a share issue can take many months. A huge amount of legal work, administration and promotion has to be carried out. Legal information may have to be provided to the Stock Exchange for example. A prospectus outlining the history of the business, its future plans and how it proposes to use the funds raised may be published. Businesses taking out long-term loans and mortgages have to make formal applications. They may have to provide financial details and documents such as accounts and cash flow forecasts. Such applications can take several weeks or sometimes months. Similarly, applications for government funding can be demanding.

Most difficult of all is obtaining finance for new businesses. Start-up capital is often difficult to come by. This is because the majority of new businesses actually fail. Entrepreneurs will have to provide a detailed business plan, showing the aims and objectives of the business and how they will be met. Fund providers may want to interview entrepreneurs. In the case of larger ventures it may be necessary for entrepreneurs to give presentations to prospective investors and answer detailed questions. Making contact with potential investors may also be a problem. However, advice about sources of finance is available. Local governments, banks and specialist websites, for example, can provide information about sources of finance. There are also registers available with contact numbers for business angels and venture capitalists.

Long-term versus short-term finance

Businesses can experience difficulties if they fund their activities inappropriately. For example, businesses that try to rely too heavily on short-term sources might run out of cash. Using bank overdrafts, HP and leasing to acquire machinery and other fixed assets for too long can raise costs and drain working capital. Similarly, if a business tries to fund rapid growth with short-term sources, it might run out of cash. This is because growth often requires heavy capital expenditure which might be better funded with long-term sources.

Using too much long-term capital may also be a problem. It is not prudent to fund the purchase of raw materials with a long-term loan, for example. The raw materials will be used to meet immediate orders and payment for them will be received fairly soon, long before the loan is repaid. However, there is a growing belief that businesses should perhaps make more use of long-term sources. They are often cheaper and provided spending is kept under control, a more solid financial foundation is built.

1. Obtain the Annual Report and Accounts of two companies.
2. Look at the balance sheets of each company and identify the amount of loan capital and the amount of share capital each is using.
3. Draw two pie charts like those in Figure 5.
4. Decide which is the most highly geared and write a brief report suggesting reasons why this is the case.

Research task

Meeting the assessment criteria - examiners' guidance

You need to write a report analysing the financing needs of your chosen business including both short-term and long-term finance and an analysis of the finance used.

Business example - Radstone Technology PLC

Radstone Technology PLC has two core businesses.
- The embedded computer business supplies the defence industry with computing subsystems. They specialise in the design of subsystems adapted to survive the most extreme military environments.
- The electronic manufacturing services business manufactures batches of complex electronic products for a range of international customers.

During the last financial year the company expanded by acquiring Bracknell-based Octec Ltd, for £10.8m. To help finance the acquisition about £6.5m was raised through the issue of some new shares. These were placed on the stock market. Brief details of the sources of finance used by Radstone are shown in Table 2.

Mark Band 1 *Your report must identify the type of business and describe in simple terms the types of finance available to that type of business. You also need to provide a basic description of the types of finance actually being used.*

Radstone Technology is a public limited company (plc). This means that it will have a wide variety of finance options. The only sources of finance not available to plcs is that provided by business angels. This is because business angels tend to invest in much smaller companies. Radstone Technology has used a bank overdraft and trade creditors to provide short-term finance. Most of the company's long-term finance is provided by shareholders. £46,472,000 is provided from capital and reserves. This will include ordinary share capital and retained profit. A further £17,099,000 of loan capital has also been used. Much of this has been borrowed from a bank. Finally, the company made an acquisition during the year. This was funded by issuing some more shares.

Table 2

Short-term finance	
Bank (including overdraft and other borrowings)	£3,759,000
Other creditors (including trade creditors)	£11,366,000
Long-term finance	
Bank and other borrowings	£17,099,000
Capital and reserves	£46,472,000

Source: adapted from Radstone Technology, *Annual Report and Accounts*, 2004.

Mark Band 2 *You must make a clear distinction in your report between financing in the short-term and the long-term. The focus here is the types of finance used by the company.*

Radstone Technology is a Hi-Tec company making complex electronic products. It is a public limited company (plc) and therefore has a wide variety of finance sources to choose from. Businesses use both short-term and long-term sources of finance. Short-term sources are normally used to fund revenue expenditure like wages, utility bills and raw materials. Long-term sources are used to fund capital expenditure. Money borrowed in the short-term must be repaid within one year. In this case Radstone has used a bank overdraft and trade credit as its main short-term sources. Long-term finance is borrowed for more than a year. In this case Radstone's main source of long-term finance is capital and reserves. This is permanent capital and is not likely to be redeemed. Radstone has also borrowed £17,099,000 from banks and other sources. This represents about a quarter of its long-term capital. This means Radstone is low geared. During the year Radstone bought Octec Ltd for £10.8m. Part of the money was raised by selling some new shares. The main advantage of this is that no interest has to be paid. However, control will be diluted and existing shareholders will have to share the profit with the new shareholders.

Mark Band 3 *You need to show a detailed understanding of financing needs and discuss when short-term and long-term finance is appropriate. You also need to discuss the risks or problems associated with each.*

Radstone Technology is a public limited company (plc). Plcs can raise finance from nearly all the sources available provided they are solvent and have a good credit history. The only source not available to them is business angels. This is because they only invest small amounts (up to £100,000) in businesses. This would be too small for a large plc. Radstone uses a combination of both short-term and long-term capital to finance its activities. A bank overdraft and trade credit, for example, is used to finance revenue expenditure. Radstone has around £15m of short-term finance. Long-term finance is provided by banks and similar institutions and shareholders. Around 75% of Radstone's long-term capital is permanent capital, i.e. not likely to be redeemed. Because Radstone's long-term capital is mainly equity, the company is low geared. This means that it is not heavily in debt. During the year the company expanded by purchasing Octec Ltd for £10.8m. This acquisition was partly funded by selling some new shares. This was a highly appropriate method of funding. Growth should be funded by long-term sources because growth is a long-term business activity. The return on the Octec investment will be generated over the life of the company. However, issuing new shares can be costly and control will be diluted. Existing shareholders may not be entirely happy with this. They will have to share the profit with more shareholders.

Portfolio practice · The Morstowe Fitness Centre

The Morstowe Fitness Centre operates as a partnership. It is currently owned by two former sportspeople who converted an old barn into a modern fitness centre. When the company was set up they both invested £60,000 of their own money and used a mortgage to borrow a further £80,000. The centre has been very successful and wants to expand. In particular it wants to build an extension to house a much larger social area where the bar facilities can be expanded and food supplied from a new kitchen. The expansion would cost £100,000. About £40,000 can be raised from retained profit and the partners are contemplating the introduction of a new partner to provide the other £60,000.

The business uses trade credit, a bank overdraft and credit cards to finance revenue expenditure. However, the company is often heavily overdrawn, particularly at the end of the year before membership fees are due. One of the partners reckons that in the future some of the equipment and fitness apparatus should be leased and not purchased outright.

(a) Using this case as an example explain the difference between trade credit and credit cards.
(b) Explain how leasing equipment in the future could help to avoid the business being overdrawn.
(c) Evaluate the advantages and disadvantages of introducing a new partner to help fund the expansion of the Morstowe Fitness Centre.

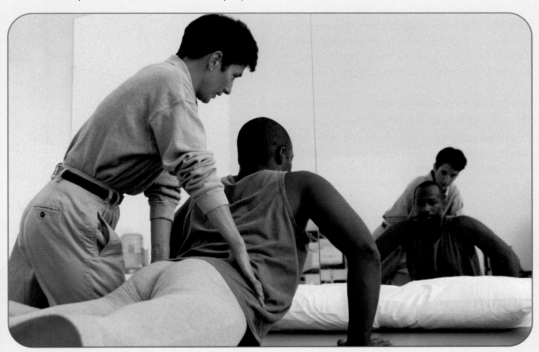

33 Working capital

What is working capital?

The money used by a business to fund revenue expenditure is called working capital or circulating capital. Working capital is used to buy resources, such as raw materials, components and fuel, and to meet other costs, such as wages, utility bills, accountancy fees and insurance. Working capital is not normally used to fund capital expenditure. The working capital of a business is the amount of money left over after all short-term debts have been met. It is the quantity of **liquid assets** owned by a business less the amount of money owed by the business in the short-term.

Liquid assets are those assets that are expected to be converted into cash within one year. The main examples of these are shown in Table 1, listed in order of liquidity, with the most liquid first.

The amount of stock held by a business varies considerably. It usually depends on the nature of the business. Figure 1 shows an example.

Money owed by a business in the short-term must be repaid by the end of the year and may include the following.

Bank overdraft Businesses do not normally remain overdrawn indefinitely. Overdrafts should be used to cope with fluctuations in expenditure. Consequently the money will be repaid within one year. For example, it is possible for a business to go overdrawn just for a few days.

Money owed on credit cards Ideally, this should be repaid as soon as it is due, typically about 25 days after the statement has been received. If it is not, the interest rates charged are very high – approaching 20% pa in some cases.

Table 1 Liquid assets

- Money in the bank.
- Investments such as shares in other companies or bonds owned by the business. However, it only includes shares and bonds that the business is able to 'cash in' within 12 months.
- Debtors. This is money owed by customers. This is likely to be received at least within 90 days. However, it depends on the credit period a business allows its customers.
- Prepayments. This is where a business pays for a resource in advance. For example, insurance premiums are often paid in advance.
- Stocks of finished goods. These may already be sold or are expected to be sold to customers very soon.
- Work-in-progress. Some products take time in the production process. For example, beer takes more than a week before it can be sold to customers. The value of any partly completed product is classified as a liquid asset.
- Stocks of raw materials and components. These are likely to be used up fairly soon by the business to make products. Businesses do not normally keep large quantities of such stocks for longer than is necessary.

Figure 1 *The amount of stock held out of liquid assets by Northern Foods and Reg Vardy, 2005*

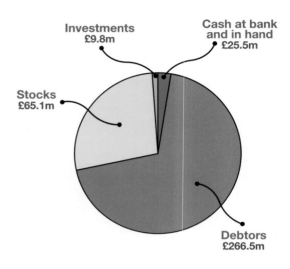

Northern Foods

Investments £9.8m
Cash at bank and in hand £25.5m
Stocks £65.1m
Debtors £266.5m

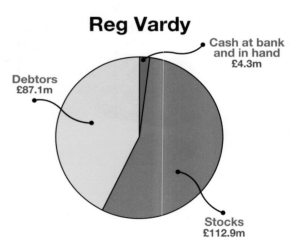

Reg Vardy

Cash at bank and in hand £4.3m
Debtors £87.1m
Stocks £112.9m

Reg Vardy's core business involves selling new and used cars from showrooms. Northern Foods is one of the UK's leading food producers. The pie charts show clearly that the are different amounts of stock held by the businesses. More than half of Reg Vardy's liquid resources are held in stock. In contrast, Northern Foods holds less than a quarter of its liquid resources in stock. The main reason for this is because Reg Vardy is a retailer and Northern Foods is a manufacturer. By its very nature, retailing involves holding stocks of goods for customers to see before they decide to buy.

Source: adapted from Northern Foods and Reg Vardy, *Annual Report and Accounts, 2004*

Trade credit Most businesses buy goods and services and pay for them later. For example, utility bills are usually sent out every three months and a further two weeks is allowed before they must be paid. The credit period offered by suppliers is typically 30 - 90 days.

Accruals An accrual is an amount of money due in an accounting period which is unpaid. It could be an electricity bill or an auditor's bill, for example. Accruals are often estimated because invoices have not been received stating the amount owed.

Taxes and National Insurance contributions Businesses collect income tax and National Insurance contributions from employees. There is usually a delay before it is eventually paid – perhaps up to a month.

Corporation tax Limited companies have to pay this tax on their profit. It is common to delay this payment for as long as possible – perhaps a few months.

Short-term bank loans By their nature, short-term bank loans are taken out for one year or less.

Hire purchase Some HP agreements can be short-term, such as one year or six months.

Dividends proposed Limited companies usually delay the payment of dividends for a period of time – perhaps a few months. There is usually a time lag between the dividend being finalised and payment to shareholders. This is because an AGM is usually held before dividends are sent out.

Calculating working capital

A simple calculation can be used to determine the value of working capital held by a business. This is shown in Figure 2.

Figure 2 *Calculating working capital*

Working capital = current assets − current liabilities.

Current assets are the liquid resources owned by a business outlined above. Current liabilities are the short-term borrowings of a business explained above. Current liabilities are sometimes referred to as Creditors: amounts falling due within one year. In a balance sheet the value of working capital is shown clearly. It is often referred to as **net current assets**. Figure 3 shows the balance sheet for Winters Timber Ltd.

The working capital cycle

The working capital cycle, sometimes called the operating cycle, is shown in Figure 4. It shows the movement of cash and other liquid resources into and out of a business. In many types of business, particularly manufacturing, there are delays or time lags between different stages of business activity. For example, there is a lag between buying resources such as raw materials and components

Figure 3 *Balance sheet for Winters Timber Ltd, 2005*

Winters Timber Ltd is a timber merchant. The value of working capital has been calculated in the balance sheet. It is referred to as net current assets. In 2005, the value of working capital was £235,000. It is calculated by subtracting creditors: amounts falling due in one year from current assets (£475,000 - £240,000). The balance sheet shows that the value of working capital has increased over the two years. The increase from £130,000 to £235,000 is quite significant. It is due mainly to a build-up of stock and an accumulation of cash.

Winters Timber Ltd
Balance sheet as at 31.12.05

	2005 £000s	2004 £000s
Fixed assets		
Tools, equipment & machinery	1,200	1,400
Vehicles	340	310
	1,540	1,710
Current assets		
Stock	230	160
Debtors	65	80
Cash at bank	180	100
	475	340
Creditors: amounts falling due in one year		
Trade creditors	120	105
Accruals	20	25
Taxation	100	80
	240	210
Net current assets	235	130
Creditors: amounts falling due after one year		
Mortgage	(500)	(500)
Net assets	1,275	1,340
Capital and reserves		
Share capital	200	200
Other reserves	115	540
Profit and loss account	960	600
	1,275	1,340

Figure 4 *The working capital cycle*

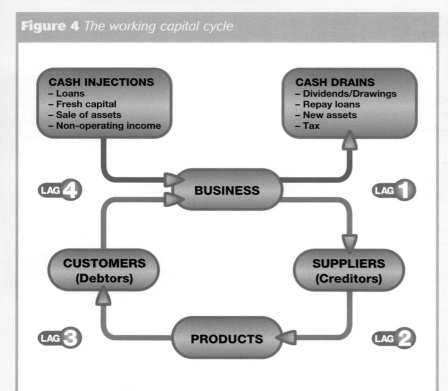

goods immediately because storage costs are high. However, this may not be possible because some firms have to keep stocks of finished goods to deal with sharp fluctuations in demand. For example, a toy manufacturer may stockpile products ready for the busy Christmas period. It is also possible that a business is struggling to sell its products.

Lag 4 The final delay in the working capital cycle is the time it takes for customers to pay for what they have bought. Many businesses sell goods on credit which means they may have to wait up to 90 days before payment is received. The length of this time lag will vary according to the nature of the business. For example, a taxi driver will not experience this time lag because customers pay what they owe at the end of the journey.

Cash injections The working capital cycle also show that cash comes into the business from sources other than revenue. Even when a business is established it is likely to borrow money and inject fresh capital. This might be used to fund expansion or develop new products, for example. A business may also sell some assets. It is quite common for large limited companies to sell parts of their organisation to provide an injection of cash. Figure 5 gives an example. Some businesses also receive non-operating income. Examples of this might be interest from bank deposits or dividends from shares owned.

Cash drains The working capital cycle also shows that cash will leak from the business in addition to payments made for resources. In limited companies dividends are likely to be paid to shareholders. In the case of sole traders and partnerships, owners may take money from the business for their own personal use. This is called drawings. A business will eventually have to repay loans to banks and other money lenders and pay tax to the Revenue and Customs. Cash is often used to buy new fixed assets such as machinery and equipment.

Recognising how the working capital cycle operates is important when managing working capital. This is explained in section 34.

and converting them into finished products ready for sale. Similarly, there is likely to be a delay between delivering goods to customers and receiving payments. These time lags occur in four distinct stages in the working capital cycle.

Lag 1 In order to make products or deliver services a business needs to acquire a range of resources. For example, a breakfast cereal manufacturer will need resources such as wheat, oats, sugar, flavourings, additives, dried fruit, electricity, water and other services. Many of these resources can be obtained from suppliers on credit. This means the manufacturer can obtain resources without having to pay for them immediately. It may be possible to delay payment for up to 90 days depending on the terms agreed with the supplier. When a business first starts trading, trade credit may not be granted until a sound trading record has been established.

Lag 2 Another time lag exists in the working capital cycle while resources are converted into products. This delay is caused by the production process which uses machinery, equipment, labour and other resources to make goods or deliver services. The length of this time lag will vary depending on what products are being made. For example, in agriculture it takes around nine months to produce cereal crops. This would be the time needed to prepare the land, plant the seeds, wait for them to grow and harvest the crop. However, many products can be made very quickly. For example, with modern technology it is possible to manufacturer a motor car in several hours. When supplying services this time lag is often quite short.

Lag 3 Once the production process has been completed goods are ready for customers. However, sometimes there may be a delay before finished goods can be delivered. This is because they are waiting to be sold. Most businesses would prefer to deliver

Figure 5 *Disposals by Unilever, 2004*

During the 2004 financial year Unilever, the global manufacturer of leading brands in food, home care and personal care, sold a number of assets to raise cash. In total, 492m euros was raised from the sale of a range of assets. Businesses sold included Puget Oils in France, its frozen pizza and baguette businesses in various European countries, Final Touch and Sunlight in North America, Capullo and Dalda Oils in Pakistan. In addition to various other fixed assets, trade marks were sold including Brut in the US and Latin America and a number of oral care brands in the US.

Source: adapted from Unilever, *Annual Reports and Accounts*, 2004.

Figure 6 *St Ives and Next working capital*

...ves is the UK's leading independent printer and operates in ...en main markets - books, direct response, financial, general ...mmercial printing, point of sale, magazines and multimedia. Next ... chain store marketing fashionable clothes. The table below ...ows the value of current assets, current liabilities and working ...pital for both companies. St Ives seems to be operating with an ...equate level of working capital. The value of its current assets is ...out 1.6 times the value of its current liabilities. This is within the ...eal' range often quoted. However, Next appears to have rather ...ss working capital. Its current assets are higher than its current ...bilities, but not as high as one and a half times their value. This ...robably does not matter though. Next is a retailer and all of its ...ales are probably for cash. It does not have to wait for customers ... pay. This is a big advantage in business and allows companies to ...perate with less working capital.

	Next plc	St Ives plc
Current assets	£710.2m	£149.8m
Current liabilities	£576.6m	£92.8m
Working capital	£133.6m	£57m

Source: adapted from Next, St Ives, *Annual Report and Accounts*, 2004.

How much working capital should a business hold?

The amount of working capital held by a business will vary according to the nature of the business. For example, retailers will tend to hold less because most of their sales are for cash which is immediately available for making payments. As a rule it is suggested that current assets should be between twice and one and a half times the size of current liabilities. Figure 6 shows two companies with different amounts of working capital.

The difference between cash and profit

It is important for a business to recognise the difference between cash and profit. In the short-term a business can survive without making a profit but it cannot survive if it has no cash. Profit and cash are not the same. At the end of the trading year the value of a firm's profit will not be the same as the amount of cash in the bank. There is a number of reasons for this.

- During the year a business may sell £1m of goods which cost a total of £750,000 to produce. This means that profit will be £250,000 (£1,000,000 - £750,000). However, if the business sells goods on credit some of the goods will not have been paid for. For example, if £30,000 is still owed by customers the amount of cash in the bank will be £220,000 (£250,000 − £30,000).
- A business may receive cash at the beginning of the financial year from credit sales made in the previous year. This will boost the bank balance but not increase profit. Also, a business may buy goods on credit from suppliers and not pay for them until the next trading year. This means that costs will not be the same as cash paid out.
- During the year fresh capital might be introduced by the owners. This will obviously boost the cash position but not affect profit. Capital is not included in the profit and loss account. The effect will be the same if the business raises finance from other sources.
- Purchases of fixed assets will reduce the cash balance but not affect profit. Again, this is because the purchase of fixed assets is not shown in the profit and loss account. Similarly, the sale of fixed assets will boost cash but not increase profit (unless a profit is made on disposal).
- The amount of cash in the bank at the end of the year will be different to profit because the bank balance at the beginning of the year is unlikely to be zero.

1. Obtain two Annual Reports and Accounts for two different types of business.
2. Look at the value of working capital for both companies and decide whether they are sufficient.
3. Write a brief report about the amount of working capital each company has and explain any differences that exist.

Research task

Meeting the assessment criteria - examiners' guidance

You need to write a report assessing the working capital management of a chosen business based on a recent set of accounts. You need to identify the components of working capital, calculate key ratios and interpret them, assess the adequacy of working capital management and make suggestions for improvement. This section focuses on the different components of working capital.

Business example - McBride plc

McBride is an established international company, with manufacturing operations throughout Europe, specialising in private label and contract manufacturing of laundry, household cleaning and personal care products. Examples of their UK brands include Clean Fresh, Surcare, Nova and Dentimint. Contract manufacturing involves making products for other companies such as the supermarkets own label brands. Table 2 shows the current assets and current liabilities for McBride in 2004.

Mark Band 1 *You need to identify correctly the components of working capital.*

McBride has £151m of short-term borrowings. It seems to be relying very heavily on trade credit and accruals for its short-term finance. This means that McBride is obtaining resources for production and delaying payment for them. This is quite a good source of finance because there is no interest. However, the company might be missing out on cash discounts. A big proportion of McBride's liquid resources are debtors. This means that the company is owed a lot by customers. This is one of the main lags in the working capital cycle but is acceptable if they pay on time. However, if there are bad debts this might leave the company short of working capital. The amount of

cash owned by McBride is also small in relation to other current assets. The working capital of a business can be calculated by subtracting the current liabilities from the current assets. The working capital for McBride is £2.9m (£153.9m - £151m).

Mark Band 2 *You need to comment on the types of working capital used by the business and whether or not it has adequate levels of working capital.*

McBride is a plc and has £153.9m of liquid resources. A significant amount of these liquid resources (about three quarters) relate to debtors. This is money owed by customers. It represents one of the time lags in the working capital cycle. This might be a problem for the company if customers are slow to pay or if they fail to pay. McBride has just £2.9m of working capital (£153.9m - £151m). This may be a bit low. Normally it is suggested that the value of current assets should be between twice and one and a half times the size of current liabilities. In this case current assets are only just greater than current liabilities. This means that the business may have liquidity problems. For example, if customers are slow to pay, McBride may struggle to pay off its short-term borrowings. Fortunately though, a lot of the working capital is funded by trade credit and accruals. Not only is this a cheap source of finance but it may also be possible to delay repayments. McBride is a manufacturer and sells its goods on credit. It could be argued that the company is operating with limited working capital, particularly if customers are slow to pay.

Table 2 *Current assets and current liabilities for McBride, 2004*

Current assets	£m
Stocks	38.8
Debtors	114.9
Cash at bank and in hand	0.2
	153.9
Current liabilities	
Bank overdrafts	2
Bank loans	1.2
Finance lease	0.3
Trade creditors	84.1
Corporate tax	1.2
Other tax and social security	10.9
Other creditors	16.2
Accruals	30.1
Dividends proposed	5
	151

Source: adapted from McBride *Annual Report and Accounts*, 2004.

Mark Band 3 *You need to evaluate the information relating to working capital.*

McBride is a manufacturer of household cleaning and personal care products. It supplies goods on credit to its international customers. This is evident because so much of the firm's working capital is tied up in debtors. About 75% of the company's entire current assets is accounted for by debtors. The time it takes customers to pay for what they have bought is one of the key time lags in the working capital cycle. This may not be a problem in itself but when you take into account the amount of cash the business has some would argue that the firm's working capital is inadequate. According to the information the company only has £200,000 cash. McBride has just £2.9m of working capital (£153.9m - £151m). As a general rule it is argued that a company's current assets should be between twice and one and a half times the size of current liabilities. In this case current assets are only just greater than current liabilities. It could argued that McBride is operating with insufficient working capital. Fortunately though, McBride uses cheap sources of finance to fund its working capital. Around £114.2m of its short-term borrowings are trade credit and accruals. This means that McBride is obtaining key production resources without having to pay for them immediately. Consequently the company may be able to operate comfortably with such a small amount of working capital. However, it would be prudent to monitor the situation because its cash resources are particularly small at the moment.

Portfolio practice · **Persimmon plc**

Persimmon is a construction company. It builds a variety of homes ranging from one bedroom apartments to five bedroom detached houses. In 2004 the company turned over £2.131bn and made an operating profit of £486m. The balance sheet on 31.12.04 showed that creditors: amounts falling due in one year, was £672.5m. More than half of this was borrowed from suppliers of materials and land. Figure 7 shows the current assets for Persimmon.

Source: adapted from Persimmon plc, *Annual Report and Accounts*, 2004

(a) **How much working capital does Persimmon have?**
(b) **Explain the pattern of current assets for Persimmon.**
(c) **In relation to the working capital cycle, which time lag is the longest for Persimmon? Explain your answer.**
(d) **Evaluate the components of working capital used by Persimmon.**

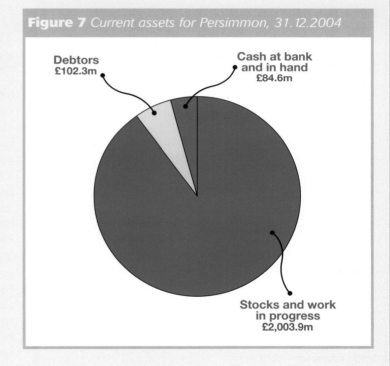

Figure 7 *Current assets for Persimmon, 31.12.2004*

Debtors £102.3m

Cash at bank and in hand £84.6m

Stocks and work in progress £2,003.9m

The importance of working capital management

The financial control of a business is vital. There are many aspects to financial control but the management of working capital is particularly important. This is because if a business runs out of cash it cannot survive. Managers must ensure that the business has enough liquid resources to meet payments when they become due. Certain payments are crucial and if they are not met the business could be forced to close. For example, if wages cannot be paid to staff they are not likely to work and the business may not be able to operate. Figure 1 shows an example of a business which experienced working capital problems.

> **Figure 1** *Running out of working capital*
>
> SWE FLY is a small airline based in Sweden. In June 2005, the airline began operating a new route between Leeds/Bradford and Lahore(Pakistan). However, in September the company was forced to cease operations. The notice below was posted on its website.
>
> Monday 26th September
> As previously stated, SWE FLY has suspended all payments and as a consequence has had to stop all flights from 2 September 2005. All SWE FLY aircraft have been repossessed and are now under the control of the respective owners outside of Sweden. SWE FLY therefore currently has no aircraft to operate. SWE FLY is actively investigating if other airlines are able to assist stranded passengers. Regretfully, SWE FLY has no funds and is still unable to help passengers financially. The owners and the management of SWE FLY regret having to bring such negative news to the public attention.
> SWE FLY management
>
> Source: adapted from SWE FLY website.

A business operating with inadequate working capital may lose out in other ways. For example, if a large and lucrative order is received from a customer, a business with insufficient working capital may not be able to afford the resources needed to meet the order. This may result in the order being turned down.

On the other hand, if the business has too many liquid resources, it could be argued that profitable opportunities are being missed. For example, the resources could be used to expand the business. This is discussed in more detail later.

The traditional approach to working capital management

Most businesses use short-term sources of finance to provide their working capital. For example, trade credit is used to obtain raw materials, a bank overdraft might be used to pay utility bills and credit cards might be used to pay an insurance premium. The reason for this is because such resources have either been used already (as in the case of utility bills) or will be used fairly soon. It therefore makes sense to fund such payments with short-term sources of finance, i.e. money that will be repaid fairly soon. It ma not be prudent to buy raw materials, for example, using a long-term bank loan. This is because repayments on the bank loan will continue long after the resources have been used and paid for by customers. Thus the resources purchased with the loan cannot sustain the repayments.

The modern approach to working capital management

In recent years a growing number of businesses have taken a different approach to managing working capital. The method is in contrast to the traditional approach and involves using more lon term sources of finance to pay for the day-to-day running of the business. Some of the reasons why this approach is used are explained below.

The permanent nature of some current assets The moder approach recognises the permanent nature of some current assets. Over a period of time, say a full trading year, many businesses have money tied up in current assets all of the time. A example is shown in Figure 2.

The costs and risks of short-term finance One of the main advantages of using long-term funds is that they are often cheape For example, the interest paid on a mortgage is much lower than that paid on a bank overdraft. Also, the costs and risks of some short-term capital can be a problem. Some short-term sources a hugely expensive. Debt factoring, unsecured bank loans, HP and credit cards (if the payment date is missed) can attract huge charges. These charges will reduce profit. Another problem with some short-term sources is that they can be withdrawn very quickly leaving a business without the resources it needs to operate. For example, a farmer missing some payments on a hire purchase agreement could find that a vital machine such as a tractor is repossessed. This might mean that the farmer is no longer able to run the business. It is also possible for a bank to 'c in' a bank overdraft. This means that the business has to pay back what it owes immediately. If it is not able to, the business could b forced into liquidation. Consequently, with more long-term fundi such costs and risks might be avoided.

Sale and leaseback More and more businesses are relying on leasing rather than purchasing for fixed assets. Leasing is usually

Figure 2 *Working capital for Crawford Ltd – extracts from the balance sheets*

[Cra]wford Ltd manufactures furniture in High Wycombe. Over the [thr]ee years shown the company has an increasing amount of [mo]ney invested in current assets (£7,480,000 in 2002 to [£9,]070,000 in 2004). If this money is invested all of the time then it [cou]ld be argued that the money invested should come from long [ter]m sources.

	2002 £000	2003 £000	2004 £000
Current assets			
Stock	2,780	3,110	3,320
Debtors	3,800	4,110	4,770
Cash at bank	900	1,050	980
	7,480	8,270	9,070
Current liabilities			
Trade credit	1,600	1,980	2,100
Short-term borrowings	1,000	1,200	1,320
Other creditors	2,100	3,050	3,890
	4,700	6,230	7,310
Working capital	**2,780**	**2,040**	**1,760**

Figure 3 *Novo Nordisk Ltd*

Novo Nordisk Ltd is the UK affiliate of Novo Nordisk A/C, with headquarters in Denmark. The company is a world leader in insulin and diabetes care and manufactures a range of other pharmaceutical products. In order to improve the management of its car fleet and release some valuable working capital, Hitachi Capital Vehicle Solutions were contracted to organise a sale and leaseback of their 160 - 170 car fleet. Norvo Nordisk's facilities manager, Neil Britland, said 'Carrying out a sale and leaseback has achieved several aims. We wanted to bring our fleet policy in line with other affiliates – all of whom lease their vehicles – and it also enabled us to release some capital. We have been able to simplify the administration of our fleet and budget forecasting has become a lot easier, because we have fixed costs'.

Source: adapted from www.novonordisk.com.

[cl]assified as short-term finance. However, if assets are being leased [in]definitely then there is a strong argument for using long-term [s]ources of finance to meet their expenditure. An increasing [n]umber of firms are selling their fixed assets to specialists and [le]asing them back. This helps to release valuable working capital, as [s]hown in Figure 3.

Funding problems faced by small businesses It is often said [t]hat small businesses in particular are undercapitalised. This means [t]hat they do not raise enough money from the owners when they [fir]st set up. Consequently they are forced into using the more [e]xpensive short-term sources of finance to fund their activities. If [o]wners were able to contribute more capital, the need to use [e]xpensive and more risky short-term sources would be reduced [s]ignificantly.

Working capital management tools

[It] is often said that working capital management is all about timing [–] making sure that the business has enough money to pay [im]portant bills when they arrive. In relation to the working capital [c]ycle discussed in section 33, it is about optimising the time lags. [F]or example, the time it takes to:

* produce and deliver products;
* sell them;
* and collect money from customers;

[s]hould all be minimised. On the other hand, the time taken to pay [s]uppliers for resources bought on credit should be maximised. [W]hen managing working capital a number of tools are available. [T]hese are summarised in Figure 4.

Credit control

Many businesses often have little choice but to offer their customers trade credit. Ideally, they would prefer customers to pay for their goods as soon as they are delivered. However, this may not be possible because of competitive pressure or common accepted business practice. If trade credit is offered to customers it is important to have a credit control system. This will help to make sure that only suitable customers are granted trade credit and ensure that they pay promptly. Figure 5 shows an example of a credit control procedure.

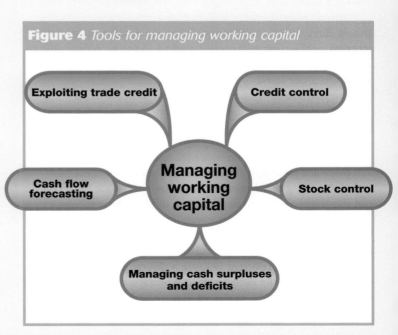

Figure 4 *Tools for managing working capital*

Figure 5 *Credit control procedure*

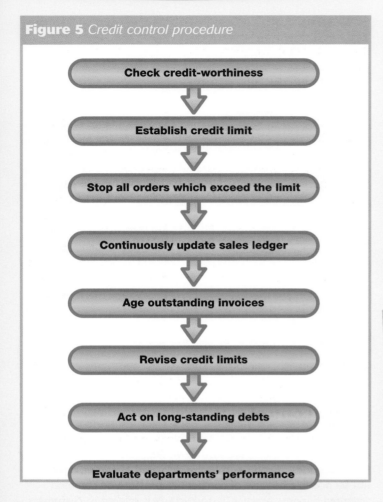

Check credit-worthiness

↓

Establish credit limit

↓

Stop all orders which exceed the limit

↓

Continuously update sales ledger

↓

Age outstanding invoices

↓

Revise credit limits

↓

Act on long-standing debts

↓

Evaluate departments' performance

Many firms are likely to check whether or not a new customer is creditworthy. They may do this by asking for supplier or bank references. Alternatively they may employ a specialist agent to do a check on their behalf. From the information gathered a business will set a credit limit according to the risk involved.

When an order exceeds the credit limit, the credit controller should carry out an investigation. Following this, the order may be stopped or the customer could be asked to pay an outstanding debt before the order is processed. Alternatively, it may be decided to let the order stand.

It is important to keep up to date records of customer transactions. For example, sending out another reminder when a bill has already been paid could damage customer relations. Every month the credit controller may 'age' all outstanding debts. This will identify customers who owe money over 30, 60 and 90 days.

If there are persistent debts the credit controller must take action. Assuming that statements and reminders have been sent out this might involve a telephone call to the debtor followed by a personal visit. As a last resort it may be necessary to take legal action. However, this may affect customer relations. Some firms employ debt factors to 'chase' customer debts. This helps to maintain customer relations because a different organisation attempts to claim the debt. Finally, the performance of the credit control function can be evaluated. This might be done using quantitative methods such as calculating the debt collection period

– the number of days on average it takes to collect debts. This is explored in section 35.

Finally, one way of encouraging prompt payment by customers is to offer cash discounts. If customers are offered, say, a 5% discount if they settle their account as soon as goods are delivered, they may be tempted to pay and cash flow will improve. Some firms offer 'staggered discounts'. This means that accounts settled immediately might get a 5% discount, accounts settled with 30 days might get a 2% discount and those settled within 60 days get 1%.

Stock control

Having too much money tied up in stock will drain working capital resources. There is a number of costs when holding stock. Figure 6 provides a summary.

Figure 6 *Costs associated with holding stock*

Opportunity cost - capital tied up in stock earns a zero financial return.
Storage and handling - e.g. warehousing space, lighting, heating and labour.
Spoilage - risk of stock perishing or becoming outdated.
Administration - placing and processing orders from stores.
Insurance - stocks may have to be insured against fire, damage or theft.
Out-of-stock costs - loss of revenue when stocks run out.
Theft and shrinkage - unfortunately large stock holdings may become targets for theft by staff and others.

Because of the cost disadvantages of holding high levels of stock, businesses have adopted a number of approaches to keep stock levels under control.

Economic order quantity (EOQ) Some businesses take a scientific approach to controlling stock. This involves calculating the level of stock that minimises costs. It takes into account the costs of holding stock, which rise with the amount of stock held, and the average cost of ordering stock, which fall as the size of the order increases. These two costs are balanced out when using a specific formula to calculate the EOQ.

Computerised stock control One way of keeping a tight control on stock levels is to use information technology. Computers can be used to decide when and how much stock to order. Entire details of stock holdings can be held on a computer database. All additions to and issues from stocks are recorded and up to date stock levels can be found instantly. Some systems are programmed to automatically order stock when the re-order level is reached. In most supermarkets, computerised check-out systems record every item of stock purchased by customers and automatically subtract items from stock levels. The packaging on each item contains a bar code which is passed over a scanner at the check-out. Store managers can check stock levels, stock values and the store's takings at anytime during the day.

ust-in-time approach A modern approach to stock control nvolves reducing stock levels almost to zero. It is based on two rinciples. First, stocks of raw materials and components arrive at he factory only when they are needed. When deliveries arrive, aterials are taken straight to the production line where they are eeded. They are not stored in warehouses. This means that it is ot necessary to hold stocks of raw materials and components. econd, goods are not produced unless they have been ordered. When production is complete the finished goods are transported traight to customers. This means that no stocks of finished goods re held. Since stock holdings are zero all stock holding costs are liminated. This means that working capital is not tied up in stock.

xploiting trade credit

usinesses that buy resources on trade credit can improve their vorking capital position by delaying payments to suppliers. Ideally, a usiness should try to ensure that the trade credit period it offers ustomers is shorter than the trade credit period it gets from uppliers. In practice this is difficult. Ensuring prompt payment from ustomers is notoriously a problem. The government has ddressed this problem and introduced the **Late Payment of ommercial Debts (Interest) Act, 1998**. The Act gives usinesses the right to charge interest on unpaid commercial ebts. It was hoped that these financial penalties would speed up ustomer payments. There is also the danger that suppliers will top deliveries if payments to them are delayed too much. This ould result in operating difficulties for a business.

Managing cash surpluses and deficits

One aspect of working capital management is dealing with cash urpluses and deficits. The investment of cash surpluses is xplained later in this unit. Cash deficits occur when cash outflows xceed cash inflows. Swift action is required if the business runs short of cash. Figure 7 shows the possible action that can be taken to deal with cash deficits. In all cases action must be taken quickly. Once cash deficits have been eliminated it is important to identify the cause and take measures to prevent it happening again.

Cash flow forecasting

Cash flow forecasts can be used to help identify times in the future when the business is likely to be short of cash. Cash flow forecasts show the expected cash inflows and outflows each month for a future period. Based on these cash flows, and the money that the business had to start with, it is possible to calculate the expected monthly cash balances. Consequently managers can take measures now to avoid cash difficulties later. For example, if the cash flow forecast shows that the business will be short of cash in seven months' time, managers can make arrangements to deal with the situation such as inject fresh capital, raise borrowing or cut expenditure. Preparing cash flow forecasts encourages managers to plan ahead and results in much better working capital management.

Dealing with surplus cash

Once a business is established and enjoying success it is possible that cash will accumulate. Surplus cash can be:
- returned to the owners, i.e. dividends can be increased;
- used to reduce borrowings which will improve gearing and lower costs;
- placed in reserve in case the business encounters difficulties in the future;
- reinvested in the business to meet capital expenditure or finance growth;
- used to buy back shares (this reduces the number of shares in circulation and means that existing shareholders receive a larger share of the profit in the future);
- invested in financial assets such as shares in other companies.

The investment of surplus cash can meet with problems. Conflict may arise if stakeholders disagree with the way cash is used. For example, the directors of a company may want to invest the cash in the business to fund expansion. However, the shareholders might prefer the cash to be returned to them or used to buy back shares. There may also be a wide range of investment opportunities and the business will have to decide which is the best option. They may have to undertake investment appraisal. This is discussed in sections 36 and 37.

Figure 7 *Dealing with cash deficits*

Sell off stocks of materials and components, below cost if necessary

Sell debts to a debt factor

Borrow money

cel all non-vital expenditure

Cash deficits

Step up action to collect debts

Extend credit with suppliers

Sell off unwanted fixed assets

Reduce drawings from business

Sell assets and lease them back

Generate cash sales, offering big discounts if necessary

---

1. Visit two local businesses and find out about the methods they use to manage working capital.
2. Prepare a questionnaire before your visit to help gather useful information.
3. Write a brief report comparing the methods used.

Research task

Meeting the assessment criteria - examiners' guidance

You need to write a report assessing the working capital management of a chosen business based on a recent set of accounts. You need to identify the components of working capital, calculate key ratios and interpret them, assess the adequacy of working capital management and make suggestions for improvement. This section focuses on managing working capital.

Business example - Molins plc

Molins is an international business providing high performance machinery and services for the production and packaging of consumer products. The company operates three divisions:

- **Tobacco Machinery** develops and manufactures secondary tobacco processing machinery for the global cigarette industry. They also supply spare parts.
- **Packaging Machinery** manufactures a range of packaging machinery such as cartoning machinery, case packers, flow wrapping machinery and vertical form fill and seal bagging machines.
- **Scientific Services** develops, assembles, sells and maintains process and quality control instruments for the tobacco industry.

2004 was a disappointing year for the company, mainly because of the poor performance of the Tobacco Machinery division. Underlying profit fell from £12.1m in 2003 to £2m in 2004. Some financial information is shown in Figure 8.

Figure 8 *Financial information for Molins, 2003 – 2004*

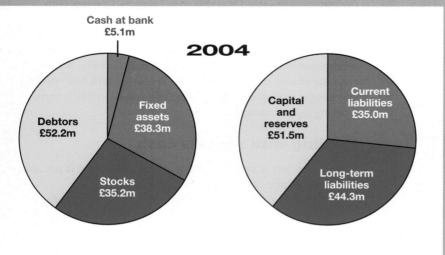

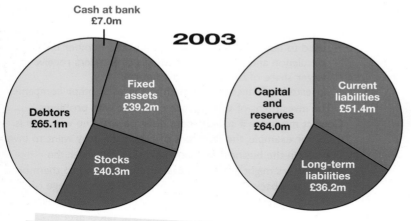

	2004	**2003**
Fixed assets	£38.3m	£39.2m
Stocks	£35.2m	£40.3m
Debtors	£52.2m	£65.1m
Cash at bank	£5.1m	£7.0m
	£130.8m	**£151.6m**
Current liabilities	£35.0m	£51.4m
Long-term liabilities	£44.3m	£36.2m
Capital & reserves	£51.5m	£64.0m
	£130.8m	**£151.6m**

Source: adapted from Molins, *Annual Report and Accounts*, 2004.

Mark Band 1 *You need to comment on the working capital position of the company.*

Over the two years the working capital for Molins has fallen slightly from £61m to £57.5m. Working capital is calculated as current assets - current liabilities. In 2004, for example, it was (£35.2m + £52.2m + £5.1m) − £35m = £57.5m. However, more important is the amount of working capital tied up in current assets. Generally, current assets are not as productive as fixed assets. Molins has a lot of money tied up in stock and debtors – about two-thirds of all assets. This does not earn any return for the business. Perhaps the company should take measures to reduce stock holding and encourage customers to pay more promptly. Finally, Molins seems to make more use of long-term sources of finance. The value of long-term liabilities is higher than current liabilities. This suggests that the company is using a modern approach to funding working capital.

Mark Band 2 *You need to comment on the working capital of the business with understanding shown of the type of business.*

Molins is a plc and its main business activity is the manufacture of machinery for packaging and the tobacco industry. Between 2003 and 2004 the value of Molins' working capital fell a little from £61m to £57.5m. Working capital is calculated as current assets - current liabilities. In 2004, for example, it was (£35.2m + £52.2m + £5.1m) − £35m = £57.5m. This is not a very significant change but the amount of cash in the bank fell from £7m to £5.1m. More striking is the amount of money Molins has invested in current assets. Around two-thirds of all Molin's resources are tied up in current assets, most of which are stock and debtors. Since Molins manufactures large and complex machinery it is likely that they will have quite a lot of work-in-progress which is unavoidable. However, according to the notes in the accounts about half of the stocks are in finished goods. This may reflect the fact that the company has not performed so well this year. The company is also owed a lot of money and could consider ways to tighten its credit control. Finally, Molins appears to be taking a modern approach to managing working capital. This is because a large proportion of its finance is long-term. This will help Molins avoid the costs and risks associated with short-term sources.

Mark Band 3 *You need to evaluate the information relating to working capital and form some reasoned judgements. Reasonable suggestions for improvements should be made, showing an understanding of the problems presented by the different components of working capital.*
Examining the liquidity position of the business, over the two years working capital fell only slightly, from £61m to £57.5m. This is a fairly insignificant change. Working capital is calculated as current assets - current liabilities. In 2004, for example, it was (£35.2m + £52.2m + £5.1m) − £35m = £57.5m. The pie charts also show clearly that Molins has a great deal of money invested in current assets. Only one-third of its funds are

invested in fixed assets. This may be surprising since Molins is a manufacturer. However, it is possible that Molins leases some of its fixed assets. The amount of money tied up in current assets could be a worry for the company. Current assets are not as productive as fixed assets. For example, money tied up in stock and debtors does not earn any financial return. Molins may consider taking measures to release some of the working capital tied up in these current assets. For example, it could tighten its credit control system. It might consider ways of encouraging customers to pay more promptly – by offering cash discounts, for example. However, in this case collecting money from customers may be more complicated since their customers are international. Another option might be to cut down on stock holding. Molins might make more use of JIT methods, for example. According to the notes to the accounts more than half the stock is in finished goods. Perhaps the company should only make goods to order (if they are not already). However, the pie charts show that Molins has actually reduced the amount tied up in stock and debtors between 2003 and 2004, from a total of £105.4m to £87.4m. This is quite a significant reduction. Finally, the majority of Molins' finance is long term. Much of the working capital used by Molins is funded by long-term borrowings or the shareholders. This is a more modern approach to working capital management and reduces the costs and risks of using short-term sources.

Portfolio practice · Benjamin Ltd

Callum Benjamin owns Benjamin Ltd, a 24-hour service for household emergencies such as burst pipes, leaking roofs, floods and breakdowns of central heating and domestic appliances. The company is successful and growing fast. It owns a small fleet of vans employing 12 service staff and has increased its turnover by 80% or more in each of the last three years. However, the company is now overdrawn at the bank and is running very short of working capital. Figure 9 shows some financial details for Benjamin Ltd.

(a) **Explain the importance of effective working capital management to Benjamin Ltd.**
(b) **What evidence is there to suggest that Benjamin Ltd is perhaps growing too quickly?**
(c) **How might Benjamin Ltd improve its working capital position?**

Figure 9 *Financial information for Benjamin Ltd, 2004 - 2005*

	2005 £000s	2004 £000s
Fixed assets	1,200	890
Stocks	130	70
Debtors	760	470
Cash at bank	0	200
	2,090	**1,630**
Current liabilities	980	560
Long-term liabilities	200	200
Capital & reserves	910	870
	2,090	**1,630**

Ratio analysis and working capital

What is ratio analysis?

The financial position of a business can be analysed using **accounting ratios**. An accounting ratio can be calculated by comparing two values from the balance sheet or the profit and loss account. The comparison might involve expressing one value as a percentage of the other or simply one value divided by the other. For the ratio to be meaningful the two values must be related. For example, the amount of profit made by a firm (shown in the profit and loss account) is linked to the amount of capital invested in the firm (shown in the balance sheet). Ratios on their own are of little use. They need to be compared with other ratios. There are several ways in which comparisons can be made.

Over time An obvious comparison to make is to look at this year's results and compare them with last year's. This will help show whether the firm's financial position has improved over the year. However, ratios can be compared over any time period.

Inter-firm comparison Stakeholders are likely to be interested in how well the company is doing in comparison with others in the same industry. This might draw attention to particular strengths and weaknesses. It is very important to compare 'like

Table 1 *Different types of accounting ratios*

Ratio	Use for business
Performance/profitability ratios	Show how well the business is doing. Focus on profit, turnover and the amount of capital employed in the business. Some are known as activity ratios which look at how well a business uses its resources such as stock.
Liquidity ratios	Help to show whether the business is solvent. They look at the firm's ability to pay its immediate bills. Focus on current assets and current liabilities.
Gearing ratios	Examine the relationship between loan capital and share capital or fixed interest bearing debt and total capital employed.
Shareholders' ratios	Can be used to analyse the returns shareholders get on their investment in the company. Focus on earnings, dividends and share prices.

Table 2 *Accounts for Winters Timber Ltd*

Winters Timber Ltd
Profit and loss account Y/E 31.12.05

	2005 £000	2004 £000
Turnover	2,300	1,980
Cost of sales	920	810
Gross profit	1,380	1,170
Administration expenses	830	750
Operating profit	550	420
Net interest payable	30	30
Profit before tax	520	390
Taxation	100	80
Profit after tax	420	310
Dividends	60	40
Retained profit	360	270

Winters Timber Ltd
Balance sheet as at 31.12.05

	2005 £000	2004 £000
Fixed assets		
Land and property	1,200	1,400
Machinery, equipment and vehicles	340	310
	1,540	1,710
Current assets		
Stock	230	160
Debtors	65	80
Cash at bank	180	100
	475	340
Creditors: amounts falling due in one year		
Trade creditors	120	105
Accruals	20	25
Taxation	100	80
	240	210
Net current assets	235	130
Creditors: amounts falling due after one year		
Mortgage	500	500
Net assets	1,275	1,340
Capital and reserves		
Share capital	200	200
Other reserves	115	540
Profit and loss account	960	600
	1,275	1,340

'with like' when making inter-firm comparisons.

Inter-firm comparisons over time The two approaches described above can be used together. This might help to identify trends in performance, for example.

Results and forecasts Firms often set financial objectives. Ratios can be used to see whether objectives have been met. This involves comparing actual results with any targets set at the beginning of the financial year.

A number of different ratios can be calculated by a business. All of them will fall into one of the categories shown in Table 1. This section deals with ratios that can be used to analyse working capital. Sections 40 and 41 look at other ratios a business may use.

The ratios in this section are calculated from the information in Table 2. It shows financial details of Winters Timber Ltd, which operates as a timber merchant. The family run business stocks and supplies timber to local builders, joiners, carpenters and sometimes to the public. Winters buys its timber on 30 day trade credit terms but most of its sales are for cash. Only a few customers are allowed to buy on credit.

Current ratio

The current ratio is sometimes called the working capital ratio. This is because it is used to examine how much working capital a business has. It is calculated using the formula shown in Figure 1.

Figure 1 *Current ratios*

$$\text{Current ratio} = \frac{\text{Current assets}}{\text{Current liabilities}}$$

The value of current assets and current liabilities are shown in the balance sheet in Table 2. The current ratios for Winters in 2005 and 2004 are:

$$2005 \quad \text{Current ratio} = \frac{£475,000}{£240,000} = 1.98$$

$$2004 \quad \text{Current ratio} = \frac{£340,000}{£210,000} = 1.62$$

What do these values show? It is often suggested that the current ratio for a business should be between 1.5 and 2. If the ratio is below 1.5 it might be argued that the business is operating with inadequate levels of working capital. If the ratio is above 2 it might be said that the business has too many non-productive liquid resources and should look for investment opportunities. However, there are many exceptions to this rule. For example, retailers are often able to operate effectively with much lower levels of working capital. This is because most of their sales are for cash. In this case, for both years, Winters has about the right level of

working capital since the current ratios lie between 1.5 and 2. Over the two years working capital has increased because the ratio rises from 1.62 to 1.98.

Acid test ratio

The acid test ratio or quick ratio is a more severe test of liquidity. This is because stocks are not treated as liquid resources. Stocks are not guaranteed to be sold, they may become obsolete or deteriorate. They are therefore excluded from current assets when calculating the ratio. Figure 2 shows the formula for calculating the acid test ratio.

Figure 2 *Acid test ratios*

$$\text{Acid test ratio} = \frac{\text{Current assets - stocks}}{\text{Current liabilities}}$$

The information required to calculate the acid test ratio are found in the balance sheet for Winters in Table 2. The ratios for 2005 and 2004 are:

$$\text{For 2005} \quad \text{Acid test ratio} = \frac{£475,000 - £230,000}{£240,000} = 1.02$$

$$\text{For 2004} \quad \text{Acid test ratio} = \frac{£340,000 - £160,000}{£210,000} = 0.86$$

If a business has an acid test ratio of less than 1 it means that its current assets do not cover its current liabilities. This could indicate a potential problem. However, as with the current ratio, there is considerable variation between the typical acid test ratios of businesses in different industries. Again, retailers with their strong cash flows, can operate comfortably with acid test ratios of less than 1. In the case of Winters, the acid test ratio has improved over two year and in 2005 the ratio was close to an 'ideal' level of 1.

Debt collection period

This ratio measures how effectively a business is able to collect money owed by customers. The debt collection period is the average number of days it takes to collect debts from customers. Figure 3 shows the formula for calculating the debt collection period.

Businesses often vary the amount of time they give customers to pay for what they have bought on credit. Credit periods may be 30, 60, 90 or even 120 days. Obviously businesses prefer a short debt collection period because their cash flow will be improved. Retailers will have a very low debt collection period, perhaps just a few days. This is because most of their sales are for cash. This appears to be the case for Winters. In both years the collection period is well below 30 days. This suggests that the company is

Figure 3 Debt collection periods

$$\text{Debt collection period} = \frac{\text{Debtors}}{\text{Turnover}} \times 365$$

This ratio uses information from both the balance sheet and the profit and loss account. The value of debtors is found in the balance sheet and the turnover comes from the profit and loss account. The debt collection periods for Winters in 2005 and 2004 are.

$$\text{For 2005 Debt collection period} = \frac{\pounds 65,000}{\pounds 2,300,000} \times 365 = 10 \text{ days}$$

$$\text{For 2004 Debt collection period} = \frac{\pounds 80,000}{\pounds 1,980,000} \times 365 = 15 \text{ days}$$

selective when advancing trade credit. Most of its sales must be for cash with trade credit being reserved for special customers. Over the two years the company has also improved its debt collection period. It has fallen from 15 days in 2004 to just 10 days in 2005.

Credit payment period

The credit payment period shows how long it takes a business to pay its suppliers for goods that have been bought on credit. The formula for calculating the credit payment period is shown in Figure 4.

Figure 4 Credit payment periods

$$\text{Credit payment period} = \frac{\text{Trade creditors}}{\text{Credit purchases}} \times 365$$

The value of trade creditors will be found in the balance sheet under 'creditors: amounts falling due within a year'. The value for credit purchases will be the cost of sales. However, any cash purchases or payments for resources other than stock must be excluded. In this case all of Winters' purchases are on credit terms. The credit payment periods for 2005 and 2004 are:

$$2005 \text{ Credit payment period} = \frac{\pounds 120,000}{\pounds 920,000} \times 365 = 48 \text{ days}$$

$$2004 \text{ Credit payment period} = \frac{\pounds 105,000}{\pounds 810,000} \times 365 = 47 \text{ days}$$

A business will benefit if it can extend the credit payment period for as long as possible without damaging relations with suppliers. In this case, Winters buys its timber on 30 day credit terms. However, according to the calculations above, it takes a further 17 or 18 days to process the payment to suppliers (unless the company deliberately delays payment for a further two weeks). When analysing this ratio it is also useful to look at the debt collection period at the same time. A business will be in a strong position if the debt collection period is shorter than the credit payment period. In contrast, a business will experience shortages of working capital if the debt collection period is longer than the credit payment period. In this case Winters is in a very comfortable position. In 2005 the debt collection period was 10 days and the credit payment period 48 days. This means that the company is collecting money quicker from customers than it is paying suppliers.

Stock turnover

The stock turnover ratio measures how quickly a business uses or sells its stock. It is generally considered desirable to sell, or 'shift', stock as quickly as possible. One approach to stock turnover is to calculate how many times during the year a business sells its stock. The formula for stock turnover is shown in Figure 5.

Figure 5 Stock turnover

$$\text{Stock turnover} = \frac{\text{Cost of sales}}{\text{Stocks}}$$

The stock value for the ratio is listed in the balance sheet while the cost of sales will be found in the profit and loss account. The stock turnover for Winters in 2005 and 2004 is:

$$\text{For 2005 Stock turnover} = \frac{\pounds 920,000}{\pounds 230,000} = 4 \text{ times}$$

$$\text{For 2004 Stock turnover} = \frac{\pounds 810,000}{\pounds 160,000} = 5.1 \text{ times}$$

Another approach to stock turnover is to calculate the number of days it takes to sell the stock. This formula is shown in Figure 6.

High stock turnovers are preferred (or lower figures in days). A higher stock turnover means that profit on the sale of stock is earned more quickly. Thus, businesses with high stock turnovers can operate on lower margins. A declining stock turnover ratio might indicate:

- higher stock levels;
- a large amount of slow moving or obsolete stock;
- a wider range of products being stocked or;
- a lack of control over purchasing.

Stock turnover differs considerably between different industries.

Figure 6 *Stock turnover (by days)*

$$\text{Stock turnover} = \frac{\text{Stocks}}{\text{Cost of sales}} \times 365$$

The stock turnover in days for Winters in 2005 and 2004 is:

$$\text{For 2005 Stock turnover} = \frac{£230,000}{£920,000} \times 365 = 91 \text{ days}$$

$$\text{For 2004 Stock turnover} = \frac{£160,000}{£810,000} \times 365 = 72 \text{ days}$$

upermarkets, such as Tesco, Morrisons and Sainsbury, may have a elatively quick stock turnover of around 14 to 28 days. This means that they sell the value of their average stock every two to our weeks. Manufacturers generally have much slower turnover ecause of the time spent processing raw materials. However, in ecent years, many manufacturers have adopted just-in-time

production techniques to reduce stock holding. This involves ordering stocks only when they are required in the production process and, therefore, stock levels tend to be lower. As a result, stock turnover is faster. Businesses which supply services, such as banks, travel agents and transport operators, are not likely to hold very much stock. Therefore this ratio is not likely to be used by service industry analysts.

In the case of Winters, stock turnover is quite poor. In 2005 it took three months to sell the entire stock holding. Also, over the two years, stock turnover has worsened. This might be because the business is holding a much larger quantity of stock in 2005. However, to determine whether Winters' stock turnover was acceptable, comparisons with other timber merchants would have to be made.

1. Obtain two sets of company Annual Reports and Accounts for businesses operating in different industries.
2. Calculate the stock turnover for both companies in both years.
3. Make inter-firm comparisons over time and write a brief report commenting on your findings.

Research task

Portfolio practice · **Busselton Steel Stockists (BSS)**

BSS stocks a wide range of steel products and supply engineering companies in the North West. The company has been struggling recently. Although turnover increased in 2005, it was necessary to attract and retain customers by offering generous credit terms. This had a detrimental effect on the company's working capital position. Table 3 shows some extracts from the accounts.

Table 3 *Extracts from the accounts 2004 and 2005*

	2005	2004
	£000	£000
Turnover	12,349	11,987
Cost of sales	8,992	8,342
Current assets		
Stock	2,177	2,009
Debtors	2,220	1,654
Cash at bank and in hand	10	105
Current liabilities		
Trade creditors	1,200	1,009
Other creditors	3,998	2,887

(a) **Explain the difference between the debt collection period and the credit payment period.**
(b) **(i) Calculate the debt collection period and the credit payment period for BSS in 2004 and 2005.**
   (ii) Comment on your results in (i).
(c) **Evaluate the measures BSS might take to improve its financial position.**

Meeting the assessment criteria - examiners' guidance

You need to write a report assessing the working capital management of a chosen business based on a recent set of accounts. You need to identify the components of working capital, calculate key ratios and interpret them, assess the adequacy of working capital management and make suggestions for improvement. This unit focuses on the use of ratios to assess working capital management.

Business example - Bellway

Bellway is one of the nation's leading house builders. It started out as a family business in 1946 and turned over £1 billion for the first time in 2004. During the year it sold 6,610 homes at an average price of £161,400. Some extracts from the balance sheet are shown in Table 4.

Table 4 *Extracts from Bellway balance sheet*

	2004 £	2003 £
Current assets		
Stocks	1,025,764	857,984
Debtors	38,176	33,420
Cash at bank and in hand	111,042	88,392
	1,174,982	**979,796**
Current liabilities	**336,818**	**269,360**

Source: adapted from Bellway, *Annual Report and Accounts*, 2004.

Mark Band 1 *You need to analyse working capital by calculating the key ratios and make simple comments based on the results.*

Bellway is a construction company and builds houses. The information in the accounts can be used to calculate the current ratio and the acid test ratio. These ratios can be used to analyse the company's working capital position. The ratios for 2004 and 2003 are shown below.

$$2004 \text{ Current ratio} = \frac{\text{Current assets}}{\text{Current liabilities}} = \frac{£1,174,982}{£336,818} = 3.5$$

$$2003 \text{ Current ratio} = \frac{\text{Current assets}}{\text{Current liabilities}} = \frac{£979,796}{£269,360} = 3.6$$

$$2004 \text{ Acid test ratio} = \frac{\text{Current assets} - \text{stocks}}{\text{Current liabilities}} = \frac{£1,174,982 - £1,025,764}{£336,818} = 0.44$$

$$2003 \text{ Acid test ratio} = \frac{\text{Current assets} - \text{stocks}}{\text{Current liabilities}} = \frac{£979,796 - £857,984}{£269,360} = 0.45$$

Over the two years there is very little change in the two ratios. But the current ratio for both years appears high. It is way above 2 and suggests that too much working capital is being held. However, the acid test ratio shows the opposite. It is way below 1 and suggests that not enough working capital is being held. This is probably because Bellway, a house builder, has a lot of work-in-progress (WIP). When WIP is taken away from current assets the effect on the ratios is significant.

Mark Band 2 *You need to analyse working capital using appropriate ratios and comment on your results. You need to take into account the type of business when interpreting your results.*

Ratio analysis can be used to help assess the working capital position of Bellway. The current ratio and the acid test ratio are the most appropriate ratios. The ratios for 2004 and 2003 are shown below.

$$2004 \text{ Current ratio} = \frac{\text{Current assets}}{\text{Current liabilities}} = \frac{£1,174,982}{£336,818}$$

$$2003 \text{ Current ratio} = \frac{\text{Current assets}}{\text{Current liabilities}} = \frac{£979,796}{£269,360}$$

$$2004 \text{ Acid test ratio} = \frac{\text{Current assets} - \text{stocks}}{\text{Current liabilities}} = \frac{£1,174,982 - £1,025,764}{£336,818}$$

$$2003 \text{ Acid test ratio} = \frac{\text{Current assets} - \text{stocks}}{\text{Current liabilities}} = \frac{£979,796 - £857,984}{£269,360}$$

The current ratios for Bellway are very high. In both years they are above the recommended maximum of 2. This suggests that the company has too many liquid resources. However, the acid test ratio shows the exact opposite. In both years they are well below 1. This suggests that working capital is inadequate. These results can be explained by the nature of Bellway's activities. Bellway builds houses and would expect to have a large proportion of its working capital tied up in WIP (houses under construction). This is indeed the case. According to the notes to the accounts the majority of Bellway's stock was accounted for by WIP. Since Bellway has a significant amount of money in the bank, the fact that it has a lot of working capital tied up in WIP may not matter. In fact, it may be unavoidable due to the nature of Bellway's activities.

Mark Band 3 *You need to calculate ratios to help evaluate the working capital of the company. You need to form reasoned judgements and make suggestions for improvements showing an understanding of the problems presented by the different components of working capital.*

Bellway is a national house builder and built over 6,000 homes in 2004. The working capital of the business can be analysed using accounting ratios. The current ratio can be used to look at the relationship between current assets and current liabilities.

$$\text{2004 Current ratio} = \frac{\text{Current assets}}{\text{Current liabilities}} = \frac{£1,174,982}{£336,818} = 3.5$$

$$\text{2003 Current ratio} = \frac{\text{Current assets}}{\text{Current liabilities}} = \frac{£979,796}{£269,360} = 3.6$$

$$\text{2004 Acid test ratio} = \frac{\text{Current assets - stocks}}{\text{Current liabilities}} = \frac{£1,174,982 - £1,025,764}{£336,818} = 0.44$$

$$\text{2003 Acid test ratio} = \frac{\text{Current assets - stocks}}{\text{Current liabilities}} = \frac{£979,796 - £857,984}{£269,360} = 0.45$$

The acid test ratio can also be used. This is a more severe test of liquidity because stocks are excluded. These two ratios are shown for Bellway in 2004 and 2003 below.

The two ratios show different things. The current ratio in both years is very high. An ideal value for the current ratio would be between 1.5 and 2. In this case, in 2004 it is 3.5 – way above 2. This suggests that Bellway has too many liquid resources. However, in stark contrast the acid test ratio is only 0.44 in 2004. This is well below the 'ideal' of 1. This suggests that the company could have inadequate working capital. However, the position is explained by the nature of Bellway's activities. Bellway is in the construction business and at any point in time will have houses under construction. This is WIP and according to the notes to the accounts most of Bellway's stock is accounted for by WIP. This is to be expected and may not be a problem. If houses are built to order then as soon as they are complete money will flow in. It is also possible that Bellway receives deposits from customers when houses are sold. This will help improve cash flow. The amount of cash in the bank suggests that Bellway does not suffer from working capital problems. However, if it wanted to improve working capital it might try to speed up construction time by offering bonus payments to staff for example, make more use of JIT methods and increase the size of deposits when orders are placed.

36 Investment appraisal 1

What is investment?

In business much investment is to do with the purchase of capital goods. Capital goods are the fixed assets used by a business to make goods and deliver services. Examples include premises, machinery, tools, equipment and vehicles. Investment might also refer to expenditure on research and development, staff retraining, promotional campaigns and the purchase of another business. When a business is first set up a lot of the expenditure is devoted to investment. The business will have to buy crucial fixed assets that they need to operate. However, even when the business is established the need for investment continues. The reasons for this include the following.

- Machinery, tools and equipment will depreciate and eventually wear out. Consequently they will need replacing from time to time.
- Some fixed assets will become obsolete and need replacing. For example, computers are often replaced, not because they do not work any more, but because they are inefficient compared to the new models. Businesses have to 'ditch' their old computers and buy the new ones to remain competitive.
- As a business grows it will need to buy more fixed assets to build up capacity. For example, a hotel might expand by extending its premises. Also, once the new rooms have been built they will need to be furnished.
- Most businesses launch new products as they develop. Old products are replaced with new ones and product portfolios are extended over time.
- Business growth is often undertaken through acquisitions. This means a company will buy other businesses. Such investments can be on a very large scale.

Some examples of investment by companies are shown in Figure 1.

Features of investment

Investment has a number of important features.

Long term The return on all investment is received over a period of time after the initial outlay. Some investment projects generate returns for many years. For example, the laser cutting machine bought by Dewhurst in Figure 1 may last for 10 years or more. Some investment projects will generate revenue for as long as the firm continues to trade. For example, when a supermarket chain opens a new store it would expect the store to operate indefinitely.

Expensive Most capital expenditure requires a large outlay of funds. In Figure 1 eBay bought Skype for £2.23bn. This is a massive amount of money to commit to one investment project. Such large capital outlays often require a business to raise additional funds which can affect the cash flow and liquidity of a business. This is discussed later in this section.

Irreversible In some cases, once a business has committed funds

Figure 1 Examples of business investment

Dewhurst plc

Dewhurst plc manufactures and supplies components to the lifts, keypads and rail industries. The company is probably best known for its high quality pushbutton products sold under the Dupar brand. The company's main manufacturing plant is located on the outskirts of London and is full of the latest machine tools. Dewhurst is committed to heavy investment in new production equipment. In 2004, the company spent £769,000 on additions to fixed assets. This included a laser cutting machine, a new turret punch press, a linishing machine and two new hydraulic presses. There was also investment in fitting out new premises in Australia. Next year the company is committed to the implementation of a new group computer system.

Source: adapted from Dewhurst, *Annual Reports and Accounts*, 2004.

eBay

In September 2005, eBay, the online auction site, bought Skype, the Internet voice company. The investment cost eBay £2.23bn. Skype supplies a small computer programme that allows users to make free telephone calls over the Internet. Skype has 54 million members registered worldwide and is adding 150,000 new users each day. Its software has been downloaded 164 million times in 225 countries. eBay hopes to close in on Yahoo and Google in the growing Internet advertising market. By integrating with Skype's voice calling technology into eBay's markets, making it easier for buyers and sellers to communicate, the company would be able to lower 'friction' in online transactions and increase the overall value of its services.

Source: adapted from the *Financial Times*, 13.9.2005.

Scottish & Newcastle plc

Scottish & Newcastle, the giant international brewer, is committed to investment in its brands. It believes that investing in brands is critical to developing revenues in the future. In 200 the company increased expenditure on advertising and promotion by 17%. In the UK there were successful new campaigns for Foster's, Kronenbourg 1664 and Strongbow and two more of the award-winning advertisements for John Smiths were released. Investment in advertising was also prominent in overseas markets such as Portugal and Russia.

Source: adapted from Scottish & Newcastle plc, *Annual Reports and Accounts*, 2004.

o an investment project it cannot recover them if the project is
ot successful. For example, the decision to raise billions of
ounds to construct a tunnel linking Britain and France was
rreversible. Once the Channel Tunnel was built it could not be
unbuilt'. Since its construction the operators of the tunnel have
onsistently lost money and struggled to meet their debt
epayments.

Risk Business investment is fraught with uncertainty. This is
ecause the returns on investment can never be guaranteed. The
Channel Tunnel example illustrates this point. Investment and risk
 discussed in more detail later in this section.

mplications of investment

ecause of the features of investment discussed above, owners
nd managers need to be aware of the implications of investment
or the business.

The effect on cash flow and liquidity The large outlay of
apital to fund investment projects can have a significant effect on
he cash flow and liquidity of a business. Heavy capital expenditure
vill drain a company's liquid resources if there is no new funding.
Vithout new funding to pay for capital expenditure a company's
quid resources may be stretched and the survival of the business
ossibly jeopardised. New businesses often have cash flow
roblems when they first start trading because capital expenditure
 so heavy. This might be avoided by leasing some fixed assets to
egin with. Alternatively a new business should seek to raise more
apital. Although capital expenditure will reduce cash flow in the
eriod that it is undertaken, if the investment is successful future
ash flows should be boosted. This will obviously help to improve
he liquidity of the business in the future. Figure 2 shows an
xample of the effect of capital expenditure on cash flow.

The effect on profit A lot of investment is undertaken by a
usiness to increase future profit. For example, a sole trader
unning a successful hair salon might decide to expand the
usiness by opening another salon in a new location. If the
xpansion was successful the owner might expect that the profit
nade by the business would eventually double. It is the prospect
f higher profits in the future which often inspires business
wners to invest. However, if investment projects fail the effect on
uture profit could be negative. In the above example, if the new
air salon was a 'flop' and had to be closed down, the money lost
n the investment would eventually have to be offset against the
rofit made by the original salon. This would obviously reduce the
verall profitability of the business. Finally, capital expenditure does
ot appear in the profit and loss account. Consequently, the
urchase of some expensive machinery by a business will not
educe profit in the year that it is purchased. However, there will
e a depreciation charge that will appear as a cost in the profit
nd loss account over the life of the machine. This will have the
ffect of reducing profit slightly each year over this period.

Risk and variability of returns The uncertainty associated with
usiness investment makes the investment decision a very difficult
ne. One aspect of this uncertainty is that businesses are often
aced with choice when investing. For example, an engineering
ompany purchasing a new CNC shaping machine will have to

decide which supplier to buy from. There may be lots of different
suppliers offering slightly different machines, with varying prices,
specifications, delivery times and terms and conditions. The
company will have to select the one which it thinks will generate
the greatest return. Firms often have to choose between different
investment projects due to limited funds. For example, a company
may want to invest in a staff training programme, launch a new
product, launch a takeover bid for a rival and extend its factory. If
the company can only afford one of these projects a difficult
choice has to be made. If all the cost and revenue data for each
project were available this may not be too much of a problem.

Figure 2 *Harbir Singh – the effect of capital expenditure on cash flow*

Harbir Singh runs a taxi business in Huddersfield and has decided to buy some new vehicles in September. A six month cash flow forecast is shown below and the effect of buying the new vehicles is clear. The new vehicles cost the business £30,000 and in September the closing cash position is negative. There is a cash deficit of £13,500. Although the cash position is expected to improve in subsequent months, unless the business has an overdraft to cover the deficit in September the business will need an injection of capital.

£

	JUL	AUG	SEP	OCT	NOV	DEC
Receipts						
Cash sales	59,000	61,000	60,000	59,000	56,000	105,000
Total cash receipts	**59,000**	**61,000**	**60,000**	**59,000**	**56,000**	**105,000**
Payments						
Wages	18,000	18,000	18,000	18,000	15,000	28,000
Fuel	12,000	12,000	12,000	12,000	12,000	18,000
Vehicle maintenance	3,000	3,000	3,000	3,000	3,000	14,000
Office expenses	9,000	9,000	9,000	9,000	7,000	11,000
Other expenses	10,000	10,000	10,000	10,000	8,000	14,000
Drawings	4,000	4,000	4,000	4,000	4,000	8,000
New vehicles			30,000			
Total cash payments	**56,000**	**56,000**	**86,000**	**56,000**	**49,000**	**93,000**
Net cash flow	3,000	5,000	(26,000)	3,000	7,000	12,000
Opening balance	4,500	7,500	12,500	(13,500)	(10,500)	(3,500)
Closing balance	**7,500**	**12,500**	**(13,500)**	**(10,500)**	**(3,500)**	**8,500**

Note: brackets equal negative numbers.

Figure 3 *External factors that might affect costs and revenues for investment projects*

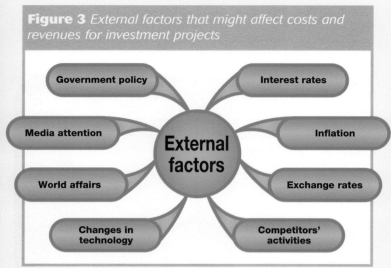

However, predicting future costs and revenues is very difficult. They are likely to be affected by a range of external factors which can be difficult to estimate. Some of these external factors are summarised in Figure 3. For example, if interest rates rise in the future the cost of borrowing will rise. This would increase the cost of investment (if borrowed money is used to fund the expenditure) and reduce the predicted returns. The variability of future revenues due to external factors makes investment highly risky. It is not uncommon for investment projects to fail, causing serious losses for companies. An example is shown in Figure 4.

Investment appraisal

When choosing between different investment opportunities, or deciding whether or not to invest at all, a business has to evaluate the investment options. The evaluation process is called investment appraisal. Investment appraisal involves comparing the capital cost

Figure 4 *Coca-Cola and Dasani*

Coca-Cola is a huge and successful business organisation. However, in 2004 the company lost a lot of money, including £7m spent on marketing, when it launched a new product in the UK. On February 10, 2004, Dasani was launched, a brand of bottled water. Unlike many of its rivals, Dasani was not natural spring water, it came from the tap. The tabloids drew on the parallel with the episode in the BBC sitcom 'Only Fools and Horses', in which Del Boy and Rodney take ordinary tap water from their Peckham flat and bottle it up to sell as Peckham Spring Water. The irony couldn't have been worse. Dasani was sourced and bottled in a factory in Sidcup, just a few miles down the road from Peckham. Coca-Cola was eventually forced to withdraw the brand.

Source: adapted from www.bbc.co.uk.

and expected net cash flows from investment projects. The net cash flow is the revenue from an investment project less the running costs. Most investment appraisal techniques involve looking at the relative profitability of different investment projects. There is a number of quantitative appraisal techniques which might be used. They are explained in this section and section 37.

Payback

The payback method of investment appraisal involves calculating the payback period. This is the amount of time it takes to recover the initial cost of an investment project. For example, if a business invests £10,000 in a project that generates net cash flows (i.e. income from the investment - running costs) of £2,000 a year for 10 years, it will take 5 years to recover the cost (5 x £2,000 = £10,000). Therefore, the payback period is five years. When using this method to choose between different investment projects, the project with the shortest payback period should be selected. To illustrate this, an example is shown in Figure 5.

Figure 5 *Allen's Ltd*

Allen's Ltd is a baker supplying local retailers in Kent with bread products. The largest oven in the bakery needs to be replaced. However, new technology in the food industry means that there are a wide range of ovens to choose from. Katie Allen, the owner, has identified three suitable ovens. Details about their capital cost and expected net cash flows over the next five years are given in the table below. It is important to Allen's Ltd to recover the cost of the new oven as quickly as possible. Consequently, Katie has decided to use the payback method of investment appraisal. Oven 1 has a payback period of exactly two years. After two years the outlay of £5,000 has been recovered (£2,000 + £3,000 = £5,000). The payback period for Oven 2 is three years and Oven 3 two years and four months. Therefore, using this method of appraisal Oven 1 would be purchased because it has the shortest payback period.

Oven	Cost (£)	Expected net cash flows (£)					
		Year 1	Year 2	Year 3	Year 4	Year 5	Total
1	5,000	2,000	3,000	4,000	5,000	6,000	20,000
2	4,000	1,000	1,500	1,500	3,000	6,000	12,000
3	8,000	3,000	3,000	6,000	8,000	6,000	26,000

Advantages of the payback method

- It is quite simple to apply.
- The method is appropriate when technology is changing rapidly such as in computing. New, more efficient and more powerful computers are being developed all the time. It is important for a business to recover the cost of computers quickly before a new generation comes along.
- This method may be helpful if a business has cash flow problems. This is because the project selected will return cash to the business more quickly than the others.

- It could be argued that the risk in investment is reduced if projects with shorter paybacks are selected. Projects with short paybacks have less time to go wrong.

Disadvantages of the payback method

- The method ignores all the cash flows after the payback period. This could lead to more profitable options being ignored if cash flows are very high for projects with longer payback periods.
- The overall profitability of investment projects is ignored. This is because the speed of repayment is the criteria used to evaluate investment options.
- The timing of the cash flows within the payback period are ignored.

Because of the drawbacks associated with the payback method it is unlikely that it would be used on its own to make investment decisions. However, it might be used in a screening process where projects with very long payback periods are dropped immediately.

1. Look in the financial section of a recent newspaper and identify an example of business investment.
2. Write a brief report describing the nature of the investment and discuss the implications of the investment for the business.

Research task

Meeting the assessment criteria - examiners' guidance

You need to write a report evaluating two proposed investment projects. You need to include a discussion on the suitability of the methods used and an analysis of the estimated future cash flows.

Business example - Burton Construction plc

Burton Construction is a well established company that carries out contract work for local authorities. About 75% of its business involves road construction. In the last two years the business has been leasing a bulldozer for heavy earth movement. After some consideration it has been decided to stop leasing and buy a new bulldozer for the company. Details about the capital costs of two available models and the expected future cash flows over their seven year life are shown in the table below. The payback method of investment appraisal will be used to evaluate the two options.

Investment	Cost (£)	Expected net cash flows							
		Year 1	Year 2	Year 3	Year 4	Year 5	Year 6	Year 7	Total
Model 1	140,000	40,000	40,000	30,000	30,000	20,000	20,000	15,000	195,000
Model 2	180,000	35,000	35,000	35,000	35,000	30,000	30,000	30,000	230,000

Mark Band 1 *You need to show a basic understanding of investment appraisal techniques evidenced by accurate calculations. Some attempt to discuss the suitability of methods and the advantages and disadvantages of each should also be described. This unit will focus on the payback method.*

Burton Construction has to decide which model of bulldozer to invest in. One method of appraisal it could use is the payback. This involves working out how long it takes to recover the capital cost of each option. In this case the payback for Model 1 is exactly four years. £40,000 + £40,000 + £30,000 + £30,000 = £140,000 which is the cost of this model. The payback period for Model 2 is five years and four months. Therefore, Model 1 is the best option for the business because it has the shortest payback period. The main advantage of this method is that it is simple. It is also a suitable method of appraisal if a business has cash flow problems. However, it does have some disadvantages. For example, it ignores all the cash flows after the payback period. This could be a problem if cash flows are particularly high after the payback period.

Mark Band 2 *You need to consider the suitability of appraisal methods with more reference given to the scenario. For example, conflicts and problems should be addressed.*

Burton Construction has recently decided to buy a bulldozer instead of leasing it. This should help to reduce the long-term cost of this particular fixed asset. In order to decide which model to purchase the company uses the payback method of appraisal. This involves calculating the payback period. This is the amount of time it takes to recover the capital cost of an investment project. For Model 1 the capital cost is £140,000. The payback period for this model is exactly four years. This is because it takes four years to get back the cost (£40,000 + £40,000 + £30,000 + £30,000 = £140,000). The capital outlay for Model 2 is £180,000 and the payback period is five years and four months. Consequently, according to this method of appraisal, Model 1 should be selected because it has the shortest payback period. This method of appraisal is very simple to use and in this case might be an appropriate method. This is because modern bulldozers use advanced technology and new, more efficient models may become available fairly soon. Consequently, it is important to get back the money invested as quickly as possible. However, payback is not without problems. The main one is that it ignores the cash flows after the payback period. This could lead to an investment option with high cash flows after the payback period being overlooked.

Mark Band 3 *You need to draw clear conclusions regarding the acceptance of projects and the limitations of the appraisal methods used should be discussed in detail.*

Businesses can use a number of quantitative investment appraisal techniques when evaluating investment projects. In this case, Burton Construction plans to use the payback method when deciding which model of bulldozer to invest in. The payback method involves calculating the payback period. This is the amount of time it takes to recover the capital cost of the investment. It is a simple method and can be applied if the cost and expected net cash flows are known for any given investment project. In this case the capital cost of Model 1 is £140,000 and it takes exactly four years to recover this cost (£40,000 + £40,000 + £30,000 + £30,000 = £140,000). The capital cost of Model 2 is £180,000 and it takes five years and four months to recover the cost (£35,000 + £35,000 + £35,000 + £35,000 + £30,000 + £10,000/£30,000 x 12 = £180,000). Based on these calculations Burton would choose to invest in Model 1 because it has the shortest payback period.

   This method of appraisal may be a good method to use. This is because when buying modern technology, as in this case, it is important to recover the cost as quickly as possible. New and more efficient models of bulldozer may become available fairly soon. However, the payback method does have some limitations. It ignores all the cash flows after the payback period. This could lead to more profitable options being

overlooked if cash flows are very high for projects with longer payback periods. In this case the cash flows after the payback periods are similar - £55,000 and £50,000 respectively. The overall profitability of investment projects is ignored. This is because the speed of repayment is the criteria used to evaluate investment options. Finally, the timing of the cash flows within the payback period is also ignored. To conclude, the payback method may be quite appropriate in this case and Model 1 appears to be the clear favourite.

Portfolio practice · UniCom plc

UniCom manufactures components for the electronics industry. It has an international customer base and is expanding quite rapidly. An important part of its corporate strategy is a commitment to capital investment. In 2006, the company plans another big investment programme and has lined up four specific projects. However, funds will be limited and only one project can be considered. UniCom plans to use a screening process to eliminate two of the projects. The two with the longest payback periods will be dropped. Some financial details relating to each project are shown in the table below.

(a) **Using this case as an example explain what is meant by the payback method of investment appraisal.**
(b) **Calculate the payback period for each of the investment projects and state which two projects should be dropped.**
(c) **Analyse the disadvantages of the payback method to UniCom.**
(d) **Evaluate the implications to UniCom of the investment project chosen.**

Investment	Cost (£)	Expected net cash flows (£)						
		Year 1	Year 2	Year 3	Year 4	Year 5	Year 6	Total
Introduce Total Quality Management	45m	5m	10m	20m	30m	35m	10m	110m
Purchase an overseas rival	40m	10m	10m	10m	15m	15m	15m	85m
Launch a new product	35m	15m	15m	10m	10m	10m	5m	65m
Upgrade the entire computer system	60m	20m	20m	20m	10m	5m	5m	80m

37 Investment appraisal 2

Accounting rate of return (ARR)

One of the disadvantages of the payback method of investment appraisal discussed in section 37, was that the profitability of investment projects was ignored. The accounting or average rate of return (ARR) overcomes this problem. The method involves comparing the average annual profit of an investment project with the capital cost. To calculate the ARR the following formula can be used.

$$ARR = \frac{\text{Average annual profit}}{\text{Capital outlay}} \times 100$$

If a business invested £100,000 in a project which returned an average profit of £20,000 per annum over 10 years, the ARR would be:

$$ARR = \frac{£20,000}{£100,000} \times 100 = 20\%$$

The ARR can be used to compare different investment projects. When choosing between alternative investment projects the one with the highest return will be selected, as shown in Figure 1.

Strengths of ARR

- The method focuses on the profitability of investment projects rather than the payback period. This is more helpful since most businesses want their investments to yield a profit.
- It is relatively easy to compare different investment projects. The higher the ARR, the better.
- The method can be used to compare the return on a particular project with the return on the capital employed in the whole business, i.e. the ROCE. This is discussed later in this section.

Weaknesses of ARR

- The method does not take into account the timing of the cash flows. This might be a problem for businesses that suffer from poor or irregular cash flow.
- Since the average profit is used to calculate the ARR, it is not possible to determine whether a project is more or less

Figure 1 *Rowe Ltd - investment appraisal using the ARR*

Rowe Ltd is an advertising agency operating from an office in West London. It has some very high profile corporate clients. It undertakes a lot of creative work, designing TV adverts for example, and manages advertising budgets for companies. In 2005, Sakinah Branch the marketing director, identified three investment needs.

- Project A Refurbish the reception and client areas.
- Project B Upgrade the entire computer system.
- Project C Replace four executive cars.

The costs and expected cash flows from these investments over five years are shown in the table. Also shown is the total profit, the profit per annum and the ARR.
- The total profit is calculated by subtracting the cost of the project from the total expected cash flow. For project A this is £20,000 (£60,000 - £40,000).
- The profit per annum each year is calculated by dividing the total profit by the number of years the investment runs for. In this case all three projects are expected to generate a return for 5 years. For example, the profit per annum for project A is £4,000 (£20,000 ÷ 5).
- Finally the ARR is calculated using the formula above. For project A the ARR is 10% (£4,000 ÷ £40,000 × 100).
- In this case Rowe is likely to opt for the computer upgrade. This generates a return of 14% - the highest of the three projects.

	Project A	Project B	Project C
Cost (£)	40,000	50,000	70,000
Expected net cash flow (£)			
Year 1	12,000	30,000	20,000
Year 2	12,000	25,000	20,000
Year 3	12,000	15,000	15,000
Year 4	12,000	10,000	15,000
Year 5	12,000	5,000	10,000
Total	60,000	85,000	80,000
Total profit (£)	20,000	35,000	10,000
Profit pa = Profit ÷ 5 (£)	4,000	7,000	2,000
ARR	**10%**	**14%**	**2.9%**

profitable in its early or later stages. For example, in the first year of an investment project the return may be negative because total costs may outweigh total revenue.

- It ignores the time value of money, i.e. that an amount of money is worth more now than the same amount in the future.

Discounted cash flow (DCF)/net present value (NPV)

This method can also be used by businesses to evaluate investment.

The time value of money and present value The NPV method of investment appraisal takes into account the 'time value' of money. This is important because all the money generated by investment is received in the future. Money received in the future is worth less than the same amount of money today. Why? Because money in hand today can earn interest if it is placed in a bank. For example, if £1,000 is placed in a bank and the interest rate is 5%, at the end of the year the money will be worth £1,050 ([£1,000 + 5%] × £1,000). £1,000 received today is worth £50 more than £1,000 received in a year's time. Therefore, £1,000 received in a year's time will be worth about 5% less. This lower amount is called the present value.

To calculate precisely what it is worth discount tables can be used. These are special mathematical tables which show the present value of £1 at the end of a number of years at a particular rate of interest. An extract from these tables is shown in Table 1. Using the appropriate value from the discount table, the present value of £1,000 to be received in one year if the rate of interest is 5% is:

Present value = 0.95 × £1,000 = £950

Table 1 *An extract from discount tables*

Year	5%	6%	8%	10%
0	1.0	1.0	1.0	1.0
1	0.95	0.94	0.93	0.91
2	0.91	0.89	0.86	0.83
3	0.86	0.84	0.79	0.75
4	0.82	0.79	0.74	0.68
5	0.78	0.75	0.68	0.62

The present value of money will get less and less the higher the rate of interest and the longer into the future the money is to be received. For example, if the £1,000 in the above example was to be received in 5 years' time and the interest rate was 10%, the present value would be:

Present value = 0.62 × £1,000 = £620

Discounting cash flows When using this method of appraisal, the expected net cash flow has to be discounted to get the present value of the entire cash flow. When the present value of the cash flow has been calculated (PV) the net present value

(NPV) of an investment project can be determined. It is given by:

NPV = PV – capital outlay

When choosing between different investment projects the one with the highest NPV will be selected. An example is shown in Figure 2.

Figure 2 *Amstelle Carriers Ltd*

Amstelle Carriers Ltd is a haulage company specialising in the transport of fuels. In 2005 the company needed a new lorry. Two models were identified and their costs and expected cash flows are shown in the table below.

Investment Cost (£)		Expected net cash flows (£)					
		Year 1	Year 2	Year 3	Year 4	Year 5	Total
Model 1	90,000	30,000	25,000	23,000	22,000	20,000	120,000
Model 2	85,000	25,000	24,000	23,000	22,000	21,000	115,000

Assuming that the rate of interest is going to be 5% over the time period, the present value of the cash flow for each project calculated and shown in the table below. The NPV is also calculated for both models. For example, the PV of the £30,000 which is to be received by Model 1 in year one is £28,500. The PV of the entire cash flow is found by adding the PV for all of the five years. It is £104,640. Finally, the NPV is found by subtracting the capital cost of Model 1 (£90,000), from this PV. In this case NPVs of both Models is very similar. However, Model 2 has a slightly higher NPV at £14,790. Another attractive feature of Model 2 is that the capital outlay is lower.

	Model 1	**Model 2**
Year 1	£30,000 × 0.95 = £28,500	£25,000 × 0.95 = £23,75
Year 2	£25,000 × 0.91 = £22,750	£24,000 × 0.91 = £21,8
Year 3	£23,000 × 0.86 = £19,780	£23,000 × 0.86 = £19,78
Year 4	£22,000 × 0.82 = £18,040	£22,000 × 0.82 = £18,0
Year 5	£20,000 × 0.78 = £15,600	£21,000 × 0.78 = £16,3
Total PV	= £104,640	= £99,7
NPV	£104,640 - £90,000 = £14,640	£99,790 - £85,000 = £14,7

Strengths of NPV

The method takes into account interest rates and the timing of cash flows.

The returns from different investment options can be compared easily.

The opportunity cost of investment is taken into account. In other words, the investment decision is based not simply on the net cash flow but on the interest 'foregone' by not depositing the money in the bank.

Weaknesses of NPV

Calculating the NPV may be time consuming if a computer cannot be used.

The method does not provide an accurate means of comparison if the initial outlay on projects is significantly different. For example, a NPV of £40,000 on a £4m investment would generally be considered not as good as a NPV of £30,000 on a £1m investment, even though the NPV is higher.

The future rate of interest is likely to vary unpredictably over time. Consequently, the NPVs of investment projects are also likely to vary unpredictably (because the NPV is determined by the interest rate). This makes calculation and comparison extremely difficult and uncertain.

Return on capital employed (ROCE)

The return on capital employed (ROCE) is a financial ratio which is used to assess the performance of a business. However, it might also be used to appraise certain types of investment. ROCE compares the profit made by a business or venture with the amount of money invested in it. When calculating the ROCE it is standard practice to define profit as net profit (or operating profit) before tax and interest. This is sometimes described as earnings before tax and interest. The long-term capital employed includes shareholders' funds plus any long-term loan capital. ROCE can be calculated using the formula:

$$ROCE = \frac{\text{Profit before tax and interest}}{\text{Long-term capital employed}} \times 100$$

The ROCE is expressed as a percentage and will vary between different industries, however, the higher the better. It is also possible to compare the ROCE with the interest rate in the economy. For the ROCE to be adequate it would have to be higher than interest rates to compensate for the risk involved when investing in business. The ROCE for a business is calculated for a company in Figure 3.

ROCE and investment appraisal

The ROCE is more commonly used to evaluate the performance of the whole business. However, it could be used to evaluate the performance of specific investment projects. For example, if a company is looking to make acquisitions, it could use the ROCE to evaluate the performance of target companies when choosing which ones to buy. Companies with higher ROCEs are likely to be

Figure 3 *Helphire ROCE 2004 and 2003*

Helphire, founded in 1992, is the market leader in the provision of assistance to motorists following accidents that were not their fault. The company currently provides over 1 million car hire days per annum.

	2004	**2003**
Turnover	£75.297m	£55.791m
Operating profit	£8.334m	£5.477m
Long-term capital	£48.185m	£41.093m

$$\text{In 2004 ROCE} = \frac{£8.334m}{£48.185m} \times 100 = 17.29\%$$

$$\text{In 2003 ROCE} = \frac{£5.477m}{£41.093m} \times 100 = 13.32\%$$

The calculations show that ROCE for Helphire rose over the two years from 13.32% to 17.29%. This is a healthy increase on what was already a very good return. The return is considerably above the interest base rate of 4.75% in 2004. However, the ROCE would have to be compared with companies in the same industry to determine how good it was.

Source: adapted from Helphire, *Annual Report and Accounts.*

more expensive to buy.

The ROCE might also be used in conjunction with the average rate of return (ARR). For example, if a company expects to achieve a ROCE of 15% generally, it would not normally consider individual investment projects that generate an ARR of less than 15%.

Strengths of ROCE

- ROCE is a very useful way of evaluating the performance of the whole business.
- ROCE relates the return on investment (profit) to the size of the investment (capital employed). This makes it possible to

1. Obtain the Annual Report and Accounts of three companies and calculate the ROCE for each one for the latest year and the previous year.
2. Write a brief report commenting on the performance of each company and, if possible, give reasons for any significant differences.

Research task

compare investments of different sizes.
- It is fairly simple to calculate.

Weaknesses of ROCE

- It is not an ideal method for appraising investment in capital equipment. For example, it may be difficult to identify the profit

made by a photocopier.
- It is more commonly used for evaluating historic performance rather than future performance.
- Comparisons may be undermined if different measures of capital employed are used by companies. For example, capital employed could be interpreted as net assets or total capital employed.

Meeting the assessment criteria - examiners' guidance

You need to write a report evaluating two proposed investment projects. You need to include a discussion on the suitability of the methods used and an analysis of the estimated future cash flows.

Business example - Xynvane plc

Xynvane operates a chemical plant on Teeside. The company produces a range of chemicals such as acrylates for adhesives, paints, coatings, textiles and cleaning products. In 2005 the corporation identified four specific investment needs. However, funds were only available for one. The four investment projects, their capital costs and expected cash flows are shown in the table below. Xynvane proposes to screen the four projects using the payback method. It plans to eliminate two and then use the NPV method of appraisal to make the final choice. It is assumed that the rate of interest will average 6% over the next five years.

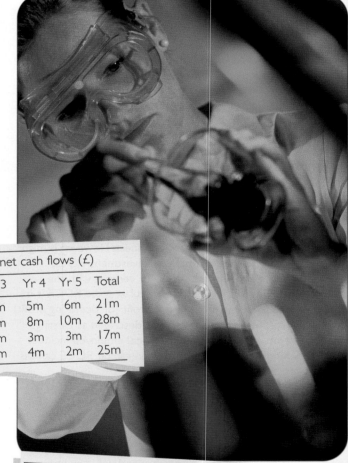

Investment project	Cost (£)	Expected net cash flows (£)					
		Yr 1	Yr 2	Yr 3	Yr 4	Yr 5	Total
1 Joint venture with a French company	10m	2m	4m	4m	5m	6m	21m
2 Research & development project	14m	0	2m	8m	8m	10m	28m
3 Purchase an Italian manufacturer	12m	4m	4m	3m	3m	3m	17m
4 Invest in a huge marketing campaign	15m	10m	5m	4m	4m	2m	25m

Mark Band 1 *You need to show a basic understanding of investment appraisal techniques evidenced by accurate calculations. Some attempt to discuss the suitability of methods and the advantages and disadvantages of each should also be described.*

Xynvane proposes to use the payback method to screen the four investment projects shown above. The payback periods for the four projects are 3 years, 3 years 6 months, 3 years 4 months and two years. This means that the research and development project and the purchase of the Italian manufacturer will be dropped. The NPVs of the remaining two projects are then calculated. According to the calculations the joint venture with the French company seems to be the best investment option for Xynvane. It has a greater NPV than the marketing campaign. Using this method of appraisal means that the 'time value' of money is taken into account. It is also easy to compare different investment projects. However, in this case it is assumed that the interest rate will average out at 6% a year over the investment period. However, in reality there may be a great deal of variation.

	Joint venture (£)	Marketing campaign (£
Yr 1	2m × 0.94 = 1.88m	10m × 0.94 = 9.40m
Yr 2	4m × 0.89 = 3.56m	5m × 0.89 = 4.45m
Yr 3	4m × 0.84 = 3.36m	4m × 0.84 = 3.36m
Yr 4	5m × 0.79 = 3.95m	4m × 0.79 = 3.16m
Yr 5	6m × 0.75 = 4.50m	2m × 0.75 = 1.50m
Total PV	= 17.25m	= 21.87m
NPV	17.25m - 10m = 7.25m	21.87m - 15m = 6.87m

Mark Band 2 *You need to consider the suitability of appraisal methods with more reference given to the scenario. For example, conflicts and problems should be addressed.*

Xynvane is a chemicals manufacturer and has identified four investment needs. However, the company proposes to eliminate two projects using the payback method before using the NPV method of appraisal to make the final selection. The payback for the four projects is as follows:

1. 3yrs (£2m + £4m + £4m = £10m)
2. 3yrs 6 months (0 + £2m + £8 + £4m ÷ £8m x 12 = £14m)
3. 3yrs 4 months (£4m + £4m + £3m + £1m ÷ £3m x 12 = £12m)
4. 2 yrs (£10m + £5m = £15m)

According to these calculations the research and development project and the plan to purchase the Italian company should be dropped. They have longer paybacks than the other two. The NPVs of the remaining two projects are then calculated. The NPV of the Joint venture is £7.25m and the NPV of the marketing campaign is £6.87m. Consequently the Joint venture is the best investment option for Xynvane. Interestingly, if the payback period had been the only method of investment appraisal, project four would have been selected because it had the shortest payback period. One of the weaknesses of the payback method is that it does not look at the profitability of

the projects. The NPV method does focus on profit and it also takes into account the time value of money.

Mark Band 3 *You need to draw clear conclusions regarding the acceptance of projects and the limitations of the appraisal methods used should be discussed in detail.*

In its approach to investment Xynvane uses two methods of appraisal. The payback method is used as a screening process to 'weed out' projects with a slow payback. In this case the two projects with the longest payback are the R & D programme and the Italian acquisition. The payback periods for all four projects are as follows.

1. 3yrs (£2m + £4m + £4m = £10m)
2. 3yrs 6 months (0 + £2m + £8 + £4m ÷ £8m x 12 = £14m)
3. 3yrs 4 months (£4m + £4m + £3m +£1m ÷ £3m x 12 = £12m)
4. 2 yrs (£10m + £5m = £15m)

Xynvane then uses the NPV method to select the most profitable project. In this case the Joint venture is the most profitable because it has the highest NPV. The NPV of the Joint venture is £7.25m compared to £6.87m for the marketing campaign. The difference is £380,000. The NPV method has some good advantages. It takes into account interest rates and the timing of cash flows, the returns from different investment options can be compared easily and the opportunity cost of investment is taken into account. However, it also has limitations. For example, calculating the NPV may be time consuming if a computer cannot be used. The method does not provide an accurate means of comparison if the initial outlay on projects is significantly different. For example, in this case the difference in the two NPVs is only £380,000, yet the difference in cost is huge. The marketing campaign costs a further £5m than the joint venture (50% more). This is not taken into account by the NPV method. Finally, the future rate of interest is likely to vary unpredictably over time. Consequently, the NPVs of investment projects are also likely to vary unpredictably. This makes calculation and comparison extremely difficult and uncertain. In this case the interest rate is estimated to be 6% over the time period.

Portfolio practice · Frampton Holdings

Frampton Holdings owns a number of businesses in the leisure industry. One is the North Senfield Golf Club (NSGC). Each business runs its own affairs but must reach a target of 15% ROCE to satisfy the parent company. In the last two years the NSGC has achieved ROCE of 12% and 8%. In 2005, Frampton said that changes to the management of NSGC would be made if ROCE did not reach 15% in 2006. As a result NSGC looked at two investment projects to help boost profit. Details of the costs and expected net cash flows are shown opposite.

(a) (i) **Calculate the ARR for the two investment projects.**
(ii) **Which of the two projects gives the best return?**
(b) **Discuss whether the NSGC should go ahead with the investment.**
(c) **Analyse the advantages and disadvantages of the ARR and the ROCE methods of investment appraisal.**

Investment project	Cost (£)	Expected net cash flows (£)					
		Yr 1	Yr 2	Yr 3	Yr 4	Yr 5	Total
Extend club house bar facilities	80,000	25,000	25,000	25,000	30,000	30,000	135,000
Purchase 20 golf buggies	60,000	25,000	25,000	25,000	20,000	20,000	115,000

Factors affecting business investment

Sections 36 and 37 looked at the different methods of investment appraisal where a business looked at the costs and expected cash flows when deciding which projects to invest in. However, a number of other factors might also be important when making investment decisions. Examples of these factors are summarised in Figure 1.

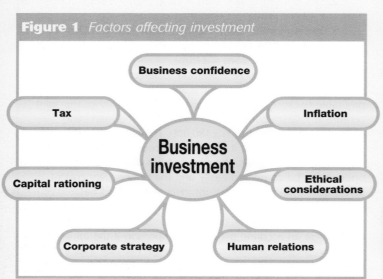

Figure 1 *Factors affecting investment*

- Business confidence
- Tax
- Inflation
- **Business investment**
- Capital rationing
- Ethical considerations
- Corporate strategy
- Human relations

Capital rationing Capital rationing occurs when a business has a number of profitable investment opportunities it would like to undertake but insufficient capital to fund them. Therefore, some projects that should be accepted are excluded because financial capital is limited. There are two types of capital rationing.
- **Hard capital rationing**. Hard capital rationing will occur if the capital shortages are the result of external influences. This means that the business is limited in the amount of money it can raise from external sources. This might be because a business is considered to be in financial distress, financial institutions and other money lenders are operating a 'tight' credit regime or the competition for funds is particularly intense. Banks also have a tendency to limit lending to small and medium-sized businesses.
- **Soft capital rationing**. Soft capital rationing occurs as a result of internal constraints. This is where the firm's own management impose limits to capital expenditure. Limits might be imposed because a firm fears losing control. For example, funds may be available from business angels or by issuing more shares. However, this could result in the loss of control as new owners are introduced. Limits might also be imposed by senior managers because the overall corporate strategy involves allocating each division in the organisation a certain amount of money. Such allocations are likely to be inflexible regardless of the investment opportunities within each division. Funds may also be rationed because of a firm's gearing. Managers may

decide against taking on more debt because they want to avoid high interest payments.

Inflation When prices are rising rapidly, investment decisions become even more difficult. This is because inflation can distort monetary values and create uncertainty. Rapid inflation reduces the value of money and as prices rise the value of money received in the future from investment projects will be worth less. This could discourage businesses from undertaking investment. It can be difficult to predict what will happen to inflation rates in the future. Also, if prices rise sharply, interest rates are also likely to rise as will the cost of other resources. This uncertainty is likely to lead to investment projects being postponed or cancelled. Inflation was quite a serious problem during the 1970s and 1980s when rates were in double figures. However, in recent years inflation has been low and steady. This has reduced uncertainty and investment in the economy has increased. Figure 2 shows inflation rates and investment levels respectively in the UK.

Taxation Businesses have to pay tax on their profits. Sole traders and partners pay income tax and limited companies pay

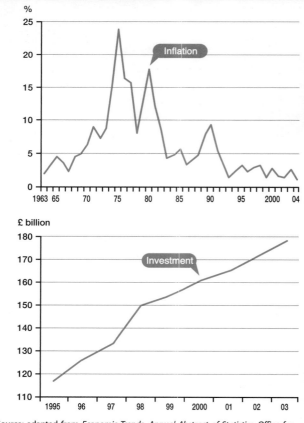

Figure 2 *UK inflation rate 1963-2004, UK investment 1995-2003*

Source: adapted from *Economic Trends, Annual Abstract of Statistics*, Office for National Statistics.

orporation tax. In recent years taxes on business profit have been educed. For example, corporation tax has been reduced from 0% to 30% and for some firms is as low as 19%. This means that ompanies get to keep more of their profit. Consequently they ave more funds available for investment which might encourage nem to undertake more investment in the future. This might also ontribute to the investment trend shown in Figure 2. Businesses an also offset the cost of investment against tax. This reduces neir tax liability and serves as another incentive to invest. ienerally, the government would like businesses to invest more nd as a result they have made business investment more 'tax riendly'.

luman relations It is not uncommon for investment projects to ave a significant impact on staff in an organisation. For example, nvestment in plant and machinery might mean that staff have to e retrained. This might take time and delay production to some xtent. Some staff might be resistant to new technology because ney may be afraid that they cannot cope with it. There is also the ossibility that investment in plant and machinery will be at the xpense of jobs. This will also raise staff anxieties. However, a lot of nvestment is to help the business grow. This might create new bbs and improve future job security.

Corporate strategy The views that companies take on nvestment decisions often reflect their overall objectives. For xample, a business that is growing rapidly through acquisitions night prefer to invest in the takeover of a close rival rather than pend money introducing total quality management.

Business confidence John Maynard Keynes, the economist, rgued that business confidence was one of the most important nfluences on investment decisions. Business owners and managers ave to take a long-term view when making investment decisions. they are optimistic about the future and feel confident about rading conditions and the progress of their business, they are nore likely to risk money for investment. On the other hand, if ney are pessimistic, they are likely to shelve or abandon nvestment plans. Business confidence may be influenced by a range f factors. They are shown in Figure 3.

thical considerations Increasingly, businesses want to be 'good orporate citizens'. This means they have to be socially responsible vhen making investment decisions and take into account the

views of all stakeholders. They may do this because they believe it is the right thing to do or because it is likely to improve their image. So, for example, a business might avoid building a new factory in a location that is environmentally sensitive even though financial costs would be minimised.

The costs associated with investment

When making investment decisions it is important to focus only on the relevant costs.

Capital outlay This is the cost of setting up the project before it becomes operational. The capital costs of investment projects can be very high and place a strain on a firm's financial resources. The problem is made worse because during the setting up of an investment project such as building a new supermarket, there is no income. Revenues will not be generated until the supermarket has been built, fitted, stocked and finally opened. The capital cost of investment projects is highly relevant and will influence the final investment decision.

Operating costs Once an investment project is up and running further costs will be incurred. In the supermarket example above, operating costs will include heating, lighting, insurance, cleaning, staff wages and depreciation. These are ongoing costs and will be

Figure 4 *The new Wembley Stadium*

In May 2000, Aston Villa and Chelsea were the last two teams to play in an FA Cup final at Wembley Stadium. Since then the old stadium has been demolished and a new one is under construction. The new Wembley Stadium will cost £757m to build and have an all-seat capacity of 90,000. It will be the biggest football stadium in the world with every seat under cover. According to Wayne Rooney 'We're all looking forward to the chance to play in front of 90,000 England fans at the new Wembley – it will be the greatest stadium on earth'. A breakdown of the cost is as follows:

- Land and design   £120m
- Construction costs   £352m
- Demolition of the old stadium and refitting the new one £99m
- Contribution to the local infrastructure   £21m
- Financing, management and other costs   £165m

These costs are sunk costs. Once the stadium is complete they cannot be recovered. Any further investment by the FA in relation to the stadium, such as building hotels, restaurants and other facilities, should not take into account these sunk costs.

Source: adapted from the Wembley website.

Figure 3 *Factors that might affect business confidence*

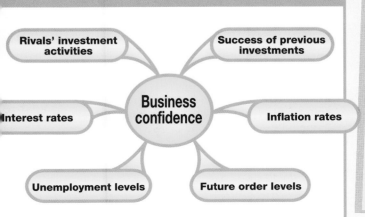

- Rivals' investment activities
- Success of previous investments
- Interest rates
- **Business confidence**
- Inflation rates
- Unemployment levels
- Future order levels

used when calculating the expected net cash flows. Operating costs will be subtracted from estimated future revenues and are therefore highly relevant when appraising investment projects.

Sunk costs With some investment projects the money spent setting them up cannot be recovered. If this is the case the costs associated with the setting up of the project are said to be sunk costs. A good example would be the construction of a railway tunnel. Once the tunnel has been built, to provide a railway service to make use of the tunnel, further investment would be required. Track, rolling stock and signalling would be needed for example. Sometimes businesses go ahead with investment simply because they have already spent a lot of money on sunk costs. However, sunk costs should be ignored when evaluating investment. In this case, only the additional costs of providing a railway service should be taken into account. Another example of a sunk cost is shown in Figure 4.

General business costs Investment appraisal does not involve looking at any other costs except those relating to specific investment projects. For example, a business investing in a staff training programme should not consider the cost of providing staff meals during training if these are provided under normal circumstances. Any business cost that is not linked to the investment project should not be taken into account. Also, where a resource is used both for the investment project and other business purposes, it is important to allocate only part of the resource's cost to the investment project. For example, if a senior manager spends one day a week working on a new investment project, only a fifth of their wages should be treated as an investment cost.

Lease or buy decisions

Businesses are sometimes faced with a choice when deciding how to fund investment projects. For example, a plc may choose between using share capital or loan capital when buying another company. When purchasing fixed assets such as plant, machinery, equipment, vehicles and tools, a business may choose between buying or leasing them. There are advantages and drawbacks to both methods. However, the circumstances of the business may influence the decision. Some examples are given below.

- If a business has poor cash flow and difficulties raising finance, leasing may be preferred. The payments for fixed assets are spread over a longer period of time so cash flow will be improved. Also, the need to raise a large amount of money to fund a purchase is avoided.
- Leasing may also be preferred when a business first starts trading. This is because heavy capital expenditure will use up too many financial resources at a time when the business may be struggling to establish itself.
- Leasing may be the best option if certain assets are only required for short periods of time. For example, a farmer may prefer to lease a combine harvester because it is only needed for 5 weeks of the year.
- When investing in property, buying may be preferred because the asset can be used as security for a mortgage. Also, a business that decides to buy property has the legal right to make changes to its physical nature such as refurbishing and extending. This may not be possible with property that is leased.

Generally, over a long period of time leasing tends to be more expensive than buying. However, an increasing number of

Figure 5 *London Taverns plc*

London Taverns plc operates a small chain of pubs in the Greater London area. It specialises in buying run-down pubs an developing them. It attracts customers by offering good ales an affordable food. In 2005, the company identified a huge pub in North London that it was interested in buying. It had been closed down for two years and needed extensive refurbishment. The capital outlay and expected net cash flows for the first five years of the investment are shown in the table below.

Capital outlay	YR 1	YR 2	YR 3	YR 4	YR 5	TOTAL
£3.5m	£1m	£1.2m	£1.4m	£1.7m	£2m	£7.3m

London Taverns evaluates investment projects using the NPV method. It aims to generate a NPV of £2m after 5 years with every investment. In this case, assuming that the rate of interest is 5%, the NPV is £2.688m ([£1m × 0.95 + £1.2m × 0.90 + £1.4m × 0.86 + £1.7m × 0.82 + £2m × 0.78] − £3.5m). Therefore, this investment will reach the £2m target quite comfortably and could be undertaken. However, London Taverns often uses sensitivity analysis to look at the effect on the NPV if there is a downturn in the market. In this case, the company will buy the pub if the NPV > £2m, even when revenues are down by 10%. The estimated net cash flows, if revenue dips by 10%, are shown below.

	YR 1	YR 2	YR 3	YR 4	YR 5	TOTAL
10% lower revenue	£0.9m	£1.08m	£1.26m	£1.53m	£1.8m	£6.57m

The NPV is now £2.0692m ([£0.9m × 0.95 + £1.08m × 0.9 + £1.26m × 0.86 + £1.53m × 0.82 + £1.8m × 0.78] - £3.5m). Since the NPV is still greater than £2m, London Taverns is likely to go ahead with this investment. Sensitivity analysis has helped London Taverns to look at the effect of a dip in revenue on the NPV of an investment.

usinesses are selling some of their assets and leasing them back. his suggests that leasing charges are lower than they used to be r perhaps the money tied up in some fixed assets can be used ore productively by a business.

ensitivity analysis

ensitivity analysis may be used to analyse the effects of changes in ome of the variables that influence investment returns. It allows

businesses to ask 'What if?' questions when appraising investment projects. For example, what will happen to the NPV of an investment project if estimated cash flows are 10% lower? Generally, the method is used to find out how sensitive the returns on investment projects are to changes in expected costs and revenues. For example, is an investment project still viable if there is a 20% fall in net cash flow? An example is given in Figure 5.

Meeting the assessment criteria - examiners' guidance

You need to write a report evaluating two proposed investment projects. You need to include a discussion on the suitability of the methods used and an analysis of the estimated future cash flows.

Business example - The Herriot Group

The Herriot Group runs a chain of hotels in Europe. The company has grown steadily in recent years through acquisitions. However, the scope for acquisitions has started to dwindle and the company is looking at building a brand new hotel complex in Eastern Europe. Two sites have been earmarked by the company, one in Poland and another in Slovenia. Details of their costs and expected net cash flows are given below. It is proposed to use the payback method of appraisal to decide which project to invest in. However, the company also wants to conduct a sensitivity analysis to see how the payback varies if net cash flows are 20% higher or 20% lower.

Mark Band 1 *You need to show a basic understanding of investment appraisal techniques evidenced by accurate calculations. Some attempt to discuss the suitability of methods and the advantages and disadvantages of each should also be described.*

The Herriot Group will use the payback method to appraise the two investments. The Polish complex has a payback period of 3 years and 6 months while the Slovenian site has a payback period of 4 years and 2 months. Therefore the Herriot Group would choose the Polish site because it has the shortest payback. The payback method of investment appraisal is quite simple to apply and appropriate when technology is changing rapidly. This method may also be helpful if a business has cash flow problems. This is because the project selected will return cash to the business more quickly than the others. It could also be argued that the risk in investment is reduced if projects with shorter paybacks are selected. Projects with short paybacks have less time to go wrong. However, the payback method of appraisal has some limitations. It ignores all the cash flows after the payback period. This could lead to more profitable options

being ignored if cash flows are very high for projects with longer payback periods. The overall profitability of investment projects is also ignored. This is because the speed of repayment is the criteria used to evaluate investment options. However, in this case the Polish site makes £10m more profit over the 10 years than the Slovenian site.

Mark Band 2 *You need to consider the suitability of appraisal methods with more reference given to the scenario. For example, conflicts and problems should be addressed. A basic understanding of sensitivity analysis should also be shown.*

If the Herriot Group uses the payback method to choose between the two hotel developments the Polish site would be chosen. This has the shortest payback period. The £100m investment in the Polish site would be recovered in 3 years and 6 months. The £85m Slovenian development would take a little longer – 4 years and 2 months. It could be argued that this method of appraisal is not the best to use. Although it is simple and appropriate if a business has cash flow problems or when technology is changing quickly, it does have some serious inadequacies. For example, it ignores all the cash flows after the payback period. This could lead to more profitable options being ignored if cash flows are very high for projects with longer payback periods. The overall profitability of investment projects is also ignored. This is because the speed of repayment is the criteria used to evaluate investment options. However, in this case the Polish site makes £10m more profit over the 10 years than the Slovenian site - although the Polish site does require a larger capital outlay. If the ARR or the NPV methods were used the profitability of the two projects could be identified. The Herriot Group also uses sensitivity analysis when appraising investment projects. Sensitivity analysis may be used to analyse the effects of changes in some of the variables that influence investment returns. It allows businesses to ask 'What if?' questions when appraising investment projects. For example, in this case, what will happen to the payback period if estimated cash flows are 20% higher or lower?

Country	Cost (£)	Expected net cash flows (£m)										
		YR 1	YR 2	YR 3	YR 4	YR 5	YR 6	YR 7	YR 8	YR 9	YR 10	Total
Poland	100	25	30	30	30	35	35	30	30	25	25	295
Slovenia	85	20	20	20	20	30	30	30	35	35	30	270

Mark Band 3 *You need to draw clear conclusions regarding the acceptance of projects and the limitations of the appraisal methods used should be discussed in detail. You should also make reasoned judgements concerning sensitivity analysis, supported by accurate and appropriate calculations.*

		Expected net cash flows (£)										
	YR 1	YR 2	YR 3	YR 4	YR 5	YR 6	YR 7	YR 8	YR 9	YR 10	To...
Poland	25	30	30	30	35	35	30	30	25	25	29
20% higher	30	36	36	36	42	42	36	36	30	30	35
20% lower	20	24	24	24	28	28	24	24	20	20	23

According to the payback method of investment appraisal the Herriot Group should select the Polish site for the hotel development. The payback period for the Polish site is 3 years 6 months. This is shorter than the payback period for the Slovenian site which is expected to be 4 years and 2 months. The payback method of investment appraisal is very simple to use and is particularly appropriate if a business wants to recover the cost of an investment quickly. Herriot Group might favour this method because the investments are overseas and may be considered quite risky. However, there are some drawbacks with this method. It ignores all the cash flows after the payback period and could lead to more profitable options being ignored if cash flows are high for projects with longer payback periods. The overall profitability of investment projects is also ignored. This is because the speed of repayment is the criteria used to evaluate investment options. However, in this case the Polish site makes £10m more profit over the 10 years than the Slovenian site -

although the Polish site does require a larger capital outlay. The Herriot Group also uses sensitivity analysis when appraising investment projects. This may be used to analyse the affects of changes in some of the variables that influence investment returns. It allows businesses to ask 'What if?' questions when appraising investment projects. For example, in this case, what will happen to the payback period if estimated cash flows are 20% higher or 20% lower? The table over shows the revenues from the Polish project if they were 20% higher and 20% lower.

If the revenues from the investment were 20% higher the payback would be slightly shorter at just under 3 years (2 years and 11.3 months). However, if the revenues were 20% lower than predicted the payback would obviously be longer – 4 years 3.4 months. With this information the Herriot Group can reflect on whether the investment is still attractive.

Portfolio practice · Moreton Health Care

Moreton Health Care runs 20 nursing homes and care establishments in the UK. It has a number of contracts with local authorities and health care trusts to provide care for the elderly. The company has struggled to expand in recent years as financial institutions have been reluctant to lend the company money. In 2005, Moreton identified two sites for new homes that were believed to be profitable. One was in Leamington Spa and one in Banbury. However, because of the shortage of funds only one could be considered. Details of their costs and expected net cash flows are shown below.

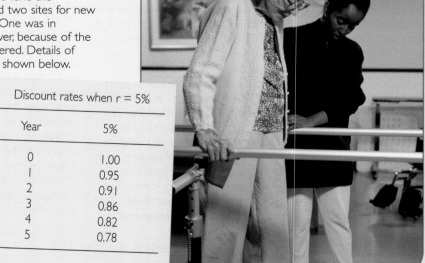

(a) **Using this case as an example, explain what is meant by hard capital rationing.**

(b) **Calculate the net present values of the two investment projects and state which one should be selected. (Assume that the rate of interest is 5% over the period.)**

(c) **(i) Moreton Health Care will only consider investment projects if Net Present Value (NPV) >£4m. Use sensitivity analysis to see whether the project would still be accepted if revenues were 20% lower. (ii) How might business confidence affect this investment decision?**

Discount rates when r = 5%	
Year	5%
0	1.00
1	0.95
2	0.91
3	0.86
4	0.82
5	0.78

Site	Cost (£)	Expected net cash flows (£m)					
		YR 1	YR 2	YR 3	YR 4	YR 5	Total
Leamington Spa	20	4	5	6	7	8	30
Banbury	24	6	6	7	7	8	34

39 Investing in other companies

Financial assets

Section 31 explained that successful businesses may accumulate cash over a period of time and use it in a number of ways. For example, it could be used to reduce borrowings, invested in new projects or placed in reserve in case the business encounters difficulties in the future. One of the options mentioned was that it could be used to buy financial assets. Financial assets are claims on real assets that are likely to earn a financial return. Figure 1 shows some examples of financial assets that a business might invest in with surplus cash.

Figure 1 Examples of financial assets

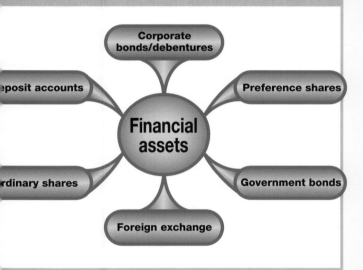

Ordinary shares

These are sometimes called equities and are the most common type of share. In addition to being a part owner of the company, shareholders may enjoy two financial returns from holding ordinary shares.

Dividends. This is a share of the profit made by a company. Dividends are variable and discretionary. This means that company directors decide on the size of dividend payments. The amount paid will depend on how much profit the company makes and how much is needed for future investment and other uses by the business. However, the directors of companies like to remain loyal to shareholders and often maintain dividends even when profits fall. Figure 2 shows an example of this.

Capital gains. Many investors buy shares in the hope of making a capital gain. A capital gain arises when a shareholder sells shares for a higher price than was paid for them. For example, in June 2003 the price of shares in Close Brothers, the merchant bank in Figure 2, was 600p, by January 2004 they had risen to 800p. Therefore, a shareholder would have made a

capital gain of 200p per share if they had bought and sold at these times.

Ordinary shares are the riskiest type of shares to buy in a company. This is because dividends are discretionary and may not be paid. There is also the chance that share prices could fall. This might result in shareholders making a capital loss if they have to sell their shares. Also, if the company collapses, ordinary shareholders could lose their entire investment in the company. Finally, since ordinary shareholders are part-owners of the company they have voting rights – one vote for each share owned. Shareholders are invited to vote each year at the Annual General Meeting (AGM) when electing directors.

Figure 2 Dividends paid by Close Brothers

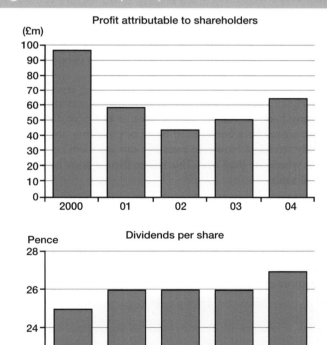

Close Brothers is an independent merchant banking group founded in the City of London over 125 years ago. The group's activities comprise asset management, corporate finance and market-making, together with investment banking and banking. The two bar charts show the profit attributable to shareholders and dividends paid over a five year period. Clearly dividends have been maintained even when the profit made by the company has fallen.

Source: adapted from Close Brothers, *Annual Report and Accounts*, 2005.

Preference shares

These shares are less risky. This is because preference shareholders are paid their dividend before ordinary shareholders. Dividends on preference shares are usually fixed. For example, the owners of 3% £1 preference shares would be paid 3p (3% x £1) for every share they own, assuming a dividend is paid. Because dividends are fixed, the prices of preference shares are less volatile than those of ordinary shares.

Another reason why preference shares are less risky is because preference shareholders usually carry preferential rights if the company is liquidated, i.e. if it ceases to trade and its assets are sold. This means that capital is repaid to them before ordinary shareholders, providing there is some money left. In most cases, preference shareholders do not have any voting rights at the company's AGM.

There are several different types of preference share.

- **Cumulative preference shares.** These entitle shareholders to receive any dividends not paid in previous years. For example, if a dividend is not declared for one year, cumulative preference shareholders are entitled to the arrears in the next year that a dividend is paid.
- **Participating preference shares.** These entitle the holder to extra dividends in addition to the fixed rate. The extra payment is made only after ordinary shareholders have received their dividend.
- **Redeemable preference shares.** The issuing company has the right to redeem these shares. This means that shareholders receive back the money for their shares at a later date.

Once shares have been issued by a company they are not normally refunded. However, investors can sell them on the stock market whenever they wish. This makes them a fairly liquid financial asset.

Corporate bonds

Corporate bonds are issued by companies as a way of raising money to invest in their business. They are loans, earn a fixed rate of return and may be bought by anyone including businesses. The key features of corporate bonds are summarised in Table 1.

Government bonds or Gilts

Gilts are bonds issued by the government. Because of this they are regarded as safe investments as the government is unlikely to go bust or to default on the interest payments. However, investors are not guaranteed to get all their capital back under all circumstances. Gilts, like corporate bonds, are traded on the stock market where their price can go up or down. Their prices can be affected by interest rates, inflation and the prices of, and returns on, other investments. Government bonds are also issued with different maturity dates like corporate bonds. Gilts can be bought and sold through brokers, high street banks or through the government's Debt Management Office (DMO) who produce a guide to buying gilts.

Foreign exchange

Some companies might invest some of their surplus cash in foreign currency. The price of currency (the exchange rate) will vary on the foreign exchange markets. This means that companies could make capital gains if the exchange rate rises. For example, if a company buys £1m of US dollars when the exchange rate is £1 = £1.80, a capital gain of £100,000 would be made if the exchange rate rose by 10% to £1 = $1.98. However, it is likely that most businesses that hold foreign currency are not speculators in this way. The currency is more likely to be held to pay for imports. But if a company strongly believes that the exchange rate is likely to rise in the future, it would be prudent to buy some foreign currency at today's prices. Investment in foreign currency is quite risky because exchange rates can be volatile.

Deposit accounts

Many firms choose to hold their cash surpluses in bank deposit accounts. This is the safest form of investment. Money held in a deposit account cannot be lost and will earn a modest but certain return. Money held in a deposit account is also very liquid. In many cases, access to it can be immediate. Table 2 shows the interest rates offered by a selection of financial institutions on deposit accounts.

Table 1 *Key features of corporate bonds*

- There is no guarantee that the money invested will be returned in full - the organisation issuing the bond might go out of business or face difficulties in meeting its interest payments.

- The maturity date for bonds may vary. For example, an investor may buy 10 year bonds or 30 year bonds. However, investors do not have to wait all that time to get their money back. They can sell them on the stock market for cash if necessary. This makes them a fairly liquid asset like shares.

- Bonds have a nominal value (usually £100) but, because bonds are traded on the stock market, the price varies and investors could make a capital gain or capital loss.

- The price of a bond can be affected by interest rates. For example, if a bond is issued with a fixed interest rate of eight per cent and interest rates are generally below 8 per cent, then eight

per cent will look like a good return and the price of the bond will tend to rise.

- Inflation can also affect the price of bonds. If inflation rises, the interest rate on some bonds might start to look less attractive compared with other investments.

- Companies have different credit ratings and a company with a high credit rating is regarded as a safer bet than a company with a lower credit rating. Market analysts might take the view that a particular company's bond no longer qualifies for a high rating and the price of the bond might fall.

- Corporate bonds are considered less risky than shares because they earn a fixed return and their prices tend not to fluctuate as much. Bonds are also loans which the company eventually repays.

Table 2 *Interest rates offered by a selection of financial institutions in October 2005*

Institution	Gross	Minimum	Type
Portman	5.10%	£1,000	90 days' notice
Northern rock	5.01%	£1	Internet only
Anglo Irish Bank	4.85%	£500	7 days notice
Most consistent schemes over three years			
Nationwide	4.75%	£1	Internet only
Halifax	4.65%	£1	Internet only
Intelligent Finance	4.50%	£1	Tel/Internet

Financial assets and the balance sheet

The financial assets owned by companies are shown on the balance sheet. If the investment is long-term in nature it will appear as a fixed asset. If the investment is only short-term then financial assets will appear as a current asset. In both cases they are listed as 'investments'. Figure 3 shows an example.

How does a business choose which company to invest in?

When a business invests money in other companies it wants to maximise its return. However, choosing a suitable company to invest in might be difficult. There are many to choose from and managers will have to evaluate the suitability of each one identified as a possibility. A number of factors will have to be taken into account.

Figure 3 *Astra Zeneca – investments*

Astra Zeneca is a large pharmaceuticals company that researches, develops and markets a wide range of pharmaceutical products. An extract from the 2004 balance sheet is shown below. There are two entries which relate to financial investments. According to the notes to the accounts the $267m fixed asset investments relate to shares owned in other companies. Since they are fixed the shares are not likely to be sold in the next 12 months. The $4,091 short-term investments relate mainly to $4,077m held in deposit accounts and the rest in other listed investments and securities.

Fixed assets	$m
Tangible fixed assets	8,083
Goodwill and intangible assets	2,826
Fixed asset investments	267
Current assets	
Stocks	3,020
Debtors	6,274
Short-term investments	4,091
Cash	1,055

Source: adapted from Astra Zeneca, *Annual Report and Accounts*, 2004.

Profitability Inevitably, the amount of profit a company is making is an important factor. Businesses will look at the historical performance of the company, the current performance and the potential that the company has for the future. The historical performance of a company will be easy to analyse. For example, the annual reports and accounts usually give a five year history of a company's turnover, profit and dividends. Figure 4 shows an example.

There will also be information available about the current trading performance. For example, there will be media reports and press releases relating to current performance. However, evaluating the future potential of a company is much more difficult. Businesses will have to rely on the media and perhaps make visits to companies that are under consideration. The chairperson's statement in the Annual Report and Accounts might outline, to some extent, how the company is expected to perform in the future. But the report may be a little biased because it is written by someone with a self interest. The future plight of a company is subject to so many unpredictable external factors that it is difficult to gauge future profitability. Finally, some investors specialise in recovery stocks. These investors buy shares in companies that are not doing particularly well at the moment but are expected to improve in the future. The price of shares in these companies are likely to be lower than those in companies that are currently doing well.

Liquidity A business will generally want to invest in companies that are financially stable. To evaluate the liquidity of a business it will be necessary to look at the amount of current assets a company has in relation to its current liabilities. If the current assets are between 1.5 and 2 times the size of current liabilities most would argue that the company has sufficient liquid resources. Retailers, however, can operate effectively with fewer liquid resources. A business may also undertake credit searches to ascertain how creditworthy a company is. A company's credit

Figure 4 *Five year history of James Fisher and Sons plc*

James Fisher and Sons is a leading provider of marines services with its business divided across three sectors – Marine support services, Marine oil services and Cable ships. The table below shows the financial performance of the company over a five year period. This information could be used by managers of a business when deciding where to invest surplus cash. Historically the company has performed well. Both turnover and the dividend payment have risen consistently.

	2000	2001	2002	2003	2004
Turnover (£000s)	60,577	67,567	71,111	77,215	78,753
Profit before tax (£000s)	5,007	8,077	9,718	5,380	13,091
Dividend payment (£000s)	2,248	2,484	2,836	3,254	3,754

Source: adpated from James Fisher and Sons plc *Annual Report and Accounts*, 2004.

rating would tend to reflect its financial position. Another factor to take into account is the ability of the firm to generate cash. For example, does the company sell its products for cash or does it offer trade credit? Is the company able to collect money from customers easily? Does the company need to hold high levels of stocks? Can stocks be sold quickly?

Gearing The long-term financial structure of a company will also be an important consideration when deciding whether to invest in a company. A company's balance sheet will show the relationship between share capital and loan capital. Generally, shares in companies that are highly geared may not be attractive. This is because they are heavily in debt and have large interest payments to meet. This will reduce the scope for paying dividends in the short term. However, in the longer-term, if debt can be reduced, the future dividend payout may be very attractive. Highly geared companies may also find it difficult to attract funding in the future. This could hamper its growth and future performance.

Competition and market considerations When choosing which companies to invest in it will also help to look at the general trading conditions in the market. If a market is particularly

competitive it may be one to avoid. It obviously makes sense to invest in companies that are operating in growing markets where there is less threat from competition. For example, in the UK many manufacturing companies are struggling to compete with competitors from China and other Asian producers. On the other hand, during 2004 and 2005 the price of oil across the world rose very sharply and investing in oil companies would have paid handsome dividends.

1. Obtain the Annual Report and Accounts of four companies.
2. Look at their historical performance of the last five years. Focus on turnover, profit, dividends and cash generation.
3. Based on this historical performance alone, determine which company looks to provide the best investment opportunity.
4. Write a brief report explaining why you would invest in your chosen company.

Research task

Portfolio practice · **Shares in ITV**

ITV is one of Britain's leading media companies, owning all channel 3 licences in England and Wales. The company has operations in television broadcasting and production, pay and digital TV and leasing. ITV also owns the market-leading cinema screen advertising business in Britain. According to fund manager Tim Steer, at New Star, it is best to buy shares in companies whose sales are rising and avoid those in companies where sales are flat or falling.

On this basis, ITV shares should be avoided. Its sales have hovered just above the £2bn mark for three years. Also, the company appears to be more focused on cost cutting than increasing revenue. About £120m of costs are expected to be cut - but this is only to be expected after a recent merger between Carlton and Granada. ITV's share of viewing is falling. Seven years ago its share of the viewing market was 24% - it has fallen to 17%. The number of TV channels is growing fast. For example, on October 10, 2005, Channel 4 launched its More 4 channel. This means that viewers and advertising business and are spread more thinly. ITV has seen its advertising revenues fall by 3% in the last quarter alone.

Steer argues that ITV needs to produce more programmes that people want to watch. He says 'Sky Sports and Channel 4 are eating ITV's lunch'. Channel 4 has had success with The Ashes, Lost and Desperate Housewives while ITV launched Celebrity Wrestling which had to be withdrawn and is still showing Who Wants to be a Millionaire - although it has had success with the X Factor. Steer believes the future relies heavily on developing revenues with ITV 2, 3 and 4. One bright spot on the horizon is that the next round of regulatory changes should work in ITV's favour with less emphasis on public broadcasting.

Source: adapted from the *Sunday Times*, 9.10.2005.

Figure 5 *ITV PLC share price*

Absolute share price

Source: adapted from www.itvplc.com.

(a) **Calculate the capital gain for an investor that bought 1m of ITV shares at their lowest point at the beginning of 2003 and sold them on 1.07.05.**
(b) **Analyse the factors that should be taken into account by any business when deciding how to invest cash surpluses.**
(c) **Discuss whether shares in ITV were worth purchasing in 2005.**

Meeting the assessment criteria - examiners' guidance

You need to produce a report which evaluates a proposed investment in a limited company. You need to include the differences between debt and equity investment and consider the viability of the investment using appropriate financial ratios.

Business example - Branshot Travel plc

Branshot Travel is a chain of travel agents. The company owns over 100 shops in Ireland and England and has enjoyed a great deal of success in recent years, especially in holidays to newer destinations in countries in Eastern Europe. Its success has been helped greatly by the development of its online business and the company is in the process of scaling down its high street shop presence by selling outlets to property developers. This has generated a large cash surplus (about £4m) which the company is looking to invest. Two options have been identified.

- Corporate bonds. Portwill Holdings, a large plastics manufacturer, is issuing £50m of 7% 10 year bonds. The company has a very high credit rating and the issue is expected to be a success. The current rate of interest in the economy is 4.5%.
- Ordinary shares. Advisers to Branshot Travel have recommended a number of companies as investment targets but one company, Hillarth Group, an aircraft components manufacturer, looks particularly attractive. Turnover and profit have risen by 100% in three years and dividend payments have increased accordingly. The share price is currently 80p but analysts expect this to rise to about £1 in the next two years.

Mark Band 1 *Outline the key differences between equity and debt investments.*

Both of the investment options available to Branshot Travel look attractive. Corporate bonds are loans to a business and in this case the money is being lent to Portwill Holdings. The bonds are likely to be the safest investment because the money will be repaid when the bonds mature. However, if Branshot Travel decides to dispose of them, they can be sold for cash on the stock market. The return is also quite attractive. The 7% paid to bond holders is 2.5% higher than the current rate of interest in the economy. The ordinary shares in Hillarth Group are a much riskier investment for Branshot Travel. The dividends paid to shareholders are not guaranteed. They can vary significantly and the prices of shares are more volatile than the prices of bonds.

Mark Band 2 *When deciding between the investment opportunities consideration of trends should be taken into account and any causes for concern should be identified.*

Branshot Travel has identified two different investment opportunities. Portwill Holdings is issuing some 10 year bonds with a 7% fixed rate of return. The company has a very high credit rating and the issue sounds as though it is going to be a success. Corporate bonds are a fairly safe investment because the money is a loan to the company and will be repaid. The return is also guaranteed. So, for example, if Branshot bought £4m of these bonds it would get £280,000 (7% x £4m) interest per annum. However, investment in shares might earn both a dividend and a capital gain. Hillarth Group is currently a successful company and dividends have been rising. Also, the share price is expected to rise by 25% over the next two years. This means that if Branshot

bought £4m of these shares it would make £1m (25% x £4m) capital gain in just two years. This excludes dividends. However, share prices can also fall because they are subject to a range of external factors. For example, if the state of the economy worsens or there is a drop in the demand for

aircraft, shares in Hillarth might fall in price. This would be a cause for concern for Branshot. Before a final decision is made Branshot should also look at trends in the returns on bonds, bond prices, Hillarth's profitability and the state of the aircraft market. This will it to make a more informed decision.

Mark Band 3 *Your report should make reference to risk and reward and outline how these relate to the different kinds of investment. You need to draw reasoned conclusions regarding the viability of the proposed investment. Limitations should also be highlighted with any requirements for further information.*

Branshot Travel has accumulated a cash pile of £4m which it wants to invest. One simple option would be to put it into a bank deposit account where it would earn 4.5% pa. This would generate a return of £180,000 pa (4.5% x £4m). There would be no risk at all in this option and the money would be immediately available if needed in an emergency. However, by investing in bonds a higher reward can be obtained. Portwill Holdings is issuing some 7% 10 year bonds which Branshot could buy. This would generate a return of £280,000 for Branshot - a £100,000 more than the return on a bank deposit. However, there would be some risk. If the company collapsed Branshot might not get its money back. Also, bond prices can fall as well as rise, so a capital loss could be made. In this case though, Portwill Holdings has a good credit rating and the bond issue is expected to be a success. The riskiest option of all is buying shares in Hillarth group. Buying ordinary shares is risky because share prices can fall and the dividends are variable and discretionary. This means that the directors are not legally obliged to pay dividends, if the company starts to struggle, for example. However, according to the information Hillarth is doing well. Analysts expect the share price to rise by 25% in just two years. This means that Branshot could make a capital gain of £1m (25% x £4m). The return from dividends would also have to be added to this. However, share prices can be extremely volatile. They are not just linked to the performance of the company. They can be affected by a wide range of external factors. If share prices fell, Branshot could end up losing a lot of its money.

Branshot should consider its attitude to risk before investing. If the £4m is not earmarked for anything in the next few years it may be worth investing in Hillarth. When making investment decisions it is important to gather as much information as possible. Branshot may want to look at Hillarth's accounts for the last few years, examine closely the situation in the aircraft industry and analyse a range of economic indicators. The information given in this case may be limited. For example, share prices of other companies may be expected to rise by 50% or more. This would make the Hillarth investment less attractive.

Company performance and ratio analysis

The value of ratio analysis

Ratio analysis was introduced in section 35. It was used to analyse the working capital position of a business. However, financial ratios can be used to examine a much wider range of performance indicators such as profitability, efficiency in resource use, capital gearing and the returns investors get on their shareholdings. Ratio analysis provides a quantitative approach to financial analysis. This is scientific and provides a sound and clear basis for comparison. Ratios can be compared over time and between different firms. For example, one supermarket chain can use financial ratios to compare its performance with other supermarket chains to see how well they are doing in the industry. Ratio analysis can be used by a business, like other investors, when deciding which shares to buy.

Performance or profitability ratios

These can be used assess how well the business is doing. They tend to focus on profit, turnover and the amount of capital employed in the business. However, when using performance ratios it is important to consider the objectives of a company. For example, using a performance ratio which focuses on profit may not be appropriate if the company is pursuing other objectives such as social responsibility. Some performance ratios are known as activity ratios which look at how well a business uses its resources such as stock. The ratios in this section are calculated from the financial information shown in Table 1. It shows financial details about Scott's Books, a small chain of bookshops. Its outlets are located mainly in the north and east of England.

Return on capital employed (ROCE) ROCE is one of the most important ratios used to measure the performance of a company. It is sometimes referred to as the primary ratio and compares the profit made by a company with the amount of capital invested. The advantage of this ratio is that it relates profit to the size of the business. When calculating ROCE, it is standard practice to define profit as net profit (or operating profit) before tax and interest. This is sometimes called earnings before interest and tax (EBIT). Tax is ignored because it is determined by the government and is therefore outside the control of the company. Interest is excluded because it does not relate to the business's ordinary trading activities. The ROCE can be calculated using the formula shown in Figure 1.

When a ratio has been calculated, it requires interpretation. The return on capital employed will vary between industries, however, the higher the ratio the better. Over the two years Scott's Books has seen its ROCE increase from 20% to 22.3%. Whether this is good depends on the ROCE other book stores, such as Waterstones, are enjoying. Also, investors might compare the ROCE with the potential return if the capital were invested elsewhere. For example, if £6,720,000 was placed in a bank deposit account in 2005, it might have earned a 4.5% return. Consequently the 22% ROCE in 2005 appears impressive. However, an investor

Table 1 *Balance sheet and profit and loss account for Scott's Books*

Scott's Books
Balance sheet as at 31.12.05

	2005 £000s	2004 £000s
Fixed assets		
Land and property	3,500	3,700
Fixtures and fittings	1,200	900
	4,700	4,600
Current assets		
Stock	1,560	1,090
Debtors	200	300
Cash at bank	1,010	890
	2,770	2,280
Creditors: amounts falling due in one year		
Trade creditors	780	540
Accruals	120	100
Taxation	300	250
	1,200	890
Net current assets	1,570	1,390
Creditors: amounts falling due after one year		
	(1,000)	(900)
Net assets	**5,270**	**5,090**
Capital and reserves		
Share capital	1,000	1,000
Other reserves	1,800	1,890
Profit and loss account	2,470	2,200
	5,270	**5,090**

Scott's Books
Profit and loss account Y/E 31.12.05

	2005 £000s	2004 £000s
Turnover	7,800	6,560
Cost of sales	4,300	3,890
Gross profit	3,500	2,670
Administration expenses	2,100	1,470
Operating profit	1,400	1,200
Net interest payable	100	90
Profit before tax	1,300	1,110
Taxation	300	250
Profit after tax	1,000	860
Dividends	730	690
Retained profit	270	170

Figure 1 *Return on capital employed (ROCE)*

$$ROCE = \frac{\text{Profit before tax and interest}}{\text{Long-term capital employed}} \times 100$$

To illustrate how financial ratios can be used to examine the performance of a business, the balance sheet and profit and loss account for Scott's Books will be used. The profit before tax and interest in 2005 was £1,400,000. Long-term capital employed was £6,270,000. Long-term capital employed is shareholders' funds plus any long-term creditors, i.e. £5,270,000 + £1,000,000.

$$\text{For 2005 ROCE} = \frac{£1,400,000}{£6,270,000} \times 100 = 22.3\%$$

$$\text{For 2004 ROCE} = \frac{£1,200,000}{£5,990,000} \times 100 = 20\%$$

the company will also wish to be rewarded for the risk involved. Money invested by shareholders in Scott's Books is at risk if the business fails. Therefore, for the investment to be worthwhile, the ROCE must be substantially above the return that could be earned in a 'safe' investment.

Gross profit margin The gross profit margin, also known as the mark-up, shows the gross profit made on sales turnover. It is calculated using the formula shown in Figure 2.

Higher gross margins are preferable to lower ones. However, they vary a lot in different industries. Generally, a fast stock

Figure 2 *Gross profit margin*

$$\text{Gross profit margin} \frac{\text{Gross profit}}{\text{Turnover}} \times 100$$

For Scott's Books in 2005 gross profit was £3,500,000 and turnover was £7,800,000.

$$\text{For 2005 Gross profit margin} \frac{£3,500,000}{£7,800,000} \times 100 = 44.9\%$$

$$\text{For 2004 Gross profit margin} \frac{£2,670,000}{£6,560,000} \times 100 = 40.7\%$$

turnover is associated with lower gross margins and vice versa. For example, a supermarket with a fast stock turnover is likely to have a lower gross margin than a car retailer with a much slower stock turnover. The gross margin for Scott's Books has improved slightly over the two years. Comparisons with other booksellers would help to confirm whether this was a satisfactory performance.

Net profit margin This ratio helps to measure how well a business controls its overheads. If the difference between the gross margin and the net margin is small, this suggests that overheads are low. This is because net profit equals gross profit less overheads. The net profit margin can be calculated using the formula in Figure 3.

Again, higher margins are better than lower ones. The net profit margin for Scott's Books is little changed over the two years although it has fallen slightly. Net margins over 10% are generally considered to be very good. However, comparisons with other booksellers would have to be made before drawing a final conclusion.

Figure 3 *Net profit margin*

$$\text{Net profit margin} \frac{\text{Net profit before tax and interest}}{\text{Turnover}} \times 100$$

For Scott's Books in 2005 net profit before tax and interest was £1,400,000 and turnover was £7,800,000.

$$\text{For 2005 Net profit margin} \frac{£1,400,000}{£7,800,000} \times 100 = 17.9\%$$

$$\text{For 2004 net profit margin} \frac{£1,200,000}{£6,560,000} \times 100 = 18.3\%$$

Activity ratios

Activity ratios are a type of performance ratio. They look at how well a business uses some of its resources such as stock and net assets.

Asset turnover The asset turnover ratio looks at how much turnover is generated by the assets employed in the business. The formula is shown in Figure 4.

The ratio shows that, in 2005, for every £1 invested in net assets by Scott's Books, £1.48 of turnover was generated. Over the two years the asset turnover improved by a few pence. The asset turnover varies considerably in different industries. It tends to be higher in retailing and services than in manufacturing. Manufacturers have a lot of money tied up in fixed assets and asset turnover might be less than 1. In retailing it can be over 3. In this case, since Scott's is a book retailer, 1.48 might be considered low.

Figure 4 *Asset turnover*

$$\text{Asset turnover} = \frac{\text{Turnover}}{\text{Net assets}}$$

The turnover for Scott's Books in 2005 was £7,800,000 and the net assets were £5,270,000.

$$\text{For 2005 Asset turnover} = \frac{£7,800,000}{£5,270,000} \quad 1.48$$

$$\text{For 2004 Asset turnover} = \frac{£6,560,000}{£5,090,000} = 1.29$$

However, comparison with other bookshops would be necessary before making a final judgment.

Stock turnover Stock turnover measures how quickly a business uses or sells its stock. It can be calculated as: cost of sales ÷ stocks. A detailed explanation of stock turnover is given in section 35. The stock turnover for Scott's Books for 2005 and 2004 is shown in Table 2. In 2005, for example, stock turnover was £4,300,000 ÷ £1,560,000 = 2.75.

Table 2 *Stock turnover and debt collection period for Scott's Books*

Ratio	2005	2004
Stock turnover (times)	2.75	3.57
Debt collection period (days)	9	17

Debt collection period This ratio measures how effectively a business is able to collect money owed by customers that have bought goods on credit. The debt collection period is the average number of days it takes to collect debts from customers, as explained in section 35. It can be calculated as: debtors ÷ turnover x 365. The debt collection period for Scott's Books is shown in Table 2. In 2005, for example, the debt collection period was £200,000 ÷ £7,800,000 x 365 = 9 days.

Liquidity ratios

Liquidity ratios help to show whether the business is solvent. They look at the firm's ability to pay its immediate bills and focus on current assets and current liabilities. They are covered in detail in section 35. For example, the current ratio shows the working capital of a business. It can be calculated by: current assets ÷ current liabilities. The current ratio for Scott's Books in 2005 was £2,770,000 ÷ £1,200,000 = 2.3.

Gearing ratios

Gearing ratios look at the relationship between loan capital and share capital or fixed cost capital and total capital employed. Gearing ratios can be used to see whether a business is likely to be burdened by its loans. This is because highly geared companies still have to pay their interest when trading becomes difficult. The formula for the gearing ratio is shown in Figure 5.

If the gearing ratio is less than 50% the company is said to be low geared. This means that the majority of the capital is provided by the owners. If the ratio is greater than 50% the company is highly geared. In contrast, this means that a much higher proportion of total capital is borrowed. With a gearing ratio of around 15% in both years, Scott's Books is low geared.

Figure 5 *Gearing ratios*

$$\text{Gearing ratio} = \frac{\text{Fixed cost capital}}{\text{Long-term capital}} \times 100$$

Fixed cost capital includes long-term loans from banks, certain preference shares and debentures. Long-term capital includes shareholders' funds and long-term loans. For Scott's Books in 2005 the fixed cost or interest ÷ dividend bearing debt, according to the balance sheet, is £1,000,000 (creditors: amounts falling due after one year). The value of shareholders' funds was £5,270,000.

$$\text{For 2005 Gearing ratio} = \frac{£1,000,000}{£5,270,000 + £1,000,000} \times 100 = 15.9\%$$

$$\text{For 2004 Gearing ratio} = \frac{£900,000}{£5,090,000 + £900,000} \times 100 = 15.0\%$$

1. Obtain the Annual Report and Accounts of two companies in the same industry.
2. Calculate the return on net assets, the net profit margin and the interest cover for both companies in both years.
3. Write a brief report explaining which of the two companies has performed the best over the two year period.

Research task

Interest cover

The gearing ratio is a balance sheet measure of financial risk. Interest cover is a profit and loss account measure. The ratio assesses the burden of interest payments by comparing profit and interest payments. It is calculated using the formula shown in Figure 6.

If interest cover is 1, this means that all of the firm's profit would be used to pay interest. This is obviously not sustainable in the long term. In the case of Scott's Books, the cover is little changed in the two years. The company can pay its interest 14 times over. This is a very comfortable position for the company and reflects the fact that it is low geared.

Figure 6 *Interest cover*

$$\text{Interest cover} = \frac{\text{Profit before interest and tax}}{\text{Interest}}$$

The profit before tax and interest for Scott's Books in 2005 was £1,400,000 as shown in the profit and loss account. The amount of interest paid during the year was £100,000.

$$\text{For 2005 Interest cover} = \frac{£1,400,000}{£100,000} = 14 \text{ times}$$

$$\text{For 2004 Interest cover} = \frac{£1,200,000}{£90,000} = 13.3 \text{ times}$$

Portfolio practice · Gemal Ltd

Xeffir.com	2004 (£)	2005 (£)
Turnover	3.23m	6.87m
Net profit before tax and interest	0.13m	0.67m
Interest paid	0.4m	0.5m
Fixed interest capital	3.5m	5m
Shareholders' funds	4m	5m
Current assets	1.27m	1.52m
Current liabilities	1.31m	1.48m

Gemal Ltd is a family engineering company. It has recently sold part of its business to a rival for a price of £5m. The family wants the £5m to stay in the business and have decided to invest it. Two investment options have emerged.

- A high profile plc is issuing some 20 year corporate bonds which pay a fixed return of 8%. The company has an excellent credit rating and the current rate of interest in the economy is 4.5%.
- Xeffir.com sells cars on the Internet. The company has only been trading for four years but has recently started to make a profit. It has been tipped by a number of analysts to grow very quickly, however, others are less convinced. Some financial information for xeffir.com is shown in the table.

(a) Explain the value of ratio analysis to Gemal Ltd.
(b) Calculate the ROCE, net profit margin, gearing ratio, interest cover and the current ratio for 2004 and 2005.
(c) Evaluate the investment options for Gemal Ltd.

Meeting the assessment criteria - examiners' guidance

You need to produce a report which evaluates a proposed investment in a limited company. You need to include the differences between debt and equity investment and consider the viability of the investment using appropriate financial ratios.

Business example - GT7

GT7 is a high profile employment agency based in London. It specialises in the recruitment of senior managers in the retail sector. The company has been successful in recent years and has accumulated a large cash pile. It is now looking to invest £20m in shares. Two companies have been short-listed as possible investment opportunities.

- Tullow Oil plc is one of the largest independent oil & gas exploration and production companies in Europe. The group's main offices are in London, Dublin and Cape Town and Tullow employs over 200 staff.
- Punch Taverns owns over 7,300 pubs in the UK. During the year the company paid £1.2bn for Pubmaster, the UK's third largest pub chain, and purchased InnSpired Group Ltd, another chain with around 1,000 pubs. The company is growing fast and saw turnover rise 49% in just one year.

Some financial details are shown for both companies in Table 3 below. All figures are for 2004.

Table 3 *Financial information of two companies*

	Tullow Oil (£)	Punch Taverns (£)
Turnover	225.3m	637.6m
Gross profit	94.2m	396.7m
Profit before interest & tax	67.5m	303.0m
Shareholders' funds	379.1m	799.6m
Long-term creditors	244.0m	2,862.5m
Current assets	142.7m	323.5m
Current liabilities	119.3m	335.0m

Source: adapted from Tullow Oil and Punch Taverns, *Annual Report and Accounts*, 2004.

Mark Band 1 *Key ratios should be calculated accurately and some attempt should be made to relate these calculations to the investment decision.*

GT7 can use financial ratios to help decide which of the two companies to invest in. Five ratios are calculated below for both companies in 2004.

The ratios show that both companies are performing well. The gross profit margins and net profit margins are particularly high. According to these two ratios Punch Taverns appears to be the best investment. However, Tullow Oil generates a higher return on capital employed and has much less debt than Punch Taverns. It also has more working capital. GT7 might prefer to invest in Tullow Oil because there may be less risk.

ROCE

$$\text{Tullow Oil} = \frac{£67.5m}{£623.1m} \times 100 = 10.8\%$$

$$\text{Punch Taverns} = \frac{£303m}{£3,662.1m} \times 100 = 8.3\%$$

Gross profit margin

$$\text{Tullow Oil} = \frac{£94.2m}{£225.3m} \times 100 = 41.8\%$$

$$\text{Punch Taverns} = \frac{£396.7m}{£637.6m} \times 100 = 62.2\%$$

Net profit margin

$$\text{Tullow Oil} = \frac{£67.5m}{£225.3m} \times 100 = 29.9\%$$

$$\text{Punch Taverns} = \frac{£303m}{£637.6m} \times 100 = 47.5\%$$

Gearing

$$\text{Tullow Oil} = \frac{£244m}{£623.1m} \times 100 = 39.2\%$$

$$\text{Punch Taverns} = \frac{£2,862.5m}{£3,662.1m} \times 100 = 78.2\%$$

Current ratio

$$\text{Tullow Oil} = \frac{£142.7m}{£119.3m} = 1.20$$

$$\text{Punch Taverns} = \frac{£323.5m}{£335m} = 0.97$$

Mark Band 2 *Your report should show an understanding of the impact of the ratios on the possible investment, both in terms of return and eventual repayment.*

GT7 has £20m to invest in shares. Two companies have been identified as possible options - Tullow Oil, which is one of the largest independent oil & gas exploration and production companies in Europe and Punch Taverns which owns over 7,300 pubs in the UK. To help decide which might be the best company to invest in, ratios have been calculated. The gross and net profit margins are both very high indeed. This suggests that both companies are operating efficiently and are enjoying good returns on their sales. Punch Taverns has the highest gross and net margins which gives them the edge over Tullow Oil. However, when looking at the ROCE Tullow Oil is performing better. A 10.8% return on Oil production is better than the 8.3% return on running a pub estate. There may also be some doubts about the capital structure of Punch Taverns. The company is quite highly geared and clearly has a lot of debt to repay. This debt may have been taken on to help fund the big acquisitions during the year. GT7 may prefer to invest in Tullow Oil because it appears less risky. However, in the future, if Punch Taverns repays its debt quite quickly, the ROCE could rise sharply. Consequently, in the longer term Punch Taverns might be a better option.

Table 4 *Financial information of two companies*

	Tullow Oil	Punch Taverns
Return on capital employed	10.8%	8.3%
Gross profit margin	41.8%	62.2%
Net profit margin	29.9%	47.5%
Gearing	39.2%	78.2%
Current ratio	1.20	0.97

Mark Band 3 *Your report should make reference to risk and reward and outline how these relate to the different kinds of investment. You need to draw reasoned conclusions regarding the viability of the proposed investment. Limitations should also be highlighted with any requirements for further information.*

GT7 has £20m which it intends to invest in shares. Shares are a risky form of investment because dividends are not guaranteed and share prices could go down which means GT7 could lose some of their £20m. A less risky investment option might have been bonds but the returns on them are limited. In this case two companies have been identified as possible investment options. They are both profitable companies and seem to be doing very well. Indeed, according to the table of ratios below, both the gross and net profit margins are very high indeed. However, the profit is before interest and if interest payments were high the net margins will be a lot lower. Based on the profit margins Punch Taverns is clearly the most profitable company. However, the ROCE for Tullow Oil is higher than that of the pub chain. A ROCE of 10.8% is significantly better than 8.3%. This means that Tullow is generating more profit with the amount of money invested. Another problem with Punch Taverns might be the amount of debt it is burdened with. It is much more highly geared than Tullow. In fact it has twice as much debt. This could be a problem in the short term – particularly if interest rates rose. Tullow also has more working capital so in the short term the oil company might be the best investment. However, in the longer term, if the pub chain can repay its debt, interest payments will fall and ROCE will rise sharply. GT7 would need to consider how long it expects to invest the £20m in shares. If it is looking for a quick return perhaps Tullow would be the best option. However, if it is more patient Punch Taverns may be a better long-term investment. Finally, the decision here has been made on limited information. The calculation of other ratios would have been helpful and a five year trading history for both companies might have helped to detect trends over the period.

Table 5 *Financial information of two companies*

	Tullow Oil	Punch Taverns
Return on capital employed	10.8%	8.3%
Gross profit margin	41.8%	62.2%
Net profit margin	29.9%	47.5%
Gearing	39.2%	78.2%
Current ratio	1.20	0.97

Investing in other companies and ratio analysis

Shareholders' ratios

Shareholders' ratios, sometimes called investor's ratios, provide information to help investors to make decisions about buying or selling shares. They help to assess the returns investors might get from owning shares in companies. They focus on profit, dividends, the number of shares issued and share prices. To illustrate how shareholders ratios can be used to examine the performance of a business, the balance sheet and profit and loss account for Scott's Books will be used. These are shown in Table 1. Some additional financial information is also shown.

Earnings per share

The earnings per share (EPS) measures how much profit each ordinary share earns after tax. It does not, however, show how much money is actually paid to ordinary shareholders. This is because companies usually retain some profit for the business. The EPS is generally shown at the bottom of the profit and loss account in the published accounts of plcs. EPS is calculated using the formula shown in Figure 1.

Figure 1 Earnings per share

$$\text{Earnings per share} = \frac{\text{Profit after tax}}{\text{Number of ordinary shares}}$$

For Scott's Books in 2005 the net profit after tax was £1,000,000 as shown in the profit and loss account. (Note that if the company had any preference shareholders, any dividends paid to these would have to be subtracted from profit.) According to the additional information shown in Figure 1 the number of ordinary shares issued in 2005 was 20m.

$$\text{For 2005 Earnings per share} = \frac{£1,000,000}{20,000,000} = 5.0p$$

$$\text{For 2004 Earnings per share} = \frac{£860,000}{20,000,000} = 4.3p$$

Over the two years the EPS for Scott's Books has improved. However, on its own, this does not necessarily indicate a satisfactory performance. Only when the EPS is compared with the company's share price and with the EPS of companies in the same industry is it possible to make an informed judgment.

Table 1 Balance sheet, profit and loss account and other information for Scott's Books

Scott's Books
Balance sheet as at 31.12.05

	2005 £000s	2004 £000s
Fixed assets		
Land and property	3,500	3,700
Fixtures and fittings	1,200	900
	4,700	4,600
Current assets		
Stock	1,560	1,090
Debtors	200	300
Cash at bank	1,010	890
	2,770	2,280
Creditors: amounts falling due in one year		
Trade creditors	780	540
Accruals	120	100
Taxation	300	250
	1,200	890
Net current assets	1,570	1,390
Creditors: amounts falling due after one year	(1,000)	(900)
Net assets	**5,270**	**5,090**
Capital and reserves		
Share capital	1,000	1,000
Other reserves	1,800	1,890
Profit and loss account	2,470	2,200
	5,270	**5,090**

Scott's Books
Profit and loss account Y/E 31.12.05

	2005 £000s	2004 £000s
Turnover	7,800	6,560
Cost of sales	4,300	3,890
Gross profit	3,500	2,670
Administration expenses	2,100	1,470
Operating profit	1,400	1,200
Net interest payable	100	90
Profit before tax	1,300	1,110
Taxation	300	250
Profit after tax	1,000	860
Dividends	730	690
Retained profit	270	170

Additional information

	2005	2004
Number of ordinary shares issued	20m	20m
Share price at 31 December	81p	76p

Price earnings ratio

The price/earnings (P/E) ratio is one of the main indicators used by investors in deciding whether to buy or sell particular shares. The P/E ratio relates the current share price to the EPS. It is calculated using the formula shown in Figure 2. The ratio is often expressed as the number of times by which the share price can be divided by the EPS.

Figure 2 *Price earnings ratio*

$$\text{Price earnings ratio} = \frac{\text{Share price}}{\text{EPS}}$$

In the case of companies which are listed on the Stock Market, their share price is published daily in the *Financial Times* and other newspapers. The share prices for Scott's Books on 31 December are shown as additional information in Figure 1. In 2005 the share price was 81p. The EPS was 5.0p as calculated above.

$$\text{For 2005 Price earnings ratio} = \frac{81p}{5p} = 16.2 \text{ times}$$

$$\text{For 2004 Price earnings ratio} = \frac{76p}{4.3p} = 17.7 \text{ times}$$

The P/E ratio of 16.2 means that the market price of the share is 16.2 times higher than its current level of earnings. Assuming that nothing changes, it would take 16.2 years for these shares to earn their current market value. The P/E ratio for Scott's Books fell over the two years from 17.6 to 16.2. However, the fall is not very significant. In general, P/E ratios of between 10 and 20 are usual. A P/E ratio of less than 10 probably means that the share price has fallen sharply and firms with very low P/E ratios may be best avoided. P/E ratios above 20 suggests that a company is high profile, is expected to do very well in the future or has an inflated share price.

P/E ratios provide a useful guide to market confidence and can be helpful in comparing companies. However, a general rise or fall in share prices will clearly affect P/E ratios, so care must be taken when interpreting changes.

Dividends per share

The dividend per share is the ratio that shows how much money ordinary shareholders' receive per share. It is calculated using the formula in Figure 3.

The dividend per share paid to Scott's shareholders increased from 3.45p per share to 3.65p over the two years. This suggests that the company's trading position and profitability is improving.

Figure 3 *Dividend per share*

$$\text{Dividend per share} = \frac{\text{Dividend (ordinary shares)}}{\text{Number of shares}}$$

For Scott's Books the dividend paid to shareholders in 2005 was £730,000. This is shown in the profit and loss account.

$$\text{For 2005 Dividend per share} = \frac{£730,000}{20,000,000} = 3.65p \text{ per share}$$

$$\text{For 2004 Dividend per share} = \frac{£690,000}{20,000,000} = 3.45p \text{ per share}$$

However, to determine whether or not it is satisfactory the dividend per share must be compared with the share price. This involves calculating the dividend yield.

Dividend yield

The dividend yield is the dividend per ordinary share expressed as a percentage of the current share price. The formula used to calculate the dividend yield is shown in Figure 4.

Figure 4 *Dividend yield*

$$\text{Dividend yield} = \frac{\text{Dividend per share}}{\text{Share price}} \times 100$$

For Scott's Books the share price is shown in Figure 1 under additional information. On 31.12.05 it was 81p. The dividend per share was calculated above and is 3.65p.

$$\text{For 2005 Dividend yield} = \frac{3.65p}{81p} \times 100 = 4.5\%$$

$$\text{For 2004 Dividend yield} = \frac{3.45p}{76p} \times 100 = 4.5\%$$

Over the two years the dividend yield is unchanged for Scott's, even though the dividend per share rose slightly. The reason for this is that the share price also rose (from 76p to 81p). Whether a dividend yield of 4.5% is adequate depends on what might be earned in other companies and other forms of investment. However, in 2005 the average dividend yield on the stock market was about 3%. So a yield of 4.5% for Scott's Books is good. It must also be remembered that dividends are not the only reward for holding shares. Investors may make a capital gain if the shares are sold for a higher price than when they were bought.

Dividend cover

The dividend cover measures how many times a company's dividends to ordinary shareholders could be paid from net profit. The formula needed to calculate the dividend cover is shown in Figure 5.

Figure 5 *Dividend cover*

$$\text{Dividend cover} = \frac{\text{Profit after tax}}{\text{Dividends (ordinary shares)}}$$

For Scott's Books the profit after tax in 2005 was £1,000,000. The dividend paid to ordinary shareholders is shown in the profit and loss account and was £730,000 in 2005.

$$\text{For 2005 Dividend cover} = \frac{£1,00,000}{£730,000} = 1.37 \text{ times}$$

$$\text{For 2004 Dividend cover} = \frac{£860,000}{£690,000} = 1.25 \text{ times}$$

For Scott's Books the dividend cover has increased slightly over the two years. A cover of 1.37 means that the dividends could have been paid 1.37 times over in 2005. If the cover is too high, shareholders might argue that more dividends should be paid. If it is too low, it may mean that profits are low or that the company is not retaining enough profit for new investment. In this case it could be argued that the directors have been generous in awarding such a large proportion of profit to shareholders. However, high dividends may attract investors in the future if some new shares are issued.

It is possible for a business to pay dividends even when there is not sufficient profit in the current year to cover the payment. A company might do this to help retain the loyalty of shareholders. The money to cover the payment would have to come from reserves.

Limitations to ratio analysis

Although ratios offer a useful method of analysing business performance, they do have several limitations. The following factors all affect their usefulness.

The basis for comparison It is important when analysing differences between businesses to compare 'like with like'. This means that valid comparisons can only be made between businesses in the same industry. Even then, differences in the size of

the business, in their accounting policies, product ranges and in their financial year ends can make comparisons difficult.

The quality of final accounts Ratios are usually based on published financial statements and therefore depend on the quality of these statements. One factor that can affect the quality of accounting information is the change in monetary values caused by inflation. Rising prices distort comparisons made between different time periods. For example, in times of high inflation, asset values and turnover might rise rapidly in monetary terms. However, when the figures are adjusted for inflation, there might be no increase in real terms. There is also the possibility that accounts have been **'window dressed'**. This means that the financial position of a business is not reflected accurately by the accounts. It is possible for accountants to present information in such a way that the true financial circumstances are disguised. For example, it is possible for accountants to change some of the accounting techniques they use such as estimating depreciation, during the financial year. This would result in different costs and profit levels and therefore ratios become distorted.

Limitations of the balance sheet Because the balance sheet is a 'snapshot' of a business at the end of the financial year, it might not be representative of the business's circumstances throughout the year. If, for example, a business experiences its peak trading activity in the summer and has its year end at a time when trade is slow, in the New Year, balance sheet figures for stock and debtors may be unrepresentative.

Qualitative information is ignored Ratios only use quantitative information. Some very important qualitative information may have a bearing on the performance of a business. For example, in the service industry the quality of customer service may be an important indicator. Ratio analysis cannot take this into account very easily.

Figure 6 *Motives for holding shares in other companies*

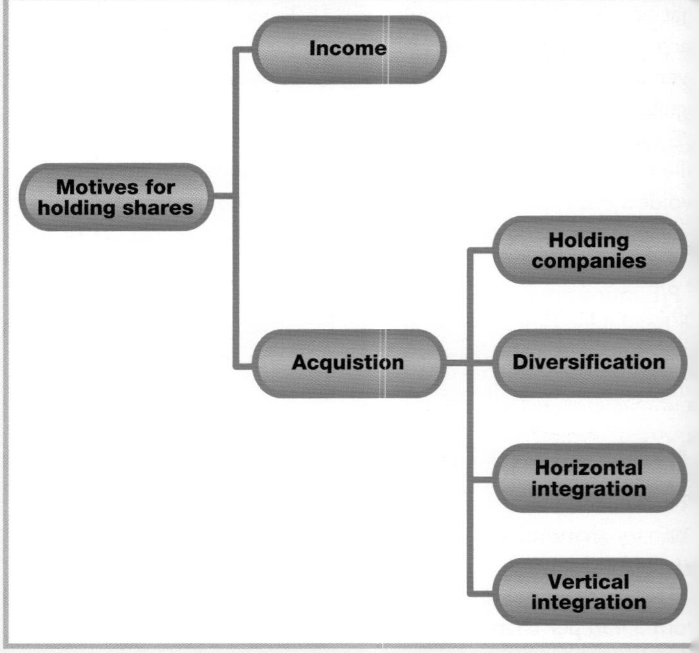

The level of investment in companies

It is common for businesses to hold shares in other companies. Why do they do this? Figure 6 provides a summary of the motives for holding shares in other companies.

- To generate an income. If a business has surplus cash it could be left in a bank deposit account. However, although the money will be safe the income (interest) is likely to be modest. Much higher returns are possible if shares are purchased. Over a long period of time the returns on shares are much higher than the income from deposit accounts.

- To exert some control over another company. In some cases, a business might take complete control. Holding companies, such as Kingfisher which owns Woolworths, Superdrug, B&Q and others, specialise in buying other companies and controlling them completely. In some cases, companies are bought, broken up, and parts sold off at a profit. This activity has been described as asset stripping.

- Buying into other companies to diversify. This involves getting involved in a different business activity to reduce the risk of business enterprise. Some firms buyout their rivals. This is called horizontal integration and is a fast way of growing. It eliminates competitors and often results in economies of scale.

- Companies may also buy into their suppliers or customers. This is an example of vertical integration.

The level of investment in other companies can vary and is classified according to the size of the shareholding. There are three levels.

Subsidiary If a business owns more than 50% of the shares in another company that company is said to be a subsidiary. A holding this size means that complete control can be exerted over its affairs. Subsidiaries operate with strong links to the parent company and their aims and objectives are likely to be the same. They may also share important resources such as an administrative centre. In some cases a company might be involved in a joint venture. This is where two companies, for example, share the costs, organisation and profits of a specific enterprise. The enterprise may have a name and operate as a company. If a business owns 100% of the shares in another company that company is said to be a wholly owned subsidiary.

Associated company If a business owns between 20% and 50% of another company then it is called an associated company. A stake this size in another company is quite significant. For example, it is possible to exert control over associated companies even though the actual ownership is less than 50%. This may happen if the other shares are held between a very large number of shareholders. Even though a business may not have complete control of an associated company, its holding is likely to be big enough to influence decision making. Strong links are likely to exist between a business and associated companies. They may be suppliers or provide important services such as distribution, for example.

Trade investments When a business holds less than 20% of the shares in another company the holding is said to be a trade

investment. This probably means that the shares are held for income purposes and there is no real desire to influence decision making. However, it is still possible to exert control even when the stake is less than 20%. Again, if the remaining shares are widely distributed among large numbers of shareholders, a company with, say, a 10% stake might exert some control. An example of a business that holds shares in another company is shown in Figure 7.

Figure 7 *Cambridge Mineral Resources (CMR) plc - investments*

Cambridge Mineral Resources is a junior exploration and mining company quoted on the Alternative Investment Market (AIM) of the London Stock Exchange under the stock symbol CMR. CMR is principally engaged in exploration for gold and base metals in Europe and the Andes Mountains of South America. The company has a strong portfolio of mineral projects with a strategy to provide shareholders with an upside opportunity for both discovery and development of these projects. Investments of £2,664,300 are shown under fixed assets on the balance sheet. Some examples of these are as follows.

- In Bulgaria CMR holds five exploration permits which contain a number of attractive gold deposits and targets. Four of the five permits are under joint venture with a subsidiary of Ivanhoe Mines Ltd (Ivanhoe), the international mining and exploration firm.
- In Peru CNR holds a 50% interest in the Patacancha claim group in the Ayacucho gold belt of southern Peru.
- In the Falkland Islands CMR holds a 7.34% equity interest in the AIM quoted company Falkland Gold and Minerals Limited which is exploring for gold throughout the Falkland Islands.

Source: adapted from Cambridge Mineral Resources (CMR) plc, *Annual Report and Accounts*.

Search through some Annual Report and Accounts to find some companies that own shares in other companies. You need to look at the balance sheet and search for 'Investments'. There will be a number next to the entry which will direct you to the notes to the accounts. Here you will find out information about the shares held in other companies. Write a brief report that explains the nature of these investments. For example, are they subsidiaries or associated companies.

Research task

Meeting the assessment criteria - examiners' guidance

You need to produce a report which evaluates a proposed investment in a limited company. You need to include the differences between debt and equity investment and consider the viability of the investment using appropriate financial ratios.

Business example - Bellvue Oil plc

Bellvue Oil plc is a large oil refinery. In 2005 it made record profits due to high global oil prices. As a result the company has accumulated a cash pile of £50m. It proposes to invest this in shares for a long-term return. The company has been advised by a financial consultant and two recommendations have been made for possible investments.

- Q-Stores is a national clothes retailer. It owns a large chain of outlets in the UK and sells mid-priced clothes. Its financial performance in the last few years has been steady but consistent. However, the share price fell during 2005.
- SK Media is a large media company. It owns newspapers, magazines and provides up-to-date financial information online. It has operations all over Europe and has grown fast in the last four years due to its online business. Some financial information is shown for both companies in Table 1 for 2005.

Mark Band 1 *Key ratios should be calculated accurately and some attempt should be made to relate these calculations to the investment decision.*

Shareholders or investors ratios can be used to help determine which of these two companies are likely to be a better investment. According to the ratios calculated there is not too much difference in the returns to shareholders. Both companies are performing well. Q-Stores has a higher dividend yield and dividend cover than SK Media but their P/E ratio may be on the low side. It is possible that the share price in Q-Stores has fallen recently causing the P/E ratio to fall. This might mean that the company has encountered some problems. The EPS and the dividend per share do not say anything about company performance on their own.

Table 1 Financial information of two companies

	Q-Stores	SK Media
Net profit after tax	£87m	£41m
Dividend payment	£28m	£14m
Number of shares	250m	100m
Share price	301p	474p

Earnings per share

$$Q\text{-Stores} \frac{£87m}{250m} = 34.8p$$

$$SK\ Media \frac{£41m}{100m} = 41p$$

P/E ratio

$$Q\text{-Stores} \frac{34.8p}{301p} = 11.6$$

$$SK\ Media \frac{41p}{474p} = 8.6$$

Dividend per share

$$Q\text{-Stores} \frac{£28m}{250m} = 11.2p$$

$$SK\ Media \frac{£14m}{100m} = 14p$$

Dividend yield

$$Q\text{-Stores} \frac{11.2p \times 100}{301p} \times 100 = 3.72\%$$

$$SK\ Media \frac{14p}{474p} \times 100 = 2.95\%$$

Dividend cover

$$Q\text{-Stores} \frac{£87m}{£28m} = 3.1\ times$$

$$SK\ Media \frac{£14m}{£14m} = 2.93\ times$$

Mark

Band 2 *Your report should show an understanding of the impact of the ratios on the possible investment, both in terms of return and eventual repayment.*

Bellvue Oil has a large amount of cash which it wants to invest to generate long-term returns. The information in Table 2 can be used to calculate shareholders' or investors' ratios. The table shows a summary of ratios for both companies. Q-Stores has a

Table 2 *Ratios for Q-Stores and SK Media*

Ratio	Q-Stores	SK Media
Earnings per share	34.8p	41p
P/E ratio	11.6	8.6
Dividend per share	11.2p	14p
Dividend yield	3.72%	2.95%
Dividend cover	3.1	2.93

lower EPS than SK Media. However, the EPS on its own does not say anything about a company's performance. The P/E ratio, which uses the EPS, shows how long it would take for current earnings to pay for a share. Companies with P/E ratios of between 10 and 20 are said to be sound. In this case, Q-Stores has a P/E ratio of 8.6. This may be caused by a recent fall in the share price. If this is the case, it may be worth avoiding the shares. However, Q-Stores has a higher dividend yield than SK Media. But again if the share price has fallen this would inflate the dividend yield. Both companies have a good dividend cover. Their dividend payments are met comfortably from net profit. Dividend payments represent about one-third of their profits which means that two-thirds have been retained for business use. To decide which of these companies to invest in it would be prudent to calculate the ratios of both companies over a longer period of time – say five years. This would help to detect trends.

Mark Band 3 *Your report should make reference to risk and reward and outline how these relate to the different kinds of investment. You need to draw reasoned conclusions regarding the viability of the proposed investment. Limitations should also be highlighted with any requirements for further information.*

Bellvue Oil has decided to invest a large cash surplus in shares. The company is looking for a long-term investment and has identified two possible investment opportunities. The information above has been used to calculate shareholders' ratios. They are shown in Table 3. Both companies appear to be performing well. For example, the dividend yields for both companies are around, or above, the stock market average for 2005 (3%). Also, the dividend cover shows that they are able to pay dividends to shareholders easily out of current profits. The EPS and dividends per share cannot be used to make judgements about financial performance on their own. One possible problem may be the P/E ratio for Q-Stores. It is below 10, which suggests there has been a loss of confidence in the company causing the share price to fall. There is no information to explain this, but it is a possible reason why an investment in SK Media might be preferable to one in Q-Stores. However, before making a final judgement it would be prudent to use performance, liquidity and gearing ratios to analyse other aspects of both companies' performance. It is also important to recognize that ratio analysis has its limitations. For example, it is important when analysing differences between businesses to compare 'like with like'. This means that valid comparisons can only be made between businesses in the same industry. Even then, differences in the size of the business, in their accounting policies, product ranges and in their financial year ends can make comparisons difficult. It is also important to recognise that accountants can 'window dress' accounts. This means that it is possible for accountants to disguise a company's true financial position. Finally, ratios only use quantitative information. Some very important qualitative information may have a bearing on the performance of a business, for example the quality of the workforce or the senior management team.

Table 3 *Ratios for Q-Stores and SK Media*

Ratio	Q-Stores	SK Media
Earnings per share	34.8p	41p
P/E ratio	11.6	8.6
Dividend per share	11.2p	14p
Dividend yield	3.72%	2.95%
Dividend cover	3.1	2.93

Portfolio practice · FAStar

FAStar is a firm of financial advisors. It specialises in financial analysis. In particular it advises companies on acquisitions, mergers and company investments. One of its regular clients has asked the business to analyse the performance of three companies it is considering for an investment. Some financial information about the three companies is shown in the table.

(a) **Calculate the EPS, P/E ratio, dividends per share, dividend yield and dividend cover for each company.**
(b) **How might FAStar advise its client in the light of your answers in (a)?**
(c) **Analyse the limitations to ratio analysis in this situation.**

Company	Jay's Ltd	FKY plc	Impy plc
Sector	Retail	Engineering	Food
Net profit after tax	£12m	£23m	£1.9m
Dividend payment	£6m	£8m	£0.6m
Number of shares	50m	200m	10m
Share price	280p	150p	431p

The importance of international trade and international business

The importance of international trade

In 2005 the UK exported over £310 billion of goods and services and imported about £350 billion of goods and services. Exports formed nearly 27% of total UK production (GDP) and imports accounted for about 30% of total purchases. For the UK, international trade is clearly very important and has been for a very long time. Figure 1 shows imports and exports as a percentage of Gross Domestic Product (GDP) from 1948 to 2004.

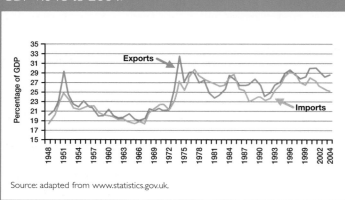

Figure 1 UK imports and exports as a percentage of GDP (1948 to 2004)

Source: adapted from www.statistics.gov.uk.

For the world as a whole international trade in 2004 was approximately £5 trillion (£5,250,000,000). That is £5 trillion exports and £5 trillion imports, because, of course, one country's exports are another country's imports.

For some countries exports and/or imports form a high level of their economic activity. Figure 2 shows the importance of international trade for three countries, two of which are in the European Union (EU) – Malta and Ireland.

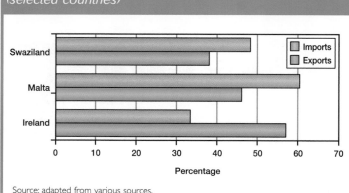

Figure 2 Imports and exports as a percentage of GDP (selected countries)

Source: adapted from various sources.

Figure 3 shows that some countries can even have import and export figures that are greater than their total GDP figures. This is because these countries import goods and then export the same goods adding only limited value to them. Hong Kong's figures are so high because many products from China also pass through. For these countries international trade is absolutely vital.

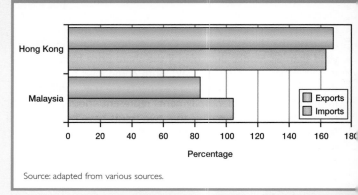

Figure 3 Imports and exports for Hong Kong and Malaysia as a percentage of GDP

Source: adapted from various sources.

The importance for individual businesses

For many countries imports and exports form a very important part of the economy. This is also true for many businesses. With very few exceptions, businesses start life in one country. Many then expand into other countries, both in terms of where they sell their goods and services, and also in terms of where they produce. Many of the well known names of businesses, such as McDonald's, Coca-Cola, Toyota and HSBC, sell vastly more outside their country of origin than in it. The same is true of many UK businesses, as is shown in Tables 1 and 2 with BP and Unilever.

BP is a major multinational business, with not only sales in a

Table 1 BP sales* and employment by geographical area, 2004

Geographical area	$ million	% of total	Employees
UK	52,826	17.9	17,400
Rest of Europe	47,790	16.2	26,000
USA	127,261	43.2	36,950
Rest of World	66,972	22.7	22,550
Total	294,849	100.0	102,900

* Sales are to third parties and by joint venture.
Source: adapted from *BP Company Report*, 2004.

huge range of countries reaching about 13 million customers every day, but also with exploration and production units across the world. Table 1 shows the distribution of sales and the numbers of employees in different parts of the world.

Table 2 *Unilever sales and employment by geographical area, 2004*

Geographical area	£ million	% of total	Employees
Europe	17,409	43.1	52,000
North America	8,992	22.3	18,000
Asia & Pacific	6,474	16.0	73,000
Latin America	4,217	10.4	29,000
Africa, Middle East & Turkey	3,274	8.1	51,000
Total	40,366	100.0	223,000

Source: adapted from *Unilever Company Report*, 2004.

Unilever sells its products in over 100 countries with over 150 million individuals buying products every day. The very wide product range includes well known branded food and home and personal care products, such as Knorr, BirdsEye, Flora, Domestos, Omo, Comfort, Sunsilk, Dove and Signal. As with BP, Unilever also produces its products around the world, as is shown by its distribution of employees.

Why international trade occurs

The main reasons why countries trade with each other are:
- the country cannot produce the resources it needs itself. Many countries have no gold or oil, for example;
- it costs too much to produce. The UK could grow bananas in greenhouses but they would be very expensive;
- one country has the comparative advantage compared to another country (see section 46);
- many types of goods and services are invented in one country and, initially, they can only be bought from there;
- international trade rules mean that some products can only be made in certain places, for example, Parma ham (Italy) and Champagne (France) (see sections 46 and 48-50).

Section 46 will look in more detail at the theories behind international trade. These theories tend to explain why countries import some goods and services and export others. For individual businesses the reason why they trade internationally generally comes down to the main objectives of business and that is to make profits and to expand. These, and the other aims and objectives that lead businesses to be international, will be dealt with in section 44.

For BT its stated aim has for some years been focused on the international, as shown in Figure 4.

Types of international businesses

This unit focuses on businesses with a clear and significant international presence. This may be through selling into a significant number of countries, i.e. **international businesses**,

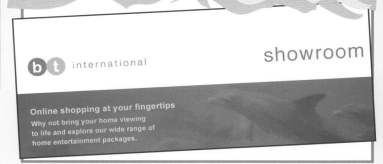

Figure 4 *BT's aim*

BT's aim is to be the most successful worldwide communications group. To achieve this, we have to generate shareholder value by seizing opportunities in the communications market worldwide, building our current business and focusing on high growth segments, while playing our part in the community and achieving the highest standards of integrity, customer satisfaction and employee motivation.

Source: adapted from *BT Business Review*, 1999, www.btplc.com.

or through having sales outlets or production units in several countries, i.e. **multinational businesses**. These are also known as **transnational businesses**. Details and examples of these businesses are given in section 70 (The importance of the global economy), which needs to be read as part of this section.

These businesses can also be classified by who owns them and whom they sell to or trade with, as shown in Figure 5.

Generally it is thought that businesses and consumers make up the bulk of international trade. In reality governments and state-owned businesses continue to be major players because it will normally be governments that buy, or fund the buying, of such items as military weapons, supplies and equipment for the health and education systems and, in some countries, for the transport and communications systems.

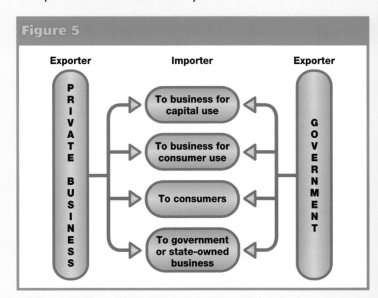

Figure 5

Business to business This covers the major part of international trade. Businesses will buy goods and services from other businesses for two main reasons.

- So that they can sell these goods and services on to consumers. An example includes Unilever selling soap powders to American supermarket chains so that they can sell them to their customers.
- Businesses also buy goods and services from other businesses which help them to produce their own goods. For example, the German firm Schweikert GmbH has bought measuring equipment from Derby based LK Ltd to help it accurately measure the sides of cars it was making for Porsche.

Business to consumers This refers to businesses that sell direct to consumers in other countries. This can be done in two ways.

- The businesses may have outlets in other countries, for example Tesco which has stores in 12 countries outside the UK.
- A manufacturing or service business may sell to consumers direct. Today the most likely way of doing this will be through e-commerce. Dell Inc, the computer multinational, for example, advertises its products through a range of media including newspapers, magazines and its websites. This allows consumers to order and buy online or by phone. Products are then supplied from its range of production centres in Austin, Texas; Nashville, Tenn.; Winston-Salem, North Carolina; Eldorado do Sul, Brazil (Americas); Limerick, Ireland (Europe, Middle East and Africa); Penang, Malaysia (Asia Pacific and Japan) and Xiamen, China (China).

Business to government This includes sales to governments and to public sector organisations such as health and education. In most countries government organisations buy a wide range of products. In July 2004, for example, Delta Power Services in Stockport was awarded the Royal Netherlands Navy contract to supply 12 Fast Patrol Craft following stiff competition with other EU suppliers and following the success of these boats when sold to the Yemeni government in 2003.

Government to business This takes place when state-owned organisations are supplying goods or services. In many countries, and even in the UK, this is still a common situation. In the UK, for example, the BBC is still a state owned business, but it does sell programmes and services to businesses in other countries. In 2003/4 BBC Worldwide Limited contributed £141 million to the BBC.

Government to government This takes place when both the buyer and the seller are part of the state organisation. Generally these sales are totally 'above board' and 'in the open' but there are also agreements for sales between governments that are very secretive.

Government to consumer This is fairly rare in international trade. This is because governments do not tend to be in direct contact with foreign consumers. State organisations are, however, interested in selling to foreign consumers. UK universities earn a large amount of income from offering courses to foreign students at very much higher cost than for UK students.

Some major UK players

There are many measures that are used to decide which are the world's biggest companies. The Forbes 2000 ranks companies on a combination of sales, profits, assets and market value. Table 3 shows the ranking of the top UK companies in each of the largest 10 categories. This does not give the second biggest in each section, for example 6 of the top 10 are banks, but only the top one, HSBC, is shown.

Table 3 *Top UK companies in top 10 categories (2004)*

World rank	UK rank	Name	Category
5	1	BP	Oil & gas operations.
7	2	HSBC Group	Banking.
80	7	GlaxoSmithKline	Drugs & biotechnology.
93	8	BT Group	Telecommunication services.
105	9	Prudential	Insurance.
120	11	Tesco	Food market.
137	12	Anglo American	Materials.
155	13	BATs	Food, drink & tobacco.
182	14	National Grid Transco	Utilities.
341	20	Compass Group	Hotels, restaurants & leisure.

Source: adapted from Forbes 2000, www.forbes.com/lists/.

All of these companies are multinationals, although National Grid operates mainly in the UK and the USA. Some details of the first five companies are given below.

BP BP, also see Table 1 above, produces 2.6 million barrels of oils and NGLs a day and 8.4 billion cubic feet of gas. It refines 5.8 million barrels a day, runs 28,500 petrol stations worldwide and owns 19 refineries. It explores for oil in 26 countries and produces in 23 countries. It is a major multinational business.

HSBC HSBC has over 9,500 offices in 76 countries and territories in Europe, the Asia-Pacific region, the Americas, the Middle East and Africa. From September to November 2005 it received the following awards.

- Best Consumer Internet Bank & Best Corporate / Institutional Information Security Initiatives - *Global Finance* magazine.
- Best Global Financial Adviser - Dealogic Project Finance league table.
- Global Bank of the Year - *The Banker* magazine.

GlaxoSmithKline (GSK) GSK employs over 100,000 people in 116 countries researching and producing pharmaceutical products. In its sales GSK is a global company with the following impressive statistics:

- more than 1,100 prescriptions are written for GSK products every minute;
- more than 200 million people around the world use a GSK brand toothbrush or toothpaste every day;
- GSK factories produce 9 billion tablets and 600 million tubes of toothpaste every year.

BT Group In the UK, BT serves more than 20 million business and residential customers with more than 30 million exchange lines. But what used to be a state-owned UK business is now a privately owned multinational business. BT Global Services employs around 30,000 people in 50 countries and delivers services in 170 countries. It also has a global Internet protocol infrastructure, which is used in 71 countries and is expected to be extended to 160 countries by the end of 2007.

Prudential Prudential has over 21,500 employees around the world and more than 18 million customers. It operates under the following names:

● Prudential in the UK, Ireland and India;
● M&G Investments in the UK, Germany, Italy, France, Australia and South Africa;
● Jackson National Life Insurance Company in the USA;
● Prudential Corporation Asia in China, Hong Kong, India, Indonesia, Japan, Korea, Malaysia, The Philippines, Singapore, Taiwan, Thailand and Vietnam;
● Egg, the on-line service, in the UK.

Source: adapted from various sources, company websites.

1. Select one of the following companies.
   Cadbury Schweppes ConAgra Kraft
   Nestlé PepsiCo Unilever
   Coca-Cola Carrefour Compass
   McDonald's Ahold Danone
2. Use its website, company reports, company fact files or business reports to identify the following points.
   (i) Which industry or industries it is involved in (there may be more than one).
   (ii) Which parts of the world it produces products in and where it sells them.
   (iii) Whether it sells to businesses or consumers, or both.
   (iv) Whether it is a multinational or a global business.

Research task

Portfolio practice · Tate & Lyle

The Tate & Lyle Group is 1,256th on the Forbes 2000 list. It manufactures food and industrial ingredients for customers in the food, drinks, pharmaceuticals, cosmetics, paper, packaging and building industries. It has over 6,000 customers worldwide. As well as manufacturing products in many countries Tate & Lyle has joint ventures with other companies such as Johnson and Johnson, DuPont and Unilever. The Group employs 6,700 people in its subsidiaries and 4,800 in joint ventures.

As well as producing raw materials for other industries, Tate & Lyle produces goods for the retail consumer market. These include the retail brands of Tate & Lyle (UK), Sidul and Sores (Portugal), Redpath (Canada) and Melli (Vietnam). Table 4 shows where the business's production plants are located.

Source: adapted from *Corporate Fact Book 2005 – Bite Size*.

Table 4 *Tate & Lyle*

Food and industrial ingredients	
Country/region	Plants
USA	9
South America	1
EU	7
Morocco	1
Sugars	
Canada	2
EU	2
Sucralose	
USA	1
Singapore	1

(a) **Explain what evidence there is that Tate & Lyle is a multinational company.**
(b) **Explain whether Tate & Lyle operates on the basis of business to business, business to consumer or business to government.**
(c) **Tate & Lyle also operates joint ventures.**
    (i) What is a joint venture?
    (ii) What is likely to be the nature of Tate & Lyle's joint ventures?
    (iii) Assess the benefits and drawbacks of running joint ventures for Tate & Lyle.

Meeting the assessment criteria - examiners' guidance

The assessment criteria for this unit are set against the *What you need to learn* parts of the specification so that for each part all of the Assessment Objectives (AOs) are being tested. For each of the sections in this unit the Meeting the Assessment Criteria will look at only one row of the assessment criteria, but it will consider all of the AOs for that part of the specification.

In this section, guidance is provided for row (a) and will consider what is needed in terms of providing details of businesses with a European and wider global presence. No specific case study details will be given because the data about businesses mentioned in this section and from unit 14 will be used instead. The issues being considered here are which businesses to select and how much detail should be given for each mark band.

AOs	Mark Band 1	Mark Band 2	Mark Band 3
(a)	The minimum requirement is for two businesses that can be compared, but even at this level it is expected that details of a number of businesses will be given before the two are selected. All of the businesses must be transnational or global and should reflect three minimum conditions. 1. A range of different markets, as shown on Table 3. 2. Businesses that trade with other businesses, with consumers, with governments, etc. as with BP which sells petroleum and gas products to businesses and governments and runs petrol stations selling direct to consumers. 3. Businesses with a European presence and businesses with a wider global presence. All of the businesses in Table 3, except National Grid, have both. Details of all of the businesses covered are likely to be mainly a list of basic facts with limited scope for in-depth comparisons.	At this level it is necessary to explain the aims and objectives of the multinational businesses, the kinds of markets they are in and factors such as legal status. It is, therefore, very important which businesses are chosen. For the two selected businesses there should be clear contrast in terms of what is produced, which countries they operate in, possibly their size and how far they are developed in terms of being multinational and even global. It would be wrong to select HSBC and the Royal Bank of Scotland, Barclays, HBOS or Lloyds TSB because, although they are all in the top six UK companies, all are banks. On the other hand, selecting BP (see above), the top UK company and, say, Waterford Wedgwood (see section 70) would provide two very contrasting companies that would allow for interesting comparisons.	At this level a thorough knowledge and understanding of both the types of international businesses, and more specifically the two chosen businesses is vital. The details of businesses given in this section would provide a starting point but very much greater research and details would be expected. To access this data, careful research is required for all businesses selected and that should cover a wide range of different multinational companies, from the UK and from other countries. For the two chosen businesses, thorough research is needed and the two businesses should only be chosen after initial research that shows that all the required data can be found. All of the businesses listed in Table 3 have a great deal of data on their websites and in company reports, but additional sources such as news reports, business forums, etc. can provide very useful additional information.

International businesses

Section 42 provided some details of international businesses in terms of whether they were business to business or business to consumer. The examples of businesses also provided details of location of production units, customers and numbers of employees. Section 70 provides details of local, national, international, multinational and global businesses.

This section will look at other specific details that should be described when meeting the assessment criteria for this unit. These details will include:

- legal format;
- target market;
- sector and product range.

As these are being described reference to the type of international business, e.g. multinational or global, will be made.

Legal format

Multinational businesses have production units in more than one country and that means that they must comply with the legal requirements in those different countries. In terms of their legal format they are likely to take one of three approaches shown in Figure 1.

Figure 1 Legal format

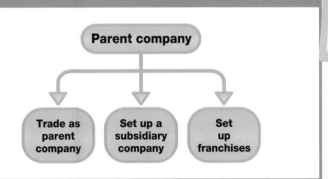

Parent company

- Trade as parent company
- Set up a subsidiary company
- Set up franchises

Trading as the parent company This will mean that in legal terms when the company is operating in another country it will simply be a branch of the existing company. An example is shown in Figure 2. This method of operation has benefits and drawbacks.

Normally the establishment of a branch in another country will require registration and the business will then need to meet the country's company laws in terms of the way that it conducts its business. It will be a foreign registered business but it may need to pay taxes and National Insurance contributions. That will depend on whether the host country and the country of the parent business does or does not have an agreement whereby profits are only taxed in the parent company's country.

Many countries see the inward investment of foreign companies setting up in their countries as beneficial because it brings employment for locals, use of local suppliers and payments for the use of local transport, land, and possibly local commercial services such as banking and marketing. The host country will also benefit because some taxes will have to be paid to the country, such as employees' income tax and National Insurance contributions and business rates.

In some countries establishing businesses can be very difficult. In Russia companies that are 100% foreign owned need to have signing power for their bank documents. They can therefore be prevented from being set up. If the company is set up as a company only in Russia – not as a branch or representative office – employees from outside Russia will need a work permit and that may well be limited to only one.

Figure 2 The Charles Kendall Group

The Charles Kendall Group provides a wide range of services including procurement, consultancy services, freight forwarding, export packing, education, recruitment, travel service and supply centres. In the UK it operates as a private company (Ltd) with 8 services. It also has offices around the world at:

- Manama in Bahrain;
- Dubai in the United Arab Emirates;
- Al Khuwair in Muscat;
- Kowloon in Hong Kong - trading as Charles Kendall Freight (Hong Kong) Ltd.

Source: adapted from www.charleskendall.com.

Setting up a subsidiary company When this is done the business is registering a separate company within the host country (see Figure 3). This means that, generally, the subsidiary will be subject to the same laws and regulations as companies in the country. The main exception is in terms of the taxation of profits, which, as was stated above, will depend upon whether there is an agreement between the two countries involved (a Double Taxation Agreement). The UK has a comparatively high number of such agreements with other countries. The legal status of the subsidiary will be the same as that of national companies. So, for example, even though Coca-Cola's parent company is American, it is registered in the UK as 10 separate companies dealing with production, sales, exports, finance and pensions.

Trading through franchises A franchise occurs when one business sell the rights to use its name and products to other businesses. The **franchisor** uses this as a method of expanding its products and production into other countries by letting national businesses in the host country actually set up and run the business. The benefit for the franchisor is that the costs of

Figure 3 Lotus and Tesco

Tesco Lotus registered as a separate company with the Thailand Ministry of Commerce. It was set up as a joint venture between Tesco and the Thailand firm Charoen Pokphand Group. It runs hypermarkets, supermarkets and express stores as well as providing Tesco products to small independents in Thailand. Charoen Pokphand used to run the chain for Tesco but it is slowly selling its interests (down to just 5% in 2005) to Tesco because it prefers to be just a supplier.

Source: adapted from www.tescolotus.com.

Figure 4 McDonald's

McDonald's fast food restaurants are probably the best known example of a franchise business, although less than 40% of McDonald's outlets in the UK are actually franchises. The rest belong to McDonald's itself which runs three UK registered companies in the UK:
- McDonald's Hamburgers Ltd
- McDonald's Restaurants Ltd
- McDonald's Europe Ltd.

The legal format of McDonald's in the UK depends on what part of the business is being looked at.
1. Some activities will be directly controlled by the USA parent company.
2. The UK restaurants that are owned by McDonald's are part of a UK registered subsidiary.
3. Franchises are negotiated with a different UK registered subsidiary.
4. The franchises themselves are owned privately by UK franchisees and are most likely to be private limited companies.

setting up the business and the risks of failure are usually taken by someone else. It is also less likely to be resisted by the country because it is a national business that is actually employing people and running the business. The **franchisee** will also pay normal national taxation.

For the franchisee the benefits are that the name of the business is already well known and normally the agreement will be that the franchisor pays for national advertising and usually offers training and financial support, and sometimes supplies the raw materials. The franchisee does, however, have to buy into the business and has to pay over part of the profits.

An example of a franchise is shown in Figure 4. McDonald's normally sells restaurants it already owns to people who want franchise. It does not offer finance to help with the purchase but it does offer a Business Facilities Lease whereby someone who wants a franchise but cannot initially afford it takes a lease for three years after which it is expected that it will be able to buy the franchise. McDonald's demonstrates many different legal formats in the way that it conducts its international trade.

Selecting the target market

When businesses move into new international markets there must be some target groups that they are trying to reach. In deciding on which countries to expand into the businesses will consider a range of important factors. Examples are shown in Figure 5.

Size of population The size of the population that might buy business's products is vital and will need to be large enough to make the expansion into the country worthwhile. In terms of who the product might be sold to, what will be important is the number of people in the segment that the business makes product for, as shown in the customer profiles comments below.

The size of the population will also be important in terms of potential workforce. Here, however, the more important factor is the skill needed to operate the business and whether or not that can be provided locally. Figure 6 shows the ten countries with the highest populations in the world, with the UK for comparison.

Figure 5 Factors to consider when expanding abroad

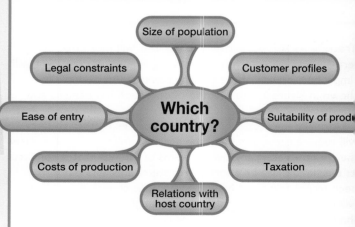

Figure 6 *Top ten countries by population (mid-2005 estimates)*

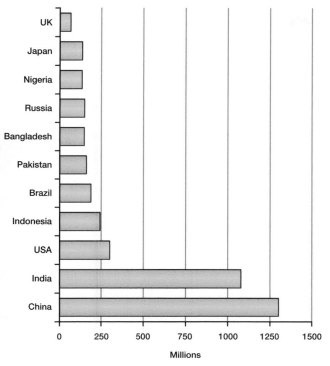

Source: adapted from US Census Bureau.

Figure 7 *GDP/head of the same countries in £s (mid-2006 estimates)*

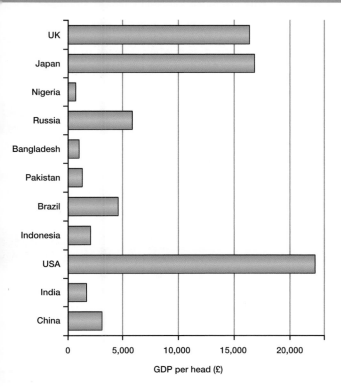

Source: adapted from IMF.

Customer profiles Businesses will produce products for particular segments of the market and the country will need to have customers which fit these profiles. All the demographic features, such as age, gender and income levels, will need to be considered to ensure that the products will sell successfully. In addition, the psychographic features will have to be considered, taking into account differences in lifestyle, interests and social and religious attitudes. Products may need to be changed in order to meet the different customer profiles.

Figure 7 shows the same ten countries and the UK as Figure 6, but in terms of the average income that each person in the country has. A quite different picture is shown. The purchasing power (PP) of people within the country itself was used, so it reflects the fact that goods and services in China, for example, are very much cheaper than in the UK or the USA.

Suitability of product Customer profiles in other countries and even such factors as weather conditions may mean that products will need to be adapted in order to appeal to the new markets. When that happens there will be additional costs and these need to be taken into consideration when choosing the right countries.

In the two businesses shown at the end of this section this will be necessary. Many Muslim countries do not allow the drinking of alcohol so if Diageo, for example, wants to sell products to them it will have to develop non-alcoholic versions of its drinks. When Cadbury sells chocolate products in very hot countries where products are not kept in chilled cabinets it has had to change the composition of the chocolate to stop it melting.

Taxation Taxation levels vary considerably in different countries. These will affect both the costs of production and profits. Costs of production will be affected by such taxes as income tax, National Insurance contributions and land taxes, e.g. rates. If these increase the costs then prices will rise and that may make it more difficult to sell the end products.

Businesses generally expand so that their profits will increase. If taxes on profits are very high in one country then it may defeat the purpose of going there. Businesses also need to consider how much of the profits they will be allowed to take out of the country.

Legal constraints Legal formats have been considered above, but there are other legal constraints such as how much profit can leave the country, what minimum payments have to be made to employees, whether there are tariffs placed on exports and whether work permits are needed for staff who have come from the parent company. These kinds of legal constraints are dealt with elsewhere in this section, or in other sections.

Costs of production The companies being considered here will be setting up production units in other countries and therefore the costs of production there become a vital consideration. All of the following costs need to be considered.
● Costs and time taken to register and set up the business.
● Buying or renting the land or buildings.
● Preparing the land and buildings ready for production.
● Local staffing costs compared to the costs of bringing staff over from the parent company.

- Transport costs both within the country and the costs of exporting to other markets.
- Taxation (see above).

Ease of entry As a member of the EU it is relatively easy for UK companies to set up in European Union countries, as explained in section 48. In other countries the regulations and costs of setting up can vary considerably, see regulations below. There will also be some countries which object to foreign companies entering and will put obstacles in their way or may even ban them.

The ease of entry will also depend on which type of business is being planned. Although France has one of the least restrictive regimes for foreign investment in the world, it does impose restrictions on foreign businesses in the industrial sectors shown in Table 1.

Table 1 *French industries - restrictions placed on foreign investment*

- Agriculture
- Aircraft production
- Insurance
- Air transport
- Atomic energy
- Tourism
- Audiovisual
- Telecommunications
- Publishing
- Defence industry
- Maritime transportation
- Radio and television
- Road transportation
- Banking/Financial services/Accounting services

Relations with host country Sometimes host nations welcome foreign businesses and provide incentives for them to come. Sometimes countries expect the new business to pay for the privilege of producing in their country. These issues are dealt with in section 47.

Country regulations In addition to the legal status a company has, any business setting up in another country will need to meet certain regulations that relate to forming a company, running a company, hiring and firing staff and paying taxes. Below are details of the ease, or difficulty, of doing this in three countries, the UK, France and China. The details come from the World Bank which provides similar details for most countries through its 'Doing Business' website.

The basic details in Table 2 show that France and the UK have fairly similar basic profiles, but that China is substantially different. Both the UK and France are developed countries and part of the EU which has tried to develop common trading practices. China, on the other hand is a developing country which has only recently opened its markets to competitive trade. Some of the differences shown might, therefore, be expected. Others may come as a surprise. The data refers to the

Table 2 *Country details*

Country	Population (million)	Average annual income/person
UK	59.3	£19,108
France	59.8	£18,630
China	1,290.0	£726

Source: adapted from World Bank, *Doing Business.*

Table 3 *The ease of setting up and running a company in selected countries*

	UK	France	China
To start a business			
Number of steps needed	6	7	13
Number of days needed	18	8	48
Cost	£134	£203	£99
To run a business			
Number of steps needed	19	10	30
Number of days needed	115	185	363
Cost	£13,414	£13,264	£915

Source: adapted from World Bank, *Doing Business.*

setting up of businesses within the country.

Table 3 shows the time and cost involved with setting up and running a company in each of three countries. It shows that although the costs are much lower in China the number of steps and the time needed are very much greater.

The amount of tax to be paid is a major consideration for businesses trading abroad, as is when it needs to be paid and how easy this is to do. Although the UK has relatively high businesses taxes they are also relatively easy to pay. Table 4 confirms this.

For businesses trading in other countries, many other issues will be very important including how easy it is to hire and fire employees, what happens if the business has to close, and how easy it is to import or export from that country. Details are provided by the World Bank, which also shows the relative ease of enforcing contracts so that a company will be paid for what has done, as shown in Table 5.

Table 4 *Paying taxes, selected countries*

	UK	France	China
Number of payments	8	29	34
Time taken to pay (hours)	Minimal	72	584
% of tax paid on profits	52.9%	48.2%	46.9%

Source: adapted from World Bank, *Doing Business.*

Table 5 *The ease of enforcing contracts in selected countries*

	UK	France	China
Number of steps needed	14	21	25
Number of days needed	288	75	241
Cost as % of the debt	17.2%	11.7%	25.5%

Source: adapted from World Bank, *Doing Business*.

Trading sectors and product range

Most international businesses produce and trade within just one sector of industry, e.g. McDonald's which trades exclusively in the restaurant sector. There is, however, a growing number of international businesses that trade in a number of sectors, e.g. Tesco which retails food and other household products but now offers finance and insurance services, telecommunications services and extras such as providing the cheapest gas and electricity supplies, online ordering of contact lenses and downloads of music.

When businesses expand into new countries the majority of companies will be targeting specific sectors of industry, even if they produce in different markets at home. Given time, companies such as Tesco will then expand their other products as Tesco has now done in Thailand. Businesses will need to make two important decisions.

- Which sector to enter, especially if they operate in more than one at home or in other international markets.
- Which parts of their product ranges to enter with if not with the whole range.

For some businesses this is a relatively easy decision because there is only one sector and the product range is fairly limited. For example, when Pilkington plc set up its float glass plant in 2005 in Ramenskoye in Russia as a 50:50 joint venture with AIG Emerging Europe Infrastructure Fund L.P., it was staying in the sector for which it is world famous. Its product range was also typical of what it produces elsewhere – float glass products, automotive glass products and speciality glass.

The Tata Tea Group, which includes the India-based Tata Tea and the UK-based Tetley Group, is the world's second largest global branded tea operation. The group concentrates on growing tea and now coffee, processing these beverages and distributing them. These stages are done in different international locations with subsidiaries in India, the UK and the USA and with plantations in Assam, West Bengal, India and Sri Lanka.

The product ranges provided to different countries and by different subsidiaries vary depending on the target markets. Tetley's range includes Black, Green, Fruit & Herbal Teas, Iced Ready-to-drink Teas and an extensive range of exotic Speciality Tea. Tetley has offices in Australia, Canada, Poland, Russia, South Africa and the US, as well as joint ventures in Pakistan and Bangladesh.

1. Using online news media and/or newspapers and business magazines, research the businesses that are setting up new production units, branches or offices in different countries.
2. For each business note down the following details if they have been provided in the article:
   (i) what type of business is being set up – new plant or office, branch or subsidiary, etc.
   (ii) what role will be carried out by the new facility;
   (iii) details of what will be produced there, how many employees, products for sale in the country or for export, etc.
3. For each business, if this is not explained in the article, check how the new production varies from the business's existing production at home and in other international centres.

Research task

Meeting the assessment criteria - examiners' guidance

You are required to investigate a range of businesses that are either transnational or global and to investigate two of these in depth so that they can be compared. This will require description, application, analysis and evaluation and will involve consideration of whether the businesses meet their aims and objectives through their international presence.

Business example - Diageo trading around the world

Diageo is the world's leading premium drinks business with an outstanding collection of alcohol beverage brands across spirits, wine and beer categories. These brands include: **Smirnoff, Johnnie Walker, Guinness, Baileys, J&B, Captain Morgan, Cuervo, Tanqueray, Crown Royal** and **Beaulieu Vineyard** and **Sterling Vineyards** wines.

Diageo is a global company, trading in over 180 markets around the world. The company is listed on both the London Stock Exchange (DGE) and the New York Stock Exchange (DEO).

We employ over 20,000 people worldwide with offices in around 80 countries. We have manufacturing facilities across the globe including Great Britain, Ireland, United States, Canada, Spain, Italy, Africa, Latin America, Australia, India and the Caribbean.

Diageo was formed in 1997, following the merger of Guinness and GrandMet and is headquartered in London. The word Diageo comes from the Latin for day (dia) and the Greek for world (geo). We take this to mean every day, everywhere, people celebrate with our brands.

Our brands offer consumers unique ways to make their days and nights special, to mark big events in their lives and brighten small ones.

Source: adapted from Diageo website – Diageo at a glance, www.diageo.com.

AOs	Mark Band 1	Mark Band 2	Mark Band 3
(a)	Basic details will be required for most, and preferably all, of the factors listed in the specification under information about the business. For Diageo this would include the following. **Legal format** – the details shown in the Diageo at a glance data. • Companies in the UK and the USA. • Offices in around 80 countries. • Manufacturing in the listed countries. **Target market** – would recognise this as a business in the alcoholic drinks industry and the need to target similar markets worldwide. **Sector and product range** – the sector recognised (the alcoholic drinks industry) and the range, with details of the brands shown in the extract above.	At this level it is necessary to explain the listed factors. Reasons should be given for why Diageo is registered in two countries, has offices around the world and manufactures in the UK, USA, Ireland, Canada and Spain. Basic reasons would be given such as the ease of running the business and the costs of transporting bottles and cans of beer. An understanding should be shown of the products themselves and how well known the brands are, allowing Diageo to expand fairly easily into many countries with its full range of products. If this is one of the two companies chosen for comparison then the details collected and explained need to cover most aspects of the business and its international presence.	Here both the study and the explanations need to be in depth. There should be clear explanations of why Diageo, a UK based company, decided to also register in the USA. An understanding of its history is important with such facts as Johnnie Walker starting in Scotland, Baileys in Ireland and Smirnoff first in Paris and then in the USA. It is also important to understand the structure of the company and the decision in 2004 to set up three divisions (Diageo Europe, Diageo North America and Diageo International) and before that the acquisition of Distillers and Bells by Guinness and then the merger of Guinness and GrandMet, then the formation in 1997 of Diageo itself. These in part explain the legal format and how and when new products were introduced. The separate production centres also explain why some products were introduced into countries around the world at different times.

Portfolio practice · Cadbury's 2006 goal

'Profitably and significantly increase global confectionery share'

Cadbury Schweppes operates in four regions: Americas, Europe, Middle East and Africa (EMEA) and Asia Pacific. Each region deals with its own geographical area and product lines although products from one region may be supplied to other regions directly or through distributors.

Cadbury has factories in the following countries as well as the UK: Australia, New Zealand, Canada, Malaysia, India, Indonesia, Japan and several countries in Africa. It also has a franchise arrangement with Hershey in the USA. In Europe subsidiary companies include Hueso in Spain, Poulain and Bouquet D'Or in France, De Faam and Frisia in Holland and Piasten in Germany. Stani in Argentina has been recently taken over and there are new factories in Peking, China and Wroclaw, Poland.

Cadbury Whole Nut is sold by a Cadbury Schweppes owned business in 73 different countries but many of

Cadbury's chocolate products are supplied directly in much fewer countries, as shown on Table 6.

Source: adapted from Cadbury Schweppes website, www.cadburyschweppes.com.

(a) **What market sector is the main company of Cadbury Schweppes involved in? Use examples to justify your answer.**

(b) **Cadbury Schweppes has many subsidiary businesses in other countries. Explain the advantages and drawbacks of using subsidiaries.**

(c) **Cadbury has a franchise agreement with Hershey in the USA. What are likely to be the benefits for Cadbury and for Hershey of this arrangement?**

(d) **Considering the examples shown on Table 6 and the rest of the data, explain why different products are sold in different numbers of countries.**

Table 6 *Selected Cadbury chocolate products sold via Cadbury Schweppes owned businesses to countries*

Product	Countries
Breakaway	Australia, Japan, and Singapore.
Creme Egg	Antigua & Barbuda, Australia, Argentina, Bahamas, Barbados, Bermuda, Canada, Canary Islands, Cayman Islands, C.C.C.I., China, Cyprus, Faroes, Hong Kong, Indonesia, Ireland, Jamaica, Japan, Malta, Netherlands, New Zealand, Portugal, Singapore, Tonga, UAE and UK.
Top Deck	Australia, China, Ireland, Japan, Singapore and South Africa.
Roses	Argentina, Australia, Bahamas, Barbados, Bermuda, Cayman Islands, Canada, Canary Islands, Ceuta, Costa Rica, Curacao, Cyprus, Faroes, Iceland, Ireland, Israel, Jamaica, Japan, Jordan, Lebanon, Malaysia, Malta, New Zealand, Netherlands, Singapore, Spain, Sudan, Tonga, UAE and UK.
Tokke	Japan, Germany, Portugal, and Spain.

Aims and objectives

Many of the common aims and objectives that businesses have will also apply to businesses with an international presence. There will, however, also be aims and objectives that are specific to businesses that are producing and trading internationally, as shown in Figure 1. This section will look at both the common and the specific aims and objectives but consider them in an international context.

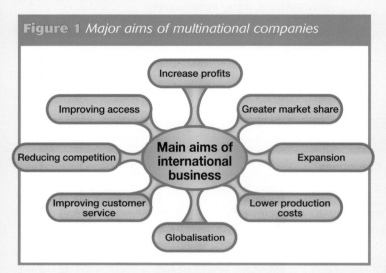

Figure 1 *Major aims of multinational companies*

In order to achieve its aims the business will have a set of objectives that will help it to do this.

Increasing sales and profits

Most companies are in business to make profits for their shareholders. There are exceptions and these are considered elsewhere below. Businesses can increase their profits by selling more or by reducing their costs. Producing and selling in other countries can achieve both of these aims.

Increasing sales The UK market presents a finite limit for businesses. Table 1 shows examples of these limits for particular types of businesses which will have a major stake in these markets.

When businesses move into international markets they will increase the potential size for all of these. The figures for the EU are also shown on Table 1.

Lower production costs The United Kingdom is a developed country in which the labour force expects to have a good standard of living and hence relatively high rates of pay. For many businesses labour costs are a major part of the overall production costs and, therefore, they may be able to cut costs considerably by producing their products in other countries. Figure 2 shows the benefit in terms of labour costs of a UK,

Table 1 *Population in specific sectors (UK mid-2006 estimates)*

Sector	UK millions	Products	EU millions
Total population	60.6	• General food items • Birthday cards • Freezers	456.9
Women	30.6	• Women's clothing • Women's magazines • Female health care	233.4
Retired	4.1	• Medicines • Stair lifts • Reading glasses	75.4
0-14 year olds	10.6	• Toys and games • Baby/Junior clothing • Educational materials	73.2
Births	0.65	• Baby clothes • Baby food • Prams and push chairs	4.6

Source: adapted from the CIA World Factbook, www.cia.gov.

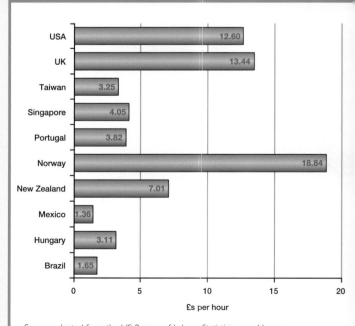

Figure 2 *Hourly compensation rates for manufacturing in £s (2004)*

Country	£s per hour
USA	12.60
UK	13.44
Taiwan	3.25
Singapore	4.05
Portugal	3.82
Norway	18.84
New Zealand	7.01
Mexico	1.36
Hungary	3.11
Brazil	1.65

Source: adapted from the US Bureau of Labour Statistics, www.bls.gov.

American or Norwegian business producing in various countries in the world.

There will also be reduction in costs if land is cheaper, taxes are lower and money can be borrowed more cheaply in other countries. Where businesses sell products around the world transport costs may also be lower if a production unit is set up in the country where the products are being sold.

Expansion, greater market share and globalisation

Expansion of a business is often a major aim because this is likely to lead to increased sales and higher profits. It also gives a business more market power and generally enhances the corporate image. This aim of expansion reaches certain barriers inside a single country which is why expansion then needs to take place internationally. These barriers include:

- **market saturation** where the business is already selling to the whole target market;
- powerful competitors so expansion nationally is difficult and probably costly;
- national competition policy, where the government (or EU) has restricted the size or market share allowed;
- lack of affordable factors of production such as land and labour.

Natural growth stages There are also natural stages of growth that really big multinational businesses generally go through as they achieve their aim of expansion. These are shown in Figure 3.

Figure 3 *Stages from local to global business*

Local	Limited market so expansion is through finding similar markets nationally.
National	National barriers such as market saturation, fierce competition and competition laws, so sales made into new markets abroad.
International	Sales in many countries allowing expansion, but costs in UK may be high and there are transport costs.
Multinational	Offices, sales systems and production units set up abroad. This reduces costs and provides a physical presence in the country so higher sales, expansion and increased market share are all possible.
Global	Sales take palce in more and more countries, often with offices, production and distribution centres in many countries. The product is known and purchased in most countries giving the business a global status.

Section 70 shows the different types of business, from local to global, and these are the stages that businesses pass through, although many businesses now miss out the local stage.

Market share Increasing market share not only increases sales but it also gives a business more power. When businesses cannot increase market share nationally they may look for new markets where they can achieve this. If it is successful they will gain benefits of additional profits and greater status in the international arena. It may then be possible to use these advantages to try to improve market share at home, or to move into yet new countries.

Globalisation Some businesses are not content just to be international or multinational companies. They want to be world leaders and to have their products sold, and sometimes made, in most countries in the world. Some examples are shown in Table 2.

Table 2 *Businesses and globalisation*

Coca-Cola's Vision for Sustainable Growth (2006):
'Bringing to the world a portfolio of beverage brands that anticipate and satisfy people's desires and needs'.

Microsoft's Mission Statement (2005):
'At Microsoft, we work to help people and businesses throughout the world realize their full potential. This is our mission.'

General Motors from letter to shareholders (2004):
'We've been the global automotive sales leader since 1931, but we know we have to work hard to earn the right to maintain that leadership. We're doing that day after day.

Our challenges on the road ahead are many. To address them, we are picking up the pace by combining and fully leveraging GM's resources on a truly global basis…for the first time in our nearly 100 years of history.

We've set the stage for that move with a track record of steady improvement in our operating capability around the world.
This is a journey rife with opportunities. We're driving hard to take advantage of them to reach our goal of becoming the best automaker in the world'.

Source: adapted from company websites.

Improving service to the market

Better customer service When products are made in, or provided from, other countries, this can mean that customers do not receive the best service possible. When ordering goods there may be time delays and when receiving services it may be difficult to contact the business if there are problems. There may also be language problems.

Setting up an office or production unit in the target country can get round some of these problems and help to achieve what is many companies' aim of providing first class customer service.

Better access There will be some forms of production where it would be impracticable to sell the products internationally unless the business had a presence in the country. It would not, for example, be possible for McDonald's to run restaurants other than in the countries where the customers are.

Where a production centre exists within the country it will also be easier in terms of access to get replacements, repairs and spare parts. Where services are provided within the country customers will usually have access to expert staff who can advise them and deal with any queries. Staff working in these centres are frequently nationals and that will mean that they can speak the language and understand national culture and conventions, all of which also provide better access for the customer.

Non-profit making and not-for-profit businesses Non-profit, or not-for-profit, organisations, such as charities, generally have aims that relate to supporting other people. For them customer service is usually a very important aim and if this can be improved by having separate businesses in different countries, and if they can afford to do this, they often will.

The World Wildlife Fund (WWF) has the aim 'to stop the degradation of the planet's natural environment and to build a future in which humans live in harmony with nature'. It has nearly 4,000 people across the world and to ensure that they operate most effectively the WWF has separate business centres in 42 countries. Each has its own company structure and specific aims and objectives that relate to that country and the other countries that it serves. For example, the WWF South Pacific Programme's headquarters is in Suva, Fiji, with country

offices in Fiji, Solomon Islands and Papua New Guinea, as well a a project office in the Cook Islands.

Achieving aims and objectives

Most of the examples given in this section are related to aims and it should be remembered that each of these aims will have a set of objectives that will help them to be achieved. A busines that wants to be global may first have objectives to expand into specific countries. The WWF's primary aim is to help protect the natural environment, but in order to achieve this it targets specific environmental problems in the world. It currently runs 300 on-the-ground projects with the objective of finding solutions to the problems and threats facing the world's forests

1. Using the Internet or company reports, identify the major aims of two UK companies.
2. For each aim identified, explain how being a multinational or global company would help to achieve that aim.
3. From the Internet, or the company report, identify any evidence that indicates how successful the businesses have been in achieving their aims.

Research task

Meeting the assessment criteria - examiners' guidance

You are required to investigate a range of businesses that are either transnational or global and to investigate two of these in depth so that they can be compared. This will require description, application, analysis and evaluation and will involve consideration of whether the businesses meet their aims and objectives through their international presence.

Business example - Metro aiming global

The Metro Group includes a chain of self-service wholesale stores (cash and carrys) which now includes the Makro stores, which in the UK alone had a 2005 turnover of more than £1 billion. It has a stated vision of:

'Domination of Cash and Carry wholesale segments globally, unique business formula, improves competitiveness of customers.'

The first Metro Cash & Carry Centre opened in Germany in 1964, the first centre abroad in 1971. In 2006 it has 506 centres in 30 countries (see Table 3). Today, Metro Group is the third largest trading and retailing group in the world. The company employs around 247,000 staff in 30 countries. And the group is continuing to grow. In the year 2005 Metro Group generated net sales of nearly €55 billion, of which over 49% of total sales came from outside Germany.

Table 3 Distribution centres by country

Country	Centres	Country	Centres	Country	Centres	Country	Centres
Austria	12	France	83	Japan	02	Russia	14
Belgium	08	Germany	114	Moldova	01	Serbia	01
Bulgaria	07	Great Britain	33	Morocco	06	Slovakia	05
China	23	Greece	06	Netherlands	16	Spain	31
Croatia	03	Hungary	13	Poland	21	Turkey	09
Czech Republic	11	India	02	Portugal	10	Ukraine	04
Denmark	04	Italy	42	Romania	21	Vietnam	04

Source: adapted from the Metro Group and Makro websites.

AOs	Mark Band 1	Mark Band 2	Mark Band 3
(a)	Basic details of Metro's international presence as a multinational and possibly global business will be given with the basic aims shown in the vision statements. Details would show what the business does and that it is operating in different countries, with examples given from the table. Evaluation will say little more than that the aim is to be global in its field and 506 centres in 30 countries show this. If this is being used as one of the two main businesses, the comparison would be limited to stating the main international aims and stating whether or not they had been achieved.	At this level it is necessary to explain the aims, in terms of having an international presence. The description should recognise the development of Metro from a national German firm to a multinational firm and the move towards being global. Details should be given of how this has been achieved, with the merger of companies in 1996 and the acquisition of Makro. There should be analysis of data to confirm the extent of the business's move towards being global which will consider the countries involved and the status of the business as the third largest in the world in its market sector with sales of €55 billion in 2005. It should also be recognised that to be global the business should be well represented in many parts of the world, but that here 22.5% of the centres are in Germany and only 6 countries outside Europe are represented.	At this level a detailed analysis of the extent of the business's international presence should be made, noting the countries where there is a presence and the number of units in these countries. It would also be noted that Table 3 is dealing with the cash and carry part of the business and that the Metro Group has other activities such as the Real hypermarkets, the Extra supermarkets and brands of consumer electronics. A reasoned evaluation would then be made of whether or not this was a global business, and if not, what progress had been made to become one. The other stated aims in the vision statement should also be considered and assessed in terms of whether Metro's multinational presence helps to achieve them. Is the unique business formula being enhanced by expanding into other countries and does this help to improve competitiveness for customers?

Portfolio practice · Guiding principles at Toyota

As part of its 'Vision and Philosophy' Toyota stated seven guiding principles for how it operates on a multinational and global scale.

1. Honour the language and spirit of the law of every nation and undertake open and fair corporate activities to be a good corporate citizen of the world.
2. Respect the culture and customs of every nation and contribute to economic and social development through corporate activities in the communities.
3. Dedicate ourselves to providing clean and safe products and to enhancing the quality of life everywhere through all our activities.
4. Create and develop advanced technologies and provide outstanding products and services that fulfil the needs of customers worldwide.
5. Foster a corporate culture that enhances individual creativity and teamwork value, while honouring mutual trust and respect between labour and management.
6. Pursue growth in harmony with the global community through innovative management.
7. Work with business partners in research and creation to achieve stable, long-term growth and mutual benefits, while keeping ourselves open to new partnerships.

In the 2005 Chairman's statement, Hiroshi Okuda gave the following commitment to the company's aims:

'Toyota will realise sustainable growth while contributing to the development of the automobile industry worldwide guided by an overriding belief in the value of competition and cooperation.'

Source: adapted from www.toyota.co.jp/en/vision/philosophy/index.html.

(a) **Explain how operating as a multinational and global company helps to achieve the aims stated in the Chairman's statement.**
(b) **Explain why each of the guiding principles listed above help to ensure that the aims in the Chairman's statement will be achieved.**
(c) **How might the competitive nature of the world automobile industry make it difficult for Toyota to achieve the aims in the Chairman's statement?**

Competition

When businesses sell their products they are usually in competition with other businesses. The level of competition that they face will affect many of their decisions, from what and where they sell to the kind of promotion and pricing strategies that they will use. The main types of market conditions are shown in Figure 1.

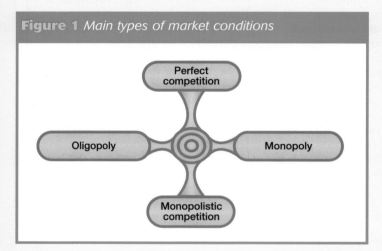

Figure 1 *Main types of market conditions*

The market conditions will explain why businesses behave in the way that they do, but they may also explain why some businesses decide to move from being simply national businesses to being international, multinational and even global businesses.

Perfect competition

Perfect competition exists when there are no barriers to producing and selling products. This means that all of the businesses are competing on the same basis and that the price at which they are able to sell their products will be determined by market forces and not by the business. Individual businesses will have similar costs of production and the product that they sell will be very similar (homogeneous). This will have the following effects:

- prices will be fixed by the market;
- it will be easy to enter the market and costs of entry will be low;
- all businesses know what the other businesses are doing so if any one business raised prices competitors would take away its customers;
- there are likely to be many businesses in the market;
- businesses will therefore be relatively small;
- it will be difficult to earn high levels of profit.

All of these factors mean that this is good for the customer, but it is not what most businesses would be happy with because they want high profits, high market share and customer loyalty.

In the UK there are very few examples of markets where there is full perfect competition, but some features exist in certain markets. In Eastleigh in Hampshire, for example, there are 9 charity shops registered with the Association of Charity Shops. They all sell essentially the same kind of items and they also sell them at very similar prices. When one has a sale, the others rapidly follow suit.

Because there are limited profits to be made in trading in the few perfect markets that do exist it is highly unlikely that multinational businesses will be found in these markets. However, it may explain why they became multinational businesses. There are two main reasons for this.

- They may have a perfect, or partly perfect, market in the national economy, possibly created by government intervention, and the business is looking for somewhere where it can gain the benefits or being in monopolistic competition, oligopoly or even in a monopolist situation in another country.
- There may be perfect competition in the target country and the business knows that it can enter the market easily and then use its business expertise to capture market share and start to dominate the market.

Monopoly

Monopoly is at the opposite end of the types of market, where there is very little competition. There are three accepted definitions of monopoly:

- where there is only one business in the market, which is where the term comes from;
- definitions set by national governments, which in the UK is a business with 25%+ market share measured by sales;
- where a business has monopoly power and dictates how the market will operate.

When a business is in a monopoly position it gives the business a great deal of power and this is often used to help meet the aims of making as much profit as possible, dominating the market through its market share and driving competitors out of the market. With pure monopolies, customers have nowhere else to go if they want the product and this allows the monopolist to charge what it wants, so it can exploit the customers.

Many countries have controls that are aimed at stopping any abuse of power by the monopolist. This is also part of UK and EU law (see section 48) and is strongly supported by the principles of the World Trade Organisation (see section 49). When businesses find these kinds of controls in the national market they may try to move into markets where they can be monopolists and gain the benefits of monopoly power. The benefits include;

- the business can decide the pricing policy and set prices to make maximum profits;

● it is very difficult for other businesses to enter the market to compete;

● there are no close substitutes so customers will remain loyal to the business.

When businesses choose which countries they will enter they need to consider the market structure in the country. Where there are monopolies it can be very difficult to get into the market as shown in Figure 2.

Figure 2 *Monopoly position of fixed line telephone operators in Brazil (2005)*

Though broadband's reach is increasing, penetration is still only 8%. In July 2005, fixed line operator Telefonica announced it was investing US$21 million to promote its broadband service Speedy. Limited competition, though, may be hampering broadband's growth. Telefonica, Telemar and Brasil Telecom combine for 80 percent market share, but they use their near-monopoly control of local access in their regions to deter competition. Only one mirror operator, GVT, has established a meaningful broadband presence.

Source: adapted from www.focusbrazil.org.br/.

Monopsony occurs when there is only one buyer in the market. This gives the buyer a great deal of power because if the business cannot sell to that customer there is no other customer. Monopsonies are often found when it is the government, or a government department or nationalised industry, that is doing the buying. This is fairly common in the arms industry. It can, however, occur when there is a monopoly and the business is a supplier to that monopoly.

If this is happening nationally then moving into international markets will mean that there will be alternative customers for the business and that it will no longer have to rely solely on the monopsonist for its sales and profits.

Oligopoly

The definition of oligopoly is that there are only a few major businesses in the market. That could occur with a monopoly situation, but oligopoly has certain characteristics that distinguish it from monopolies:

● there are few businesses in the market;

● they sell similar products;

● there are usually many buyers;

● there is interdependence in the sense that what one business does will affect how the others react.

The interdependence means that these businesses have to accept the market conditions. If one business tried to put up prices the others would not and therefore that business would lose customers. However, if one business decided to cut prices the other businesses would react and lower their prices so there would be no benefit to the businesses. If oligopolies are

going to make reasonable profits they will need to avoid getting into price wars and try to compete using non-price competition, such as effective advertising, good customer service and branding.

In the UK the major supermarkets might be thought of as being in an oligopoly position. There are only four major supermarket chains, Tesco (30.4%), Sainsbury (15.9%), Asda (Walmart) (17.0%) and Morrison (11.5%). These figures were for food sales in 2005. Other, smaller chains had the other 25.2%, and included Aldi, the Co-op, Iceland, Lidl, M&S, Somerfield and Waitrose.

There are business commentators who argue that Tesco is moving into a monopoly situation, and it certainly does have a great deal of power in the market. However, there are controls on monopolies in the UK and Tesco was, for example, prevented by the Competition Commission from buying the Safeway chain of stores. This was eventually bought by Morrison.

For Tesco, UK expansion has been very strong for a number of years, as shown in Figure 3, but now it may have expanded as much as the government will allow it to. It has therefore moved into the international arena, opening chains in Ireland, Poland, the Czech Republic, Slovakia, Hungary, Turkey, China, Japan, South Korea, Thailand, Malaysia and Taiwan.

Figure 3 *Tesco's growing share of supermarket food sales, 1970 to 2005*

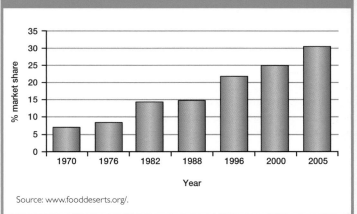

Source: www.fooddeserts.org/.

Monopolistic competition

Monopolistic competition describes a market where there are many firms but they are all producing products that are slightly different. It has some features of monopoly and some features of perfect competition;

● many firms in the market;

● fairly easy to get into and out of again;

● product differentiation with businesses producing similar but slightly different products.

There are examples of small scale businesses in this kind of market, for example, hairdressers, bed and breakfast providers and restaurants. There are also large national and multinational businesses such as car producers, film makers and magazine publishers. For these larger producers there are potentially high entry costs but they are not prohibitive and businesses that want to enter the market find few barriers.

Figure 4 *The music industry*

Next month Planet Funk will become the first band to release a single exclusively via mobile phones. This month, the song Crazy by Gnarls Barkley became the first track to hit No.1 on the strength of digital downloads alone. With the Internet, mobile phones and multi-channel TV all vying for their attention, teenagers clearly aren't keen to fork out on CD singles too often.

Source: adapted from www.smh.com.au/news/entertainment/ (April 2006).

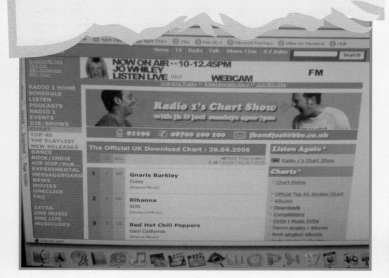

The main characteristic of the market is product differentiation. The businesses are in very close competition with each other and they are constantly trying to find an edge that their competitors do not have. The car industry is a very good example because each car maker is trying all the time to come up with some innovation that will make their product the most attractive. Car producers have developed assisted breaking systems, power steering, automated windows, short cars that are easy to park and hybrid cars that can switch between petrol and electric power sources.

However, each time one manufacturer comes up with a really good innovative idea the other manufacturers will respond by developing their own versions. For businesses faced with this constant need for innovation and monitoring of their competitors, a new market in another country, where there is limited competition, can be highly attractive.

Markets also change, as can be seen in Figure 4. The music industry has tended to be one of monopolistic competition with many firms competing but it started to move towards oligopoly as some of the major players merged or took each other over. Today, with many artists choosing to produce their own music and distribute over the Internet, the industry is back in a condition of monopolistic competition.

Strategies for business

Businesses need to think very carefully about what type of market they are currently in and what type of market they will be entering if they start producing in other countries. These are the kind of questions they will need to be asking themselves if they are planning to expand into other countries.

- Are the market conditions the same as for the markets we are currently in?
- If they are different how will we need to change our production and marketing to ensure that we will be successful?
- Are markets in some countries easier to get into than others and, if so, should we be targeting them first?
- How are the firms already in the market likely to react to our entry and should that alter how we enter the market?
- What laws apply in the country in terms of competition policy and how will they affect our entry and our expansion once we are there?

Using supermarkets or other major retail chains carry out the following tasks.

1. Select a range of products that you know will be sold by this kind of business.
2. Visit different supermarkets or other major retail chains in your nearest town or city. Alternatively, use their websites.
3. Note down the prices of the products, any special offers, and any non-price competition being used to sell them.
4. Compare the prices and the strategies being used to sell these products.
5. Decide what type of market these businesses are trading in, monopoly, oligopoly or monopolistic competition and write a justification for your decision.

Research task

Meeting the assessment criteria - examiners' guidance

You are required to investigate a range of businesses that are either transnational or global and to investigate two of these in depth so that they can be compared. This will require description, application, analysis and evaluation and will involve consideration of the type of competition that the business faces in its domestic and overseas market.

Business example - News Corporation

Rupert Murdock's News Corporation is one of the world's largest media conglomerates. The origins of the business come from Murdock's single Australian paper, the Adelaide News, in 1952. In Australia he progressively acquired other Australian papers. In Sydney he bought the *Daily Mirror* which allowed him to successfully compete against the other two main Sydney daily papers, the *Sydney Morning Herald* and the *Daily Telegraph* (Sydney).

In the 1960s he began to buy UK papers and in the mid-1960s he moved to the UK, owning the *News of the World*, *The Sun*, *The Times* and *The Sunday Times*. In 1973 Murdock started to buy papers in the USA. His media empire included buying television stations and broadcasting, including Sky (now BSkyB). The movement into new forms of media including, books, satellite television, cable television (e.g. Fox) and the Internet

(e.g. Grab.com) has meant that the Corporation's presence in the newspaper industry has diminished, but it is still very significant in certain countries.

Table 1 *Newpapers owned by News Corporation, numbers of publications, local and national (2006)*

Country	National	Regional/specialist	
Australia	2	Queensland	
		New South Wales	2
		Victoria	4
		South Australia	2
		Western Australia	1
		Tasmania	2
		Northen Territories	2
United Kingdom	4	Specialist	2
United States	1		0
Fiji	1		0
Papua New Guinea	1		0

Source: adapted from News Corporation website.

AOs	Mark Band 1	Mark Band 2	Mark Band 3
(a)	Basic details of News Corporation's international presence as a multinational media business will be given with details of the range of media businesses in which it is involved and the countries in which it operates. There should be an understanding that the business is involved in distinctly different industries, newspapers, magazine, television broadcasting, cable and books. There should be some assessment of the market conditions, noting some of the competitors, but there is unlikely to be any justified identification of whether the business, or the market, is in a position of monopoly, oligopoly or monopolistic competition.	At this level a good basic understanding of the likely market conditions for the business should be shown, with some justification being given. For example, in terms of newspaper publications News Corporation has only one publication in the USA and that is likely to make it part of monopolistic competition in a highly competitive market. The *New York Post* is in fact only the 12th largest paper in the USA. To make a reasoned assessment of News Corporation's position in the UK, with two daily newspapers and two Sunday newspapers, further research would be required into what other major papers were published in the UK, preferably with details of the relative circulations. The other main interests of the business also need to be considered as well as the market so that when pay-for-satellite TV in the UK is considered it should be possible to explain that BSkyB is essentially in a monopoly position. Details should be given of how News Corporation moved into new markets, mainly through acquisition. There should also be some recognition, but little explanation, of the fact that the type of market would affect the strategy of the business as it expanded into new countries.	At this level it should be recognised that News Corporation is operating is many different market conditions depending on which media industry is being considered and which country is being considered. To establish what the different market conditions are research will need to go beyond simply looking at News Corporation. Details will be required of the markets themselves so that it is possible to see how the market operates and where the business fits into it. This kind of detail is often difficult to find precise information about and it would therefore be acceptable to provide conclusions about the types of market on the basis of well reasoned arguments. For example, it would be reasonable to assume that the *Fiji Times* was a major publication in what is a relatively small country, without finding details of the major other publication the *Fiji Post*. There should be an explanation of how the type of market affected the expansion of the News Corporation into new countries, for example an oligopoly situation in the UK which made creating a new paper difficult and was the main reason why Rupert Murdock bought existing newspaper businesses.

Portfolio practice · Car production in India

In the 1930s, India became one of the first countries in the developing world to manufacture automobiles. However, since the 1950s, the automobile has been viewed as a luxury item by Indian policymakers, and the automobile sector has been heavily licensed, controlled, and punitively taxed. The duties on imported vehicles, even second-hand ones, continue to be prohibitive. Indeed, the latest scam in India's automobile sector is the import of luxury cars, supposedly as tourist taxis, which attract significantly less import duty, but actually for use by the rich and powerful.

The automobile sector has seen gradual deregulation over the past two decades, and about a dozen international car manufacturers now operate in India. In a country of one billion and counting, the annual sale of automobiles is around 900,000 vehicles, around three-quarters of them in the small-car segment. Of the 65 million vehicles on Indian roads today, two-thirds are two-wheelers; the rest include cars, buses, and trucks.

India has one of the lowest vehicle densities in the world. Most Indians still cannot afford cars. In addition, the public transport sector is dominated by loss-making public-sector corporations, which are a further burden on the taxpayers. Consequently, there is a tremendous and largely unfulfilled demand for transportation, particularly in rural areas.

Source: adapted from 2006 Index for Economic Freedom, www.heritage.org.

(a) **What type of market does the data suggest that the Indian car industry has, perfect competition, monopoly, oligopoly or monopolistic competition? Justify your answer.**

(b) **Explain what barriers to entry there might be for a car manufacturer thinking of setting up production in India.**

(c) **Assess whether India is likely to be a profitable country to produce and sell cars in.**

46 Theory, restrictions and strategies

Strategic objectives and international trade

Sections 42-45 looked at some of the strategies that businesses need to consider when they are faced with particular legal structures, market conditions and aims and objectives. Business strategy will also depend on why international trade occurs in the first place and the restrictions placed on international trade. This section considers the reasons behind international trade including the theory, the general barriers to international trade and how these affect business strategy when expanding into new countries.

Section 42 considered the main causes of international trade:
- the country cannot produce the resources it needs itself;
- they cost too much to produce;
- one country has the comparative advantage compared to another country;
- many types of goods and services develop first in only one country;
- international trade rules mean that some products can only be made in certain places.

This section will deal with the main theory of international trade, comparative advantage theory.

Comparative advantage theory

The theory of comparative advantage explains that countries, and the businesses within them, will trade with each other because both countries benefit from this process. A theoretical example with cars and wine in the UK and Germany shows how comparative advantage works and how both countries can benefit from trade.

Assuming that Germany can produce cars and wine more efficiently than the UK, the amount of production that each country can produce with the same input of labour, raw materials and land might be as shown in Table 1.

It would appear that Germany would gain no benefit from trading with the UK because it is better at producing both products. Germany has the **absolute advantage** in producing cars and wine.

Comparative advantage considers which country gives up least to produce each of the products. If Germany wanted to produce 200 more cars it would have to give up producing 300

Table 1 *Germany with an absolute advantage for both products (number of units)*

	Cars	Wine
Germany	200	300
UK	100	100
Total production	300	400

units of wine, or for each 1 car that would be 1.5 units of wine. The UK, on the other hand, can produce 1 extra car by only giving up 1 unit of wine. In terms of what has to be given up, the UK is more efficient than Germany in the production of cars, i.e. it has the **comparative advantage** in the production of cars.

This also means that Germany has the comparative advantage in the production of wine. To produce 1 unit of wine Germany must give up producing 0.67 of a unit of cars, but the UK would have to give up producing 1 unit of cars.

If the UK stopped producing wine altogether if could produce 100 more units of cars. If Germany gave up producing 80 units of cars it could produce another 120 units of wine. Table 2 shows that if this was to happen total production for the two countries would rise.

Table 2 *Production after specialisation*

	Cars	Wine
Germany	120	420
UK	200	-
Total production	320	420

In total, car production and wine production have each increased by 20 units. However, the UK now has no wine and Germany may have less cars than it needs. This will be sorted out by importing and exporting. The UK can sell cars to the Germans and buy wine from them and both countries will be better off.

Comparative advantage shows why countries benefit from trade, but not why individual businesses would benefit. The theory shows that total production will increase and the countries and their businesses will specialise in certain products. This will help to increase expertise and create economies of scale which should lower costs. At the same time there is less production in the other country, which should help to increase demand. For the individual businesses both situations will make it easier for them to sell their products abroad.

Limitations to the comparative advantage theory

In the real world this theory is rather simplistic and there are four main reasons why it should be questioned.

1. **Transport costs** The UK and Germany are fairly close together, but if the two countries being considered were the UK and Australia then it may be cheaper for the UK to produce, say, cars but there will then be the additional cost of getting them to Australia. This could be so high that it would

remove any advantages.

2. Economies of scale If a country's businesses are already set up, they may already be experiencing very significant economies of scale. These will reduce costs and make it impossible for production in smaller businesses in the other countries to begin to compete economically.

3. Transferring factors The theory assumes that a country can simply take labour, land and capital from one type of production and get these factors to work effectively producing something totally different. However, industrial land is unlikely to be very useful for growing crops, much of the machinery will be specific to a particular type of production and the labour will need to be retrained.

4. Trade barriers In many countries barriers such as quotas and tariffs will be put on the import of goods and services, usually to protect national businesses. Details of these are given below.

These limitations do bring into question how reliable the theory is, but at the same time they also explain the strategies taken by multinational companies.

1. Setting up plants, distribution centres, retail outlets and offices in countries where the goods and services are being sold can help to eliminate the additional transport costs.
2. When businesses expand into other countries they will take some of the benefits of economies of scale with them, such as expert management, cheaper finance and some of the marketing and development costs. They may also benefit, as the car industries do, from mass producing parts of the production in different countries.
3. Because this is an expansion of the existing business, fewer factors will need to be transferred to new types of production. For example, managers and other staff can be moved to the new centre to run it as nationals are recruited and trained.
4. In many cases when a multinational company produces in another country it will be treated as a national company in terms of tariffs and quotas, so the barriers will be removed.

Restrictions to international trade

Sections 48 and 49 deal with policies and controls created by the European Union and the World Trade Organisation in terms

Figure 1 *Major international trade restrictions*

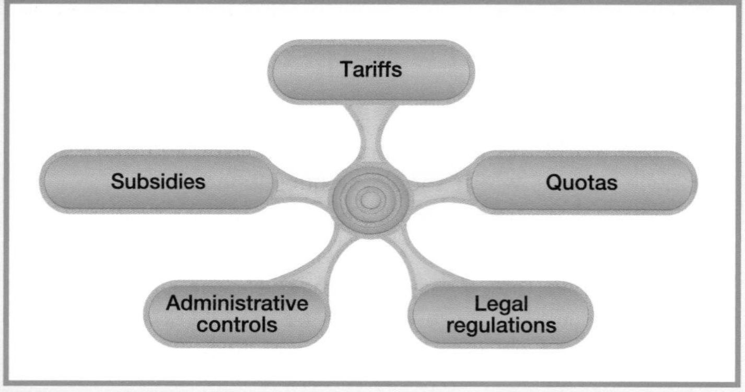

of what restrictions are, and are not, allowed in international trade. Here the types of restrictions, see Figure 1, and their effects on trade will be considered at a more theoretical level.

Tariffs Import tariffs are taxes on the import of goods or services into a country. They act as a barrier to international trade because they put up the cost of the imported products and make it more difficult for the importers to compete with home produced products.

Tariffs are generally put on products to make imports more expensive and so protect the home producers (see the 'Portfolio practice' for this section). There can be other reasons for tariffs. They can be simply retaliation against another country's import controls (see section 48).

Strategy: When businesses are faced with tariffs they will have to decide whether to either raise their prices and lose sales or keep the price the same and lose profit. Longer-term strategies might be to find ways of cutting costs, finding new markets where there are lower or no tariffs, or setting up production in the country to escape the import tariffs.

Quotas A quota places a physical limit on the amount of a product that is allowed to be imported into a country. Again this is designed to protect the national businesses. If customers cannot buy imports, because the number of these is limited, then they will demand home-produced goods and services instead. When a ban or embargo is placed on particular products, as with illegal drugs in the UK, the quota is being set at zero.

Quotas artificially limit the import of goods and some producers may not be able to import their goods even though they want to. This can lead to a black market where goods are smuggled in, as in the UK with illegal drugs, bush meat from Africa, and rare animals.

Quotas cannot be placed on products by individual EU countries, but the EU does set quotas for the whole Union (see section 48). This may be general, as with quotas that are placed on the import of eggs and poultry meat if they threaten to undermine the EU market, or they may be specific, as with the quotas placed on textile imports from Belarus.

Strategy: When businesses are faced with quotas the only legal solutions are to apply for licences to import and obey the quota limits, or set up the business in the country itself. Some countries will only allow production and sale of products produced by national businesses, especially where defence and security are involved. When this happens, the main strategy of foreign businesses will be to find other countries where they can produce and trade.

Subsidies Import tariffs increase the cost of imports and give home producers a competitive edge. This can also be achieved by subsidising the home production. This is where the government will pay part of the production costs, which allows producers to lower their prices. This also creates a barrier to international trade.

Export subsidies are subsidies given to businesses exporting the goods. The EU, for example, will pay EU producers of eggs and poultry products a refund when they export their products to countries outside the EU. This allows these businesses to lower their prices and to compete on world markets where the costs and prices are very much lower.

Strategy: Foreign businesses would need to find ways of cutting their costs in order to compete. Alternatively, if they can set up in the country they may be able to apply for the same subsidies and then compete on the same footing.

Legal regulations and controls Tariffs and quotas are legal regulations, but there are also other legal regulations placed on the production and sale of goods and services which will affect imports. There are also regulations and restrictions on exports for example, the EU has regulations in force that essentially ban the export of goods which could be used for capital punishment, torture or other cruel, inhuman or degrading treatment or punishment. The latest amendment to these controls came into force in July 2006 following Council Regulation (EC) No.1236/2005.

Legal regulations also affect the import and export of basic goods and services, for example:

- the UK law requires people to drive on the left-hand side of the road. Importers who want to compete with UK produced cars will have to put the steering wheel on the right and fit the dashboard the other way round. This increases costs;
- the EU has very tight controls on the safety of children's toys. Producers in other countries may need to change the way that they produce and check quality before they can sell in the EU;
- Australia has laws that prohibit the importation of anything that might affect the natural environment. Goods, therefore, cannot be packaged in anything that has been alive, e.g. straw or wood chippings;
- in the USA, producers are liable for almost any damage that the product might cause to the customer. This is called product liability. Exporters to the USA need to be aware of this and to take out suitable insurance;
- most countries require instructions and guarantees to be written in the language of the country where they are being sold. Producers must, therefore, pay for new labels or translations.

Strategy: It will make no difference if foreign businesses are importing products into the country or producing them in the country. They will still need to obey these regulations. The strategy must therefore be to ensure that the requirements are known and fully understood and to comply with them.

Administrative controls When goods are imported or exported there are many administrative procedures that need to be followed. Some of these are dictated by the government and may act as a barrier to trade. Some examples follow.

Import licences are required for the import of many products into the UK. Obvious examples include alcoholic drinks and tobacco, but licences are also required for less obvious products such as broad leaf mahogany. Products that need import licences can be checked at the DTI, and include all of the following categories;

- Common Agricultural (CAP) Licences;
- Department of Trade and Industry (DTI) Licences;
- Department for Environment, Food & Rural Affairs (DEFRA) Licences;
- European Commission Licences;
- Forestry Commission inspection documents;
- Radio Communications Agency (RDA) Licences.

Documentation is needed to import and export products. The number of documents and details required is decided by the countries, or trading blocks. In some countries this process can be time-consuming and costly and can discourage businesses from importing or exporting.

Inspection of goods coming into or going out of countries is also very common. This is done to prevent illegal importing and exporting, but it can be very time-consuming and used to delay getting goods into the market.

Strategy: If production takes place in the country most of these administrative procedures do not apply, although there will, of course, be procedures for setting up the business and providing tax returns. One strategy is, therefore, to produce within the country. If this is not done the licences must be applied for, the correct documentation filled out and products presented for inspection.

Using either the DTI website (www.dti.gov.uk) or DEFRA website (www.defra.gov.uk/) carry out the following tasks.

1. Identify two imports that require a DTI or DEFRA licence and identify the products that these licences apply to.
2. Describe the procedures needed to apply for the licences, noting such points as what details need to be provided, any cost involved and how long it takes to get the licences.
3. Explain why you think that a licence is needed for each kind of import.

Research task

Portfolio practice · Retailers put the boot in over EU import tariffs

Struggling British retailers accused the European Union of being 'overwhelmingly in favour of protectionism' as it prepared to slap duties on cheap goods imported from Asia. Tariffs will be imposed on leather shoes made in China and Vietnam on April 7 after EU trade commissioner Peter Mandelson found evidence of 'dumping' - shoes being sold to Europe at knockdown prices with the help of state subsidies.

The European Commission said it had not made a decision on the size of the anti-dumping duties, but it is thought they could be up to 20%. The move followed complaints from 30 EU manufacturers in countries such as France and Italy who demanded that measures were imposed to stop them going out of business amid unfair competition from Asia. But the move left Mr Mandelson on a collision course with retailers and shoppers in the UK worried that higher costs will increase high street prices and lower profit margins. And it could spark a repeat of last year's lengthy 'bra wars' dispute between Brussels and Beijing over Chinese textile exports.

Source: adapted from http://icliverpool.co.uk/ (Feb. 2006).

(a) Explain what is meant by the following terms used in the article:
(i) protectionism;
(ii) dumping;
(iii) duties.
(b) Explain the effect of the European Commission placing a tariff of 20% on the import of leather shoes made in China and Vietnam on the producers in those countries.
(c) What strategies could the producers in China and Vietnam take to reduce the negative impact of this tariff?
(d) British retailers and manufacturers in countries such as France and Italy had totally different views about the imports from China and Vietnam. State what the views are likely to have been and explain why they were so strongly held.

Meeting the assessment criteria - examiners' guidance

You are required to research and analyse the factors which have influenced one business to develop an international presence. This business must be one of the main businesses studied for '12.1' of the specification. The factors, such as market sector, aims and objectives and market conditions will have already been identified and now need to be set in the context of the strategies that the business will take in order to ensure success as a transnational or global business. This will require a consideration of the reasons for international trade and the restrictions placed on it by governments and economic limitations.

Business example - Sony in the USA

Sony has five centres in the USA, each with different productions and functions.

- **San Diego, California** is the corporate headquarters and centre for domestic sales, marketing groups and customer service.
- **San Jose, California** is a centre for design, research and development activities including semiconductor design, data storage, intelligent systems development and software solutions.
- **Park Ridge, New Jersey** is a centre for audio/video and IT solutions as well as consulting services.
- **Pittsburgh, Pennsylvania** is the centre for vertically integrated TV manufacturing.
- **Dothan, Alabama** is the centre for the production of magnetic recording media, video products, and audio voice and music grade media.

The Sony Technology Centre at Pittsburgh, set up in 1990, is the company's only U.S. television assembly plant. It builds more than 1 million televisions a year. Industrial analysts have said that manufacturing in the USA makes financial sense for Sony, considering that wages in parts of Japan and Korea can be comparable to U.S. wages in some regions.

Sony is an international company that believes in free trade but expects to compete on a level playing field. In 2005 Sony started production of new models of television at Pittsburgh, raising its workforce of 2,300 by almost 50%. Charles Gregory, president of the Pittsburgh unit put Sony's success down to various factors including the quality of the product and its ability to keep costs under control. Unfortunately, even though Sony assembles the televisions in the USA and sells them in the USA it is still affected by tariffs.

In order to make the televisions Sony imports components from plants in other countries and these are subject to import duties of $1 per unit for the high-definition cathode ray tubes for televisions, $13 per unit for the liquid crystal displays (LCDs) for the projection-type televisions, and $45 per unit for the LCD direct-view televisions. This costs Sony on average $1,300 on every 1000 televisions it produces. It could set up a plant in the USA to produce these LCD components but that would cost the company around $1 billion.

Source: adapted from various sources.

AOs	Mark Band 1	Mark Band 2	Mark Band 3
(b)	Basic details would be provided of Sony's business and its international presence as a multinational. Details here would cover the different types of production in the USA centres. The benefits of international trade in a free market should be given with some reference to comparative advantage. The limitations would be stated and a basic statement made as to why Sony is therefore producing in the USA. Comments would be expected on lower transport costs and avoiding tariffs. There should be acknowledgment that Sony still has to pay duties on imported components, with some details of the amount. Evaluation should state the benefits of locating in the USA and view this as part of the company's business strategy.	At this level the benefits and limitations of comparative advantages should be explained and related to Sony's position. Sony believes in free trade and has a high quality product so it would benefit from having no international trading restrictions. They are however there, and this should be stressed, with examples such as the LCDs. The reasons for the restrictions should be given, from the USA's point of view. There should then be details and explanations of Sony's strategies to get round these, e.g. setting up in the USA. There should also be an evaluation of why the USA is happy for Sony to set up there, with reference to employment and taxes. There should also be a basic evaluation of why Sony does not set up an LCD plant in the USA, with reference to the cost of doing this compared to the duties being charged.	The Sony situation is fairly complex and at this level the amount of research needed should reflect that, which will also allow for a more sophisticated evaluation. For example, some of these components come from Mexico which, being part of the North American Free Trade Agreement (NAFTA), means that they can be shipped duty-free, yet Sony produces other parts in Asia which automatically incurs import duties. The question should be asked as to why all the components are not made in Mexico. It would also be noted that Sony's strategy now includes putting pressure of the US government to get the tariffs cut and an explanation should be given of why the government is unlikely to change the duties. The benefits of free trade compared to restrictions should be assessed and justifications given for the strategies Sony has used to get round the restrictions. There should also be an appreciation of the benefits of economies of scale which should be explained in terms of why Sony produces its LCDs outside the USA and imports them and why it has different types of production at each of its five USA centres.

47 Interactions with the host countries

Host countries

When multinational companies set up in countries they need to create a legal format, buy or rent suitable premises, recruit staff and obtain licences if that is required. These, and many other activities, will require close cooperation and interaction with the host country. Some of these interactions have been covered in previous sections of this unit and should be checked when researching for part (b) of the portfolio. Section 50 must also be checked as this is where the impact on developing and developed countries and on governments and other stakeholders is covered.

This section will consider the following issues.
- How and why host countries attract foreign businesses to set up in their countries.
- How and why the home countries help their own businesses to set up in other countries.
- The importance to businesses of having an international presence.

The host country is the country into which the multinational business is expanding. The home country is the country where the business originated or where its main corporate head office, or plant, is now situated. Rupert Murdock's business empire, used to be based in Australia, then it moved to the UK and now it is based, as News Corporation, in the USA.

Why host nations attract foreign companies

When multinational companies set up in a country there will be benefits for the host country. Major benefits are shown in Figure 1.

Employment More employment will nearly always be created for the host country because the new business will employ nationals. It will also train staff and raise skills levels. The downside may be that managerial positions, and even skilled technical positions, may be taken by staff from the parent company.

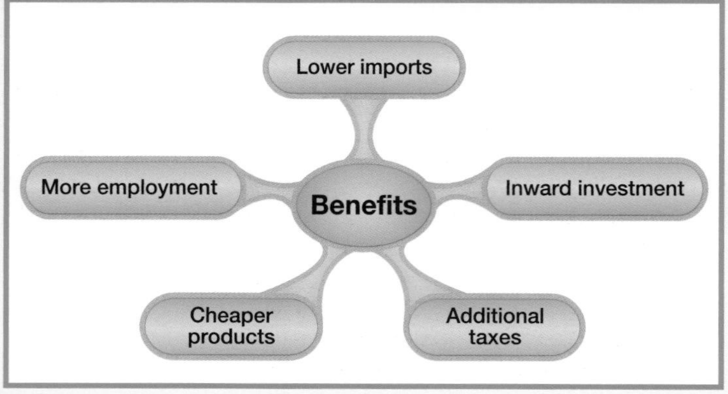

Inward investment This means that the multinational company will be investing money into the host country. It will need to do this in order to build the factory, office or distribution centre or pay for rent on existing buildings. It will also need to spend money on staff, transport facilities, basic supplies such as electricity, water and waste disposal. It may also buy raw materials from the host nation and services such as market research, banking and professional legal advice.

Taxes Additional taxes will be gained by the host country because not only will the multinational be paying taxes on its profits, but it will frequently also be paying taxes on employing staff, buying raw materials and services, the use of petrol and owning property. This would not be the case if the goods or services were simply imported, although there might be taxes to be gained through import duties.

Cheaper products Cheaper products for the host nation are likely to result because the business only has the transport costs of distributing products nationally. In poorer countries the labour and other costs may be cheaper than in the home country where imports used to come from, so this may also help to lower prices.

Lower imports Lower imports will result because the goods or services will be produced within the country. At the same time it is possible that some of the goods or services now produced in the country will be exported. The effect of lower imports and higher exports will mean that the Balance of Payments will be improved and this will help to raise the value of the currency. Some host countries do have Balance of Payments problems and will welcome multinationals because of this.

How host nations attract foreign companies

When businesses set up in other countries there is always some cost involved and often this cost can be fairly high. Businesses

Figure 1 Benefits of multinationals to the host country

Benefits
- Lower imports
- More employment
- Inward investment
- Cheaper products
- Additional taxes

Figure 2 UK Trade & Investment

UK Trade & Investment is a specialist government organisation set up to support:
- foreign companies seeking to set up or expand in the UK;
- UK companies to trade internationally.

The organisation provides details of the UK market and foreign markets and case studies on businesses that have moved into other countries. Its website is www.ukinvest.gov.uk/.

Source: adapted from www.ukinvest.gov.uk.

will therefore think very carefully about which countries to expand into. It will not just be the potential target market that influences the decision, it may also depend on **incentives** being offered by the host country.

Host countries use a range of incentives to try to attract foreign businesses, including:

* grants and subsidies to help businesses to set up in the country;
* special tax rates and possibly tax free zones;
* employment subsidies to reduce labour costs;
* information centres that provide details about the country and market profiles, what incentives are available and what procedures are required.

Examples of incentives for the UK and Morocco are given below. Most countries will have similar incentives.

Incentives in the UK There are about 250 different kinds of financial assistance on offer to companies setting up in the UK. The level of grant usually depends on which part of the country the business is locating in, with the highest grants normally in Northern Ireland and then in Tier 1, 2 and then 3, as shown in Figure 3. The grants are not automatic and will be considered in light of what the business can do in terms of long-term viability, job creation, promotion of exports or economic development.

Some examples of the aid provided in the UK are as follows.

* In Northern Ireland capital grants are available for buildings, machinery and equipment. Revenue grants are available for start-up costs, interest relief, factory rents, market entry and R&D. There are also special tax and finance arrangements.
* 18% of the project costs in West Lothian in Tier 2, plus SMART and SPUR grants from the Scottish Executive and the Scottish Enterprise Innovation Fund.
* Regional Selective Assistance is provided in all assisted areas. In Scotland Bausch & Lomb (an eye health company) received aid of £1,050,000 in April 2005 and Methode Electronics Europe Ltd received £150,000 in aid in September 2005. Both are subsidiaries of American companies.
* The Doncaster Area is a Tier 1 location which, in addition to grants, offers tailored training packages and subsidised recruitment services.

Table 1 shows the number of businesses setting up in the UK from other countries in 2004/2005.

Table 1 *UK inward investment success by country 2004/2005*

Country	Projects	New Jobs
USA	464	17,730
Canada	67	646
Germany	60	5,188
France	57	1,424
Japan	57	3,279
Australia	42	1,363
China	37	347
India	36	1,418
Ireland	34	1,681
Norway	24	209
Rest of EU	104	3,657
Rest of world	84	2,650
Total	1,066	39,592

Source: adapted from www.ukinvest.gov.uk.

Incentives in Morocco Each country will have its own reasons for wanting inward investment and its own incentives designed to achieve this. In the case of Morocco, the government is keen to encourage foreign investment as a means of job creation and technology transfer. To encourage this it has issued a new Investment Charter, which has simplified the existing administration and system of incentives. It has also established free zones where imported goods that will be processed in the country and then exported will not be subject to import duties.

The Moroccan government is also keen to maximise local content in any contract. The most beneficial agreements will be ones that ensure that there is local assembly or part manufacture of products, using local labour. As labour costs are low this will also benefit the foreign company. Incentives include:

* no restriction on taking post tax revenues out of the country;
* companies exporting goods or services will be exempt from Corporation Tax (35%) for the first five years;
* Corporation Tax at 10% for the first 15 years;
* no VAT on equipment, materials and tools acquired locally or

Figure 3 *Assisted areas in the UK*

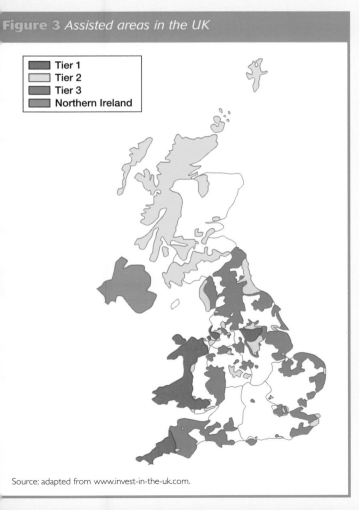

Legend:
- Tier 1
- Tier 2
- Tier 3
- Northern Ireland

Source: adapted from www.invest-in-the-uk.com.

imported;
- no urban tax (i.e. rates) on new buildings and extensions for five years after their completion.

Help and assistance given by a home country

It may seem strange that the home country would want to help businesses that are planning to expand into other countries rather than expand at home and export. The reasons why home countries support these expansions include the following.
- The businesses may expand abroad anyway and support from the home country will simply help a national business to do well, which is one of the responsibilities of governments.
- The profits from the centres abroad may return to owners in the home country and get spent there.
- Having major world companies that originate from a particular country not only gives the company greater status, but also the country.
- Some components, staff and capital may come from businesses in the home country and when these are paid for much of that money will stay in the home country and be spent there.

Again the UK will be used as an example of the kind of assistance that is available to UK businesses considering setting up abroad.

UK Trade & Investment (UKTI) This provides three areas of help for firms exporting from the UK or setting up businesses in other countries.
- Advice and support through Trade Advisors who will assess the business's needs and help plan for export or setting up businesses abroad. Advice is also provided on language and culture.
- Information about the target markets and overseas business opportunities. Links are provided to British consulates and embassies around the world which can carry out tailor-made research into potential markets for the business's products. Listed opportunities include details about overseas businesses looking for suppliers, current tenders, possible joint-ventures and manufacturing under licence. UKTI also provides a database of countries with details of population, the economy, major business sectors and other market details.
- Providing contact with the market through helping businesses to attend international trade shows and by helping the businesses to promote themselves in the overseas trade press. Grants of up to £52,000 are available for new exporting businesses when attending exhibitions.

The Export Credit Guarantees Department (ECGD) This was primarily set up to help UK businesses export by providing insurance in case the customers in foreign countries did not pay for the goods or services that had been purchased. The ECGD now provides similar guarantees for UK businesses investing in other countries and this helps to encourage businesses to set up in countries where there might be some political risk. The kinds of risks covered are expropriation, nationalisation or confiscation of the business and when there is a war or revolution.

The British Chambers of Commerce This also provides support for businesses trading abroad. The support includes:
- an export marketing research scheme with grants of up to 50%;
- visiting the market/trade missions;
- country profiles;
- training courses on a range of export practices;
- logistics, transport and export procedures.

Full details are available at the British Chambers of Commerce website, www.britishchambers.org.uk/. The site also provides case studies.

The importance of an international presence

An international presence for a business can provide it with a number of benefits. Major benefits are shown in Figure 4.

Figure 4 Benefits of having an international presence

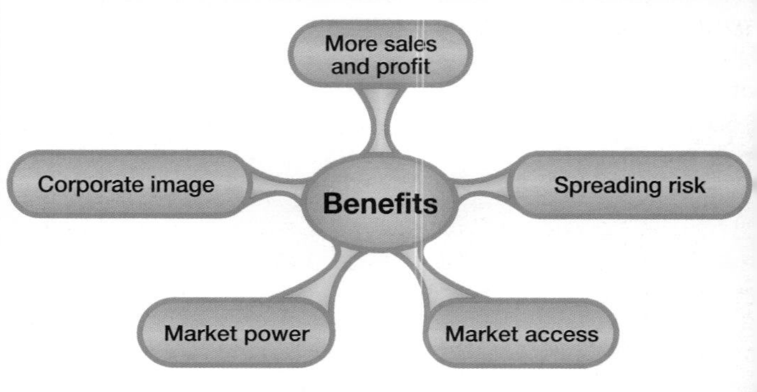

Higher sales and profits Expansion of the business into exporting or setting up and producing in other countries usually has the benefit of increased production, a wider customer base and access to new markets. All of these should result in increased sales and, through that, increases in profits. Section 42 considered the benefits in sales for various companies.

Higher profits will also have benefits for the business. The shareholders can receive higher dividends, which may make it easier to raise finances for further expansion. There will also be additional profits available to directly fund further expansion.

Spreading risk There is always a danger for a business if it only operates in one market. That market could decline due to a downturn in the business market or to an increased level of competition. When this happens it is very helpful to have other markets where demand is not falling and is preferably rising. The sales and profits from the prosperous markets can then be used to support the business in the depressed markets and hopefully keep it going there until things improve.

Market access National firms do sell products to foreign customers, but that will only happen when the foreign customers come into the country and buy products. If goods are exported to other countries then more customers will have access to them.

When businesses become multinationals and start producing goods or providing services inside other countries this often increases access because it frequently gets round many of the trade barriers that might exit. Moving into one country may then give easier access to other countries. Producing in the UK using mainly UK labour allows a foreign company to claim that its production is UK production and that means that there will be no tariffs, quotas or other external trade restrictions when it sell its products in other EU countries.

Market power Generally as businesses expand and gain more market share this gives them more power in the market place. Becoming an international business allows a business to expand and with that come economies of scale, such as bulk buying, lower interest charges on borrowing, employment of highly skilled senior management and technological economies. These economies will increase production and reduce costs which gives the business a more competitive edge and through that more power in the market.

When businesses become very large, as with many of the global businesses, the market power that they gain can mean that they not only dominate their competitors but also sometime governments and countries (see section 50 for details).

Corporate image Part of the image of a company is created by how well known it is. Many of the best known companies in the UK are not originally UK businesses and it has been the development of exports and multinational centres that have made the businesses so well known. Having an international corporate image can help a company in the following ways:

- as it is well known internationally potential customers may be more willing to try the products;

- its success internationally suggests that its products are good so this will also attract more customers;

- it may be easier to recruit staff, borrow money and enter new markets because having international status suggests that the business is reliable;

- suppliers want to supply major international businesses because they can then use this to encourage other businesses to buy their supplies;

- a well known international image gives additional power to the business when dealing with national governments.

	Company	Sales
1	Wal-Mart Stores	287.0
2	BP	285.1
3	Exxon Mobil	270.8
4	Royal Dutch/Shell Group	268.7
5	General Motors	193.5
6	Daimler Chrysler	176.7
7	Toyota	172.6
8	Ford	172.2
9	General Electric	152.9
10	Total	152.6

Table 2 *Top ten world companies by sales in $ billion*

Source: adapted from Global Business Resource Centre.

Table 2 shows the top ten businesses in the world in 2005.
1. Carry out research with a group of twenty people from different age groups asking the following questions.
   (a) Which of these businesses have they heard of?
   (b) What are the main goods and/or services produced by each business?
   (c) What nationality is the parent company of each business?
2. Use the Internet or world trade directories such as Compass to find out the answers to questions (b) and (c) above.
3. Compare your research to the results of your survey and explain why some of these businesses are better known by the general public than the others.

Research task

Meeting the assessment criteria - examiners' guidance

You are required to research and analyse the factors which have influenced one business to develop an international presence. This business must be one of the main businesses studied for section 12.1 of the specification. The factors, such as market sector, aims and objectives and market conditions will have already been identified and now need to be set in the context of the strategies that the business will take in order to ensure success as a transnational or global business. This will require consideration of how a business interacts with the host nation and its stakeholders and what incentives and support are given by the host country and the home country.

Business example - Blue Skies Holding Ltd

Blue Skies Holdings Ltd was set up in 1997 to deliver cut fruit to businesses in the UK, including Sainsbury, Budgens, Waitrose and M&S, and in the rest of Europe. Instead of importing the fruit from other countries Blue Skies set up processing plants where the fruit was grown.

The first factory was set up in Ghana at Nsawam. Before Blue Skies set up there, Nsawam had no electricity, no running water and high unemployment. There is now a factory employing nearly 1000 people with its own medical centre, library, creche and Internet cafe. Blue Skies also has plants in Egypt and South Africa

The factory in Egypt was opened in 2003 and now employs 250 people with a turnover of over £4 million. In choosing its Egypt site the company was part of a trade mission organised by UK Trade & Investment to the country in 2001, through which Blue Skies made vital contacts within the country. Blue Skies also received assistance from the British Embassy in Cairo, which helped the business in terms of understanding the Egyptian market structure and legislation.

Source: adapted from Blue Skies Holding Ltd and UKTI.

AOs	Mark Band 1	Mark Band 2	Mark Band 3
(b)	The nature of the business should be stated, preparing fresh fruit for flying to Europe, and the need for location in foreign countries where the fruit is grown, i.e. Ghana, Egypt and South Africa. The benefits to the countries should be stated, as shown for the town of Nsawam and with some indication that there were incentives given by the host countries. The role of the home country, in this case the UK, should also be identified, noting the involvement of UKTI and the British Embassy in Cairo. The strategies identified will be obvious ones, such as the original decision to set up factories where the fruit is grown, researching the countries and the available incentives and making contact with the right authorities.	At this level there should be explanations of the various elements shown in Mark band 1. The following questions should be addressed: • Why was it necessary to set up in these countries? • How did Blue Skies' presence in the three countries help the countries themselves? • What incentives were given by the host nations? • How did the support given by UKTI and the British Embassy help the business? Details should be in more depth, for example showing the kind of incentives that Egypt offer, such as Law 8 which allows 100 per cent foreign ownership, profits and capital to be taken out of the country and guarantees against confiscation or nationalisation. Evaluation of these factors would be expressed in terms of the fact that the business did set up and has been very successful. There should be evidence of some prioritising of factors, for example, did the incentives encourage Blue Skies to go to Egypt and South Africa or was it simply that these countries had the kinds of fruit that the business was looking for? The strategies the business took in relation to the decision to set up the factories and in response to the incentives and support should be explained.	Detailed research is required and all three foreign locations should be considered in terms of why the business went there, what incentives were given by the host countries and what support was provided by home country organisations. The effect on the stakeholders in the host countries should be explained and evaluated, noting details of factors such as employment, exports, the skills and technology benefits for the country. The social responsibility policy should also be considered, noting Blue Skies' commitment to understanding and fitting in with the culture, as with the mix of Christian and Muslim principles in Ghana. Details of the additional support provided beyond simply giving people jobs should be explained. At this level there should also be a clear consideration of how important the host country's incentives were and how much use was made of home country support. The strategies that the business took in relation to the choosing of the countries and to the incentives should be evaluated and both positive and negative elements should be considered. For example, how useful was the trade mission to Egypt, was there a cost and could other approaches have been used as effectively?

Portfolio practice · Changing attitudes to inward investment

In the introduction to their working paper *The economics of foreign direct investment* (2003) Blomstom and Kokko stated that:

'The attitude towards inward foreign direct investment (FDI) has changed considerably over the last couple of decades, as most countries have liberalized their policies to attract investments from foreign multinational corporations (MNCs). On the expectation that foreign MNCs will raise employment, exports, or tax revenue, or that some of the knowledge brought by the foreign companies may spill over to the host country's domestic firms, governments across the world have lowered various entry barriers and opened up new sectors to foreign investment. An increasing number of host governments also provide various forms of investment incentives to encourage foreign owned companies to invest in their jurisdiction. These include fiscal incentives such as tax holidays and lower taxes for foreign investors, financial incentives such as grants and preferential loans to MNCs, as well as measures like market preferences, infrastructure, and sometimes even monopoly rights.'

Source: adapted from http://web.hhs.se/eijswp//168.pdf).

(a) **Explain what is meant by the following terms used in the extract above:**
   (i) foreign direct investment;
   (ii) multinational corporations;
   (iii) entry barriers;
   (iv) tax holidays;
   (v) monopoly rights.
(b) **The extract lists both fiscal and financial incentives.**
   (i) Explain the difference between fiscal and financial incentives.
   (ii) Explain the difference between grants and loans.
(c) **Explain why the presence of MNCs in the host country will have the positive effects listed in lines 5 to 8 of the extract.**

The European Union

The European Union (EU) is a grouping of countries in Europe with similar aims and objectives. It was first set up by the Treaty of Rome, 1957 and included just 6 member countries. By 2006 this had risen to 25 countries, with 2 more to join in 2007/8 and further countries predicted to join in future, as shown in Figure 1.

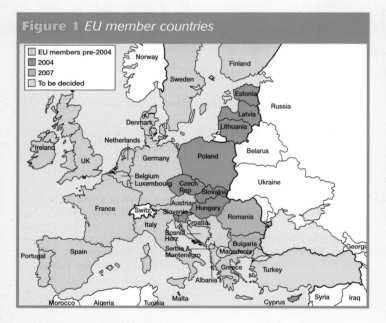

Figure 1 EU member countries

EU members pre-2004
2004
2007
To be decided

The EU has certain features.
- It is a customs union and close to a common market. Countries within the EU trade freely with each other, with no restriction on the movement of goods or services. It is known as the Single European Market.
- The free movement of factors of production, particularly labour and capital.
- There are common external tariffs on goods imported into EU countries from outside.
- Common economic, social and political policies, which affect businesses operating in EU countries.
- A common currency, the Euro. Not all countries in the EU are members of the Euro-Zone.

The EU has many rules and regulations. They are controlled by certain institutions, as explained in Table 1.

EU rules and regulations

The EU has many rules and regulations. European laws are called **directives**. The European Commission has the power to issue **regulations** based on these directives, with which member countries must comply. EU rules and regulations can affect:
- businesses which only operate in countries which are EU

Table 1 EU institutions

Institution	Area of responsibility
European Commission	Proposing policy and legislation to the European Council of Ministers. Implementing agreed policies.
Council of Ministers	Approves or rejects policies put forward by the European Commission.
European Parliament	Debates and comments on proposals put forward by the European Commission. Does not have the power to make laws like national parliaments, although this may change in future.
European Court of Justice	Individual citizens or businesses can appeal against decisions made by other bodies to the court, which bases it judgements on EU law.

members, for example Hackney and Leigh, an Independent UK Estate Agent covering South Lakeland, The Kent Estuary and The Lune Valley or Ulamo, a Dutch metal and coatings group, which operates in the Netherlands and Germany;
- businesses which sell into EU countries, for example Shiang Der Enterprise Co, Ltd., a Taiwan manufacturer and exporter of auto repair tools, winch and tow cables and hand tools, which sells to France and Germany.
- European businesses which operate in many countries, some of which are not EU countries, for example BA;
- non-EU based businesses which operate in many different countries (see other sections on multinationals), some of which are EU countries, for example McDonald's or Toyota.

This section deals with some of the major areas which affect businesses, as shown in Figure 2. However, it is important to recognise the vast amount of legislation that exists in the EU and the many ways in which it can affect a particular business. This may involve research into exactly how EU law affects a particular business or industry. Detailed information about EU legislation can be found at:
- http://europa.eu.int/ - which gives access to information (press releases, legislation and fact sheets) published by the European Union and its institutions;
- http://europe.osha.eu.int/legislation - the European agency for Safety and Health at Work;
- http://library.kent.ac.uk/library/lawlinks/european.htm - allows a search for legislation chronologically;
- news.bbc.co.uk and newspaper websites which give stories on the introduction of EU legislation and comments on how it affects businesses.

Figure 2 *EU legislation*

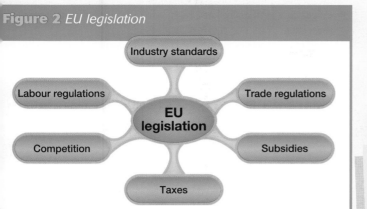

Some examples of the effects of EU rules and regulations on particular industries are explained later in this section.

Businesses can be affected in many ways by EU rules and regulations. In general terms, their compliance or non-compliance can affect:

- costs – complying with legislation can increase the costs of a business, especially if major changes need to be made, but non-compliance may lead to fines, charges and even in some cases legal action which may restrict trade;
- opportunities – rules may present opportunities for businesses to earn revenue, change production methods or products, expand trade, and increase sales and profits;
- possible dangers of increased international trade for businesses and consumers;
- possible retaliation to restrictions placed by the EU on imports.

These issues are considered throughout this section and in section 49 which deals with compliance with the regulations of a number of other international bodies.

Trade regulations

Businesses operating in the EU and those selling into the EU are governed by trade regulations. One of the major features of the EU, as explained earlier, is that countries within the EU trade freely with each other, with no restriction on the movement of goods or services. The **Single European Act, 1986** removed additional barriers to trade between member countries, creating the Single European market. Creating free trade within the EU has a number of effects on businesses.

Benefits Section 46 explained that free trade should result in an increase in trade and income for businesses and a greater variety of products for consumers. Removing restrictions to trade gives businesses within the EU a larger market into which to sell. Apart from transport costs, it should be just as easy for a Paris business to sell to a business in Rome as it is to sell to a business in Paris. Some businesses have expanded their product range or set up in other EU countries. Some businesses have even set up joint ventures with other EU countries as a result of the removal of trade restrictions. They have been able to reduce their costs by operating as a larger business and gaining **economies of scale**.

It has been suggested that creating free trade in the EU has led not only to trade creation - more trade - but also trade

diversion, where businesses change the businesses or counties into which they sell. An example is shown in Figure 3. A further benefit is that costs may fall. For example, a manufacturer of electronic goods may find that it can buy products relatively easily and cheaply from a supplier in Europe, with few costs and no restrictions.

Figure 3 *Czech and Russian farmers*

In 2004 the Czech Republic became part of the EU. Some businesses benefited, whilst others suffered.
- Farmers in the Czech Republic sold their products into nearby Germany at higher prices.
- German consumers could buy services in the Czech Republic, such as funerals, at lower prices.
- Farmers in Russia faced reduced sales as Czech consumers bought EU products at lower prices.

Source: adapted from the *Financial Times*, 13.2.2005.

Problems Opening up trade can also lead to difficulties. An obvious issue is that businesses in any EU country will now face the same trading conditions as other businesses. This will result in greater competition. A business may have to respond to this by:

- cutting the prices of its goods;
- launching new products or finding new markets;
- increasing promotion, which raises costs.

EU income and spending

Two major controversial issues concerning the EU are often said to be the EU Budget and the Common Agricultural Policy.

The EU budget Like national governments, the EU has a budget. It raises income from certain sources and spends the money in areas it considers merit spending. The EU budget cannot be in deficit, so income must always be equal to or greater than spending. Both income and spending have implications for businesses operating in the EU.

EU income comes from:
- contributions by members.
- 'own resources' such as taxes, tariffs and levies, as explained later.

Taxpayers' money is used to fund member countries' contributions. Around 1% of the EU's national wealth, equivalent to about €232 per head of the population, comes into the annual budget. If the EU wants to spend more it may raise contributions from members, which they might fund by raising taxes on consumers and businesses. Higher taxes on consumers will cut their spending on products. Higher business taxes will reduce profits.

Spending falls into various categories.
- Natural resources/Rural development and the environment - this includes spending on agriculture, including secure supplies of safe food, modernisation of production and higher

quality, rural development, fisheries, health and consumer protection in areas such as animal welfare and plant health, and protection of the environment. This is the largest area of spending, accounting for €42.9bn in 2006.

- Making the EU more cohesive by closing gaps in levels of economic, environmental and social development - this is the second largest budget item, taking €39.8bn in 2006. The money is spent on roads, bridges, motorways and airports, but other projects qualify for assistance, from small businesses to decaying city centres, wind farms to schemes to help the disabled become part of the community.
- Making the EU a global partner – involves enhancing trade and providing aid to countries in Euorpe, and in Africa, the Caribbean and the Pacific (ACP) through the European Development Fund.
- Citizenship, freedom, security and justice – for example, helping coordination between police forces.
- Administrative costs involved in running the European Commission.

Agricultural support The EU's Common Agricultural Policy (CAP) is a scheme designed to increase agricultural productivity, stabilise agricultural markets, guarantee supplies, protect consumers and ensure farmers have a fair standard of living. It has a number of features.

- A tariff placed on agricultural imports to the EU (see later).
- Setting intervention prices. The EU sets an intervention price, which is a minimum price for agricultural products. Farmers can sell their produce on the open market, but if they can not sell at a high enough price they can sell to the EU at the intervention price. The EU guarantees to buy up any excess at the minimum price.
- Quotas, or limits, on the production of products such as milk, for members countries. Farmers can sell their quota to other farmers. Limits on supply raise prices of these products.
- Set-aside for cereal farmers, who were paid by the EU for not using land. This reduces supply and raises prices of cereals.
- Subsidies and grants. In the past the EU has subsidised farmers' production, making payments based on the amount produced. Between 2005-12 the EU agreed to decouple subsidies and provide direct grants to farmers. Payments would be based on the amount of land they own, not the amount they produce.

CAP affects business and consumers in a number of ways.

- It maintains farmers' incomes.
- It supports rural areas, protecting employment.
- It helps farmers look after the environment.
- It guarantees supplies to customers and has helped the EU become almost self-sufficient in food production, importing fewer agricultural products.

However, critics disagree for a number of reasons.

- Farmers in some countries benefit more than others. Countries with a relatively large agricultural sector benefit most - France is the largest beneficiary.
- The cost is high and has to be paid for by consumers and businesses in members countries. For example, in 2002-04 the OECD found that the cost to consumers was €55,343 million and to taxpayers was €58,960 million.

- Prices are artificially kept high, which is not in consumers' interests.
- Foreign exporters complain that inefficient EU farm industry is protected and that they are not allowed to compete in a free market.

Agriculture as a proportion of the budget (35%) is now only half what it was 40 years ago as a result of agricultural reforms and an expansion of the EU's responsibilities.

The Euro

As part of the **Maastricht Treaty** (1991) most members of the EU agreed to adopt a single currency for the EU. The UK, Denmark and Sweden opted out. This meant that instead of having different currencies the other 12 members (at the time) gave up the Franc, Lira or Peseta and replaced their currencies with the Euro, in much the same way as the USA has a single currency, the US Dollar, for all of it states.

The benefits of a single currency include:

- that there are no costs involved in having to change one currency to another;
- prices are all in the same currency so that they can be easily compared;
- the currency and interest rates are controlled by the European Central Bank and that should help to create more stable economies for businesses in the EU.

The drawbacks include:

- individual countries have lost control over what their exchange rates will be and they cannot use exchange rates to protect their own businesses;
- if major EU countries are doing well the exchange rate will rise, but if weaker EU countries are not doing well that will make it more difficult to sell their products to non-EU countries.

As the EU expands the new countries have to decide if, and when, they will join the Euro-zone. Most new members have already aligned their currencies to the Euro. Table 2 shows when these countries planned to adopt the Euro.

Taxes

A number of features of EU taxation regulations can affect businesses.

Tariffs The EU has **common external tariffs**. This means that a tax is placed on the imports of goods to the EU, raising their prices. This can have a number of effects on businesses.

- EU business may face reduced competition as the prices of competitors' imports are higher.
- Trade diversion. Consumers in EU countries buy EU

Table 2 *Countries adopting the Euro from 2007*

Date	Country
2007	Slovenia
2008	Estonia, Cyprus, Latvia, Malta
2009	Lithuania, Slovakia, Czech Republic
2010	Hungary
2011	Poland

products rather than higher priced products from the USA or Japan.

● Retaliation. Countries can retaliate by placing tariffs on the exports of EU businesses or restricting the number of exports (quotas). This makes it harder for EU business to sell in other countries.

● Inward investment and location. Some non-EU businesses have avoided tariffs by setting up operations in the EU. By producing and selling in the EU without tariffs they can afford to lower prices to compete.

Tariffs and quotas are explained in section 46.

Figure 4 *Korean location in the EU*

It has been suggested that Korean electronics businesses have located in the EU to avoid tariffs. Some businesses that have located in the EU are shown below.

Regions	Company	Employment
UK (North)	Samsung Electronics	1,100
Northern Ireland	Daewoo Electronics	738
UK (North)	LG electronics	570
France (Lorraine)	Daewoo Electronics	539
Denmark (Ansberg)	LG electronics	350
Spain (Cataluna)	Samsung Electronics	950
UKL (Wales)	LG electronics	2,000

Source: adapted from www.lse.ac.uk/collections/europeanInstitute.

Tax harmonisation It was explained earlier that a large part of the EU's income comes from taxpayers in member countries. Another feature of EU rules is that, like other areas, regulations must be applied equally in member countries. In the case of taxes, there has been some harmonisation, trying to make them similar, but the tax on alcoholic drinks shows that there is a long way still to go. Even with VAT, where directives have set a minimum standard rate of 15% and a maximum rate of 25%, there are exceptions, with rates as low as 5% and some products with no VAT.

Other areas where the EU has regulations which encourage tax harmonisation include:

● taxation on company profits;
● taxation on pensions;

as well as minimum tax rates for petrol, natural gas, electricity and coal.

Tax harmonisation can affect businesses in a number of ways.

● It prevents businesses taking advantage of tax differences to gain a competitive advantage.
● It gives consumers equality of treatment in different countries.
● It helps prevent fraud, which is easier if there is a complex taxation system.

Labour regulations

Just as there is free trade in goods and services in the EU, there

Table 3 *Freedom of movement and business*

Example: a doctor moves from Estonia to the UK.

UK business – gains employee with scarce skills.
Estonia business – loses skilled worker.
Estonia business – loses worker from pool of skilled labour.

Example: an unemployed builder moves from the Czech Republic to the UK.
UK business – gains employee perhaps paid at lower wages, which reduces wage costs.
Czech business – smaller pool of unemployed workers to support.

is also freedom of movement of factors of production, such as labour. This means that workers can move from one country with limited restrictions and easily work in another country. Table 3 shows examples of how this might affect businesses in different countries.

The Social Charter of the EU is the chapter of the **Maastricht Treaty, 1991** relating to social policy. It requires member countries to adopt common social policies. The UK signed up to this in 1997.

There are many examples of EU directives which affect the rights of workers in the EU. They become the laws of members states. A comprehensive guide to European employment law can be found at http://europa.eu.int/pol/socio/index_en.htm. which includes:

● Council Directive 75/117/EEC of 10 February 1975 on the approximation of the laws of the Member States relating to the application of the principle of equal pay for men and women.
● Council Directive 98/59/EC of 20 July 1998 on the approximation of the laws of the Member States relating to collective redundancies;
● Directive 2003/88/EC of the European Parliament and of the Council of 4 November 2003 concerning aspects of the organisation of working time.

Employment legislation is covered in detail in section 67.

Competition

In order for the single market to function effectively, businesses in the EU need to compete on a level playing field. One of the roles of the EU is to create fair competition and 'a system ensuring that competition in the internal market is not distorted'. This means ensuring:

● a climate favourable to innovation and technical progress;
● the interests of European consumers are protected;
● European businesses, goods and services are competitive on the world market;
● healthy competition is not hindered by anticompetitive practices by companies or governments through restrictive agreements and practices;
● businesses do not exploit their economic power over weaker companies;
● governments do not distort competition by state aid.

Figure 5 EU investigates Internet travel joint venture

In 2001 the European Commission investigated a planned venture between German ISP T-Online and German tour operators TUI and C&N (Neckermann). It was concerned that the joint venture would be so powerful it could mean less choice for consumers of online travel services. The venture would join the two leading German tour operators with Europe's largest Internet access provider. It would be an online travel agency offering tourist products in Germany, such as leisure package trips, last minute trips and flight seats, which end-consumers could book online. The venture was eventually abandoned as a result of the investigation.

Source: adapted from www.out-law.com.

The European Commission lays down regulations and carries out investigations similar to those of the Competition Commission in the UK (http://europa.eu.int/scadplus/leg/en/s12000. htm). This can be in areas such as mergers or joint ventures, setting prices, restricting supplies or unfair trading conditions. An example is shown in Figure 5.

Industry standards

Many different businesses and industries are affected in many different ways by EU rules and regulations. As well as the effects already dealt with in this section, specific industries may be covered by particular EU regulations. An example is given in Table 4. A further example is explained in 'meeting the assessment criteria'.

Table 4 Areas where EU regulations might affect a UK airline

- Directive 2002/30/EC, 26 March 2002 - procedures on noise-related operating restrictions at EU airports - airlines face cost of reducing noise levels.
- Regulation (EC) No 785/2004, 21 April 2004 - insurance requirements for air carriers and aircraft operators - raise cost of insurance.
- Commission communication on air transport and the environment, 1 December 1999 - sets out a strategy to make air transport environmentally friendly - change operations to reduce pollution.
- Council Regulation (EEC) No 3922/91, 16 December 1991 harmonisation of procedures in civil aviation - change operations so they are the same as other airlines.

Source: adapted from http://europa.eu.int/scadplus/leg/en/s13000.htm.

EU expansion

It is suggested that the EU will continue to expand, with a growing number of member countries. The EU economy already resembles that of the USA, with many individual members operating in a large integrated market. There will be a number of effects on businesses of expansion.

- A growing market for businesses in countries which join, with few restrictions.
- Increased competition for businesses in existing member countries.
- An increase in the need for finance from the EU budget.
- A need to change legislation to cope with different business situations in new countries.

Using the website http://europa.eu.int/scadplus/scad_en.htm investigate how EU legislation affects the food industry.
1. Identify the types of business that are affected.
2. For three of these businesses explain how (a) the businesses themselves and (b) consumers might be affected.

Research task

Portfolio practice · EU imposes Asian shoe penalties

In 2006 the EU began imposing duties on imports of shoes from China and Vietnam. China exported 1.2bn pairs of shoes to Europe in 2005, while Vietnam exported 265m pairs.

The European Commission says leather shoe manufacturers in the Far East are receiving unfair government subsidies and that it has 'identified clear evidence of disguised subsidies and unfair state intervention to the leather footwear sector in China and Vietnam'. China denies this, saying the EU does not want to open up its markets to competition. The EU is concerned that a wave of cut-price imports could force European shoemakers out of the market. The tariffs will initially be low, but will rise over a five month period. In the case of China, they could rise to nearly 20%.

The action is supported by EU nations with large shoe industries, such as Italy and Portugal. But other EU members, such as the UK, oppose them because they are likely to push up prices for consumers, and could mean lower sales for retailers.

Source: adapted from http://news.bbc.co.uk, 7.4.2006.

(a) **The tariff imposed by the EU will be a common external tariff. (i) Explain what that means.**
    (ii) Explain why the EU uses this kind of tariff.
(b) **Explain why producers in the Far East have been able to keep their prices so low.**
(c) **The article identifies Italy and Portugal as having large shoe industries, but the UK being more interested in the retail sector. Why is it likely that the way the EU works will lead to this kind of specialisation?**

Meeting the assessment criteria - examiners' guidance

You are required to explore the dynamics of international organisations on one chosen business in a globally competitive environment. This will be one of the two main businesses studied for '12.1' of the specification, which should include a business with a European presence and one with a wider global presence. This will require consideration of the existence of the EU and the impact of its rules and regulations on this business.

Business example - Nissan in the EU

Nissan is a Japanese motor manufacturer.

- It operates worldwide in four regions: Japan, North America, Europe, General overseas markets. In Europe it has manufacturing plants in Sunderland, UK (set up in 1984) and Barcelona, Spain. Nissan Design Europe operates from London. It opened in 2003 and works on design strategies for future European models.
- In 1999 Nissan signed the Renault-Nissan Alliance with French company Renault. The companies set up joint project structures covering most of the companies' activities.
- An EU directive on End of Life Vehicles (ELV), issued in 2000 placed responsibility for recycling of these spent vehicles, on manufacturers or dealers. Following this, Nissan teamed up with Renault in December 2000 to set up ELV collection and a recycling network, to collect relevant information and to provide support to each EU dealership.
- In 2001 The European Commission approved the granting of £5 million aid to Nissan for the transformation of the same plant to enable the production of the new Nissan Primera.
- In 2004 Nissan announced its Almera model replacement

Table 5 *Nissan - European net sales (units)*

2001	453,697
2002	458,222
2003	548,693
2004	554,901

Source: adapted from http://www.jetro.go.jp/uk/e/pdffile/what_pdf/Nissan.pdf. www.nissan-global.com, www.hri.org, www.eiro.eurofound.eu.int.

would be built in Sunderland.

- In May 2004, a collective agreement was signed at the Spanish operations of Nissan. A four-year deal was reached, with employees accepting longer and more flexible working time, whilst gaining wage increases in line with inflation.

AOs	Mark Band 1	Mark Band 2	Mark Band 3
(c)	Basic details would be provided here of the benefits and opportunities of international organisations operating in the EU. Reference should be made to the EU rules and regulations that affect these areas. These would include rules relating to benefits such as freedom of trade within the EU area without restriction, the prevention of restrictive practices so there is a 'level playing field', and possible aid from the EU. It should be explained how these would affect Nissan and a general statement of evaluation should be given about the extent to which Nissan has benefited.	Details would be provided here of the strengths and opportunities for international business of membership of the EU. This would take into account how Nissan could benefit and have opportunities by having operations in the UK and Spain, which are members of the EU. Reference should again be made to EU rules and how these might benefit Nissan. Specific mention should be given of the avoidance of EU tariffs and the potential of alliance with EU businesses such as Renault. Reference could also be made to the possible expansion of the EU in future. The effects of these on Nissan should be analysed and an evaluation of the extent of benefits should be given, with supporting evidence.	Details would be provided here of the strengths, opportunities and drawbacks for Nissan operating in EU member countries. Specific reference should be made to the EU regulations that might affect the business, such as EU external tariffs, aid from the European Commission, the Working Time Directive and the EU directive on End of Life Vehicles (ELV). Explanation should be given on how these rules affect the business, both in terms of increases in sales or costs, changes in operations, and the effect on consumers and the environment. An evaluation should be given of the benefits against the costs, supported by evidence, and a judgement given on whether benefits outweigh the costs. Evaluation should also consider possible negative effects of Nissan's location, for example locating in the UK which is not part of the Euro-zone.

49 Free trade and the World Trade Organisation

International organisations

Section 48 dealt with the European Union and the benefits of being part of that trading agreement. It also considered the position of businesses outside of the EU and trying to sell into it. This section provides details of other international trade organisations, such as the **North American Free Trade Agreement (NAFTA)**. It also looks at the major world body that has been set up to promote international trade, the **World Trade Organisation (WTO)**.

The fundamental goal of the WTO is to 'help producers of goods and services, exporters and importers conduct their business'. In the past it was assumed that this must be done by removing all barriers to international trade. This remains an aim of the WTO but at the same time it is now recognised that international trade is a complex process and sometimes producers and countries need some kind of protection, particularly from powerful multinational businesses. However, the principle of free trade remains an important corner stone of the WTO and trading blocks such as the EU.

The case for and against free trade

Free trade exists when there are no artificial barriers of any kind to trade. This would be the position if there was a perfectly competitive market (see section 45). With perfect competition everyone knows what everyone else is doing and so businesses can compete on an equal footing and no business is artificially prevented from entering the market.

Competition would also allow for a position in which one business is better than the others and therefore rises to a position of market domination. For free trade, what is important at that stage is that if a single business does not continue to provide what is best for its customers, other businesses can come in and compete.

An ideal international trade environment would have these elements and would benefit the world as a whole. Unfortunately there are also downsides to completely free trade.

Benefits of free trade

When free trade works effectively it will lead to the following benefits.
- An increase in total world production, see section 46 on comparative advantage theory.
- Better quality of products because firms that produce inferior products will be competed out of the market.
- Lower prices caused by the level of competition.
- Labour can move more easily from job to job so unemployment is often lower.
- Free trade can stimulate new ideas and development of products so that individual businesses are in a position to compete effectively.

- Statistics show that countries that have more areas of free trade have higher production, lower costs and a higher standard of living.
- The movement towards free trade has removed barriers such as tariffs and quotas which artificially distort the marke

Drawbacks of free trade

The major problem with totally free trade is that it allows businesses to compete with no controls and when this happens it does lead to significant negative effects. These include:
- monopoly power. It is assumed that competition leads to more businesses in the market. But each of these businesses is trying to make as much profit as possible and to do this they will try to compete other businesses out of the market In the end there may only be one business left which can then exploit the market;
- businesses already in the market have access to customers, customer loyalty, and lower costs because of some economies of scale. It is then very difficult for new businesse to enter the market and compete;
- very high levels of competition can mean that businesses regularly get competed out of the market and when that happens the owners, the employees and the suppliers lose their income;
- competition makes businesses cut costs, but they may be ones that relate to protecting the environment, supporting local communities and producing in an ethical way, such as using child labour.

Because of these drawbacks to totally uncontrolled free trade i is necessary for governments to introduce controls that will in the long run help to protect the people. These controls include legislation to:
- prevent the abuses of monopoly power by having laws on anti-competitive practices (competition policy);
- protect the environment as with laws to prevent the dumping of dangerous waste products;
- protect employees from exploitation, as with the laws on minimum wages, unfair dismissal, and so on;
- allowing some trade barriers so that businesses that are new can grow or to protect businesses in less developed countries;
- ensure that products are safe for the users.

The World Trade Organisation (WTO)

The WTO started as The General Agreement of Tariffs and Trade (GATT) in 1947. At that stage it only dealt with the international trading of goods, and only industrial goods. As the name suggests, its main aim was to work towards the complete removal of tariffs and other barriers, such as quotas. Over the years not only has its name changed but also its aims. The WTO now also deals with agricultural goods and with services. It also ecognises that sometimes barriers are necessary and that what s needed is the best environment to allow trade to develop and row in the future.

The WTO is a very large organisation with many different terests and policies, many of which relate to specific dustries. In this section only an outline can be given. Students re strongly recommended to check the WTO website at ww.wto.org/ in order to research the impact that the WTO ight have on the business selected for the portfolio.

What is the WTO? The WTO is essentially an agreement etween member countries to work towards a better nternational trading environment. This will not only help the dividual countries in terms of their trade, but it should also elp to ensure that world trade as a whole is both greater in olume and of constantly improving quality. There are 149 ember countries, which include all the major trading nations f the world except Russia, although it has applied for embership. There are also 31 observer countries, including ussia, some of which have applied for membership. These bserver countries follow some, but not all, of the rules of the VTO.

The WTO states its main function as ensuring 'that trade ows as smoothly, predictably and freely as possible'. In order to chieve this, it has the basic objective of removing all nnecessary barriers to trade, such as tariffs and quotas. This ill help to ensure trade flows as freely and smoothly as ossible. To ensure that it is also predictable the WTO sets own rules that have to be followed by the member countries. his means that all members know what is or is not allowed in erms of how they trade. The benefits of the way in which the VTO works are shown in Figure 1.

Figure 1 *The ten benefits of the WTO trading system*

1. The system helps promote peace.
2. Disputes are handled constructively.
3. Rules make life easier for all.
4. Freer trade cuts the costs of living.
5. It provides more choice of products and qualities.
6. Trade raises incomes.
7. Trade stimulates economic growth.
8. The basic principles make life more efficient.
9. Governments are shielded from lobbying.
10. The system encourages good government.

Source: adapted from www.wto.org.

How the WTO achieves its main aims When the WTO tarted, as GATT, there were a great many barriers to world rade and many countries believed that protecting their usinesses from foreign competition was not only acceptable ut something that needed to be done. This was known as **protectionism**. Encouraging countries to reduce this rotection and open up their markets to competition has been

a painfully slow process and it has been achieved through a series of what are called '**rounds**'.

The WTO is like a club. It belongs to its members, the 149 countries. It is these countries that decide the rules and what changes will be made for the future. There are various levels to the WTO, see Table 1, which show how decisions are made. For the first five levels, all of the bodies are made up of all of the members which is one of the reasons why it takes so long for the WTO to make new decisions. The levels also show why it is important to check the specific details for the type of industry your chosen business operates in.

Rounds Because all members must agree to any changes in the WTO rules and to what are called the **multilateral trading**

Table 1 *The Organisational Levels of the WTO*

Body	Function
Ministerial Conference	Composed of all member countries. Meets at least every two years and makes all major decisions about trade and rules.
General Council	This operates as three bodies. • The General Council which represents the members on all WTO matters. • The Disputes Settlement Body which deals with any disputes between member countries. • The Trade Review Body makes regular checks of member countries' trading policies to ensure that they meet WTO rules.
Councils for each area of trade	Three councils cover all areas of broad trade. • The Council for Trade in Goods. • The Council for Trade in Services. • The Council for Trade-Related Aspects of Intellectual Property Rights. There are also committees for such areas as the environment and trade and development.
Committees	Each of the councils above is split into committees which deal with specific parts of trade, e.g. agriculture, textiles and subsidies.
Heads of Delegations	The Delegations are informal meetings where specific issues are discussed and initial recommendations made.
Negotiating Groups	Where there are particularly difficult issues these will be discussed in smaller groups of 20-30 members with all other members being fully informed of the discussions and decisions.

agreements, reaching agreement takes a very long time. The process of proposing changes, discussing them at the various levels shown on Table 1 and coming to a final agreement on the basis of consensus is called a 'round' and it typically takes many years to complete. The rounds are named after the location where the first meeting took place. The Uruguay round started in 1986, although decisions as to what should be included in it started in 1982. The agreement was not finally signed until April 1994. The Doha round started in 2001 and was scheduled to finish in 2005. This has now been extended to the end of 2006 and there is some concern as to whether an agreement will be signed at that time.

The last agreements stem from the Uruguay round and are summarised below. The proposals for the Doha round will also be summarised but it is important to check that these proposals have actually been agreed when the Doha round is finally completed. The Uruguay round had three parts.

GATT, 1994 The General Agreement on Tariffs and Trade, 1994 (GATT) dealt with agreements on the trade of goods and built on the 1947 agreements. The main agreement was to reduce tariff rates and non-tariff measures further applicable to trade in goods. The major achievements were:
- setting up the WTO as the replacement to GATT for administering the trade agreement;
- further reductions in tariffs for non-agricultural products;
- major reforms, including the reduction of tariffs and removal of quotas, for agricultural products. Previous rounds had failed to deal with agriculture. This also provided more access for less developed countries exporting agricultural products to developed countries and made developed countries reduce their subsidies on their agricultural exports;
- recognised the need for food safety and animal and plant health regulations and permitted these in WTO rules, trying to ensure that these were the same for all countries;
- insisting that as far as possible there are no artificial technical barriers to trade created by such requirements as specific standards for goods or specific testing and certification procedures;
- strengthening the rules on anti-dumping, i.e. when a business sells its products below market price in another country in order to get rid of them.

GATS, 1994 The General Agreement on Trade in Services (GATS) set out rules for the trade in services. This agreement included the following.
- Defining what services will be covered. This includes services supplied to other countries and services supplied within a country to consumers from another country (for example, tourism).
- Setting the basic obligation for any country which is known as the 'most-favoured-nations' rule. This says that if preferential treatment is given to any country when its businesses supply services, this treatment must immediately be given to all member countries. Note, however, the exception for members of customs unions.
- Establishing the basis for progressive liberalisation in the services through successive rounds of negotiations and the development of national schedules.

Specific agreements were also made on the movements of

labour between member countries, the telecommunications industry and the financial services industry.

TRIPS Trade-Related Aspects of Intellectual Property Rights (TRIPS) created agreements to protect intellectual property rights. These include patents and copyrights and protect businesses from other businesses stealing and using their ideas. For many businesses it is the innovative ideas and products that they come up with that makes their goods or services valuable. Now these ideas and products are protected from businesses which simply copy them and frequently sell them more cheaply because they had no costs involved in developing them. This also protects against the copying of trade marks and service marks.

Doha round The framework agreement was made in 2004, but the final agreement was not signed by mid-2006, so final details need to be checked. The framework agreement in 2004 included the measures shown in Table 2.

Table 2 *Features of the Doha round*

Agriculture
- Reduction in subsidies, with a 5% cap on subsidies which limit production.
- Export subsidies to be eliminated.
- Highest tariffs to be reduced the furthest.
- Developing countries to be given longer to implement tariff reductions.
- Least-developed countries to be exempt initially from tariff reductions.

Industrial products
- Tariffs to be reduced below a maximum ceiling.
- Some tariffs to be eliminated or brought to fixed levels.

Services
- Countries must submit offers to liberalise their service industries as soon as possible.
- No service sector should be excluded from liberalisation.
- It should be made easier for people to work abroad.
- Special attention to be given to sectors of export interest to developing countries.

Exemptions to trade rules Although the rules are designed to apply to all member countries there are reasons why some of the rules do not apply to certain blocks of countries or individual countries. Two examples are given that show this, but it is important to check if there are any specific exemptions for the countries that your chosen business trades with.

Customs unions, such as the EU, have been specifically set up to create a set of rules and privileges that apply to the member countries. It would then defeat the point of these special agreements if they had to be extended to every member of the WTO. So, for example, if the EU removes all tariffs, quotas and administrative barriers between its member countries, i.e. it gives them preferential treatment, this does not have to be extended to all WTO countries under the 'most-favoured-nations' rule.

Some countries have particular reasons for not wanting to adopt all of the WTO rules. If they can provide a well justified reason to the WTO they will not be required to. For example, Croatia has been allowed to keep measures which reserve or limit the provision of transport services and specify operating conditions, including transit permits and/or preferential road taxes on transport services into, in, across and out of the Republic of Croatia. This was allowed because of specific characteristics of the road transport services in Croatia.

Settling disputes Despite the fact that the member countries are signed up to the principles and rules of fair trade laid down by the WTO, disputes between countries still occur. A dispute arises when one country adopts a trade policy measure or takes some action that one or more fellow WTO members considers to be breaking the WTO agreements and obligations. The country affected can then complain to the Disputes Settlement Body which will investigate the dispute and make a ruling. The WTO prefers to consult with the countries involved and to settle the dispute without having to make a ruling but where a ruling is made the countries have to follow it. It also now insists that disputes are resolved fairly quickly, see Table 3.

Table 3 *Dispute procedure and duration*

60 days	Consultations, mediation, etc.
45 days	Panel set up and panellists appointed
6 months	Final panel report to parties
3 weeks	Final panel report to WTO members
60 days	Dispute Settlement Body adopts report (if no appeal)
Total = 1 year	**(without appeal)**
60-90 days	Appeals report
30 days	Dispute Settlement Body adopts appeals report
Total = 1y 3m	**(with appeal)**

Source: adapted from www.wto.org.

Following the ruling the country at fault should change what is it doing so that it is no longer breaking the rules. If it cannot immediately correct the position it should offer compensation to the country which has been affected. If this cannot or will not back down it may well be fined and if even this does not work trade sanctions, such as tariffs on its products, can be imposed.

Other trading agreements

Section 48 dealt with the European Union as a special trading block with its own rules and regulations and with agreements that help to make trade easier. In the EU most, but not all, barriers to trade have been removed and it is close to being a common market. Similar agreements have been made between other countries and these will need to be checked to see if they affect the business that is being studied for the portfolio work.

EFTA The European Free Trade Association (EFTA) was set up in 1960 as an alternative trading block to the EU. At that time the UK was a member of EFTA. Today EFTA only has four members, Iceland, Liechtenstein, Norway and Switzerland.

Three of the EFTA members (not Switzerland) have made an agreement, called the European Economic Area (EEA), with the EU whereby they gain many of the benefits of EU memberships such as the free movement of goods, services, capital, and persons between the EEA countries. Details of EFTA can be found on its website at http://www.efta.int/.

NAFTA The North American Free Trade Agreement (NAFTA) was set up in 1994 mainly because the USA was worried about the growing size and market power of the EU. The member nations are the USA, Canada and Mexico. The USA and Canada already had trade agreements and the main changes were made with Mexico with the tariff halved immediately and the rest phased out completely over the next 14 years.

NAFTA is not like the EU which has set up organisations to make laws and administer EU matters. It is simply a trade agreement between the three nations. Details of NAFTA can be found on its website at http://www.nafta-sec alena.org/ DefaultSite/index.html.

There is a number of other regional trading agreements and organisations. These are shown in Table 4.

It is also important to check whether countries are members of other major international organisations because this can give them certain rights and set down certain rules and obligations. Membership of the following organisations should be checked.

Table 4 *Other regional trading blocks*

	Full name	Full members
ASEAN or AFTA	Association of Southeast Asian Nations	10
CACM	The Central American Common Market	5
CARICOM	The Caribbean Community and Common Market	15
CEMAC	Economic and Monetary Community of Central Africa	6
COMESA	Common Market for Eastern and Southern Africa	5
CSN	South American Community of Nations	10
EAC	East African Community	3
ECOWAS	Economic Community of West African States	16
EurAsEC	Eurasian Economic Community	6
GCC	Cooperation Council of the Arab States of the Gulf	6
PARTA	Pacific Regional Trade Agreement	12
SACU	Southern African Customs Union	5
SAARC	South Asian Association for Regional Cooperation	8
SADC	South African Development Community	14

- The International Monetary Fund (IMF) which can lend countries money, but which member countries must pay money into as well. Check http://www.imf.org/.
- The International Bank for Reconstruction and Development (IBRD), also known as the World Bank. This bank will make long-term low interest loans for reconstruction and development projects. Check http://www.worldbank.org/index.html.
- The inter-governmental grouping called Asia-Pacific Cooperation (APEC). This is similar to the WTO in its aims but it works by countries coming together to discuss and agree ways of improving international trade, growth and investment in the Asian-Pacific region. There are no formal agreements and no binding commitments. Check http://www.apec.org/.

Taking the regional trading blocks listed in Table 4, carry out the following tasks.

1. Select two trading blocks and find out which countries are members. Some may be part members and others may simply be observers.
2. Identify some of the major benefits the blocks provide for members and some of the external trade restrictions they impose on countries trying to sell into the block.
3. Find out if businesses setting up a production unit in the country would escape the trade restrictions and explain the strategies such businesses would need to take to become an accepted 'national' business.

Research task

Portfolio practice · Bicycles sales benefiting from WTO environmental policy

'bikeforall.net', a UK website of the joint initiative of the Bicycle Association and the Association of Cycle Traders, published an article in which the following speculations and information were given.

(a) **Explain the meaning of the following phrases used in the details above:**
   (i) **liberalisation of trade;**
   (ii) **non-tariff barriers;**
   (iii) **environmental goods.**
(b) **Explain why making bicycles 'free from tariffs' would help businesses producing and selling bicycles.**
(c) **'The Doha round' is the latest of the WTO's rounds. What does that mean?**
(d) **Considering the nature of the WTO as an organisation of member countries, explain why it has such a positive policy towards environmental issues.**

WTO and OECD could define bicycles as 'environmentally preferable products'

If this happened bikes would be free of tariffs, making them cheaper to buy and so, in theo[ry] bought by more people leading to more cycling, and less auto-congestion. Organizations promoting bicycle use at the international level may have a new avenue to do so – throug[h] the liberalization of trade in bicycles, bicycle parts and components, and bicycle accessories that could result from the World Trade Organization's current negotiations on environmen[tal] goods and services.

The mandate for these negotiations comes from the Doha Development Agenda, issued by trade ministers at the WTO Ministerial Conference in Doha, Qatar, in November 2002. Paragraph 31(iii) of the DDA calls for the reduction or elimination of tariff and non-tariff barriers to environmental goods and services.

A decision is expected by the end of 2006.

Source: adapted from www.bikeforall.net, Cycle News,

Meeting the assessment criteria - examiners' guidance

You are required to explore the impact of international organisations on the behaviour of one of the main businesses studied for section 12.1 of the specification. That exploration will require careful research of the countries in which it trades and of the kinds of goods or services produced and sold in other countries. You will then need to research the various international organisations and agreements that might affect how the business carries out its international trade. This will require consideration of the benefits of free trade and the restriction imposed by regional trading bodies. It will also require a consideration of the rules and regulations of the WTO and if appropriate such organisations as the World Bank and the IMF.

Business example - Adidas Group

Adidas the sports clothing and equipment multinational has its corporate headquarters at Herzogenaurach in Germany. It also has 80 subsidiaries around the world. Table 5 shows where these subsidiaries are located.

In addition to its subsidiary businesses, which produce in a wide number of countries, Adidas also sells into many more countries supplying to retailers all over the world. It also imports raw materials from a range of foreign countries. Through all of these contacts, Adidas is affected by many international trading organisations.

Source: adapted from Adidas website, www.adidas-group.com/.

Table 5 *Countries in which Adidas has subsidiary companies*

Argentina	China	Hong Kong	Mexicp	Poland	Switzerland
Australia	Czech Republic	Italy	Netherlands	Russia	Turkey
Austria	Denmark	Japan	Norway	Spain	UK
Brazil	France	Korea	Panama	Sweden	USA

AOs	Mark Band 1	Mark Band 2	Mark Band 3
(c)	The nature of what Adidas produces should be identified and details of the countries in which it produces and sells. There will be a general outline of the benefits of being within particular trading groups and an appreciation of the benefits of free trade. The role of the WTO and of trading blocks will be outlined but with limited application to Adidas itself. Adidas is a highly successful global business and there should be basic evaluation of how the movement toward free trade has helped to achieve this and whether or not the benefits and barriers of trading blocks have had any effects.	At this level there should be explanations of the benefits and drawbacks to Adidas of a range of international trade organisations. Examples need to be given to support the explanations. Adidas produces, sells and obtains raw materials from a very wide range of countries and it is expected at this level that the examples are selected to represent different aspects of Adidas's trade. Reference to the WTO would be useful as it allows an explanation of the benefits of free trade. It also deals with: • agricultural goods which Adidas uses for raw materials; • manufactured goods which Adidas produces and sells; • intellectual property rights that apply to Adidas's designs. The countries Adidas produces in would allow consideration of the EU, EFTA, EEA, NAFTA, CSN, EurAsEC, and PARTA. Because Adidas's products are sold worldwide any of the trading blocks and agreements could be used to make valid points. There must be a clear recognition that the rules and regulations laid down by these international organisations bring both benefits and drawbacks and there should be an appreciation of why that balance is necessary.	At this level it is the detail and the depth of explanation and evaluation that is required. A quick look at the websites referred to in this section will indicate just how complex international trade rules are. The explanations, with examples will have been given for Mark Band 2. Here there should be much greater assessment of just how important the benefits and drawbacks have been. For example: • Germany is in the EU whereas Norway and Switzerland are in EFTA. Norway is a member of the EEA but Switzerland is not. Have any of these factors affected the way in which Adidas trades? • Adidas is committed, in every country where it produces, to follow the International Labour Organization (ILO) conventions on employment, including safety in the workplace, child labour, and hours of work. How does this affect its costs? • Adidas produces within all of the trading blocks shown in Mark Band 2. Does this mean that the business is treated as if it was a national business and how does it affect exports out of the country? Adidas will be affected by most of the international organisations referred to in this section. You cannot, and are not expected to, cover all of them. You must therefore select carefully which elements you need in order to create a good balance of effects.

Multinationals

The reasons for the growth of multinational corporations (MNCs) and the impact that they have had on international trade and the countries in which they trade have been themes that have run through all of the sections of this unit. It is important, therefore, that when this part of the portfolio is completed all of the points so far covered are considered. This section focuses more specifically on these two main aspects:

* the growth of multinational corporations;
* their impact on countries and stakeholders.

The growth of multinationals

Today it is estimated that over half of the world's trade comes from MNCs. In its *World Investment Report 2005* the United Nations Conference on Trade and Development (UNCTAD) gave figures for the world's top 25 transnational corporations (TNCs). These are essentially the same as MNCs. The figures for the total foreign assets, sales, employment and owned subsidiaries (affiliates) are shown on Table 1. This top 25 list did not included financial institutions such as banks which, are amongst the biggest MNCs in the world.

Table 1 *The world's top 25 non-financial TNCs 2003*

Foreign assets	$2,213 billion
Foreign sales	$1,393 billion
Foreign employment	2.1 million
Number of foreign affiliates	8,600

The top of the list in each category was:

* for foreign assets, General Electric with $259 billion;
* for foreign sales, British Petroleum with $193 billion;
* for foreign employment, Siemens with 247,000;
* for number of affiliates, Hutchinson Whampoa with 1900 affiliates (subsidiaries or majority owned).

In 2004 there were approximately 70,000 TNCs in the world, with about 270,000 foreign affiliates generating sales of almost $19,000 billion. This has grown significantly even from 1995 when there were only about 40,000 TNCs and 1999 when there were about 60,000 TNCs.

Reasons for the growth of MNCs

There is a number of reasons given for the growth of MNCs, and there is some dispute as to which of these really caused the dramatic growth in MNCs in the last forty years or so. It is also important to distinguish between two possible types of multinationals because they may have different reasons for their growth.

Multinationals like McDonald's experience **horizontal growth** meaning that its new businesses are all at the same stage of production, in the case of McDonald's preparing and selling food in restaurants. It is true that there are other parts to McDonald's, but this is the main way in which it has become global.

Other multinationals like Tate & Lyle and many of the car companies produce different parts of their production in different countries, concentrating on just one type of production in one place. Where this is also one stage of the production this is called **vertical specialisation**.

The liberalisation of trade With the creation of GATT and the WTO, see section 49, there have been significant reductions in the barriers to international trade. This has allowed businesses to sell into other countries with less cost and it has also enabled businesses to set up in other countries and export with less cost. Where there is vertical specialisation this has been particularly beneficial because tariffs may have been imposed at each stage of production, as partly finished products were sent from one country to the next.

In reality most MNCs are not found all over the world but in countries close to their original location. With these businesses what may have been more important than the WTO is the liberalisation of trade that has taken place within trading blocks such as the EU, NAFTA and SADC. The EU is a particularly good example because it has gone further than most, even introducing a single currency for the majority of its members, see section 48.

The liberalisation of trade and the incentives given by host countries and such organisations as the World Bank and the United Nations through its Development Programme also explain the growth of MNCs. The flow of money into countries in the form of **foreign direct investment (FDI)** is now very considerable. 2004 saw FDI inflows of $684 billion, with 36% going into developing countries.

Natural growth As has been explained in previous sections, the natural stages for the growth of MNCs include a stage when it is simply a national business. At that stage it will have a finite possible demand from the country itself, so the next logical step is to become international, selling into other markets, and then multinational, producing or having separate centres in other countries.

With improved production techniques and better communication and marketing businesses are able to grow much more rapidly than in the past. This means that more of them will reach saturation within the country so there will be more international and multinational businesses worldwide.

Economies of scale As businesses grow in size they will gain economies of scale. This will reduce their costs or improve their access into new markets, allowing them to compete with businesses in other countries.

For business with horizontal growth they will gain economies because they are duplicating what is being produced. The research and development costs can now be spread across more centres and possibly more of their products. Once the name of a business is well established, any positive promotion for one part of the business will help to promote the rest of the business at little or no extra cost. For example, Coca-Cola sponsoring the World Cup will promote its products in countries throughout the world because that is where the football is being watched.

Businesses which use vertical specialisation will gain economies of scale because parts of their production will be centred in specific plants. Economies will include spreading fixed costs, multiple machine use, specialised labour and bulk buying of raw materials.

Power As international and multinational businesses get bigger they gain more power. Very large businesses will spend significant of sums of money in the host countries, providing employment, taxes and production. If one of these businesses chooses to close down and move to another country that will negatively affect the host country so it may give in to pressures such as keeping wages low and providing tax incentives. This helps the business to keep costs down and produce more, increasing the size of the multinational in terms of world trade. Figure 1 shows an example.

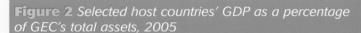
Figure 1 *Apeejay international buys Typhoo*

In 2005 Typhoo, the tea company, was sold by Premier Foods for £80m to the Calcutta-based company Apeejay International Tea, a commodity tea producer which is one of the largest exporters of tea into Britain. The chairman, Karan Paul, said: 'We wanted to get into the branded tea business and thought that Typhoo was a great brand that is profitable and has a very efficient plant.' The stability of a branded business would help to balance out the cyclical swings of the commodity side of Apeejay. Typhoo's main competitors Tetley and PG Tips have twice its UK market share. Apeejay was keen to make the investment necessary to make Typhoo a market leader.

Source: adapted from *The Guardian*, 14.10.2005.

The influence of multinationals

TNCs are now so large, powerful and operating and selling into so many countries that it is inevitable that they will significantly affect the stakeholders of the host countries. In many cases the assets of the TNC are substantially larger than the total GDP of the country. The total assets of General Electric in 2005, for example, were $673 billion. Many of the countries around the world in which GEC was producing had a fraction of this as their total GDP, as shown in Figure 2.

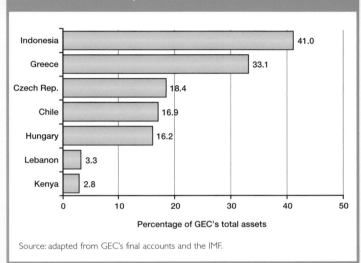
Figure 2 *Selected host countries' GDP as a percentage of GEC's total assets, 2005*

Source: adapted from GEC's final accounts and the IMF.

The effect on stakeholders The effect that multinationals have on stakeholders will depend very much on two main distinctions:
- whether the stakeholders are in the host countries, the country of origin or other countries where goods are being produced or sold;
- whether the stakeholders are in developing or developed countries.

The first distinction should be clear if employees are taken as the stakeholders and the situation is that of a UK business deciding to close its call centre in Birmingham and set up a call centre in India rather than Pakistan. This is how employees in three areas may be affected.
- In the UK employees lose their jobs and their incomes.
- In India new employees are taken on and receive wages and a rise in their standard of living.
- In Pakistan employees, or the unemployed, will be the same as before and gain no direct benefit.

The second distinction is hinted at by Figure 2. GEC also produces in the UK and when the UK's GDP is compared to the assets of GEC it comes out for 2005 at 327%. The UK's GDP is close to 100 times larger than the Lebanon's. The figures still suggest that GEC is a potentially very powerful business, even in the UK, but developing countries are both smaller and less able to make demands on businesses setting up in their countries.

From the home country's point of view the decision of a

Table 2

Stakeholder	Questions
Employees	• Will more or less employees be needed? • Will incomes rise or fall? • Will employees be exploited? • What are the long-term prospects?
Customers	• Will prices rise or fall? • Will this increase the range of products available? • Will there be better access?
Suppliers	• Will the business now be looking for new and cheaper suppliers? • Must suppliers be from the host country? • How will changes in demand for suppliers affect their ability to supply other customers?
Competitors	• Will the MNCs take away their customers? • What strategies will they need to take in order to stay competitive? • Can they put pressure on their governments to get protection?
Governments	• Will the benefits to the economy outweigh any negative effects? • How much incentive will be needed to attract the flow of FDIs? • How powerful will the MNCs be compared to the government?
The community	• Will the new factories and offices damage the environment? • Will new products change the local culture positively or negatively? • Will employees spend their incomes in the local community?

business to be international or multinational is very important. If the business remains international and produces goods or services in the country and exports them, this is likely to be more beneficial to employees, suppliers and the government than if it becomes multinational and sets up production units abroad. France Telecom, for example, has very substantial foreign assets, with over 64% of its assets invested abroad and with 44% of its affiliates abroad, but at the same time nearly 60% of its employees are in its home country, France.

When assessing the impact of multinationals on stakeholders Table 2 shows the kind of questions that should be asked.

The effect on governments Multinational companies need the support and agreements of governments in the host countries before they can set up and produce there. They,

therefore, frequently develop a special relationship with them. As was shown in section 47 it is generally the host country that offers the incentives, set the levels of taxation and sets the conditions about ownership of land, factories and so on. On the other hand, if the MNC is economically powerful and can offer the prospects of significant levels of employment, revenue and social and environmental support it may well be the MNC that dictates the conditions rather than the host government.

For the multinational there is also a need to consider how stable the government is. If there is a major change in the government, which brings in a new regime with very different views, the multinational may find itself with unexpected changes in the allowed conditions. There have also been examples where very powerful multinationals have helped to change governments, so that the new regimes will be more favourable for them.

Figure 3 *BP to expand in China?*

In February 2006 it was reported that the Chinese government may approve a possible deal for BP to make the largest investment by an overseas company in China. BP would enter into a £14bn joint venture with Sinopec, the foreign-listed arm of China Petroleum Chemical Corporation, which is China's biggest oil producer and refiner. It was suggested that BP could help the country alleviate power shortages as the country, faced with double-digit economic growth, rapidly industrialised.

Source: adapted from *The Observer*, 26.2.2006.

The effect on developing and developed countries

Of the flow of FDIs in 2004, 36% went into **developing** countries and 64% into **developed** countries. The reason why more went into the developed countries is because they are richer. This has two main effects. First, because they have more income they are more likely to buy the products being made. Second, because the incomes are higher the costs of living are higher and therefore more investment is needed to set up in a developed country than in a developing country.

The impact of MNCs in developing countries is likely to be greater than in developed countries for the following reasons.
- Developing countries have less income so inflows of capital will have relatively more effect.
- Developing countries can benefit greatly from MNCs locating there and that gives the MNCs greater bargaining power.

- Many MNCs go to developing countries because labour and other costs are low so this has a greater effect on employment than if they went to a developed country.
- Developed countries already have advanced technology and communications and so benefit less from new technologies brought in by the MNCs than developing countries do.
- Developing countries are likely to have fewer controls on protecting the environment and sometimes MNCs abuse this and cause environmental damage.
- Most developed countries already have a great deal of international trade and therefore have a range of cultural influences, whereas developing countries may have a much more national culture which can be negatively affected by MNCs.

The impact of multinationals on host and home countries is also dealt with in section 47. An example of the impact of a multinational on a country is shown in Figure 3.

Portfolio practice · Solectron

Solectron is the multinational you've almost certainly never heard of. If, however, you own a mobile phone, a video games console or a digital television receiver, there's a pretty good chance it was made by Solectron.

The California-based company is an invisible giant. With sales of around $12 billion a year, and employing 70,000 people in 23 countries, it manufactures high-tech products for big brand-name owners like Dutch electronics company Philips, as well as a lot of other firms who would prefer that their names were not divulged. Solectron operates a business where it must generate profits from margins that can be paper-thin. This requires the firm to squeeze out every cent of profit to stay afloat, and leaves it vulnerable to changing economic conditions.

In 2002, it reported a net loss of $2.6 billion. While the result can in part be attributed to the global economic downturn, Solectron must nevertheless address why its losses reached this scale. In an effort to save expenses, it has cut 30,000 jobs in places like South Wales where it used to base factories. Now it has relocated the centre of its European manufacturing operations to Romania where wage levels are around an eighth of what they are in Western Europe.

Source: adapted from www.bbc.co.uk.

(a) Considering the types of products that are made by Solectron explain how being a multinational company would help the business.

(b) Assess and explain the likely impacts of Solectron's decision to move parts of its production from Wales to Romania on:
(i) stakeholders in Wales;
(ii) stakeholders in Romania;
(iii) stakeholders of the parent company in the USA.

(c) Solectron's total assets in 2005 were $5.3 billion and Romania's total GDP for 2005 was $98.7 billion. How is this fact likely to affect Solectron's power when negotiating with the Romanian government?

Select one country in which there is likely to be significant MNC presence and then carry out the following tasks.
1. Using the country's own government databases, website or publications, identify major MNCs operating in the country.
2. Use press reports to check for positive and negative effects of these MNCs on the country.
3. Use the MNC's websites to find out what social corporate responsibilities the businesses have towards the specific country or to host countries in general.

Research task

Meeting the assessment criteria - examiners' guidance

You are required to examine and evaluate the growth and influence of multinational businesses. There should be a general perspective covering MNCs as a whole and the use of specific businesses and situations to show the impacts of MNCs on host countries.

Business example - Shell in Nigeria

Shell's commitment to the community and the environment in Nigeria
Shell Nigeria places great importance on making a difference in the environment in which people live and work, fostering and maintaining relationships with communities, taking care to be a good neighbour and contributing to sustainable development initiatives.

Community development
Health Care – e.g. support project to diminish the spread of HIV/AIDS and increase immunisation.
Education – e.g. scholarships scheme for schools and universities.
Youth Development & Sports – e.g. the Shell Intensive Training Programme and an annual football cup.
Business Development – e.g. the micro-credit scheme providing loans and support to new businesses.

Sustainable development
Local content – supporting the use of local contractors.
Technology – using the latest Shell technology to ensure efficient production.
Environment – a commitment to reduce the negative environmental effects of production.

Shell in the Niger Delta
- Area spread in nine states of the Niger Delta - 70,000 sq kilometers
- Production capacity of 1.3 million bopd, - over 1,000 producing wells
- Over 6,000 Km of pipelines & flowlines
- 87 Flow Stations & 10 Gas Plants
- 2 Terminals at Bonny & Forcados
- More than 10,000 staff
- Huge associated gas gathering network

Negative Issues
- Gas flaring is the burning off of the gas that is released when drilling for oil. This causes air pollution. Shell has agreed to end all gas flaring in Nigeria by 2008.
- The Movement for Survival of Ogoni People (MOSOP) have been campaigning for some years for the right to control and use a fair proportion of Ogoni economic resources for development purposes, and greater autonomy and control over their affairs, (including cultural, religious and environmental matters). Allocation of oil revenues to oil producing countries was raised from 3% to 13% in 2000, but it is the Nigerian government which decides if that will go to the Ogoni people.
- Where land has already been degraded as a result of oil production and oil spills, Shell now has an extensive remediation programme in place to ensure that in due course, all this land will be rehabilitated to what is agreed, by international standards, to be an environmentally acceptable condition.

Source: adapted from the Shell website, www.shell.com.

AOs	Mark Band 1	Mark Band 2	Mark Band 3
(d)	At this level there should be general comments on the development of MNCs in the last 40 or 50 years, giving reasons for this growth and details of the relative size and importance of MNCs now. There should also be details of how Shell has grown, how many countries it now produces in and its size in terms of total and foreign holdings, e.g. 67% of its $174 billion assets were in foreign countries and 61% of its 88,300 employees. The impact that Shell has on it host countries will tend to be general and the more obvious effects of employment and revenue. All stakeholders should be considered. And there should be a comment on the likely differences in impact on developing countries such as Nigeria and developed countries such as Norway, Germany, Canada and the USA where Shell also has exploration and production facilities for oil and gas.	At this level there should be explanations of the advantages and disadvantages of both the growth of multinationals and their size and power. The reasons for growth should be explained in detail and introduce such approaches as the benefits of economies of scale and the natural development from national to international to multinational. In the case of Shell it should also be explained that Shell needs to be in a range of countries because that is where the oil and gas is. There should also, however, be comment on the fact that Shell has many different businesses, from extraction to selling petrol in garages. There should be a clear explanation of the differences in impact on developing and developed countries and why they are different. There should also be a clear recognition of both the positive and negative effects. This is shown for Shell in Nigeria where pollution has been caused and large parts of the revenue taken out of the country but now these issues are being addressed and community and environment supports are helping the local people and businesses. The potential for negative effects is shown by the size of operations in Nigeria, e.g. 6,000 kilometres of pipeline in the Niger Delta. There should be some prioritising of the impacts. The decision to use local contractors is more important for local development than running an annual football competition. There should also be use of wider sources of information, particularly press reports, which in this case may provide alternative views of Shell's activities.	At this level there needs to be a much more critical evaluation of the advantages and disadvantages of MNCs. At all levels there are both good and bad points. For example, when an MNC moves its production to a low labour cost country the benefits to the shareholders, to the employees in the host country, and to the customers who have cheaper products, must be contrasted with the negative effects on the home country employees who have lost their jobs, the knock-on effects on the communities where they live because they are not spending money, and the possible exploitation of employees in the host country. For Shell in Nigeria the benefits of employment and some revenue must be contrasted with any damage done to the environment through gas flaring and oil spillages and what some have seen as the exploitation of the Ogoni People. An evaluation should also be given of whether these negative effects would have been tolerated in the developed countries where Shell produces and reasons should be given for any differences. The relative power of MNCs should be considered, with examples. Shell's total assets in 2005 were $219.5 billion whereas Nigeria's total GDP was only $99 billion, or 45% of Shells assets. Nigeria is a comparatively wealthy country because of the oil sales but Shell still has considerable power in the country. It should also be noted that world opinion can also be a major influence on MNCs and in the case of Shell it is partly this pressure that stopped oil production in the Ogoni territory and a pledge by Shell that it would not start production there again until it had the agreement of all of the Ogoni people.

What is an event?

Everyone is likely to have attended an event of some kind. Some people may have been participants, whilst others may have helped in their organisation. Events can be 'one-off', annual or more frequent occurrences. They may be open to the public or to a specific interest group and have pre-determined opening and closing dates. Businesses often hold events. For example, they hold meetings for shareholders every year, called an Annual General Meeting (AGM). They may also organise trade fairs, product launches, conferences and staff events. Other examples of events are shown in Figure 1. They have been put into different categories. There may be many other categories and it is possible that some events fall into more than one category. For example, the Football World Cup is both a sporting event and a world event.

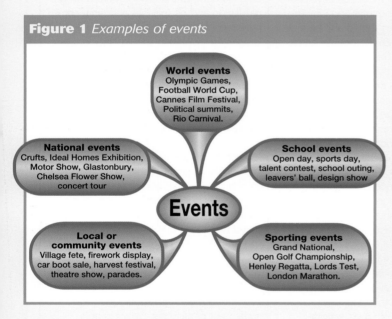

Figure 1 *Examples of events*

All events have some common features

Aims and objectives Every event has a purpose. They attract people with a common interest or cause. A local firework display will attract local people who want to celebrate 5 November - Guy Fawkes' night. Events are organised for a variety of reasons but all of them will have aims to achieve. A fund raising event for charity might aim to raise a certain amount of money. Many events are staged to provide entertainment where the aim will be to maximise the entertainment experience.

Planning and organisation All events have to be planned carefully and require good organisational skills to make them a success. Some events, such as the Olympic Games, are huge and require systematic and long-term planning. In July 2005, London won the right to hold the Olympic Games in 2012. Planning began almost immediately and it would take 7 years for the preparations

to be completed. Even much smaller events, such as organising a sponsored run for charity, require planning. For example, the event coordinator has to publicise the event, attract participants and process applications, plan a route, arrange for refreshments, organise first aid back up, recruit marshals, inform the police to control and divert traffic if necessary.

Resources Events usually cost money. This money is used to acquire resources to stage the event. The amount of money needed will obviously vary but even small events need funding. In the example above, some of the resources may be donated because the event is for charity. However, others will have to be funded. For example, a group of volunteers might provide refreshments free of charge but a paramedic team would probably need paying.

Promotion To ensure that events are successful they need to be publicised. People need to be informed that events are going to take place. They also need information about the details of the event such as dates, times, venues and prices if appropriate. For example, every year plcs send out invitations to shareholders inviting them to the AGM.

Reasons for holding events

All events are staged for a reason. Many of them are also big social occasions and most events fall into one of the following categories.

Celebration Many events are organised to celebrate achievements, milestones, religious or historic events and important occasions. Examples include weddings, staff leaving parties, Christmas, graduation ceremonies, a BAFTA Awards ceremony and St Patrick's Day.

Raise funds A lot of events are organised to help raise money for charities and other good causes. The London Marathon, which is a huge sporting event, is also used to raise money for charities through sponsorship. Clubs, societies and other organisations stage events to raise money for their activities. For example a scout group might hold a jumble sale to help raise money for a summer camp.

Provide recreation or entertainment A large number of events are staged to provide recreation and entertainment for groups of people, communities or even world audiences. Rock concerts, beer festivals, sporting events, song contests, speakers and school outings are all examples. People like to attend or participate in events because they are enjoyable. They are often big social occasions and provide opportunities for groups of people to meet, share a common interest and have a good time. Some very big events are televised and people can enjoy them in their own homes.

Business motives Many events are organised by businesses. The reasons for business events are varied. Some business events, such s an AGM and press conferences, are held out of obligation. Others, such as exhibitions, trade fairs and product launches, are sed to promote their products. Businesses might also organise vents for their staff, such as a weekend away for team-building. There are also businesses that specialise in the staging of events to nake money. Boxing promoters stage boxing contests between he top fighters in the world. Revenue is raised from admission harges, the sale of broadcasting rights and the sale of efreshments and merchandising.

Choice of event

When planning and organising an event, the choice of event is mportant. Making the wrong choice may result in a financial loss nd a great deal of disappointment for both the organisers and the articipants. A number of factors might affect the choice of event.

- The event must be substantial. This means that it must be challenging and require some of the organisational skills that people in business might need to stage an event. For example, organising a raffle to raise £1 for a charity might not be considered substantial. Such an event is too easy to organise and insufficiently demanding. Examples of substantial events might be a foreign trip, exchange trip, graduation, leavers' ball, large fund-raising event for charity, Christmas party for elderly people or skateboard competition for local youths.
- It will be helpful if the chosen event draws on the skills, preferences and experiences of the team staging the event. The event is more likely to be successful if the people organising it are motivated because they are genuinely interested. For example, if the people in the team are not interested in travelling, they might not be motivated if asked to organise a foreign trip.

- It is also important for the event to have the complete support of the team. When making a choice it might be useful to draw up a shortlist of possible events and select a winner democratically. This is a fair way to choose an event and should ensure that all team members are committed.
- Events should not be too ambitious. They must be realistic and affordable. Most events require some initial funding and this must be taken into account when making a choice. For example, staging a mini rock concert might be too ambitious because the owner of the venue, some of the bands and other suppliers might need payments in advance. Raising large amounts of money to fund the initial costs may be too difficult.
- Making the most of local amenities and opportunities should influence the choice of event. For example, if a local business provides free access to its sports facilities to young people, it might be a good idea to organise an event that utilises these facilities.

Feasibility research

Before an event is staged it is important to determine whether or not it is feasible. Events use resources and therefore cost money. If an event is not feasible money is likely to be lost. To determine the feasibility of an event it is necessary to evaluate whether the reasons for holding it are worthwhile and whether there are sufficient organisational resources such as human, financial and

Figure 2 *Evaluating interest in a possible event*

A team of students is organising a day trip to London for a group of school children. The questionnaire over was used to find out what sort of attractions the children would like to see during their visit and whether there was sufficient interest in the event.

ANNUAL SCHOOL OUTING

A day trip to London is being organised for your annual school outing. Please answer the following questions to help make the day more enjoyable.

1. Which of these attractions would you most like to visit? Tick one box only.

London Zoo ☐   The London Eye ☐
Tower of London ☐   The New Wembley Stadium ☐
Natural History Museum ☐   Science Museum ☐
Madame Tussauds ☐   Houses of Parliament ☐
Buckingham Palace ☐
Other ☐ (Please state)...............

2. Which method of transport would you prefer? Tick one box only.

Coach ☐   Plane ☐   Train ☐

3. Where would you like to go for lunch? Tick one box only.

Harry Ramsdens ☐   Burger King ☐
McDonald's ☐   Hyde Park – packed lunch ☐
Other ☐ (Please state)..............

4. Which day would you prefer to go? Tick one box only.

Wednesday ☐   Thursday ☐   Friday ☐   Saturday ☐

5. Are there other places you would prefer to visit for the day? Tick one box only.

I want to go to London ☐

I would prefer to go to:

Brighton ☐   Blackpool ☐
Lake District ☐   Oxford ☐
Alton Towers ☐   Legoland ☐
Other ☐ (Please state)...............

- What are the reasons for holding the event?
- Will there be sufficient interest in the event?
- What physical resources, such as facilities and equipment, are available or accessible to enable the event to be staged?
- What are the costs?
- Is there a reasonable chance that event objectives can be met?
- What needs to be done to overcome potential barriers to holding the event?
- Is there sufficient time for planning?
- Who might help in the organisation?
- Who might check the feasibility?
- Are there any possible legal aspects or considerations?

physical, to stage it. Information must be gathered to help determine feasibility. Data may be gathered to answer the key questions shown in Table 1.

Using primary data Both primary data and secondary data can be used to help address the issues listed in Table 1 when evaluating the feasibility of an event. Primary data is information that does not already exist. It has to be collected using field research. For example, primary data may be gathered to determine whether there is sufficient interest in an event. A team of organisers might use a questionnaire to gauge interest. Figure 2 shows a questionnaire that was used to test the interest in an event.

Once information has been gathered using field research it has to be collated, presented and analysed. Figure 3 shows how the data gathered using the questionnaire in Figure 2 was presented and analysed.

Based on the primary data presented, the team of students organising the outing felt that there was sufficient interest in a day trip to London. They also drew the following conclusions.

- The children would visit the Natural History Museum in the morning and the London Eye in the afternoon.
- The group would travel by train.
- At lunch time the party would be split into two groups. One would go to Hyde Park, the other to Harry Ramsdens.
- The trip would go ahead on Friday.

The data collected in Figure 3 is quantitative data. This means that the information is presented in numbers. It is also possible to gather qualitative data. This is information presented in words – people's comments, for example.

Using secondary data Secondary data is information that already exists. Desk research is used to gather secondary data and it may be qualitative or quantitative. It is important to use a balance of primary and secondary data and to make use of quantitative and qualitative information. When evaluating the feasibility of the school outing described above the following secondary data may have been gathered.

- Admission charges for party tours at the Natural History Museum.
- Price of a 'flight' on the London Eye.
- The group train fares for the return journey.

Figure 3 *Presentation and analysis of primary data to assess event feasibility*

One hundred children were questioned about plans for their annual school outing using the questionnaire in Figure 2. The results are shown in the graphs and charts.

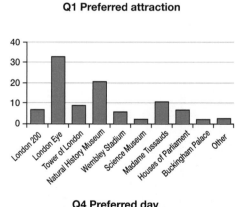

Q1 Preferred attraction

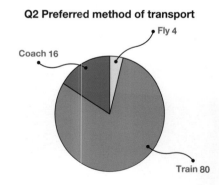

Q2 Preferred method of transport

Fly 4
Coach 16
Train 80

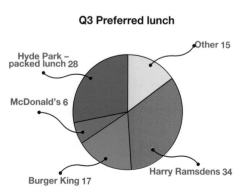

Q3 Preferred lunch

Other 15
Hyde Park – packed lunch 28
McDonald's 6
Burger King 17
Harry Ramsdens 34

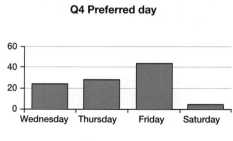

Q4 Preferred day

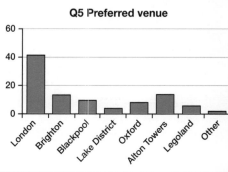

Q5 Preferred venue

- The times of trains.
- Insurance costs.
- Legal aspects, for example, how many adults would have to be present with a party of 100 children and would any adults need any special qualifications?
- Whether any of the children have special needs and how this might affect the nature of the trip.

1. In your teams suggest three events that might be staged for the following groups of people.
   - Students your own age.
   - Children at a local primary school.
   - Elderly people living in a nearby residential care homes.
2. In your teams suggest six events that might be held to raise £500 for a charity. Use the Internet and newspapers to help generate ideas.

Research task

Meeting the assessment criteria - examiners' guidance

You need to prepare a presentation and write a report which provides evidence of research into the feasibility of an event.

Event example – Car boot sale

Students in a sixth form college want to raise £600 to pay for a sound system in their common room. An Event Committee was formed and a number of events were shortlisted. After a vote the students chose to organise a car boot sale. However, the Event Committee was not convinced that a car boot sale would be successful in their small town of 10,000, so they carried out a feasibility study. Three specific tasks were carried out.

- About four hundred local residents were questioned in the high street on a Saturday morning. The results from the study are shown over.
- Two members of the committee estimated the set up costs.
- Two members of the committee met with a Womens' Institute representative from a nearby town. She had experience of organising car boot sales and was happy to talk to the students about the difficulties in their organisation.

Projected staging costs

Hire of a venue - field	£200
Promotion - posters and leaflets	£100
Other costs	£150

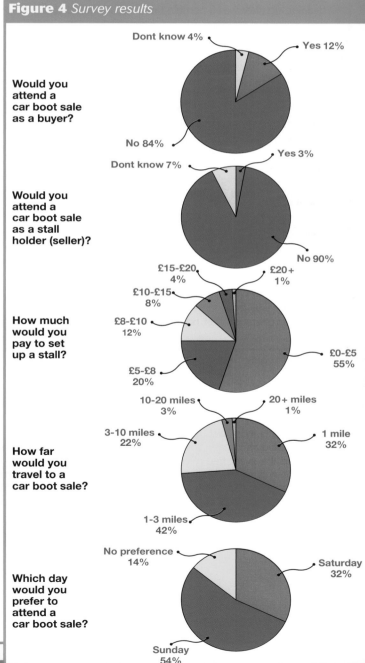

Figure 4 *Survey results*

Would you attend a car boot sale as a buyer?
- Dont know 4%
- Yes 12%
- No 84%

Would you attend a car boot sale as a stall holder (seller)?
- Dont know 7%
- Yes 3%
- No 90%

How much would you pay to set up a stall?
- £15-£20 4%
- £20+ 1%
- £10-£15 8%
- £8-£10 12%
- £0-£5 55%
- £5-£8 20%

How far would you travel to a car boot sale?
- 10-20 miles 3%
- 20+ miles 1%
- 3-10 miles 22%
- 1 mile 32%
- 1-3 miles 42%

Which day would you prefer to attend a car boot sale?
- No preference 14%
- Saturday 32%
- Sunday 54%

Mark Band 1 *You need to provide individual evidence of research into the feasibility of an event. Use both primary and secondary research and also qualitative and quantitative data.*

The feasibility of the car boot sale was evaluated using a range of both primary and secondary data. According to the survey carried out, 12% said they would be probably attend as buyers. This means that about 1,200 (12% of 10,000) might potentially turn up. However, from a feasibility point of view it would be best to assume that the real figure would be less. 3% said they would be interested in setting up a stall. This means that potentially 300 (3% of 10,000) stall holders might turn up. Again though, it would be best to assume that the real figure would be less. The Event Committee also met with someone who had experience of organising a car boot sale in another town. Her comments were helpful. For example she said that promotion was very important, the weather can have a huge influence on attendance and cleaning up after was a horrible task. She also felt that the survey was probably a bit optimistic.

Mark Band 2 *You need to provide individual evidence of research into the feasibility of an event. Use both primary and secondary research and also qualitative and quantitative data from a range of sources and draw reasoned conclusions.*

The survey provided some useful quantitative information. Based on the responses and the size of the town's population, about 300 stall holders could be expected with around 1,200 buyers attending the event. However, the survey could be inaccurate so it would be best to base estimates on lower figures. If £5 per stall was charged (the highest frequency in the results) and, say, 200 stall holders turned up then £1,000 would be raised. Set up costs are £450 so a profit of £550 would be made. This suggests that the event is feasible. It might also be possible to charge the buyers a small entrance fee to raise more revenue and organise some food stalls to make a contribution. Also, if the event was promoted in other nearby towns the number of visitors and stall holders might be higher. However, there were problems to consider. If the weather was bad the event could fail and a loss made. The lady from the WI also said that the cleaning up after was a big operation that no-one liked. It might be worth paying a group of people to do this. Although profit would be lower, at least the job would be done. Based on the information gathered, the Event Committee voted 6 - 3 in favour of going ahead with the car boot sale.

Mark Band 3 *You need to provide evidence of detailed research using a wide range of sources and data. You also need to draw justified conclusions and make appropriate recommendations.*

In the feasibility study both quantitative and qualitative information was gathered. A high street survey of 400 people provided some useful quantitative data. For example, based on the size of the town and the responses in the survey about 1,200 people were expected to attend, with 300 stall holders. The revenue generated from the stall holders could be as high as £1,500 (£5 x 300). However, a more cautious estimate might be to assume 200 stall holders. This would reduce revenue to £1,000 but still generate a profit of £550 when subtracting costs of £450. This would make the event financially feasible. Also, on the positive side a small admission charge could be made for the buyers and the event could be more widely promoted, in nearby towns for example. There were two within 10 miles (which accounted for 96% of all results related to travel distance). Extra revenue could also be raised by selling food and other refreshments. However, on the negative side the weather could badly reduce attendance figures. The lady from the WI warned about this. She provided some very useful qualitative information. For example, she explained that congestion can be a problem and that sufficient parking should be arranged (although some of the Event Committee saw this as an opportunity to generate more revenue). There was also the problem of cleaning up after. The lady from the WI warned that the mess would be unbelievable and that it was probably best to pay someone to clean up. This would obviously raise costs. The Event Committee decided to go ahead with the car boot sale after a 6-3 vote in favour. The following recommendations were also made.
- A price of £6 per pitch would be charged to stall holders.
- A 20p admission charge would be made.
- £100 would be paid to a group of students to clean up.

Portfolio practice • Christmas party for disabled children

Students in Ipswich planning to organise a Christmas party for disabled children in their local area. They have permission to hold the event free of charge in the college hall. However, money is needed to pay for food and drink, a Christmas present for each of the children, a DJ and a surprise visit from a local high profile footballer. The following information needs to be gathered.
- How many and which children will be invited.
- Details of food, drink, and activities that the children might enjoy.

- An estimated cost for the whole event.

(a) Using the case as an example, explain the difference between quantitative and qualitative data.
(b) Design a questionnaire to collect information about 'Details of food, drink, and activities that the children might enjoy'.
(c) Analyse the factors that might be taken into account when evaluating the feasibility of the event.

Aims

The reasons for holding events were discussed in section 51. Most events are staged to:
- celebrate achievements, milestones, religious or historic events and important occasions;
- raise funds for charities, clubs, societies and other organisations;
- provide recreation or entertainment. They are often big social occasions and provide opportunities for groups of people to meet, share a common interest and have a good time.
- satisfy a wide range of business needs such as promoting products, reporting to the press or shareholders or meet other stakeholder needs.

All events will have an aim. An aim is what the event hopes to achieve – its purpose. Different events will have different aims. For example, events which are staged as celebrations aim to provide pleasure for the people attending. Fund raising events aim to raise as much money as possible. The aim of most sporting events is to provide spectators with an enjoyable sporting spectacle. The aims of business events will vary. For example, the aim of a team-building event might be to improve staff morale, whereas the aim of a product launch may be to raise awareness of a new product.

Objectives

The objectives of an event are its goals – outcomes or targets which help to achieve its aims. Objectives should be the practical outcomes from the staging of an event. Choosing suitable objectives will help event organisers achieve their aims. Some examples are given below.
- The aim of an event might be to raise money for a charity. An objective to achieve this aim could be to sell 450 tickets for the event.
- The aim of a school reunion might be to organise an enjoyable social evening where old school friends can meet and catch up with what's being happening in their lives. An objective which might help to achieve this aim is to encourage 80% of a particular year group to attend the event.
- The aim of staging a concert might be to provide an exciting and accessible music evening for local teenagers. An objective to help achieve this aim might be to attract a popular and well known bands in the line-up.
- In business, the aim of a staff party might be to reward staff for their hard work and loyalty throughout the year. An objective to help achieve this aim might be for the organisers to persuade the owners to provide £20,000 to fund some spectacular food, drink and entertainment.

Figure 1 shows an example of the aims and objectives of a well known event.

The importance of aims and objectives

When teams are organising an event it is important to have clear aims and objectives. This will help to make the event a success.

Figure 1 *The Edinburgh International Festival*

The Edinburgh International Festival takes place over a three-week period in late summer each year. The Festival also has a year-round programme of work, aimed at all ages from primary school pupils to adults. Edinburgh's festivals are now of substantial economic benefit to Edinburgh and to Scotland as a whole. In 2004/05 the summer festivals alone generated around £130 million of expenditure in Edinburgh and created nearly 2,900 jobs across Scotland. 60% of the audience in 2004 came from Scotland, 26% from the rest of UK and 14% overseas. The aims and objectives of the festival are shown below. The mission is the overall aim of the event and the objectives, which are used to help achieve the aim, follow under the 'By' heading.

Mission:

To be the most exciting, innovative and accessible Festival of the performing arts in the world and thus promote the cultural, educational and economic well-being of the people of Edinburgh and Scotland.

By:

Presenting arts of the highest possible international standard to the widest possible audience.
Reflecting international culture in presentation to Scottish audiences and reflecting Scottish culture in presentation to international audiences.
Presenting events which cannot easily be achieved by any other UK arts organisation through innovative programming and a commitment to new work.
Actively ensuring equal opportunities for all sections of the Scottish and wider public to experience and enjoy the Festival.
Encouraging public participation in the arts throughout the year by collaborating with other arts and festival organisations.

Source: adapted from the Edinburgh International Festival website.

Figure 2 *How can aims and objectives help in organising an event?*

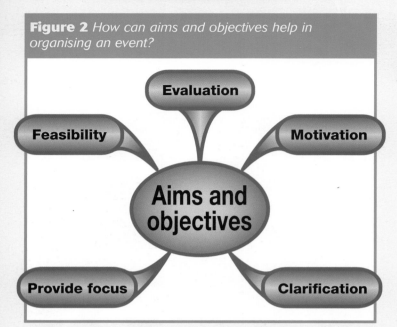

Clear aims and objectives will help in a number of ways. These are summarised in Figure 2.

Feasibility An event should only be staged if the aims and objectives can be met. For example, there is no point trying to stage a firework display for a village if there is not a safe and suitable venue. Identifying clear aims and objectives, and deciding whether they can be met, is an important part of assessing the feasibility of an event.

Focus One of the main advantages of having a clear aim and a set of established objectives is that the people involved in organising the event will know what they are striving for. If they understand what they are trying to achieve they may be able to make a better contribution. If everyone is focused on the same outcome there will be less confusion and a more concentrated effort. In a team it is important that everyone pulls in the same direction focusing on the same aims and objectives.

Clarification People like to know what they are doing and what is expected of them. Clear aims and objectives will help people understand their roles and clarify what is expected of them. For example, if one of the objectives when organising an event is to minimise costs, then everyone must take that into account when carrying out their tasks.

Motivation If teams or individuals are set objectives this can help to motivate them. This is because, when an objective is met, there is a sense of achievement. This will make people feel good and they can go on in a positive frame of mind and try to meet the next objective. Objectives are often a set of targets. Provided these targets are achievable they will serve to motivate people involved in event organisation. For example, if team members are set targets for the number of tickets each must sell for an event, they may enjoy a sense of achievement once their individual allocation has been sold out.

Evaluation Unless aims and objectives have been set it is very difficult to evaluate the success of an event. Events will be considered successful if they achieve their aims. For example, if a disco is organised to provide a 'fun night out' for local youths, the event will have failed if nearly everyone goes home after an hour because they are bored. The aim will not have been met.

SMART objectives

When setting objectives for events it might be helpful to set objectives which are SMART. This means that objectives should be Specific, Measurable, Achievable, Realistic and Timed.

Specific Objectives are easier to achieve if people understand them. They should be stated in a language that people are familiar with and avoid the use of jargon. Selling 30 tickets in five days for an event is an example of a specific objective.

Measurable If objectives are not measurable it is difficult to evaluate performance. People also need to know exactly when an objective has been achieved. Selling 30 tickets in five days for an event is also an example of an objective that is measurable.

Achievable This means that objectives should not be over-ambitious and demand things from people which are impossible achieve. Unattainable targets will serve to demotivate people. However, people need to be challenged so objectives must not b too easy either.

Relevant This means that people's roles in the planning and staging of an event must have an influence on the objectives. For example, there is little point in asking traffic marshals at a concer to help increase sales of refreshments as, it is not something they can influence whilst directing traffic.

Timed Objectives must have a time allocation and a deadline. Selling 30 tickets for an event in five days is an example of an objective with a time constraint.

The SMART acronym is widely used when setting objectives. However, some of the letters may have other meanings. For example, 'A' might mean agreed where the objectives set must b agreed by all those people who are asked to achieve them.

SMART objectives and client outcomes

The clients at an event are usually the people for whom the even is being organised. At a wedding party it will be the guests, at a sporting event it will be the spectators and at a village fete it will be the visitors. The aim of such events is generally to make sure that everyone enjoys themselves and has a good time. A number of objectives might be set to try and achieve this aim. An example is shown in Figure 3.

SMART objectives and organisational outcomes

In some cases clients are not people but organisations. For example, a group of students might take charge of running an event on behalf of their school or college, such as a musical evening for children and parents. Alternatively, a group of student might organise a promotional event for a local business. For example, a local clothes store might engage students to stage a promotional event for a new season's clothes. In these cases the aims and objectives of an event are likely to be established by the organisation. They will inevitably reflect the culture and the highe objectives of the organisation. An example is given in Figure 4.

Figure 3 *SMART objectives for a rounders tournament*

A group of students is organising a 'round-robin' rounders tournament for four primary schools in the local area. The aim of the event is to provide the children with an enjoyable sporting experience. Some examples of the SMART objectives set by the students are listed below.

- A total of £250 is raised from sponsors, donations and other sources to fund the event adequately.
- Ensure that all fixtures start promptly and are refereed fairly.
- Ensure that all results and league positions are displayed within 10 minutes of each fixture ending.
- Suitable prizes are acquired for the winners.
- A 'local hero' should be booked to make a short speech and present the winners with their prizes.

Figure 4 *SMART objectives for a promotional event*

A group of students have been employed by a local authority to stage a promotional evening for a local youth club. The aim is to raise awareness of the club and its activities in the area. The local authority is committed to increasing the provision of activities for youths in the local area. In particular it wants youths to participate more in sporting activities. The authority set the following SMART objectives for the group.

- Attract at least 150 youths to the event.
- Provide a range of no less than 15 different activities which youths can try out.
- Invite a high profile local person (e.g. sportsperson) to give a motivational speech.
- Persuade at least 50 youths to register with the club.

SMART objectives and quality standards

A successful event will require certain quality standards to be met. For example, a wedding is a very special event and the bride, groom and their guests will expect every aspect of the day to be 'perfect'. This means that the event organisers have to ensure that high quality standards are met. SMART objectives may be set to deliver high quality standards, although in some cases quality objectives may be difficult to quantify. For example, how can the quality of the food served at a wedding be measured accurately? At a wedding, the following examples will be subject to quality standards and might be met by setting SMART objectives.

- Decoration of the venue.
- The matrimonial service.
- The wedding cake.
- Standard of service by catering staff.

1. Visit the websites of some national, international or corporate events such as the Commonwealth Games, Eurovision Song Contest, Motor Show, Rugby World Cup, Crufts, Remembrance Day or AGMs. There are many others to choose from. You may have some favourites of your own which you can use.
2. Choose two events and identify the aims and objectives of each one.
3. Assess to what extent they are SMART objectives.

Research task

Portfolio practice ‣ Restaurant re-launch

A group of students at a sixth form college have been asked to assess the feasibility of a restaurant re-launch. One of the students' parents owns an Italian restaurant and wants them to organise a special promotional evening. It is intended to invite local dignitaries and business people to spend an evening at the restaurant and enjoy a free meal (drink not included). The aim of the event is to promote the restaurant after an extensive refurbishment and menu overhaul. The owner wants some media attention and can offer 60 free places for the evening. It is also intended to provide some entertainment. A budget of £100 has been provided for this.

(a) **Using this case as an example, explain the difference between aims and objectives.**
(b) **Identify FIVE possible SMART objectives for the event which can be used to assess the feasibility of the restaurant re-launch.**
(c) **Explain how the use of SMART objectives might help when organising an event.**

Meeting the assessment criteria - examiners' guidance

You need to prepare a presentation and write a report which provides evidence of research into the feasibility of an event. This section focuses on the aims and objectives of the event.

Event example – Sponsored Fun Run

Students at a college in Staffordshire organised a sponsored Fun Run to raise money to help a disaster fund after they had seen reports on the television. After appointing an Event Committee and carrying out a feasibility study, the students decided that their aim would be to raise £1,000 for the disaster fund. A 5K run was planned and the event would take place on a Sunday. Only students at the college would be eligible to run, but as many people as possible from the local community would be encouraged to attend the event as spectators and supporters. In an effort to achieve the aim a number of SMART objectives were set.

- Attract at least 50 runners who would each get an average of £20 sponsor money. Their applications must be processed two weeks before the event.
- Obtain £200 sponsorship from local businesses to fund the set up costs two months before the event.
- Promote the event in the local community using leaflets. Aim to distribute 5,000 leaflets to be completed one week before the event.
- Promote the college in the local community by using the college logo on all documentation (e.g. on sponsor forms) and promotional materials.
- Gain media interest from at least one local newspaper or radio station.
- Organise at least 20 stalls near the finishing post to help generate more income and create interest for spectators. Obtain a list of stall holders one month before the event.
- Collect 95% of all sponsorship money within two weeks of the event finishing.

Mark Band 1 *You need to provide individual evidence of research into the feasibility of an event, with stated aims and objectives.*

For an event to be feasible the aims and objectives must be achieved. A feasibility study was carried out to see whether it was feasible to organise a Fun Run to raise £1,000 for a disaster fund. Students had seen the distressing reports on the TV and felt they wanted to do something. After a simple survey the Event Committee was confident the event would be a success. A number of SMART objectives were set to help achieve the overall aim. One of the first objectives was to persuade local businesses to provide a total of £200 in sponsorship money. This was needed to cover setting up costs such as application forms and the printing of posters and leaflets. Another important objective was to attract 50 runners. This number would be needed to raise £1,000, if they each contribute £20 in sponsorship money. Most of the objectives set were SMART. This means they were specific,

measurable, achievable, relevant and timed.

Mark Band 2 *You need to provide individual evidence of research into the feasibility of an event. Use both primary and secondary research and also qualitative and quantitative data from a range of sources and draw reasoned conclusions.*

One of the ways in which the feasibility of an event can be determined is to assess whether or not the aims and objectives can be achieved. Clearly, if they are not achievable then the event is not feasible. In this case a survey was carried out to see whether the college would support a Fun Run to raise money for a disaster fund. 87% said they would, either as participants, helpers, spectators or sponsors. Such a positive response suggested that the event would be feasible. The feasibility became clearer when local businesses were asked for sponsorship. The objective was to get £200 to cover the setting up costs two months before the event. In fact £340 was raised more than 10 weeks before the event. The objectives set by the Event committee helped to achieve the overall aim of the event. For example, 50 runners had to be attracted, each contributing £20 in sponsorship money. This target helped to keep the team focused and served as a motivational force. One of the objectives which proved difficult was delivering 5,000 leaflets. This was not completed until two nights before the event took place. However, SMART objectives generally were a great help.

Mark Band 3 *You need to provide evidence of detailed research using a wide range of sources and data. You also need to draw justified conclusions and make appropriate recommendations.*

When assessing the feasibility of the Fun Run two popular students offered to give a presentation in assembly to promote the idea of raising money for the disaster fund. Most students had seen the TV reports covering the disaster and wanted to help. After a survey which followed the assembly, it was fairly obvious that the event would be feasible. 87% said they would support the Fun Run, either as participants, helpers, spectators or sponsors. To help achieve the overall aim a number of SMART objectives were set. These are objectives which are specific, measurable, achievable, relevant and timed. For example, a target of 50 runners in the race was set. It was also established that each one should raise £20 in sponsorship money. This would generate the £1,000 needed to achieve the aim. This target was met and the applications forms were processed well within the deadline. SMART objectives like this helped the team to focus. Another example was the delivering of 5,000 leaflets. Although the deadline was missed, setting the target made sure that a very important job was done to completion. Without the target people may have given up. Some of the objectives were organisational. For example, one was to promote the college by using the logo. When setting objectives it is often important to take into account the higher objectives of the organisation. The setting of SMART objectives is to be recommended when assessing the feasibility of an event and seeing through its organisation.

Financial constraints and risk assessment

Financial constraints and feasibility

When assessing the feasibility of an event inevitably the question of money will arise. Most events require funding. Some world events, such as the Olympic Games, cost billions of pounds to stage. Indeed, such a huge event usually requires government backing. But even with more modest events funding is still critical. Unless funding can be obtained an event will not be feasible. One of the biggest obstacles to staging an event is raising adequate funds. An example is outlined in Figure 1.

Figure 1 Financial constraints and feasibility

A group of students were asked to organise a swimming gala on behalf of their school. The aim was to find out who the best swimmers were in each year group and provide an afternoon of entertainment for spectators. Unfortunately the event was not feasible because of financial constraints. The only swimming pool big enough in the area to stage the event was owned by a private health and fitness club. They were happy to offer their facilities as a venue but wanted £300 in advance to secure the booking. The problem was that the pool would have to be shut to members and customers during the afternoon of the gala and the club would have to be financially compensated. It was also felt that opportunities to raise money during the afternoon of the event would be limited. The event was not feasible.

Even if an event is going to generate revenue, from the sale of tickets, for example, funding may still be a problem. This is because money is usually needed in the planning and preparation stages of the event. Money may be needed to book a venue, pay for promotional materials or carry out research into feasibility, for example. Unless, money can be raised in advance of the event to cover such costs then the event will not be feasible.

Budgets

When assessing the feasibility of an event a budget may be prepared. A budget is a financial plan which is agreed in advance. Budgets are helpful when organising events because they:
- force people to plan ahead and improve coordination;
- help to control spending and draw attention to waste and inefficiency;
- enable the event coordinator to delegate responsibility because others are expected to meet budget targets;
- may act as a review for an event, allowing time for corrective action.

However, budgets may also act as constraints in the organisation of an event. This is because a budget holder may claim that insufficient funds have been allocated for a particular activity. For example, the budget holder responsible for promoting an event may claim that the amount of money allocated for promotion is inadequate. This might result in poor promotion. In some circumstances, some budget holders might claim that a particular activity is not feasible with the allocation of funds. This might mean that the event itself is not feasible. A variety of different budgets might be used when organising an event, depending on needs and circumstances. For example, when organising a charity dinner the following budgets might be used.
- Food Budget.
- Drinks Budget.
- Entertainment Budget.
- Prizes Budget.
- Overheads Budget.

An example of a budget is shown in Figure 2.

Fixed and variable costs

The costs of an event fall into two categories. Those costs, which are not linked to the number of people who attend the event, are said to be fixed. The money paid to a band to provide live music at a party is an example. It does not matter how many people attend, the amount paid to the band will be the same. Any cost

Figure 2 Marketing budget for a concert

| | \multicolumn{12}{c}{Weeks} | £ |
	1	2	3	4	5	6	7	8	9	10	11	12	Total
Newspaper adverts						50		50	50	50	50	100	350
Radio advert										200		200	400
Posters	50						50						100
Leaflets	60				60					60			180
Other promotional costs	10		10	15	20			45				65	165
Total	120	0	10	15	80	50	50	95	50	310	50	365	1,195

A group organising a concert in Hereford allocated £1,200 for marketing and promotional expenses. A marketing budget, drawn up for the 12 week planning and preparation period is shown in the table. The budget shows that total planned spending amounts to £1,195, just £5 below the total allocated. This shows the value of using budgets to control spending.

which rises with the number of people who attend the event is a variable cost, for example, the cost of the food and drink needed at a party. The more people that attend the more food and drink will be needed. Categorising costs in this way can be helpful when organising events. It is possible to calculate how many people need to be attracted to an event to make it feasible. An example is shown in Figure 3.

Sources of funding

Money will be needed to plan and stage events before the event takes place. When the event is staged more money can be generated. Table 1 shows some examples.

Figure 3 *Assessing financial feasibility*

A group of students organising a social evening for people in a small town felt they could charge £3 per head. £200 was needed to pay for speakers, the venue and other fixed costs. Variable costs were expected to be £1 per head. This was to pay for refreshments and a programme. The number of tickets that needed to be sold for the event to be feasible is:

$$\frac{\text{Fixed cost}}{\text{Price} - \text{variable cost}} = \frac{£200}{£3 - £1} = \frac{£200}{£2} = 100$$

Thus, if 100 tickets are sold the event is feasible. This means that the total costs of the event will be covered exactly by the revenue from ticket sales. The event will break-even, both total cost (£200 + [£1 × 100]) and total revenue (£3 × 100) are £300.

It is also possible to calculate how much to charge for an event to make it feasible (i.e. for it to break-even). This can be done using the formula below, providing the number of people who are going to attend the event (Q) is known.

$$\text{Break-even price} = \frac{\text{Total cost}}{Q}$$

If an event is being organised to generate a certain amount of profit, it is possible to calculate how much should be charged for the event. The formula is given below.

$$\text{Price} = \frac{\text{Profit target} + \text{total cost}}{Q}$$

Finally, if the fixed costs of an event are very high relative to the variable costs, this can act as a constraint. This is because a lot more people have to be attracted to make the event feasible. Alternatively, the price charged for the event would be too high to attract clients.

Table 1 *Possible finance before and during an event*

Before
- Loans from parents.
- Bank loans.
- Loans from school or college.
- The sale of advertising, such as adverts in a programme.
- Sponsorship from local businesses, for example.
- Donations. Some local people, businesses and other organisations may be happy to donate money depending on the purpose of an event.
- Advanced ticket sales.
- Fundraising activities such as a raffle, bring-and-buy sale or jumble sale.

During
- Admission charges.
- Sales of refreshments.
- Programme sales.
- Merchandising sales.
- More fundraising activities such as stalls, raffles and auctions.

In some cases it is possible that money will be generated in the future, even though an event has finished. For example, some charity events involve giving out a telephone number which people can ring to make credit card donations. Finally, raising sufficient funds can act as a constraint. If a lot of money is needed to set up an event, it may be impossible to raise the amount needed. If this is the case then the event is not feasible.

Risk assessment

Arranging and running an event is defined as a 'work activity' and is therefore subject to the **Health and Safety at Work Act 1974** and the **Management of Health and Safety at Work Regulations**. Consequently, when organising an event it is necessary to carry out a risk assessment. This involves identifying and evaluating the possible risks to people who will be involved in the event and others that attend. The risks to people at an event will vary according to the nature of the event. For example, at a firework display there is a risk to people from exploding fireworks. Alternatively, at a concert there is the risk of people being crushed if they are too tightly packed by the stage. On the other hand some risks are common to a wide range of events such as minor illnesses, accidents and injuries. If the risks are too high the event is not likely to be feasible. One approach that might be used when assessing the risks to people at an event is summarised in Figure 4.

Identify hazards The first step is to identify the hazards associated with the activities. A systematic assessment must be made of the event, site, management, structures and activities. It will be necessary to produce a Risk Assessment document, which

Figure 4 *Step by step approach to risk assessment*

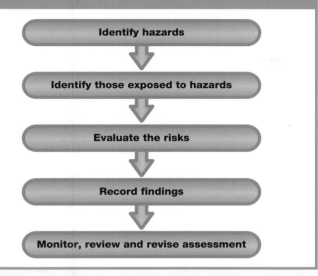

details the recognised risks and the methods to be employed to eliminate or minimise them. Examples of potential hazards that might exist for a concert are shown in Figure 5.

Identify those exposed to hazards The second step is to identify those who are likely to be exposed to the hazards identified. This should include visitors, performers, spectators, contractors, staff and any other person who is likely to be affected by the event. Particular attention should be paid to vulnerable groups, such as those with special needs, the elderly, young or expectant mothers, young staff, trainee staff and children.

Evaluate the risks Evaluating the risks involves making a judgement about the likelihood of hazards causing harm to people. Every precaution must be taken to eliminate risks or reduce them to a tolerable level. Even when precautions have been put in place a level of risk may remain. It is important to classify the risk as low, medium or high. If the risk is high it may be necessary to:
- try a less risky option;

- prevent access or reduce exposure to the hazard;
- issue protective clothing or equipment;
- provide welfare and first aid facilities.

If work needs to be done to eliminate or reduce a hazard an action plan may be drawn up to ensure that this work is carried out. Finally, if the risks are still considered intolerable then the event may not be feasible.

Record findings An important part of risk assessment is recording the process in writing. Documents must be produced that show that hazards have been identified and evaluated. There must also be records of the action taken to eliminate or minimise risks. The records must also be shown to appropriate people. According to the leaflet on risk assessment by the Health and Safety Executive, the following needs to be documented.
- A proper check was made.
- People were asked who might be affected.
- Obvious hazards were dealt with taking into account the number of people that could be involved.
- Reasonable precautions were taken and the remaining risk was low.

Some examples of the documents that might be used in risk assessment are described in the next unit. Such documents are

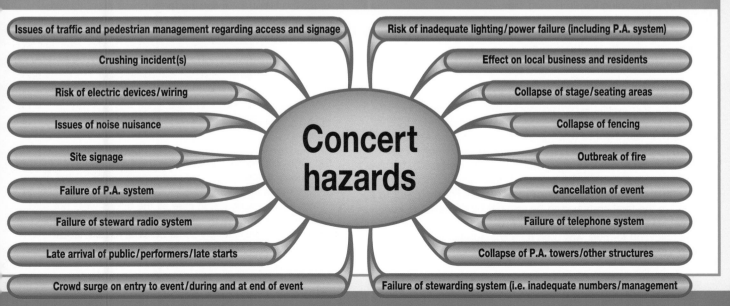

1. Find some examples of risk assessment documents. They may be available from:
   - the Internet;
   - your school;
   - local authorities;
   - local sports clubs;
   - local businesses.
2. Write a brief report outlining the main issues mentioned in the assessments.

Research task

Figure 5 *Potential hazards at a substantial event such as a concert*

- Issues of traffic and pedestrian management regarding access and signage
- Crushing incident(s)
- Risk of electric devices/wiring
- Issues of noise nuisance
- Site signage
- Failure of P.A. system
- Failure of steward radio system
- Late arrival of public/performers/late starts
- Crowd surge on entry to event/during and at end of event

Concert hazards

- Risk of inadequate lighting/power failure (including P.A. system)
- Effect on local business and residents
- Collapse of stage/seating areas
- Collapse of fencing
- Outbreak of fire
- Cancellation of event
- Failure of telephone system
- Collapse of P.A. towers/other structures
- Failure of stewarding system (i.e. inadequate numbers/management

likely to be used to gather primary data.

Monitor, review and revise assessment The final stage in the risk assessment process is to review and revise the assessment. The documents produced in the previous stage may form the basis of the review. It is important to keep the documents because they may:

- be helpful if a Health and Safety inspector asks what precautions have been taken;

- be helpful if there is any action for civil liability;
- serve as a reminder to keep an eye on particular hazards in the future;
- help to show that legal requirements have been met.

During the review stage it is important to note any problems that arose and make adjustments to the risk assessment for the next time an event is held.

Meeting the assessment criteria - examiners' guidance

You need to prepare a presentation and write a report which provides evidence of research into the feasibility of an event. This section focuses on financial constraints and risk assessment.

Event example – Cooking Demonstration

A group of sixth form students have been asked to organise a cooking demonstration by a well known local chef. The group was given permission to use the school hall free of charge to stage the event. The capacity of the hall is fixed at 200. To assess the feasibility of the event attention was paid to the financial constraints and the possible risks involved. The group identified the costs of staging the event and realised that most of them were fixed. They are summarised below. The only significant variable cost would be the cost of programmes containing an introduction and details about dishes cooked during the evening and recipes - £1 per person.

Payment to celebrity chef	£500
Marketing	£150
Hire of cooking equipment	£150
Food ingredients	£120
Other fixed costs	£80

The group held a meeting to discuss the possible hazards of the event. The information generated at the meeting would help in the risk assessment. The following are examples of hazards that were identified at the meeting.

- Outbreak of fire from the gas cookers.
- Food poisoning if visitors tried samples.
- Floor becoming slippery from condensation from cookers.
- Celebrity chef failing to turn up.
- People at the back of the audience struggling to see the demonstration.

Mark Band 1 *You need to provide individual evidence of research into the feasibility of an event. Use both primary and secondary research and also qualitative and quantitative data.*

Initially, it was thought that the event would not be feasible. The fixed costs were very high. The payment to the celebrity chef alone would be £500. But without a celebrity chef it was felt that local people would not be interested. Total fixed costs were £1,000 and variable costs were £1 per person. For the event to be feasible the total costs had to be covered by the revenue from ticket sales. To calculate the ticket price needed to achieve this, the following formula was used (Q = the number of people expected to attend the event).

$$\text{Break-even price} = \frac{\text{Total costs}}{Q} \qquad \frac{£1,000 + (200 \times £1)}{200} \qquad \frac{£1,200}{200}$$

It was thought that people would pay £6 to see a celebrity chef so the event was considered feasible. During a meeting the topic of risk assessment came up. A number of important hazards were identified. These included the possibility of fire from the gas cookers, food poisoning if visitors tried samples, the floor becoming slippery from condensation caused by the cookers and the effects of the chef failing to turn up. It was agreed to carry out a proper risk assessment.

Mark Band 2 *You need to provide individual evidence of research into the feasibility of an event. Use both primary and secondary research and also qualitative and quantitative data from a range of sources and draw reasoned conclusion.*

Before going ahead with the planning of the event the committee decided to assess its feasibility. Some quantitative data was gathered to anaylse the costs of the event. A major concern was the cost structure. Most of the costs would be fixed. This means that if people did not attend in sufficient numbers a large loss could be made. This can act as a financial constraint on the event. The total fixed costs were estimated to be £1,000. This included a £500 payment for the celebrity chef. The variable costs were low and expected to be £1 per person. To calculate the break-even price for the event the following formula was used. (Q = the number of people expected to attend the event).

$$\text{Break-even price} = \frac{\text{Total costs}}{Q} \qquad \frac{£1,000 + (200 \times £1)}{200} \qquad \frac{£1,200}{200} =$$

The event committee decided that the event was feasible. They thought that people would pay £6 to see a celebrity chef 'live' and there might also be opportunities to raise more revenue on the night of the event, just in case all the tickets were not sold.

Another issue when determining feasibility is risk assessment. A meeting was held to identify some possible hazards at the event. These included the possibility of fire from the gas cookers, food poisoning if visitors tried samples, the floor becoming slippery from condensation caused by the cookers and the effects of the chef failing to turn up. It was felt that these risks would not jeopardise the feasibility of the event but it was agreed that a proper risk assessment should be undertaken.

Mark Band 3 *You need to provide evidence of detailed research using a wide range of sources and data. You also need to draw justified conclusions and make appropriate recommendations.*

To assess the feasibility of the event a range of data was gathered. Some primary data was collected to analyse the costs of the event. Events must be financially feasible so this was an important activity. It was found that most of the costs would be fixed. This is unfortunate because unless a lot of tickets could be sold at a reasonable price, the event might make a loss. The total fixed costs, those costs not related to the size of the audience, were £1,000. Variable costs, those which increase with the size of the audience, were just £1. The price needed to cover all the costs, assuming that all tickets were sold was calculated using the formula below. (Q = the number of people expected to attend the event).

organised to generate more revenue in case the event was not a sell out.

Some attention was also paid to risk assessment. Such an event may have some unique hazards to consider. For example, a cooking demonstration using gas cookers could be a fire hazard. There would also be condensation from the cooking which could make the floors very slippery. There is also the chance that, if people sampled the food, they might get food poisoning. Even though these hazards were serious, it would be easy to take precautions to minimise the risk. However, it was clear that a proper risk assessment would have to be carried out. The following recommendations were made.

$$\text{Break-even price} = \frac{\text{Total costs}}{Q} \quad \frac{£1,000 + (200 \times £1)}{200} \quad \frac{£1,200}{200} = £6$$

It was decided that the event would be feasible. However, it was also suggested that some fundraising activities should be

- Charge £6 per visitor.
- Organise some additional fundraising activities during the night.
- Attract some advertising to be placed in the programme.
- Undertake a proper risk assessment which should be documented.

Portfolio practice · **Camping expedition**

An Event Committee was formed to organise a weekend away for a group of students. Some students expressed an interest in trying a new outdoor activity. A number of suggestions were raised, such as pot holing, white-water rafting and hang gliding. However, it was agreed that the most practical event would be a camping expedition in the Lake District. The Event Committee gathered a range of information and focused on costs and hazards in their feasibility study. The fixed costs such as hiring a mini bus and driver, petrol, maps and some equipment hire was £2,500 for the weekend. Variable costs were also high and included food, insurance, some equipment hire and other variable costs. These came to £60 per head. The mini bus had a capacity of 20 seats. It was felt that to keep the cost down for students some fundraising activities could be organised.

(a) (i) Calculate the amount each student would have to pay to cover the costs of the expedition.
(ii) Explain how fixed costs might act as a constraint when organising an event.
(b) Analyse the sources of finance that the students might use to help fund their expedition.

(c) Identify THREE possible hazards that students might be exposed to during their expedition and suggest what could be done to minimise them so that they are low.

The importance of planning

Once an event is considered feasible, its success will depend on the quality of planning. Planning an event will make it better and result in positive feedback from clients and spectators.

- Planning forces organisers to look ahead. It helps to anticipate problems for example.
- Planning will reduce the number of mistakes made. For example, important tasks are less likely to be overlooked.
- When organising an event, the day of the event is a critical deadline. The date of the event cannot be changed at the last minute. Planning will help to ensure that all preparation is completed by the deadline. Part of the planning process is to work out how long it will take to complete all the preparation tasks and make sure they are completed on time.
- Less time will be wasted with proper planning. People will know what to do and will not waste time wondering what is expected of them.

The planning process

A systematic approach to planning should help the preparation of an event run more smoothly. Figure 1 shows a very simple approach to planning.

There are certain common aspects of planning for most events.

- It is important that the aims and objectives of the event are clear. If the aim is clear and the objectives SMART, people will be able to focus more easily and will know what is expected of them.
- Planning and preparing for an event can be broken down into a

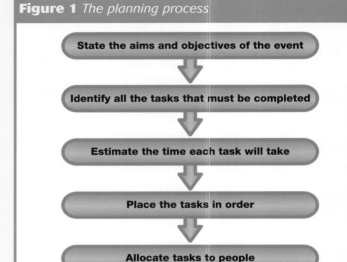

Figure 1 *The planning process*

- State the aims and objectives of the event
- Identify all the tasks that must be completed
- Estimate the time each task will take
- Place the tasks in order
- Allocate tasks to people
- Monitor progress and review plan

number of specific tasks. They should be identified and listed. The number of tasks will vary according to the size and complexity of the event – it might be hundreds or even thousands of tasks.

- It is possible to calculate how long it will take to complete the planning and preparation for an event if the completion time

Figure 2 *A simple risk assessment document*

The document below is an extract from a risk assessment carried out by Cheryl Timms, a person helping to plan a village fete. Only the first three hazards are recorded here. This document is not the complete risk assessment.

Event: Hillford Fete **Event date:** 15.12.05 **Assessment by:** Cheryl Timms **Date:** 21.10.05

Hazard/task	Who's at risk?	Risk Level	Control measures	Comments
Exposed cables running across walkways.	All	Medium	All cables to be covered with heavy duty rubber mats.	Mats can be borrowed from a local primary school.
Fire around the hot dog tent.	All	High	Provide small fire extinguisher for tent area and train stall holder to use it.	Fire extinguisher can be borrowed from local school. Need to check it's in working order.
Congestion in car park.	People arriving by car	Low	Provide clear signage, well defined parking spaces and stewards.	Might be a good idea to get further information from police.

for each individual task is known. Planning aids such as critical path analysis can be used to do this.

- Tasks will have to be completed in a particular order. For example, a marquee will have to be erected before it can be decorated for a party. Some tasks can be completed at the same time which will speed up the preparation time. This is significant and can be explored when looking at critical path analysis in section 55.
- Every task should be assigned to a particular person in the group. This will clarify what is expected of people and provides a system of accountability.
- It is likely that plans will have to be modified and adjusted when preparation gets underway. This is not a sign of weakness but a natural part of the monitoring and reviewing process in planning.

Undertaking risk assessment

One of the most important tasks in the planning process is to undertake a thorough risk assessment. Risk assessment must be documented and an example of a simple risk assessment document is shown in Figure 2.

Physical resources

Most events require a variety of physical resources. These will vary depending on the type of event organised. Some of the resources may be specialised, which means that it might be difficult to find a supplier. It is likely that a lot of resources will be hired or rented. This is because events are often 'one-off' or annual activities and it would not be cost effective purchasing resources. For example, it would cost far too much to buy a marquee for a wedding party. It would be much cheaper to hire one for the day.

Location or venue One of the most important resources required for an event is the venue or location. The type of venue needed will depend on the nature of the event. For example:

- a theatrical production or concert will need a hall with a stage (although it might be possible to construct a stage in a hall);
- an athletics meeting will need a running track or sports field which can be marked out;
- a swimming gala will need a swimming pool;
- a golf tournament will need a golf course.

A careful choice of location is important. A number of factors have to be taken into account when choosing a suitable venue. Some important examples are given below.

- Is it big enough?
- Is there sufficient parking?
- Are the utilities (gas, water and electricity) fully connected?
- Are there enough exits?
- Does the place have a fire certificate?
- Is the location well served by public transport for access?
- Will local residents be affected?
- Will furniture and other equipment be available for use?

In many cases schools, colleges and local sports clubs can provide suitable venues for all kinds of events. Some communities have places which can be hired. For example, villages and towns usually have halls which can be hired. Businesses might hire out their facilities to people who want to organise events. For example, they may own large meeting rooms, conference facilities

and sports facilities. There are also specialist event locations like the NEC or Earls Court – although these are expensive and only suitable for very large events. Finally, the venue or location is likely to be one of the most expensive resources used when staging an event. The charge will be a fixed cost and it is often necessary to pay in advance for its use. This will have implications for funding and feasibility.

Equipment Most events will require a range of equipment. Some will be common to all events such as computers, mobile phones for communication and photocopiers. However, the type of equipment needed will depend on the nature of the event. For example:

- a sound system, a fog machine and lighting will be needed for a disco;
- an outdoor wedding party might require a marquee, dining furniture, bar facilities, mobile toilets, a sound system and an electricity generator;
- a school sports day may need sports equipment such as a starting pistol, landing mats, javelins, discuses, judges scoring tent, high jump apparatus, a podium and timing devises.

Nearly all the equipment needed for an event is likely to be hired. Although in some cases, where an event is held annually for example, it may be worth buying some equipment. This is because it will be used more frequently. When acquiring equipment for events, there may be a number of suppliers who are able to meet specific needs. It is obviously important to 'shop around' and make sure that the best supplier is found. There is a number of businesses that specialise in the supply of equipment for events. The website of one such business is shown in Figure 3.

Materials A wide range of materials are likely to be needed both in the planning stages of the event and for the event itself. During the planning stages the materials needed are likely to be similar for most events. For example, stationery for making notes and drawing up plans will be needed. Flip charts, marker pens and

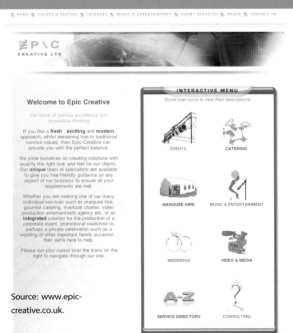

Figure 3 *An example of a business that supplies equipment for events*

Source: www.epic-creative.co.uk.

OHP transparencies might be needed for meetings. The materials needed for the event itself will again depend on the nature of the event. For example, food, drink, party-poppers, decorations, balloons, candles and materials for games are likely to be needed when organising a party.

For most events the cost of materials may not represent a significant proportion of the total cost. However, it will still be a good idea to 'shop around' and get the best possible deal for materials.

Human resources

No event can be organised without people. The success of an event will depend very heavily on the skills and attitudes of the people involved in its organisation. In most cases the people involved will be unpaid volunteers. A number of human resource issues needs to be considered when planning an event.

Team working Many events are organised by a team of people. People often work very well together when in a team. This is because they are better motivated and are likely to develop a team spirit and support each other. The advantages of working in a team are as follows.

- Greater productivity because people's talents are pooled.
- Increased flexibility because people bring a range of different skills and can cover each other.
- More ideas are usually generated by a team.
- The burden of responsibility can be shared.
- People can specialise in the areas and tasks in which they are most competent.
- People can draw on the skills and knowledge of their colleagues in the team.
- A team has a greater potential to solve problems.

However, there are some disadvantages when working in teams. For example, there may be conflict between some team members which could slow down the progress made by the team. There may also be problems if individual team members 'do not pull their weight'. This can cause resentment amongst the others. Finally, in the case of very large events there may be a large number of teams all working together but on different tasks.

Training Part of the planning and preparation of an event might involve training or briefing people about their tasks and responsibilities. It is very likely that some people are assigned tasks which they are not familiar with. For example, people assigned to stewarding traffic at an event might benefit from a briefing with a local police officer. People who will be dealing with clients or spectators face-to-face may benefit from customer service training. If people are trained they will be able to perform roles and fulfil tasks more easily. In the case of very large events staff may need to be recruited on a temporary basis. Some of these might be specialised such as chefs, first-aiders or security staff.

Allocation of tasks and roles The work needed to organise and stage an event has to be divided between team members. One important job in the planning process is to appoint or select a leader. The leader will have overall responsibility for the event and will coordinate the entire project. This job will require someone with good leadership, motivational, organisational and communication skills. If more than one person wants to be leader

then it might be necessary to have a vote. This might be preceded by all the leadership candidates giving a presentation to the rest of the group outlining the reasons why they should be selected. Once all the tasks needed to prepare and stage the event have been identified, they have to be placed in order and then allocated to people or teams. It is best if people are allocated tasks that they want to do. In some cases people may have some skill or experience that might allow them to do a particular task really well. A simple table might be used to do this. An example is shown in Figure 4.

It might also be helpful to produce an organisation chart for the planning of an event. This shows the structure of the organisation in terms of the people involved. Such charts have a number of advantages.

- The roles and job titles of people are clearly defined.

Figure 4 *Allocating tasks and roles to team members*

The table below was used to help plan an evening event where two speakers were invited to talk about a trip to Australia. The event was intended for sixth form students but anyone from the local community could attend. It was hoped that an experienced back-packer and someone from a TV travel programme could be persuaded to give a speech and answer questions. The table below is an extract from the one used in the planning process. I shows clearly who has responsibility for a particular task and how long it will take to complete.

TASK	TIME NEEDED	PERSON RESPONSIBLE
Design and print tickets	Two weeks	Jane Weston
Design and print programmes	Three weeks	Kevin Ball
Obtain advertising from local business	Four weeks	Naved-ul-Hasan
Obtain and prepare a venue	Four weeks	Greg Mitchell
Invite speakers and liaise with them	Four weeks	Paulo Diablo
Produce a promotion campaign	Three weeks	Sheila Burton
Prepare and serve refreshments	One week	Angus McBride

- The route through which decisions are made is clarified.
- Positions of responsibility are defined and it is clear who is accountable to whom.
- The relationship between the different positions in the organisation of the event is shown.
- They help spot communication problems. If information fails to arrive at its intended destination it may be possible to identify where the breakdown occurred by tracing the communication chain along the chart. An example is shown in Figure 5.

Special needs Some people involved in the organisation of an event may have special needs. For example, there may be people with hearing difficulties, people who are partially sighted or people who need assistance with mobility. It is important to accommodate people with special needs and not treat them as a planning constraint. However, measures might need to be taken in order that they are able to play a full role in the organisation of the event. For example, venues selected must have wheelchair access.

Contract supplies

It is common when staging events to use specialised contractors to provide certain services. Some common examples are catering, security and bar facilities. There are lots of businesses that compete to supply these types of services. They are likely to be local and might vary in the type of service they supply.

Catering In some cases such as weddings, parties, Sportsperson's Dinners and conferences, the food is an important part of the event. The people who are organising the event may decide to use outside caterers to provide the food. This is because they are specialists and are likely to provide better quality food than if it was prepared by the organisers. Outside caterers will have all the kitchen equipment needed to provide meals and buffets. They will also employ qualified and experienced staff such as chefs and waiters. Although outside caterers may be expensive, if employed they will reduce the burden of responsibility and work load when organising an event. Figure 6 shows an example of a business that provides catering for events.

Figure 6 *An example of a contract supplier that provides catering for events*

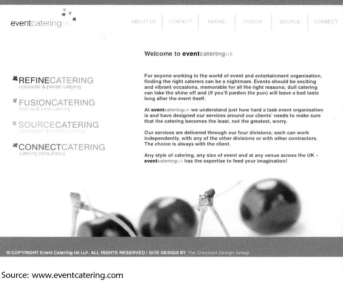

Source: www.eventcatering.com

Security Some events require proper security. This is unlikely to be provided effectively by a small group of organisers. The most common type of security is probably door security at events where an admission is charged or certain groups of people are not welcome. The main purpose of such security is to ensure that people do not gain entry without paying and to prevent entry by those who are not welcome. This is a job that is best handled by people who have been trained. Security might also be needed to protect the venue and its facilities. For example, the Southport Flower Show employs a security firm and part of their job is to prevent unauthorised entry on to the event site during the night. The site is patrolled by security officers and dog handlers. Security is also needed at certain events to help with crowd control and deal with difficult spectators and visitors.

Figure 5 *An organisation chart for an event*

The chart has been drawn up for a team of 21 students organising a leaving party for one of their teachers. Around 250 staff and past and present sixth form students will be attending. The chart shows clearly that Kim Partington is in charge of the whole event. The organisation is then divided into four functional teams, each of which has a leader. For example, the person in charge of entertainment is June Wishart. June is also responsible for two other teams, Music and Acts, which both have leaders.

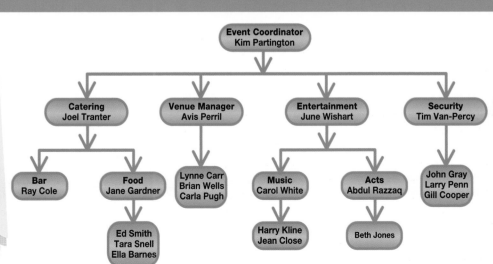

Bar facilities Many people expect to find a bar at events. Since events are often social occasions, many people would like to enjoy a drink. It is possible for a group of organisers to provide bar facilities but with larger events outside contractors are likely to do a better job. They will be able to provide a wider range of drinks, a proper bar counter, glasses and trained and experienced staff. Running a bar at events is often an important source of revenue. If an outside contractor is employed to provide the bar facility they will have to pay the event organisers for the opportunity to make money. At test matches in England, Guinness, the brewery, provide bar facilities from large mobile vans with fitted bars. It is also necessary to obtain a licence to sell alcohol. This is dealt with in section 56.

Assume that a small pop concert is being organised for a weekend evening. A maximum of 250 people are expected and there will be no seating provided.
- Identify the important features of a suitable venue.
- Search for a venue in your local area – use the Internet, *Yellow Pages* and individual research of your local area.
- Short-list three options and decide which would be the most suitable.
- Write a brief report outlining the reasons for your choice of venue.

Research task

Meeting the assessment criteria - examiners' guidance

You need to prepare a presentation and write a report which provides evidence of planning an event. This section focuses on risk assessment, physical resources, human resources and contract supplies.

Event example – Disco for youngsters

The head of year for 12 year-olds at a school has asked a group of sixth-formers to organise an end of term 'themed' disco. She has asked that refreshments are provided and a prize given for

the best dressed boy and girl. The team has six weeks to promote and organise the event and have also been asked to:
- hold the event in the school hall (max 200);
- keep the admission charge to £1;
- provide a documented risk assessment;
- allow admission by ticket only;
- ensure adequate security;
- restrict admission to members of the school only.

Mark Band 1 *Your report should provide evidence of planning and an outline of risk assessment.*

A meeting was held to set the aims and objectives of the event and draw up plans for its organisation. A list of tasks was identified and these were allocated to team members. Mary was appointed Event Coordinator – no one else wanted the job really. The table shows the tasks required in the planning of the event. It was decided to draw up a similar table for the night of the event so that everyone had a clear role to play during the course of the disco. At a later meeting it was decided to use an outside contractor for a DJ. For £150 this would be done by an experienced DJ who would bring her own equipment. Some state-of-the-art lighting would be obtained by Tengji Jiang whose father had some useful contacts. A risk assessment was carried out and the following hazards were identified.
- Fire from lots of lighting and electrical equipment.
- Exhaustion from over-exertion and heat.
- Spillage from refreshments.
- Effects of strobe lights.

Mark Band 2 *Your report should provide evidence of planning and a completed risk assessment.*

The planning stage of an event is important. Careful planning will improve the quality of the event and help avoid mistakes. At the first meeting a leader was appointed and a list of planning tasks were identified. Each important task was allocated to one of the team members. They are shown in the table above but not in any particular order. During the planning stages the team worked together very well. Cooperation and communication between team members was good and people supported each other. It was decided about three weeks before the event to use an

END OF TERM

£1

THEMED DISCO

ADMIT ONE PERSON – ADMISSION BY TICKET ONLY

TASK	TIME NEEDED	PERSON RESPONSIBLE
Design and print tickets	Three weeks	Peter Small
Produce promotion posters	Two weeks	Celia Roberts
Sell advanced tickets	Three weeks	Mary Fletcher
Decorate and prepare the venue	One day	Robin Trestle
Organise refreshments	One week	Carl Asaba
Organise security using teachers	Three weeks	Patricia Hurst
Organise a DJ and sound system	Four weeks	Melanie Clifford
Organise Lighting	One week	Tengji Jiang
Carry out risk assessment	Two weeks	Jenny Vaughan

Event: Themed Disco **Event date:** 23.3.05 **Assessment by:** Jenny Vaughan **Date:** 15.3.05

Hazard/task	Who's at risk	Risk Level	Control measures	Comments
Fire from lighting and electrical equipment.	All	Medium	Check all fire extinguishers, notify brigade of event and emphasise fire exits.	Ask head teacher to organise a school fire drill before the event.
Exhaustion from over-exertion and heat.	All	Low	Provide free water, and outside area for fresh air and a qualified first-aider.	Check out which teachers have first-aid training.
Spillage from refreshments.	All	Low	Ensure that spillages are reported and cleaned up immediately.	Carl will have responsibility for this task since he is in charge of refreshments.
Effects of strobe lights.	All	High	Warning signs. Follow proper guidelines for their use. Provide warnings. Ensure first-aid can deal with their effects.	A warning could be printed on the tickets.

outside contractor to provide a good sound system and a proper DJ. This would cost £150 but would be worth it. However, there would be pressure to raise some money from the sale of refreshments. As a result the organisation of refreshments became a bigger job and Peter and Celia offered to help. A proper risk assessment was carried out and is shown above.

Mark Band 3 *Your report should provide evidence of planning and a detailed risk assessment that correctly identifies all major hazards.*

The planning process is an important part of staging an event. Careful planning should help to ensure that the event is a success. In this case the aim of the event was to provide an enjoyable experience for youngsters at a 'themed' disco. It was decided at the first planning meeting to draw up a list of tasks and allocate them to team members. This would help to clarify people's roles and show what was expected of them. A leader was also

appointed at the first meeting. Someone with good communication, organisational and motivational skills was needed to lead the team. There was only one suitable candidate and it was Mary who rightly got the job. The tasks and the people responsible for them are shown in the table above. They are not shown in any particular order but the completion time for each is stated. To improve the quality of the event and reduce the burden of responsibility it was decided to employ an outside DJ to provide the music. Although this was an expensive option (£150), it was felt that the expense would be worth it and some extra money could be raised from selling a wider range of refreshments and perhaps some T-shirts. It was also necessary to produce a detailed risk assessment for the event. This was supervised by Jenny Vaughan and a copy of the risk assessment document is shown above.

Portfolio practice · Fund-raising ball

The Parent Teachers Association (PTA) at a school appointed a team of students to organise a Ball to raise money for the school swimming pool fund. The PTA set a target of £1,000 for the event. A number of specifications were given to the team of students. They are shown below.

- A buffet with Asian cuisine.
- A maximum price of £10 a ticket.
- Live classical music.
- A bar to be provided by an outside contractor.
- A maximum of 300 people could be accommodated.

(a) Identify SIX important planning tasks that would have to be carried out when organising this event.
(b) Analyse the physical resources that might be needed for this event.
(c) Evaluate the advantages and disadvantages of using contract suppliers for this event.

Time constraints

When organising events the time and date of the event provides a critical deadline. Once the time and date have been agreed, very rarely can an event switch to another time or day. This means that all the planning and preparation must be completed by this deadline. This is the main time constraint which organisers will have to work with. There may be other time constraints within the preparation period. For example, when organising an event in a village hall, access to the hall may be restricted to 12 hours before the event. This is because someone else might be using the hall. Also, every task in the planning process will have a minimum amount of time which it takes to complete. To make planning easier and help deal with time constraints a number of planning aids can be used.

Time lines

When planning an event time lines can be used to help clarify the order in which planning tasks should be carried out. A time line shows a series of events in chronological order along a straight line. When applied to the planning of an event the timeline will show all the tasks that need to be completed in the planning process in chronological order. An example is shown in Figure 1. The time line is vertical. However, it could easily be shown as horizontal.

What are the advantages of timelines?

- They show how long the event will take to plan.
- They show clearly the order in which tasks have to be completed.
- They show the deadlines for each task.
- Easy to draw and understand.
- Despite the advantages of using timelines, they do have drawbacks. For example, they do not show how long each task takes. Nor do they show the current status of the planning process or the progress being made.

Gantt charts

Gantt charts are a project planning tool that can be used to represent the timing of tasks required to plan an event. In a Gantt chart:

- each task takes up one row;
- dates run along the top in increments of days, weeks or months, depending on how long it will take to plan the event;
- the expected time for each task is represented by a horizontal bar whose left end marks the beginning of the task and whose right end marks the end;
- tasks may run sequentially, in parallel or overlapping;
- as the planning progresses, the chart is updated by shading in the bars to show the amount of work that has been done on a task;
- a quick reading of planning progress can be obtained by drawing

Figure 1 *Using a time line to plan an event*

The timeline used here shows the deadlines for completing tasks when organising a staff Christmas party for a local business.

Date	Task
12.10.05	First planning meeting
20.10.05	Complete risk assessment
28.10.05	Confirm venue
30.10.05	Second planning meeting
5.11.05	Meet with three prospective caterers
7.11.05	Book entertainment
9.11.05	Meet to select caterer
13.11.05	Book caterer
12.12.05	Purchase drinks and party accessories
14.12.05	Decorate and prepare venue
15.12.05	Christmas party

a vertical line through the chart at the current date. Complete tasks lie to the left of the line and are completely filled in. Current tasks cross the line and are behind schedule if their shaded section is to the left of the line and ahead of schedule if the shaded section stops to the right of the line. Future tasks lie completely to the right of the line.

An example is shown in Figure 2.

Figure 2 *A Gantt chart used in the organisation of a comedy night*

TASK	4/3	5/3	6/3	7/3	8/3	9/3	10/3	11/3	12/3	13/3	14/3	15/3	16/3	17/3	18/3	19/3	20/3	21/3	22/3	23/3	24/3	25/3	26/3	27/3	28/3
PLANNING MEETINGS																									
RISK ASSESSMENT												▼													
SIGN UP ACTS																									
PROMOTION CAMPAIGN																									
DESIGN/PRINT TICKETS																									
SIGN UP CONTRACTORS																									
RECRUIT HELPERS																									
SELL TICKETS																									
PREPARE VENUE																									

The planning of the Comedy Night is divided into nine specific tasks. These are labelled in the far left hand column. Each task is represented by a bar. The planning of the event begins on 4 March and the event takes place on 28 March. The shaded section in red in the bar shows how much of the task is complete in terms of time and the section in pink shows how much is yet to be completed. The vertical dotted line at the end of 16th March is the current date. Any block to the left of the line which is completely shaded in red shows that the task has been completed. Risk assessment and the signing up of acts are both examples of completed tasks. Any block, or part of a block, to the left which is in pink shows that the task is not complete. For example, the signing up of contractors should have started but has not. Most blocks to the right of the line are in pink. This is to be expected because the tasks are not due for completion yet. However, some blocks are partly shaded in red beyond the dotted line, which means work is ahead of schedule on those activities. In this case, promotion and ticket printing are ahead of schedule.

Often the planning of an event has important 'milestones' which might be shown on the chart. For example, the completion of crucial tasks might be highlighted. These can be shown on the chart and marked with a special symbol, often an upside-down triangle. The chart in Figure 2 shows one such 'milestone'. It is the signing up of the acts. This was completed on 15 March and is shown by '▼'. The advantages of Gantt charts are as follows.
- Time is linear and clearly shown.
- All tasks are visible in relation to each other.
- Deadlines are shown clearly as are important 'milestones'.
- The current status of a project or plan can be shown by drawing in the vertical line.
- Progress is recorded easily by shading in the blocks.

However, there are some drawbacks when using Gantt charts.
- One problem with them is that they don't indicate task dependencies. It cannot be shown how one task falling behind schedule affects other tasks.
- Gantt charts only focus on time. There is no information on the use of other resources in the planning process.
- The chart also fails to show which tasks are critical. Critical tasks are those which will hold up the completion of the planning process if delayed.

Critical path analysis

Critical path analysis (CPA) or network analysis is a planning aid which overcomes some of the problems associated with Gantt charts. CPA can be used when planning an event to:
- calculate the minimum amount of time it will take to complete the whole planning process;
- identify tasks which are 'critical', i.e. those that if delayed will hold up the entire process;
- identify tasks which can be delayed without holding up the entire operation.

Consider the planning of a Charity Auction. The individual tasks involved in the whole planning process, the order in which they must be completed and their duration is shown in Table 1.

Table 1 *The order and duration of tasks when planning a Charity Auction*

	Task	Order/dependency	Duration
A	Feasibility study	Must be done first	4 days
B	Risk assessment	Must follow A	4 days
C	Find venue	Can start after B	5 days
D	Gather Lots*	Can start after B	20 days
E	Promotion	Can start after C	14 days
F	Appoint auctioneer	Must follow D	4 days
G	Organise refreshments	Must follow F	3 days
H	Prepare venue	Must follow E	1 day

* This involves persuading local retailers to donate goods and services for auction.

Figure 3 *Network diagram for planning a charity auction*

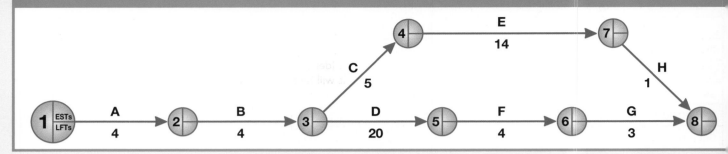

Figure 4 *The ESTs and LFTs for the charity auction tasks*

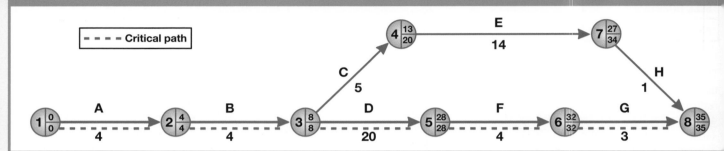

The information shown in Table 1 can be used to construct the network diagram in Figure 3. A network diagram contains a number of important features.

- The circles are called nodes. They show the start or finish of tasks.
- The tasks in the table are represented by the arrows between the nodes. For example, arrow A represents the feasibility study. The tasks use up resources as they are carried out. In this case, task A will take time and use labour.
- Nodes contain information. Figure 3 shows that nodes are divided into three sections. In the left hand semi-circle the node number is written. This is just for identification purposes. The number in the top right is the earliest start time (EST). This shows the earliest time the next task can begin. The number in the bottom right is the latest finishing time (LFT). This shows the latest time that the previous task can finish without delaying the next task. (These have not been calculated yet.)
- The arrows show the order in which the tasks can take place. The tasks are dependent on each other. For example, finding the venue and gathering 'Lots' cannot start until the risk assessment has been completed. The amount of time a task takes is written underneath the arrow.

The total amount of planning time needed for the charity auction is 55 hours. However, some of the tasks in the table can be done at the same time. For example, once the risk assessment has been carried out, finding a suitable venue and gathering 'Lots' can be done together. To find the minimum amount of time needed to complete the whole planning process it is necessary to calculate the earliest start times. These are shown in Figure 4.

Earliest start time Assuming that the earliest time task A can be started is day 0 then task B cannot start for 4 days (0 + 4), i.e. until task A has been completed. These ESTs are shown in the top

right of nodes 1 and 2 in Figure 4. Tasks C and D cannot start un A and B have been completed, this takes 8 days (0 + 4 + 4). This shown in the top right of node 3. Task E cannot start for 13 days (0 + 4 + 4 + 5). This is shown in node 4. The process of calculating the ESTs continues in this way until we arrive at node 8. Here there are two choices. Is it 28 (27 + 1) or 35 (32 +3)? The EST must always show the **highest value**, i.e. 35. This is written in th top right of node 8. The EST in the final node shows the minimum time in which the whole planning process can be completed. It is 35 days (0 + 4 + 4 + 20 + 4 + 3).

Latest finish time The next step is to calculate the latest finish time of each task without extending the planning process. Starting at node 8, tasks G and H must be completed by the 35th day. Thi LFT is shown in the bottom right of node 8. To calculate the LFT for task F, the time taken to complete task G must be subtracted from the previous LFT, i.e. 32 (35 − 3). This LFT is shown in node 6. To calculate the LFT for task E, the time taken to complete task H must be subtracted from the previous LFT, i.e. 34 (35 − 1). This is shown in node 7. This process is continued until node 3 is reached. Here there are two possibilities. Is it 15 (20 − 5) or 8 (2 − 20)? The LFT must always show the **lowest value**, i.e. 8. This is written in the bottom right of node 3. All the LFTs are shown in Figure 4.

The critical path The critical path shows all the tasks that cannot be delayed without holding up the whole planning process. To identify the critical path a line is drawn from node 1, along all the tasks, through all the nodes where the ESTs and the LFTs are the same. In this case it would be along tasks A, B, D, F and G. This is shown by a dotted line in Figure 4.

The float Tasks which do not lie on the critical path, ie C, E and H, can be delayed for a certain amount of time without holding u the entire planning process. For example, together they could be held up for 7 days. This is called float.

- **Total float** is found by subtracting the EST and the duration from the LFT. So for task C it would be 20 − 5 − 8 = 7 days.
- **Free float** measures the extra time available so there is no delay to the next task. It is found by subtracting the EST at the start of the task and the duration from the EST at the end of the task. So for task C the free float is 13 − 5 - 8 = 0.

This shows that task C can be delayed, but will interfere with tasks E and H. It is important to know how much float each non-critical task has. If a task is not critical the resources required to complete that task might be used for another purpose or shared

Figure 5 *A simple flow chart used to help plan a trip*

This flow chart shows the planning tasks involved in organising a trip for school children to a local museum.

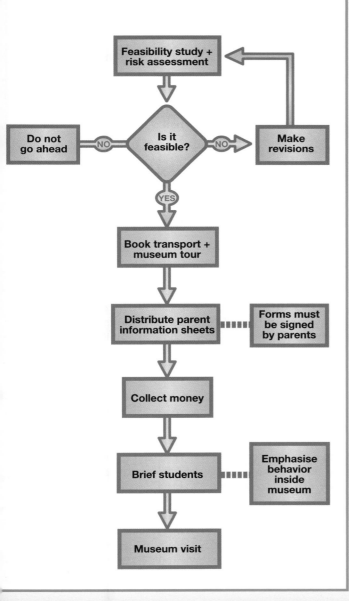

between other tasks.

There are certain advantages of critical path analysis in planning.

- Provides a visual image of the planning process.
- Forces people to look at all the tasks involved in the planning process. When drawing the network diagram all aspects of the planning process have to be included.
- It identifies clearly the critical and non-critical tasks.
- It will help to conserve cash. For example, materials will only be bought just before they are needed. So, in the example above, the refreshments will not have to be purchased for 32 days.

However, there are also disadvantages.

- The construction of the network diagram alone will not guarantee the smooth running of the planning and preparation process. The tasks themselves have to be completed on time and not go over schedule.
- The data needed to construct the network diagram must be accurate. If not then the ESTs, LFTs and critical path will be misleading.

Flow charts

It is possible to use a flow chart when planning an event. A flow chart is another method which shows how the planning process can be expressed visually. The flow chart contains information about tasks, decisions and outcomes in the planning process. The information is shown in boxes and linked by arrows. To draw a flow chart the order of the tasks must be known. An example of a simple flow chart is shown in Figure 5. The rectangular symbols contain information about tasks. They are drawn in order of completion. The diamond shaped symbol shows where a decision is made in the flow chart.

Flow charts have certain advantages.

- They provide a visual image of the planning process.
- Each task is shown and described clearly.
- The order of tasks is shown.
- They show the outcomes of decisions in the planning process.

However, there are also disadvantages.

- There is no time scale.
- They do not show any quantitative information such as the duration of tasks.
- There is no information on resource use.

1. Using contacts, such as family, friends or business contacts, carry out an interview to evaluate the time taken on a project. It might be an activity such as a new building, the fitting of a new piece of machinery or a change in work processes.
2. Research the estimated time of the project and whether there was any over-run.
3. Evaluate to what extent deadlines where met and any reasons why they may not have been met.
4. Estimate any costs of over-runs.

Alternatively, research newspaper articles to evaluate projects such as the building of the new Wembley Stadium or similar projects.

Research task

Meeting the assessment criteria - examiners' guidance

You need to prepare a presentation and write a report which provides evidence of planning an event. This section focuses on time constraints and the planning aids that might be used in the planning process.

Event example – Business studies conference

A group of sixth form students were asked to organise a Business Studies Conference for their college and other colleges in the region. Some money was made available to help funding but the students were encouraged to get some sponsors from local businesses. The planning of the conference was broken down into nine key tasks. The tasks, their order and duration are shown in Table 2.

Table 2 *Planning a conference*

	Task	Order/dependency	Duration
A	Risk assessment	Must be done first	4
B	Book speakers	Can follow A	20
C	Shortlist caterers	Can follow A	10
D	Find sponsors	Can follow A	25
E	Promote conference	Must follow B	10
F	Calculate attendance	Must follow E	2
G	Book caterers	Must follow F	1
H	Brief stewards	Must follow F	1
I	Prepare venue	Must follow G	2

Mark Band 1 *Your report should provide evidence of planning and an outline of the time constraints involved. These can be shown on a simple timeline.*

When organising events the time and date of the event provides a critical deadline. Once the time and date have been agreed, very rarely can an event switch to another time or day. This means that all the planning and preparation must be completed by this deadline. To help plan the conference a timeline was drawn to show the order in which planning tasks should be carried out. A time line shows a series of events in chronological order along a straight line. The timeline for planning the conference is shown in Figure 6. Timelines are helpful because they show how long the event will take to plan, the order in which tasks have to be completed and the deadlines for each task. They are also easy to draw and understand.

Mark Band 2 *Your report should provide evidence of planning and an understanding of time constraints. You should attempt to bring in critical path analysis in your planning.*

When planning an event there are bound to be time constraints. For example, certain tasks will need a minimum amount of time to complete and some tasks cannot begin until others have been completed. When planning the conference a network diagram was drawn to calculate the minimum amount of time it would take to organise the conference. This is shown in Figure 7. The ESTs, LFTs and critical path are all shown. According to the

Figure 6 *Planning a conference*

12.3.05	Planning meeting
16.3.05	Complete risk assessment
26.3.05	Short list caterers
31.3.05	Confirm sponsors
5.4.05	Confirm conference speakers and begin promotion
16.4.05	Calculate attendance
18.04.05	Book caterers and brief stewards
19.4.05	Finish venue preparation

network diagram the planning and organisation of the conference would take 39 days.

Mark Band 3 *Your report should provide evidence of planning and an understanding of the importance of time constraints. You should also use critical path analysis in your planning.*

Timing can be crucial when planning events. Once the date of an event has been finalised it can rarely be changed. In this case a conference has to be organised. The information shown in Table 2 above can be used to help cope with time constraints. A timeline can be drawn (as in Figure 6) to show the order in which planning tasks should be carried out. A time line shows a series of events in chronological order along a straight line. The timeline for planning the conference is shown above. The deadlines for each task are shown. However, a more useful planning tool is critical path analysis (CPA). CPA can be used when planning an event to calculate the minimum amount of time it will take to complete the whole planning process and to identify tasks which are 'critical', i.e. those that if delayed will hold up the entire process. A network diagram is shown in Figure 7. The ESTs, LFTs and critical path are all shown. According to the network diagram the planning and organisation of the conference would take 39 days. CPA has some useful advantages. For example, it forces people to look at all the tasks involved in the planning process. When drawing the network diagram all aspects of the planning process have to be included. It also identifies clearly the critical and non-critical tasks. For example, in this case tasks C, D and I are non-critical. This means they could be delayed for a while if

Figure 7 Network diagram for the planning process

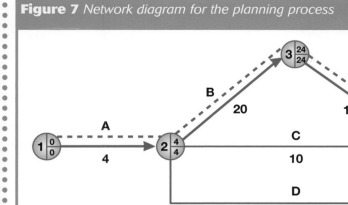

necessary. However, CPA does have some disadvantages. For example, The construction of the network diagram alone will not guarantee the smooth running of the planning and preparation process. The tasks themselves have to be completed on time and not go over schedule. Also, the data needed to construct the network diagram must be accurate. If it is not then the ESTs, LFTs and critical path will be misleading.

Portfolio practice · Skateboard competition

A group of students plans to organise a skateboard competition for youngsters at the beginning of the summer holidays. To help plan the event the Gantt chart in Figure 8 was used. The entrants had to pay £1 to take part and the winner would be selected by a panel of slightly older skateboarders. The entrance money would be used to pay for some prizes for the best three skateboarders on the day. Some light refreshments would also be provided for the contestants free of charge. On the Gantt chart the current time is represented by a vertical dotted line.

(a) **Using information in the case explain what is meant by a time constraint.**
(b) **(i) How long does the risk assessment take?**
    (ii) Which task is ahead of schedule?
    (iii) Which task is behind schedule?
(c) **Discuss the advantages and disadvantages of Gantt charts to the group planning the event.**

Figure 8 Gantt chart

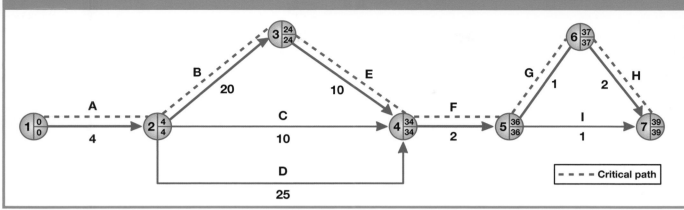

TASK	1/7	2/7	3/7	4/7	5/7	6/7	7/7	8/7	9/7	10/7	11/7	12/7	13/7	14/7	15/7	16/7	17/7	18/7	19/7	20/7	21/7	22/7	23/7	24/7	25/7
FEASIBILITY STUDY																									
RISK ASSESSMENT													▼												
OBTAIN COUNCIL PERMIT*																									
PROMOTE EVENT																									
SIGN UP ENTRANTS																									
RECRUIT JUDGES																									
OBTAIN PRIZES																									
ORGANISE REFRESHMENTS																									
PREPARE VENUE																									

Permission to use the council owned skateboard park.

Legal and working practice constraints

What are legal constraints?

The staging of many events is likely to be subject to legal constraint. This means that organisers have to ensure that certain legal requirements have been met before going ahead. For example, if an event is on private land, in the open air or in a building or temporary construction and involves public music or any other public entertainment of a like kind, then a public entertainment licence may be required. Legal constraints are likely to add to the costs of staging an event. For example, providing safety barriers to protect crowds to comply with health and safety law will cost money. Legal constraints may also restrict the activities involved, for example there may be a legal limit as to the number of people that can attend an event due to the safe legal capacity at a venue.

> THE WHOLE AREA OF HEALTH AND SAFETY IS AN IMPORTANT ONE. ANYONE ORGANISING AN EVENT SHOULD GET PROPER PROFESSIONAL ADVICE. A TEACHER OR LECTURER WILL PROVIDE INITIAL GUIDANCE FOR STUDENTS IN SCHOOLS AND COLLEGES.

Health and safety

It is obviously important to make sure that the people involved in the event, such as contestants, spectators, employees, volunteers and contractors, will all be safe when the event takes place. There are laws, regulations and guidelines designed to protect people from danger which may have to be considered when planning an event. Details of health and safety laws can be accessed from the following websites, www.healthandsafety.co.uk/haswa.htm and www.hse.gov.uk.

Some examples of areas where health and safety is a key issue are shown in Table 1.

Table 1 *Examples of areas where health and safety is a key issue*

- The use of electricity, particularly outdoors
- The use of gas cylinders or bottles
- The use of temporary structures such as seating
- Food catering
- Vehicles in and around the event area
- Emergency procedures
- Crowd control
- Inflatable bouncing devices for children
- Large items of machinery and other equipment
- Funfair rides
- Toilet facilities
- Licensing and alcohol
- Bonfires and fireworks
- Road closures

Contracts

Planning and organising an event may involve organisers entering into contracts. A contract is a legally binding agreement between two or more parties. However, it will only be legally binding if:

- it has been entered into voluntarily;
- it contains mutual considerations, i.e. both parties have something to gain;
- it is created for legal purposes;
- it is signed by the authorised parties.

Once a contract has been signed, organisers will be obliged to fulfil their part of the agreement. For example, if a contract is signed to pay £500 to a landlord to hire a venue for the day, that payment has to be made by law according to the terms and conditions stated in the contract. Even if the event is cancelled or the organisers run short of money, the payment must be made. It is easy to see that contracts can act as constraints when planning an event. However, contracts can also benefit the organisers. This is because they clarify the terms and conditions of any agreement made between two or more parties. Contracts are usually documented and difficult to dispute after being signed. Consequently the organisers of events know their legal obligations.

Examples of contracts that might be entered into when planning an event are shown in Table 2.

Table 2 *Typical contracts for events*

- Contracts with the owners of venues are possibly the most likely example. Sometimes the owners of venues will want a payment before the event starts and a percentage of the takings after the event. Such agreements may be received in a written contract.
- When taking out insurance policies with insurance companies signatures will be required to secure cover.
- Contracts with suppliers are very common. For example, contracts may be signed with caterers, security companies, drinks suppliers and marketing or staff recruitment agencies when they agree to provide their services.
- Contracts may need to drawn up with bands or other performers that promise to appear at events. Insisting on a contract is one way of making sure they turn up on the day of the event.
- If organisers plan to sell goods or services at events they themselves will be subject to consumer protection legislation such as the **Trade Descriptions Act, 1968**, the **Consumer Protection Act, 1987** and the **Sale of Goods Act, 1979**. This will also include the sale of tickets for events. Guidelines when complying with these laws may be given by the local council's trading standards section.

Negligence

It is possible that something might go wrong at an event and someone might get hurt. For example, at a firework display a person may be injured by a misdirected firework. This might result in that person making a compensation claim. When this happens it is necessary to apportion blame for the incident so that compensation can be awarded. The organisers are likely to be a target for blame since they are responsible for the event taking place and have a duty of care to the people involved. Indeed, it may be found that the organisers have been negligent. This means that the organisers have failed to take reasonable care of the people involved in the event. As a result they may have to pay compensation. In the case of students who are organising an event, if they are under 18 years old, their school or college might take overall responsibility in such cases. However, this would have to be checked and it would still be important to take every precaution to ensure the health and safety of all people involved at events. This is why risk assessment is such an important part of the planning process when organising an event. One way in which organisers can protect themselves from a negligence claim in the event of an incident is to take out insurance. This is explained in section 57.

Data protection

Another law which might restrict the planning of an event is the **Data Protection Act, 1998**. This legislation is designed to protect people such as customers from the misuse of data relating to personal details. The act covers the collection, storage, processing, and distribution of data. People organising an event may set up a data base to store names, addresses and contact details of people who have bought tickets. If this is the case they must acknowledge the Act requirements, summarised in Figure 1.

Licensing

Some activities at events may need a licence. In many cases licences may be obtained from the council, however, certain licences can only be granted in a court of law. If licences are refused this is likely to restrict the planning and staging of an event. Examples of some activities that will need licensing are given below.

The sale of alcohol in public places and some private places has

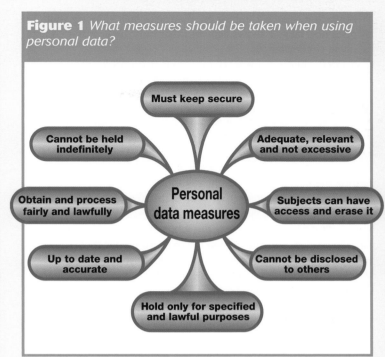

Figure 1 *What measures should be taken when using personal data?*

Personal data measures

- Must keep secure
- Adequate, relevant and not excessive
- Subjects can have access and erase it
- Cannot be disclosed to others
- Hold only for specified and lawful purposes
- Up to date and accurate
- Obtain and process fairly and lawfully
- Cannot be held indefinitely

to be authorised by licence. Even if alcohol is given away, as a prize in a raffle for example, a licence may be needed.

- A public entertainment licence may be needed if an event involves public music or dancing or any other public entertainment of a similar nature.
- Public contests, exhibitions or display of boxing, wrestling, judo, karate or any other similar sport must be licensed.
- Certain fund-raising activities may need council approval. This will be the case if fund-raising involves collecting money from the general public, on the street for example. If a house-to-house collection is being organised a permit is required from the council.
- In 1996 it became a legal requirement under **The Activity Centres (Young Persons' Safety) Act, 1995** for providers of certain adventure activities to undergo inspection of their safety management systems and become licensed. However, this licensing scheme only applies to those who offer activities to young people under the age of 18 years and who operate these activities in a commercial manner. Generally, licensing only applies to these activities when they are done in remote or isolated environments. For example, climbing on natural terrain

Table 3 *Licensable activities*

CLIMBING	WATERSPORTS	TREKKING	CAVING
Rock climbing	Canoeing	Hillwalking	Caving
Abseiling	Kayaking	Mountaineering	Potholing
Ice climbing	Dragon boating	Fell running	Mine exploration
Gorge walking	Wave skiing	Orienteering	
Ghyll scrambling	White-water rafting	Pony trekking	
Sea level traversing	Improvised rafting	Off road cycling	
	Sailing	Off-piste skiing	
	Sailboarding		
	Windsurfing		

requires a licence, climbing on a purpose built climbing wall does not. Table 3 shows activities that must be licensed under these circumstances.

In 1997 it became a legal requirement that only licensed activity providers will be able to offer activities as described above.

Licensing laws can be quite complex and it will be necessary to seek advice on whether a licence is needed. Failure to obtain appropriate licensing can result in fines or other legal action.

Working practice constraints

During the planning of an event a number of systems and procedures will be required to ensure that the planning process runs smoothly. These systems and procedures may be known as working practices, i.e. 'the way the job is done'. Working practices have to be designed and agreed for them to be effective. They also need to be established very early on in the planning process. Working practices should be designed so that they encourage effective communication, problem solving, reporting and the handling of finance. Once established, it is important that everyone involved in the planning process uses them. However, working practices may also act as constraints because they force people to use a particular method. The following issues may be important.

Booking methods The planning of events normally requires bookings to be made. For example, venues, speakers, entertainers, caterers and other resources may have to be booked well in advance of the event. Organisers may use standard booking forms for this task. This will help to ensure that all the information needed when making a booking is collected every time a booking is made. It will not matter who makes the booking if a standard form is used – the information collected will always be the same.

Recording data Working practices will have to be established for the gathering and recording of important data in the planning process. Some examples are shown in Table 4.

Meetings The planning of an event will require organisers to have regular meetings. Meetings will be needed to:
- set aims and objectives;
- agree on plans and tasks that need to be done and to determine who will carry them out;
- monitor progress against any targets set;
- coordinate tasks and activities between the different teams and individuals;
- give teams and individuals the opportunity to report back on their progress;
- solve problems and make decisions.

It is possible to waste a great deal of time at meetings. There may be a lack of direction and some people may spend too long making contributions. For meetings to be productive and run smoothly the following actions may be taken.
- Before the meeting starts an agenda should be prepared listing all the topics for discussion. The agenda should be circulated to all the people attending the meeting.
- Any information that may be used to help make decisions in the meeting should be circulated well before the day of the meeting. This will help people prepare and make a more meaningful contribution. Also, some information may be lengthy or complicated and need careful reading and analysis.

Table 4 *Recording data*

Details	Practices
Financial transactions	They must also be supported with appropriate documentation such as receipts and invoices. Financial information will be needed to produce financial documents, such as accounts to show whether or not the event made a profit. The financial information generated from these records may also be used to monitor cash flow. Some financial information may be recorded using spreadsheets.
Personal details	If a sporting event is being organised, for example, it may be necessary to record some personal details of contestants. Some of the information might be used to screen applicants for suitability. For example, if a physically demanding sporting event is being organised, such as a long distance run, it may be necessary to check that people are sufficiently healthy to take part. Also, with some events the age of contestants might be an issue. For example, young children might not be allowed to participate.
Customer details	It may be necessary to keep details of people who have bought tickets for an event. For example, contact details might be helpful if there are any changes to the venue or itinerary, for example. When holding personal data it is important to remember the requirements of the Data Protection Act. This applies to information held manually or electronically. If events are held regularly it may be useful to set up databases for contacts such as suppliers and other contacts. This will save time in the future.
Risk assessment	Information relating to risk assessment must be collected in a systematic way. This is discussed in section 53.

A meeting should be chaired by one person and that person should maintain control. An effective chairperson should be able to promote effective debate, allow everyone to make a contribution and bring discussions to a fruitful end. It is also important not to dwell too long on one agenda item. Meetings should start and end on time.

Someone should be appointed to take minutes at the meeting, write them up after and make them available to appropriate parties.

Communication Communication between organisers and others involved in an event will be crucial. Proper channels of communication need to be established to ensure a free flow of information. Communication is discussed in more detail in section 58.

1. Using your own contacts or the Internet find out what fund raising activities need to be licensed in your local area. The local council might help provide this information, for example.
2. Write a brief report explaining:
   - what types of fund-raising activities need licensing;
   - the procedure for obtaining a licence;
   - the costs involved;
   - what restrictions or constraints exist when fund raising.

Research task

Meeting the assessment criteria - examiners' guidance

You need to prepare a presentation and write a report which provides evidence of planning an event. This section focuses on legal and working practice constraints.

Event example – Mini-agricultural show

A group of students decided to organise a mini-agricultural show in their village in Norfolk. They hoped to raise money to help pay for a new church steeple which had been damaged in a severe storm. Some of the features at the show would include:
- display of agricultural machinery by local farmers;
- food stalls such as home-baked cakes and breads, locally produced cheeses, pates, honey, pickles, jams and other preserves;
- displays of farm animals where children would be invited to help with feeding and grooming, for example;
- evening entertainment from local musicians and other performers;

competitions such as guess the weight of the vicar and name the newly-born Shetland pony.

Mark Band 1 *Your report should provide evidence of planning and an outline of the legal and working practice constraints.*

Agricultural shows are very common in rural locations. They provide an opportunity for local communities to get together, and in this case, raise some money for a good cause. The nature of the event meant that a great deal of thought had to be given to legal issues. For example, a number of health and safety problems had to be resolved. It was necessary to check whether it was OK for children to get so close to farm animals. It was decided that children would not be able to touch the animals unless accompanied by a parent or guardian. It was also necessary to check the legal position regarding the sale of food at the event. Toilets and washing facilities had to be provided because the event was held in a farmer's field. A licence was also needed because live entertainment was being scheduled in the evening. There was no problem with noise because there were not any residential properties for miles.

Mark Band 2 *Your report should provide evidence of planning and reference to legal and working practice constraints.*

When organising an event it is important to investigate legal issues. In this case there was a number of legal problems which had to be resolved. Health and safety was one area of concern. For example, it was hoped that children could get inside tractor cabs and play on the agricultural machinery. However, this had to be ruled out because of the possible danger. All machinery had to be fenced off. It was also necessary to check whether it was safe for children to touch farm animals. It was decided that only children accompanied by a parent or guardian could get involved with feeding and grooming. The sale of food at the event was also a concern. The local council had to be consulted for guidance. It was also necessary to provide toilets and washing facilities. These were hired from a specialist company. A licence was also needed for the evening entertainment. However, there was no danger of causing any disturbance to local residents because the nearest dwelling was about three miles away. One contract had to be signed. This was an insurance policy. It was decided to take out public liability insurance as a precaution. This would provide protection from claims if anyone at the event was injured, for example.

Mark Band 3 *Your report should provide evidence of planning and clear understanding of legal and working practice constraints.*

The mini-agricultural show was considered feasible after a three week study. However, it was clear that a number of legal issues would have to be addressed. There was also a need for a thorough risk assessment. Health and safety was a major cause for concern. The exhibitions of powerful farm machinery were a focal point of the show and it was hoped that children in particular would have physical access to them. However, it was decided that the risk of accidents or injury was too great. Machinery would have to be fenced off. There was also a concern about interaction between children and farm animals. It was decided that only children accompanied by parents or guardians could get involved in feeding and grooming. Provision also had to be made for the clearance of animal waste on the site. The sale of food products was also a concern. Much of the food was home produced and it was necessary to seek council guidance on conditions of sale. Since the event was going to be held in a field where there were no facilities it was necessary to provide toilets and washing facilities. A hire company provided these and also advised on their positioning and maintenance. It was necessary to obtain a license for the evening entertainment. However, it was clear that no-one would be disturbed by the noise because there were no dwellings for three miles. The question of negligence was dealt with by taking out a public liability insurance policy. This would provide financial protection from any financial claim relating to the event. Finally, the working practices adopted by the organisers seemed to be very effective. Meetings were held every two weeks in the three months before the event took place. They were effectively led and productive.

Portfolio practice · **Team building day**

A group of students were asked to organise a team building day for a local business employing 12 staff. It was decided to hold the event in the Peak District which was only 19 miles from the business premises. The owner of the business wanted staff to enjoy a day of activities that would help to build team spirit. It was decided to book a motivational specialist to lead the day which would revolve around a number of outdoor pursuits. For example, the team would have to learn canoeing skills and then construct a craft from limited resources to cross a river. Hot food and drinks would also be provided by an outside caterer.

(a) **Using examples from this case, explain what is meant by a legal constraint.**
(b) **Discuss TWO important health and safety issues that might need to be considered in this case.**
(c) **A number of meetings was held by the group when planning this event. How might the quality of these meetings be improved?**

57 Financial requirements and contingency planning

Finance and planning

An important part of the planning process is working out how much money will be needed to prepare and stage an event. To do this it will be necessary to identify the total costs. It will also be necessary to ensure that funds are available when they are needed. Most events will generate some revenue. However, much of the money needed will be required to meet expenditure before the event. A systematic approach will be needed in the planning process to ensure money is available when resources have to be paid for. A possible approach is shown in Figure 1.

Figure 1 *Planning financial requirements*

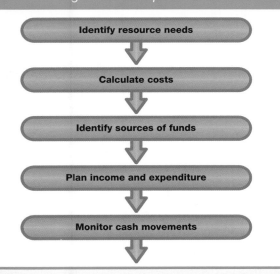

Identify resource needs

Calculate costs

Identify sources of funds

Plan income and expenditure

Monitor cash movements

Identifying resource needs The task of calculating financial requirements begins by identifying all the resources that will be needed in the planning and staging of the event. This might start by drawing up a list of resources at a meeting. However, some research later might reveal that other resources are needed and these should be added to the list. A list of all physical resources such as venue, equipment and materials, should be made. There is also likely to be a need for services, such as advertising, catering, cleaning and printing. Human resources must also be included if paid helpers, speakers, entertainers or other people are to be employed.

Calculate costs It should be possible to identify the cost of most of the resources on the list. For example, the cost of hiring a hall or a venue will be known because a quote can be obtained from the landlord. Quotes may also be obtained for other resources. The only real problem will be calculating total variable costs. To do this it will be necessary to estimate the number of people who will have to be catered for at the event. Any costs that cannot be calculated must be estimated. Once the costs of individual resources have been identified the total cost of preparing and

staging the event can be calculated.

Identify sources of funds When the total cost of staging the event has been estimated, it will be necessary to find ways of raising the money needed. Raising finance is discussed in more detail below.

Plan income and expenditure To help ensure that money is available when it is needed, the timing of receipts and payments must be planned carefully. This should help avoid running out of money. One way to do this is to prepare a **cash flow forecast** statement. This is a financial statement which lists all the likely receipts and payments over a future period of time, i.e. in the run up to the event. Cash flow forecasts are explained in detail below.

Monitor cash movements It is likely that the actual timings and amounts of receipts and payments will differ slightly to those in the forecast. For example, the amount of money from advanced ticket sales for an event on a particular day may be higher than planned. This means that the figures in the cash flow forecast will need adjusting. By monitoring payments and making adjustments the cash flow forecast will be kept up to date. When the event is finished, the actual receipts and payments can be compared with those planned in the forecast. The differences, called variances, can be analysed and this might help to account for overspending, for example.

Cash flow forecasts

When planning an event the organisers are likely to draw up a cash flow forecast using a spreadsheet. The forecast will show the likely receipts (cash inflows) and payments (cash outflows) over a future period of time. If organisers expect an event to take six months to plan they might produce a new forecast at the beginning of each month. Most of the entries in a forecast are estimated because they have not occurred yet. An example of a cash flow forecast is shown in Figure 2.

There are certain benefits of cash flow forecasts.

- A cash flow forecast will help to identify in advance whether organisers of an event are likely to run out of cash during the planning and preparation stages. For example, the closing balances at the bottom of the forecast will show whether there will be a need to generate more cash, from a loan for example.
- The planning of an event is an important process and the preparation of a cash flow forecast is a key part of that process. It forces the organisers to look ahead and helps to identify problems before they occur.
- Forecasts can help to monitor the cash flow during the planning stages of an event. For example, at the end of each forecast period organisers can calculate cash variances. These are the differences between the actual cash balances and the planned ones. The differences will be caused by overspending, underspending, higher than expected income or lower. Once the causes of the differences have been analysed corrective

Figure 2 *A cash flow forecast for an event*

The organisers of a school drama evening drew up a cash flow forecast. It is prepared for a 10 week period. This is the time it will take to organise the event. The top section shows the cash receipts that the organisers expect. For example, in the first week the school will lend them £200 to get started. The next section of the budget shows the planned payments. For example, in week 9 there will be payments of £20, £25 and £65 for an advert, food and drinks and lighting, respectively. The bottom section of the cash budget shows the net cash flow, the opening cash balance and the expected cash balance at the end of each week. For example, at the end of week 4 the net cash flow is expected to be -£70 (0 - £70). The opening cash balance is £185. This was the closing balance at the end of the previous week. The expected cash balance at the end of week 4 is £115 (£185 - £70). Over the 10 weeks the event is expected to generate a cash surplus of £175.

	1	2	3	4	5	6	7	8	9	10
Receipts										
School loan	200									
Donations/sponsors					100					
Advanced ticket sales										
Ticket sales										
Refreshment sales							50	50	50	15
Total cash receipts	**200**	**0**	**0**	**0**	**100**	**0**	**50**	**50**	**50**	**10**
Payments										
Printing		15								
Newspaper advert			45							
Food and drinks								20	20	20
Loan repayment									25	30
Lighting										200
Other costs				25		15			65	
Total cash payments	**0**	**15**	**0**	**70**	**0**	**15**	**0**	**20**		**25**
Net cash flow	200	(15)	0	(70)	100	(15)	50	40	110	275
Opening balance	0	200	185	185	115	215	200	10	(60)	(25)
Closing balance	**200**	**185**	**185**	**115**	**215**	**200**	**250**	**260**	**200**	**175**

Note: brackets equal negative numbers.

action might be taken, if this is necessary. Also, future forecasts might be more accurate.

- If organisers need to borrow money, from a bank for example, a cash flow forecast can be used to support the application.

Raising finance

Once organisers have calculated the total amount of money needed to plan and stage the event, it is necessary to search for suitable sources. Even if an event is likely to generate revenue, money will still be needed to pay for resources before the day of the event. A number of sources could be considered – loans from parents, bank loans, loans from school or college, the sale of advertising, sponsorship and donations are some of the examples mentioned. Raising money to get started is one of the most difficult tasks when organising an event. Some tips on raising finance are given in Table 1.

Contingency planning

The vast majority of events staged will be a success provided they are planned carefully and funded adequately. However, it is possible that during the planning stages or on the day of the event things could go wrong. Unforeseen circumstances may cause serious problems. For example, what would happen at a children's Christmas party if Santa Claus failed to turn up? To deal with unexpected emergencies such as this event organisers should draw up contingency plans. A contingency is an event that is liable but not certain to happen. A contingency plan outlines the actions that should be taken when such a crisis does arise. The first stage when drawing up a contingency plan is to identify all the possible crises that might occur in relation to the event. These will differ depending on the nature of the event. However, there may be some common ones, such as what to do if there is a power cut. Information gathered during risk assessment would probably be very helpful when carrying out this task. Once these have been identified it is possible to prepare a course of action that should be followed if the crisis occurs. Some examples of possible crises and their solutions are outlined below.

Running out of money Two things can be done in advance if money runs short during the planning stages of an event. One is to budget for a contingency fund. This involves putting a sum of money aside to deal with such an eventuality. A list of emergency funding might also be drawn up with the most likely providers at the top.

Bad weather Many events are held outdoors. If the weather is bad some indoor facilities can be booked as a precaution. It may also be possible to use marquees at short notice, for example. Choosing the driest month of the year might also help when arranging a date for an outdoor event.

Lost children If small children are expected to attend an event provision should be made for lost children. Stewards and other staff should be on the look out for lost children and there should be a clear course of action when a child is found or lost. At large events there may be a 'lost children tent' where children are looked after while they wait for parents.

Fire It may be possible to get advice from the fire brigade before staging an event. They can give information about the types of recautions that would be necessary, what firefighting equipment hould be made available and what to do in a crisis.

Non-appearance Speakers, entertainers, acts or bands could be elayed or not turn up at all. This could be a serious problem ecause this is what people have come to the event for. It may be ossible to delay the start, have reserve speakers or acts, refund money (a last resort) or postpone the event.

Transport disruption Many people travelling to an event may be seriously delayed by traffic congestion or disruption to public transport. If such a problem affects a large enough number of people it may be possible to delay the start of an event. For example, football clubs have been known to delay the kick-off time for matches because supporters travelling to the match have been seriously delayed.

Some general tips on contingency plans are outlined in Table 2.

Insurance

When staging an event it may be prudent to take out certain insurance policies. By paying an insurance company a sum of money in advance (a premium) it is possible to get financial compensation if something goes wrong. One type of insurance that might be recommended is public liability insurance. This is a policy which provides protection if someone sues the event organisers following an incident. For example, a spectator may be injured at an event and claim compensation. Public liability insurance will cover such a claim. Insurance companies offer a range of different cover which may be helpful for organisers. Some examples are shown in Figure 3.

Table 1 *Help with raising finance*

Help	Suggestions
Help from the educational insitution	If the event is connected to the school or college in some way, it may allocate some funds to help get started or provide a loan which can be repaid after the event. This would be the first source to explore.
Help from other organisations	If the event is being staged to raise money for a good cause, businesses and local dignitaries can be targeted for donations of money or prizes. They may also be interested in sponsorship deals where businesses pay to have their name associated with the event. When approaching business people and others for help the standard of personal presentation and conduct is very important. It is best to approach people in person after making an appointment. **Permission from teachers must also be obtained for security reasons.**
Fund raising	Simple fund-raising activities around school or college are a good way of raising finance which does not have to be repaid. They may take a lot of effort but the amounts raised might be quite surprising. Alluring and imaginative prizes will help.
Ticket sales	If tickets are going to be sold for an event everything possible should be done to generate advanced sales. Discounts for early booking and bulk purchases might be given.
Borrowing	If money is going to be borrowed it is important to make a professional application. This will involve putting together appropriate documentation such as cash flow forecasts and detailed plans for the event.

Table 2 *General tips on contingency planning*

Area	Suggestions
Responsibility	It should be clear who takes control in a crisis.
Priorities	Some tasks are more important than others when a crisis occurs. For example, ensuring people's safety is the most important task.
Information	All the information that will be needed to cope with a crisis should be circulated in advance, for example, important telephone numbers and other contacts.
Communication	Crisis can be confounded by poor communication between staff. Every person should be made aware of the problems and how the problems are to be controlled.
Public relations	If the crisis has a public impact the recovery team may be put under pressure, particularly from the media. The first rule in any crisis management and whenever a mistake is made is to be completely open.
Practice	The plan, where practically possible, should be tested. If simulations are used they should be as realistic as possible.

Figure 3 *Types of insurance cover for events*

- Abandonment
- Cancellation
- Public liability
- Postponement
- Adverse weather
- **Insurance**
- Non-appearance
- Damage to the venue
- Denial of access
- Failure of public utilities
- Theft/Accidental damage
- Terrorism (must be purchased separately)

1. Identify some insurance companies and find out if they offer cover for events. Compare the cost of cover provided by the companies for:
   - public liability insurance;
   - cancellation;
   - non-appearance;
   - accidental damage.
2. Write a brief report showing a comparison of premiums between the companies and brief details of the cover provided.

Research task

Meeting the assessment criteria - examiners' guidance

You need to prepare a presentation and write a report which provides evidence of planning an event. This section focuses on financial requirements and contingency planning.

Event example – Comedy night

A group of students is planning a Comedy Night to raise money for a local charity. The students aim to raise £1,000 by selling 400 tickets at £3.50 each. Revenue will also be generated by selling light refreshments and organising an auction. Lots for the auction will hopefully be donated by local businesses. To generate interest in the event it has been widely promoted in the town and three local comedians have been booked for the night costing £100 each. Admission will be by ticket only and access will be restricted to the over sixteen age group. The college hall has been booked to stage the event free of charge.

Mark Band 1 *Your report should provide evidence of planning and an outline of any insurance needs.*
The aim to raise £1,000 was considered to be ambitious but worthy. When persuading local business people to donate prizes for the auction they were often impressed. The cost of staging the comedy night was close to £600. However, £300 of that would not have to be paid out until the night of the event after all the revenue had been received. £100 was needed for promotion, £100 for miscellaneous expenditure such as printing and £100 for insurance. To raise the £300 needed to get started £150 was provided from donations and £150 borrowed from the college. 75% of the tickets for the event were sold in advance. It was decided to take out an insurance policy to provide cover in case any of the comedians failed to appear on the night.

Mark Band 2 *Your report should provide evidence of planning and an identification of essential insurance items together with an identification of non-essential but desirable insurance needs.*
When planning the event it was important to work out the financial requirements. This was carried out by identifying all the costs that would be incurred. After gathering some information from advertisers, insurance companies and local comedians a budget of £600 was planned for the staging of the event. The

biggest item of expenditure was £300 for the comedians. However, this would not have to be paid until they had performed on the night. £100 would be needed for promotion, £100 for insurance and £100 for miscellaneous expenditure such as printing and other materials. It was therefore necessary to raise £300 to get started. The college provided a loan for £150 and a further £150 was obtained from local business people in the form of donations. The question of insurance arose during the planning stages. It was agreed to pay £100 to protect against the non-appearance of the comedians because without these the event would be a complete flop. Public liability insurance was also considered but not taken out. It was felt that the risk to the audience during the event was extremely low.

Mark Band 3 *Your report should provide evidence of planning and an identification of essential insurance items together with an identification of non-essential but desirable insurance needs. There should also be some explanation of the reasons for inclusion and likely costs.*
Once it had been decided that the event was feasible a meeting was held to calculate the cost of staging a comedy night. After gathering some information from advertisers, insurance companies and local comedians, it was agreed that a budget of £600 would be needed to stage the event. The biggest item of expenditure was £300 for the comedians. However, this would not have to be paid until after their performance on the night of the event. The main costs were £100 for promotion, £100 for insurance and £100 for miscellaneous expenditure such as printing and other materials. To raise the £300 to get started the college kindly provided a loan for £150 and a further £150 was obtained from local business people in the form of donations. A plaque at the entrance to the hall on the night of the event would show the names of the businesses that had donated the funds. Some time was sent discussing insurance for the event. Since the event would be a flop if the comedians failed to turn up it was decided to take out some non-appearance cover. The question of public liability insurance was also raised, however, it was decided not to take out any cover because the risk of any incident was considered very low according to the risk assessment carried out. The college was already covered for damage caused by fire.

Portfolio practice · Alton Towers

A group of students is planning to organise a trip for 20 children to Alton Towers for the day. Some of the children have special needs. The trip would be supervised by four trained care workers. This means that 24 places would need to be booked by the students. The students are determined to overcome some of the obstacles such as funding and insurance. The cost of the day out would be met by using a range of financial sources.

(a) **How would the students identify the financial requirements for the event?**

(b) **How might the students raise the money needed to fund the trip?**

(c) **Discuss any contingency plans that might be necessary.**

Planning and communication

Communication is about sending and receiving information. Everyone involved in the organisation of an event will communicate with each other on a regular basis. This is **internal communication**. Event organisers will also have to communicate with people and organisations outside their team such as clients, the local community, businesses, local councils and the media. This is **external communication**. Good communications will help to ensure the smooth running of the event and its preparation.

Effective internal communication will help to:

- avoid mistakes. If a team member misunderstands some instructions when booking a marquee, the wrong size might be booked;
- speed up the completion of tasks. If a team member can contact another with a mobile phone to get vital information, this will avoid having to wait until the next time they meet;
- improve motivation. People will tend to work better if they understand what everyone else in the team is doing and know what is going on.

Good external communication will help to win the support of outsiders. For example, if the aims and objectives of a particular event are communicated to the local community, they are more likely to support it. They might attend the event if invited or make a financial contribution in another way such as a donation or sponsorship. When dealing with outsiders it will be important to ensure good quality communication such as professionally written letters and a courteous telephone manner. In many cases students will be representing their school and college and it will be important to maintain or improve the image of the organisation.

Methods of communication

There is a wide range of ways in which information can be communicated. A lot of communication will be spoken and communication will be carried out face-to-face with colleagues or clients, for example. Information will also be exchanged verbally at meetings and over the telephone. Some communication is visual, through the use of body language, signs or images such as photographs or diagrams. There are numerous electronic methods, such as e-mail, television, surveillance cameras and electronic notice boards. However, when planning an event some of the most important methods of communication will be written. Some of the key examples are outlined below.

Letter

A letter is a formal and flexible method of written communication. It is used mainly for external communication but might be used internally if it is necessary to send confidential information to a colleague. Letters are likely to be produced using a word processor where presentation, grammar, punctuation and spelling can all be checked. Some word processing packages provide standard formats for letters which can then be personalised. This will save time if a lot of letters have to be sent out when organising an event. An example of an appropriate format for a formal or business letter is shown in Figure 1.

Report

A report is a written document used to communicate information formally. Information is presented in a simple way by breaking it down into manageable pieces. This helps the reader to get a picture of what the information is about. Reports are often used to communicate information to decision-makers. Most reports are written according to a standard format. An example of a simple report is shown in Figure 2. The main advantages of using reports to communicate information are that:

- people can study the material in their own time, rather than attending a meeting;
- time that is often wasted in meetings can be better used;
- the report is presented in an impartial way, so conflict can be avoided.

Figure 1 *A example of a formal or business letter*

Crowford Colle
Multan Ro
Crowfc
Berkshire BS9 2

Caldwell Travel Ltd
12 King Street
Crowford BS2 6YH

3rd November 2005

Dear Mr Caldwell,

I am writing to thank you for the £50 donation which you made on behalf of your company. The money will be used help organise a Christmas party for disabled children in ou community.

We will add your company's name to the list of donors which will be printed on the tickets. However, should you wish your donation to remain anonymous please contact on 01776 237768.

Thank you once again for your kind donation.

Yours sincerely

Dilip Soman

(Event coordinator)

Reports often have standard features.

- The first section is formal and shows who the report is for, who has written it, the date it was written and the title.
- A short introduction will explain briefly what the report is about. In this case the report is about a feasibility study for an event.
- The main body of the report should be divided into sections. Each section should address a separate issue. Each section should be given a clear heading. In this case, because the report is a simple one, there is only one section. It is about the main findings of a feasibility study.
- Each section should be broken down into sub-sections and information should be written in short sentences. This makes it easier to read. Each important point could be numbered or presented as a bullet point as in this case.
- Numerical information such as tables, graphs and charts should be presented in an appendix at the end of the report. In this case details of pupil responses are shown in an appendix.
- The conclusion is very important and should aim at bringing together the main points in the report. No new material should be added at this stage. A conclusion is often an action plan, a list of recommendations.

Invitations

Many event organisers want VIPs and other local dignitaries to attend. Their presence helps to promote the event and raise its profile in the community. In some cases they might be invited to make a small contribution such as opening a show or saying a few words of encouragement. Invitations could be sent out in the form of a personal letter. However, if a lot of invitations are being sent out this may take too long. For some events invitations might be printed like tickets. Invitations only contain a limited amount of information. This includes:

- the name of the person being invited;
- the nature of the event;
- the date of the event;
- the event venue;
- the time of the event;
- a contact number.

Many invitations end with the letters RSVP and a name and address. This means that a reply is needed from the person invited to say whether or not they plan to attend. Replies are often important because other people may have to be invited if they are unable to attend. It may also be necessary to know who is attending so that catering can be organised for the exact number. It may also be necessary to organise a seating plan for guests. A number of companies offer invitation services online. They send out invitations electronically. A website for such a company is shown in Figure 3.

Notices

Attaching a notice to a notice board is a cheap and simple way of communicating certain types of information. To communicate internally a notice may be pinned to a notice board to pass on information to other members of the event team. Externally a notice might be placed in a shop window or on a permanent notice board to pass on information to the local community. The

Figure 2 *An example of a simple report*

To: All members of the Event Team
From: Hazel Venables
Title: Initial feasibility study
Date: 1.11.06

Introduction
People in the school were interviewed to see if they would support a talent contest. About 300 responded and the appendix shows the full results.

Main findings
- Lower school pupils said they would like to attend but hardly any of them wanted to be a performer.
- Middle school pupils were very keen. They liked X Factor on the TV and some said they would have a go at performing.
- Senior school pupils were very supportive. They thought it would be good laugh but wanted some proper judges – not teachers. Lots of them expressed an interest in performing.

Recommendations
- The event will be feasible provided it is held in school time
- Performers are likely to be attracted from the older members of the school. Therefore promotion should be directed at these pupils.
- The judges should not be teachers – some local celebrities or peers perhaps.

Figure 3 *An example of a company that sends out electronic invitations*

main problem with notice boards is that some people might miss the notice. Also, the information may not apply to everyone that reads it. Notices may also be removed or defaced before the information has been passed on. Notices cannot easily be used when feedback is required.

Information and communications technology (ICT)

The development of ICT in recent years has revolutionised communications and information handling. It is now possible to deliver messages instantly, over great distances and to a large number of people at the same time using a variety of electronic media.

The Internet The Internet is a vast source of information for people who have access to a computer. The introduction of broadband in the UK means that websites containing images and text can be quickly viewed and information can be downloaded. The Internet can be used in a variety of ways when organising an event. Some examples are shown in Table 1.

> **Table 1** *Uses of the Internet when organising an event*
>
> - Searches can be made for contractors that supply catering, security and other services.
> - Information about performers, speakers, bands, entertainers and musicians, for example, can be found.
> - A website might be set up to promote an event. For example, the London Marathon has its own website. The home page is shown in Figure 4.
> - It may be possible to take bookings for an event using a website. This will cut down on administration costs and allow people to buy tickets 24/7.
> - Information about certain types of events such as fund-raising activities might be posted on websites. This information might be helpful when planning a particular event.

E-mail Many individuals, businesses and other organisations have e-mail addresses. They allow organisers of events and other individuals to communicate with each other instantly. It is possible to send text, data, graphs, charts, photographs, audio material and video material between e-mail addresses. Information sent from one email address, via a computer, modem and telephone to another address is stored by a 'server' - a computer dedicated to storage and network facilities. It stays at that address until it is picked up by the receiver. For example, if the event coordinator was working at home in the evening, copies of a completed report could be sent to all other members of the team as soon as it was finished. Recipients might download the report later that evening or in the morning before leaving home. This would allow the report to be accessed before they all met again.

Other electronic methods of communication A wide range of other electronic methods of communication might be used when planning and preparing for an event. Some examples are shown in Figure 5.

Figure 4 *Using a website to promote an event*

Handling information electronically

When organising an event it will be necessary to collect and process information. Computers can be used to gather, collate, sort, manipulate, store, retrieve and transmit written, numerical and visual information extremely efficiently. Computers have a wide range of applications when it comes to handling information. Many of these can be used when planning and organising an event. Some examples are given below.

Figure 5 *Electronic communication*

- Fax machines
- Mobile phones
- Paging devises
- Walkie talkies
- Lap top computers
- **Electronic communication**
- Answerphon[e]
- Multi-media communications
- Electronic notice boards
- Videoconferencing and teleconferencing

Table 2 *A database showing details of people that have bought tickets for an event*

Surname	First name	Address	Town	Age	Tel no.	Ticket Nos
Rossi	Aldo	12 Hatch Way	Oxford	23	08625 998114	23-25
Ackroyd	Ian	34 Troy Lane	Oxford	43	08625 336719	43-47
Arnold	Peter	21 Field Close	Swindon	32	04528 277764	34
Best	Kari	9 Church Street	Oxford	26	08625 887791	26-30
Bellamy	Jean	78 Compton Way	Banbury	54	05678 534677	2-3

Databases and records

It may be helpful to set up databases when handling information. A database is just an electronic filing system. It allows huge quantities of data to be stored. The information is set up so that it can be stored, updated and recalled instantly when needed. Table 2 shows an extract from a database set up by the organisers of an event. It gives details about people who have bought tickets for an event. The collection of common data is called a file. A file consists of a set of related records. In the database in Table 2 all the information on Peter Arnold, for example, is a record. The information on each record is listed under headings called a field, e.g. surname, first name, address, town, age etc.

It is possible to keep a wide range of records on databases like this when organising an event. Some examples are given below.

- Details of financial transactions.
- Contact details of team members and staff.
- Mailing lists for sending leaflets to potential clients, for example.
- Details of suppliers.
- Inventory records of equipment, for example.

Spreadsheets

Certain types of numerical data can be presented using a spreadsheet. A spreadsheet allows a user to enter, store and present information in a grid on a computer screen. Most spreadsheets are used to manipulate numerical data. They may be used by event organisers to aid decision making. One well known spreadsheet programme is Excel. For example, cash flow forecasts can also be produced using Excel. One of the problems when preparing cash flow forecasts is that if one of the entries needs to be changed, a lot of other numbers in the forecast, such as the closing balances, have to be changed as well. However, when using a spreadsheet, if an entry is changed any other numbers that are affected will be changed automatically. This saves a lot of time. When preparing and organising an event spreadsheets could be used to:

- prepare cash flow forecasts;
- draw up budgets;
- compile cost schedules for resources and;
- analyse break-even information.

There is a number of advantages of spreadsheets.

- Numerical data is recorded and shown in a clear and ordered way.
- Editing allows numbers, text and formulae to be changed easily to correct mistakes or make changes to the data.
- It is easy to copy an entry or an entire series of entries from one part of the spreadsheet to another. Or from one spreadsheet to another. This is particularly useful when one number has to be entered at the same point in every column, for example.
- Numbers can be added, subtracted multiplied and divided anywhere on the spreadsheet.
- Spreadsheets calculate the effect of entry changes automatically. This is sometimes referred to as the 'what if' facility. For example, what would happen to cell X (closing cash balance) if the entry in cell D (promotion cost) increased by 10%? The answer can be found instantly.
- Many spreadsheets allow users to generate graphs and charts from the data.

Specialist software

Software producers have developed a wide range of applications for computers to help business people and others improve efficiency. It is possible to buy 'off the shelf' packages that are flexible and can be used by different types of businesses or people. Event organisers may be able to use one of the standard packages for bookings and reservations. On the other hand some software is highly specialised and developed for just one user. Some events may attract thousands of people, such as, all the different events for the Olympic Games will be held at different times in different venues over a two week period. It will be necessary to sell thousands and thousands of tickets in total for these events. To help process ticket bookings and reservations computers will be needed. In this case specialist software is likely to be developed to cope with such a complex ticket administration process. However,

Figure 6 *Booking and reservation software*

hotels, theatres, football clubs, event organisers and other organisations may buy software to facilitate the task of booking and reservations. A company which specialises in this type of software is shown in Figure 6.

Monitoring and data identification

When planning an event it will be important to monitor progress. For example, it is important to know that certain tasks have been completed on time and whether certain tasks have been delayed. This is because some tasks are critical and if held up the whole project will be delayed. Gantt charts (see section 55) and critical path analysis can be used to do this. However, with large events using these methods may be time-consuming. However, with computers and software based on Gantt charts and critical path analysis, it is much easier. The whole planning process can be monitored using such applications. Online booking can also be used to monitor progress. It can provide information about the number of seats that have been sold and how many are left to sell.

Identifying trends and features from data stored is also important. For example, it may be planned to play music from charts in the last year at an evening gathering. However, the data many indicate the average age of people will be over 40. This many mean a change in music will be necessary to cater for tastes.

Projecting

It is sometimes helpful to make predictions about the behaviour of variables in the future. For example, what might happen to attendances at Premier League football matches in the next two or three years. One way of estimating this is to use back data as a basis for projection. This involves identifying a trend in past data and projecting this trend into the future. This is called **extrapolation**. There is a mathematical technique which can be used to make such projections. Computer programmes can be used to do this. It might be helpful for event organisers to make projections about future attendances at big events to help assess their feasibility, for example.

1. Using your contacts or the Internet, identify two companies that sell computer software for project or event planning and calendaring.
2. For one or two specific programmes write a brief report:
   - stating the cost of the programme;
   - explaining the functions of the programme;
   - outlining the benefits of the programme.

Research task

Meeting the assessment criteria - examiners' guidance

You need to prepare a presentation and write a report which provides evidence of planning an event. This section focuses on communication and ICT.

Event example – Health fun day

Shoretown Youth Services asked a group of sixth form students to organise a health fun day for teenagers. The idea was to promote exercise, sport, good diet and a healthy lifestyle to local youths in Shoretown. A range of activities and attractions will include climbing wall, fencing, archery, swimming, tag-rugby, football, dance, aerobics and many others. The event would take place in Shoretown Leisure Centre which would be available free of charge. Staff at the leisure centre would also be able to supervise youths during the activities. There would be no charge for this either. It is hoped that the organisers would invite experts in the field of diet and healthy living to set up stalls, give brief talks and answer questions. The event would have to be staged on a Sunday afternoon.

Mark Band 1 *Your report should provide evidence of planning and an outline of communication methods used and any ICT.*
When planning an event effective communication will help to make things run more smoothly. It is important to keep everyone informed and exchange information freely. For internal communication meetings, mobile phones and e-mails were used.

For external communication were written. An example of one is shown in Figure 7. This was used to invite a local doctor to talk about the importance of exercise to maintain a healthy heart. The letter was produced using a computer. ICT was also used to produce a budget on a spreadsheet and get information off the Internet.

Mark Band 2 *Your report should provide evidence of planning and demonstrate a good understanding of the role played by communication and ICT.*
Effective communication is essential when people are working together as a team to achieve a common aim. They need to keep in touch to exchange important information, get help and support when needed and relay the progress that each member is making. When organising the health fun day team members were communicating on a daily basis using mobile phones and emails. Regular meetings were held and occasionally notices were used to jog people's memories. Once a fortnight the event coordinator wrote a short progress report so that everyone was up to date with what was going on. This was sent by e-mail to all team members as soon as it was finished – often at a weekend when college was closed. External communications were also necessary. The event team designed an advert for the fun day which was posted on a number of appropriate websites such as the Shoretown Leisure Centre, local schools and youth organisations. Formal letters were also sent out, like the one in Figure 7.

Figure 7

Shoretown Sixth Form College
Centenary Road
Shoretown DR3 5RT

Shoretown Health Centre
45 Tenby Street
Shoretown DR7 3RE

4 November 2005

Dear Doctor Hussain

You may be aware that a health fun day is being organised on 17.12.05 for young people in the town. The purpose of the day is to promote a healthy lifestyle for young people. We wondered if you could give a short talk during the event about the importance of exercise to maintain a healthy heart?

We would expect the talk to last about 30 minutes. Your talk would be one of a series starting at 2.00pm in a sports hall annex which seats 50 people.

We plan to telephone you next week to see if you are able to attend and, if so, make final arrangements.

Yours sincerely

Gordon Timmings

(Event coordinator)

Mark Band 3 *Your report should provide evidence of planning and demonstrate a comprehensive understanding of the role played by communication and ICT.*

Without effective communication, serious problems can arise when organising a substantial event like the health fun day. Good communication will help avoid mistakes, speed up the completion of tasks and improve motivation. The event team worked very well together and internal communication was outstanding. A range of communication methods was used such as meetings, mobile phones, e-mail and notices. Written communication was essential because it was often necessary to keep a record of the message. For example, the fortnightly progress reports sent out by the coordinator contained some important information which needed to be referred back to at a later date. The reports sometimes contained financial information, such as budgets, which were presented on a spreadsheet. All this was transmitted by e-mail, usually at the weekend. External communication was undertaken using letters, e-mail and the telephone. For example, letters were used to invite speakers. An example of a letter sent to a doctor is shown in Figure 7. This was produced using a word processing package on a computer. The Internet was also used. For example, an advert was placed on a number of key websites to help promote the event. The advert also contained a link to a questionnaire which gave young people an opportunity to give information about their lifestyle. A mark of between 1 – 10 was given to show them how healthy they were. This link was very popular and generated a lot of interest and discussion.

Portfolio practice · Friquess

Jennifer Hartley owns a boutique in Cannock called Friquess. The shop sells expensive clothes and fashion accessories for women. In the spring of 2005 Jenny invested £20,000 buying some of the latest fashion designs from Milan. She wanted to launch the new range extravagantly and raise the profile of the boutique in the town. She asked her younger sister, who was at college, to put together a team and organise an evening event to achieve these aims. Jennifer wanted to invite 150 local business women and dignitaries. It was hoped that the 150 people who attended would form the beginning of a new customer database for Jenny which she could used for mailshots in the future. It was hoped that the evening would comprise of:

- a welcome reception including canapes and pink champagne;
- a mini-fashion show where some of the Milanese outfits would be on display;
- classical background music to give an air of sophistication;
- some sales of outfits and accessories, hopefully.

(a) **Explain whether it would be better to use invitations or letters to invite guests.**
(b) **Discuss THREE methods of internal communication** that might be used by the team when planning the event.
(c) **Analyse the value of a customer database for Friquess.**

The importance of marketing

Most events need to be marketed in some way. The success of an event can depend significantly on the quality of marketing used. Arguably, the most important aspect of the marketing mix when it comes to staging an event is **promotion**. The methods of promotion used may depend on the nature of the event and the size of the advertising budget. For example, large national or international events will have huge advertising budgets and use a variety of advertising media including the television. On the other hand, the promotion of a school disco is likely to rely on notices, announcements and posters around the school. Some events may be staged for a small and select group of individuals and attendance might be compulsory. If this is the case promotion is not likely to be needed. For example, a Business Studies conference organised for three local schools and colleges, where all Business Studies students have to attend in school time, is not likely to need much promotion. However, for events that involve people donating money or paying for entertainment or other services, promotion is crucial. Figure 1 shows adverts used in local and national newspapers to promote events.

impact and may be lost amongst lots of other adverts on the same page. They also lack movement and sound. National newspapers may be used for advertising a limited number of large events.

Magazines For some types of event magazines are an ideal advertising media. Adverts in magazines are colourful, can be linked to features and people can refer back to them. They can also be directed at specific target groups because most magazines are specialised. A gymkhana could be advertised in 'horsey' magazines such as the *Horse & Hound*, *Horse*, *Eventing* and *Your Horse*. However, magazines are often crammed with adverts and lack movement and sound.

Posters and billboards A lot of events are advertised using these methods. They are useful for passing on short, sharp messages, they are seen repeatedly and can be directed at most groups. However, they can only transmit a limited amount of information and it is difficult to measure how effective they are. For small events, notices might be useful. For example, a notice pinned to a school notice board can help to give details about a forthcoming event. It is also a cheap method of advertising. Figure 2 shows an example of a poster being used to advertise an event.

Figure 1 *Advertisements to promote events*

Figure 2 *Advertising a forthcoming event using posters*

Advertising

Businesses and other organisations have a wide range of media to choose from when advertising their products and services. However, most event organisers are likely to have rather less choice.

Newspapers For local events placing adverts in local newspapers is a popular method of advertising. It is relatively cheap, people can refer back to the advert and details of the event can be communicated effectively. However, newspaper adverts may lack

Internet The Internet is a flexible method of advertising. This is because information about events can be updated very easily. It is also relatively cheap to set up and can be used to target particular groups of people. For example, a link from a school or college website could be made to give information about a forthcoming event. However, adverts on the Internet may have a limited audience and technical difficulties such as connection and viewing may be a problem. Large events are likely to have their own web site. Figure 3 shows the website for the Southport Flower Show which is a national event.

Figure 3 *Using the Internet to promote an event*

Radio Local radio is growing in popularity with advertisers. It enables the use of sound, is relatively cheap and can be used to target particular groups such as younger audiences. Local events can be promoted quite effectively using local radio stations. However, adverts are not visual, they may not capture the audience's attention and interruptions to radio shows may be irritating to some.

Television Most organisers would not consider using the television to advertise their events. It would be too expensive. Only very large national or international events such as big sporting events are likely to be promoted on television. However, when it is used the effect might be significant. Creative TV adverts can attract the viewer's attention and have an impact. They could show footage of past events, for example. They can reach a vast audience and messages can be reinforced by continuous advertisements. They can also prompt an immediate reply if a telephone number or website address is part of the advert. However, messages may be short-lived and people may ignore adverts by leaving the room when they are broadcast.

Other methods of promotion

Advertising is not the only way to promote an event. Other methods of promotion may be used.

Sales promotions These are incentives to encourage people to attend an event or make a financial contribution. Sales promotions are very popular in business and they include coupons and loyalty cards, competitions, product endorsements, product placing, free offers and special credit terms. Only some of these are likely to be used when promoting events. Money-off coupons in local newspapers, discounts for advanced tickets and bulk purchases and free gifts are some possible examples. Figure 4 shows a coupon placed in a newspaper offering £1 off per pitch at a car boot sale.

Figure 4 *Money-off coupon used to promote a car boot sale*

Public relations Organisers can often use the media to raise the awareness of a forthcoming event. Information about an event can be released to the media which they might use in their reports and programmes. For example, local newspapers are often keen to communicate information to the local community about forthcoming events, as shown in Figure 5.

Direct mailing This involves sending information about an event through the post. For most events the materials used will probably be a standard leaflet giving details of the event. They may be delivered by the event organisers or a team of volunteers. In a minority of cases a personal letter might be sent to a person telling them about an event. Direct mail is also being sent using e-mails. Annual events might make use of databases when direct mailing. Databases containing contact details of people that have attended the event in the past might be used for direct mailing purposes. One of the problems with direct mailing is that many

Figure 5 *Newspaper reports about a forthcoming events*

Figure 6 *Examples of merchandising used to help promote a film*

people object to the amount of paper that comes through their letter boxes. Many just pick it up and immediately throw it away.

Sponsorship This method of promotion plays a big role in many events. It is often an important source of finance for events. Businesses and other organisations may pay to have their name associated with the event or the organisation staging it. For example, in 2004 Travelex, the foreign exchange company, spent around £5m sponsoring the Toyota Formula One racing team, the Cricket World Cup coverage on Sky, the Travelex season of £10 tickets at the National Theatre and the Rugby World Cup coverage on ITV. Sponsorship does not have to be in the form of money. Businesses might make donations of goods and services for prizes, equipment and other resources. For example, a business might donate a set of football shirts sporting their name or logo for a team entering in an event. Sponsors will pay a lot of money if an event is televised. They see it as a cost-effective means of getting widespread exposure.

Merchandising It is quite common at events to sell products which are associated with the event. This might include T-shirts, other clothing, mugs, toys, pens, models and books. The products will carry the event's logo or name. Sales of these products help to generate more revenue for the event and raise its profile. In some cases these products are given away free purely as a means of promotion. Some examples of merchandising are shown in Figure 6.

Factors influencing the choice of promotion

It is likely that organisers will use a combination of the methods described here. The use of several different methods will help to have a bigger impact. However, there is a number of factors that will influence the choice of method.

The size of the event Large events that are trying to generate interest right across the nation may use some of the national advertising media such as national newspapers or even television. On the other hand local or regional events are likely to use local newspapers or local radio for example. Small events are more likely to use leaflets and posters.

The nature of the event Some promotional methods are better suited to certain types of event. For example, business sponsors often favour sporting events and fund-raising events. Some events may be exclusive. For example, a school disco would only be promoted within the school community and the methods chosen would reflect this, such as posters and notices around the school being favoured perhaps.

Advertising budget and cost The more money an event allocates to advertising and other forms of promotion, the more choice it will have. Also, some advertising media, such as television is so expensive that only a few events could ever afford it. Many cheap forms of promotion such as leaflets and posters are very popular.

Technology Increased ownership of personal computers has seen a huge increase in advertising on the Internet in recent years. Event organisers are likely to exploit technological developments as they become available at the right price.

Invitations and guest lists

Invitations are really a form of direct mail. However, they are more formal and personal. Some invitations will be in the form of a letter whereas others may be specially printed cards like wedding invitations. They are likely to be used for two reasons.

- If an event is organised for a relatively small and select group of people, like a party or a business event like a product launch or exhibition, invitation cards might be used. These may be printed on good quality card but personalised by having people's names hand-written on them. With some events invitations might be given out like free tickets. This is to encourage attendance and is more of a promotion.
- At many events it is likely that local dignitaries, officials and other VIPs will be invited, such as the Mayor, the Chamber of Commerce, School Governors or Celebrities. These people might help to raise the profile of an event if they attend. They might also be asked to make a small contribution, such as

opening the event, making a short speech or presenting awards and prizes. These guests are likely to receive a letter of invitation. The letter will contain more detail than a printed invitation card and will aim to make the guest feel more important.

Many events have guest lists drawn up by the organisers. This is simply a list of people who have been invited to an event and are likely to attend. They might be used by people working on the door to prevent unauthorised entry. They could also help with security issues or just to check the arrival of guests so that the organisers know who has turned up.

Meeting the assessment criteria - examiners' guidance

You need to prepare a presentation and write a report which provides evidence of staging the event and evaluating your own contribution. This section focuses on the contribution made to promotion.

Event example – West Budbury Fishing Competition

West Budbury is a small town close to the River Trent in Nottinghamshire. Sixth form students at the small secondary school in the town have decided to organise a fishing competition. They plan to make it an open competition and offer prizes for different age groups. This will be the first time such an event has been organised but the students want to establish it as an annual event, hoping that it will grow in the future. To make it a success the event team believe that promotion is very important. They also think that good prizes will attract entrants and hope that local businesses will provide sponsorship in the form of cash, goods and services. It is proposed to invite a 'famous' angler to award prizes to the winners.

Mark Band 1 *You must demonstrate active participation in the staging of the event together with a basic description and subjective evaluation of your own performance.*

A special meeting was held to discuss the promotion of the fishing competition. There were six students at the meeting and one of my jobs was to keep the minutes. A lot of time was spent discussing the different promotion options. There was a £100 budget for advertising and promotion. After a lengthy debate it was decided to spend £80 on some large posters which could be positioned around the town on notice boards, in shop windows and in public buildings, such as libraries, doctors' surgeries and public houses. It was also proposed to set up a database to keep a record of all the entrants. This could be used in future years if the event is held again. In addition to taking the minutes at the meeting, I helped to pin up the posters around the town and was therefore actively involved in the promotion of this event.

Mark Band 2 *You must demonstrate a positive and sustained contribution to the staging of the event together with an explanation of your own role and an objective evaluation of your own performance resulting in a reasoned conclusion.*

During the planning process a meeting was held to discuss the issue of promotion. The event team believed that promotion would be really important because the event being organised was the first of its kind in the community. If it was a success first time around it might become an annual event. Various promotion methods were discussed at the meeting but we finally decided that £80 of the £100 advertising budget should be spent on posters which would be displayed around the town. I took responsibility for the design of the poster since graphic design is a hobby of mine. I spent two weeks on the task and came up with four potential designs. They were all bright and colourful and included a fishing theme. At another meeting there was a vote on which design should be printed. Fortunately my favourite one was chosen and after a few modifications it was sent off to be printed. My lead with the poster design provides evidence of my positive and sustained contribution to the staging of the event. I think that my contribution was very good because my work has gone to print.

Mark Band 3 *You must demonstrate a significant sustained participation in the staging of the event together with a detailed explanation of your own role and an objective evaluation with justified conclusions.*

A meeting was held to decide how the £100 advertising budget should be allocated. Various promotion methods were discussed, such as local radio, local newspapers, leaflets and sponsorship. It was agreed that local businesses would be asked to sponsor the event by donating money, goods and services for prizes. It was also decided to spend £80 on some well designed and brightly coloured posters that would be professionally printed. I also suggested that some free publicity could be obtained by giving some information to the local press. The event coordinator asked me to write a short article about the event which could be passed on to the *West Budbury Chronicle*. It is shown here.

My article appeared in the local newspaper with hardly any changes. I felt very proud to have some work published and think that this shows a significant contribution to the promotion of the event. As result of the article a number of letters appeared in the paper the week after saying that they would support the event.

West Budbury will hold its first ever Annual Fishing Competition on Saturday June 18th, at Long Meadow. The event is being organised by a group of sixth form students from West Budbury High School as part of their Applied 'A' Level Business Studies course. The competition, which starts at 7.30 am, is open to all-comers but children under the age of 11 must be accompanied by adults. Prizes will be awarded for the under 11s, 11 to 13, 14 to 16, 17 to 19 and the over 19s. Mike Bamber, a local angler, said 'This is a great idea from the students ... . It will be good for the community to get together and enjoy a bit of fun'. The event is being sponsored by a number of local businesses and prizes will be awarded by Charlie Booker, the ex-football player, who is a keen angler and a local hero.

Portfolio practice · College Reunion

Calthorpe Sixth Form college was contacted by some ex-students to see if a reunion could be organised at the end of the summer term. The job of organisation was placed in the hands of a student event team. They did some research by investigating how other colleges organised such an event. This was very helpful. The college hall was chosen as a venue, a catering company was approached and some entertainment booked. To promote the event the following measures were taken.

- Invitations were sent out to the last known addresses of 512 students who left in 1998.
- The event was advertised in the local newspaper.
- The event was advertised on an Internet link on the college website called Old Calthorpians.
- An article was sent to the local newspaper about the reunion including contact numbers for anyone interested.

(a) Describe the details that would be included on the invitations that were sent out.

(b) What are the advantages and disadvantages of using the Internet to promote the event?

(c) What influenced the choice of promotional methods used in this case?

The day of the event

As the day of the event approaches, and on the day itself, people involved in the planning and organisation of the event are likely to feel nervous. This is natural and a positive thing. It means that people are taking the job seriously and are alert and focused. During the event the role of the organisers is likely to change. Before the day of the event most of their work involves planning and preparation. On the day of the event organisers may be involved in a range of different activities depending on the role they are playing. For example they may be:

* looking after guests and VIPs;
* stewarding;
* handling cash and keeping records;
* supervising children;
* dealing with contractors;
* dealing with client or customer problems;
* supervising other staff;
* collecting litter and cleaning up;
* participating in the event, in a sponsored walk for example.

Organisation

During the event a number of operational issues have to be addressed to ensure that it runs smoothly.

Teams Being well organised on the day of the event is often the key to success. Many organisational issues will have been covered during the planning stages. For example, event organisers and their staff or helpers are likely to be divided into working teams. Provided a team has a strong leader and clear aims and objectives, people tend to work better when organised in this way. They will support each other, come up with more ideas and are better motivated. Communication might also be more effective.

Briefing Before the event starts it will be important for the event coordinator to hold a final briefing. For a small event everyone involved in the organisation and preparation might attend. However, for a large event it might be better for team leaders to meet with the coordinator and then hold team briefings to 'trickle down' information. The purpose of a final briefing is to:

* check that everyone has turned up on the day;
* motivate and galvanise the team or teams;
* pass on information regarding last-minute changes, for example;
* provide an opportunity for last-minute questions or queries.

Allocating individual roles During the planning process people involved in the organisation of the event will have been allocated tasks to complete or roles to play. For example, one team member may have been responsible for keeping records of all financial transactions and handling cash. On the day of the event some people will have different roles as explained above. It is important that everyone knows what is expected of them on the day. To help clarify people's roles a simple checklist can be drawn up. Table 1 shows an extract stating the roles and tasks allocated to a group of students who organised a charity auction to raise money for a local hospice. Notice that some tasks require more than one person.

Breaks and relief It is important that the people who organise the event also enjoy it. To help ensure that they have a good time a system of breaks from work should be organised. The system must be fair so that everyone has the same opportunity to enjoy the event. If people are organised into teams each team can draw up its own work schedule. A rota system might be used. It is important to ensure that all stations are covered when someone

Table 1 *Individual roles and tasks during the day of an event*

Task or role	Name	Comment
Greet and host VIPs and other distinguished guests	Amanda Li Phillip Watson	Ensure that everyone is formally introduced and wears name badges.
Greet and assist auctioneer	Greg Carter	Check before arrival that all the documentation needed is available.
Cashiers	Susan Williams Pavel Novotny	Store cash in cash box and keep locked at all times.
Stewards	Shane Hooper Sharon Bee	Must wear stewards' badges.
Recorder	Helen Sharpe	Record the names and addresses of all successful buyers along with the lot numbers.
Catering	Abdi Bili	Only allow authorised people into kitchen area.

is off on a break. Equally, everyone in the team should stick to the schedule and return to a station at the agreed time.

Communication

On the day of the event effective communication will be essential. If the venue is small, such as a school hall, communication among team members should not be a problem. For much of the time they will be able to see each other and communicate face-to-face. However, as the size of the venue grows communications may become more difficult. For example, if a 10K sponsored run is being organised, communications along the route and at different sites near the route, may be more demanding and require a number of communication channels and methods. Some tips on communication during the event are shown in Table 2.

Table 2 *Tips on effective communication during the event*

- Have a clear chain of command so that everyone knows who they are accountable to.
- Use formal communication channels and ensure that everyone understands how to use them. Train people if necessary.
- Check that all communication aids such as mobile phones, pagers and PA systems are in working order before the event begins.
- If an event is organised on a single site, 'walkie talkies' or mobile phones are recommended as good methods of communication.
- Do not argue in front of guests VIPs, spectators and other people that are there to enjoy the event.
- For large events it may be useful to appoint someone to control and coordinate communications.
- Have a contingency plan ready if communications begin to break down.

Customer service

On the day of the event many of the organisers, helpers and staff will deal with customers or clients. These will be the people who participate in the event or attend as spectators. Everyone who comes into contact with customers must understand the importance of customer service. Customer service is all about

---

Table 3 *Examples of customer service at an event*

- Giving some directions to baby-changing facilities.
- Conducting transactions at a stall, e.g. serving refreshments.
- Helping people to their seats.
- Giving extra assistance to people with special needs.
- Giving advice, e.g. explaining where the best place is to get a taxi home.
- Helping someone to fill in their application form when registering for a sponsored run, for example.
- Reassuring a lost child.

---

looking after customers and meeting their needs and wants. To help people enjoy themselves more at an event the organisers might aim to exceed customer expectations. What are the features of good customer service?

- Making sure that people get what they are paying for.
- Being courteous, friendly and helpful to customers.
- Dealing with problems sensitively and in a practical way.
- Reassuring customers when they have doubts.
- Making sure customers feel important and cared for.

Some examples of customer service at an event are shown in Table 3.

Customer service issues

There are certain issues relating to customer service that must be dealt with if an event is to be successful.

Training It is possible that many of the people involved in the organisation and staging of an event have no experience in customer service. Because customer service is so important, it may be necessary to train people. This will help people deliver better customer service at the event and also equip them with new skills. Since an event is likely to be a 'one-off' experience, on-the-job-training cannot be used. It may be necessary to bring in a specialist to provide training. This may be expensive unless someone from a willing company can be persuaded to provide training free of charge. However, allocating some money to pay for training in customer services may be money well spent.

Handling complaints If things go wrong at an event, organisers and their helpers and staff have to be prepared. Some examples of the types of things that customers might complain about at an event are outlined below.

- Queuing is a common problem. People can get agitated when they have to queue to get in at events. At large events there could also be health and safety issues to consider if queues are large.
- Overbooking might occur if the number of tickets sold is greater than the number of places available. People may think they are going to lose out.
- The quality of entertainment might be questioned. For example if customers have paid money to see some comedians and they are not funny, they may want their money back.
- Delays during an event can be a source of irritation. For example, if people have turned up to listen to a speaker and the speaker is an hour late, this could cause inconvenience to many customers. They may get bored waiting or have other engagements later.

Handling complaints requires staff to be composed and sympathetic. Handling face-to-face complaints can be particularly difficult if customers become angry or abusive. Handling complaints is likely to be an important part of any customer service training. One approach to handling complaints is summarised in Figure 1.

Personal presentation If someone is likely to be involved in providing customer service, it is important to look presentable.

- Dress. Appearance is important because it is the first thing customers will notice. Customers may make judgements on the quality of an event when they see and deal with staff. It is important that staff at events can be distinguished from other

Figure 1 *Handling complaints*

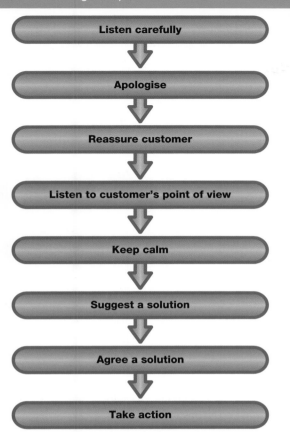

people. Even though it may not be cost-effective for an event to provide all organisers, helpers and staff with a uniform, it will help if everyone wears the same type of clothing. It may be possible to get a sponsor to pay for some printed T-shirts which everyone could wear. Some staff might wear specialist clothes. For example, a steward might wear a yellow fluorescent jacket.

*   Personal hygiene. Appearance is not just to do with what clothes are worn, it can also depend on personal hygiene and cleanliness. For example, on the day of an event it is important to take a bath or shower, use an anti-perspirant deodorant, wear clean and ironed clothes and ensure that teeth, fingernails and hair are all clean. This is important because when giving

Table 4 *Examples of positive behaviour when dealing with customers*

*   Attending to customers immediately.
*   Greeting customers with a smile.
*   Showing interest in what customers say.
*   Treating customers as individuals and making them feel important.
*   Being patient with difficult, awkward and demanding customers.
*   Making every effort to give customers exactly what they want.
*   Supporting colleagues at the event.

customer service it is possible that customers will be physically close.

*   Attitude and behaviour. People who come into contact with customers must show that they care. Customers are very sensitive to the attitude of staff and the way they behave. Examples of positive behaviour when dealing with customers are shown in Table 4.

Problem solving

During the event most things will go well if everything has been carefully planned. However, minor problems are bound to arise. In some cases an individual organiser or member of staff may be able to deal with it single handed. For example, if a supplier fails to deliver the bread rolls for a hotdog stall, this may be dealt with by the person running the stall, by telephoning a new supplier or using an alternative bread product. However, more difficult problems may need some thought, discussion and debate. One approach to problem solving is summarised in Figure 2.

Figure 2 *An approach to problem solving*

Stay calm/don't panic

Share the problem ┈┈▷ Call in an expert

Look at the facts

Identify possible solutions ┈┈▷ Refer to contingency plan

Decide on a solution and take action

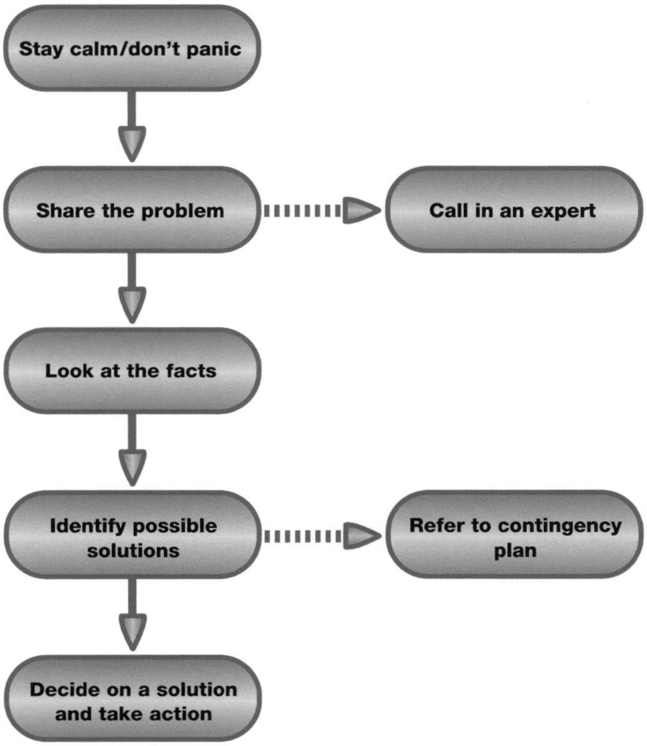

*   When a problem arises it is important to remain composed. It is much more difficult to solve a problem if people panic and lose focus. Staying calm will also send a positive message to other people such as customers.
*   Minor problems may be resolved individually. However, for more serious problems it is often said that 'a problem shared is a problem halved'. A group of people may be better equipped to solve a problem than an individual. This is because the burden of the problem will be shared and more ideas for solutions can be generated. Some problems, such as a computer system crashing, may be technical and need the

services of a technician or other expert. Good planning will ensure that key telephone numbers are at hand.

- An important part of problem solving is gathering information and looking at the facts. Irrelevant information should be ignored. Solving problems often involves looking at causes and effects. Careful thought and systematic analysis will help to get to the root of serious problems. Many problems at events will involve people. Thus, it is important to consider carefully the health and safety aspects of any problem or solution. It will often be important to act quickly.

- After analysing all the information available it may be possible to identify a number of solutions. In some cases it is possible that none of the solutions are entirely satisfactory. It is therefore necessary to choose the solution that derives the most benefit in relation to its cost. Certain types of problems will have been foreseen in the planning stages. In this case there should be a contingency plan which can be referred to immediately.

- Once a solution has been agreed the necessary action must be taken. Again, speed of implementation is likely to be important. Throughout the entire process of solving a problem strong and confident leadership will be required.

Contingency plans

Contingency plans are back-up plans if things go wrong or problems arise. They will have been drawn up when planning the event. It is possible to predict many problems and if a contingency plan is already in place resolving the crisis will be a lot easier. An example of a contingency plan is shown in Figure 3.

Final adjustments

On the day of the event it is possible that some last minute adjustments will have to be made to the day's arrangements. For example, at a village fete it may be necessary to accommodate another two stalls that have arrived at the last minute. Last minute adjustments are common, but need to be dealt with swiftly. They may be addressed at a staff briefing just before the event starts. Some examples of final adjustments are given below.

- Some staff may be absent due to sickness. This may require changes in roles and schedules. It may also mean that some people have to do more than one task. However, the extra workload resulting from staff absence should be shared slowly. Quite often event organisers will plan for absence and have some reserves for cover.

- For outdoor events it may be necessary to set up tents and other covers if rain is forecast. In some cases it may be necessary to move the whole event indoors. Such a radical adjustment will have been prepared for in a contingency plan.

- Adjustments may have to be made to the timing of various activities to cope with last minute changes caused by performers, entertainers or other key people changing their schedule.

- Bigger than expected crowds might arrive. This may require extra supplies of food and drink to be acquired at the last minute. Extra stewards may also be needed.

Figure 3 *An example of a contingency plan*

The plan below has been drawn up to cope with the non-appearance of a speaker at an event. A group of students have arranged for three speakers to give 40 minute talks on their experiences working as accountants. The event is part of a careers convention for 265 sixth form students.

Contingency plan
Non-appearance of a speaker

- It has been arranged for all speakers to arrive at the same time. If a speaker does not appear at the agreed time contact him/her to see if they are on their way.

- If they are going to be late, rearrange the timing or order of the talks so that the late speaker is last. This must be agreed with the other speakers.

- If they are not coming or there is no reply there are three options. They are listed in order of preference.
  1. Prepare a list of questions about a career in accountancy and ask if the two remaining speakers would mind spending 40 minutes answering questions. There may be other questions from the audience.
  2. Show the careers film 'Life as an Accountant'.
  3. End the session 40 minutes early.

1. Obtain some information about customer charters, from businesses, contacts or company websites. These are documents which outline what customers are entitled to when they buy a product from a particular company.
2. Using these charters draw up a customer charter for an event. It could cover things such as:
   - customer service quality;
   - queuing times;
   - refunds;
   - who to contact if help or information is needed;
   - who to contact if a complaint needs to be made;
   - services for people with special needs.

Research task

Meeting the assessment criteria - examiners' guidance

You need to prepare a presentation and write a report which provides evidence of staging the event and evaluating your own contribution.

Event example – Christmas concert

Every year a group of students at Bibury Sixth Form College organise a fund-raising activity. In 2005 it was decided to raise money for children in need so that they could have a more enjoyable Christmas. It was agreed to hold a Christmas concert in the college hall and open it up to anyone in the community. The college orchestra agreed to play a significant part and a group of local musicians offered to support. Refreshments would be provided during an interval and there would be an opportunity to buy hand-made Christmas gifts from a stall.

Mark Band 1 You must demonstrate active participation in the staging of the event together with a basic description and subjective evaluation of your own performance.

On the night of the event one of the stewards was absent. I was asked to join the team responsible for stewarding at the last minute. We had to wear badges to show that we were there to help people when arriving. We had to answer simple questions and give directions. We also had to give assistance to people with special needs. For example, we allowed wheelchair users to access the hall from the fire exit which was right next to the college car park. I enjoyed the role and did a good job.

Mark Band 2 You must demonstrate a positive and sustained contribution to the staging of the event together with an explanation of your own role and an objective evaluation of your own performance resulting in a reasoned conclusion.

One of the important roles during the event was to greet and look after the VIPs and distinguished guests during the evening.

They were greeted at the entrance and shown to a reception room where they were served drinks and nibbles. They were formally introduced to each other and had reserved seats at the front of the hall. During the interval they were invited back to the reception room where they mingled and were served with more drinks and nibbles. They were also introduced to the Principal of the college. I was in charge of this operation and had three assistants. It was important that we looked smart and communicated well with these people. I thought the evening went very well because at the end of the concert one of the VIPs said a special thank you to our team for the high quality of our hospitality.

Mark Band 3 You must demonstrate a significant sustained participation in the staging of the event together with a detailed explanation of your own role and an objective evaluation with justified conclusions.

At the briefing, an hour before the audience was due to arrive, someone mentioned the possibility of mobile phones interrupting the music during the concert. This was something that had been overlooked but needed to be addressed. I suggested printing off some notices and putting them up around the hall. This was agreed and I was given responsibility for quickly designing a notice on a computer and putting them up. It was also suggested that before the concert started the compere should ask the audience politely to check that their phones had been switched off. As a result of these actions, during the event, not one single phone rang. Another problem arose during the interval. The demand for refreshments had been underestimated and queues formed very quickly. I was part of the refreshment team and it became very stressful. People were becoming irritated and worst of all, some people were late returning to the hall because they had been delayed in the refreshment area. Also, at one point some of team, including myself, argued in front of customers. This was unprofessional and demonstrated poor customer service.

Portfolio practice · Day trip to France

A shopping trip to Calais was organised for senior citizens in a Devon village. People paid £45 for their coach fare, ferry crossing and free refreshments on the coach. Unfortunately, the coach broke down on the motorway before reaching the ferry port. This meant a delay while a breakdown service made some roadside repairs to the coach. The result was that the coach party missed their ferry. Another crossing was organised but the time spent in Calais would be reduced by 3 hours. A couple of the party complained but were told quite bluntly that nothing could have prevented the breakdown. 'These things just happen' said one of the organisers.

(a) **What communication measures might be taken during the trip?**
(b) **How might the complaint in the above case be dealt with more effectively?**
(c) **Prepare a contingency plan to deal with a member of the party failing to turn up when the coach was due to return from Calais.**

Contracts

On the day of the event all the plans made in the preceding planning period will come to fruition. To some extent the success of the event will depend on whether contracts are fulfilled by other parties. With large events contracts are very important. For example, at large pop concerts contracts will exist between the promoters (event organisers) and the bands. Some of the details that might appear in such a contract are shown in Figure 1.

Figure 1 *Details that might appear in a contract between a promoter and a band*

- The dates and times of a performance.
- The length of time for a performance.
- Financial arrangements, such as payment details.
- Band's requirements at the venue.
- Get-out clauses – these are conditions which allow either party to withdraw from the contract.
- Penalty clauses – these are usually payments for non-compliance, e.g. how much a band would have to pay to the promoters for non-appearance.

Contracts are useful because they remove a lot of the uncertainty associated with business agreements. For example, when organising an event, such as the pop concert mentioned above, one of the worst things that can happen is for the bands not to turn up. Contracts make this a lot less likely. They also help to avoid disputes, conflict, disagreement and bad feeling.

Contracts for the venue One of the most important contracts of all is likely to be with the owner of a venue. This may be the largest cost of staging an event and there may be a lot of details to agree. The owners of venues may want to secure bookings by contract because they do not want to be left with an empty stadium, for example, because an event organiser has cancelled at the last minute. Equally, the organisers of an event may require a contract because they want a guarantee that the venue will definitely be available on the date of the event. Some examples of details that might appear in a contract between event organisers and the owner of a venue are outlined below.

- dates and times that the venue will be needed;
- insurance liability and details, i.e. who is responsible for damage, fire, etc;
- access details, e.g. when will the venue be available for preparation;
- cost structure, e.g. details of commission on the day or other financial matters;
- payment details, e.g. how much in advance;
- conditions of hire, e.g. who is responsible for cleaning, security, stewarding and ticketing;
- any special requirements e.g. wheelchair access.

Contracts with suppliers In some cases it will be necessary to draw up contracts with suppliers. This might be the case if:
- the value of the goods or services being supplied is very high;
- quality standards or standards of performance are important;
- the details of a business agreement are numerous and complex;
- either, or both, parties want security of agreement.

Also, in an environment where regulation and litigation (legal claims) are increasing, contracts may provide protection for event organisers.

One approach when searching for suppliers at an event is to use **tendering**. This involves inviting suppliers to bid for a contract. For example, an event organiser might require some temporary seating for spectators at a sports event. The organiser will outline the specifications for the contract and invite a number of businesses to give written quotes or bids. The business with the lowest price and best terms will get the contract.

Contracts with personnel When employing staff at an event they may be given contracts of employment. There is no legal obligation to offer casual labourers contracts of employment but they may serve to clarify both the rights of staff and what is expected of them during the event. The details such a contract might include are:
- names of the employer and employee;
- the date on which employment will begin;
- the job title;
- the terms and conditions of employment (this might include a job description).

Contracts of employment do not necessarily have to be written down. There may be a verbal agreement or an 'implied' agreement. Even without contracts of employment personnel still have rights when working. Some examples of the laws that protect workers are shown in Figure 2.

Figure 2 *Examples of laws that cover the employment of staff*

The Health and Safety at Work Act 1974
Sex Discrimination Act 1975
Race Relations Act 1976
Race Relations (Amendment) Act 2000
Disability Discrimination Act 1995
Employment Equality (Religion or Belief) Regulations 2003
Employment Equality (Sexual Orientation) Regulations 2003
Working Time Regulations 1998
Numerous UK/EU health and safety regulations

quality of access

ne important issue when staging an event is equality of access. his means that there should be no discrimination when it comes participation in an event or attending an event. Most forms of scrimination are illegal. For example, it is against the law to revent someone attending an event on grounds of race or nder. There are penalties for breaches in such legislation. In ractical terms organisers must take measures to ensure that eryone, regardless of their personal circumstances, is able to in access to the event. This means that provision must be made r people with special needs. Some examples are given below.

It will be necessary to ensure that wheelchair users can gain access. This might mean providing ramps, lifts, reserved and wider car parking spaces, wider entrances and assistance with mobility.

The visually impaired may need spoken information, information in Braille, enlarged printed information, guidance around facilities and special or adapted equipment.

The hearing impaired may need staff to face them directly and speak very clearly (but not shout) so they can lip read. They may need visual aids, information in sign language and special telephones.

Some people may have difficulties with reading, writing and recognising numbers. For example, they may need help completing application forms to participate in an event.

Some people attending or taking part in an event may not be able to speak English. This is because there are many ethnic groups living in the UK for whom English is not their first language. Consequently provision must be made to assist them. This might involve recruiting some staff who can speak another language. For example, if an event is being organised in an area where there is a large Pakistani community, it would make sense to recruit some staff or helpers that can speak Urdu.

Provision might be made for mothers with babies or very young children. For example, a crèche and baby-changing facilities might be provided. Some events attract a lot of children and their needs must be catered for effectively.

With very large events it may be necessary to recruit staff with xperience of dealing with people with special needs. Generally, ese groups need staff to give them a little more time, respect and patience. It is particularly important not to patronise them by offering help if it is not needed.

Financial recording

Most events will involve spending money and generating revenue. This means that someone will have to take responsibility for keeping records of all financial transactions. This is an important task and requires diligence and accuracy. The following information will have to be recorded.

- Details of all purchases made by the organising team. This includes, the amount paid, a description of the goods or services bought, the date, possibly the name and address of the supplier and possibly an invoice number. All purchases made by the organising team must be supported by a document such as a receipt or an invoice. These documents provide proof of purchase.
- Details of all cash receipts, from the sale of tickets, for example. Ideally, there will be a record kept of the buyer with some contact details. These may be useful if it is necessary to make changes which affect customers.
- Details of any loans, donations, sponsorship or other cash inflows received by the organising team. They must all be recorded.

The records of financial transactions may be sorted and summarised to produce financial statements such as an income and expenditure statement. These are like profit and loss accounts and will show whether the event has generated a surplus or profit. Financial transactions may be recorded using a computer. For very large events, where the amounts of money are substantial, it may be necessary to employ auditors. These are specialist accountants that check the authenticity of the records kept.

Security

One of the reasons why auditors are employed is to ensure that money is used for legitimate purposes. This is to help prevent fraud. People who have access to money cannot use it for their own personal purposes. Auditors will make a series of checks to ensure that expenditure is for business purposes only.

Another security issue is handling cash. At a lot of events cash is collected from entrance fees, payments for refreshments, payments for other activities and fund-raising activities. This cash must be taken to a central point, counted and recorded. It must then be kept secure before it can be banked or taken to a safe. Documentary evidence must be kept relating to the amounts of cash collected. It is important that at least two people are present to verify the amounts and that the room where money is being counted is kept locked. Cash should be banked or taken to a safe as quickly as possible. If the amounts of cash are very large it may be necessary to employ specialist security staff to deal with the movement of cash between a venue and a bank.

Health and safety issues

On the day of the event the health and safety of all the people involved is of great importance. During the planning stages a risk assessment will have been carried out, various laws, regulations and guidelines consulted and the appropriate provisions will have been made, to ensure that the event goes ahead without any danger to people.

> THE WHOLE AREA OF HEALTH AND SAFETY IS AN IMPORTANT ONE. ANYONE ORGANISING AN EVENT SHOULD GET PROPER PROFESSIONAL ADVICE. A TEACHER OR LECTURER WILL PROVIDE INITIAL GUIDANCE FOR STUDENTS IN SCHOOLS AND COLLEGES.

Some examples of the measures which may have to be taken to comply with health and safety legislation are given below.

First aid Many events will require first aid or paramedical facilities. For example, if a sporting event is being organised there may be injuries to contestants that need medical attention. If large crowds are expected at an event the chances of illness or injury to spectators or others will increase. The Ambulance Service and voluntary organisations such St. John Ambulance and the Red Cross may give guidance on what might be required for a particular event. It may also be necessary to ensure that emergency vehicles can gain easy access to an event site.

Trips When organising a trip for school children there is a great deal to consider. There has to be a 'safe' ratio of adults to children in the party, parents have to give permission for their children to attend by signing consent forms, parents must be given adequate information about the trip, adequate insurance must be taken, contingency plans must be made to cope with unforeseen incidents and proper channels of communication established between the organisers and parents. Anyone organising an event involving children should seek professional advice on health and safety. One source of information can be found on the following website, www.schooltravelforum.com/planavisit.pdf.

Stewards Organisers will have to provide a sufficient number of stewards to cater for the size and nature of the event. Good stewarding can improve safety at venues. Stewards can keep crowds of people moving by giving out helpful information and directing people to their destinations. The timing of an event, site characteristics, weather conditions, availability of alcohol, entertainment, crowd surges or the presence of large groups of vulnerable people will increase the need for supervision.

Fire Close attention will have to be paid to the threat of fire. Whenever a crowd is placed in any confined space, an evacuation procedure must be part of the plan. In many cases, particularly if events are held indoors, the premises will already have a plan. However, it may need to be reviewed if a larger number of people than normal are expected. It is also important to ensure that appropriate firefighting equipment is available and that organisers, staff and helpers are trained to use it. The level of provision will obviously depend on the size of the event. Guidance should be sought from the Fire Brigade.

Catering When using outdoor catering services, it is important to ensure that contractors are registered under the **Food Safety Act, 1990** and carry the appropriate any insurance. Food stalls are best positioned away from the main access to an event and densely populated areas. Local councils may give advice on food

providers in their Environmental Health Section.

Toilet facilities Event organisers will be normally obliged to provide toilet, washing and baby-changing facilities for spectators and other people involved. Figure 3 shows the health and safety guidelines recommended for the provision of toilets at an event.

Figure 3 *Health and safety guidelines for the provision of toilets at an event*

The provision of toilets at most events is considered essential, however, without careful thought to health and safety they can create hazards. For example, at a concert in Birmingham, toilets were positioned too close to the stage. A number of people climbed on to the roof for a better view.

Some guidelines include the following.

- Toilets should be sited correctly on flat, even ground.
- Toilets should be positioned away from main attractions, such a stage, to discourage people from climbing on to the roof.
- Disabled toilets must be provided.
- Enough toilets should be provided. The old Wembley stadium had about 300 toilets for a 100,000 people. The new Wemb stadium will have over 3,000 for 90,000 people.
- Toilets should be clean, hygienic and have running water.
- The structure should be safe and all necessary hand rails an steps fitted securely.
- Lighting should be provided when appropriate.
- Sewerage disposal must be adequate – contractors will usu be responsible for this.
- The toilets should be serviced and maintained throughout event.
- Notices distinguishing between ladies and gentleman must clearly visible.
- Direction signs to the toilets must be positioned around th

Source: adapted from Birmingham City Council guidelines.

1. Find out what health and safety measures would be required if a sponsored run was being organised, where part of the course was on a public highway.
2. Write a brief report outlining your findings. Council websites might be a helpful source of information as might charities with links to fund-raising activities.

Research task

Meeting the assessment criteria - examiners' guidance

Event example – Westbourne Carnival

Students at Westbourne Technical College are planning a carnival to celebrate the college's centenary. A significant proportion of the community is expected to turn out to watch a procession of floats, dancing groups, parades and take part in a range of 'fun' activities. It was also planned to have street parties at night and set up food stalls selling a variety of different foods from around the world. There would also be fund-raising activities to help make a sizable contribution to the college swimming pool fund.

Mark Band 1 *You must demonstrate active participation in the staging of the event together with a basic description and subjective evaluation of your own performance.*

The organisation of this event was huge. We started planning at least nine months before the day of the event. One of the tasks I was involved in was helping to get suppliers for certain goods and services. A method called tendering was often used. For example, we wanted a company to supply a number of bouncy castles and similar products for children during the day. Six companies were asked to provide details of how much they would charge and what they would provide. I was responsible for collating all the information from the companies and presenting it at a meeting where the decision was going to be made. I produced some charts and tables which showed the information clearly.

Mark Band 2 *You must demonstrate a positive and sustained contribution to the staging of the event together with an explanation of your own role and an objective evaluation of your own performance resulting in a reasoned conclusion.*

The carnival procession was going to last two hours and wind its way through the streets of Westbourne. It was necessary to get permission from the local council to close some streets for a time. I had to liaise with the council and organise a number of safety measures. For example, some areas would have to be 'coned off' and at one or two 'tight' spots on the route some barriers would be needed to prevent spectators spilling into the procession. The council was very helpful and even offered to supply some of the safety equipment free of charge. I also had to walk along the route and identify any possible hazards such as trees or other obstacles which might 'knock' people off their floats during the procession. The job I had was a very responsible one because it involved health and safety. I think I performed well because I followed the guidelines from the council. I kept everyone informed and there were no complaints from people when the roads were closed. I made sure that an announcement was made in the press about the closure to warn people.

Mark Band 3 *You must demonstrate a significant sustained participation in the staging of the event together with a detailed explanation of your own role and an objective evaluation with justified conclusions.*

I was responsible for financial control during the planning and staging of the event. In the nine months leading up to the event I kept records of financial transactions. Details of every single transaction were recorded on a computer. I developed a security system to ensure that all spending was legitimate. I designed a form which had to be signed by a teacher and one person from the finance team before any purchase over £5 could be authorised. Also, every single purchase had to be supported by a receipt or other business document. On the day of the event my main role was to supervise the collection and counting of donations from spectators and others. Every float taking part in the carnival procession collected money in buckets. After the procession these were brought to the college office where it was counted and bagged up. The money was then put into the college safe ready for banking on Monday morning. Money was also collected from the various fund-raising activities, sponsors, donations from local businesses and revenue from stall holders. Receipts were issued every time an amount of money was received. At the end of the day one of the registered floats had not returned any money. After an investigation it was discovered that the float had not turned up to take part in the procession due to a breakdown. I spent the week after the carnival producing an income and expenditure statement which showed that the event had raised £1,467 for the college swimming pool fund. I enjoyed my role as financial director and felt that the financial recording was undertaken professionally and transparently. All monies were accounted for and our team worked well together. However, I felt that if a target had been set for the fund-raising, more money could have been raised.

Portfolio practice · A day at the test match

A trip was organised for 40 school children to see England play a test match at Old Trafford. A coach was booked and 50 tickets purchased. Two teachers, three other adults and five members of the organising team attended. Two of the children were wheelchair users and a special provision had to be made to meet their needs.

(a) What factors may have been taken into account when selecting personnel to supervise the event?
(b) Analyse the provisions that might have to be made in this case to ensure equality of access.
(c) Discuss the health and safety issues which may have been considered when staging this event.

The end of the event

After an event has been staged it will be necessary to tie up a number of loose ends. The following tasks may need to be completed.

Site clearance The venue used for an event must be left in the same condition as it was before the event. For example, it may be necessary to clear litter and dispose of refuse, remove resources such as lighting, stalls, furniture, and make repairs to any damage done during the event. Failure to restore the venue to its original condition may result in penalty charges. This task of clearing up afterwards should be included in the planning process.

Settle accounts and make final payments After an event it is likely that a number of suppliers, contractors, entertainers or contract staff will have to be paid. In some cases payments may be based on the amount of money taken at the gate. For example, a band may require an initial payment before the event and then a percentage of the takings. Such payments, by their nature, have to be made after the event. It is also common to pay many contractors and suppliers after they have provided their services. It may also be necessary to tie up other financial loose ends such as closing a bank account. If an event has been staged to raise money for a good cause or a charity, arrangements must be made to hand over the money. A formal presentation could be organised which might be attended by the media.

Sell off unused resources It is possible that some of the resources bought by the organisers may not have been used up during the event. If they can be sold then extra money can be raised. For example, leftover drinks bought for a party may be sold off.

Accounts Once all final transactions have been completed a set of final accounts can be prepared. For example, a profit and loss account might be produced which provides a summary of all revenue and expenses and shows how much profit or loss has been made from staging an event. Accounts are also needed to show how money has been spent by the organisers.

Thank you letters It may be necessary to thank people or organisations for their contribution in the planning or staging of the event. This may involve writing letters of thanks to speakers, entertainers, groups that have made donations for example, and other helpers. It is important to thank such people as a matter of courtesy and because you may be representing your school or college. An example of a letter of thanks is shown in Figure 1.

Celebration party The organisers of events often plan to have a party after the event. This allows them to celebrate the end of all the hard work they have put into organising and staging the event. In some cases organisers are not able to enjoy the event itself because they have to work or are burdened with responsibility. A party might help to reward these people for their efforts.

Evaluation The final stage in the whole process of organising an staging an event is evaluation. This involves looking at whether or not the event was a success. It will be necessary to gather information from a range of sources and analyse it so that conclusions can be drawn. It may also be appropriate to make recommendations for the future if the event is to be repeated. A report should be written to record the outcome of the evaluatio process.

Figure 1 *An example of a letter of thanks*

Northfield Sixth Form College
Worcester New Road
Hereford
HE12 ES1

12 December 2005

Dear Mrs Tremlett

I am writing to thank you very much for the donation you made to the prize pool for our Christmas raffle. The quality of the prizes donated were impressive and helped to make the event a resounding success.

A total of £850 was raised for the hospice and a cheque was presented to a reception party last Wednesday.

Thank you once again.

Yours sincerely

Melvyn Watts

Melvyn Watts
(Event coordinator)

The importance of evaluation

The main purpose of evaluation is to learn lessons that can help to improve future performance. During the evaluation process the organising team need to identify both the positive and negative aspects of the event. By doing this the organisation of future events might be improved. It is important to learn from any mistakes and build on the positive aspects. Ideally, evaluation will take place, not just after the event but at key times during its organisation. If evaluation is ongoing throughout the whole organisation period, it may be possible to improve performance. Ongoing evaluation will also help to:

- identify problems early on so that corrective action can be taken;
- provide progress information for clients;
- reaffirm the team's commitment to the event;
- provide an opportunity for individual team members to evaluate their own personal contribution.

Evaluating success

How can the success of an event be evaluated? Generally, if the aims and objectives of the event have been achieved then the event will have been a success. For example, if the object of an event is to raise £1,000 for a local charity and the amount raised came to £1,109, it is reasonable to conclude that the event has been a success. When objectives are SMART, it is relatively easy to determine whether an event has been a success or not. However, the success of some events may be more difficult to measure. For example, how might the success of a day trip to the coast, organised for a group of underpriviliged children, be evaluated? Generally, such an event would be regarded as a success if the majority of the children had a good time. But how is this measured? It would be necessary to collect some feedback from the children and compare it with some performance criteria. The gathering of feedback from relevant parties is discussed in the next unit. Figure 2 shows how the success of a particular event was evaluated.

Meeting client needs

In some cases an event is organised for a client such as a business,

an organisation or a group of people. For example, a group of students might organise a promotion evening for a local business. In such cases, the success of the event will depend on whether the needs of the client have been met. In this case, the evaluation process will focus on the client. It is likely that certain objectives will have been set by the client and the evaluation process will involve discussing with a client the extent to which the objectives were met. An example is shown in Figure 3.

Fitness for purpose

Events are organised for a purpose and it is important to evaluate whether the event actually fit the purpose for which it was designed. For example, a comedy night organised for youngsters might be unsuccessful if the wrong sort of comedians were employed – comedians whose material was too political perhaps. Careful thought must be given in the planning stages to ensure that the nature of an event is appropriate for its purpose. Then, after the event, part of the evaluation process may involve assessing whether or not the nature of the event was fit for its purpose. To do this information may have to be gathered from the people involved. The process of gathering information is discussed in the next unit.

Fitness for purpose may also have a financial dimension. For example, was the money spent on the event justified? Or, did the expenditure fall within the budget target? The use of budgets is very useful when evaluating the success of an event. Variances (the difference between actual and budgeted spending) can be calculated to determine whether targets have been met, exceeded or missed.

Figure 2 *Evaluating the success of a holiday auction*

Monmouth Life is an insurance company which sells life assurance. Most of the company's policies are sold over the telephone from a small call centre. The company employs 58 staff and every year the personnel department organises an event to raise money for the local community. In 2005 a holiday auction was organised in a function room at a local pub. This involved staff bidding for extra time off work which had been donated by the company. The holidays were auctioned off in the following ways.

- 1 full fortnight
- 2 full weeks
- 3 long weekends
- 10 single days

The company paid for all food and drink consumed during the evening. The objectives of the event were to:

- raise £1,000 for a local charity or good cause;
- provide a 'fun night out' for all staff;
- promote the company as a good corporate citizen;
- reward staff for their efforts by providing extra holidays and a free night out.

After the event the manager of the personnel department spent some time evaluating the event and wrote a report. The conclusion of the report is shown below.

Conclusion
The holiday auction proved to be a real success. All of the objectives were either met or exceeded. The auction itself raised £1,240 and 85% of the staff attended. In the past attendance at company social events has averaged about 80%. Informal feedback from staff was very positive. Many people asked if the same event could be repeated next year. People who had bought the extra holidays thought it was a great way of raising money for charity and rewarding staff for their efforts. A reporter from the local newspaper took some photographs and a positive report appeared in the next edition. Monmouth Life was shown in a good light.

Figure 3 *Meeting client needs – an evaluation*

A group of students was asked to organise an event to launch a new business. A local entrepreneur planned to open a shop selling specialist imported coffees and teas, wines, condiments, as well as kitchenware in the town's high street. The purpose of the event was to raise awareness, meet prospective customers, talk about the products and their origins, attract some media attention and hopefully make a few initial sales. Some specific objectives were set by the client.

- A budget of £400 for food and drink must not be exceeded.
- At least 150 people should attend between 4pm and 9pm.
- Some free publicity in the local newspaper was an important requirement.
- A sales target of £1,000 was set.

The week after the event the group met with their client to evaluate the success of the evening. The client had mixed feelings. She felt that some aspects of the evening had not gone well. Only 120 turned up during the evening. She suggested that the event had not been promoted sufficiently around the town. Since the number of people attending was below expectations quite a lot of the food and drink was wasted. Money could have been saved if a lower number had been catered for. The sales of products during the evening had also been a disappointment with only £510 being generated. However, this was to be expected given that the attendance was below expectations. However, on a positive note some good photographs appeared in the local newspaper and many of the people that attended the event showed genuine interest and said they would return at a later date to make purchases.

When organising events for clients, the evaluation process must involve an input from that client. If their needs are met and their aims are achieved, clients will generally be happy and the event can be considered a success.

Figure 4 *Self-evaluation*

The form shown here was completed by a student involved in organising a sponsored swim for charity.

Self-evaluation form

Personal role/job title: Financial Director

Personal targets:
- Ensure that 95% of the money pledged to swimmers is collected within two weeks of the event.
- Produce an income and expenditure statement within two weeks of the event.
- Keep up-to-date records of all financial transactions.

Personal role in feasibility assessment:
I helped to set the financial target for the amount of money to be raised and worked out the individual targets for each swimmer.

Personal role in planning event:
I kept a record of all the financial transactions and made sure that money was spent for legitimate purposes only. I also attended all meetings and helped make decisions on many planning aspects. For example, it was my idea to award the swimmer who got the most sponsor money with a special prize.

Personal role in staging the event:
During the event I played a low profile. Most of my work was undertaken during the planning stages. However, I did help out entertaining some guests and served refreshments to swimmers at the end.

Personal role in review of the event:
My main duty here was to review the financial planning and the targets set. The event raised £457 which was £57 above the target. This was after all the costs had been covered. Fortunately we were able to use the school swimming pool free of charge.

What might you do differently if you played the same role again?
- Make more use of the computer when keeping financial transactions.
- Redesign the sponsor forms used by the swimmers.
- Organise more people to help collect sponsor money.
- Organise my time more effectively. I tended to waste time, especially when working at home.

Signature: *Jake Tranter*   **Date:** 18.12.05

Self-evaluation

An important part of the evaluation process involves looking at one's own performance. People need to review their own contribution so that they can identify their strengths and areas for development. Exploiting strengths and working hard on areas for development will help to improve future performance. An example of a self-evaluation is shown in Figure 4.

1. Find out two recent events in local newspapers.
2. List the appropriate criteria that might be used to evaluate the events.
3. Compare the success of the events in terms of these criteria.

Research task

Meeting the assessment criteria - examiners' guidance

You need to produce a report reviewing and evaluating the event.

Event example – Quiz night

Ten Sixth Form students organised a quiz night for their peers and teachers just before the Christmas holidays. It was also planned to auction a night out with one female and one male member of staff. The aims of the event were to:

- provide a fun night for students and teachers;
- attract 30 teams of three;
- raise £200 for charity.

Students and teachers were invited to form groups of three and pay a £4.50 entrance fee. This money would be used to pay for prizes and refreshments during the evening. The event was held in the college sixth form common room which was decorated especially for the evening.

Mark Band 1 *You need to provide a basic evaluation of the success of the event.*
I was involved in buying the prizes for the quiz winners. We had a budget of £120 to buy three prizes. Unfortunately there was a lot of disagreement about what should be bought. We finally decided to buy some gift vouchers for CDs or computer games. The event went very well indeed. The aims were exceeded. Everyone had a great time and £280 was raised for charity. 41 teams took part in the quiz. The only real complaint was that some of the questions were too hard. There was also a problem with the sound system which 'screeched' sometimes.

Mark Band 2 *You need to provide a sound evaluation of the success of the event.*
The quiz night was a resounding success. Everyone was talking about it the next day at college. The auctions for a night out with a teacher were particularly popular and helped to push the amount raised for charity to £280. This was far more than expected. I was

involved in writing the questions. This took up a lot of time and was more difficult than expected. We devised six rounds of 15 questions – music, sport, TV, films, general knowledge and geography. For the TV and film questions we used video clips. These questions were particularly popular. However, there were a few complaints that about a third of the questions were too difficult and excluded some people. This resulted in the marks for teams being very 'bunched'. In fact, three teams tied for the lead at the end. We had to devise a sudden death competition to find an eventual winner. This was OK because we had some questions in reserve as part of our contingency plan.

Mark Band 3 *You need to provide a detailed evaluation of the event.*
It was quite clear that the event had been a success. The next day at college everyone was talking about it in a very positive light. At least four teachers thanked and congratulated the organising team for their efforts. There was also a mention in assembly. However, to evaluate the event properly a meeting was held to review the organisation and staging of the event. All the aims of the event were exceeded which provided proof of success. Everyone had a good time, 41 teams entered and the amount raised for charity was £80 higher than the target. However, there were lessons to be learnt if the event was to be repeated. More thought needed to be given to the questions. It was clear that about one-third of them were too difficult – even for teachers. This resulted in some bunching of the final scores – 29 teams scored between 55 and 60. It was also felt that even more money could be raised for charity and in future a more challenging financial target should be set. Another suggestion was that people should be allowed to bring their partners or a close friend. This would boost the numbers involved and make the event even more sociable. Finally, there was a complaint from the caretaker that the sixth form common room had not be cleared up properly after the event. This was actually overlooked in the planning stage.

Portfolio practice · Talent contest

Students at a school were set a challenge to organise a talent contest for the entire school. The event would be held at the end of the summer term and would be attended by all pupils in the main hall. The organisers invited pupils from each year group to an audition so that a short list could be drawn up for the final event. It was decided to offer a prize for each year group and a short list of 3 acts per year would be allowed to perform on the day of the finals. This meant a total of 18 acts would be seen by the audience. From these the audience would vote for the winner for each year group. Members of the audience would be given a voting slip to cast their votes. The aim of the event was to provide pupils with an opportunity to demonstrate their talents and provide an end-of-term show for everyone to enjoy.

After the contest some observations were made.

- Counting the votes took too long and the audience became restless while they waited.
- The gap between acts was sometimes too long.
- The compere was poor.
- Some pupils complained that the panel of judges involved in the initial auditions were biased and unqualified.

(a) **Explain why the evaluation of an event is important.**
(b) **Explain the importance of aims and objectives when evaluating the success of this event.**
(c) **In addition to aims and objectives, what other factors might be taken into account when evaluating the success of this event?**

The need for feedback

Part of the evaluation process is likely to involve the organising team meetings to discuss how successful the planning and staging of the event was. They will look to see if their objectives have been met and discuss the contributions made by each individual. The quality of evaluation will be improved if the team has gathered some information from clients, if appropriate, and from people who attended the event. It is important for the evaluation to be objective. This means that judgement about the success of the event is based on information that is not coloured by the views of the people involved in making that judgement.

Gathering feedback

Feedback can be gathered from clients or people that have attended the event. There are different ways of doing this.

Questionnaires It is possible to design a questionnaire which people can complete after an event. This is a common method of gathering feedback and is often used by businesses to get feedback from their customers after selling them products. For example, tour operators often ask holidaymakers to complete an evaluation sheet during their return flight. However, in some cases this might be impractical. For example, after a concert or a sporting event people return home and may not be interested in completing questionnaires. One way of overcoming this problem is to use postal surveys where people complete a questionnaire in the comfort of their own homes and return it to the sender by post.

It may also be possible to encourage people to complete online questionnaires. Some thought must be given to the design of questionnaires. They should not be arduous for the people confronted with them and they should contain a combination of open and closed questions. Closed questions are useful because the answers can be quantified more easily. However, open questions allow a wider range of responses. An example of a questionnaire used to gather feedback after an event is shown in Figure 1.

Interviews It may be possible to interview clients or people that have attended an event after it has been staged. Personal interviews could be arranged where members of the organising team organise a structured interview to get feedback. The advantage of interviews is that more detailed information can be gathered. However, it is important to prepare properly for an interview with a list of meaningful questions and appropriate discussion points. It will also be necessary to record the information collected. This might be done using a tape recorder provided permission is obtained from the interviewee.

Focus groups This involves bringing together a group of people to discuss the success of an event. Clients or people who have attended the event can be invited to a convenient venue to provide useful feedback on the event. It is important though that the individuals invited are representative of the entire audience. With a small group of people discussions can be involved and detailed information can be gathered. However, it may be necessary to provide the people attending with some sort of

Figure 1 *A questionnaire used to gather feedback after an event*

Students were asked to complete this form after they had attended a summer ball organised by a group of peers.

Event evaluation sheet

Please complete the following questions.

	Very much			Not at all
1. How much did you enjoy the event overall? Circle one number.	1	2	3	4
2. How much did you enjoy the food? Circle one number.	1	2	3	4
3. How much did you enjoy the music? Circle one number.	1	2	3	4

4. Was the venue suitable? Tick one box. YES ☐ NO ☐

5. Was the venue decorated appropriately? Tick one box. YES ☐ NO ☐

6. Was the £25 ticket price value for money? Tick one box. YES ☐ NO ☐

7. How would you improve the event for people next year?

....

8. Do you have any other ideas for social events in the next academic year?

....

Thank you for your time.

Figure 2 *Newspaper reports on local events*

incentive because they will be giving up their time.

Complaints Hopefully an event will be successful - aims will be met and people will enjoy themselves. However, things might go wrong and people might have cause for complaint. It is important to take complaints seriously because important lessons can be learned. It might be appropriate to organise a system whereby people can make complaints freely. For example, in business it is often possible to complete a complaints form if customers are unhappy with the quality of products or customer service. People may also write letters of complaint. Complaints should be dealt with swiftly and courteously and the information gathered when a complaint is made used in the evaluation process.

Media It is common for the media to report on events. Major events such as the London Marathon and other sporting events get live television coverage. They are also reported in national newspapers, radio and on TV news bulletins. Their reports are likely to express an opinion on the success of an event and can therefore be used in the evaluation process. Local events are likely to be reported in local newspapers and perhaps on local radio. Some examples of reports on events are shown in Figure 2.

Recommendations and improvements

One of the main reasons for evaluating the success of an event is to learn from the experience. An evaluation report should normally conclude by making a number of suggestions or recommendations for improvement in the future. Individuals may also like to think about how they can improve their own personal performance. By identifying areas for development future performance can easily be improved. An example is shown in Figure 3.

Figure 3 *Example of recommendations for improvements after an event*

A group of students organised a five-a-side football tournament for youths in their local town. On the whole the event was a success, but during the evaluation a number of recommendations were made for improvements if the event were to be repeated next year. They are based on feedback from a sample of 10 youths that took part in the event. An extract from their evaluation report is shown below.

Recommendations for improvements

- The standard of the refereeing needs to be improved. To avoid disputes and the possible escalation of conflict it would be cost-effective to employ qualified referees. Teams said that they would be happier to pay a higher entrance fee if qualified referees were employed.
- Hot water in the changing rooms should be provided. A number of complaints were received when it was discovered that people could not get a proper shower after their games.
- The car park should be roped off to prevent cars parking too close to the football pitches. This is also a health and safety issue which was overlooked in the planning process. Employing a car park steward would also be helpful to ensure that cars are parked in appropriate places.
- Arrangements need to be made to clear the site properly after the tournament. There was a complaint from the parks manager that litter had been left in the changing rooms, the car park area and near the refreshment tent. Again, this was overlooked in the planning stages and a team of litter collectors would need to be employed in the future.

Using the research task from section 62, suggest improvements that may be made to the organisation of events you have researched. Indicate how these changes might improve the organisation of the event.

Research task

Meeting the assessment criteria - examiners' guidance

You need to produce a report reviewing and evaluating the event making clear any recommendations for future improvements.

Event example – Café launch

Students at a Further Education College were asked to organise an event to launch a new catering facility at the college. The café, which was going to be run by the catering department in the college, asked the group to organise a two hour lunchtime event where college students could sample some of the food and drinks that would be available at the café during college hours. The aim was to get at least 50% of the college students through the doors during that two hour period. Some form of entertainment was also required and a competition to encourage students to come back to the café to see if they had won.

The evaluation process after the event involved speaking at length to the head of the catering department. The meeting took two hours and a number of issues were raised. The catering department hoped to open a restaurant next year and provided certain improvements were made the same group would be responsible for its launch.

Mark Band 1 *Provide a basic evaluation of the success of the event with simple recommendations.*

After the café launch quite a lot of time was spent evaluating its success. The process involved meeting with the client, the head of catering, to get her views about the event. We also spoke to some of the students that attended the launch to get their views. It was agreed that the event was a success (more than 56% of students visited the café) but should a similar event be organised in the future, the following improvements are recommended.

- Design some more creative promotion materials.
- Arrange for a more constant flow of customers – everyone arrived at the same time and there was a lot of overcrowding for an hour.
- The competition organised was a bit weak – more creativity was needed.
- More staff would be need to be employed in the café to shorten the queues.

Mark Band 2 *You need to provide a sound evaluation of the success of the event that makes recommendations from the data collected and analysed. This will help explain the viability of the event.*

To evaluate the success of the café launch a meeting was arranged with the client – the head of the catering department. She raised a number of issues. She was happy that more than 56% of students at the college attended the launch but felt that the numbers could have easily been increased. She also

criticised the random nature that students arrived during the two hour period. However, she agreed that the event was viable. We also spoke to some students that attended the event. They enjoyed it and most said that they would return to the café. Improvements for the future include the following.

- Design some more creative promotion materials. For example, the posters were hand drawn. They could have been a lot more professional and colourful.
- Arrange for a more constant flow of customers. Everyone arrived at the same time and there was a lot of overcrowding for an hour. In the last half an hour the café was virtually empty.
- The competition organised was a bit weak – more creativity was needed. One good idea would have been to organise a 'name the café' competition.
- More staff would need to be employed in the café to shorten the queues. However, this would have to be agreed with the client.

Mark Band 3 *You need to provide a detailed evaluation of the event making appropriate recommendations drawn from the data collected. There will be realistic proposals for improvement.*

In the evaluation process data was collected from a meeting with the client and a sample of students that attended the café launch. The meeting with the client was recorded and the students were asked to complete a simple questionnaire. The main aim of the event was achieved. More than 56% of the college students visited the café during the launch. However, it was felt that a lot more could have been encouraged to attend with some more powerful promotion. There were a few areas for development and the following improvements were recommended for future, similar events.

- The promotion materials could be easily improved. For example, the posters were hand drawn. They could have been a lot more professional and colourful.
- Arrange for a more constant flow of customers – everyone arrived at the same time and there was a lot of overcrowding for an hour. In the last half an hour the café was virtually empty. This could be achieved by issuing tickets stating arrival times which could be staggered for different groups of students.
- Not very many people were interested in the competition. A better idea would have been to organise a 'name the café' competition. The winner could receive free coffee in the café for a year and have the satisfaction that he or she came up with the name.
- More staff would need to be employed in the café to shorten the queues. However, this would have to be agreed with the client.

Portfolio practice · **Fashion and design show**

A group of sixth form students decided to organise a fashion and design show at their college to raise money for a local children's hospital. The show would be organised by the college's design department. However, all other aspects of the event such as promotion, pricing, ticketing and stewarding would be handled by the organising team. The aims of the event would be to:

- raise £1,000 for the hospital;
- invite some disadvantaged children in the local area free of charge;
- provide some refreshments for the audience during the interval;
- organise a party for the cast and organising team after the event.

To evaluate the success of the event it was decided to use a questionnaire to get feedback from the audience and perhaps arrange for a focus group to meet.

(a) Explain the difference between an interview and a focus group.

(b) Design a questionnaire that could be used to gather feedback from the audience.

(c) Explain why it is important to make recommendations for future improvements.

External influences

Unit 14 looks at the external influences that can affect businesses and how businesses should adjust to and plan for these external influences. They are described as external influences because they do not come from the business itself but from the environment in which it is producing and selling. This unit requires students to select a specific business and to identify which external influences are the most important for that business, how they affect the business and what strategies should be in place to deal with them.

Four main external influences have been chosen.

- Legal.
- Economic.
- Environmental.
- Technological.

PEST analysis

Many business studies textbooks start from what is called a PEST analysis approach. Generally this covers the same external influences as listed above, but they are given slightly different names, as shown in Figure 1.

Political This would cover actions taken by governments, including legislation which is the main way in which governments control a country. **Legal** influences specifically cover how businesses are affected by the laws of the countries in which they trade.

Economic This covers changes that occur in the economy of a country including changes that come from government, such as taxation and managing the economy. It would also cover changes that come from the behaviour of other businesses and international organisations, such as the World Trade Organisation (WTO).

Social This covers the way in which we live our lives and would include demographic features, such as age and gender distribution in the country, and psychographic features, such as the interests that we have and what we feel is important to us. As these change they will affect the markets that businesses sell into. Some of these aspects are covered in this unit, for example changing income levels under economic influences. Generally, however, this unit does not consider the purely social external influences.

Technological This covers changes that affect businesses because of the introduction of new technologies. For example, today there are few businesses that do not use computers for some parts of their production, even if it is only for record keeping or sending messages.

What are not directly included in PEST, but are required for this unit, are **environmental** influences. Environmental influences cover any influences that affect the environment in which we live and in which businesses operate. That includes laws that control such negative effects as pollution and the changes in lifestyle that we have made in order to accept the need to recycle waste. Environmental influences are therefore covered under PEST in the political and social categories. The methods of controlling pollution and recycling waste are covered under technology and the effects on businesses' costs are covered under economic influences.

When a PEST analysis is carried out for a business all of the major external influences will be considered. The business will need to consider what the current external influences are and what changes are likely to occur in the future. It will then need to react to these external influences to ensure that it remains in business and meets its primary objectives.

PEST to STEEPLE

A business will tend to carry out the analysis of external influences that is most appropriate to the business itself. The business is unlikely to worry about what title is given to this analysis. Academics, on the other hand, like to invent new terms for this

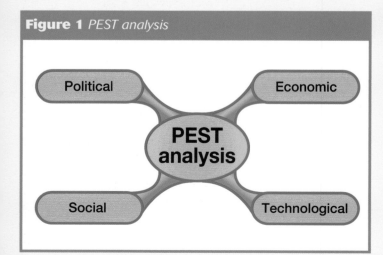

Figure 1 PEST analysis

Political — PEST analysis — Economic

Social — Technological

Table 1 Elements for analysing external influences

Title	What it stands for
PEST	**P**olitical, **E**conomic, **S**ocial, **T**echnological
STEP	**S**ocial, **T**echnological, **E**conomic, **P**olitical
SLEPT	**S**ocial, **L**egal, **E**conomic, **P**olitical, **T**echnological
STEEP	**S**ocial, **T**echnological, **E**conomic, **E**nvironmental, **P**olitical
PESTLE	**P**olitical, **E**conomic, **S**ocial, **T**echnological, **L**egal, **E**thical
STEEPLE	**S**ocial, **T**echnological, **E**conomic, **E**nvironmental, **P**olitical, **L**egal, **E**thical

...ind of analysis and it is therefore possible that all of the terms in ...able I may be used to describe what is essentially the basic PEST ...nalysis.

Ethical covers what people think is morally 'right'. For some ...usinesses this is very important. The Body Shop, for example, has ...lear ethical policies of not using animals to test its products on ...nd of offering third world producers fair prices so that they can ...eed, clothe and educate their families.

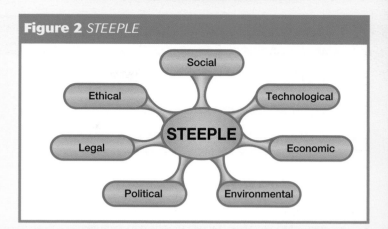

Figure 2 *STEEPLE*

Meeting the assessment criteria - examiners' guidance

When choosing which of the external influences are most important and should be included in the portfolio work, the decision will depend very much on which business is being studied. The minimum that must be included are the four specific influences listed in the specification – legal, economic, environmental and technological. The chosen business may, however, be strongly influenced by political, social and ethical external factors and if that is the case these should also be included.

When choosing a suitable business to study it is very important that all of the following steps are thought about in advance, otherwise parts may be missed out or vital data may be impossible to get hold of.

1. Choose a business that you know you have good access to or which has a wide range of published data about it.
2. Carefully study what the business does in terms of what it produces, who it sells to and where it is located. The more you know about the business the easier it will be to identify relevant external influences.
3. Check all of the listed influences given in each section of the specification, and check all those referred to in the sections of this textbook.
4. List all the likely external influences, noting which part of the business they are likely to affect.
5. Research all possible influences carefully. Actual contact with the business is highly recommended.
6. Make comments on all external influences that you have found data about, but also prioritise your comments so that the most important influences have most written about them.
7. Check what strategies the business already has for dealing with these external influences and what strategies it is planning.
8. Recommend and justify any additional strategies that the business could take that would be beneficial for it.

Examples of the approach that can be taken are given at the end of each of the other sections in unit 14.

The 'Meeting the assessment criteria' at the end of each section in this unit will provide guidance as to how the Assessment Criteria for the Mark Band levels and for Assessment Objectives (AOs) can be met, but this unit also requires that the evidence is presented in a form similar to that found in a chairman's report to the company. Below is some advice on how that might be achieved. This advice should be considered as applying to each of the sections although it will not be repeated in each section.

The first piece of advice is a warning about taking the term 'chairman's report' as the basis of how your report should be presented. The problem is that many chairman's reports are very superficial and would not include many of the details that you will need to include. The same is often true of the other recommended sections of companies' annual reports, namely 'chief executive's reports' or 'review of operations'.

Table 2 shows some of the external influences covered in different reports of a business.

Table 2 *Details from Scapa Group PLC Annual Report, 2005*

Part of the report	External influences referred to
Chairman's Report	<ul><li>Rising raw material costs</li><li>Lower demand</li><li>The weakness of the US dollar</li><li>Personal injury claims in the US</li></ul>
Operating Review	<ul><li>Reactions to a downturn in many international economies</li><li>Rising raw material costs</li><li>Increased competition</li><li>Weakness of the US$</li><li>Weak economic indicators for many European markets</li><li>The Registration, Evaluation and Authorisation of Chemicals (REACH) legislation passed by the EU</li></ul>
Environmental Review	<ul><li>Policies to ensure care of the environment</li><li>Recognition of meeting the legal requirement as an absolute minimum</li><li>Targets for air and solvent emission, oil, gas and electricity consumption and use of packing materials</li></ul>

Source: adapted from Scapa Group PLC, *Annual Report and Accounts*, 2005.

What is really needed for this unit is that you present the results of your study:

- in the form of a report;
- in a form that would be acceptable in an official company report.

In order to ensure that you are doing this you need to carry out the following research.

- Check a range of company reports as recommended in the unit. These can be found in libraries, at the companies own websites or on the very wide range of reports that are provided free at www.ftannualreports.com.
- Read different sections of the reports to find where external influences are being referred to and how they are being presented, e.g. text, tables, graphs and pictures.
- Check other publications that the business produces, for example its website, to see if these explain how the business deals with external influences. Many other sources do have reference to external influences, especially under the heading of 'corporate responsibility'.
- Check press, television, and Internet coverage of the business as external effects, and the business's response, are often highlighted there.

You will be covering a wide range of possible external influences that many company reports would not make any mention of. You will need to research what these influences are and then present them as though they were being included in a company report.

Unit 14 allows students to look at either one business or a whole industry. It is likely that taking a whole industry will give more scope for finding a wide range of external factors but if that is the approach taken students must weigh up the benefits against the possible need for much wider research. Whichever approach is taken the results of the research must still be written up in a form suitable for a company report.

Consumer legislation

Consumer protection

This is a particularly difficult section of the syllabus to find the right information for. This is because there are a great many parts of law that relate to different aspects of selling goods and services to consumers. The laws dealt with below cover the main aspects of consumer legislation, but it will also be necessary for students to consider the specific product or industry chosen for the portfolio work and research the laws that apply to that specific product or industry.

Consumer legislation refers to laws passed by the government designed to protect consumers from businesses that take advantage of them. Consumers need this protection for the following reasons.
- Businesses are generally larger and more powerful than individual consumers.
- Businesses often have expert knowledge that consumers do not have.
- Some businesses simply do not take enough care in the way they make their goods or provide their services and this can put consumers in physical danger or in danger of receiving a substandard good or service.
- Some businesses are only interested in making as much profit as they can and are quite happy to cheat consumers if they can get away with it.

Because consumer legislation is the law, businesses have to react to it otherwise they can be sued by their customers or prosecuted by the State. Generally consumer legislation does help to make the balance between the business and the consumer fairer.

The major areas of consumer law

This unit only asks for a consideration of consumer law in terms of how it affects the sale of goods and services. In reality, however,

that covers most of the parts of consumer law. The main elements of consumer law are shown in Figure 1.

A huge number of laws relates to the protection of consumers. Some of the laws have been brought together into single major acts, e.g. the **Sale of Goods Acts**. Others are amendments and regulations that are added to existing laws, e.g. the **Consumer Protection Act**, **1987** which has had over seventy additional regulations added in separate pieces of legislation between 1987 and 2004. Yet other laws are designed to deal with specific elements of selling, e.g. **The Christmas Day Trading Act**, **2004** which prohibits large store from trading on Christmas day.

Selecting the legislation and laws that relate to the specific business or industry chosen for portfolio work can be difficult. This section will deal with some of the major Acts of Parliament and mention some other, more specific, pieces of legislation. This unit also requires students to consider changes in the legislation that have occurred in the last five years, which may only apply to specific industries, businesses or products.

Details of UK Acts of Parliament can be found in public libraries or at http://www.opsi.gov.uk/acts.htm. Details of bills that are in front of parliament can be found at:
http://www.publications.parliament.uk/pa/pabills.htm.
A full list of legislation, by topic can be found at
http://www.tradingstandards.gov.uk.

The three main areas of consumer law that will be covered in this section are:
- the sale of goods and services, including pricing;
- description of goods and services, including labelling and advertising;
- consumer protection in terms of quality, ingredients and safety.

The sale of goods and services

Some parts of consumer law are relatively old. The first **Sale of Goods Act** was passed in 1893 and the first Act which made it illegal to use a trade mark to make it look as though the goods were being produced by a well known business was passed in 1887 (**The Merchandise Marks Act**). Since then the major elements of consumer law have been brought together into single Acts, although many have also been amended a number of times.

In England, Wales and Northern Ireland legislation has been passed to cover many aspects of the sale of goods and services. Scotland has a separate system of law and much of its consumer law is based on what is called Common Law, rather than legislation, so some of the basic rules are slightly different.

The Sale of Goods Act

The **Sale of Goods Act**, **1979** set the basic conditions that govern the sale of goods although amendments were made in the **Supply of Goods and Services Act**, **1982**, the **Sale and Supply of Goods Act**, **1994** and the **Sale and Supply of**

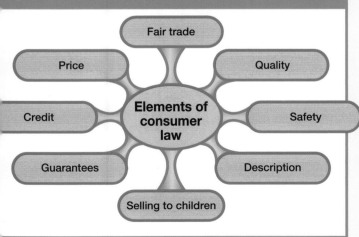

Figure 1 *Elements of consumer law*

- Fair trade
- Price
- Quality
- Credit
- Elements of consumer law
- Safety
- Guarantees
- Description
- Selling to children

Goods to Consumers Regulations, **2002**. These Acts lay down that:

- goods must be 'as described';
- goods must be of 'satisfactory quality';
- goods must be 'fit for purpose'.

If any of these conditions are breached consumers can:

- ask for their money back within a reasonable time;
- claim damages for up to six years (five in Scotland) if the product should have lasted that long;
- ask for replacement or repair if that is possible.

From the **Sale and Supply of Goods Act**, 1994 the requirement for satisfactory quality and fitness for purpose would include:

- appearance and finish;
- freedom from minor defects;
- safety;
- durability.

An example is shown in Figure 2. The Act also extended consumer rights to the hiring of goods.

Figure 2 *How the Sale of Goods Act might affect the sale of a product*

The Honda commercial tiller FG510 is supplied by Mowers UK. The FG510 is ideal for users requiring rigged performance and versatility. With 3 forward and 1 reverse gears and a range of optional attachments this machine will make light of most horticultural tasks.

Source: adapted from Mowers UK website, www.mowers.uk.com.

To meet the **Sale of Goods Act** it would have to be:

- as described – e.g. with 3 forward and 1 reverse gears;
- of satisfactory quality – with a 5.5hp 4 stroke engine and costing £1,299 satisfactory quality would include the ability to take on heavy rotovating work and last for many years;
- fit for purpose – this is designed for horticultural work so it should be capable of rotovating fairly large areas of land in most conditions.

The **Sale and Supply of Goods to Consumers Regulations**, **2002** allow consumers to ask for goods to be repaired if they can be. They also deal with the following situations, where:

- installation by a retailer is unsatisfactory;
- installation instructions have serious shortcomings;
- goods do not match any public statements made about them, e.g. in advertisements;
- a specially commissioned product has relevant failings.

The Supply of Goods and Services Act

The **Supply of Goods and Services Act**, 1982 essentially extended the protection that consumers receive when they buy goods to when they buy services. The Act requires a supplier of a service to:

- carry out that service with reasonable care and skill;
- carry out that service within a reasonable time;
- make no more than a reasonable charge.

If the supplier of the service fails to meet these conditions consumers can:

- continue with the contract but also claim compensation for any damages suffered;
- rescind (cancel) the contract.

Where individuals find that any of the conditions have been broken under the **Sale of Goods and Services Acts** they should initially contact the supplier. If that does not provide a satisfactory solution they can take the supplier to court. They can also complain to the Office of Fair Trading (OFT) which has two significant enforcement roles:

- ensuring that consumer legislation and regulations are properly enforced;
- taking action against unfair traders.

Figure 3 shows an example.

Figure 3 *OFT wins landmark ruling in Scottish court*

Interim enforcement orders have been granted against a Scottish-based double glazing supplier for providing poor goods and services to consumers, following OFT action. In the first court action of its kind in Scotland by the OFT the Court of Session granted the interim enforcement orders under Part 8 of the Enterprise Act 2002 against MB Designs (Scotland) Ltd and its directors for breaches of the Supply of Goods and Services Act 1982 and the Sale of Goods Act 1979 while selling and installing conservatories and replacement windows and doors. The move follows a number of complaints which were referred to the OFT by trading standards departments in Scotland.

The OFT's case was that MB Designs had supplied goods of unsatisfactory quality and which were unfit for their purpose, as well as supplying goods that did not match the original description or contract. The company also failed to take reasonable care when installing goods or appointing third party installers.

The interim enforcement orders mean that MB Designs will be required to improve its trading practices to supply conservatories and replacement windows and doors that are fit for their purpose, are as described and are fitted to a satisfactory standard. If the interim enforcement orders are breached, this could lead to further action for contempt of court.

Source: adapted from OFT press release (June 2005).

Prices Acts

The control of prices has been introduced so that consumers know exactly what they should be paying for goods and services, and so that they will not be fooled by claims of special offers or sale prices which are not genuine. Table 1 gives details of four Acts and the main requirements in terms of prices.

Table 1 *Impact of prices Acts*

Legislation	Main requirement
Development of Tourism Act, 1969	• Prices of accommodation must be displayed by hotels and guest houses.
Prices Act, 1974 & 1975	• Controls how certain prices must be displayed. • Requires price information to be given to consumer. • Regulates the use of sales prices.
Consumer Protection Act, 1987	• Prohibits the giving of misleading price indications to consumers.
Price Marking Orders	See details below.

Price marking for specific ways of selling goods and services is often changed with statutory instruments called orders which do not create full Acts of Parliament. It is therefore important to check on the regulations for the specific industry or product being sold.

For example, the **Price Marking Order**, **1999** introduced the requirement that the selling price must be indicated for all products offered by retailers to consumers. Goods supplied 'in the course of the provision of a service' are exempt because of an EU directive (98/6/EC).

The Price Marking (Food and Drinks Services) Order, **2003** requires restaurants, bars, cafeterias, take-away and similar outlets to display information about the prices of goods and services. The details required can be very specific as shown in the extract from the DTI in Figure 4.

Figure 4

The price of food must be given by description (e.g. fish and chips; coq au vin) unless the item is sold by quantity or weight (e.g. a pint of beer, six oysters). If the price is given by quantity or weight and other prices are directly proportionate to that price, one indication of price is sufficient. Thus if half a pint of beer costs half the price of a pint, or a dozen oysters twice the price of six oysters, the prices for a pint and for six oysters would suffice.

Source: adapted from Department of Trade and Industry (DTI).

Trade Descriptions Acts

The **Sale of Goods Acts** require that goods must be as they have been described. This has, however, been extended by specific Acts that refer to how products for sale can be described and how they can be advertised.

The **Trade Descriptions Act**, **1968** This made it a criminal offence to:
- make a false description about goods including:
  - details of quantity or size;
  - how they were made;
  - their strength, performance or accuracy;
  - where they were made and who made them.
- supply any goods about which a false decription had been made;
- make certain false statements about services, accomodation and facilities including:
  - when and how they will be provided;
  - who will provide them.

The Trading Standards authorities are required to enforce this Act and breaches of this Act can lead to fines and even inprisonment.

Labelling

As part of ensuring that consumers have full descriptions of what they are buying there has been a great deal of legislation on how products are labelled so that customers know exactly what the product is made of. This has been particularly important with food products.

The **Food Labelling Regulations**, **1996** dealt with many requirements of accurate labelling including for any foods that are ready for provision to the consumer:
- the name of the food;
- the ingredients;
- sell buy and use by dates;
- storage and use instructions;
- the name and address of the producer, packer or seller.

Since the 1996 regulations there have been 17 additional regulations up to 2005 which have amended the 1996 regulations or added to them, for example on the labelling of genetically modified (GM) foods in 1999 and the need to state that food has added substances in 2004. There are also EU regulations that need to be followed. Details of all of these can be found at the University of Reading's School of Bio-science website, www.foodlaw.rdg.ac.uk/.

Descriptions in advertisements

In the past businesses felt that they could say pretty much what they wanted to in their advertisements. The law now restricts what can be said. Many of these restriction are covered under other laws such as the **Sale of Goods Acts** where what is described in advertisements becomes part of the description. The **Food Safety Act, 1990** covers the quality, standards and claims made for food as well as its description, advertising and labelling.

Some products have specific laws made for them that restrict or ban advertising. **The Tobacco Advertising and Promotion Act**, **2002** bans the advertising and promotion of tobacco products including when the brand name is being used to sponsor cultural and sports events. The Act was introduced in stages so tobacco companies and sellers of tobacco had to change their advertising practices year by year.

- Feb. 2003 advertising banned on billboards and in newspapers and magazines.
- May 2003 advertising banned when using direct mail.
- July 2003 tobacco sponsorship of domestic sporting events banned.
- Dec. 2004 only one A5 advertisement allowed where tobacco products were being sold at point of sale directly to consumers.
- July 2005 tobacco sponsorship of international events, e.g. Formula One motor racing, banned.

In addition to laws that regulate advertising there are also voluntary codes that govern advertising in the media. **The British Code of Advertising**, **Sales Promotion and Direct Marketing** sets standards for most forms of advertising other than radio and television. There is a separate **Radio Advertising Standards Code** and a **TV Advertising Standards Code.**

Details of these codes are provided through the Advertising Standards Authority (ASA) website (www.asa.org.uk/asa/) which has the role of monitoring advertisements to ensure they meet the code. This is also done by the Office of Communications (Ofcom).

Further consumer protection

All of the above laws, regulations and codes are designed to protect the consumer when goods are sold or advertised. There are a great many other laws that affect particular aspects of businesses when selling to consumers. Examples of these are given below.

Product Liability

When producers of goods make their goods they need to ensure that they are safe for consumers to use. This requirement was introduced by the **Consumer Protection Act**, **1987**. This Act:

- made businesses liable for damage caused by defective products;
- prohibited the supply of unsafe goods;
- gave powers to seize unsafe goods and stop the sale of goods that were suspected of being unsafe;
- could make providers of goods which were found to be unsafe publish notices warning consumers;
- prohibited misleading price indications.

The Act covers most goods, their components and raw materials. It did not cover services. The **Supply of Goods and Services Act**, **1982** helped to address that by insisting that service providers have a 'duty of care' to those they work for and work carried out must be 'to a reasonable standard'.

As with many of these pieces of legislation amendments have been introduced and for the **Consumer Protection Act** the following amendments have been made for different parts of the UK:

- Northern Ireland - the **Product Liability (Amendment) Act (Northern Ireland), 2001**;

- Scotland - the **Consumer Protection Act 1987 (Modification) (Scotland) Order, 2001** (Statutory Instrument 2001 No. 265);
- England and Wales - the **Consumer Protection Act 1987 (Modification) Order 2000,** (Statutory Instrument 2000 No. 2771).

Consumer credit

A huge number of sales to consumers is made when the buyer cannot afford, or does not wish to, buy the good or service outright. When this happens the consumer will be buying the good or service using borrowed money, i.e. buying on credit. In the past the businesses lending the money may have taken advantage of the borrowers. Consumer credit legislation has been introduced to correct that situation.

The **Consumer Credit Act**, 1974 set down the basic acceptable conditions for credit agreements, including:

- the need for the lender to have a licence;
- how credit could be advertised;
- how the interest to be paid was calculated;
- what documents should be used;
- controls on debt-collecting and credit reference agencies.

Other legislation

The **Consumer Protection (Distance Selling) Regulations 2000** relate to businesses that sell goods or services to consumers using the Internet, digital television, mail order, fax or phone.

They require the following actions.

- Consumers must be given clear information about the goods or services offered including the seller's name, the price, when payment is due and delivery details.
- Consumers must be sent confirmation after making a purchase.
- Consumers must be allowed a cooling-off period of seven working days.

Part 8 of the **Enterprise Act**, 2002 gives the organisations which enforce the consumer protection laws greater powers, through the courts, to make businesses follow the law. The enforcement authorities include the Office of Fair Trading (OFT), the Trading Standards Service in Great Britain and the Department of Enterprise, Trade and Investment in Northern Ireland.

This Act gives no additional rights to consumers but it does give considerable additional powers to ensure that businesses obey the laws. The laws covered by this Act are listed in it and include most of the laws mentioned in this section. For businesses this means that if they break these laws they can be forced to obey them or be stopped from trading and they are more likely to get fined. Businesses, therefore, need to ensure that all aspects of their selling of goods or of services to consumers meet the requirements of consumer legislation.

Examples of legislation since 2000

Many amendments to the law and new laws are very specific, especially with the growth of new methods of selling, such as through the Internet. Some examples of these recent specific laws

...re given below, but it is important that the right pieces of ...gislation are found for the product, business or industry being ...udied.

The Mobile Telephones (Re-programming) Act, **2002** makes it illegal to re-programme the unique mobile phone identity number and makes the stealing of mobile phones less likely.

The Private Hire Vehicles (Carriage of Guide Dogs etc.) Act, **2002** extends the **Disability Discrimination Act**, **1995** requirement that guide dogs can travel in taxis with no additional charge to private hire vehicles.

The Copyright, etc. and Trade Marks (Offences and Enforcement) Act, **2002** increases the range of offences involved in copying other people's and businesses' products, e.g. music CDs. This builds on the **Copyright, Designs and Patents Act**, **1988**.

- The **Fireworks Act**, **2003** provides specific regulations for the production, sale and use of fireworks that were not covered in the **Consumer Protection Act**, **1987**.
- The **Poultry Meat, Farmed Game Bird Meat and Rabbit Meat (Hygiene and Inspection) (Amendment) (England) Regulations**, **2005** prohibit the sale of fresh poultry meat where agents have been used to retain water in the meat.

---

1. Using libraries or the Internet identify the main controls created by the following legislation in relation to the sale of goods to children and young persons:
   - **The Children and Young Persons (Protection from Tobacco) Act, 1991**.
   - **Licensing Act, 2003** (Sections 145 – 154).
   - **The Firework (Safety) Regulations, 1997**.
   - **Children's Food Bill** – this is proposed legislation.
2. For each of the above pieces of legislation state which businesses are likely to be affected by the regulations it imposes on the sale of goods to children and young persons.

Research task

Portfolio practice · Benjys

Benjys started as a London based sandwich retailer. In London it has already started to challenge more established fast-food outlets such as McDonalds, Burger King, Subway and the many sandwich, bagel and café outlets that provide basic ranges of foods and drinks for consumers who want take-away meals or meals that can be quickly consumed on the premises. It is now expanding into many other parts of the UK.

Part of Benjys 2006 sales campaign was to offer consumers a Meal Deal which would save up to half the price. The offer was for any sized hot drink and any savoury muffin for £1.49 and was to last from the 13th February – 26th March 2006.

Source: from original research.

(a) **Explain how the following legislation would control what was being offered or how it was being offered.**
   (i) **The Sale of Goods Act.**
   (ii) **The Trade Descriptions Act.**
   (iii) **The Prices Act.**
   (iv) **The Supply of Goods and Services Act as it would apply to Benjys providing a service.**

(b) **If consumers asked for a bacon and egg muffin as part of their Meal Deal but were given a bacon and sausage muffin instead would:**
   (i) **they have the right to ask for a replacement? Specify the law that covers this;**
   (ii) **the business have broken the Trade Descriptions Act because it provided the wrong product?**

(c) **How would the Price Marking (Food and Drinks Services) Order 2003 affect Benjys? Explain your answer.**

Meeting the assessment criteria - examiners' guidance

For your chosen business you are required to produce a Chairman's report which describes, applies, analyses and evaluates the effects of external influences on a business. This will involve a consideration of the impact of consumer legislation.

Business example - Dell

As part of its March 2006 newsletter Dell made the offer shown here for its Dimension 3100 computer. The advertisement gave details of the product, price and warranty. The website link also offered credit facilities with a 'buy now pay in 2007' offer.

To meet the assessment criteria it is necessary to consider the impact that consumer legislation will have on this business. This advertisement alone indicates that the following pieces of legislation could be considered.

- The **Sale of Goods Act**, 1978 – because goods are being sold.
- The **Supply of Goods and Services Act**, 1982 – if a service of lending money is being provided by the business.
- The **Supply of Goods to Consumers Regulation**, 2002 – because this gave consumers additional rights in terms of how the goods perform and in terms of guarantees and what was shown in advertisements. It might also apply if installation in the home was carried out on behalf of Dell.
- The **Sale and Supply of Goods Act**, 1994 – because appearance, safety and durability are important aspects of home computers.
- The **Prices Acts**, 1974 & 1975 – because prices for the computers are being displayed.
- The **Trade Descriptions Act**, 1968 – because details of the product are being described, especially in terms of size and performance.

Dimension™ 3100
- Intel® Pentium® 4 Processor 521 with HT Technology (2.80GHz, 1MB L2 cache, 800 FSB)
- Genuine Windows® XP Media Center Edition 2005
- 80GB Serial ATA Hard Drive
- 16x DVD+/-RW#
- Internal Analogue TV Tuner and Remote
- 1 Year Collect & Return Service
- Free Double Memory, Now 1024MB (Was 512 MB)

Was £549
Now **£499****

- The **Consumer Protection Act**, 1987 – because there are clear safety issues with electrical equipment.
- The **Consumer Credit Act**, 1974 – because this business is offering credit terms.
- The **Consumer Protection (Distance Selling) Regulations**, 2000 – because the sale is being offered over the Internet.
- The **Trade Marks Act**, 1994 and the **Copyright and Trade Marks (Offences and Enforcement) Act**, 2002 – because the business is using trade mark names of other businesses.

AOs	Mark Band 1	Mark Band 2	Mark Band 3
AO1	Details should be provided of why legislation is needed in general for Dell and its products and there should be identification of some of the major pieces of legislation such as The Sale of Goods Act, The Trade Descriptions Act and the Consumer Protection Act.	Details should be given of what some of the Acts listed above entail. A wider range of appropriate Acts should be identified and the details given should clearly relate to the nature of Dell's business. The nature of Dell's business should be outlined in detail so that it is clear what the business sells and how it sells its products.	The most important Acts should be selected and there should be thorough knowledge shown of the main points of each Act. The reasons for the selection of these Acts should be given with specific reference to what Dell is selling and the service that it provides. This should show a good understanding of both the business and its products and the range of different, but appropriate, legislation.

AOs	Mark Band 1	Mark Band 2	Mark Band 3
AO2	There should be clear application of the requirements of the Acts to Dell's products and way of selling. At this level it is likely that only the main general Acts are considered and that the application is very general, rather in the way that the Acts have been referred to above.	Details of how the legislation relates to Dell's products should show clearly why the legislation applies. For example, details could be given of the kind of appearance, safety and durability that consumers might expect from Dell as it meets the requirements of The Sale and Supply of Goods Act, 1994.	Here the most relevant legislation should be applied accurately to the business and its products. The most up-to-date legislation should also be used. A great deal of legislation could be applied and there should be evidence of careful selection. The advertisement is offering goods for direct sale and delivery so the Consumer Protection (Distance Selling) Regulations, 2000 will apply and, for example, the sale and delivery of goods (unless otherwise agreed) will have to be completed within 30 days of the order.
AO3	At this level only limited sources will be used, for example Internet advertisements for what Dell sells and textbooks for the legislation. The basic sources must, however, provide details of some of Dell's products and how it sells them and details of the main requirements of the major pieces of legislation.	A wider range of sources is required and this should provided details of the range of products that Dell sells and a good range of appropriate current legislation. Both parts need to be analysed so that the appropriate legislation and requirements can be matched with what the business sells and how it sells. For example, because Dell sells electrical products that should be matched to the requirements of the Consumer Protection Act, 1987.	Here there should be evidence of thorough research and it would be expected that different sources confirmed what Dell actually does in terms of selling their goods. It would, for example, be expected that the research would identify if Dell or another company provides the loans when consumers buy on credit. It is also expected that research will identify if there have or have not been new pieces of legislation that specifically affect this business selling its products. Details of that research should be given. For example, what will be the effect on Dell of the General Product Safety Directive (GPSD) 2005?
AO4	The evaluation here will be simplistic. It should have identified the main pieces of legislation and the main requirements of these and should have stated the most obvious impacts that those requirements will have. There will be limited evaluation of how Dell has responded to the requirements.	At this level the impact of the legislation should be explained and the way that the business responds identified. Dell, for example, will be aware of the requirements of the Consumer Protection (Distance Selling) Regulations, 2000 and will make sure that it has provided all of the details needed about the product for sale, with its name and the price clearly displayed, what the price includes and when the offer ends.	A detailed evaluation is required at this level with clear justifications being given for the impact that the chosen pieces of legislation will have on the business. This should include an evaluation of any changes Dell will need to make to keep in line with new, and even proposed, legislation. The justifications should be clearly linked to the type of business and products being sold. For example, the legislation relating to prices is particularly important because Dell frequently offers its products at sale prices so the Prices Acts and the Consumer Protection Act would apply.

Protecting data

Businesses collect a great deal of data on individual people and data protection legislation is designed to ensure that the businesses do not misuse this data. Business might keep data on individuals for the following reasons.

- They are employees and the business needs the data so that it can keep its staff records up to date, pay staff and identify suitable training and promotion prospects.
- They are customers and this allows the business to contact them, send invoices and inform them about special offers.
- They are customers and the data provides useful market research in terms of what customers buy, what interests they have or where they live, and this builds up buyer profiles.
- They are customers, such as the patients of doctors and dentists, where records need to be kept for the direct benefit of the customers.

Data protection legislation has also been put in place to ensure that individuals, and the general public, have access to data that is about themselves or data of public interest. Businesses need to know what this legislation is and conduct their business in such a way that it does not contravene these acts and regulations.

Businesses also keep data on other businesses but there are generally less restrictions on this data. This does depend on what type of business the data is about. Sole traders and partnerships, because of their legal status, tend to be treated as though they were individuals.

The regulatory body that has been given the task of ensuring that the legislation is followed is the Information Commissioner's Office (ICO).

The ICO's aims are to ensure that:
- public information is out in the open, unless there are good reasons for non-disclosure;
- personal information is properly protected.

Full details of the ICO's role and reference to the legislation can be found on the ICO website at www.ico.gov.uk.

The Data Protection Act, 1998

The **Data Protection Act**, 1984 (DPA) created the basic legislation that deals with data protection and has since been replaced by the 1998 Act which also replaced the **Access to Personal Files Act**, 1987 as well as sections of a number of other acts. The earlier legislation mainly covered electronically stored data. This has now been extended to all data kept in 'relevant filing systems', in other words, electronic or paper based.

The **Data Protection Act**, 1998 lays down eight main controls that businesses must follow.

1. Personal data should be obtained fairly and lawfully.
2. Personal data can only be held for specified and lawful purposes.
3. Personal data cannot be used or disclosed in any manner which is incompatible with the purpose for which it was held.
4. The amount of data held should be adequate, relevant and not excessive.
5. Personal data should be accurate and kept up to date.
6. Personal data should not be kept for longer than is necessary.
7. An individual should be entitled to:
   (a) be informed by any data user if he or she is the subject of personal data and should have access to that data;
   (b) where appropriate, have data corrected or erased.
8. Security measures must be taken by the data user to prevent unlawful access, destruction or loss of personal data.

Each of these controls lays very strict requirements on businesses and any business holding data on individuals needs to ensure that all of these requirements are met.

The Act does require that the individuals whom the data is about are given the opportunity to consent to the collection and processing of their data. In other words they should know about and agree to its collection, preferably in advance. Such an agreement is made when, for example, customers take out a Tesco Clubcard, as explained in Figure 1.

The Act has even stronger protection for sensitive information, such as data about ethnic origins, political opinions, religious beliefs, trade union membership, health, sexual life and any criminal history.

Figure 1 *Tesco Clubcard - Data Protection Statement*

We would like to use your details from the application form, plus details on how you use your Clubcard and what you buy in our stores, to:
- Help manage Tesco Clubcard and improve the way we run it
- Understand our customers' shopping habits to improve our service
- Unless you indicate otherwise, contact you with offers and information about products and services of interest to you and your family.

We will share your details among Tesco companies at home and abroad (e.g. Tesco Personal Finance), and businesses that process Clubcard information on our behalf (e.g. printers who need certain details to print our mailings).

We may also use and share information relating to groups of customers, without identifying individuals, to learn more about customer behaviour and find ways of enhancing our service.

Source: adapted from www.tesco.co.uk.

All individuals have a right to see the data collected about them and when a business is asked for the information it must reply within 40 days and must then supply a copy of the data. There are some exceptions to this, namely if it would:

- affect the way crime is detected or prevented;
- affect the catching or prosecution of criminals;
- affect assessing or collecting taxes and duties;
- disclose data that was provided in confidence, as with a reference for a job.

In some cases the data held by health and social organisations may have restricted access.

There are also clear rules governing releasing data about individuals to other people or businesses. Generally this is not allowed without the permission of the individual except where it is required:

- by law or statutory instrument;
- to prevent or detect crime;
- to assess or collect tax or duty.

Controls on the use of data for direct marketing

The **Data Protection Act (DPA)** also gives individuals the right to stop organisations using personal information for direct marketing purposes. However, the DPA only applies if the data that a business is using for direct marketing is about an actual named individual. If, for example, the business is simply using telephone numbers, street numbers or e-mail addresses the DPA does not apply. To protect individuals who do not want unsolicited marketing new legislation has been passed (see below).

An individual can register free with four preference services to prevent businesses from sending them marketing information that they do not want. The services are:

- the Mailing Preference Service (MPS);
- the Telephone Preference Service (TPS);
- the Fax Preference Service (FPS);
- the E-mail Preference Service (EPS).

Once an individual is registered businesses should not use that system for unsolicited marketing. Indeed the **Privacy and Electronic Communications (EC Directive) Regulations, 2003** make it illegal for a businesses to make unsolicited direct marketing calls or faxes to individuals who have indicated that they do not want to receive such calls or faxes. The MPS and EPS lists are only voluntary lists but most businesses do take notice of them.

Privacy and Electronic Communications (EC Directive) Regulations, 2003

These regulations apply to the sending of direct marketing messages by electronic means such as by telephone, fax, e-mail, text message and picture (including video) message and by use of an automated calling system. They also apply to new technological methods as they are invented. They have replaced and added to the requirements set down in the **Telecommunications (Data Protection and Privacy) Regulations, 1999**.

For telephone and fax marketing The following rules apply.

- If a business has been told by an individual that they are not to be contacted by phone for marketing purposes it must not do this.
- A business must not contact by phone, for marketing purposes, anyone on the TPS or FPS list.
- The business's employees must identify the name of the business when making a telesales call. If asked, they must provide a valid business address or freephone telephone number for contact purposes.
- For marketing by fax the business must have consent in advance from the individual to do this.

For electronic mail marketing The following rules apply.

- The individual must consent to receive unsolicited marketing by electronic mail before the business can send it.
- If consent has been received the marketing information must include a valid address so that the individual can opt-out for the future if they wish to.

The rule about opting out can be complex and businesses often use what has been called a 'soft opt-in' to get around this. It would be assumed that an individual had opted in if the business had:

1. Placed a tick box on their web site that said 'If this is not ticked we will assume you are willing to receive marketing information.'
2. If the contact details of the individual have been given to the business when it sold them something else.
3. If the business has already sent information about something similar to the individual.

Business to business When businesses are using direct marketing to companies there are far less restrictions in terms of what they can or cannot do. They must, however, give their identity and offer the opportunity to opt-out. If a company does opt-out the business using the direct marketing can still send information and it would not be breaking the law. It would, however, be a foolish thing to do as the other business is likely to annoyed and ignore it.

Sole traders and partnerships are treated in English law as individuals and they have the same protection under this 2003 regulation as ordinary individuals.

Other important legislation

The **Freedom of Information Act, 2000**, which came fully into force in 2005, allows people to gain information that is held by public authorities. Generally anyone can ask for information that is held by a public authority, which includes central and local governments, the police, health services and schools. It also makes it a criminal offence for a public authority to alter, deface, block, erase, destroy or conceal any record it holds in order to prevent its disclosure.

There are however exceptions to the right to disclosure similar to those for the **Data Protection Act**, including:

- if it is against the public interest to disclose information;
- where there is a national security issue;
- where information relates to court records;
- personal information;
- where information could prejudice law enforcement.

Knowing that this right of disclosure of information now exists is likely to mean that public authorities will in future be very careful about what is, or is not, recorded in their paper based or electronic records.

Meeting the assessment criteria - examiners' guidance

For your chosen business you are required to produce a Chairman's report which describes, applies, analyses and evaluates the effects of external influences on a business. This will involve consideration of the impact of data protection legislation.

Business example - Comet Jobs Privacy Policy

Comet's retail section employs more than 6,000 permanent full-time and part-time staff with another 2,000 joining for the busy October to January period. One way in which Comet recruits new employees is through its online recruiting service Comet Jobs. To ensure that it meets the requirements of the Data Protection Act it follows a strict Privacy Policy for this service. This policy is

summarised as:

'We will use information you provide us on Cometjobs.co.uk for recruitment purposes only, and this information will not be shared with third parties for purposes other than Comet recruitment.'

The policy also includes details of the following.

What personal data will be collected	Name, address, e-mail, etc. Age, nationality, etc. Past experience, etc. th will help assess suitability for the job.
Storage of data	Stored in secure facilities which only a access to authorised personnel and w are regularly tested for security.
Retaining data if not employed	Data will be kept on the system for up to six months so that applicants can be informed of any other jobs tha might be suitable for them. Individuals be regularly asked if they want to rema on the list.
Other data that might be stored	The applicant's domain name and IP address, operating system, browser, version, cookie details and the website that you visited prior to our site.
Access to the data stored	Access to all the information is available for a small charge and any inaccurate information will be corrected.

Source: adapted from cometjobs.co.uk.

AOs	Mark Band 1	Mark Band 2	Mark Band 3
AO1	There should be basic details of the business in terms of what Comet does and, in this case, the role of the online jobs section. The basic requirements of the Data Protection Act (DPA) should be given but there would be limited application to the business or the recruitment process being carried out by Comet Jobs.	Much fuller details of the business should be given with reference to numbers of employees, the need to recruit and keep details on record for six months, especially for the Oct – Jan period. The requirements of the DPA should be put into context so the description of what data the business holds should include an explanation of why the data is needed and how the eight rules of the DPA could be broken.	It should be clear at this level that the requirements of the DPA are fully understood and the Privacy Policy of Comet Jobs should be matched against those requirements. There should be clear explanations of why Comet Jobs needs the data it is collecting, e.g. address, so that it can contact people to ask them for interviews. It should also be clear that the operation of the DPA allows such things as charging for access (up to £10), and what procedure would take place if there was a breach, e.g. contacting the business first and then the ICO.

AOs	Mark Band 1	Mark Band 2	Mark Band 3
AO2	The basic effects of the DPA on Comet Jobs will be described but the approach will be fairly general. There will be little consideration of what Comet Jobs needs the data for, nor of how its Privacy Policy ensures that the requirements of the DPA are being met.	A good understanding of what data is being held by Comet Jobs and for what general purposes it is needed. It would then be possible to take the basic requirements of the DPA and show how they are being met through the Privacy Policy. Some data must be held if Comet Jobs is to carry out its functions and it has made it very clear what will be held, for how long and what it will be used for.	Application here does require reference to two examples of each type of legislation so there should also be consideration of, say, the Privacy and Electronic Communications (EC Directive) Regulations, 2003. Consideration might include why this legislation would not apply to Comet Jobs but would apply to the Comet retail sector and any direct marketing. Application of the DPA to Comet Jobs should be detailed and show a good understanding of what the business does with the data and why, for example it likes to hold on to the data for up to six months.
AO3	At this level only limited sources will be used, for example the cometjobs.co.uk website and one source that gives the general details of the DPA. Basic analysis should show what Comet Jobs does, the main points of the Privacy Policy and the main requirements of the DPA.	A wider range of sources is required and should include the ICO and links from the Comet Jobs website to check on the main business of Comet itself. Legislation other than the DPA should also have been checked to see if it is likely to affect the business. There should be clear evidence of selecting the most relevant information from the different sources.	The research at this level should be thorough, comprehensive and up-to-date. There should be no obvious sources that have not been checked. Analysis should be of a high standard so that only the relevant information is included, but it should also show evidence of other potential avenues of investigation For example, the Privacy Policy explains that it is part of Comet Group Plc which itself is part of the Kesa Electricals Group. Can the data be passed on to these other bodies?
AO4	The evaluation here will be simplistic. It should have identified the main requirements of the DPA and given a basic assessment of whether or not Comet Jobs is meeting these. This might be done by taking each of the eight main controls in turn and seeing if they are covered by the Privacy Policy.	At this level the impact of the DPA should be explained and the way that the business has responded identified. This would include: <ul><li>why the Privacy Policy was created and posted on the website;</li><li>the extent to which each requirement of the DPA has been met;</li><li>whether or not other legislation applies to Comet Jobs and if this is covered in the Privacy Policy.</li></ul>	A detailed evaluation is required at this level with clear justifications being given for the impact of the DPA on the business. It is likely that this would need to be explained on a what-if? basis because Comet Jobs does have a comprehensive Privacy Policy in place. The evaluation could include what would need to be changed if the policy had to apply to the permanent employees and to consumers of the retail products. It might also question some elements of the data that 'might' be collected, such as 'the website visited prior to our site'.

Portfolio practice · Marketing using more than one media

In his **Guidance on The Privacy and Electronic Communications (EC Directive) Regulations**, 2003 the Information Commissioner gave the following question and answer to illustrate how the regulation could affect a business marketing by more than one media.

(a) **Explain what is meant by a 'consent option' and how the extract shows the way in which a business could get this.**

(b) **This business wants to use individuals' details for marketing purposes. Write out a suitable section for its form, remembering that there is limited space, which would ensure that this business is not breaking either the Data Protection Act, 1998 or the Privacy and Electronic Communications (EC Directive) Regulations, 2003.**

(c) **Explain what rights an individual would have to see the data that had been collected on them.**

We collect individuals' addresses, telephone numbers, mobile numbers and email addresses for marketing purposes on a paper form. We have limited room on the form and we have to provide other information in order to comply with other legislation. What is the minimum amount of information we have to provide in order to comply with data protection rules?

Under DPA, the bare minimum that you are obliged to tell people is who you are and what you plan to do with their information, including any unexpected use such as processing for marketing purposes and/or disclosures to third parties. Because you plan to market by electronic means, you also need to provide consent options. The very highest standard would be to provide the individual with the opportunity to solicit information from you e.g.:

'Please contact me by post ❑, by telephone ❑, by text/picture/video message ❑ by e-mail ❑ with further information about your products and services (tick as applicable).'

However, if you use this wording, you cannot send marketing material to them by post, telephone, text message or e-mail unless the individual ticks the box to invite further contact from you.

Source: adapted from www.ico.gov.uk.

Many businesses and public organisations hold data on individuals. This is likely to include students and their families.

1. Make a list of businesses that you believe have data on you or your family.
2. Select some of these businesses and write down a list of the data that you think they are likely to hold about you or your family.
3. Prepare a letter, detailing that information, and send this to the businesses requesting that they send you the data that they hold on you. Remember that some of these businesses may want to charge you up to £10. Others may provide the data free, and those are the ones to target. Also remember that if this is data about some other family member they should be making the request.
4. Consider how you or your family gave the business permission to hold this data.

Research task

Protecting employees

There is a great deal of employment legislation that has affected the way in which businesses operate. Many of the Acts and regulations have simply been amended and built on previous legislation, so it is often difficult to find out exactly what the law is. There have also been a huge number of European Union treaties, regulations and directives that have had to be incorporated into law in the UK. Figure 1 shows some of the areas covered by employment law.

Figure 1 *Elements of employment law*

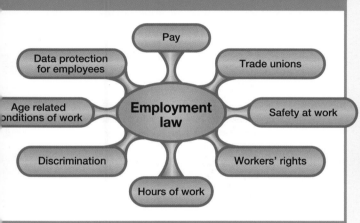

This section will consider most of these under four headings.
* Discrimination in employment.
* Employment rights.
* Employment relations.
* Health and safety at work.

Businesses that do not comply with the legislation can be taken to an employment tribunal or court, fined, and made to pay compensation. It is, therefore, very important for businesses to find out exactly what these laws require and to ensure that they meet these requirements. The details given below show the major requirements of the legislation.

Discrimination in employment

Discrimination in employment occurs when one person is treated differently than another simply because of differences that have nothing to do with their work, for example discrimination because of their race, gender or disabilities. Laws to deal with this discrimination have been built up over a number of years and will continue to grow as additional discriminations, such as discrimination on the basis of age, are legislated against.

Discrimination can be direct or indirect. **Direct discrimination** occurs where an employer or prospective employer treats, for example, one sex less favourably than the

other on the grounds of sex. An example would be where a job advertisement was only for a male or only for a female even though the job could be done equally well by either.

Indirect discrimination will occur where a requirement or condition is applied, for example, equally to men and women, but in reality it is harder for one sex to meet this condition. An example would be where only a full-time post was offered because many women find that harder to do because of family commitments.

The Equal Pay Acts, 1970 & 1983 These Acts make it illegal to pay men and women different rates if they are doing the same job, a very similar job or one that has equal value. The Acts give details of how the jobs will be measured against each other and details of how and when to claim for a breach of the Act. The **Equal Pay Act 1970 (Amendment) Regulations**, 2003 have made some minor changes to when claims can be made which might apply to specific businesses.

Despite over 35 years in which the **Equal Pay Act** has been in force, there are still significant differences in the average rate of pay for men and women, as shown in Figure 2.

Figure 2 *Average rate of pay for women compared to each £100 paid to men (2005)*

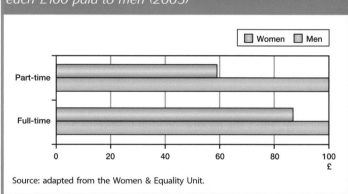

Source: adapted from the Women & Equality Unit.

The Sex Discrimination Act, 1975 This Act makes it unlawful to discriminate on the grounds of gender, marital status or gender reassignment in recruitment, promotion and training. The Act also covers education, the provision of housing, goods and services and advertising. **The Sex Discrimination Act**, 1986 made some important amendments to the original Act, including:
* making it unlawful to set different retirement ages for men and women;
* extending the law to employers with five or fewer employees;
* removing the restriction on women's hours and times of work (e.g. shift work and night work).

There was a **Sex Discrimination Act 1975 (Amendment) Regulations**, 2003 but this dealt mainly with the police authorities as employers.

The need to ensure that men and women are treated the same is even more important now as women have a much greater role in the workforce than they did in 1975, as shown in Table 1.

Table 1 *Changing role of women 1975 & 2005**		
	1975	**2005**
Employment rates: Women (aged 16 – 59) Men (aged 16 – 64)	60% 90%	70% 80%
Working women with dependent children	47%	67%
Hours worked compared to men (full-time)	87%	92%
Percentage of self-employed jobs compared to men	20%	28%
Percentage of managers compared to men	1.8%	33.1%

* Dates are approximate.
Source: adapted from various sources.

The Race Relations Act, 1976 This Act makes it illegal to discriminate on the grounds of race, colour, nationality or ethnic or national origin, as illustrated in Figure 3. This Act covers recruitment, promotion and training as well as education, the provision of housing, goods and services.

The requirements of this Act are very similar, in general terms, to the **Sex Discrimination Acts**. As with those Acts there are exceptions where favouring one candidate for a job above another may not be considered discrimination. This could include:

- where the job expects people from a particular racial group, for example, a Chinese waiter/waitress in an ethnic Chinese restaurant;
- where there is positive discrimination designed to make the balance of employees from different racial groups more accurately reflect the national or local balance of people.

Figure 3 *The cost of race relations legislation*

'In 2003/2004, race was the main element in 2,830 claims registered by employment tribunals. At an average cost to an employer of £5,813 to defend a claim of racial discrimination or harassment, the total cost to employers each year is around £16,451,000.'

Extract from Trevor Phillips' address to the BT Business Breakfast event (2006). Trevor Phillips is the Chair of the Commission for Racial Equality (CRE).

Source: adapted from www.cre.gov.uk.

There have been two recent amendments to the **Race Relations Act**. The **Race Relations Amendment Act, 2000** mainly dealt with possible discrimination by the police and also with matters of national security. The **Race Relations Act 1976**

(Amendments) Regulations 2003, made many technical changes including changes related to the definition of 'indirect discrimination' and 'harassment' in racial discrimination situations and to the burden of proof needed in proceedings.

The Disability Discrimination Act 1995 This Act made discrimination on the basis of disability essentially the same as that for sex or race. There is, however, a complication with disability because it clearly does affect how suitable a person may be for a particular job. What this Act, and the 2003 amendment, also did was to require businesses to change their work environments so that disabled people could work there.

This Act now covers:

- all employers, whatever size the business;
- all employees;
- all occupations with the exception of the armed forces;
- the responsibility of employers for the discriminatory actions of their employees unless practical steps, such as training, have been taken to prevent this.

As with the sex and race discrimination, what constitutes discrimination can be very wide and the Act, or a summary of it, should be studied with the chosen business in mind. It is, for example, illegal to 'violate the disabled person's dignity'.

The requirement that a business must make reasonable adjustments to the work environment would include all of the following:

- ensuring easy access to buildings, rooms, etc.
- changing the way tests are run at interview, e.g. oral or in brail for blind applicants;
- modifying computers so that disabled people can use them effectively;
- reallocating some minor duties to other non-disabled work colleagues.

Clearly it is not reasonable to expect everything to be changed to accommodate every disability and the cost and difficulty of the changes would be taken into account. There will also be some jobs that some disabled people simply cannot do, for example, a blind person driving a van or lorry, so it would not be against the law to exclude them.

The Human Rights Act, 1998 The Human Rights Act is primarily about our basic human rights and is therefore much wider than just employment law, but it does affect it.

Article 8 provides the 'right to respect for private and family life'. This could affect businesses. They do not have the right to intercept private calls or e-mails, although they can stop them if there is time wasting.

Article 10 provides the 'right to freedom of expression'. This could have an impact on dress codes within organisations. For example someone who in their private life chooses to wear a nose ring may claim the right to wear it in the office.

The Employment Equality (Sexual Orientation) Regulations, 2003 & The Employment Equality (Religion or Belief) Regulations, 2003 These two regulations implemented law from the EU and provided these two additional categories of people similar rights to those covered by the other discrimination legislation.

The **Sexual Orientation Regulations** apply to discrimination on grounds of orientation towards persons of the same sex lesbians and gays), the opposite sex (heterosexuals) and the same and opposite sex (bisexuals). The **Religion or Belief Regulations** apply to discrimination on grounds of religion, religious belief or similar philosophical belief.

As with the other discrimination laws, these regulations deal with direct and indirect discrimination, harassment and victimisation.

The Equality Act, 2006 This Act has widened the areas of discrimination covered by legislation, particularly in terms of sexual orientation, religion and belief. It has also set up a Commission for Equality and Human Rights and outlined its duties. This will replace the Equal Opportunities Commission, the Commission for Racial Equality, and the Disability Rights Commission. The duties will cover all of the areas of discrimination and rights shown in Table 2.

Table 2		
Age	Disability	Religion or belief
Race	Gender	Sexual orientation
The promotion and monitoring of human rights		

Employment rights

All of the legislation referred to above gives rights to employees, but they generally relate to discrimination. Below other pieces of legislation are considered that give more general rights, although some may still relate to discrimination as with the right of women to take maternity leave. If they were not allowed to, it would be clear discrimination against women.

The Employment Rights Act, 1996 The Act provides employees with the following rights:
- a written statement of employment, within 8 weeks of starting work, giving the main details about name of employer, rate of pay, location, hours of work, holidays, etc.;
- an itemised pay statement;
- protection of wages;
- protection from being made to work on Sundays;
- time off work for public duties and employees' representatives;
- time off work to look for work and arrange training and for ante-natal care;
- when suspended from work on medical and maternity grounds;
- maternity rights;
- rights related to termination of employment: notice periods, written reasons for dismissal;
- not to be unfairly dismissed (and the remedies if a person is unfairly dismissed);
- redundancy provisions and payments.

The National Minimum Wage Act, 1998 This Act set minimum wages for people in employment with four main categories:
- employees 22+ (except those within the first six months of their job and receiving accredited training);
- employees aged from 18 to 21 (plus those 22+ within the first six weeks or on accredited training);
- employees aged 16 and 17 who had finished compulsory education;
- no minimum wage for people below school leaving age.

Benefits such as redundancy payments, employers' pension contributions, loans, or awards are not generally counted as pay.

Because national wages rise each year the national minimum wage is also raised each year with a new regulation or order. Minimum wage rates in 2005/06 are shown in Figure 4.

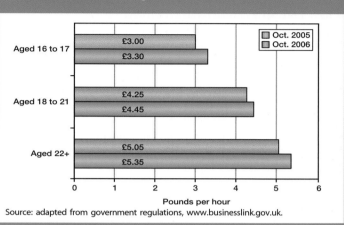

Figure 4 *Minimum wage rates October 2005/2006*

Source: adapted from government regulations, www.businesslink.gov.uk.

Working time The European Union has been responsible for a huge number of pieces of employment legislation, many of which have been introduced into UK law as statutory instruments. These include legislation on:
- redundancy payments (1999);
- maternity and parental leave (1999);
- part-time workers (2000);
- fixed term workers (2002).

The most well known is the **Working Time Regulations, 1998**, which has been amended in 1999, 2001 and 2002. The main requirement of this legislation was that employees could not be forced to work more than 48 hours (on average) a week. They could, however, work more hours if they wanted to. The legislation also introduced other requirements on working time:
- four weeks' paid annual leave;
- a daily rest period of 11 hours;
- a daily rest break of 20 minutes;
- a weekly rest period of 24 hours;
- restrictions on the amount of night work that can be required;
- a limit to young people's (16 to 18) work to 8 hours a day and 40 hours a week.

Employment Act, 2002 This Act deals with a range of issues, many of which had been covered in previous legislation but now needed to be updated. These issues include:
- help for working mothers allowing a year's maternity leave, half of which would receive maternity pay;
- two weeks' paid leave for working fathers;
- the right to flexible working for mothers and fathers with children under 5 years of age;
- measures and recommendations to help to resolve disputes between employees and employers;
- additional rights for fixed term employees;
- time off for trade union representatives to train in that role.

Employment relations

Generally employers and employees work well together, but occasionally disputes do arise and this can lead to action taken by the employees, such as strikes and go-slows, and by the employers, such as lock outs and sacking employees. What is or is not permitted for both sides is governed by legislation that has been built up through many Acts.

The law now requires actions by employees:

- to be part of a trade dispute;
- only to take place after the union which called for it has first held a properly conducted secret ballot;
- only to take place after the trade union has provided the required notice of official industrial action to the employers;
- not to be for the purposes of promoting closed shop practices, or of preventing employers using non-union firms as suppliers;
- not to be in support of any employee dismissed while taking unofficial industrial action;
- not to involve unlawful picketing.

Although these rules apply to unions and employees taking industrial action, it is also important that businesses understand the rules. If employees follow the rules then it becomes illegal for the employer to dismiss them for the first 12 weeks because the employees have taken action. Even after this period the employer cannot discriminate by dismissing only some of those taking action.

The Employment Relations Act, 1999 This Act includes the following elements of employment relations:

- the requirement that organisations employing 21 or more workers recognise individual trade unions if the majority of the workforce want this;
- the requirement that employers must not discriminate on the basis of whether a person is or is not in a trade union;
- the rights for maternity and parental leave (note other legislation that also covers this);
- the right for workers to be accompanied by a fellow worker or a trade union official during disciplinary and grievance hearings;
- the right for part-time workers to be treated the same as full-time workers in their terms and conditions of work.

The Employment Relations Act, 2004 The Act makes various technical changes to previous Acts, mainly the **Employment Relations Act**, 1999. Whilst it is important for businesses to be aware of the changes, it is very likely that the business chosen for study will not be affected. It does, however, specifically clarify the following:

- how trade unions can get recognition from the employer and what procedures should be followed if the employer will not recognise the union;
- when an employer can apply to end an agreement to recognise a trade union;
- procedures that must be followed before and during industrial action;
- protection for employees who are on strike;
- additional rights for trade union members, employees and workers (which mainly amend the **Employment Rights Act**).

Health and safety

Businesses are also responsible for the health and safety of their employees whilst they are at work and legislation has been passed to ensure that employees are protected.

The Health and Safety at Work Act, 1974 This is the main piece of legislation dealing with health and safety at work and, although there have been many additions and amendments, it provides the basic regulations. These include for the employer that

- there must be a written policy on health and safety on public display to all workers;
- managers and employees must comply with this policy;
- managers must give employees training, information and supervision on health and safety issues;
- safety representatives must be appointed;
- safety equipment and clothing must be provided free;
- personal protective equipment must be provided;
- safe handling, storage and transportation of substances is ensured;
- welfare facilities are provided.

For the employees, they must:

- obey the requirements of the Act;
- take reasonable care of themselves and others;
- not misuse items;
- report damaged items.

The Health and Safety Executive and Health and Safety Commission are responsible for ensuring that the Act is carried out. Inspectors have the power to visit businesses and investigate. Businesses that do not comply with the law can be taken to court and fined.

The 1974 Act has been amended by various other pieces of legislation including the **Management of Health and Safety at Work Regulations, 1992 and 1999**. These are fairly general regulations that affect many industries but there have also been many regulations that affect specific industries and need to be checked if that is the industry being studied because they lay down specific requirements for safety of employees in those industries. Examples include:

- the **Railways (Safety Case) Regulations, 1994**;
- the **Construction (Design and Management) Regulations, 1994**;
- the **Mines Miscellaneous Health and Safety Provisions Regulations, 1995**;
- the **Gas Safety (Management) Regulations, 1996**;
- the **Control of Substances Hazardous to Health Regulations, 1994 & 1999 (COSHH)**;
- the **Quarries Regulations, 1999**;
- the **Prohibition of Smoking in Certain Premises (Scotland) Regulations, 2006**.

There are also industries where specific health and safety laws have been created because of the potential additional risks involved. These include the food industry where all of the following pieces of legislation will affect employment legislation:

- **Food Safety Act, 1990**;
- **Food Safety (General Food Hygiene) Regulations, 1995**;
- **Food Hygiene (England) Regulations, 2006**.

For all of the pieces of legislation it is important to relate them to the specific business or industry being studied and to consider the impact that they will have on the way that the business or industry must operate.

Meeting the assessment criteria - examiners' guidance

For your chosen business you are required to produce a chairman's report which describes, applies, analyses and evaluates the effects of external influences on a business. This will involve consideration of the impact of employment legislation on the business.

Business example - Pilkington's Policy on Employment

Pilkington is one of the world's largest manufacturers of glass and glazing products for building, automotive and related technical markets. It employs around 23,800 people worldwide.

Its approach to its workforce is that it believes that the range of nationalities, skills, qualifications and experience available in its many areas of operations are a positive benefit to the Group's business. A strict equal opportunity policy prohibits discrimination on the basis of 'race, colour, creed, religion, age, gender, sexual orientation, national origin, disability, union membership, political affiliation or any other status protected by law'. This policy operates in all employment-related decisions.

The health, safety and well being of all employees, contractors, visitors, neighbours and customers remain in the forefront of our business activity. Pilkington's safety policy is based on the premise that all accidents are preventable. Our primary measure of safety performance is the lost time accident rate (LTAR) – recording any work-related injury or illness resulting in one or more day's absence from work.

Source: adapted from Pilkington website, www.pilkington.com.

Key features of the Pilkington Code of Conduct.
- Working safely.
- Responsibility towards the environment.
- Operating within the Law.
- Cultural and ethical responsibilities.
- Human rights and employment standards.
- Avoiding conflicts of interest.
- Rules regarding gifts, favours and payments.
- Relationships with customers, suppliers, business partners and competitors.
- Retention of accurate and complete records.
- Relationships with the community.
- Protection of personal and confidential information.
- Responsibilities of individuals.

AOs	Mark Band 1	Mark Band 2	Mark Band 3
AO1	There should be basic details of the business in terms of what Pilkington does, numbers of employees and where the factories and offices are based. Basic details such as the total number of employees, 23,800 worldwide, and recognition of the main employment legislation on anti-discrimination and general employment rights, would be expected.	Much fuller details of the business should be given with, for example, a clear breakdown of employees into UK based and others. The nature of the business should also be considered and, for example, the likely importance of health and safety and hazardous materials because this is a manufacturing business. Reference to specific legislation would be expected with examples of how that would affect the business. A sound knowledge of the main points of the legislation is required.	The knowledge of the business, its employment processes and the way that it meets employment legislation should be shown in detail. For Pilkington the appropriate legislation should be identified and examples provided of how the business meets the requirements. For example, the approach to its workforce states that it considered that a range of nationalities, skills, qualifications and experience is important. Details should be provided of what Pilkington does to ensure that range and how this matches the requirements of various Acts. The same should be done with the employment parts of the list of 'Key features of the Pilkington Code of Conduct.'

AOs	Mark Band 1	Mark Band 2	Mark Band 3
AO2	Pilkington makes clear its commitment to anti-discrimination and health and safety legislation. The appropriate legislation should be identified and applied to the stated commitments. Pilkington's commitments and the legislation will be matched and should include simple examples of how the business does this, e.g. in the way it recruits staff.	Details at this level must give an accurate description of the relevant legislation and the effects that the legislation is having on the business. For example, the main requirements of the legislation on equal opportunities should be given. This should then be matched against Pilkington's 'strict equal opportunity policy'. A basic explanation should be given of how the policy meets the requirements.	Application here does require reference to two examples of each type of legislation and there should be details of anti-discrimination legislation and other employment rights. The stated policy is very clear in terms of Pilkington's commitments to its employees and to meeting the requirements of employment legislation. Both the legislation and how Pilkington meets the requirements should be given in detail. Clarification of the commitments, e.g. to 'human rights' will be needed and there could also be some consideration of where the business goes beyond the requirements.
AO3	At this level only limited sources will be used, for example Pilkington's website, the Code of Conduct and textbooks that show the main requirements of employment legislation. The analysis should be sufficient to ensure that all details from the legislation are relevant to Pilkington and that most of the details about the business for this section refer to employment.	Sources for the legislation must be accurate and should be cross checked. Most acts of parliament are very detailed and the appropriate major requirements need to be selected. The need to be up-to-date with legislation means that sources other than textbooks should also have been checked. For details of the business and how it meets the employment legislation contact should be made with the business itself as well as checking its website, company reports, etc.	The research at this level should be thorough, comprehensive and up-to-date. Sources must provide both the basic requirements of the major pieces of employment legislation that are still in force, such as the Equal Pay Act, the Employment Rights Act and the Discrimination Acts, and also more recent legislation such as the Equality Act and any major legislation passed since the publication of this textbook. Recent statutory instruments should also be checked to see if there are any that relate specifically to how Pilkington produces its goods. The selection of all of the legislation must be appropriate to Pilkington and should be prioritised in terms of which are most important.
AO4	The evaluation here will be simplistic. The requirements of one major Act will be taken and the likely impact on the way Pilkington operates will be given. For example, the main requirements of the Anti-discrimination Acts would be listed with comments on how Pilkington would need to react. There should then be a basic evaluation of how the business has reacted, as shown, for example, by its policy statements.	At this level the evaluation of how the employment legislation has affected Pilkington should include a basic judgement on the effects of the legislation and on how well the business has met the major legal requirements. The policy commitments provide part of the answer but some evaluation of what is happening in the actual workplace is also needed. Details such as the number of women in management positions, the effectiveness of trade unions and minimum rates of pay could provide very valuable data for the evaluation.	A detailed evaluation is required at this level with clear justifications being given for the impact of the employment legislation. The legislation lays down basic requirements and a good evaluation would look at the extent to which Pilkington has gone beyond those basic requirements. How much higher, for example, is the lowest wage compared to the required minimum wage? The policy says the business works 'on the premise that all accidents are preventable'. Is that the case in practice? There should also be some recognition that employment laws and other laws may be linked, for example protecting employees' right to privacy through the Data Protection Act.

Using reports from papers, other media or the Internet about an industrial dispute that has been in the news, carry out the following tasks.

1. Outline the details of the dispute.
   (a) The parties involved, i.e. the business, the trade union, other affected groups such as other businesses, customers, etc.
   (b) What the dispute is about, pay, conditions, job losses, etc.
2. Check the requirements of legislation that relate to industrial action.
3. Identify from the reports any details of how the trade union, employees and the employer followed, or did not follow, the legislation in the way that the industrial action was carried out.
4. State what the outcome of the dispute was or, if it has not finished, what the outcome is likely to be.

Research task

Portfolio practice · Flexible working

As part of its role of providing information to employers and employees, the Department of Trade and Industry (DTI) has produced guidance on flexible working.

(a) **What is the meaning of the term 'flexible working' in terms of UK law?**
(b) **What would be typical job roles and businesses in which flexible working would be common?**
(c) **In the column 'What kind of changes can be applied for?' there are examples of different work patterns. What does each of these mean?**
   - **annualised hours**
   - **compressed hours**
   - **home working**
   - **job-sharing**
   - **self-rostering**
   - **staggered hours**
   - **term-time working.**
(d) **Looking at the 'Who can apply?' column, why are these people likely to want, or need, flexible working?**
(e) **What are the practical implications for businesses as they respond to employees' rights to flexible working?**

Who can apply?	What kind of changes can be applied for?
In order to make a request under the new right an individual will: <ul><li>be an employee</li><li>have a child under six, or under 18 in the case of a disabled child</li><li>be either - the child's mother, father, adopter, guardian or foster parent, or - married to or the partner of the child's mother, father, adopter, guardian or foster parent</li><li>have worked with their employer continuously for at least 26 weeks at the date the application is made</li><li>make the application no later than two weeks before the child's sixth birthday or 18th birthday in the case of a disabled child</li><li>have or expect to have responsibility for the child's upbringing</li><li>be making the application to enable them to care for the child</li><li>not be an agency worker</li><li>not be a member of the armed forces</li><li>not have made another application to work flexibly under the right during the past twelve months.</li></ul>	Eligible employees will be able to request: <ul><li>a change to the hours they work</li><li>a change to the times when they are required to work</li><li>to work from home.</li></ul> This covers working patterns such as annualised hours, compressed hours, flexitime, homeworking, job-sharing, self-rostering, shift working, staggered hours and term-time working (further information on different types of flexible working and the potential business benefits is available).

Source: adapted from *Flexible working - a right to request: A basic summary*, DTI.

367

Changes in the economy

This section considers the changes that are occurring in both the UK economy and the wider world economies and how these changes are likely to affect specific businesses. In order to understand how changes in the economy affect businesses it is necessary to understand what the important parts of the economy are.

For businesses the major concern will be 'is there a demand for what the business is making?' But that is really only part of the picture. Businesses will, for example, also need to consider what their competitors are doing, whether they can get enough employees and whether they have sufficient capital to invest in new machinery. All of these factors will depend on what is happening to the economy as a whole.

When the government examines the health of the economy it will look at certain specific indicators. The most important are:

- economic growth;
- unemployment;
- inflation;
- the Balance of Payments and exchange rates;
- interest rates.

For each of these, this section will show how it is measured, what that measure indicates and how businesses can use this data to make their decisions. The importance of changes over time in each of the indicators will be looked at in more detail in sections 69 and 70.

GDP and economic growth

Gross Domestic Product (GDP) measures the total amount of goods and services, in money terms, produced in a country during a specific time period, usually a year. Figure 1 shows how much GDP was produced in the UK for each year between 1994 and 2004. In 2004 the value of the total production in the UK was over £1,163,000 million.

GDP figures are useful for businesses because they provide three major sets of data: production; income; and expenditure (see below). These are all different measures of the **national income**.

Economic growth Each year the size of the GDP changes, usually getting larger. When it gets larger this is called **economic growth**. If it gets smaller, which it does in some years, this is called **negative growth**. Economic growth is usually shown as a percentage. For example, the UK had a growth rate of 3.1% in 2004 and 1.8% in 2005. This indicates that output, income and spending had risen by 3.1% between 2003 and 2004 and 1.8% between 2004 and 2005. Further details on economic growth are given in section 69.

Production or output The production or output figures show how much has been produced in the country. It splits this down into all of the major industrial and business sections. Businesses can therefore study these figures to find out how big the market is for their type of products and how the production has been changing in that sector. It should also help to inform businesses about which products are being supplied by other UK businesses and which may need to be imported.

Figure 1 shows that total production (GDP) for the UK has risen, after taking account of inflation, every year from 1994 to 2004. Businesses also need to know what is specifically happening in their sectors. Figure 2 shows what happened in three sectors, leather manufacturing, communications and education, compared to all sectors.

The leather manufacturing industry has clearly suffered a major collapse whereas education is close to the average and growing slightly. On the other hand the communications industry has done very well, helped by such developments as mobile phones and 3G.

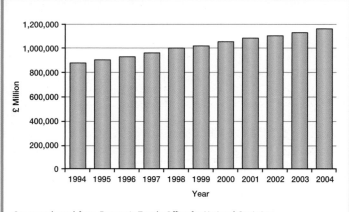

Figure 1 *GDP for UK 1994 to 2004 (£ million)*

Source: adapted from *Economic Trends*, Office for National Statistics.

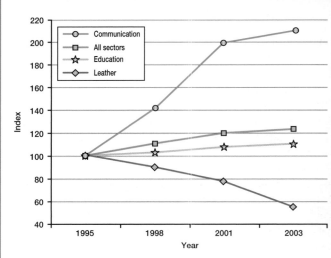

Figure 2 *Changes in output in selected UK sectors 1995 to 2003 (1995 = 100)*

Source: adapted from *Economic Trends*, Office for National Statistics.

Income When GDP is measured in terms of incomes it shows which sections of the economy received income from the sale of goods and services. This is divided into incomes from employment, incomes from self-employment, profits for businesses and rent.

These figures provide businesses with details of how much income the population has and therefore how much it has available to spend. With 59.8 million people in the UK in 2004, and a total national income of £1,163,000 million, that means that on average each person had £19,448 pounds to spend. That of course ignores the fact that some people have high incomes whilst others have low incomes and that the government takes a very large percentage of this income and spends it. But all of these figures are available through the national income statistics. Figure 3, for example, shows the amount of income received per person working in Warwickshire compared to the national average. Over this period Warwickshire incomes have gone from being £155 below the national average to being £613 above the national average. This might show that Warwickshire is a good potential market for businesses to target.

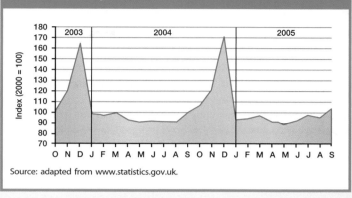

Figure 4 *Sales of books, newspapers and periodicals, Oct. 2003 to Sep. 2005 (2000 = 100)*

Source: adapted from www.statistics.gov.uk.

Figure 3 *Income per head (£s) in Warwickshire compared to national average (1995 to 2002)*

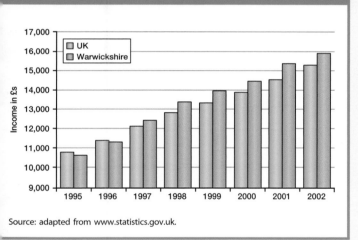

Source: adapted from www.statistics.gov.uk.

Expenditure Knowing what is being produced and who is earning the income will be useful for businesses because it will help them to compare their own performance against national averages and may help them to know which sections of industry, or which parts of the country to target. What is probably more important for businesses is for them to know how the national income is being spent. That will indicate if there is a demand for the kind of products that they are making, or thinking of making.

The national expenditure figures provide details of what people, and businesses, have spent their incomes on. They also include details of imports and exports so that businesses can see what foreigners are buying from the UK and what UK citizens are spending their money on abroad.

As Figure 4 shows, the statistics are very detailed and can apply to individual industries. Businesses producing books will find it very useful to know that sales rise just before Christmas, peaking in December. This might tell them the best time to launch new books.

Employment, unemployment, pay and skills requirements

Employment and unemployment figures provide data about the labour market. This is potentially very useful to businesses as it will provide them with details of the kinds of people who are or are not employed, how many there are, how long they have been unemployed, how much they are paid, and so on. Below some of these statistics are considered with an explanation of why they may be useful to businesses.

Unemployment This will provide details of all of the following.
- How many people are looking for work. This could tell businesses how easy it will be to recruit additional staff.
- What age groups they are in. Some businesses will want to recruit long-term staff who will stay with the business for many years.
- What part of the country they are in. This may help businesses to decide where the best place to locate will be.
- How long they have been unemployed. This is likely to indicate the level of training unemployed people may need before they can work effectively again.
- Vacancies by industry. This will help business see how many other businesses in their type of industry are also looking for employees and hence how difficult recruitment is likely to be.

The levels of unemployment are also a major indicator of how well the economy as a whole is doing (see section 69).

Employment Employment figures provide details of how many people are employed in each industry, their age groups, the number of men and women and the average hours they work. Businesses can use this data to consider their balance of employees against businesses producing similar products.

Pay and productivity Employment statistics also provide details of a range of measures that can tell businesses how well their employees are performing compared to the national average and to the averages for their type of production. These include the following.
- Rates of pay. This will allow businesses to assess their own rates of pay and may help them in terms of wage bargaining, attracting new staff and keeping their staff motivated.
- The size of bonus payments. This can be used to ensure that staff are not attracted to competitors who provide better deals on pay.

- Productivity and unit wage cost. This will allow businesses to compare the efficiency of their employees with the national average and their competitors.

Skills and training Employment statistics also provide details on skills levels in the economy and the levels of training given by firms. Skills and training are vital elements in the success of most businesses. Where a business finds that its competitors are more effective in these areas it will need to plan and implement changes in order to deal with this.

Employment data is very wide indeed. Figure 5, for example, shows where school leavers in Scotland go when they leave school. This would help businesses plan recruitment strategies and help them to decide whether they should be approaching schools, colleges, universities or the job centre when trying to recruit young employees.

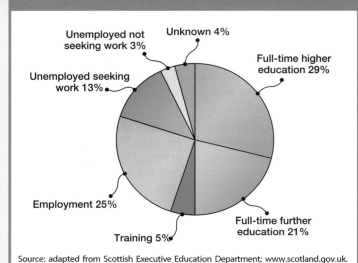

Figure 5 *Destinations for school leavers in Scotland, 2003/2004*

Unemployed not seeking work 3%
Unknown 4%
Unemployed seeking work 13%
Full-time higher education 29%
Employment 25%
Training 5%
Full-time further education 21%

Source: adapted from Scottish Executive Education Department; www.scotland.gov.uk.

Where there is a shortage of skills, that is likely to affect the business in two ways. First, it may have to pay more for skilled staff because it will have to compete against other businesses that want these skills. Second, it may need to train staff so that they gain these skills and that will create an additional cost.

Inflation

Inflation is a measure of how prices change. Normally, in the UK, overall prices rise, and that is why this is called **inflation**. Occasionally general prices fall, and quite frequently prices for individual products will fall. When this happens this is called **negative inflation**. For businesses inflation is a very important measure.

First, if the costs of raw materials, machinery, labour, and anything else a business needs in order to produce its products rise then it will be faced with two options. Either it will have to absorb these extra costs and lose profit, or it will have to pass the higher costs onto its customers in higher prices and probably upset these customers and possibly lose sales.

Second, rising prices may mean that customers are unable to buy everything that they want and therefore some businesses will lose customers, sales and profit. When this happens it is often the luxury markets that suffer and businesses providing necessities continue to sell well and make profits. Rising fuel prices and worries about the future led to a fall in spending on some products in 2005, as shown on Figure 6.

Figure 6 *New lows on the high street*

Year-on-year growth in high street sales has slowed to its weakest rate in two years – 2.3% – with many high street retailers reporting difficult trading conditions.

'It's not a good time to be a retailer,' said retail analyst Debbie Harrison. 'Despite Tesco's continued amazing performance many of the big names are having a tough time of it.'

'Clothing store Next, for example, has warned that the slowdown in underlying sales has accelerated in recent months. If you strip out food, we are seeing significant weakness.'

Source: adapted from www.yourmoney.com, May 2005.

Inflation also causes problems for businesses on the wages side. Staff will know that if prices are rising they will need higher rates of pay in order to pay for the higher prices. When prices are rising and the cost of living is getting higher, staff may well put pressure on their employers to pay them more. Where staff have some power over their employers the employers may have to give in to these demands or face losing staff or find their production affected through industrial action, for example strikes or a go-slow. This is most likely to happen in the following business situations.

- Where there is a strong trade union presence.
- Where the staff have skills that the business cannot do without and staff would be difficult to replace.
- Where the final product is in high demand and the business cannot afford any delays in production or delivery.

The Balance of Payments and exchange rates

Balance of Payments statistics provide details of the imports and exports for the UK. For the government these figures are important because if the total value of imports is greater than that of exports that will cause pressure for the value of the Pound (the exchange rate) to fall. This happens because the UK sells Pounds so that it can buy foreign products with, say, Euros, but not as many foreigners want to buy Pounds so that they can buy UK

Figure 7 *Effect of changes in the value of the Pound on UK businesses*

	UK importers	UK exporters	Domestic UK businesses competing with foreign producers
Value of Pound rises	Raw materials from abroad will be cheaper to buy so costs will be lower	Customers in other countries with Euros, Dollars, etc. will find it more expensive to buy UK products so sales may fall	UK customers will get more Euros, Dollars, etc. for their Pounds so they may decide to buy abroad rather than from UK businesses
Value of Pound falls	Raw materials from abroad will be more expensive so costs will rise	Customers in other countries with Euros, Dollars, etc. will be able to get more Pounds for their currency and so can afford to buy more UK products	Products priced in Euros, Dollars, etc. will be more expensive in terms of Pounds so UK customers may well buy UK products instead of foreign ones

exports. This creates a surplus of Pounds on the foreign exchange markets and so their value goes down. If the total value of imports [is] less than that of exports the value of the Pound is likely to rise [in] value.

For UK businesses, changes in the value of the Pound are very [im]portant. The effects will depend on whether the UK business is [im]porting, exporting, or is a domestic UK business that faces [c]ompetition from foreign businesses selling in the UK. Figure 7 [s]hows the likely effects of rises and falls in the value of the Pound.

The Balance of Payments figures also provide details of what is [im]ported and exported and where the products are coming from [a]nd going to. This can help businesses when they are making [d]ecisions about where they might sell their products and even in [t]erms of which countries it may be profitable to expand into or [r]elocate to.

Interest rates

[In]terest is what is paid when borrowing money or received when [le]nding money. The percentage that is paid or received on the [m]oney that is borrowed or lent is known as the interest rate. [C]hanges in the interest rates will affect businesses in three ways, [th]rough their borrowing or lending, through the borrowing and [le]nding of their customers and through the effects on the [e]xchange rate. These are shown in Figure 8.

The direct effect on businesses Most businesses will borrow [m]oney at some time, with some businesses borrowing very large [su]ms of money. For these businesses when the interest rate rises [it] means that the cost of borrowing money has risen and that [in]creases the overall cost for the business. The business is then [fa]ced with the decision of raising prices for their customers and [p]ossibly losing them, or keeping their final prices the same and [lo]sing profits.

For some businesses large rises in interest rates can mean that [th]ey cannot afford to pay the interest on their loans and if they [ca]nnot repay them the business can be forced to close down.

Effect through the businesses' customers Many individuals borrow money. Mainly this is so that they can afford expensive items such as houses, cars and furniture. There is, however, also an increasing number of people who buy more day-to-day items on credit, with borrowing on credit cards and store cards reaching £55.7 billion in May 2005.

At the beginning of 2005 mortgage debt for people borrowing money to buy houses passed the one trillion mark, £1,000 billion. Most of these people have variable rates of interest on their mortgages so that when interest rates in the country rise they have to put more money aside to pay their mortgages and that leaves less to spend on other products.

Borrowing by individuals can lead to inflationary pressures in the country as a whole as individuals then spend this borrowed money. In the 1980s borrowing did get out of control and caused high inflation. The reaction of the then Conservative government was to raise interest rates from 7.5% to 15% in just over one year. As a result individuals could not afford to borrow and so greatly reduced their spending causing many businesses to go out of business.

Figure 8 *Effects of changes in interest rates*

	Effect on business	Effect on customer	Effect on Pound
Rising	Costs will rise	Borrowing more expensive	Value of Pound will rise
Interest rate			
Falling	Costs will fall	Borrowing less expensive	Value of Pound will fall

Interest rates and the exchange rate When interest rates in the UK rise compared to rates in other countries it attracts international investors to save in the UK. What is known as 'hot money' flows in. In order to save in the UK these speculators must first change their Euros, Dollars, etc., into Pounds. This increases the demand for Pounds so its value rises. This will affect UK business in the way that was shown in Figure 7.

When the interest rate falls, hot money will flow out of the country, reducing the demand for Pounds and causing the exchange rate to fall.

Other important indicators

The indicators listed above are those that the government is likely to feel are particularly important. There are, however, many other indicators that businesses may consider equally important because they have direct effects on their particular type of business. Below are some examples of these indicators.

Consumer confidence This is measured by asking consumers how confident they are about the future in terms of job security, how much income they will be receiving and what they feel about such factors as future house prices or interest rates. If consumers are not confident about the future they are likely to cut down their expenditure and save more.

In both cases businesses are likely to have less demand for their products and less sales. There will, however, be some businesses that benefit from this lack of confidence as consumers switch from more expensive luxury items to cheaper standard products. Even when confidence is very low, people will continue to buy basic necessities so businesses selling these may not be affected.

Business confidence Business confidence measures the general confidence of businesses themselves, as shown in Figure 9. This is measured by asking business leaders what they think about current and future prospects for their businesses. The Confederation of British Industry (CBI) produces regular reports on the confidence of UK businesses. These reports can affect what businesses feel about the state of the economy and may well affect the decisions they make in terms of expansion, bringing out new products and generally planning for the future.

Population statistics For many businesses details of what is happening to the population is very important. Table 1 shows examples of features of the population and the kinds of business that would want to know what is happening in terms of this feature. For each feature the businesses will be interested in the current numbers of people and the likely changes to those numbers in the future.

Table 1 *Population trends and business*

Population feature	**Examples of businesses that would want to know these figures**
Numbers in each age group	• Pension providers • Producers of baby products • Producers of educational products • Providers of health care
Numbers in each gender group	• Shops selling just men's or women's clothes • Magazine publishers • Hospitals providing maternity facilities
How many people live in each part of the country	• Chain stores considering expansion into new areas • Manufacturing firms needing a large labour force • Market research businesses carrying out surveys

Figure 9 *CBI cuts economic growth estimate*

The CBI has cut its forecast for UK economic growth in 2005 to 2.5% from its previous 2.7% estimate.

The business organisation's decline in confidence for the UK economy comes after its latest manufacturing survey showed a big growth in pessimism.

Source: adapted from http://news.bbc.co.uk, May 2005.

Using national statistics online at http://www.statistics.gov.uk or library based statistics sources, such as the *Monthly Digest of Statistics* or *Social Trends*, carry out the following tasks.
1. For the latest year shown, record the categories of spending by households on different products, and how much was spent on each category.
2. Display the data in the form of a pie chart or bar chart, fully labelled and showing the percentages of total expenditure for each category.
3. Identify a range of businesses that would want to know how much was spent in each section. For this you should include obvious and less obvious types of business, for example hotels do want to know how much is spent on transport because without that guest could not get to the hotels.

Research task

Meeting the assessment criteria - examiners' guidance

For your chosen business you are required to produce a chairman's report which describes, applies, analyses and evaluates the effects of external influences on a business. This will involve consideration of the major economic factors.

Business example - Scottish & Newcastle meeting changing market conditions

Scottish & Newcastle (S&N) saw 5.6% growth in sales of its beer and cider brands between July and September 2005 against a national trend of only 1.8% increase. Despite this increase it raised concerns in November that sales may be affected in the run-up to Christmas as Britons may not celebrate as lavishly as in previous years. There were also concerns that supermarkets and other retailers would slash their prices of alcoholic drinks during the festive season as competition in the sector intensified.

Taking 2005 as a whole it has been a year of weak demand with consumers tightening their belts as economic conditions worsened. There have also been additional costs due to the rising price of oil. To remain competitive S&N is spending more on advertising and promotion but also keeping a tight control on costs. The Tyne Brewery in Newcastle has been closed as has a brewery in Edinburgh. It is also expanding its business abroad with good sales in the USA and Russia and greater involvement in production in China.

Source: adapted from RedOrbit.

AOs	Mark Band 1	Mark Band 2	Mark Band 3
AO1	This would explain what S&N does and identify external economic influences, e.g. consumer confidence and rising costs, but little else.	Here an explanation of the influences is required so details should be provided of why consumer confidence affects the business and how higher oil prices lead to increased cost in brewing.	The RedOrbit article provides limited detail of what is actually occurring in the industry and at this higher level details of how consumer spending habits were changing and what the supermarkets actually did would also be expected.
AO2	Basic application of the facts to the business is required so that details of how changing consumer confidence, increasing costs and new markets are affecting S&N should be given.	Here the application should be more targeted with specific products being cited and explanations given as to why they would be particularly affected by the external changes.	External changes should be carefully selected here with the main emphasis being given to those which are most important to the business. Profits at S&N have continued to rise in 2005 so it should be recognised that the effects of rising costs and falling demand are offset by additional sales in the USA and Russia.
AO3	There will be limited research at this level, but more than one source. Analysis will be little more than extracting relevant elements from the data.	A wider range of sources should be used at this level, such as: - consumer confidence data - wholesale prices for oil - changing prices in supermarkets - comments from S&N itself. The data should then be analysed and conclusions justified.	All appropriate sources should be checked and the data analysed carefully to ensure that the details provided are correct and relevant to the situation S&N finds itself in. Current sources should be used and older sources only used for comparisons. The effects of changing demand, costs and new markets can be gauged from company reports and press releases.

AOs	Mark Band 1	Mark Band 2	Mark Band 3
AO4	Here the actions that S&N has taken to meet the new challenges would be recorded, such as closing plants and expanding into China. There would also be a brief evaluation mainly on the basis of whether or not these were sensible reactions.	Here the evaluation of S&N's reactions to the external influences should be justified with clear reasoning. For example, the expansion into China should be justified in terms of the falling limited growth in the UK and continental Europe, but also questioned in terms of the cost of going into China, an additional £36 million.	At this level the evaluation and justifications should be detailed. For this to be effective there needs to be data for a range of sources that can be used to support or question the points being made. There also needs to be a good understanding of how the business actually operates. For example, if supermarkets are lowering prices of alcohol why cannot S&N do this, especially considering that the supermarkets are being supplied by the brewers in the first place?

Portfolio practice · Meeting possible skill shortages in the NHS

In September 2004 the NHS, in conjunction with the Learning and Skills Council and Jobcentre Plus, started a new initiative to help the unemployed in Merseyside to get jobs in the NHS. The project, called 'Ambition: Health', helps the local area which has high unemployment levels. There are also skills shortages in the hospitals. The programme includes intensive training which consisting of a mixture of up to 26 weeks technical training and work placement - working towards NVQ Level 2 and/or employer equivalent qualification.

In May 2005, Lord Owen, the Chancellor of Liverpool University, officially opened the Wirral Hospital Education Centre at Arrowe Park Hospital. The Centre has a large library, a 163-seat Lecture Theatre, eight Seminar Rooms of varying sizes, a dining room and exhibition space. It is available to all health care staff for educational purposes.

Arrowe Park Hospital on the Wirral also supports staff who study through the Learning through Work (LtW) initiative which allows them to gain diplomas and degrees without leaving the workplace. The programmes are custom made and build on existing skills and knowledge.

Source: adapted from www.wirralhealth.org.uk.

(a) **How are skills shortages in the NHS likely to affect the hospital trusts that have responsibility for providing patient care and treatment?**
(b) **Three initiatives are mentioned.**
   - **Ambition: Health.**
   - **The Wirral Hospital Education Centre.**
   - **Learning through Work (LtW).**
   For each of the three initiatives explain:
   (i) **how it will help deal with potential skills shortages;**
   (ii) **what planning will need to be made by the hospitals to support the initiative.**
   (Further research on each of these initiatives will help you provide detailed and justified answers.)
(c) **Explain any problems that these initiatives might cause for the hospitals.**

Changes in the economy and business

Section 68 examined some of the main economic indicators that the government and businesses consider are important. For businesses these indicators will help them to understand the market conditions that they are facing and are likely to face in the future, and it will help them to decide what actions are necessary in order to remain profitable and expand.

This section examines how changes in these economic indicators may affect individual businesses and the economy as a whole.

The business or trade cycle

Sometimes there can be confusion when using the terms business cycle and trade cycle. For this unit, however, they should be considered as being the same thing and they will be referred to as the business cycle.

The business cycle affects many parts of the economy and, through these, many aspects of business. When considering the effects of the business cycle it is important to recognise that all of the parts of the economy shown in Figure 1 are being affected.

Figure 1 Parts of the economy affected by the business cycle

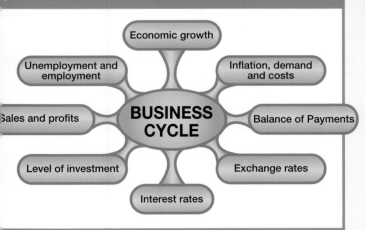

As shown in Section 68, 'economic growth' is a measurement of how much, in percentage terms, Gross Domestic Product (GDP) has increased by in a set period of time, usually a year. In the UK this growth varies on average over a ten year period between 2% to 3% per year. But this is not steady growth. In some years it can be as much as 9% and in other years it can actually be negative.

There is, however, a pattern to this high and low level of growth. This pattern follows a very predictable path - up, down, up, down - and so on. It is this up and down pattern that is called the business cycle. Figures 2 and 3 show this pattern for the UK's GDP.

Figure 2 UK Gross Domestic Product 1967-2004 at market prices (chained volume measure)

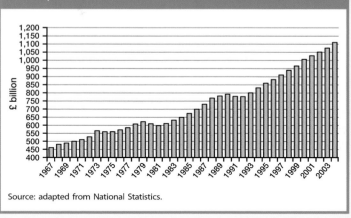

Source: adapted from National Statistics.

Figure 2 shows that the general trend for GDP is rising, which means that there is growing production of, and demand for, good and services in the UK. It is not, however, a smooth rise and in some years GDP actually fell. It is easier to see this if just the yearly percentage increase is taken, as in Figure 3.

Figure 3 Annual percentage growth in UK Gross Domestic Product, 1967-2004

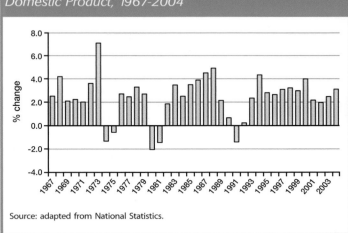

Source: adapted from National Statistics.

Figure 3 shows very clearly the annual fluctuations in how fast GDP grows. Even in the more stable period of growth from 1993 to 2004 there are still very significant fluctuations in the level of growth each year. For businesses these fluctuations can be very important because they affect how much can be sold, how many employees are needed, plans for new investment and so on.

Figure 4 shows a highly stylised business cycle and the typical stages that the economy goes through. In most countries the business cycle reflects what is happening to the demand for goods and services and the cycle will go through the stages: boom -

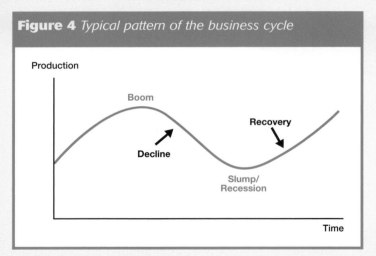

Figure 4 *Typical pattern of the business cycle*

decline - slump - recovery - boom, and so on. Each stage has distinct characteristics and impacts on business, as shown in Table 1.

The terms 'slump' and 'recession' are used to means slightly different things. Recession has a very specific government definition.

- **Recession** means that there have been two consecutive quarters when the growth in GDP have been negative. In the UK this occurred in 1970, 1974/5, 1979/80 and 1990/91.
- A **slump** is a downturn in the growth rate which may or may not have negative growth. It is defined as a short period of economic or financial weakness. Since 1991 there have been two significant slumps, in 2001-2002 when growth fell to only 2% and 2005 when growth fell to 1.8%.

When the business cycle moves from boom to slump to boom it affects all of the major indicators as shown in Figure 5. When economic growth is high more employees are needed so unemployment is low. In a slump the reverse will be the case. When economic growth is high and there are less people available for work, costs and prices will rise so inflation will be high. When prices are high it is more difficult to sell products abroad so there are less exports. With high UK prices, UK citizens may switch to buying cheaper imports. The Balance of Payments, therefore suffers. In a slump prices are lower and the balance of payments improves. Business confidence also suffers, as shown in Figure 6.

The business cycle and interest rates

As was pointed out in section 68, interest rates are very important to businesses because most businesses are borrowing money. They are also important because many

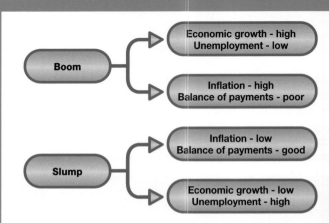

Figure 5 *The effect of the business cycle on the major economic indicators*

Table 1 *Characteristics and effects of the business cycle*

Stage	Characteristics and effect on businesses
Boom	• Demand is high – businesses are able sell many products and make good profits. • Employment is high – people have the income to buy additional products. • Unemployment is low – businesses may find it difficult and costly to recruit staff. • Prices are high – can cause loss of sales in other countries where demand is not high. • Consumer confidence is high – people can be persuaded to buy more products than usual.
Decline	• Demand is not rising as fast or is even falling – businesses have to change their plans to be ready for lower sales, lower profits, etc. • Sales stop increasing or fall – businesses may need to reduce their workforce, reduce their level of stocks and consider lowering prices.
Slump	• Demand is low – businesses have difficulty selling products and some will have to close. • Profits are low – businesses find it difficult to invest and produce new products. • Unemployment is high – people's incomes have fallen so many stop buying luxuries. • Consumer confidence is low – businesses need to keep prices low and competitive and use effective promotion. • Prices are low – businesses may be able to take advantage of selling internationally to markets where demand is still good.
Recovery	• Demand starts rising – businesses need to plan for rising demand and sales by increasing stock levels, recruiting more staff, making investments in new products and new ways of producing. • The slump may have removed competitors – expansion into their markets is now possible as customers have more money and confidence.

Figure 6 Business opinions and trends, July 2005

UK companies' business confidence is weak going forward into the second half of the year. Companies expect slower UK economic growth to negatively affect their sales, while a lack of pricing power is preventing higher producer input prices from being passed on to customers.

Looking out to the second half of 2005, the balance of companies expecting higher rather than lower orders fell back to 14% from 24% last January and a recent peak of 33% a year ago. This survey reports that 35% of companies expect higher orders and 21% expect lower orders in the second half of 2005, compared with 40% of companies expecting higher orders and 16% expecting lower orders in the first half of this year.

In addition, the balance of companies expecting higher rather than lower sales over the next six months declined to 18% in this survey from 34% last December.

Source: adapted from Lloyds TSB survey - *Business in Britain* (July 2005).

individuals borrow money and when interest rates rise they have less money to spend on goods and services. They are also very important because interest rates are used to control how much growth and spending there is in the economy.

Figure 7 shows what will happen when there is a boom with unacceptably high inflation and what will happen with a slump, or recession, when unemployment is high and growth rates are very low.

In a boom interest rates are raised to make it more expensive to borrow. This reduces demand and lowers inflation. At the same time, however, it reduces sales and causes negative effects for businesses and employment.

In a slump or recession inflation is usually low so it is safe to stimulate the economy by lowering interest rates. This encourages borrowing and spending which means more sales, so more economic growth, and less unemployment.

In the past the government decided what the interest rate would be, but since 1998 this responsibility has been passed over to the Bank of England. It now sets the main interest rate in the UK. Once this basic rate is set all the major banks follow suit and change their interest rates to reflect this. The Bank of England's basic rate is known as the **base rate** or **repo** rate.

The Bank of England has been given complete control of setting interest rates on the understanding that it carries out the following major objective:

'... to deliver price stability – low inflation – and, subject to that, to support the government's economic objectives including those for growth and employment.'

The recent target for inflation set by the government has been a 2% rise in the Consumer Price Index (CPI). The problem for businesses is that if the inflation rate starts to move away from 2%,

Figure 7 How interest rates work to control the economy

Boom

Higher interest rates needed to control inflation

For the individual
Mortgage rates rise
Cost of borrowing rises
Less money to spend
Less demand
Price falls
Inflation and growth fall
Unemployment rises

For the business
Cost of borrowing rises
Pressure to raise prices
Customers have less to spend
Prices kept the same or fall
Less sales
Inflation and growth fall
Unemployment rises

Slump

Lower interest rates needed to stimulate growth

For the individual
Lower mortgage rates
Cost of borrowing falls
Encouraged to spend
Greater demand
More produced and sold
Growth rises
Unemployment falls

For the business
Costs of borrowing falls
Firms can lower prices
Customers spend more
Sales and output rise
Increased level of profits
Growth rises
Unemployment falls

Figure 8 UK annual CPI % change and Base Rate % (Jan 1996 to Aug 2005) – both given for each month.

Source: adapted from National Statistics.

or the Bank thinks that it might, it then changes the interest rate. This then directly affects businesses which are borrowing and it may affect them indirectly if people decide to stop spending. Figure 8 shows how frequently the inflation rate has changed and how frequently, even when CPI was below 2%, the Bank has changed the interest rate.

Table 2		CPI	Base Rate
2003	O	1.4	3.50
	N	1.3	3.75
	D	1.3	3.75
2004	J	1.4	3.75
	F	1.3	4.00
	M	1.1	4.25
	A	1.2	4.25
	M	1.5	4.25
	J	1.6	4.50
	J	1.4	4.50
	A	1.3	4.75

Figure 8 does show the base rate generally falling as CPI does and then rising with CPI in 2003-04. However, movements in interest rates also take place because of other changes in the economy such as the level of consumer spending and the value of the Pound.

For businesses interest rate movements can be very difficult to predict and they need to be watched very carefully. Between October 2003 and August 2004 the CPI was always well below the 2% target but the Bank still raised the base rate from 3.5% to 4.75% in just ten months, as shown in Table 2. For a business borrowing, say, £100,000, that would mean a possible increase in annual charges for borrowing of £1,250.

For a business an extra £1,250 may or may not be a serious additional cost. For individuals with mortgages, many of which will be for £100,000 or more, an extra £1,250 in a year is a considerable additional sum. It is therefore important for businesses to know why the Bank of England changes interest rates and then make their plans on that basis.

Each month the Bank publishes minutes of the meetings that decide whether or not to raise the interest rate. In November 2003 these were the reasons given for starting the rise in rates shown in Table 2.

- Interest rates were rising in other countries.
- Most experts expected a rise in the repo rate.
- Lending to individuals had been increasing.
- House price inflation was rising.
- Business confidence levels were rising.
- Unemployment was low and stable and economic growth good so that a rise in interest rates would not affect these but would help to keep inflation low.

This list of reasons indicates that the Bank of England considers many economic indicators when it makes its decisions and businesses need to consider these as well when planning for the future.

House prices

Figure 3 showed that economic growth was actually very weak in 2001 and 2002, when the economy was in a slump. Despite that fact the price of houses, as shown in Figure 9, increased dramatically. This shows that actually people had a lot of money to spend but they preferred to put it into houses, which tend to increase in value over time, rather than to spend more on other

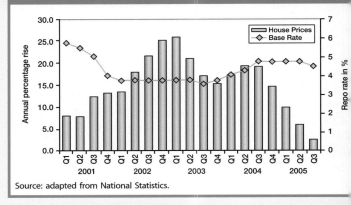

Figure 9 *Annual percentage change in house prices and base rate Q1 2001 to Q3 2005*

Source: adapted from National Statistics.

major expenditures such as cars, holidays and luxury items.

This is also something that the Bank of England watches carefully and it will put up interest rates to try to reduce house price inflation. Figure 9 shows that the base rate was being lowered whilst house price inflation was relatively low in 2001. It then levelled out in 2002-03 as house price inflation rose to over 25%. As house price inflation remained high, above 15%, the base rate was then raised and has only started to come down again with the huge drop in house price inflation in 2005.

Figure 10 shows the total amounts of money lent by financial institutions such as banks and building societies to individuals and still outstanding in January of each year. Most of this is in the form of mortgages, which between 2001 and 2005 rose from £529 billion, to £882 billion, a rise of 67% in four years.

Which businesses are affected?

When changes take place in the economic indicators shown in sections 68 and 69 the effects that these changes will have on businesses depends very much on what the businesses are producing. Some examples are given in Table 3 for the indicators covered in this section. This shows how some firms will benefit and some will suffer from the same change.

The way in which businesses are affected, or are likely to be affected, by changing economic conditions will also determine what strategies they should take in order to minimise the effects of negative changes and benefit from the effects of positive changes.

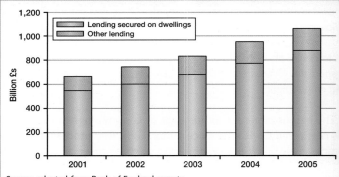

Figure 10 *Lending to individuals (£s billion), Jan 2001 to Jan 2005*

Source: adapted from Bank of England reports.

Table 3 *Businesses affected by changes in major economic indicators*

Indicator and or change	Businesses affected negatively	Businesses not affected or affected positively
Slump or recession	Those producing luxury items such as new cars, expensive jewellery and cruise holidays.	Those producing necessities such as food, gas and electricity and cheaper clothes.
Higher interest rates	Those borrowing money, those selling to consumers with mortgages.	Banks and other lenders of money who can now charge a higher interest rate.
High house prices	Those who build and sell houses if this causes lower demand for houses.	Producers of other expensive products such as cars and holidays.
High rates of inflation	Those buying expensive UK raw materials or trying to sell to consumers with low incomes such as students or OAPs.	Those importing low priced goods from abroad or those selling to people whose incomes are rising as their pay rises.
Rising levels of unemployment	Those selling to people who are losing their jobs.	Those providing retraining courses for the unemployed.

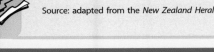

UK manufacturing sector in dangerous tailspin

Manufacturing in Britain took a nosedive last month while spending on credit cards posted its smallest rise in four years, according to figures released yesterday which point to a widespread economic slowdown.

The Chartered Institute of Purchasing and Supply (Cips) said output fell for the first time in two years, new orders fell back, while firms were forced to cut both jobs and prices. Roy Ayliffe, a director of Cips, said: 'Manufacturers reported a decline in output for the first time in over two years and in spite of a marked easing in cost inflationary pressure, output prices declined for the first time in 20 months.'

The survey comes a few days after the Office for National Statistics said factory output in March slumped by 1.6 per cent, the worst fall for a decade excluding the impact of the 2002 Golden Jubilee. The headline index has now tumbled by 7.5 index points since its recent peak in December, the steepest six-monthly fall since mid-1998, when the Bank reacted by cutting rates aggressively.

There was mixed evidence on the health of the British consumer, with unsecured borrowing and retail sales showing continued weakness but an upturn in mortgage approvals pointing to stabilisation in the housing market.

Source: adapted from the *New Zealand Herald*, 2.6.2005.

(a) **State and explain what evidence there is in the extract above that shows that UK manufacturing was suffering from recession in the end of 2004 and the beginning of 2005.**

(b) **(i) Identify TWO ways in which UK manufacturers have responded to this situation.**
(ii) For each way you have identified explain why businesses have responded in that way and how it should help to keep the businesses profitable.
(iii) State and justify ONE other action, not mentioned in the article, which these businesses could have taken to ensure that they survived the recession in their industries.

(c) **Identify ONE positive factor for manufacturing businesses in the article and explain why it is positive for them.**

Access the latest copy of the *Monthly Digest of Statistics*, either through a library or online at www.statistics.gov.uk/. Carry out the following tasks.
1. Using the figures for Final Household Consumption Expenditure, record the monthly or quarterly expenditure (not seasonally adjusted) for different types of products, e.g. alcohol and tobacco, transport, and housing.
2. Display the data in the form of line graphs.
3. Identify which types of products have the greatest seasonal fluctuations in sales.
4. Evaluate the effect that will have on (i) the retailers and (ii) the producers of these products.
5. Suggest, and justify, what strategies (i) the retailers and (ii) the producers should take to minimise the effects of these fluctuations.

Meeting the assessment criteria - examiners' guidance

For your chosen business you are required to produce a Chairman's report which describes, applies, analyses and evaluates the effects of external influences on a business. This will involve a consideration of changes in economic conditions.

Business example - Monsoon bucks the retail sales trend

Figure 11 shows the annual percentage increase for each month for UK retail sales. The graph shows that after reasonable increases at the start of 2004 with up to 6.8% in May, increases in retail sales declined steadily. In 2005 there were rises but they were very much smaller with no rise at all in September and falls in sales (compared to 2004) in April and May. Table 4 shows major changes for the clothes and accessories chain Monsoon.

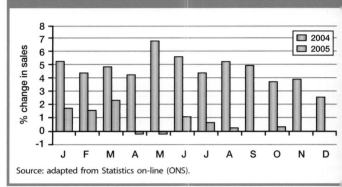

Figure 11 *Retail sales by value, annual percentage increase by month (Jan 2004 to Oct 2005)*

Source: adapted from Statistics on-line (ONS).

Table 4 *Monsoon, business information*

	2003/04	**2004/05**
UK turnover	£251.3 million, up 17.2 %	£332.6 million, up 32.3%
Profit after tax	£30.0 million, up 12%	£34.6 million, up 15%
New stores opened & total	28 new stores – total 303 stores	39 new stores – total 336 stores
New acquisitions	21 stores from Dixons	Stores acquired from Arcadia
Interest and similar receipts and interest payments	£1.56 million received £0.11 million paid	£2.2 million received, £0.08 million paid
Cash in bank and at hand	£54.5 million with 91.5% earning a (floating) interest rate	£58.7 million, with 86.8% earning a (floating) interest rate
Number of staff and average yearly payroll cost	Staff: 2668 Cost: £18,591	Staff: 3745 Cost: £17,842
Major new launch	March 2004 – transactional website available	October 2004 – Monsoon Men launched
Final dividend for shareholders	Nil	Nil

Source: adapted from Monsoon, *Annual Report and Accounts*.

AOs	Mark Band 1	Mark Band 2	Mark Band 3
AO1	The main trend of the retail figures would be identified. Monsoon's main interests of selling women's and children's clothing and accessories, homeware and gifts would be described. The main details of the 2003/04 and 2004/05 report listed, as for Table 4.	Details of the changes in the retail sales would be expected and particularly the decline in 2005. The significance of Monsoon's figures should be commented on, e.g. a 40% rise in staff, and turnover, pre-tax post-tax profit and number of stores all increasing.	At this level it should be clear what the retail figures are showing, i.e. retail sales for each month compared to the previous month one year before. No seasonal fluctuations are, therefore, shown. The likely effect on Monsoon could also be given, e.g. a similar down turn might be expected in its performance. For Monsoon's figures comments should be made as to how 2004/05 is even better than 2003/04, e.g. more stores opened, even higher turnover.

AOs	Mark Band 1	Mark Band 2	Mark Band 3
AO2	A basic comparison of the retail figures to Monsoon's results would be expected. Comment on the fact that Monsoon is performing well despite the falling retail growth would be expected but little other comment.	Here details should be provided as to why it would be expected that the overall retail figures would affect Monsoon, e.g. because of lower growth in consumer expenditure, and which elements of the reports show that Monsoon is not being affected by the general trend, e.g. more stores opening and new lines.	Application at this level would need additional details of national statistics (see AO3). This would allow a more detailed comparison to consumer spending, incomes, and retail sales for clothes. There should also be speculation as to why Monsoon has been able to buck the trend with, for example, comments on the introduction of a website for ordering and payments and a range of clothes for men. A justified explanation should be in (AO4).
AO3	At this level it may well be that little more than the details shown in Figure 11 and Table 4 are presented, with the addition of basic details of the business itself. Analysis should show the data clearly so that conclusions can be drawn from it.	To ensure that a full evaluation is possible a much wider range of data should be accessed. This would include figures for incomes, consumer spending and confidence and most useful of all a break down of retail spending into different categories, and especially for clothes sales.	To allow detailed evaluation even more sources of information might be necessary and the performance of competitors would provide valuable data, e.g. in terms of sales, market share, prices, etc. This would help to explain why Monsoon has been able to perform so well and expand whereas general retail sales are poor and many direct competitors have not performed very well.
AO4	The evaluation here will be basic, noting that Monsoon has bucked the trend and providing a basic explanation such as the fact that it has more stores, new products and a new way of marketing its goods. A statement would be expected that no additional response is needed and that Monsoon should continue with its present strategies.	Here the evaluation should be supported by good basic reasoning and confirmed by the data. If clothing and footwear figures were taken they would show that in 2004 the trend was even worse than general retailing, but for 2005 it was better. The evaluation should therefore concentrate more on Monsoon's performance compared to its competitors and the fact that it has more shops, more staff but lower wage costs, new products, etc. The report should then justify why that has lead to increased sales and profits even though the retail sector is weak. The present strategies should be identified and commented on.	For really detailed evaluation, a full understanding of the data and the way the business works is required. At this level it would be expected that students had noticed that the business has given no dividends for the last two financial years, that is earned a net £1.45 m and £2.12 m in interest in 2003/04 and 2004/05 respectively, and that it has managed to increase staff numbers at the same time as lowering staff's average pay. More detailed study of the business would show that it does not borrow money to expand, and indeed had over £50 m in the bank to buy new shops, invest in new ranges and set up internet sales. To ensure this liquidity it has not paid dividends and earns high interest. However, the savings are on a floating rate and could be affected by changes in the base rate. The strategies should be evaluated and justified and possibly others considered.

The importance of the global economy

The global economy

Almost all UK businesses will be affected, in some way or another, by what is happening in the wider world economy. They can be affected for the following reasons.

- They sell their products abroad.
- They import raw materials from abroad.
- Part of their production takes place in other countries.
- They produce and sell in the UK but face competition from abroad.
- Their customers are visitors to the UK.

In all of these situations changes in international economic conditions, such as exchange rates, can affect the businesses and they will then need to watch for these changes and have strategies available to deal with them if they occur.

This section looks at these international dimensions, how they are likely to affect UK businesses and how this will affect planning. Section 71 covers international events such as wars, terrorism and natural disasters, which also can have major economic effects on UK businesses. Unit 12 deals with the 'International Dimensions of Business' and details of the effects of the European Union (EU) and international organisation such as the World Trade Organisation (WTO) should be checked in that unit.

Types of UK businesses

The effect that changes in international business conditions will have on UK businesses will depend fairly heavily on what type of business the UK firm is involved in. This is true in terms of what it sells but also in terms of its international status. The types of business, shown in Figure 1, are likely to influence how international economic conditions affect the business.

Local businesses Local businesses selling in one local part of the UK can still be affected by international conditions because they are bound by EU and international laws, but also they may rely upon imported raw materials and may face competition from international businesses.

Figure 1 *Types of business*

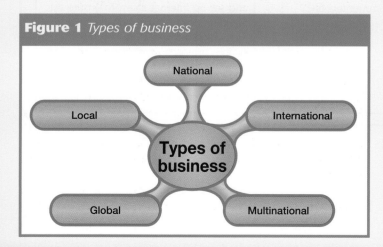

For example, Jenny's Restaurant in Andover sells hot and cold beverages and basic meals such the traditional English breakfast. Coffee, tea and cocoa are all imported, as may be the bacon, the cookers and the furniture. Jenny's also faces competition from a McDonald's outlet round the corner. McDonald's is an American owned business affected by international conditions.

National businesses National businesses sell in many parts of the country and are therefore more likely to come across international competition. Depending on what they sell they may well have imported raw materials, machinery or equipment.

For example, Café Nero and Coffee Republic, both UK national businesses, face competition from Starbucks from the USA and Costa, an Italian business. As they mainly sell coffee, tea and hot chocolate they will be affected by import costs. For their equipment they may also import products such as Wega Pegaso, Gaggia or Jura coffee machines from Italy and Switzerland.

International businesses International businesses are companies based in one country which sell their products in more than one country. They will therefore be affected not only by what is happening in their own country, in this case the UK, but also the economic conditions in the other countries where their products are sold, including the countries' business cycles, levels of consumer spending and competition from national firms.

For example, Walkers Shortbread Limited, located in Aberlour Speyside, originally sold its shortbread and other products only locally, then nationally and, in the 1970s, internationally. Around half of its products are now exported to over 60 widespread overseas markets.

Multinational businesses Multinational businesses are firms which produce and sell in more than one country. Because they are producing in different countries they can be affected by many different economic conditions in those countries, including labour costs, taxation levels, land prices and all of the conditions that affect international businesses.

For example, see details about Wedgwood and Waterford Wedgwood in the 'Meeting the assessment criteria' at the end of this section.

A **global** business was defined by the *Financial Times* as one that

' ... *operates, or actively aspires to operate on a global scale. It thinks and acts in terms of world market share, not just local or regional penetration.*'

Its ultimate objective will be to operate and sell in every country in the world. As it does so it will then be affected by all of the individual national economic conditions, although it will have the major benefit that when one country's sales are doing badly it can still benefit from those countries where the economic conditions and sales are good.

For example, McDonalds and Coca-Cola are recognised global companies, producing and selling in a very large number of ountries in the world. Both now have UK-registered subsidiary ompanies. Global companies that originated in the UK are more fficult to find, but BP plc does fit the bill with operations in over 00 countries and active exploration in 26 countries. For a ompany such as BP, global economic conditions are highly fluential, such as the oil price dictated by OPEC or terrorist tivities that blow up pipelines in Iraq.

The strategies that these different types of business take to deal ith changing international economic conditions will depend on e type of business but also on which economic conditions are anging. Strategies will be considered later in this section.

rends in the global economy

rends in the global economy can refer to changes in the dicators that were covered in sections 68 and 69 but also to anges in the way that international trade is being affected by olitical agreements about trade, e.g. the establishment and xpansion of the:

European Union (EU);
World Trade Organisation (WTO).

heck details in unit 12 and especially sections 48 and 49.

xchange rates For UK businesses importing raw materials, quipment and goods for resale, or exporting products to other ountries, the exchange rate for the Pound is a vital part of ternational economic conditions. The exchange rate indicates the umber of Euros, Dollars, Yen, etc. that can be bought for each ound sterling. Figure 2 shows what happens if the rate of the ound falls or rises against other currencies.

Figure 2 *How changing exchange rates affect imports nd exports*

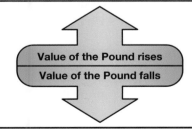

- Imports of raw materials, equipment, etc. will be cheaper.
- Foreign firms importing will be able to sell their products at a lower price.
- Exports will be more expensive for people in other countries.
- It may be cheaper to produce in other countries than in the UK.

Value of the Pound rises
Value of the Pound falls

- Imports of raw materials, equipment, etc. will be more expensive.
- The price of imported foreign products will rise and be less competitive.
- Exports will be less expensive for people in other countries, so more sales.
- There will be less advantage to UK firms producing in other countries.

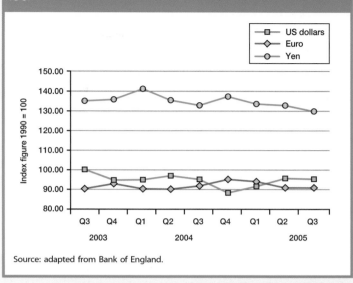

Figure 3 *Effective Exchange Rate Index of the Pound Sterling against the US Dollar, Euro and Yen (1990 = 100)*

Source: adapted from Bank of England.

The changes in the exchange can vary dramatically in a relatively short space of time. Figure 3 shows how the value of the Pound against the US Dollar, the Euro and the Yen has changed between 2003 and 2005. The index of 100 was set in 1990. From 1990 the Yen has risen by 30% against the Pound meaning that 30% less Yen could now be bought for the same amount of Pounds. That should mean Japanese goods are comparatively much more expensive to import, but it will be easier for UK firms to export to Japan.

It the short term there have also been major changes. In Q3 of 2003 the exchange rate with the US dollar was £1 = $1.66 but by Q4 of 2004 the value of the Pound had risen so that £1 = $1.92, a rise in the value of the pound of 15.7%. For a UK business trying to sell to customers in the USA and keeping the price the same in Pounds that would make the product very much more expensive, for example:

Q3/2003 UK price = £500, would in USA = $830.
Q4/2004 UK price = £500, would in USA = $960.

On the other hand a USA business keeping its price the same in Dollars would be able to undercut businesses in the UK.

Q3/2003 USA price = $830, would in UK = £500.00
Q4/2004 USA price = $830, would in UK = £432.29

This second set of figures also shows what would have happened if a UK business sold its products but priced them in Dollars and then changed these Dollars into Pounds. It would have received £67.71 less for each item it sold. All of this has happened in just over a year and by the end of Q3 2005 the exchange rate had fallen back to £1 = $1.77, so an $830 product would then be worth £468.93.

These fluctuations make it hard for businesses to plan ahead because they need to know how much they will be getting back from their sales abroad if they are pricing in Dollars and how many sales they will lose or gain when they price in pounds. To try to help them get round these fluctuations, major international businesses will **hedge** against currency fluctuations. They do this by buying or selling the rights to future currency at special rates. For example in Q3 of 2003 a UK firm might have sold the Dollars it was going to get paid in Q4 of 2004 at a better rate than $1.92 = £1. This would ensure that they would not be too badly affected by major fluctuations in the currency values.

It is not just international businesses that are affected by exchange rates. Businesses in the UK that cater for foreign tourists will be affected by the exchange rate because that will determine whether or not foreign tourists want to come to the UK and, if they do, how much money they will bring with them. Also, when UK citizens spend their incomes abroad they are not spending them in the UK so local and national UK firms are likely to be affected.

Figure 4 shows how the changes in the value of the Pound against the Dollar can affect purchases by UK tourists of US products.

Figure 4 *With a fistful of dollars*

It's a sterling time for consumers. Lastminute.com is flying the equivalent of nine jumbo jets full of Brits on shopping trips to the US; Thomson has all but sold out of holidays to Florida; British Airways' profits rose on the back of a recovery in transatlantic travel. The plunging dollar is cutting a further 20 per cent or so off already-cheap prices and we are rushing to take advantage.

For companies, however, sterling's strength is rather less welcome. Last week alone, it cut earnings growth at drug group GlaxoSmithKline from 10 to 5 per cent, knocked around 8 per cent off profits at consumer products group Unilever and cut £30 million from the revenues of Yell's US directory information business.

Source: adapted from *The Observer*, 2004.

International business cycles

All countries have businesses cycles but, because countries trade with each other, one country's business cycle can, and usually does, affect the countries that it trades with. There are also more global effects with many, or most, countries going into boom or slump at the same time. So, even when the UK economy is doing well, it may well be that it is how the rest of the world is doing that determines how well UK businesses can do.

The Organisation for Economic Co-operation and Development **(OECD)** produces statistics for all of the major countries of the world. These statistics cover the 30 member countries and 70 other countries, providing a very clear picture of what is going on in individual countries and the world as a whole.

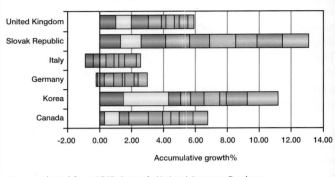

Figure 5 *Accumulated GDP growth figures for selected OECD countries (2003 Q3 to 2005 Q3)*

Source: adapted from OECD Quarterly National Accounts Database.

Figure 5 shows that even in the OECD countries GDP growth varies considerably from one country to another. Low rates of growth, as in Italy and Germany, are likely to mean low incomes and hence low demand for products from the UK. High rates of growth, as in Korea and the Slovak Republic, would suggest rising incomes and increased demand for products. At the same time high growth may also indicate increased production at very competitive prices and a threat to UK businesses.

Over the longer period of 1994 to 2004 the average annual growth rate for all OECD countries was 2.6% per year. Table 1 shows how different the growth rate was for some of the OECD countries. The table shows the top and bottom three countries, the UK and the USA.

Major trading partners

Table 1 and Figure 6 suggest that the USA has not done particularly well in terms of GDP growth between 1994 and 200 and that UK business should be thinking about countries such as Ireland, Korea and Luxembourg. The reality is, however, that the USA is the most powerful economy in the world and what happens in the USA affects the rest of world whether or not the rest of the world likes it. Prudent businesses with any major international element in their production will therefore watch ver carefully what is going on in the USA in terms of its GDP and interest rates.

Table 1 *Annual average GDP growth 1994 to 2004*

Country	Annual % GDP growth
Ireland	7.9
Korea	4.9
Luxembourg	4.8
USA	3.3
UK	2.8
OECD Average	2.6
Germany	1.5
Switzerland	1.3
Japan	1.2

Source: adapted from *OECD in Figures*, 2005.

Figure 6 *USA Annual growth in GDP per capita*

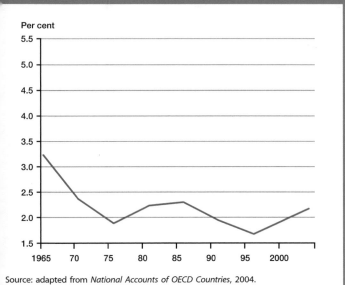

Source: adapted from *National Accounts of OECD Countries*, 2004.

Figure 7 *The estimated potential annual growth rate for the Chinese economy*

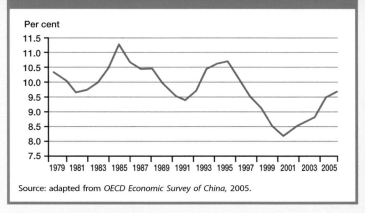

Source: adapted from *OECD Economic Survey of China, 2005.*

Another country that should demand careful consideration is China, because this is now a country which has over 1.3 billion people or one fifth of the world's population. It is also has an economy that is rapidly industrialising and an economy with consistently high GDP growth, as shown in Figure 7. The lowest annual figure shown is about 8%, which is way above the 2% to 3% being achieved in the UK.

China is also now far more willing to trade with other countries than it was and this offers major opportunities for UK firms to:

● sell tools, equipment and finished products;
● sell their expertise in terms of supporting Chinese businesses;
● import cheap, but now well made, products for re-sale in the UK;
● set up businesses within China itself.

For UK businesses, countries in the EU are also very important because of their geographical closeness but also because we are all members of an economic union that sets common rules, regulations and benefits.

International trading organisations

Details of major international trading organisations are given in

Table 2 *Strategies to cope with changing conditions*

Situation 1
A local business facing competition from a new international business expanding into the UK because the value of the pound is low.
Strategies
● Find ways of cutting costs, e.g. cheaper sources of raw materials.
● Lower prices to remain competitive.
● Relocate away from competitor business.

Situation 2
An international business which prices its products in pounds and sells only into Euro countries in the EU, faced with a rising value of the Pound.
Strategies
● Price in Euros and hedge against changes in the value of the pound.
● Find ways of cutting costs so that the price in Euros can be lowered so as to remain competitive.
● Look for markets in other countries where the Pound has not risen in value, or where GDP growth and income levels are very strong.

Situation 3
A multinational business faced with falling rates of growth in some of the countries where it produces goods and in some where it sells its goods.
Strategies
● Concentrate marketing and sales in countries where the GDP and incomes are not badly affected.
● Consider producing more in the countries that are suffering because stable or falling incomes and wages may help to keep production costs low.
● Use the profits from the prosperous sectors of the business to support those under pressure.

Situation 4
A UK national business with rising labour costs in its call centre business facing increased competition from other UK businesses with lower costs.
Strategies
● Try to find less labour intensive ways of running the call centre, i.e. with more technology.
● Move the call centre facility to a cheap labour country such as India.
● Consider selling and producing in countries where there is less direct competition.

unit 12. When considering the influence that these organisations have upon specific businesses it is important to recognise which countries are members and what rules and influence these organisations have on businesses, countries and trade. Students are reminded of the resources and links available through Geosource, at http://www.library.uu.nl/geosource/cat4.html#4.

Strategies to cope with changing conditions

The strategies that businesses use for coping with changes in international economic conditions will depend on:
- the type of business — e.g. local, national or international;
- what products they are selling;
- which countries they are selling into;
- what competition they face and where that is based;
- which economic conditions exist and which are changing.

Because these conditions are so wide and variable only some examples can be given, as shown in Table 2.

Select the latest company report for an international or multinational UK business and then complete the tasks listed below. Company reports should be available in public libraries, school or college libraries, or on the Internet.
1. Make a note of the countries or areas of the world where the business sells and, if it is a multinational, produces its products.
2. Make a note of any comments made in the report that relate to economic conditions in these countries, or in the world in general, such as changing GDP levels, consumer spending, interest rates, exchange rates and taxation rates.
3. Where the company report outlines plans for the future, list these plans and assess, considering the conditions you have identified in (2), whether or not these plans are sensible or unwise.

Research task

Meeting the assessment criteria - examiners' guidance

For your chosen business you are required to produce a chairman's report which describes, applies, analyses and evaluates the effects of external influences on a business.

Business example - Wedgwood moving from national to international and multi-national.

Wedgwood was founded in Stoke-on-Trent in 1759. Its reputation grew rapidly and it expanded its range of products to include ceramic cookware, earthen ware and china ware. Its reputation also ensured that it sold products into other countries very early on. Between 1966 and 1973, it also expanded by acquiring some of the leading names in the English tableware industry including Coalport, Mason's Ironstone, Midwinter and Johnson Brothers.

Wedgwood was a UK international business. In 1986 it was acquired by the Irish company Waterford, famous for its crystal glassware, to form Waterford Wedgwood PLC. In 1997 the company acquired the majority stakeholding of Rosenthal the German ceramics and porcelain firm and in 2005 took over UK rival Royal Doulton. It now produces two-thirds of its products in Ireland, the UK and Germany and out sources the rest for manufacture in Germany, other European countries and Asia. The percentages of its sales of £831.9 million for 2003/04 are shown in Figure 8.

In June 2003 Waterford Wedgwood announced the closure of its two Johnson Brothers earthenware factories in Stoke-on-Trent with the loss of 1,000 jobs, with the work being transferred to China. Following the takeover of Royal Doulton, Waterford Wedgwood and its various businesses have been hit heavily by the sinking dollar and competition from Asia and in May 2005 it

announced that it was to lose 1,800 jobs and close one of its factories in Ireland.

For preparing a report for this section the details given below relate specifically to the external effects that would come from the fact that Waterford Wedgwood operates in an international environment.

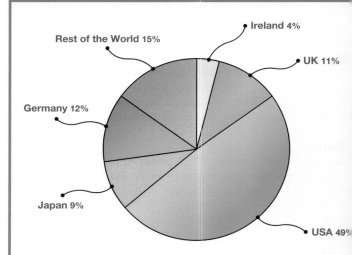

Figure 8 *Percentage sales by destination for Waterford Wedgwood products (Year ending March 2004)*

Rest of the World 15%
Ireland 4%
UK 11%
Germany 12%
Japan 9%
USA 49%

Source: adapted from Waterford Wedgwood's corporate profile, www.waterfordwedgewood.com.

AOs	Mark Band 1	Mark Band 2	Mark Band 3
AO1	A short history of the move from a national and almost local business to an international and multinational firm should be given. This should include details of the countries in which sales and production are taking place. There should be a description of likely external influences such as exchange rates, labour costs, etc.	The description of the business here should have much more detail with some indication of the relative standing of the business in national and international terms. An understanding of the importance of the international conditions should be shown and especially those that will affect Waterford Wedgwood such as exchange rates, the growing world competition and the fact that production takes place in a number of countries.	At this level explanations of the importance of each international condition should be detailed. The changing value of the pound, euro and dollar should be considered as well as the changes that are occurring inside the business itself e.g. the acquisitions of competitors and the movement of some of the production to Asia. Changes in international conditions should be recognised and highlighted, ready to explain how the business has been affected and why that explains the way in which the business has reacted.
AO2	The main conditions and changes should be identified here. It would be expected that figures would be provided to show the changing value of the Pound, Euro and Dollar, the position of the business in terms of product and sales (as in Figure 8). It should also be noted that this is a multinational business and some attempt should be made to link that fact to the changing international conditions.	Here all conditions selected, including the multinational status, should relate to the business, what it sells, where it sells and produces and the position of its competitors. Waterford Wedgwood has expanded both nationally and internationally and needed to change its production processes and the number of direct employees it used. This is all needed if sound explanations are to be provided for the evaluation in AO4.	Here all of the major international influences and trends should be identified and applied. In 2005 it was the sinking Dollar, competition from Asia and the takeover of Royal Doulton that were causing problems. Each of these factors needs additional detail with charts for the sinking Dollar, clear details of how the Asian competition is growing and details such as the cost of the Royal Doulton takeover, about £40 million. It is also vital in assessing the impact of international changes that there is up to date data on what is produced where, as shown in the second paragraph of the data.
AO3	The details given in the data above would easily cover this level. It represents three or four sources and reference to news items. It allows for comments in all of the AO sections and, because it has been separated into sensible paragraphs with data presented as a pie diagram, there is basic analysis.	To ensure that a full evaluation is possible a much wider range of data should be accessed and direct contact with the business should be made. All sources should be acknowledged. Additional sources here could include ones that would provide details of exchange rate changes, world market share in this industry and labour costs in the different countries identified. Selection of data and analysis should be supported by the reason for this.	Research at this level should be comprehensive and use up-to-date information. That requires careful selection of the data and some consideration about possible future changes if that is appropriate. For example, the offer for Royal Doulton was at one stage being considered at £70 million, whereas the final figure was only about £40 million. The value of the Dollar was sinking in 2004, but it has recovered in 2005. Analysis should have identified, extracted and displayed the most relevant data for the business and for the evaluation in AO4.

AOs	Mark Band 1	Mark Band 2	Mark Band 3
AO4	The evaluation here will be simplistic and do little more than acknowledge that production and sales are in a number of countries and indicate the benefits and drawbacks that are likely to be created. It would also note the problems that Waterford Wedgwood has been having recently and give basic statements as to causes, such as the sinking Dollar, but without explanation.	Here any conclusions should be reasoned although that is likely to be at a relatively basic level. If the sinking Dollar is used to explain why Waterford Wedgwood needed to cut jobs and close a factory it should be explained in terms of the weakening Dollar raising the price of the business's goods in Dollars. It would be expected that the very high exposure to USA sales also causes problems. The very low growth shown on Figure 5 could be used to explain why sales in Germany might be poor.	For really detailed evaluation all important aspects of the collected data need to be considered and a balanced evaluation given. For example, here Waterford Wedgwood suggested the growing competition from Asia as a negative influence. This should be weighed against the benefit that it is receiving because it produces some of its output in Asia. There should also be a careful evaluation of the business's strategies. Should it have taken over Royal Doulton knowing it was under these external pressures which have now resulted in the loss of 1,800 jobs?

Portfolio practice · Dorset Cereals

Dorset Cereals was started in 1989. It produces all of its muesli products in Poundbury in Dorset using cereals from around the world. It also now sells the finished muesli products in 60 foreign countries in 4 continents. Its website supports these sales by providing details of products in French, German, Spanish, Italian, Chinese, Japanese, Russian and Arabic. Sales in 2004 were £8.5 million and growth for this company looks very healthy, despite new producers and competition in a number of countries.

The recently appointed Export Sales Manager has identified several key areas, including the US, Australia and New Zealand, where new marketing and sales growth will be targeted. In Europe it has markets in all of the countries shown in Table 3.

For this portfolio practice it will be useful to refer to the details given on international trade and the European Union (EU) in unit 12.

Source: adapted from various sources.

(a) **Identify from Table 3 (i) which countries are in the EU and (ii) which are in the Euro zone.**
(b) **Outline the benefits for Dorset Cereals of selling into (i) EU countries and (ii) a number of countries which all have the Euro as their currency.**
(c) **Other than different currencies, describe the problems that Dorset Cereals might have because of the number of different countries it sells its products in.**
(d) **Dorset Cereals already had sales in the United States (US).**
(i) Explain why it might consider increasing sales in the US as a major priority.
(ii) Using Figure 6, explain why there might be problems with doing this.

Table 3 *Dorset Cereals' markets*

Austria	Belgium	Bosnia	Bulgaria	Czech Republic	Denmark
Estonia	Finland	Greece	Greenland	Hungary	Iceland
Ireland	Isle of Man	Italy	Latvia	Liechtenstein	Lithuania
Luxembourg	Macedonia	Monaco	Netherlands	Norway	Poland
Romania	Serbia	Slovenia	Slovakia	Switzerland	United Kingdom

Other major external economic factors

Other economic influences

The economic factors in sections 68-70 are ones that most businesses are aware of and expect to be affected by at one time or another. This section will consider other major factors that are less predictable but still affect economies and specific businesses. Four main factors, shown in Figure 1, will be considered.

Figure 1 *Other major external economic factors*

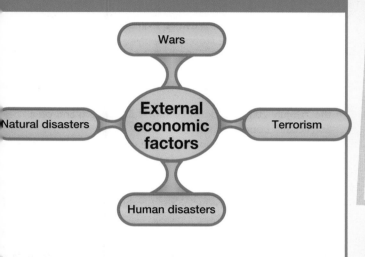

Some of these factors, such as the threat of terrorism, are global factors and affect a wide range of businesses. Others are more localised, as with some wars and many of the disasters. Some will affect certain businesses mainly because of the type of products that they sell.

Wars and other military conflicts

Wars normally affect business negatively because of the destruction and disruption that they cause. However, there will be some businesses, such as weapons suppliers, which do benefit from these military conflicts. It may be thought that the effect of wars on businesses are both rare and remote, but that is not always the case, especially as more and more businesses have an international presence.

The UK Foreign Office provides information to individuals and businesses about the safety of travelling to foreign countries. In December 2005, for example, the Foreign Office was advising against all travel to the Ivory Coast, because of likely demonstrations during the elections, and to Somalia, because of terrorist threats and strong anti-western feelings in the country. In addition, the Foreign Office advised against travel to parts of 27 other countries for a variety of reasons including military conflicts, terrorist and insurgent threats. These countries included Afghanistan, Eritrea, Iraq, Israel and the Philippines.

The wars that were given most coverage between 2000-2005 in the UK press were the Iraq war and the military action in Afghanistan, but there were also conflicts in Azerbaijan, Sri-Lanka, Somalia, Chad, Eritrea and Ethiopia, and Darfur in the Sudan.

It can be argued that wars have both negative and positive effects on business. The expected effects of the Iraq War on UK businesses are shown in Figure 2.

Figure 2

Even before the war had started a poll conducted by BusinessEurope.com revealed that 55% of UK small businesses thought a war in Iraq would have a negative influence on them. Of these, 31% said it would have a marked impact. On the 1st of April 2004 *Accountancy Age* reported that, following its survey of Financial Directors, 73% believed the threat of a terrorist attack was higher in the UK than elsewhere in Europe because of the UK's support of the United States in the Iraq war.

Source: adapted from various sources.

Figure 3 *Fall in Iraqi GDP 1980 to 2004*

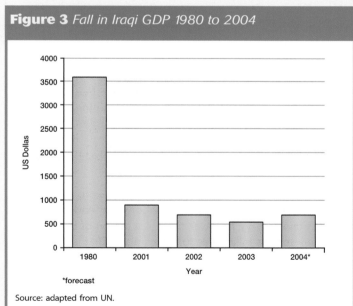

*forecast

Source: adapted from UN.

Negative effects of the Iraq War Businesses producing or selling in Iraq were unable to do so whilst the war was on.

- Businesses involved in travel and tourism to and from Iraq were unable to continue because of travel restrictions and lack of demand.
- Many businesses in Iraq were destroyed and so there was no demand for imports from the UK.
- Sanctions placed on Iraq before the war and the destruction

during the war saw the Iraqi GDP fall by over 75% between 1980 and 2001 and then fall by 12% in 2001, 21% in 2002 and another 22% in 2003. Unemployment rose to over 50% and incomes fell as shown in Figure 3.

- Estimates suggested that it would take £55 billion to reconstruct Iraq after the damage created by the war and that this was money that could have been used for other expenditures in the USA, the UK and other donor countries.

Businesses in demand Some businesses found that their products and services were in demand.

- Businesses that sell military equipment and arms may have benefited. In the first 12 days over 700 Tomahawk missiles were fired costing over £556 million alone to replace. Also see Table 1.
- Businesses involved in the reconstruction after the war. For example, UK firms Parsons-Brinkerhoff and Foster Wheeler have shared in contracts worth £24 million and £4.7 million respectively.

Table 1 *Sample hardware costs of the Iraq war*

Type of armament	Cost for one
M2 Bradley Armoured Troop Carrier	£1.8 mil.
M1 Abrahms Battle Tank	£2.4 mil.
M270 Rocket Launcher	£1.3 mil.
Advanced Attack Helicopter	£7.9 mil.
M109 Paladin Self-propelled Howitzer	£1.0 mil.
Tomahawk Missile	£0.8 mil.

Source: adapted from *Time Magazine*, March 2003.

Indirect effects Many UK businesses may have been indirectly affected by this war. These include:

- businesses affected by the change in oil prices. Iraq has the world's second largest proven oil reserves and the amount it can produce affects the world price for petroleum;
- businesses affected by increased terrorist threats. It is accepted by most commentators that this war increased, rather than reduced the threat of terrorism.

Business strategies It is difficult for businesses to plan for wars or conflicts because, generally, nations are working to prevent them. Usually, however, there is a period of build up before any serious military action takes place. That is the time for businesses to think really carefully about how they are likely to be affected and plan some actions that will limit the effects if the war or conflicts take place. Those businesses that will be negatively affected might, for example, look for supplies in other countries, target other countries when selling products or prepare for less sales by not taking on new staff. Those businesses that could gain more trade might, for example, consider increasing production.

Terrorism

Terrorism is defined by the United States Department of Defense as:

'the calculated use of unlawful violence or threat of unlawful violence to inculcate fear; intended to coerce or to intimidate governments or societies in the pursuit of goals that are generally political, religious, or ideological.'

The attack upon the Twin Towers of the World Trade Centre in New York on the 11th Sept 2001 and on the Pentagon signified a new dimension to terrorist activities and was described as 'The day the World changed'. The terrorists had, essentially, announced that no target was safe. This has now been confirmed with attacks across the globe.

Terrorism in today's society is increasing and UK businesses can be a target for terrorist activities, which may have direct and indirect effects. Direct effects come from businesses themselves being targets for terrorist activities. Examples include:

- Feb. 2005 when BOC stopped supplying products to Huntingdon Life Sciences after animal rights activists attacked BOC staff;
- the 20th Dec 2005, attack on the Anglo-Dutch oil business Shell in Nigeria killed 8 people;
- the 7th July 2005 attack on London Tube system and on a Stagecoach London bus.

Indirect effects come when there are other targets, but these then affect UK businesses, for example:

- between Jan. 2005 and Oct. 2005 there were over 88 bomb, mortar and rocket attacks on Iraqi oil pipelines, wells and processing factories, reducing the production of oil and affecting world prices;
- the 7th July 2005 bomb attacks on the tube and bus systems in London have heightened fears of future attacks affecting tourism in London and sales in retail outlets in London;
- the 1st Oct. 2005 attack on 3 restaurants in Bali affected UK travel agents selling holidays to Bali.

The cost of terrorism Terrorism and the threat of terrorism cause huge losses to businesses. Table 2 shows the costs of some terrorist attacks in recent years.

Table 2 *Costs of terrorist actions*

Terrorist action	Estimated costs
11th Sep. 2001 attacks in the USA	More than $100 billion
1993 Bishopsgate bomb in London	About £1 billion
1996 London Docklands	Cost insurers £170 million
1996 Manchester bomb	Cost insurers £411 million
7th July 2005 London bombs	Estimated at £300 million

Source: adapted from press reports.

The figures in Table 2 relate to the costs to businesses of damage to buildings, loss of trade, insurance costs and damage to tocks. In addition to these costs there is also the huge loss in terms of human suffering, both to those killed and injured, but also to their families and friends.

The whole purpose of terrorism is to make people frightened and even the threat of terrorism can and does create considerable additional cost for businesses. Where there is a threat of terrorism businesses need to take additional precautions to ensure that no attacks take place. These precautions include additional surveillance costs, camera, detectors and also higher insurance premiums.

Where there have been terrorist attacks there are also additional costs of encouraging customers to come back as shown in Figure 4.

Figure 4 *Sales slump in London after bomb*

Shop sales in central London dropped sharply in the wake of the July terror attacks, according to figures published in 2005. Retail sales in the capital fell 8.9% last month compared with last year, the worst drop since monitoring started in October 2002. Trade was hit hard on July 7 and 21 when the bombings occurred, according to retailers lobby group the London Retail Consortium. Sales picked up slightly during the rest of the month but were still blighted by tube disruption, security alerts and consumer anxiety.

Source: adapted from *The Guardian*, 16.8.2005.

Business strategies In areas where there is a clear threat of terrorist activity businesses need to take precautions to prevent their businesses being attacked. In shops, for example, the premises should be periodically checked to ensure no packages have been left and they should ensure that customers do not have access to parts of the building, such as the cellars, which are not regularly checked. On transport systems customers are warned to be vigilant and to keep luggage with them at all times.

In some cases ensuring that there is no terrorist attack is almost impossible. In other cases it might be possible to reduce the likelihood of an attack by using very invasive measures, such as searching everyone who comes into a shop. In both cases the business must weigh up the benefits against the costs and inconvenience. Strategies need to be effective, but at the same time not prohibitively expensive or so dramatic that they stop the business from continuing to provide the goods and services that the customers want.

Natural disasters

On Boxing Day 2004 an earthquake in the Indian Ocean created a tsunami (tidal wave) that devastated coastal areas of Indonesia, Sri Lanka, South India and Thailand and even reached, and killed, people on the east coast of Africa. In all some 275,000 people were killed including 9,000 foreign tourists. The economic impact for the countries involved has been massive, with, for example, 66% of the fishing fleet in Sri Lanka destroyed on which 250,000 people's incomes depended.

The insurance costs for the Asian tsunami were estimated at over £34 million. Total reconstruction costs for the areas affected have been estimated at £6.65 billion. For UK businesses involved in the reconstruction there are benefits, but for many other businesses, including those providing insurance cover these kinds of natural disasters can cause major negative effects. In January 2005 UK travel agents which were members of the Association of British Travel Agents (Abta) offered tourists due to travel to the disaster region in January refunds or new dates. The additional costs of arranging these were paid for by the travel agents.

The major natural disasters in the world have tended to affect other countries, with UK businesses being indirectly affected. However, the UK itself has also been affected by potential, and sometimes actual, major natural events. Some examples are shown in Table 3.

Table 3 *Effects of natural disasters*

- 1987 the remnants of Hurricane Floyd hit the UK causing damage in the UK estimated at £1.25 billion.
- Storms in 1990 caused damage estimated at £2 billion.
- Flood damage following torrential rain in October 1998 was estimated at £400 million.
- Floods in autumn 2000 caused damage to 10,000 properties with a total cost of more than £1.3 billion.
- August 2004 a flash flood hit Boscastle in Cornwall causing damage estimated at over £50 million and possibly as much as £500 million (see Portfolio Practice).
- July 2005 a tornado ripped through Birmingham causing up to £25million worth of damage to buildings in its path.

Business strategies Most natural disasters are, by their nature, fairly unpredictable and even the scientific experts can generally do no more than guess, with varying degrees of uncertainty when (or if) the next 'event' will occur. For businesses this uncertainty can cause serious strategic problems.

- Should they, or should they not, take precautions against something that might not happen?
- How much will the precautions cost and how much might they lose if they did not take precautions?
- If a disaster occurs, will potential customers react to the actual dangers involved, and/or the media hype, or work out the risks for themselves?
- What are the insurance implications for the business if no insurance has been taken out for the specific disaster that occurs?

Human-created disasters

Some major disasters are not natural but come from the activities of people and businesses. Some are accidents, as with the Buncefield oil depot fire in Hertfordshire in December 2005. Others are caused by our lifestyle, as with global warming which experts blame on the amount of carbon dioxide released into air from factories or car exhausts. The effects of these mistakes are generally on the environment and this is covered in sections 72 and 73.

1. Using a trade directory or the Internet identify three UK public limited companies (plcs) that supply military equipment or support materials. This could range from aircraft, warships or tanks to missiles and guns or to uniforms and military rations.
2. For one of these businesses check its company reports, website, or publicity material and list what it produces and to whom it sells these produces.
3. Identify any military conflicts that its equipment has been used in and any plans that it has for the future.

Research task

Meeting the assessment criteria - examiners' guidance

For your chosen business you are required to produce a chairman's report which describes, applies, analyses and evaluates the effects of external influences on a business.

Business example - It's up to all of us – new security campaign

Transport for London (TfL) is responsible for the main public transport systems in London including London buses, the Underground and the Docklands Light Railway. Following the terrorist attacks on the tube and bus services in July 2005 TfL has had to re-evaluate its security procedures.

Security procedures now include the following.

- Evacuation plans for each of the 275 tube stations with every member of staff trained for this.
- British Transport Police (BTP) patrols increased with police in both high visibility clothing and undercover.
- BTP numbers increased from 450 in 2003 to 650 by the end of 2005.
- Checks of all public areas of the train undertaken by train crew before during and after each trip.
- All buses are checked by the drivers at the end of each trip.
- All stations checked on a continual basis.
- Searches of road vehicles entering depots.
- Plans to increase the number of CCTV cameras on London Underground from 6,000 to 12,000 in the next five years.
- Publicity campaigns to make customers more security

conscious, including posters and PA announcements.

Despite these measures and the huge publicity that the bomb attacks received, the general public still ignores safety warnings, with packages left on trains and buses often leading to delays and fear as the packages are checked.

Source: adapted from TfL press releases.

AOs	Mark Band 1	Mark Band 2	Mark Band 3
AO1	Details of the role of TfL in providing transport facilities for London should be given. The basic threats and effects of terrorism should be covered and details given of the July 7th bombing.	Details of TfL role should be in much greater depth including such detail as the scale of its services. Each day journeys include 6.3 million by bus, 3 million by tube, 1.4 million by rail and 11 million by car or motorbike. Details on terrorism should recognise that July 7th was only one of several attacks on London transport, including a failed attempt on July 21st 2005.	The likely impact of terrorism in general terms should be fully covered with an understanding of both actual attacks and the threat of attacks shown. For TfL there should be a clear understanding of the likely impacts that this might have in terms of actual loss of custom, additional costs, the need for good PR to make people aware of the dangers, but also not to frighten them. The nature of the business should also be appreciated and comments made on why this makes TfL a target.
AO2	Application of terrorist acts to TfL will be basic with the most obvious identified, such as the closing of parts of the underground, increased numbers in the BTP and increased checks on tubes, trains and buses. Details of the impact of such attacks on TfL will be limited, with basic statements rather than reasoned effects, e.g. evacuation plans in all 275 tube stations, but no details of what these plans are.	Here details of the impact of terrorism on TfL will recognise the nature and size of TfL's business. Where impacts are shown, for example the plan to double the CCTV cameras, these will be clearly related to the changed situation that TfL finds itself in since the 7th of July. A wide range of impacts should be considered as shown in the bullets in the case study. For each, the nature of the business should be clearly applied, for example the need for customers to be encouraged to hold on to their luggage so as not to cause unnecessary scares.	Details of how terrorist activities have affected TfL should be carefully selected so that the major impacts are clearly identified and distinguished from more minor effects. TfL is responsible for 580km of main roads and all of London's 4,600 traffic lights as well as the central London Congestion Charging scheme. The July 7th bombs had very little effect on roads, traffic light or congestion charging, but it had major, and costly, effects on the trains and the underground network that were destroyed and on the cost of providing increased security. Loss of income from network closures was estimated to have cost TfL in the region of £20 million.
AO3	Obvious sources should be used including TfL itself and news reports for the July 7th attacks. Little attempt will have been made to find more detailed reports on impacts and costs so that the basic data provided will deal mainly with headline details relating to casualties, changed procedures, etc.	A wider range of sources should be accessed here with a range of news reports and a full study of TfL's own press releases. In addition there should be contact with the organisation (TfL) itself. Because the impact of terrorism is a result of targeting London other London sources should also be consulted, for example the Mayor of London's office.	For a full appraisal of the effects of terrorism on TfL it is necessary to consider how the threats and responses have changed over time. The type of terrorism in the July 7th attacks, suicide bombing, should be compared to earlier attacks. In order to make this comparison, older sources will need to be accessed and appropriate data selected and analysed.

AOs	Mark Band 1	Mark Band 2	Mark Band 3
AO4	The evaluation here will be simplistic. It should recognise the increased threat of terrorism for TfL and recommend increased security and surveillance. It will probably relate only to the July 7th attacks and simply list changes that have been made with perhaps comments on which of these changes are likely to be the most important.	At this level the changes should have reasoned explanations, for example explanations of why doubling the number of CCTV cameras is likely to help prevent terrorism. There should be clear prioritisation of the measures taken with explanations of why some are likely to be more effective than others. There should also be some recommendations about measures that have not been taken and justifications of why they should, or should not, be considered, e.g. the use of electronic scanning of passengers.	A detailed evaluation should recognise the change in the nature of terrorism with the July 7th attacks and compare these to previous attacks and threats. It should then examine the changes that have been made and consider their likely effectiveness in this new environment. The changes should be assessed in terms of the impact that they will have on the terrorists, the general public and the TfL itself. The report should also recognise the impossibility of completely preventing terrorist attacks on all parts of the transport system and the balance that will have to be made between cost, practical measures and the convenience of the customers.

Portfolio practice · Boscastle devastated by a flash flood

Boscastle is a village on the North Cornish Coast with a small number of fishing boats. About 90% of its livelihood comes from tourism. In August 2004 it was hit by a flash flood with an estimated two million tonnes of water flowing through the village during the day. This washed away boats, cars and shops and damaged building by the harbour side. Most of the village was evacuated, including the tourists, and 20 accommodation providers were forced to shut.

The cost of the damage was originally estimated at between £50 million to £500 million with some buildings needing to be replaced, other needing major re-construction work and work needed on the roads, car park and flood defences. In addition there was the loss of the tourist trade as customers were at first prevented from staying in the village and later came for day visits but did not stay overnight.

By September 2004 there had been some recovery with the lower half of the car park open, a temporary visitors centre open two days a week in a portacabin and some shops and accommodations re-opened. There were other businesses that were still closed or finding cash flow a major problem. It was also recognised that considerable additional marketing would be needed to inform potential customers of what was available and to encourage them to come to an area that had suffered such a catastrophic flood.

Source: adapted from various sources.

(a) **Outline the negative effects of the August 2004 flash flood on the businesses in Boscastle.**
(b) **Why might there have been positive benefits for businesses both inside and outside of Boscastle because of the flood?**
The marketing undertaken following the floods and the rebuilding of businesses in Boscastle focused on three elements:
(i) **that businesses and the village were re-opened;**
(ii) **that Boscastle and the surrounding areas were safe and an attractive and welcoming place to visit;**
(iii) **details of what had happened during the flood and afterwards.**
(c) **Explain why it was important for Boscastle's marketing to include all of these three elements.**

Business activity and the environment

When businesses produce goods and services they almost inevitably affect the environment in which we live. Sometimes this can be beneficial, as with the creation of an attractive golf course, which also has footpaths for the general public. In most cases, however, the effect on the environment is negative, as with dirty smoke from factory chimneys and the sound of heavy lorries passing by residential houses as they go to and from factories and regional distribution centres.

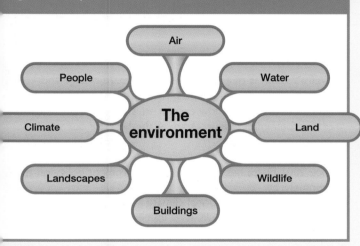

Figure 1 *Aspects of the environment*

Figure 1 shows aspects of the environment that can be affected by the way in which businesses carry out their production. This can happen during all of the following phases of production.

- Extraction of raw materials from the land, sea, rivers and air, e.g. coal mining causing subsidence in local houses.
- Processing of raw materials into finished products, e.g. the production of iron and steel causing smoke pollution.
- Distribution of raw materials, semi-finished and finished products, e.g. heavy delivery vehicles damaging buildings through vibrations.
- The sale of products in wholesale and retail businesses, e.g. out-of-town supermarkets using land that used to be a place of recreation.
- The disposal of used products, packaging and waste, e.g. car manufacturers designing cars that will not last and which will need to be disposed of.
- Communication between businesses and between businesses and consumers, e.g. placing base stations for mobile phone transmission in unsightly locations.

Sulphur dioxide – an example

The effects on the environment will depend on what damaging bi-products are produced by business and which businesses create

them. When government makes regulations to control the harmful effects of these bi-products it will be the businesses that created them that are most directly affected.

In the past sulphur dioxide (SO_2) gas was considered a major cause of pollution. It affected the environment in the following ways.

- The gas combines with water in the air to produce sulphuric acid which can kill trees, pollute water systems and kill fish and damage buildings.
- The gas can directly affect human health as the fumes and particles are inhaled. This can lead to breathing difficulties.
- The gas can travel hundreds and even thousands of miles away from where the SO_2 was released into the atmosphere and damage the environment in other areas and even other countries.

Efforts to reduce the emissions of SO_2, from all sources, have been very effective, as is shown on Figure 2. Figure 2 also shows that the major cause of SO_2 emissions has been from the production of power such as electricity and gas. It has, therefore, been those industries that have been most affected by regulations.

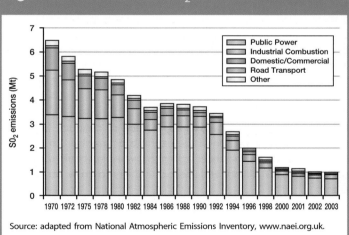

Figure 2 *Reduction in UK SO_2 emissions*

Source: adapted from National Atmospheric Emissions Inventory, www.naei.org.uk.

The emissions of SO_2 have not been completely eliminated, which would be a difficult thing to achieve because of the continuing need to use fossil fuels for making power. The effects of this on local communities will differ depending on what part of the country is taken. Figure 3 shows the SO_2 pollution that has affected three locations for the month of March 2006. It also shows that there is a wide fluctuation from day to day.

Why is regulation needed?

It would be good if businesses automatically took measures to ensure that the environment is not negatively affected by what and how they produce. Some businesses do try to voluntarily limit the negative effects. This approach to business will be looked at in

Figure 3 *SO₂ measurements (cubic gms) for selected parts of the UK, March 2006*

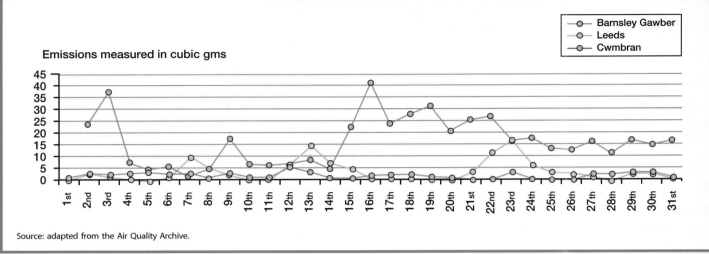

Source: adapted from the Air Quality Archive.

section 73 The problem is that reducing the effects on the environment generally has a cost and so affects profits. Businesses, therefore, frequently do not try to reduce the negative effects voluntarily and that is why the government has to step in and force businesses to meet certain minimum standards.

It has been recognised for some time that the way in which humans produce products, exploits the natural environment and pollutes the air, water and land is causing unacceptable damage, both to people and to the balance of nature itself. This pollution can be as apparently minor as people dropping chewing gum on the pavement or as major as changing the ozone layer or global warming.

In the first case travel magazines can, and do, comment on the unsightly look of London's streets, for example, with endless discoloured blobs of dirty gum, which both discourages some tourists from coming and costs a great deal to clean up. In the second case the depletion of the ozone layer may lead to increased risks of skin cancer and global warming could totally change the UK's climate and affect our ability to grow certain crops.

Faced with this very wide range of environmental challenges, and ones that businesses are not voluntarily addressing, it is understandable that the government has first developed an environmental policy and has then enforced it through legislation and regulation.

Government environmental policy

In the UK the Department for Environment, Food and Rural Affairs (Defra) has been given the task of ensuring that businesses, and the general public, meet the regulations that have been laid down by both UK law and EU law. The full range of its areas of influence and the way in which it works can be found at its website, http://www.defra.gov.uk/, or through its Information Resource Centre at Lower Ground Floor, Ergon House, c/o Nobel House, 17 Smith Square, London, SW1P 3JR.

Defra was set up in 2001 and in an early report in 2002 it stated

its vision as:

'Defra's vision is of a world in which climate change and environmental degradation are recognised and addressed by all nations and where low carbon emissions and efficient use of environmental resources are at the heart of our whole way of life.'

Since 2001 Defra has implemented government policy on the environment by:

- supporting the international climate change negotiations in 2001 and creating the UK legal framework for the Kyoto Protocol, (see below);
- working with the Department of Trade and Industry and the Department for Transport in setting a target of a 60% cut in the UK's carbon emissions by 2050;
- supporting local authorities to increase recycling of household waste and setting required targets for this.

The policy for the future is to:

- make local environments cleaner, safer and greener;
- improve air and water quality further and to further cut greenhouse gas emissions which contribute to global warming;
- support businesses, farmers and individuals in changing their behaviour so that they do not damage the environment;
- work to remove the threat of climate change at national, EU and global level;
- work for sustainable development which will allow economic growth without damaging the environment.

All of these policy commitments and plans have, and will have, effects on how businesses produce their goods and services.

UK environmental legislation

The environment covers a great many different aspects of the world in which we live and therefore the legislation that has been passed to protect the environment is also very wide. There is no overall legislation that covers all aspects. Examples of the legislation will be given below but students will need to check for legislation that relates to the particular business or industry being studied.

The Kyoto Protocol The main general commitment that the UK has made to environmental protection has come through it signing up to the Kyoto Protocol. This was an amendment to the United Nations Framework Convention on Climate Change (UNFCCC) made in 1997, with countries of the world signing up to it in 1998 and 1999. When they signed up they agreed to reduce their emissions of carbon dioxide and five other greenhouse gases. They could, however, use 'emissions trading' whereby they could buy the right to continue emissions and even increase them if they could buy these rights from countries which had emissions below the levels agreed by Kyoto. The idea was to ensure that in the world as a whole the emissions of these harmful gases would not increase.

The UK took the approach of cutting emissions rather than trading and agreed to reduce greenhouse gas emissions by 12.5% below 1990 levels by 2008-2012. The UK government went further than this with a commitment to cut carbon dioxide (CO_2) emissions by 20% by 2010 and 60% by 2050.

These commitments will affect businesses that cause these emissions. For the CO_2 emissions the main business sectors causing these were recorded by the European Pollutant Emission Register (EPER). This is shown on Table 1. CO_2 emissions also come from vehicles and in the long-run there will need to be alternative ways of transporting goods and people or vehicles that do not run on petrol, diesel or gas.

Table 1 *Major business sectors causing CO_2 emissions (% share)*

Business activity	%
Combustion, e.g. power stations, cars	64.9
Cement and lime	9.5
Refineries, e.g. oil	8.7
Metal industry	7.6
Organic chemicals	4.0
Inorganic chemicals	1.8
Pulp and paper	1.3
Waste from towns and cities	1.3
Slaughter houses, milk production	0.4
Landfill sites	0.4

Source: adapted from *EPER Review Report* (June 2004), http://eper.cec.eu.int.

The other greenhouse gases identified by the Kyoto Protocol are shown on Table 2 with the top three business sources of emissions. These will also have targets for reduction that will have to be met by businesses.

To control possible damage to the environment a very wide range of legislation is in place in the UK. Some of the legislation is fairly general and some of it is very specific. It is specific to either the type of environmental danger or to the types of production. The 'Meeting the assessment criteria' below deals with onshore hydrocarbon production as an example. Here some specific pieces of legislation are considered, but students need to identify and

Table 2 *Major business sectors causing other greenhouse gas emissions (% share)*

Business activity	%
Methane (CH_4)	
Non hazardous waste and landfills	88.1
Hazardous/municipal waste	6.5
Poultry and pigs	2.3
Hydrofluorocarbons (HFCs)	
Inorganic chemicals	48.0
Organic chemicals	41.1
Combustion	3.4
Perfluorocarbons (PFCs)	
Metal industry	95.7
Surface treatment	2.2
Inorganic chemicals	1.4
Nitrous oxide (N_2O)	
Inorganic chemicals	40.9
Combustion	27.9
Organic chemicals	25.7
Sulphur hexafluoride (SF_6)	
Metal industry	80.9
Inorganic chemicals	10.4
Surface treatment	6.4

Source: adapted from EPER Review Report (June 2004), http://eper.cec.eu.int.

research the legislation that applies to their chosen business or industry.

Environmental Protection Act, 1990 This Act defined many aspects of what was meant by the 'environment' and how it might be damaged by business, and by individuals. It also re-enforced the requirement that businesses which might cause environmental damage had to register (and obtain a licence), providing details of their production processes and the likely emissions, or waste, that might be created because of this. It also allowed the secretary of state responsible to:

● establish limits for the total amount of specific emissions which could be released into the environment;

- allocate quotas for these emissions for particular businesses or industries;
- progressively reduce the limits of the emissions that would pollute the environment.

The Act also set out which authorities would be responsible for regulating and enforcing the controls, passing significant controls and responsibilities to local authorities. It outlined the powers that the authorities had to control and even close down businesses that did not meet the limits set down by the secretary of state.

Part II deals with 'waste on land' and set down requirements for what is or is not acceptable for the disposal of waste, from both businesses and households.

Part III deals with the control of nuisances such as noise and air pollution, defining a wide range of things that would be considered as causing an environmental nuisance, e.g. the levels of noise that would be considered too loud for a discotheque.

Part VI deals with Genetically Modified Organisms (GMOs) and is designed to prevent or minimise any damage to the environment which may arise from the escape or release from human control of genetically modified organisms.

Other legislation Environmental legislation is very wide and each of the environmental areas listed below has its own specific legislation that needs to be checked if that is involved. Details of all legislation is provided by the Environment Agency through its NetRegs website at www.netregs.gov.uk/netregs/legislation/
- Air Legislation.
- Chemicals Legislation.
- Energy Legislation.
- Land Legislation.
- Noise and Statutory Nuisance Legislation.
- Pollution Prevention & Control (PPC) Legislation (including IPC).
- Plant Protection Legislation.
- Radioactive Substances Legislation.
- Waste Legislation.
- Water Legislation.

Research task

1. Using the Environment Agency's website at www.netregs.gov.uk/netregs/legislation/or media stories about future changes in environmental legislation, select one piece of proposed environmental legislation.
2. Give an outline of what the new legislation would require.
3. Identify the types of business that are likely to be affected by the legislation.
4. Describe how the businesses would be affected and how this might change the way in which they produce and what they would produce.

Portfolio practice · A new car

As we become wealthier as a nation our demand for cars becomes ever greater, with most households owning a car and often two or three cars. All vehicles that use the internal combustion engine create polluting emissions including nitrous oxide, carbon monoxide, carbon dioxide, particles that affect humans and even noise pollution. Legislation has been brought in to deal with these emissions and car manufacturers have had to change their production processes in order to meet the legislation.

Now, with lower and lower levels of emissions being set by new regulations, car manufacturers are having to redesign the engines so that they will meet these new lower limits. The lean-burn engine and even hydrogen driven cars have been looked into, but these take time to research and develop. New research is now focusing on either running cars on hydrogen, electricity or very much lower quantities of petrol. Without these developments, and with ever lower permitted emissions, the car of today could be illegal in the not too distant future.

(a) Which type of environmental damage is being reduced by the following parts of a car? The:
(i) bumpers; (ii) exhaust pipe; (iii) silencer;
(iv) catalytic converter; (v) pneumatic tyres;
(vi) engines which use lead free petrol.
(b) Explain why the Kyoto Protocol has led to the situation described in the two paragraphs above.
(c) (i) Identify ONE piece of environmental legislation, an Act or regulation, which affects the way in which car manufacturers must produce cars.
(ii) State the main environmental requirements of this legislation and explain how that affects the manufacturers.
(d) Assess how the continuous lowering of permitted emissions will affect car manufacturers in terms of:
(i) cost;
(ii) the design of cars in the future.

Meeting the assessment criteria - examiners' guidance

For your chosen business you are required to produce a chairman's report which describes, applies, analyses and evaluates the effects of external influences on a business. This will involve consideration of the impact of environmental legislation on the business.

Business example - Legislation for onshore hydrocarbons production

The Department of Trade and Industry (DTI) has provided a detailed summary of the legislation that would affect businesses involved in the production of hydrocarbons in England, Wales and Scotland. Parts of these requirements are shown in Table 3.

Table 3 *Key EC and UK environmental legislation for onshore hydrocarbon production*

Legislation	Main requirements	Regulator
Town and Country Planning Act 1990 (England and Wales), Town and Country Planning (Scotland) Act 1997, Environment Act 1995	Planning permission is required for all hydrocarbon developments.	Local authorities / county councils
Petroleum Act 1998 and The Petroleum (Production) (Landward Areas) Regulations 1995	A licence is required for exploration, development, production of fields.	DTI
Pipelines Act 1962 and Pipe-line Works (Environmental Impact Assessment) Regulations 2000	Requires pipelines over 16 km in length to prepare an Environmental Statement.	DTI
EC Directive (92/43/EEC) Conservation of natural habitats and of wild fauna and flora and Conservation (Natural Habitats) Regulations 1994	Requires developments to take account of Special Areas of Conservation in their environmental impact assessment.	Local authorities
EC Directive (96/82/EC): Control of major accident hazards and a) Planning (Control of Major Accident Hazards) Regulations 1999 [2000 in Scotland] b) Control of Major Accident Hazards (COMAH) Regulations 1999	A licence is required for storage of listed hazardous substances. Requires operators to implement certain management practices and report to the competent authorities.	Local authorities Environment Agency / SEPA
EC Directive (80/68/EEC) Groundwater and Groundwater Regulations 1998	Discharges of listed substances which could pollute groundwater require to be authorised through the issue of a licence.	Environment Agency / SEPA
Energy Act 1976 and The Petroleum Act 1998	Consent is required for flaring or venting or hydrocarbon gas. Requires licensees of an onshore field to ensure that petroleum is contained both above and below ground.	DTI
Environment Act 1995, Part IV and Air Quality Regulations 2000	Sets emission limits for certain substances and requires authorities to take action where quality parameters are exceeded.	Local authorities
EC Regulation (3093/94): Substances that deplete the ozone layer and Environmental Protection (Controls on Substances that Deplete the Ozone Layer) Regulations 1996	A licence is required for the production, supply, use, trading and emission of certain 'controlled substances' that deplete the ozone layer.	DEFRA
Control of Pollution Act 1974, Part III Environmental Protection Act 1990, Part III and Environment Act 1995, Part V.	Requires local authorities to take action where noise limits are exceeded.	Local authorities

Source: adapted from DTI, www.og.dti.gov.uk.

AOs	Mark Band 1	Mark Band 2	Mark Band 3
AO1	Details of the business or industry should be provided with reference to it being an onshore hydrocarbons producer, e.g. extracting and/or producing of oil and gas. Reference to environmental legislation will be fairly general but should consider policy, the Kyoto Protocol, and some appropriate legislation, such as the Environmental Protection Act.	Details at this level should show what is involved in the setting up and production of hydrocarbon products. This would then show the need for a wider range of environmental legislation to be considered by the business. This would run from planning restrictions to control of waste products. More legislation should be referred to but will have limited details of what is required and how that would affect the business or industry.	There should be a good understanding shown of all the major stages involved in setting up and running an onshore hydrocarbon business. Some major legislation should be identified for each of these stages and some of the basic requirements of that legislation should be outlined. Examples of these are given in the second column of Table 3.
A02	Application here is likely to be very general and will focus on major environmental concerns such as the Kyoto Protocol and global warming. There will be limited explanation of how that relates to onshore hydrocarbon production.	Here the main impacts of onshore hydrocarbon extraction and production should be identified with details of how the environment may be affected, for example pumping facilities causing unacceptable levels of noise, laying of pipelines digging up the countryside, leakages affecting natural water systems and processing releasing pollution into the air. For the identified problems the relevant legislation should also be identified and the main requirement(s) outlined.	All details should be accurate and the major stages involved in the setting up and production of onshore hydrocarbons should be correctly matched with the major requirements of the relevant legislation. Where the environment is being affected details should be given of how it is being affected and how the legislation reduces that effect. There should also be some assessment of how the business is affected in terms of, for example, cost, time to set up the business and the ways of ensuring that the effect on the environment is minimised.
A03	Sources chosen should provide basic details of the business and how it is likely to affect, and be affected by, the environment. Sources for legislation should include the Environment Agency and Defra.	Sources at this level should include access to the main environmental legislation that affects the business. This should be through the Acts and regulations themselves or through good summaries of these. There should be sound knowledge of the business and how it operates so sources need to be selected that will show how it actually produces, what waste products there are, etc. Contact with the business itself is recommended.	Sources need to be wide enough to provide all of the important details of how the business produces and what environmental impact it has. Details are also needed of how it deals with the legislation so contact with the business itself is important. As Table 3 shows, there is a great deal of relevant legislation and a significant amount of this needs to be checked. In addition to the Environment Agency and Defra, www.opsi.gov.uk gives access to the legislation itself.
A04	The evaluation here will be fairly general. It should give details of the main environmental issues involved, e.g. air, water and land and identify some of the likely impacts of these on producing hydrocarbons. There will also be a basic evaluation of how policy and legislation might affect the businesses, e.g. with the Kyoto Protocol, Defra's vision and the Environmental Protection Act.	The impact of the business's activities on the environment and of environmental policy and legislation on the business needs to be outlined, but these impacts also need to be explained. For example, if pipelines affect the countryside it should be explained how. And, when the legislation dictates what the business must do about this, details should be given of how pipelines are buried and how the business ensures that the pipelines will not break and pollute water systems.	Evaluation at this level should consider how important the impact of the business on the environment is and the relative importance of different legislation on the business. If, for example, the business extracts petroleum miles away from any houses then noise pollution is not likely to be important. Table 3 shows many potential pieces of legislation that could affect this business. Some are less important than others, e.g., the Petroleum Act deals mainly with offshore petroleum extraction.

Voluntary environmental actions

Businesses environmental policy

Section 72 considered government policy and legislation on the environment and how this affected businesses. This section will look at the voluntary action that businesses take to protect the environment and to reduce waste.

Businesses need to follow government regulations and legislation because if they do not they may be:

* unable to get a licence to carry out their business;
* taken to court and fined;
* in extreme cases, sent to prison;
* forced to stop production which causes damage;
* forced to make changes that will remove or reduce the environmental damage.

In addition, however, many businesses have introduced their own environmental policy. Figure 1 shows an example.

Figure 1 *Tarmac's environmental policy statement*

Tarmac Topblock is committed to minimising the impact of its operations on local communities and the natural environment, and implements this though a demanding environmental management system.

Key measures include ensuring that up-to-date and proven technology is used, compliant with all statutory requirements, permissions and authorisations.

Raw materials are used in the most efficient way possible, incorporating appropriate opportunities for waste minimisation and to reuse and recycle. All sites, fixed and mobile plant, and vehicles, and their immediate environment are subject to a regular cleaning and maintenance regime.

Direct transport drivers are expected to exhibit particular care to minimise noise, particularly during unsocial hours, and to be considerate drivers and to comply with any designated routing requirements. Management and staff are encouraged to seek positive improvement in environmental performance.

Source: adapted from Tarmac Topblock's website, www.topblock.co.uk.

Figure 2 shows the main reasons for businesses taking their environmental commitments beyond what the legislation demands.

Social conscience The owners of many businesses appreciate that the environment is extremely important and that they should try to ensure that their businesses do not damage it unnecessarily. To help to protect the environment these businesses will try to achieve the following kinds of outcomes:

* minimise the pollution their methods of production, or

Figure 2 *Reasons for environmental commitment*

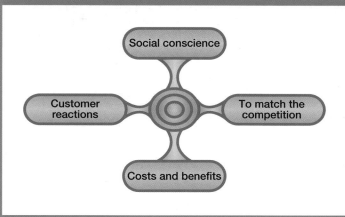

products, might cause;

* use raw materials that are sustainable, e.g. paper from renewable timber plantations;
* minimise waste or use bio-degradable packaging;
* make products that can be recycled and encouraging their customers to recycle;
* produce products that will last rather than have to be regularly replaced;
* operate at hours that cause least disturbance to the local community.

The Body Shop has long been associated with producing products that reflect its social conscience. Table 1 show the targets that it has set for protecting the planet through what it does in its own business.

Table 1 *Body Shop targets to protect the planet*

By	Target
2006	Ensure a 5% reduction in the total CO_2 emissions for electricity use in stores and offices.
2010	Eliminate articifial musks from all product formulations.
2006	Eliminate phthalates (a group of man-made chemicals) from all product formulations.
2008	90% of company fleet to be hybrid models which combine petrol and electric sources to reduce pollution.
2010	Achieve 100% wood products and shop-fits from Forest Stewardship Council (FSC) certified sources.

Source: adapted from the *Body Shop Values Report 2005*, http://valuesreport.thebodyshop.net/.

Matching the competition If a major competitor is committed to an environmental policy and if it makes certain that its customers know this then it would be foolish of other businesses to ignore this. Most major UK businesses now have an environmental policy as part of their corporate social responsibility commitments. Table 2 shows an example from supermarkets.

Table 2 *Major UK supermarkets' environmental policy Statements*

Supermarket	Environmental policy statement
Tesco	Tesco endorses and aims to apply the principle of sustainable development, which means meeting the needs of the present without compromising future generations.
Sainsbury	We recognise that virtually all the activities of an organisation or an individual have some impact on the environment. Our aim is to reduce the impact of our own organisation through a programme of continuous improvement.
Asda/ Wal-Mart	Focusing on the environment is key to our mission to improve the quality of life for people around the world. Environmental leadership is critical to our future ability to grow and thrive as a company.
Morrisons	The priorities for our Corporate Social Responsibility programme include Operational Environmental Management - Avoiding waste - Saving energy - Preventing pollution - Conserving natural resources - Sustainable sourcing.

Sources: adapted from supermarkets' websites.

Cost and benefits Most businesses have the objective of making a profit and if helping to improve or sustain the environment also reduces costs or increases sales it makes sound business sense to do this. Increasing sales is likely to come because of positive reactions from customers. This is dealt with below. Lowering costs will come from good waste management, recycling and using renewable resources. These are dealt with in the second part of this section.

Customer reactions It is not just businesses that have a social conscience and care about what they are doing to the environment. There is also growing awareness and concern from the general public. Many people take such threats as global warming, depletion of the ozone layer, increased air, water and land pollution and the sustainability of natural resources very seriously. When faced with a choice of products from a business that tries to do something about these issues and a business that does not seem to care, such customers are likely to choose the first kind of business.

A survey of public attitudes to the environment in Scotland was carried out in 2002. The main findings that affected business were as follows.

- Raw sewage in the sea and nuclear waste were the main concerns.
- 89% felt that litter was a big problem in Scotland.
- With a door-step collection service, 88% said they would recycle paper, 85% said they would recycle glass and 79% said they would recycle cans.
- 62% said the world's climate is definitely changing.
- Public preference was for half of Scotland's electricity to be produced from renewable sources (such as hydro, wave and solar power).

A survey for England was carried out by Defra in 2001, details of which can be found at the Defra website at www.defra.gov.uk/environment/statistics/. Another survey for England was being planned in 2006.

Methods and benefits of waste management

The Defra study of waste in 2003 showed that businesses contributed the major part of waste and even household waste usually came from products bought from industry.

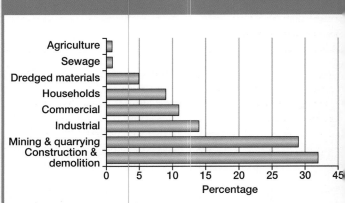

Figure 3 *UK waste by sector (2002)*

Source: adapted from *Defra Key Facts*, www.defra.gov.uk.

For the two major contributors to waste, shown in Figure 3, construction and demolition and mining and quarrying waste is unfortunately part of the production process. In order to build roads or mine for coal it is necessary to move a great deal of unwanted materials, which then create waste. For other businesses waste can be managed so that less of it occurs and costs for the business can actually be cut. Table 3 shows the major sectors of industry responsible for particular types of waste.

Table 3 shows that both manufacturing businesses and businesses in the commercial sector create waste. All industries in the UK create some waste, as is shown by the inclusion of education in the table.

Dealing with this waste can be beneficial for businesses for the following reasons.
- It helps to ensure that the business is not breaking any environmental laws.
- Dealing with waste often costs money, so if there is less waste there will be less costs.

Table 3 *Percentage of wastes contributed to by specific UK industries*

Sector of industry or commerce	Oil & solvents	Paints, varnish, etc.	Paper & card	Discarded equipment	Food	Combustion wastes
Food, drink and tobacco					66.0	
Manufacture of pulp, paper and paper products		22.4				
Publishing, printing and recording			15.4			
Production of coke, oil, gas, electricity, water						57.7
Manufacture of chemicals and chemical products	31.5	35.9				
Manufacture of basic metals						38.5
Retail - motor vehicles, parts and fuel; wholesale; other retail	25.1		42.2	42.3	26.7	
Transport, storage, communications	19.1					
Travel agents, other business, finance, real estate and computer related activities			13.7	17.4		
Education			1.9		1.7	1.7

Source: adapted from *Defra Key facts*.

- Some waste can be used for other purposes so a potential costs can be turned into a revenue earner.
- Having policies for reducing waste and achieving these is good public relations.

Figure 4 shows how waste could be used to create power sources. This would benefit both the businesses that used the waste and the environment that would not be polluted by it.

Figure 4

Up to 17% of the UK's electricity supply could be powered by common household rubbish by 2020, according to a report.

More than half of the 30m tonnes of rubbish sent to English landfills could power 2m homes a year, it says.

The Institution of Civil Engineers and the Renewable Power Association report says most of this waste is named in EU law as sources of renewable energy.

Source: adapted from BBC News (April 2005), http://news.bbc.co.uk

Recycling

One of the major ways in which waste can be avoided is to recycle products. In reality many of our major purchases as householders are already recycled. New cars are often sold on later as second hand cars, most houses are bought second hand, some household waste is put on the compost heap and unwanted toys, furniture or clothes are sold at auctions or given away to charity shops. In addition to these, we are now encouraged to separate our rubbish and put glass, metal, plastic and paper into the recycling bins.

Businesses can be involved in recycling in three ways. These are shown below with examples of businesses and products.

1. Producing products that they use again themselves
- Businesses that accept back empty printer cartridges which are then re-filled.
- Car showrooms selling new cars with part exchanges and then selling the other car as second hand.

In these cases the business saves on costs because it does not need to buy in as much raw material or it has something additional to sell.

2. Producing products that their customers can use again
- Body Shop re-fills empty plastic bottles of grapefruit shower gel.
- Some producers of Dijon mustard pack the mustard in containers that are glasses and can be used for drinking out of afterwards.

In these cases customers are encouraged to buy the products because they feel they are getting something extra for nothing.

3. Using the waste from other businesses or households to produce new products

- Recycling of paper and cardboard from households and businesses and creating new paper and cardboard for packaging or toilet paper.
- Leeds City Council is using old oil from local chip shops which has been turned into bio-diesel to fuel their vehicles.

In these cases the businesses creating the waste may be able to sell it, or save on having to pay for it to be disposed of. The businesses processing the waste into new products will make money from selling these.

Sustainable development

Businesses and people want economic growth because this means that the businesses will be able to make more sales and profits and the individuals will have a higher standard of living. At the same time it is very important that our generation does not achieve a higher standard of living by using up raw materials, which will mean that future generations suffer.

Sustainable development describes a situation where economic development is achieved and the ability to maintain or increase production and the standard of living in the future is not affected. Businesses will play a significant part in ensuring that this happens.

Many raw materials will run out as we produce more and more and many raw materials will run out if we do not replace them. Some parts of the natural environment will not be sustainable unless we reduce the levels of pollution.

The most important raw materials that will run out are the fossil fuels that are used to create our power and allow us to run transport systems, e.g. coal, gas and petroleum. In the long run these will have to be replaced by renewable energy sources such as solar, wind, water, nuclear, biomass and, for transport, electricity. The businesses that produce power will have to find new raw materials and the businesses that use power may have to change their products ready for this.

Businesses that make their products from raw materials will continue to have these raw materials if they are properly managed and replaced. For example:

- timber that is cut down to make furniture, joists for houses and paper can be replanted so that wood will continue to be available;
- fish stocks in the North Sea will continue to provide fish in the future if they are not over-fished now and if new sources, such as fish farming, are used.

Many businesses are now committed to using only renewable sources for their raw materials.

Select a range of products that are in the home or that are being bought and for each carry out the following tasks.

1. Check for and record any details on the packaging, instructions, etc. that indicate actions that the business is taking, or that the consumer is recommended to take, in order to protect the environment. This would include such details as 'dolphin friendly' on tins of tuna, made from recycled paper' on packaging, or instructions to place wrappings from sandwiches in a bin.

2. For each record explain how this is helping the environment and how it affects the way in which the business carries out its production.

Research task

Meeting the assessment criteria - examiners' guidance

For your chosen business you are required to produce a chairman's report which describes, applies, analyses and evaluates the effects of external influences on a business. This will involve consideration of the impact of voluntary controls by the business on the effects of its activities on the environment.

Business example - Boots environmental policy

As part of its Corporate Social Responsibility Policy, Boots plc is committed to reducing its impact on the environment. It does recognise that achieving sustainable development is a demanding task but it is determined to find a way of doing this. It has identified six major ways in which this can be achieved. These are shown on Table 4, with examples of specific commitments.

Table 4 *Boots' commitments to protecting the environment*

Title of Policy	Examples of the policy in use
Biodiversity	• Wood and pulp and paper products only come from independently accredited sources, accredtied by, for example, the Forest Stewardship Council (FSC). • Sponges and loofahs are only sourced from renewable sources. • It does not sell any products from endangered species listed in Appendix I of the Convention for International Trade in Endangered Species (CITES).
Chemicals	• Where there are reasonable grounds for concern that a chemical used could be harmful to human health or the environment there is a commitment to take appropriate precautionary measures.
Energy	• Reducing CO_2 emissions through work with the Carbon Trust. • Encouraging all staff working in Boots to make energy efficiency a part of their daily routine.
Waste and recycling	• Receiving, sorting and recycling over 22,000 tonnes of materials from its business each year. • Recovering cardboard boxes for re-use in the business or in other businesses.
Transport	• Using larger vehicles so that less journeys are made and CO_2 emission are reduced. • Greater use of duel-fuel vehicles to reduce harmful emissions.
Sustainable products	• Working with experts to find products that will ensure sustainability.

Source: adapted from *Boots Corporate Social Responsibility Policy*.

AOs	Mark Band 1	Mark Band 2	Mark Band 3
AO1	Details of Boots' main business and of the products being sold, where they are sold, etc. should be given. These details form the basis for explaining how and why Boots' policy and actions will help the environment. It would be expected that basic environmental issues are identified and that it is recognised that the policy primarily refers to voluntary actions.	Details at this level should show the most obvious potential environmental problems caused by the products Boots produces and sells and how its does this. Specific environmental problems should be linked to a specific causes, e.g. delivering goods from warehouse to stores will cause emissions of CO_2, etc. and use up limited petroleum stocks. There should also be a clear recognition of the potential impact that this will have because of the business's size and number of outlets.	There should be a good understanding of all aspects of Boots' business that are likely to affect the environment, from the raw materials sources used to the disposal, or recycling of waste. There should also be some assessment of how big the potential environmental problems might be, e.g. because of the size of the delivery fleet of lorries. All six parts of the environmental policy should be considered and form part of the report.
A02	Application here is to point out general potential environmental dangers, such as use of electricity, fuel and creation of waste. The policies will be given but with limited application to the specific potential environmental problem, providing statements similar to those given in Table 4, but with no development or explanation.	Here the specific environmental issues will be identified. The correct policy will be applied and an explanation will be given as to why that policy will help to reduce the environmental issue. For example, elements of the waste and recycling policy would need details of why the waste that Boots creates could cause a problem because of cost of disposing of cardboard, old shelving, etc. Details should then be given of the policy of recycling, for example what is recycled and how this helps to reduce costs or earn revenue through selling to other businesses.	All policies should be applied here with details of the kind of environmental problems each sector is designed to reduce. Each element of the policy should be explained so that it is clear how it helps to reduce the danger to the environment. The detail provided should be sufficient to show the likely impact of each element of the policy on the environment. For example, 22,000 tonnes of potential waste being recycled, a 2.1% improvement in CO_2 emissions, and the requirement for suppliers to inform Boots if they change their sources for palm oil.

AOs	Mark Band 1	Mark Band 2	Mark Band 3
AO3	Sources for the potential environmental impacts are likely to come from textbooks or general sources on the environment such as encyclopaedias. The details for Boots' policy will come mainly from the general page of the policy on Boots' website. There will be little additional research and limited analysis to identify which points are most important.	Sources here should include some follow up sources so that what the policy says is clear. For example, the policy on biodiversity refers to the FSC accreditation of sources of wood, etc. and the CITES list of endanger species. What these involve needs to be checked so that examples can be given of what Boots is actually doing with its policy commitments.	A wide range of sources is needed here. Boots' website does provide a great deal of detail but it also refers to elements that are not explained, such as FSC, and some of these should be checked. The website also provides links that allow for more in-depth research. As always, contact with the business is advised and would allow additional questions to be asked, for example, how the business would prioritise the six parts of the policy.
AO4	The evaluation here is likely to do little more than state what the policy is trying to achieve and give details of where progress has been made in reducing potential environmental threats.	The evaluation here should give details of how effective meeting the policy has been in terms of reducing the threats to the environment. It should also consider the impact that the different parts of the policy have had on the way that Boots runs its business, such as identifying new practices or assessing the cost.	Evaluation at this level should be looking carefully at each element of the policy and assessing how well it is meeting potential environmental issues. It should also be considering both sides, for example using larger vehicles means less journeys and lower CO_2 emissions, but how does it affect road surfaces, vibration in building and road congestion?

Portfolio practice · Energy efficient buildings

Alliance of global companies to develop energy self-sufficient buildings

United Technologies and Lafarge Group have joined together with the World Business Council for Sustainable Development (WBCSD) to create an alliance to show how buildings can be designed and constructed to run effectively without using energy from external power grids and with zero carbon emissions.
 Other companies are expected to join the project to transform how buildings are built and operated.
 According to the WBCSD, buildings today account for 40 percent of energy consumption in developed countries. The project contends that by 2050 all new buildings could be produced to a standard so as to consume zero externally supplied energy with no resultant carbon emissions. The target would be achieved with a mix of onsite power generation and ultra-efficient building materials.

Source: adapted from *Business Respect Newsletter* (April 2006). www.mallenbaker.net.

(a) **Explain why businesses which used these types of buildings would create benefits for:**
   (i) the business;
   (ii) the environment.
(b) **What drawbacks might there be for existing businesses located in the centre of towns and cities?**
(c) **Would these kinds of developments be more effective for businesses in the primary, secondary or tertiary sectors of industry? Justify your answer.**
(d) **Businesses that used these types of buildings would do so voluntarily. Explain why they would do this if there was no legislation forcing them to do it.**

Computer technology and computer hardware

Technological developments

Developments in technology are taking place at an ever-increasing rate. New products are being developed, such as high definition flat screen televisions and MP3 players. New drugs are being developed to help with illnesses that have been deadly in the past. Solar and wind power are now being used as alternatives to solid fuels.

Two areas which have seen rapid development in business are the use of computers and communications technology. Sections 74 and 75 consider the impact of computer hardware and software on businesses. Section 76 examines how technological developments have changed the way in which businesses and their employees communicate with each other.

Computer hardware

Computer hardware is the physical part of a computer, including the drives, the motherboard and the physical circuitry, as distinguished from the computer software that instructs the hardware and runs such programmes as Word and Excel.

The computer hardware that most people are familiar with is the personal computer, which has an interface between the user and a screen, as explained in section 75. However, there are many other examples in business of computer hardware. This is usually not seen, but is found in equipment shown in Table 1.

As the prices of computers have fallen, many businesses have

Table 1 *Computer hardware usually not obvious in business*

Equipment	Type of business operation
Microwave ovens	Factory and office kitchens, cafes and restaurants.
Electrocardiograph machines	Monitor heart rates in hospitals.
Compact disc players	Bars, nightclubs, cafes.
Navigation and satellite systems	Company cars or vans.

taken the opportunity to purchase them, with the aim of improving the efficiency of their operations. Even the smallest businesses may have a basic computer to carry out simple operations, such as word processing letters or invoices, keeping records or carrying out calculations. The introduction of computers into businesses will have a major impact on their operations. This is discussed later in this section.

Human-computer interface technology

Computers and peripherals, such as printers, modems and scanners, are complex pieces of equipment as is the software that is run through them. In order to allow people to use them efficiently it is necessary to have interfaces that make this process manageable for non specialists. Software interfaces, such as the graphic user interfaces (GUI), will be considered in section 75. In this section some of the hardware interfaces will be considered. First, it is necessary to appreciate the kind of hardware that may be used for different business activities. Examples are given below.

Marketing
- Creating an advertisement to be used in a radio promotion using digital sound software with speakers, mikes and a MIDI synthesizer.
- Designing a poster to be printed as part of a marketing campaign using a mouse, keyboard and graphics tablet.
- Producing leaflets created with graphics software and printed on a LaserJet colour printer.
- Producing a moving image presentation for a product launch using video capturing software with digital camcorder and video and audio capture cards in the computer.

Producing goods and services
- Automated soldering and painting using robotic arms in a car assembly plant.
- Precision engineering using computer aided manufacturing (CAM) machines.
- Telesales with automated telephone dialling systems using PCs, modems and broadband connections.
- Teaching using a computerised whiteboard.

Human resource management
- Calculating employees' pay using accounting software which then uses a printer to create pay slips.
- Using EPOS systems to record the speed of checkout staff using the scanners at the tills.
- Recording hours worked using swipe cards and time attendance recorders linked to a computer.
- Using CCTV in stores to reduce the need for surveillance staff.

Human-computer hardware interfaces

Many of these interfaces are used with little thought about what they are doing, but without them using computers and peripherals would be very difficult. Typical interfaces include the following.
- A **keyboard** allows letters, numbers and symbols that can be seen on the keyboard to be transferred onto the monitor for users to process. Keyboards also have special function keys and the software can be programmed to set up specific functions that would be useful for a specific business.
- The **mouse** allows drawing movements to be carried out, as does a **light pen** and a **graphics tablet**.

● The **monitor** allows users to see what the results of their actions are.

In addition to these more obvious interfaces the computer is also creating interfaces with many other pieces of hardware, often with very little input required by the user. When the computer is being used, if it is correctly set up it will also recognise and interact with speakers, printers, modems, webcams, scanners, digital cameras, CD and DVD drives, automated machines and so on.

Hardware is now also frequently available for customers to use as part of their activities. Examples are shown in Table 2.

Table 2 *Customer/computer activities*

Business	Activity
Cinemas/Railway stations	Ticket machines for buying or collecting pre-ordered tickets.
Supermarkets	Use of home computers and modems for ordering groceries on line from the website.
Banks	Cash machines for taking out cash, checking balances and requesting statements.

Integrated hardware

Working computer systems are made up of various pieces of hardware, disks, motherboards and wiring and these are connected with peripherals such as printers and scanners. There are also more developed integrated systems used by businesses whereby the computer technology is linked to machinery and other parts of the production process.

Computer integrated manufacturing (CIM) This is the linking of a variety of computer related operations in the production of manufactured goods. Typically a product is designed using computer aided design (CAD) on a computer and the design information transferred to a computer aided manufacturing (CAM) machine, such as a computer numerically controlled (CNC) lathe or a milling machine. Sometimes large organisations have many

related activities and the entire system of production is controlled by computers.

EPOS systems and computerised stock ordering Electronic point of sale (EPOS) systems use computers, combined with cash registers, bar code readers, scanners and magnetic strip readers to capture information about a transaction when it takes place. This information can be transferred to a main computer to provide a variety of data about customers. EPOS can also be linked to:

● stock control systems so that stock information is kept up to date and goods that need replenishing are identified and re-ordered;
● linked to suppliers' extranets or websites so they know when to supply goods and can track them.

The impact of computer technology

Sections 75 and 76 deal with the impact of particular aspects of software and communications on business. Overall, there are some general effects on business of introducing new technology that can be identified.

Costs of hardware The introduction of computer hardware and integration systems into a business can have a high initial cost, especially if the business is large or its operations are complex. There will also be the ongoing costs of maintaining and replacing and updating equipment.

Efficiency and cost savings Businesses introduce computers into their operations to improve efficiency. They hope that activities will be carried out more quickly and accurately. They would hope that computers will reduce costly mistakes. They would aim to carry out large numbers of operations more quickly and reduce operational costs. Computers may even save on labour costs, as fewer workers may need to be employed. Improved efficiency may also come from linking operations together and through links with suppliers.

Changing work organisation The introduction of computer hardware will affect the organisation of an office or factory. Space will need to be found for the equipment. In some cases the organisation of the work process may need to change, for example the layout of a factory floor when using computer aided manufacturing. There will also be a period of adjustment needed as operations change and people get used to new systems.

Arrange an interview with the manager of a branch of a supermarket/DIY/Electrical Goods chain.
1. Identify all the different computers and peripherals used in the business, both in the local branch and those linked to other branches and head office.
2. Identify the main functions of these computers and peripherals.
3. Explain how the use of computer technology benefits (i) the business and (ii) consumers.

Research task

Effects on employees The demands made on employees are likely to change. New skills will need to be developed, which may require training. New employees may need to be brought in with specialist skills. Job descriptions will change. Some employees may even lose their jobs. Computer technology can also affect motivation. Some employees will be motivated by the changes, whilst others may not. Employees may find that they have improved chances of promotion or can earn higher salaries as a result of the new technology, whilst others may feel that their jobs are threatened.

Meeting the assessment criteria - examiners' guidance

For your chosen business you are required to produce a Chairman's report which describes, applies, analyses and evaluates the effects of external influences on a business. This will involve consideration of the impact of introducing computer hardware and integration systems on the business.

Business example - Systems (Telcoms) Limited

Andrea Jones is managing director of Liversedge-based Systems (Telecoms) Limited. It is a business that specialises in the next-day delivery of refurbished telecommunications equipment.

What I did - Invest in a computerised system
'We bought our computer system with its accounting software, Sage Line 100, when we were turning over £500,000 a year. It cost a lot of money but I got it on a five-year lease and I only paid £50 a week. I couldn't have got anybody to do the stock work for £50 a week. I chose this system because I wanted something that integrated all my accounting functions - my stock control, my buying … basically, to have everything under one roof, as it were. And, importantly, I wanted barcoding. I did a lot of phoning around software companies before making my choice. As an item comes in it gets barcoded and then it's logged on to the system under a purchase order with the serial number, stock code and details of the product. The product then goes down to our test room for refurbishing. The system can tell you whether any item has been tested or not and exactly where it's located in the warehouse.'

Hold enough equipment to fulfil customer orders
'For the refurbished products side of my business there's no such thing as having too much stock. We can't ask people to wait a week if they want something so I buy anything that comes up for sale if it's cheap enough and I know it will move. I wouldn't buy stuff if there was no demand for it but that doesn't happen. I know my market very well. We sell new installation products too and we re-stock that on a demand-led basis. We set minimum and maximum stock levels on the Sage system and when the stock hits the minimum level the screen lights up telling me to reorder. But I prefer to print a report on stock levels every Friday. That tells me what we're low on and I always top up to the maximum level.'

What I'd do differently - Install a computer connection from work to my home earlier than I did
'When I get home I can click on two buttons and I'm basically sitting in my office. This means I can keep an eye on my stock at all times and I do a lot of bidding for products from home, for example on eBay. I can also complete purchase orders from home.'

Source: adapted from www.businesslink.gov.uk

AOs	Mark Band 1	Mark Band 2	Mark Band 3
AO1	Details of the business and of the products being sold, where they are sold and how they are sold, should be given. Description should be given of the computer hardware and integration packages introduced that might affect the business.	Details at this level should show the main computer technological developments that can affect the business with illustrations, including relevant business and technical terms, such as stock control and barcoding scanners. Details must be given of the hardware needed to run this software, for examples PCs, scanners and modems.	There should be a good understanding and explanation of all the computer hardware, integration packages and human-computer interface technology that are likely to affect the business. The most important factors will be outlined with examples of the effects. It should also be recognised that some of these systems will only work if they are compatible with systems that suppliers have.

AOs	Mark Band 1	Mark Band 2	Mark Band 3
AO2	Application here is to point out general computer hardware that affects the business. There may be some confusion between hardware and software and there will be limited analysis that identifies the functions of specific types of hardware. Basic changes in computer technology over time may be given.	Here the specific use of computer hardware in this business will be outlined and explained, for example the hardware needed to run stock control, re-ordering and accounting systems. The functions of the computers, scanners and printers need to be explained in the context of running the business. The report should also show a good general understanding of changes that have occurred since the mid-1990s.	All aspects of the introduction of computer hardware, integration packages and human-computer interfaces should be outlined here. Each should be explained so that it is clear how it affects the business. Some originality of thought might be used. Details should be clearly applied to the business so that, for example, the hardware in the office, in the test room and even in Andrea Jones's home is described and the required hardware links outlined. The benefits of changes over time should also be applied, as with the low cost of leasing the systems.
A03	Details of the potential impact of computer hardware are likely to come from a limited number of sources, such as just the statements from the managing director shown here. There will be little additional research and limited analysis to explain exactly how the business has been affected.	Sources here should include a range of appropriate data taken from a variety of acknowledged sources. Information is presented which analyses the impact of computer hardware, integration packages and human-computer interface technology on the business in a number of areas, including costs. Once the specific types of hardware have been identified, suppliers or the Internet could be used to find details of what the hardware actually does.	A wide range of sources is needed here, such as interviews, articles and primary and secondary research. It is very important that a good understanding of exactly what hardware the business has and how it is used is achieved and that will require good access to the business itself. The research must be up-to-date and would be expected to go beyond simply what the business has done so that alternatives could be considered, for example, how much it would cost to buy rather than lease and what changes in capacity or speed may be needed in the computers as newer versions of software such as Sage are developed. These kinds of technologies changes very rapidly.
A04	The evaluation here is likely to do little more than state whether the introduction of computers has been successful or not, with little evidence to back this up.	The evaluation here should give details of the extent to which the introduction of computer technology has been of benefit to the business. This will be backed up by evidence from certain sources, such as statements from stakeholders or figures.	Evaluation at this level should be looking carefully at all aspects of the introduction of computer technology and its effects on the business. Figures, comments and analysis of data will be used to support conclusions. For example, judgements on effectiveness should take into account suggestions for improvements that could be made. There will also be evaluation of interrelationships, for example between home computers and work computers and ordering systems and testing and the effects of this technology on employees, suppliers and managers.

Portfolio practice · The introduction of computer hardware

A designer and manufacturer of hydraulics components, selling to the European aircraft industry, found customers wanted shorter lead times and 'just in time' deliveries. The company allows customers and suppliers on-line access to its computerised manufacturing information. This means that everyone in the supply chain can see what the customers are planning and adjust production to suit. Customers can also see when there is spare capacity, which they might use at special prices. This solution also reduced stock levels.

A crane manufacturer facing a smaller home market had to export to survive. To compete against foreign competition it uses computer-aided design to standardise its products, reduce stock holding and speed quotation, design and delivery. It can now quote for a crane in minutes, when its competitors can take weeks. This has attracted new overseas clients and turnover has trebled in the past decade within its existing factory.

A plastics manufacturer wanted to improve the scheduling of manufacturing operations on the shop floor. Its procedures were a mixture of different paper-based systems, and were hard to manage. The solution was a computerised integrated resource planning system. By scheduling operations on the shop floor, depending on the level of orders and the ability of sub-contractors to deliver raw materials, the company increased productivity by 28% and halved materials stocks.

Source: adapted from www.is4profit.com.

(a) Identify the hardware that is likely to be needed to run these systems.
(b) Describe the ways in which computer hardware and integrated systems have been used in these businesses.

(c) Examine the impact on (i) the businesses and (ii) their stakeholders of the introduction of these computers and systems.

Types of software

Section 74 explained how businesses are increasingly using cheaper, more powerful computer hardware. On their own, computers have limited scope. They require computer software, defined in Figure 1, to carry out operations. Software can take many forms, but the main software applications used in business are shown in Figure 2.

Figure 1

Computer software is 'that part of a computer system that consists of encoded information (or computer instructions), as opposed to the physical computer equipment (hardware) which is used to store and process this information.'

Source: adapted from http://en.wikipedia.org.

Figure 2 *Computer software*

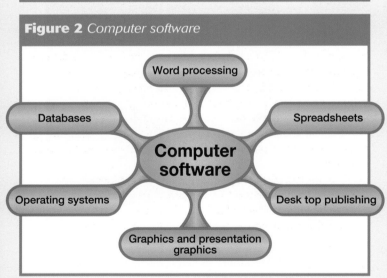

Word processing

Word processing is perhaps the most straightforward software application. It has replaced the typing of those materials shown in Table 1 which was previously carried out on a typewriter.

Sometimes when computers are bought they are already loaded with a word processing application installed, although, if not, one will need to be purchased separately by the business. This could be a 'stand alone' word processing package or integrated suites of programmes. Familiar software includes Microsoft Word, Microsoft Works and Microsoft Office for PCs or AppleWorks for Apple Macs. The most generally used word-processing programmes, such

Table 1 *Operations suitable for word processing*

- Letters.
- Memos.
- Reports.
- Job descriptions and person specifications.
- Production orders.
- Marketing copy.
- Minutes of meetings.

as Microsoft Word, now include database, spreadsheet and graphics facilities.

Benefits of word processing

Word processing packages usually include many inbuilt features which help in the production of those materials shown in Table 1.
- Errors can be removed instantly and replaced.
- A spell check can be used to find and replace spelling mistakes in text and grammar. Care must be taken to 'double check' as a spell check will not pick up errors such as repeated words in text.
- Text can be copied and 'pasted' into other parts of the text. This allows small or large parts of the text to be changed and moved easily.
- The layout, size and look of a page can be amended, for example into single or two column, or with various sizes of margin.
- Text can be saved to use again at a later date.
- Text can be saved as files and transferred to other computers via disks and e-mail (see section 76).
- Text can be printed out in the forms shown in Table 1.

All of these and other features of word processing allow typed materials to be quickly and easily changed, saving time and cost for a business.

Graphics and presentation graphics

Computer software applications allow a variety of graphs, charts and images to be drawn. They can then be printed out, saved, transferred or used as presentations in the same way as text produced on word processing software. Well known drawing software used by businesses includes Corel Paint Shop Pro and Microsoft Draw for PCs and Adobe Illustrator for Apple Macs.

Software is also available that allows the business to manipulate photographs or moving images. Digital cameras can take photos or videos or images can be scanned in from a scanner. These can be saved as files and 'taken-in' to a software application such as Adobe Photoshop in the case of photographs. The business can then amend the image in a number of ways, including making the image larger or smaller, changing the colours or cutting out (cropping) part of the image. This is very useful if the business wants to

Table 2 *Graphics presentations*

Type of image	Use for business
Pie chart	Show market shares and competition.
Line graph	Show expected rises in sales in next 5 years.
Bar chart	Compare sales in different regions for a retail chain throughout the UK.
Photograph	Show locations of possible new premises.
Moving images	Illustrate the operation of a new product in the development stage to identify defects.
PowerPoint presentation	Show report of market research surveys.
Posters	Advertisements for forthcoming products.

hange the image to suit its own purposes. As with text, graphics
nd images can be saved and sent to other computers.

Text, graphics and images may also be used in a presentation.
owerPoint software allows slides to be made or images created
om text graphics, or images. These materials can be moved on
creen or moving images may be created. Figure 3 shows part of a
owerPoint presentation by Coca-Cola HBC, a non-alcoholic
everage bottling business.

Possible examples of graphics and presentations that might be
sed by a business are shown in Table 2.

Using graphics software has all the benefits for a business of
sing word processing software.

Desk top publishing

esk top publishing (DTP) software allows a business to produce
ll detailed designs, often used in publications. DTP makes use of

Figure 3 *A PowerPoint presentation*

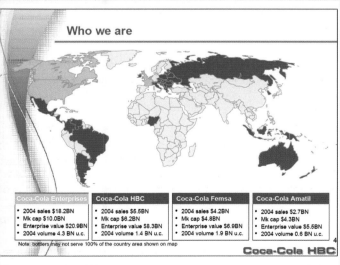

Source: www.coca-colahbc.com.

artwork, graphs, images, scans, downloads and text produced in
other software. For example, a farm may have created a new
service which involves a zoo for young children, a play area, a cafe
and a tour of a windmill on its site. The business may want to
produce a brochure to illustrate the opening of a new service. This
could include photos of the farm, text stating the opening hours
and the aim and objectives of the farm, a colourful design to
attract customers and a logo to brand the farm in the eyes of
visitors. These components will be created in other software and
then incorporated into the design.

The use of DTP can have a great impact on a business.
● It can improve communication, both internally and externally.
● It can be used for improved promotions to customers.
● It can enhance the reputation and quality of the business.
Examples of publications that a business might produce using a
DTP package, such as Quark Xpress, are shown in Table 3.

Table 3 *Examples of materials produced using DTP*

● Websites for customers.
● Business magazines for employees.
● Annual Reports and Accounts for stakeholders.
● A business plan to show to a bank to raise finance.
● A brochure showing the latest products to customers.
● A catalogue showing prices to customers or suppliers.
● Trade magazines.
● Books.

Related to DTP is the production of **websites** by businesses.
Software such as Microsoft Word, for basic sites, or more detailed
web authoring software such as Macromedia Dreamweaver or
AdobeGoLive is used. Most major software programmes have the
ability to convert what has been created into HTML which can
then be used in website design. Software can be used to design
websites that allow interaction with a wide variety of business
stakeholders. The impacts of websites on a business are discussed
in section 76.

DTP materials, such as reports, are sometimes included on
websites to be downloaded. This involves creating files called
portable document files or PDF files. They can be downloaded
from a website and viewed using Adobe Acrobat software.

Spreadsheets

Many businesses now make use of spreadsheet software, such as
Lotus 1-2-3, Quattro Pro and Excel. Spreadsheet software allows a
business to:
● store large amounts of numerical data in cells and organise it
into a useful order:
● carry out complicated calculations from the data using
formulae;
● present graphics from the data.
Making use of formulae, calculations on entire rows or columns
can be carried out instantly. Further, changing one cell can
automatically change other cells which are affected. So, for
example, a business may have calculated the effect of a 10% rise in
price on the sales revenue of 500 products. It can calculate the

Table 4 *Uses of spreadsheet software*

Department	Use
Human resources	Calculation of wages.
Accounting	Calculation of cash flows, budgets, balance sheets and profit and loss accounts.
Marketing	Forecasting of sales.
Production	Calculation of critical paths.

effect of a 20% rise on the revenue of all products simply by changing the 10% to 20%. Table 4 shows some of the ways in which spreadsheet software can be used by a business.

There are certain benefits for a business in using spreadsheet software.

- Time can be saved compared to making large numbers of individual calculations.
- Errors in calculation may be removed, although human errors in inputting data will still take place.
- Large amounts of data can be easily manipulated and graphs can be drawn to show exactly what a business wants.
- Changes can be made constantly to take into account changes in the market.

Databases

A database is a filing system which stores information on a computer in common data, known as files. Files will contain related records. For example, a business selling machinery might set up a database to show information about its customers, who are other businesses. All the information about a particular business will be a record. This information will be listed under headings known as fields, such as name, location, regularity of purchase, average spending and payment record.

Databases have a number of uses for a business.

- They can be placed in rank order, for example to show which customers spend the most in a year.
- They can be searched, for example to show all clients who spend less than a certain amount.
- They can be updated so that accurate information is retained.

Data held in databases can be used for a variety of reasons. Table 5 shows some examples.

Integration packages

Integration packages are computer-based activities which involve a number of computer operations taking place. Integration packages allow activities to be linked together. Examples that might be used in an office are:

- links between e-mail and fax, so that faxes can be accessed from anywhere;
- the management of incoming telephone calls, to identify numbers dialled from telephone calls and link them with automatic voice response;
- pulling lists of names and addresses held on computer and creating large numbers of different mailing labels.

Computer management information systems (MIS), for example, involve the collection, recording, storing and processing of business data. MIS allow a business to:

- record and store accounting records, such as sales, investment and payroll data and produce financial statements from these records;
- record and store inventory data such as work in progress, maintenance data and information about the supply chain and process these records into production schedules and monitoring systems;
- record and store human resources data such as salaries and employment history and produce performance reports from these;
- record marketing data such as customer profiles and market research information and produce marketing plans from the data;
- record business intelligence data such as industry data and corporate objectives and produce industry reports and strategic plans.

Operating systems

For different packages to communicate with each other they need a common format. That is provided by what is called the operating system. The operating system is, in effect, the engine of the computer, without which the hardware and software will not work. There are many different systems but some of the best known are Windows, Mac OS and Linux. These operating systems also allow the software packages to interact with the hardware so that when the user, for example, clicks on the icon for 'print' it will send the file to the print queue and activate the printer.

Because Microsoft is now the major software provider for mos

Table 5 *Examples of uses of databases*

Data	Use
Employees' records	- To monitor absenteeism and staff turnover so that they can be reduced. - To examine the ages of staff to see when retiring staff may need to be replaced. - To assess how far staff travel to work when working out rotas. - To check staff skills, qualifications and experience when considering promotions.
Customer records	- To investigate whether a product is selling to a target market. - To target new products at particular customers. - To identify the average spending of customers.

small computers it is Windows that businesses are most likely to be using. Software firms also tend to create programmes that use the Windows interface because that is what the customers will be used to. Larger businesses and ones that create specialist programmes, such the Revenue and Customs and Sony for its PlayStation, will either have specialised software created for them or create their own. The specialist software will include the businesses' own operating systems.

Human-computer interface

As with the hardware, see section 74, there will also be a need to create good human-computer interfaces because most users have very little idea of how software packages work. These are provided with such facilities as a Graphics User Interface (GUI) and What You See Is What You Get (WYSIWYG).

The **GUI** facility displays visual elements such as icons, windows and drop down menus at a relatively simple level and the interactive movements found in computer games at a complex level. When architects and other designers use CAD software to design houses or new cars it is the GUI that will allow them to swivel the pictures around so that they can be viewed from different angles.

WYSIWYG is a user interface that is designed to display what has been created, up-loaded or downloaded into a software package in the way that it will look if printed out, sent out by e-mail or posted on a website. This allows the business user to see what the end-product will look like and to edit work-in-progress, using the screen, so that the images and presentation can be improved and displayed in exactly the way the user wants. Usually it will also be possible to see the work in more than one mode, so that for example with Microsoft Word, the work can be seen in different sizes using zoom, in print layout and web layout with or without ruler, task panes and toolbars.

The impact of introducing software on a business

The majority of businesses today make use of some form of software applications. Introducing any form of software into a business has certain implications.

Cost Although, perhaps, there is the cost of buying software, such as a word processing package, this is likely to be relatively small compared to the cost of the hardware. DTP packages tend to cost more and may be prohibitive for a small business, which could use the services of a design business. A further cost is likely to be the

regular upgrades needed for software to ensure that they are compatible and effective with the current operating system of the computer.

Training, recruitment and hiring services Training will be required in the use of computer software. This might involve simply keying-in skills, but it is likely to be more effective if it involves a full course covering all aspects of the use of word processing software, for example. The training of a skilled graphics, DTP or website designer is likely to be more involved. A business designing in-house may want to recruit its own design team. However, it may be easier, as explained above, to hire the services of a specialist design business. Where specialised software which is created just for the business is concerned, expert programmers and systems analysts may be required or consultancy firms used.

Compatibility issues Unless a business has an integrated software package, there could be compatibility issues. For example, text produced on an Apple Mac may not be readable in Windows. To take from one application to another may require saving and importing, which then loses the style and format. Reformatting may then take time.

Monitoring and protection issues It is important that software is monitored. This is not only to make sure that software is up to date. A business must make sure that it complies with regulations regarding use of software, such as licences. It must also ensure it complies with data protection legislation. Further, a business must make sure that it has adequate virus and spam protection, to prevent major problems such as loss of data and prevent hacking into a computer from an outside source.

Arrange to carry out an interview with a small business, perhaps with only a few employees or a sole trader.
1. Using the information in this section, identify software that is not currently available in the business.
2. Examine the reasons why the software is currently not being used.
3. Place the possible introduction of different software in rank order of importance for the business. Evaluate the benefits to the business and its customers of the introduction of the software with the highest priority.

Research task

Meeting the assessment criteria - examiners' guidance

For your chosen business you are required to produce a Chairman's report which describes, applies, analyses and evaluates the effects of external influences on a business. This will involve consideration of the impact on the business of introducing software.

Business example - Tesco's use of software

How has Tesco been so successful? As Britons have become more middle class, Tesco has followed them up-market. It has also made better use of technology than its rivals. Tesco is always hungry for data. Most of its information comes from the Tesco Clubcard, a customer loyalty scheme that records what people are buying. 12m Clubcards are used in Britain. This gives Tesco a massive amount of pieces of data about shoppers. It can then explore links between purchases of different items and market them together in the store. 'We believe we have one of the largest databases anywhere in the world,' says Martin Hayward of Dunnhumby, the company that handles it for Tesco. The knowledge about customers allows Tesco to do two things.

- It gives customers discounts on things that they buy routinely. Each cardholder gets a letter at the end of each quarter containing vouchers worth 1% of what they have spent. They also get coupons that entitle them to discounts on products that Tesco's database suggests they might like.
- Tesco can adjust its shelves to suit the profile of the local area, or even the time of day. Tesco in Brixton, an area of south London settled by immigrants from the Caribbean, sells

plantains, a kind of savoury banana that can also be found for sale on market stalls outside. Tesco stores in central London don't. They sell sandwiches to office workers at lunchtime and then ready-meals to them in the evening.

Source: adapted from www.economist.com.

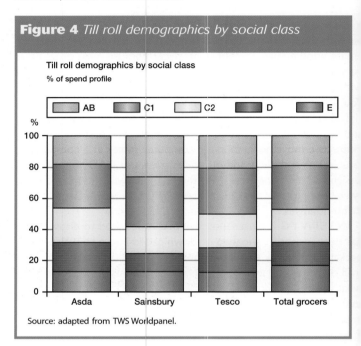

Figure 4 *Till roll demographics by social class*

Till roll demographics by social class
% of spend profile

Source: adapted from TWS Worldpanel.

AOs	Mark Band 1	Mark Band 2	Mark Band 3
AO1	Details should be given of the business and of the products being sold, where they are sold and how they are sold. Major types of software used by Tesco should be identified, for example the EPOS system. There should also be a basic appreciation of any major changes since the mid-1990s.	Details at this level should show the main software developments that can affect the business with illustrations, including relevant business terms, such as the target market. Tesco will have a very wide range of types of software and a reasonable range should be identified with sufficient detail to indicate that their main functions are understood. For example the role of EPOS in collecting and recording data and how this relates to the cards and the potential for marketing should be shown.	Tesco uses all of the main types of software listed in this unit and details should be given of how these will benefit the business. It also has dedicated software and some details of that should also be provided so that it can be seen how Tesco has effectively used computer technology to be the leading supermarket chain in the UK. For example, Tesco's website has been specifically designed jointly with Accenture to deal with the very heavy usage that it receives.

AOs	Mark Band 1	Mark Band 2	Mark Band 3
AO2	Software facilities and developments will be identified and applied in general terms that might apply to most businesses. The benefits and usages should, however, be appropriate for Tesco. Even at this level the nature and size of the business should be appreciated and the need to have software packages that will deal with customers, staff and suppliers, such as databases and up-dating the website.	At this level details of the software packages should be applied specifically to Tesco and there should be a clear recognition that a business of this size will be using general software packages for some of its staff and dedicated packages for other staff. For example, staff in the customer service department dealing with complaints are likely to be using standard word processing packages and possibly databases, whereas staff in the accounts department will be using dedicated accounting packages rather than basic spreadsheet programmes.	A good range of software applications used by Tesco should be outlined here. There would need to be some priorities here as Tesco has a very wide range. The EPOS system linked to customer and supplier databases and the website are major software systems which could be examined in greater detail, with clear indications of how the business uses them and how this benefits various stakeholders.
AO3	Sources will be limited and are likely to rely on textbooks for the basic software functions and sources such as the one newspaper article shown here and the Tesco corporate website for details of the actual software used by Tesco. There will be limited analysis to explain exactly how Tesco has been affected.	Sources at this level should be sufficient to give some details of how Tesco actually uses the software and what benefits it gains from this. Where a range of software packages is being identified, there should be some analysis to ensure that ones that are particularly important to Tesco are selected. All sources used should be clearly identified.	At this level a wide range of sources is needed. Newspaper articles, business profiles and Tesco's corporate website do provide important data but contact with the business itself is likely to be very helpful. Research must be up-to-date but also sufficient to provide details of how the use of software has developed over time at Tesco. There should be careful analysis and selection of the most appropriate data so that some software applications can be examined in detail and the benefits to Tesco and its stakeholders clearly stated and justified.
AO4	The evaluation here is likely to do little more than state whether the introduction and use of software has been successful or not, with little evidence to back this up. Generalised statements are likely to be made that could apply to most businesses.	The evaluation here should apply specifically to Tesco and should give details of the extent to which software has been of benefit to the business. The points made should be supported with details, for example the success of using the data collected through the loyalty card system to stock specific goods in certain Tesco outlets.	Evaluation at this level should be looking carefully a range of software uses and their effects on Tesco. It should not be assumed that Tesco's dominance of the market comes purely from its use of software and therefore there should be some evaluation of just how important the use of software has been and some assessment of which applications have been the most important. Conclusions should be justified with supporting data and good arguments. For example, when Tesco targeted immigrants from Caribbean in Brixton did that come from the Clubcard or other research? Registering for a Clubcard does not include filling out any data about ethnic origins so it is likely that it came from some other source.

Portfolio practice · James Meeles

James Meeles is a property development business based in The North West. It specialises in finding properties for development for clients both in the UK and abroad. The business often spends a great deal of time with clients so that their exact needs are recorded. However, as the market changes rapidly it is concerned to ensure that its information is up to date. This not only includes clients' details but calculation of costs. If costs suddenly increase on projects, then clients may pull out and a great deal of time put in by the company may be wasted.

The business tends to aim its marketing at clients who have sold their own home or have savings available to spend on a second home. It wants to develop a brand image that shows it offers a unique service of high quality. However, despite discussing its requirements with a number of advertising agencies, it feels that the marketing of its corporate image should be kept in-house. So all future advertisements for the business will be produced by the marketing department.

Source: adapted from company information.

(a) **Identify THREE types of software that the business might make use of to meet its objectives.**
(b) **In each case explain the possible benefits to the business of introducing the software.**
(c) **Discuss how a business might evaluate whether the use of software has been successful.**

Communications technology

The need for effective communication in business

Businesses need to communicate effectively. They need to pass and receive information from the external business environment in which they operate. They need to liaise with their stakeholders. Employees within a business need to communicate information and instructions to each other. The growth of globalisation and the trading of businesses into other countries, where centres of communication are also geographically separated, make effective communication even more important.

Without effective communication:

- incorrect details or instructions may be given;
- decisions and actions taken on these may be incorrect;
- delays may take place, which could lead to problems such as lost orders;
- information may be sent to the wrong source which may lead to problems such as disclosure of important data or even the breaking of data protection legislation.

Developments in communications technology are helping businesses to solve these problems. This section examines how communications methods such as those shown in Figure 1 impact on a business and its decisions.

Figure 1 Communications technology

Websites

The Internet as a medium of communication is becoming increasingly important in business. Many businesses now have their own websites and trade through e-commerce. The process of marketing electronically has become more and more important as customers have gained access to computers and information technology. It could be argued that, in future, a business without a website could struggle to reach its target audience. Operating a website can affect a business in a number of ways.

Communicating with customers This is perhaps the most important feature of a website. It allows a business to pass information directly to any customers with a computer that has Internet access. Table 1 shows some of the ways in which a business can make use of its website to communicate with customers.

Table 1 Benefits to a business of using a website to communicate with customers

Use	Benefits to business
Online shopping	Improve sales, cash flow and profit.
Information	Update customers about changes in prices or products.
Online surveys	Gather information about the profile of the market.
Contact the business	Feedback from customers.
Banner advertising	Attract funds from other businesses.
Develop a corporate image	Improve company recognition and brand loyalty.

Operating a website gives a business a constant, 24 hour access link to its customers. The website never 'closes' in the way that a shop does and it can be constantly and quickly updated more effectively than, say, printed material.

Flexibility Operating a website allows business flexibility, particularly in terms of where it is located. A business does not need, for example, to locate in London simply to attract customers in that area. Similarly, with the growth of international trade, operating a website is an effective way in which a business can sell into other countries without a physical presence there.

Changing job roles The operation of a website will also affect the nature of the job roles of personnel employed in a business. A business operating a website will need to employ designers to operate and update the site or hire the services of a specialist business that can do this for them. Sites need to be constantly updated to be effective.

Communicating with potential employees A website allows a business to change its methods of operation, for example its recruitment process. A business may make use of its site to recruit employees. It can advertise posts for which it wants to recruit and it can use the site to obtain applicants' details.

Efficiency and costs Operating a website can have a major impact on the efficiency and costs of a business. Run well, a website can greatly improve efficiency. It allows information to be passed to customers whenever they choose to access it, it can be edited rapidly to take into account changes in the market, customers can be targeted and sales and profits can be improved. Run badly, however, it can be a wasted exercise in marketing. If it is not updated, is badly designed, or is difficult to find and access, it may be of limited use.

There are also cost implications to running a website. The costs involved include:

- its design;
- the cost of registering the site on search engines;
- the cost of updating;
- the costs of computers to run the site;
- training involved for staff;

or the costs of employing a specialist business to do these. However, businesses that run websites would hope that the benefits outweigh the costs. They may also find that the way they operate changes because of the website, making the business more efficient and reducing costs over time.

Security and updating Security is major issue with the Internet. A business running a website must make sure that it takes steps to make its website safe from intrusion, viruses and fraud. This is particularly the case if payments are being made and customers' details are being held in a computer. A business must also regularly update with the latest software (see section 75) to prevent unlawful access. Regular updating is also necessary to make sure that applications are compatible with the current operating system of the computer.

Businesses also make use of other websites for a number of reasons.

- Researching the market. A business may be able to monitor changes that competitors are making, such as the introduction of new products or changes in prices via their websites.
- Collecting data. Many websites offer information about markets in which businesses operate. This can be general information from such sites as the Office for National Statistics, which provide information about factors such as the ageing of the population or the income of different groups. Or it might be a specialist website which needs to be subscribed to and paid for, such as Mintel where detailed reports can be downloaded about specific markets.

E-mail

E-mail is now, perhaps, almost as important as the telephone as a method of communication in business. It is like sending a letter or note to another person, but electronically using a computer. E-mail can be used for both internal and external communication as shown in Figure 2. Using e-mail can have an impact on a business in a number of ways.

- Employees in the business will need a computer terminal with e-mail facilities.
- Employees need to be trained how to use e-mail effectively.
- Employees must regularly check e-mails or messages may not be received in time.
- E-mails must be responded to within a reasonable time in order to ensure the efficiency of their operation.
- Care must be taken that information sent in e-mails remains confidential. A business must therefore ensure it has adequate facilities to protect e-mails and comply with data protection legislation.

Figure 2 *Internal and external e-mail*

Sender	Message	Receiver
Internal Manager	Date of next week's meeting	Department staff
External Customer	Inquiry about where to send goods for repair	Customer services department

There are certain benefits that e-mail can give to a business.

Sending a variety of information E-mail can send a relatively large amount of information instantly to a receiver. It may also include attached files with images, photos or other data in them.

Sending to many people Messages can be communicated to many people via one e-mail by using the database facility in the software in the same way as mail merge works. This makes it a very effective communication method for any single message that needs to be given to many people.

Large businesses It is particularly useful for large, international organisations that operate over many countries. It provides instant information transfer and feedback.

Mobile phone technology

Many businesses now issue their employees with mobile phones. As the name implies, these are telephones which can be used without the need to use a 'land line' fixed telephone.

Using mobile phones will tend to increase costs for a business. First, they have to be bought and second, charges for their use are generally very much higher than for land lines. However, the use of mobile phones by business can make communications more efficient. Employees who are out of the office or workplace can be contacted instantly. In the past a person wanting to make contact with another may have had to wait until they returned or they may have been 'paged' to contact the office. This is particularly

Figure 3 *Employees who might make use of mobile phones*

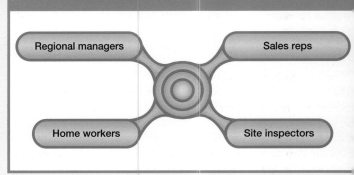

useful for employees who work away from an office or factory. Some examples are shown in Figure 3. Instant contact can help if urgent decisions need to be made. This may be particularly important for small businesses or businesses in fast changing markets.

Mobile phones also have other uses.

- They can be used as a medium of advertising, as shown in Figure 4.
- They may incorporate camera and video technology. This may help if an employee needs visual evidence to back up a report, for example.
- Texting is now an accepted communication method. It allows short messages to be sent instantly from one mobile phone to another, without the need for e-mail or a computer.

Figure 4

Text messages used to be the main method for companies wanting to market via mobile phones. Chocolate maker Cadbury's and cinema chain Warner used small message campaigns to promote particular products. Warner Village Cinemas used Short Messaging Service (SMS) to promote the Lord of the Rings movie.

2006 is predicted to be the year of mobile advertising. 3G technology allows messages to be much more innovative. So now full multimedia adverts can be sent to and downloaded from mobile phones.

Source; adapted from news.bbc.co.uk and www.3g.co.uk.

Teleconferencing, videoconferencing and web conferencing

Teleconferencing allows people in different rooms, in different locations to talk to each other via a phone link. They can communicate as if they were in the same room and all people in the room can hear what is being said through speakers. Internally this can be done with an intercom system.

Videoconferencing is similar but makes use of images as well. It involves the use of cameras in rooms which send images to receivers in other locations. This can be particularly useful if meetings need to take place between people in locations in very different parts of the world. It can save travel time, cost and can allow decisions to be made more quickly, although the facilities have to be available in all locations for this to take place. It could be suitable, for example, if a multinational company had locations in five countries and regular management meetings were necessary.

Internet technology has developed so that it is possible for teleconferencing, videoconferencing and web conferencing to be carried out over the Internet. Web conferencing allows projects to be worked on from a variety of locations and applications to be shared. Even small businesses can use the benefits of Internet links through web cams and Internet facilities such as MSN or Skype to communicate face to face at very little cost.

Figure 5 *Broadband technology*

'Broadband comes from the term 'broad bandwidth'. It is used to describe a high-capacity, two-way link between an end user and access network suppliers capable of supporting full-motion, interactive video applications.'

Source: adapted from largebande.gc.ca/pub/technologies/bbdictionary.html.

Figure 6 *Sales of single-track downloads by volume, UK, 2005*

In 2005, 26.5m tracks were legally downloaded in the UK – a 355% increase on the total in 2004.

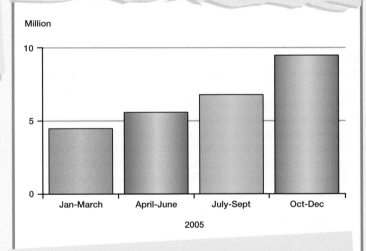

Million

2005

Download share of single sales
2004	52%
2005	75%

Source: adapted from *The Guardian*, 13.02.3006.

Broadband technology

Broadband technology refers to the development of Internet access which sends more information than available over the standard telephone line as explained in Figure 5. It has allowed relatively large amounts of data and moving images to be sent to computers quickly.

This has presented a number of opportunities for businesses.

Image transfer within a business Relatively large amounts of data can now be sent electronically from one computer to another. For example, a business can scan an image of a report and send it as a file to another computer instantly. This saves time. It also allows exact detail to be sent compared to a photocopy, for example. This is particularly useful when detailed plans, diagrams or even video materials are being sent.

Marketing It also presents opportunities for marketing. Online streaming allows moving images to be accessed from a computer. This is particularly effective for promoting products that require moving images such as promotions of films.

New sales Downloading directly from the Internet has now become a recognised medium for certain businesses. Sales of downloaded music are one area that appears to be growing as a result of broadband access. This has now become the main way in which the single music charts are decided. Film rental also seems to be a business that could benefit. Without broadband, downloading would be so slow that potential customers would not bother.

Businesses need to consider the potential that broadband offers and to plan for how they can use this new high speed technology. Where they are in competitive markets and their competitors are using this facility, they would be foolish to ignore it. Figure 6 shows how rapidly this market is developing.

Networking

Networking is the communication between computer systems. There are different methods of categorising networks, but one is to look at the extent of the coverage.

- A personal area network is a computer network used to communicate between computers close to one person. An example might be **Bluetooth** technology used to connect a camera or printer to a computer via a radio transmission.
- A local area network (LAN) covers a small area. An example might be computers connected to a central server in an office.
- A metropolitan area network covers computers linked in a campus or city, such as all buildings in a university.
- A wide area network (WAN) covers a wide area and an array of computers, such as the Internet.

Business operations can be affected in different ways by networking. For example:

- people can work together, on projects, linked by computers. This team work can prevent delays if one member of a team has free time to work on the project;
- different parts of a business can access common information and change it easily (businesses often set up **intranets** to allow only parts of the business to access their own information);
- suppliers and other stakeholders can access the information. For example, a business may set up an **extranet** to allow suppliers to view stock levels at a supermarket, so that stocks do not run out.

Other communications technology

Communications technology is constantly developing and businesses with their fingers on the pulse will be checking and making use of these new developments. Examples of new developments will include the following.

- **Wireless technology**, which allows users of computers to connect to the computer without needing to be actually sitting at the computer terminal.
- **Podcasting**, involves the distribution of multimedia files, visual and audio over the Internet. This has now become an important way of promoting and distributing entertainment products but is likely to expand into many other business areas.
- **750 gigabyte drives** which will be able to store 10,000s albums worth of music. Initially these will be internal hard drives but eventually they will be available as mobile ipods and will revolutionise what consumers and business employees can carry around with them without the need for a fixed, or even laptop, computer.

Communication technology is constantly changing and it is important that businesses are up-to-date so that they can benefit from the new technologies.
1. Use a search engine to find out and record what each of the following technologies do.
- Smart phones.
- Wireless Fidelity (WiFi).
- Personal Digital Assistants (PDAs).
- Voice over Internet Protocol (VoIP)
2. Explain how each of these new technologies could help a business.

Research task

Meeting the assessment criteria - examiners' guidance

For your chosen business you are required to produce a Chairman's report which describes, applies, analyses and evaluates the effects of external influences on a business. This will involve consideration of the impact of communication technology methods.

Business example - Music retailing businesses

In 2006 HMV revealed poor Christmas trading figures. Part of its poor performance was blamed on the growth of online retailers. Alan Giles, the boss of HMV, resigned, stating that there had been 'a quantum jump' in online sales in recent months. Profits at HMV's 200 music stores in Britain slumped £300,000 into the red in the six months to the end of October. During the same period in 2004 they had made a profit of £13.5m. Over Christmas - when HMV makes 90% of its profits - the sales decline slowed, but it was still nearly 9% lower. Mr Giles had dismissed downloading as posing little threat to his business. 'A year ago I was saying the Internet would plateau at about 10% of this market, now I say that I was wrong. I just don't know now how far it will go. This is a brave new world for retailers.'

HMV has been criticised for failing to embrace the Internet early enough. It only launched a download site in autumn last year and, while its Guernsey-based online store is growing fast, it is still smaller than one of its Oxford Street stores.

HMV also faced competition from supermarkets. It combated this by selling back catalogue ranges which supermarkets do not stock. Now, however, online retailers, led by sites such as Amazon and Play.com, have moved in on that part of the business. Stuart Rowe, the managing director of online Play.com, said the Internet was now the mass market. Play.com is the second largest online entertainment retailer after Amazon and its Christmas sales were in contrast to HMV's: music sales were up 37%, DVDs up 8% and video games up 50%. 'This Christmas has been the turning point and now it will just grow and grow. Two or three years ago online shoppers were early adopters, but now they are people who realise it is just a more comfortable way of shopping and checking prices. People have become more comfortable with technology now they use Sky+, eBay and broadband' said Mr Rowe.

Source: adapted from *The Guardian*, 13.1.2006.

AOs	Mark Band 1	Mark Band 2	Mark Band 3
AO1	Details of the business and of the products being sold, where they are sold and how they are sold, should be given. Descriptions should also be given of some of the developments in communications technology that might affect businesses.	Details at this level should show the main communications factors that can affect businesses with illustrations, including relevant business and technological language, such as the stating of particular communications technology methods and the different business operations that may be affected.	There should be a good understanding and explanation of all the developments in communications technology that are likely to affect a music retailing business. The most important factors will be outlined with examples of the effects. Business language such as the impact on target markets, marketing strategies, sales revenue and profits will be used.
AO2	Application here is to point out general communications technology and developments that affect the music retail industry. The factors are stated, but with limited application to the music retail industry and with no development or explanation.	Here the specific developments in communications technology will be outlined and two will be explained, with particular reference to businesses in the music retailing industry, such as downloading via the Internet and the use of websites to promote the business. Other areas will also be mentioned, such as the use of mobile phones, although perhaps more descriptively.	Sound explanation is given of all the main areas of developments in communications technology and how they impact on the businesses in the music retail industry. Some originality of thought might be used, such as how the pace of development might influence consumers in future.
AO3	Sources for the potential communications technology factors are likely to come from a limited number of sources, such as the one newspaper article shown here. There will be little additional research and limited analysis to explain exactly how the business has been affected.	Sources here should include a range of appropriate data taken from a variety of acknowledged sources, such as the newspaper article and the data in Figure 6 of this section. Information is presented which analyses the impact of the technology on the business in a number of areas, including sales, profits and target markets.	A wide range of sources is needed here. This will involve areas such as newspaper articles and research of the Internet market through reports, primary research and surveys. A thorough understanding is given of the way in which changes in a variety of developments in communications can affect the business. This will include websites, Internet sales and broadband downloading, but also wider areas such as stock control through networks. The impact on the business of these changes will be clearly explained.

AOs	Mark Band 1	Mark Band 2	Mark Band 3
A04	The evaluation here is likely to do little more than state whether communications technology has affected a business greatly or not, with little evidence to back this up.	The evaluation here should give details of the extent to which a chosen business has been affected by changes in communications technology. This will be backed up by evidence from certain sources, such as figures showing that sales have fallen or grown. It may also include some judgement on the strategy used by the business, with evidence to support this.	Evaluation at this level should be looking carefully at each development and assessing exactly the extent to which a business has been affected. Figures, trends and other conclusions will be used to support the argument. There will also be some attempt at understanding interrelationships, for example that increasing use and familiarity of a website might also encourage greater downloading. It should evaluate using data whether the strategy used by the business given the changing trends is justified or not.

Portfolio practice · PPS distribution

PPS Distribution is a small-medium sized distribution operation which makes 24 hour deliveries for businesses to anywhere in the UK. It employs drivers in vans who are allocated jobs when they arrive in the morning. They then drive to pick up the parcels and deliver them the same day to the required destinations. Businesses often pay premium rate for such deliveries, as it is vital that they are delivered the same day. The business prides itself on its record on deliveries, and has very few complaints from customers. However, always looking to improve efficiency of the distribution, management has suggested that internal communication between staff and external communication to customers can be improved. Two suggestions have been raised at a meeting to improve communication.

- Customers should be able to find information about what is happening to their parcel, such as when it left the depot, when it arrived and any other useful information such as the person who signed for it.
- Drivers should be able to be contacted 'en route' if there is a possibility of picking up another parcel and making a second delivery to a nearby address the same day.

Source: adapted from company information.

(a) State ONE method of communication technology that could be used to improve efficiency in each case.

(b) Explain the impact on the business of introducing these methods of communication.

The business is considering merging with another operation in another part of the country. Again, the business is concerned about communication. If the merger takes place the managing director wants managers to have regular meetings to coordinate activities.

(c) Discuss whether the business should use video conferencing for these meetings.